Instructor's Manual with Test Bank

A History of Modern Psychology

TENTH EDITION

Duane P. Schultz
University of South Florida

Sydney Ellen Schultz

Prepared by

Chimborazo Publishing, Inc.

WADSWORTH
CENGAGE Learning™

Australia • Brazil • Japan • Korea • Mexico • Singapore • Spain • United Kingdom • United States

ISBN-13: 978-1-111-35368-1
ISBN-10: 1-111-35368-9

Wadsworth
20 Davis Drive
Belmont, CA 94002-3098
USA

Cengage Learning is a leading provider of customized learning solutions with office locations around the globe, including Singapore, the United Kingdom, Australia, Mexico, Brazil, and Japan. Locate your local office at: **www.cengage.com/global**

Cengage Learning products are represented in Canada by Nelson Education, Ltd.

To learn more about Wadsworth, visit **www.cengage.com/wadsworth**

Purchase any of our products at your local college store or at our preferred online store **www.cengagebrain.com**

Printed in the United States of America
1 2 3 4 5 6 7 15 14 13 12 11

Table of Contents

1. The Study of the History of Psychology   1
2. Philosophical Influences on Psychology   30
3. Physiological Influences on Psychology   68
4. The New Psychology   98
5. Structuralism   131
6. Functionalism: Antecedent Influences   158
7. Functionalism: Development and Founding   189
8. Applied Psychology: The Legacy of Functionalism   240
9. Behaviorism: Antecedent Influences   281
10. Behaviorism: The Beginnings   313
11. Behaviorism: After the Founding   341
12. Gestalt Psychology   385
13. Psychoanalysis: The Beginnings   418
14. Psychoanalysis: After the Founding   469
15. Contemporary Developments in Psychology   521

Chapter 1

The Study of the History of Psychology

Why study the *history* of psychology? One reason is that the past is relevant for the present. For example, researchers in 1999 asked psychology students to watch a one-minute video of two teams of basketball players passing the ball to their teammates. Students were asked to count the number of times the ball bounced during a particular team's passes. Towards the end of the video, a person dressed in a large gorilla costume came out, stopped amidst the players, and pounded his chest. When asked if they saw anything besides the basketball players, only about half of the students could identify the gorilla. The study of *The Invisible Gorilla* suggests that people may find it difficult, if not impossible, to pay attention to more than one stimulus at a time. Similar results on the usefulness and effectiveness of multitasking were demonstrated in 1861 by a German psychologist. Thus, the history of psychology often informs the nature of psychology in the 21st century. In other words, history is important is because studying the evolution of psychologists' thought will help students understand contemporary psychology.

In addition, this course is being offered because faculty believes it to be an important contribution to the field. Courses about the history of psychology have been offered since at least 1911, and are currently offered in 93% of 311 psychology departments surveyed in 2010. Other sciences typically do not offer such a course. Furthermore, there are specialized journals, research centers, and even a division of APA dedicated to the history of psychology. Because there is no single form, approach, or definition of psychology on which all psychologists agree, present day psychology has become so diverse that our history is perhaps the one thing that provides order and imposes meaning to the seemingly chaotic field.

Psychology can be considered both one of the oldest fields of study and one of the newest. It can be considered one of the oldest because its subject matter, the mind, can be traced back to the Greek philosophers in the fifth century BC. On the other hand, we can also view psychology as being about 200 years old if we mark our beginnings with the merging of physiology and philosophy. Psychology distinguished itself as a formal discipline in the last quarter of the nineteenth century when it shed philosophical tools of speculation and intuition and adopted the tools used in biology and physical sciences. While the questions addressed by early psychologists were similar to their philosophical predecessors, carefully controlled observation and experimentation set psychology apart as a field with increased precision and objectivity.

History is quite different than psychology, so this course merges two distinct disciplines. The methods used to study history, broadly termed historiography, are quite different than those of science. History cannot be replicated, but is instead constructed from the scraps of information found and interpreted by the historian, and historical data can be incomplete and incorrect for a variety of reasons. Some data have become lost, for example John Watson burned his letters, research notes, and unpublished manuscripts before he died. In other cases, data have been found decades or even centuries after having been lost, such as when some papers written by Hermann Ebbinghaus were found in 1984 or when missing letters written in 1641 by Rene Descartes were later recovered in 2010. Other times, information is purposefully withheld in order to protect the reputation of an individual, such as when Freud's biographer, Ernest Jones, purposefully downplayed Freud's cocaine use.

Some data will be made available at a later time, for example, the Library of Congress in Washington D.C. is holding papers and letters from Freud's estate with instructions not to release them until a certain time.

Sometimes information is distorted, which is often seen in faulty translations, and can cause errors in either the meaning of the term or the emotions attached to them. For example, Freud's original systems of personality were translated into Id, Ego, and Superego. A better translation of these ideas from their original German might be It, I, and above-I. Likewise, his idea translated as free-association is more accurately translated into something that conveys the idea of an invasion or intrusion of thought. Other historical data is inaccurate because individuals recount a biased perception of their lives to protect themselves or enhance their public image. In his autobiography, B. F. Skinner portrayed his graduate student days as being filled with nothing but work. Twelve years after the account was published, Skinner recanted his statement as being a "pose" rather than a reality. Some distortions can be resolved by consulting other sources. In this example, graduate student colleagues of Skinner remember him for finishing his work quickly in order to spend his afternoons playing ping pong.

Contextual forces such as the Zeitgeist of the time often shape the nature and direction of psychology. Every age has a Zeitgeist, which is the intellectual climate or spirit of the times. During the early years of the twentieth century, increased economic opportunities coupled with changes in America's demographic composition lead to a fundamental shift in emphasis. The focus of psychology went from the academic laboratory to using psychology to solve issues related to teaching and learning. World War I and II implemented another contextual shift as psychology extended its influence into personnel selection, psychological testing, and engineering psychology... During World War II, European researchers and theorists escaped to America, thereby relocating the forefront of the discipline to the United States.

Finally, prevailing discrimination also shaped the field, with its impact on women, Jews, and African Americans. Women were often denied admission to graduate school or conferment of degrees, and later had a difficult time finding jobs particularly if married. Eleanor Gibson, who later won a number of professional awards for her work in perceptual development and learning, was restricted from certain courses and areas on campus when she attended Yale. Such discrimination extended into 1960, when Sandra Scarr was told by the officer interviewing her for admission that most women don't finish their degrees, and the ones that do amount to nothing anyway. Despite such obstacles, women did attain doctoral degrees in psychology. One champion for the education of women was James McKeen Cattell, who supported women frequently, urging scientific societies to include women. Largely because of his efforts, the APA was the first scientific society to admit women as members. Mary Whiton Calkins became the first female president of APA in 1905.

Discrimination extended to Jewish psychologists as well. A study of discrimination of Jews at three universities—Harvard, Yale, and Princeton—found widespread practices that excluded Jews from admission. Those Jews who were admitted to colleges were often separated and socially ostracized. Many colleges and universities, including two important to psychology (Johns Hopkins and Clark), had explicit policies to disallow Jewish students. In the face of such discrimination, some Jewish psychologists changed their names, which helped them secure jobs. Isadore Krechevsky became David Krech, David Bakanovsky became David Bakan, and Harry Israel (even though he was a protestant) changed his name to Harry Harlow.
Some chose not to do this, for example Abraham Maslow refused to change his first name to something "less Jewish".

African Americans also faced an enormous amount of discrimination. When Black students were allowed to attend predominantly White universities, they were often not allowed to live on campus or mix socially with White students. Howard University in Washington D.C., a traditionally Black school, provided an education in Psychology for many Black students. Kenneth Clark graduated from Howard with his bachelor's degree and was refused admittance to graduate school at Cornell. He received his doctoral degree from Columbia University, married Mamie Phipps Clark, and they both went on to perform their landmark study about the self-concept of Black children that was cited in the 1954 U.S. Supreme Court decision that ended racial segregation in schools. For those Black students who did receive their doctoral degrees, finding a job was the next obstacle, and many found work at the traditionally Black universities. Because so many of these universities were under funded, it was difficult for these psychologists to do research that received wide attention, therefore their work is less visible. Although the history of psychology is dominated by White male psychologists, it is important to bear in mind that we can only focus on a few individuals. The overwhelming majority of psychologists, no matter what race or sex, receive no attention at all.

There are two ways to conceptualize how history happens; the personalistic theory and the naturalistic theory. The personalistic theory is the view that the contributions of individuals is what fuels progress. With this theory, if these special individuals had not done their work, their fields would not have progressed. The naturalistic theory is the idea that the times draw out ideas from people. For example, Charles Darwin and Alfred Russel Wallace developed the idea of the theory of evolution independent of (and half way around the world from) each other, indicating that the time was right for that idea to emerge. As further support, sometimes ideas are presented before their time. The Scottish scientist Robert Whytt presented the idea of the conditioned response in 1763 but was largely ignored by his contemporaries. A century later, Ivan Pavlov expanded on Whytt's ideas when the Zeitgeist was more receptive. The Zeitgeist may be directed by some individuals. Oftentimes journal editors can act as gatekeepers of mainstream ideas and refuse to publish papers that are revolutionary. Psychologist John Garcia tried to publish a paper that challenged prevailing thought on stimulus-response theory. Although the research was solid, he was only able to publish in journals that were less known. This book uses both the personalistic and naturalistic viewpoints, while highlighting the importance of the Zeitgeist in defining the history of psychology.

Wilhelm Wundt, a German physiologist working in the last quarter of the nineteenth century, is often credited as the founder of psychology because he determined its goals, subject matter, research methods, and topics of investigation. Although Wilhelm Wundt first defined and promoted psychology, challenges to his conception began quickly. By 1900, there were several organized positions that rose in opposition to Wundt's psychology and to each other. Each of these was a "school of thought", and a series of them emerged, rose, and fell in succession as psychology developed over time.

Thomas Kuhn wrote a book about how sciences develop over time called *The Structure of Scientific Revolution*. According to Kuhn, when a science has produced an accepted way of thinking and has matured, this way of thinking is called a paradigm. Paradigms are present in other science, for example for about 300 years the paradigm in physics was the Galilean-Newtonian framework. Paradigms can also change, in what Kuhn calls a scientific revolution, such as when Einstein's model of physics became the paradigm..

Because psychology remains divided, it is considered to be "preparadigmatic"—there is no prevailing school of thought. In fact, many contemporary psychologists criticize the field because of its fragmentation.

To some extent, it has always been fragmented, because competing schools of thought have always been present. Oftentimes, new schools of thought are proposed and championed by younger psychologists. The schools of thought described in this book began with Wundt's psychology and structuralism, followed by functionalism, behaviorism, and Gestalt psychology, all three of which opposed structuralism. At about the same time, psychoanalysis developed independent from (instead of in opposition to) these other schools. Later, humanistic psychology develops as a reaction to both psychoanalysis and behaviorism. The last formal school discussed in the text is cognitive psychology which opposes behaviorism. Contemporary new foci in psychology include evolutionary psychology, cognitive neuroscience, and positive psychology.

Outline

I.   The Invisible Gorilla
  A. Study of multitasking and attention (Simon & Chabris, 1999)
  B. Conclusions similar to 1861 study
  C. Example of the past informing the present
II.   Why Study the History of Psychology?
  A. History of psychology: common requirement for majors
  B. Unique among the sciences in the focus on our history
  C. An area of status within psychology
      1. journals
      2. formal organizations
          a.   APA Division 26
          b.   The Archives of the History of American Psychology)

  D. Rationale for studying the history of psychology
      1. recognizes diversity within psychology
      2. provides a framework for solidarity
      3. emphasizes the relationships that make the whole cohesive
      4. integrates topics and issues
      5. is interesting in its own right
III.   The Development of Modern Psychology
  A. Paradox: Psychology is both
      1. a 2,500 year-old discipline
          a.   traced to 5th century B.C. speculation about human nature and behavior
          b.   Greek philosophers such as Plato and Aristotle wrestled with issues with issues still covered in introductory psychology classes.
      2. a new discipline began 200 years ago
          a.   formed when it emerged from
                (1) theories of philosophy
                (2) tools used in other biology and physical sciences
  B. Historical roots
      1. philosophical in character
      2. principal methods were speculation, intuition, and generalization

C. Modern distinct from the old
    1. a primary scientific field
    2. applies tools and methods from biology and physiology
    3. relies on controlled observation and experimentation
    4. objectivity and precision are continually sought and refined
D. represents a union of philosophy and physiology that emerged with its own character, status, and popularity
E. a better starting point is the nineteenth century
    1. psychology becomes independent
    2. early philosophical approaches can be considered psychology's "prehistory"

IV.   The Data of History: Reconstructing Psychology's Past
A. Historiography: "the principles, methods, and philosophical issues of historical research"
B. The data of history are different than the data of sciences like psychology
    1. there is no laboratory for historians in which situations are controlled and manipulated
    2. there is no replication or independent verification of results
C. The data of history
    1. materials used to reconstruct lives, events, eras
    2. unique: not replicable, conditions not controlled
    3. data fragments: the shards
D. Lost or suppressed data
    1. lost permanently: Watson burning his papers
    2. lost temporarily: found papers by Hooke, Ebbinghaus, Fechner
    3. suppressed: Freud's materials to be opened in the 21st century
    4. altered
        a.   self-interest: Freud's cases, Skinner's youth
        b.   to protect: Köhler's papers, Freud's cocaine use
E. Data distorted in translation
    1. Freud's use of Es (it), Ich (I), and Über-Ich (above-I)
    2. Freud's Einfall, translated as free association, but meant intrusion
F. Self-serving data
    1. Skinner's report as wholly "nose to the grindstone"
    2. Freud's self-depiction as a martyr to his cause

V.   Contextual Forces in Psychology
A. The Zeitgeist: "The intellectual and cultural climate or spirit of the times."
B. Economic opportunity as a contextual force
    1. turn of the century: more PhDs than academic positions
    2. rapid increase in U.S. immigration leads to swelling public school enrollment
    3. American pragmatism: interest in the practical utility of psychology
    4. result: shift in theoretical focus of psychology, increased application of psychology to "real-world" problems in education
C. War as a contextual force
    1. World War I:
        Application of psychology to personnel selection, psychological testing, and engineering psychology demonstrated the usefulness of psychology to the community at large

2. World War II
    a.   leading European psychologists fled to the U.S.
    b.   clinical psychologists: assessment and treatment
3. influence on theories: Freud's Thanatos
D. Prejudice as a contextual force
    1. women denied admission to schools, denied jobs
    2. Jews barred from many schools, difficulties finding academic positions so some change their names to secure positions
    3. African American largely denied graduate study altogether, with rare exceptions
    4. 1960-APA made an effort to increase diversity through funding opportunities
    5. effects of prejudice: to this day minorities and women as underrepresented on psychology faculties

VI.   Conceptions of Scientific History
A. The personalistic theory of scientific history: "The view that progress and change in scientific history are attributable to the ideas of unique individuals"
B. The naturalistic theory of scientific history: "The view that progress and change in scientific history are attributable to the Zeitgeist, which makes a culture receptive to some ideas but not to others"
    1. Simultaneous discovery: Darwin and Wallace
    2. Sometimes the discovery made before its time: Whytt
    3. Dominant theories may stifle new thought: journal editors as gatekeepers
C. This text uses both personalistic and naturalistic viewpoints
D. Highlights the importance of the Zeitgeist in the analysis of history

VII.   Schools of Thought in the Evolution of Modern Psychology
A. Wundt
    1. drew together the various philosophical and scientific lines to found psychology
    2. psychology was shaped by his vision
B. The term school of thought "refers to a group of psychologists who become associated ideologically, and sometimes geographically, with the leader of a movement"
C. Thomas Kuhn (1970) The Structure of Scientific Revolutions
    1. paradigm: "an accepted way of thinking within a scientific discipline that provides essential questions and answers"
    2. preparadigmatic phase: the "stage in the development of a science when it is still divided into schools of thought"
    3. paradigmatic phase: "The more mature or advanced stage in the development of a science...when the majority of the scientists agrees on theoretical and methodological issues....a common paradigm or model defines the entire field"
D. Fragmentation characterizes psychology: it is preparadigmatic
E. Schools of thought as protests against the current order that correct the predecessor's errors and then incur their own protest

VIII.   Plan of the Book
    A. Philosophical antecedents of experimental psychology
    B. Physiological antecedents of experimental psychology
    C. Wundt's psychology
    D. Structuralism
    E. Functionalism
    F. Behaviorism
    G. Gestalt psychology
    H. Psychoanalysis
    I. Humanistic psychology
    J. Cognitive psychology
    K. Contemporary developments
        1. evolutionary psychology
        2. cognitive neuroscience
        3. positive psychology

Lecture prompts/Discussion topics for chapter one

- Use a salient recent event and ask your class how that event might currently shape the field of psychology (what gets funded, what gets studied). For examples, the terror attacks of 9/11 may have spurred interest and research in the psychology of terrorism, post-traumatic stress syndrome, psychology of fear, etc. The subsequent invasion of Iraq may have spiked interest in effective repatriation of soldiers, psychological warfare, effective recruiting techniques, etc.

- Have the class suppose that one of them in the room will become a future eminent psychologist. What types of information might future historians of psychology use to piece together their current lives? How might this information differ from the information used to study an eminent psychologist who lived 100 years ago?

Internet Resources for chapter one

Today in the History of Psychology
http://www.cwu.edu/~warren/today.html
    This site provides a listing of a number of historical events in psychology for any day of the year you submit. You can find out what has happened in psychology on your birthday in the past.

Women in Psychology History
http://psychology.okstate.edu/museum/women/cover2.html
    This site provides a listing of a number of women in psychology history, along with photographs and a listing of their accomplishments.

Association for Women in Psychology
http://www.awpsych.org/
    This is a site that provides networking for women in psychology, as well as a list of resources for women psychologists and an email discussion list.

Association for Black Psychologists

http://www.abpsi.org/

>This is a site that provides networking for Black Psychologists, and is an organization whose goal is to have a positive impact on the mental health of Black Americans.

Thomas Kuhn

http://www.des.emory.edu/mfp/Kuhnsnap.html

>This site provides a summary of Kuhn's life and works, and has a nice collection of links including some that summarize *The Structure of Scientific Revolutions.*

Potential answers to chapter one discussion questions

1) What can we learn from studying the history of psychology?

The history of psychology has become a discipline in its own right; psychology departments offered history of psychology courses as early as 1911, there are journals dedicated to publishing history of psychology papers, APA has division 26 (History of Psychology), and 93% of 311 surveyed psychology departments offer a course in History of Psychology. Understanding the history of and therefore the evolution of thought preceding contemporary psychology will help one to understand contemporary psychology. Furthermore, contemporary psychologists differ widely in the topic areas they study, but all psychologists share the history. A study of the history of psychology will bring cohesion to the diverse discipline as a whole.

2) Why can psychologists claim that psychology is one of the oldest scholarly disciplines as well as one of the newest? Explain why modern psychology is a product of both nineteenth-century and twentieth-century thought?

Psychology can trace its roots to the fifth century BC, to the Greek philosophers such as Plato, Aristotle, and Socrates, because we grapple with the same questions they attempted to answer. On the other hand, we could view psychology as emerging when philosophy and physiology merged to include experimentation and empirical methods to answer those questions about 200 years ago. Modern psychology can be considered a product of nineteenth-century thought because this is the time when the field developed its own independent methods and became its own independent discipline. One can also see the influence of the historical context on the formation of the field. The Zeitgeist of the time can have a tremendous influence on what the focus of psychology is at any given time. For example, during the world wars, psychological testing, personnel selection, and engineering were emphasized.

3) In what ways do the data of history differ from the data of science? Give examples of how historical data can be distorted.

History is different from science because historians must find, interpret, and assimilate scraps of information from a variety of sources to try to understand a complete picture. Such data cannot be reconstructed in a laboratory like a scientific experiment can. John Watson burned his letters, manuscripts, and notes before he died. Some papers written by Hermann Ebbinghaus had been lost but were recently found. Another problem relates to the distortion of data through translations. Some of the terms Sigmund Freud used to label phenomena within psychoanalysis lost the original meaning intended by Freud when the terms were mistranslated into English.

Some data of history are best described as being distorted to promote a particular impression of a person. In his autobiography, B.F. Skinner portrayed himself as doing nothing but work while he was a graduate student, although his classmates remember his Ping-Pong playing.

4) In what ways have contextual forces influenced the development of modern psychology?

Psychology has been shaped by historical events. Economic conditions toward the late nineteenth century lead to more psychologists being trained than there were academic positions to employ them. At the same time, the increase in immigrants caused an increase in the number of students needing public education. Psychologists sought to apply their skills to educational settings. Thus, applied psychology mushroomed in America. Wartime has also shaped the field. World war II lead to the migration of researchers and theorists from Europe to the United States and thus the forefront of psychology moved as well. Prejudice and discrimination also shaped the field, as women, African Americans, Jews, and other groups were systematically denied education and employment in psychology.

5) Describe the obstacles faced by women, Jews, and African Americans in pursuing careers in psychology, especially during the first half of the twentieth century.

Women were often denied admission to graduate school or conferment of degrees, and later had a difficult time finding jobs particularly if she was married. Eleanor Gibson, who later won a number of professional awards for her work in perceptual development and learning, was restricted from certain courses and areas on campus when she attended Yale. Such discrimination extended into 1960, when Sandra Scarr was told by the officer interviewing her for admission that most women don't finish their degrees, and the ones that do amount to nothing anyway. Despite such obstacles, women did attain doctoral degrees in psychology. One champion for the education of women was James McKeen Cattell, who supported women frequently, urging scientific societies to include women as members. Largely because of his efforts, the APA was the first scientific society to admit women as members. Mary Whiton Calkins became the first female president of APA in 1905.

Discrimination extended to Jewish psychologists as well. A study of discrimination of Jews at three universities—Harvard, Yale, and Princeton—found widespread practices that excluded Jews from admission. Those Jews who were admitted to colleges were often separated and socially ostracized. Many colleges and universities, including two important to psychology (Johns Hopkins and Clark), had explicit policies to disallow Jewish students. In the face of such discrimination, some Jewish psychologists changed their names, which helped them secure jobs. Isadore Krechevsky became David Krech, David Bakanovsky became David Bakan, and Harry Israel (even though he was a protestant) changed his name to Harry Harlow.

Some chose not to do this, for example Abraham Maslow refused to change his first name to something "less Jewish".

African Americans also faced an enormous amount of discrimination. When Black students were allowed to attend predominantly White universities, they were often not allowed to live on campus or mix socially with White students. Howard University in Washington D.C., a traditionally Black school, provided an education in Psychology for many Black students.

6) How does the process of writing history in any field necessarily restrict the number of people whose work can be singled out for attention?

What gets highlighted in histories are a few individuals or events that have had an impact. By definition, this is a very small percentage of total individuals in a particular field. For example, many contemporary psychologists might be therapists, or might work for corporations. Unless they take the unusual step of publishing their work and ideas, their work will remain invisible to later psychology historians and won't move beyond a small group of colleagues.

7) Describe the differences between personalistic and naturalistic conceptions of scientific history. Explain which approach is supported by cases of simultaneous discovery.

The personalistic conception of scientific history states that science advances because of eminent individuals whose work creates an impact on the field. The naturalistic conception of scientific history is the viewpoint that the intellectual climate (the Zietgeist) fosters the creation of a particular idea. If one person does not discover the idea, another person is likely to. There are many instances of simultaneous and independent discoveries which lends support to this naturalistic conception. For example, Wallace developed the shell of evolutionary theory independent of Darwin and halfway around the world from him.

8) What is the Zeitgeist? How does the Zeitgeist affect the evolution of a science? Compare the growth of a science with the evolution of a living species.

The Zeitgeist is the intellectual spirit of the times, and may be directed by some individuals. Oftentimes journal editors can act as gatekeepers of mainstream ideas and refuse to publish papers that are revolutionary. Psychologist John Garcia tried to publish a paper that challenged prevailing thought on stimulus-response theory. Although the research was solid, he was only able to publish in journals that were less known. The Zeitgeist can inhibit or promote methods of investigation or a discipline's subject matter. Just like species adjust to the demands of the environment, a science will change depending on the Zeitgeist.

9) What is meant by the term "school of thought"? Has the science of psychology reached the paradigmatic stage of development? Why or why not?

A school of thought is when a group of psychologists agree on a subject of study, on methods to use, and approaches to psychology. Thomas Kuhn wrote a book about how sciences develop over time called *The Structure of Scientific Revolution*. According to Kuhn, when a science has produced an accepted way of thinking and has matured, this way of thinking is called a paradigm. Paradigms are present in other science, for example for about 300 years the paradigm in physics was the Galilean-Newtonian framework. Paradigms can also change, in what Kuhn calls a scientific revolution, such as when Einstein's model of physics became the paradigm. Because psychology remains divided, it is considered to be "preparadigmatic"—there is no prevailing school of thought. In fact, many contemporary psychologists criticize the field because of its fragmentation. There is no single view of psychology upon which a majority of psychologists agree.

10) Describe the cyclical process by which schools of thought begin, prosper, and then fail.

In the history of psychology, the early schools of thought rose in opposition to the prevailing schools. Emerging schools would criticize the weaknesses of the previous schools and would address these weaknesses and attempt to redefine psychology, its methods, and its topics of study. If enough people agreed with the new school, the old school was rejected. Some early schools of thought (structuralism, functionalism) no longer exist while other schools (behaviorism, psychoanalysis) still do.

Key terms from chapter one

- **Behaviorism** This school of thought is most associated with Watson and Skinner, which grew in opposition to those interested in conscious experience. Behaviorists were interested in studying only visible and therefore objective behavior. Studies were carefully controlled and experimental as opposed to observational.

- **Cognitive psychology** This is the most recent school to form; its members also study conscious processes, particularly how the mind organizes thoughts.

- **Data Distorted in translations** Translations can lead to a change in meaning of a concept. For example, Freud's *Einfall* was translated into English as *Free Association*, which does not convey the idea of intrusion/invasion Freud intended.

- **Functionalism** The school of psychology that grew in opposition to structuralism, and like structuralism focused on conscious experiences as it relates to evolutionary adaptation. To functionalists, conscious experience should be studied as it happens, and the goal is to determine the utility of consciousness.

- **Gestalt psychology** This school of thought began in Germany then came to the United States. With Gestalt, there is a focus on learning and perception in the context of the real world, and a focus on the wholeness of experience.

- **Historiography** The methods and techniques used to study history, shaped by the fact that the data of history (fragments of what has been left behind and found) are quite different than the data of science (which allows replication).

- **Humanistic psychology** This school of thought grew in opposition to both behaviorism and psychoanalysis, and emphasized the wholeness of human nature and communicated the ability to overcome the past.

- **Lost/Suppressed data** Some historical data has become lost over time (John Watson burning his papers), and some is purposefully suppressed (Freud's biography downplaying his cocaine use).

- **Naturalistic theory** This is the idea that science progresses not because of the work of extraordinary individuals, but rather because the time is ripe for the progression. The Zeitgeist, or intellectual climate, can be both accepting of new discoveries or can dampen a new discovery if it is too revolutionary.

- **Paradigm** A paradigm is an accepted way of thinking in a particular discipline. In physics, for example, Einstein's theories are broadly accepted. This is in contrast to psychology, where there is no broadly accepted psychological ideology.

- **Personalistic theory** This is the idea that the skills and discoveries of specific individuals is what creates new information

- **Psychoanalysis** Most associated with Freud, the focus of psychoanalysis is on the unconscious mind, with application to therapy.

- **School of thought** When a group of psychologists agree on a subject of study, on methods to use, and approaches to psychology we can call this group a school of thought.
- **Self-serving data** The idea that historical participants are motivated to shape how they are presented. For example, in his autobiography Skinner wrote that he did nothing but work in graduate school. At the same time, his graduate student colleagues remember his ping-pong skills.
- **Structuralism** The school of psychology most associated with Titchener, whereby conscious experience is dissected using introspection.
- **Wilhelm Wundt** Broadly known as the father of psychology, he defined what early psychology should be.
- **Zeitgeist** The prevailing spirit of the times which influences the flow of new thought. Sometimes the Zeitgeist is 'right' for an idea and more than one individual has the idea at once, such as Darwin and Wallace developing the theory of evolution independently. At other times the Zeitgeist is 'wrong' for an idea, such as when the Scottish scientist Robert Whytt suggested the idea of the conditioned response in 1763.

TESTBANK

ESSAY

1. Why is it important for psychology students to study the development of psychology?

   ANS:
   Answer not provided.

   PTS: 1

2. Argue that Psychology's roots began 2000 years ago. Now argue that they began 200 years ago. What fields came together to form Psychology?

   ANS:
   Answer not provided.

   PTS: 1   MSC: WWW

3. Define historiography. How do the data of history differ from the data of science? Name and describe the three major difficulties involved in recalling and presenting the data of history.

   ANS:
   Answer not provided.

   PTS: 1

4. Discuss and give one example of each of the contextual forces that influenced the development of psychology.

ANS:
Answer not provided.

PTS: 1

5. Describe, compare, and contrast the personalistic and naturalistic theories as conceptions of scientific history. How could the contributions of Darwin be used to illustrate both?

ANS:
Answer not provided.

PTS: 1   MSC: WWW

6. Define "school of thought" and discuss it in terms of Thomas Kuhn's concept of paradigms in scientific evolution.

ANS:
Answer not provided.

PTS: 1

MULTIPLE CHOICE

7. Psychology is unique among the sciences in its requirement that its students _____.
   a. have a minor in the natural sciences
   b. learn the experimental method
   c. use carefully controlled observations in its procedures
   d. study the history of psychology
   e. have a liberal arts background in the humanities

   ANS: D   PTS: 1   REF: Why Study the History of Psychology?

8. What conclusions can be drawn from the study of the Invisible Gorilla?

   a. All psychology students can multitask when presented with multiple stimuli at one time
   b. Extraordinary events can induce extreme stress when presented to unsuspecting people
   c. It is difficult for people to pay attention to more than one stimulus at a time
   d. Doing homework and watching television at the same time are as efficient as if the two are done separately
   e. Counting can be a difficult task when one is being watched

   ANS: C   PTS: 1   REF: The Invisible Gorilla
   MSC: WWW

9. Division _____ of the American Psychological Association is concerned with the study of the discipline's history.
   a. 1
   b. 2
   c. 26
   d. 32
   e. 42

   ANS: C   PTS: 1   REF: Why Study the History of Psychology?

10. In what year was the American Psychological Association founded?
    a. 1892
    b. 1932
    c. 1952
    d. 1969
    e. 1979

    ANS: A   PTS: 1   REF: Why Study the History of Psychology?

11. Psychology is marked by diversity and divisiveness. The one aspect of the discipline that provides cohesiveness and a common ground for discourse is its _____.
    a. reliance on the experimental method in all its research
    b. focus on the study of overt behavior
    c. use of the hypothetico-deductive method
    d. national organizations (APA and APS)
    e. history

    ANS: E   PTS: 1   REF: Why Study the History of Psychology?
    MSC: WWW

12. Perhaps the most valuable outcome of the study of the history of psychology is that one will learn the _____.
    a. relationships among psychology's ideas, theories, and research strategies
    b. contributions of the classic Greek philosophers
    c. origins of the experimental methods
    d. evolution of the scientist-practitioner model of clinical psychology
    e. issues at the root of the pure versus applied research conflict in psychology

    ANS: A   PTS: 1   REF: Why Study the History of Psychology?

13. According to Schultz & Schultz, a course in the history of psychology is useful because _____.
    a. it helps us to understand why modern psychology has so many different movements
    b. it helps to integrate the areas and issues that constitute modern psychology
    c. it provides a fascinating story on its own
    d. All of the choices are correct
    e. None of the choices are correct

    ANS: D   PTS: 1   REF: Why Study the History of Psychology?

14. As a scientific discipline, psychology is _____.
    a. one of the newest
    b. one of the oldest
    c. the only one to have started in the United States
    d. one of the newest and one of the oldest
    e. None of the choices are correct

    ANS: D   PTS: 1   REF: The Development of Modern Psychology

15. Greek philosophers studied issues involving _____.
    a. motivation
    b. abnormal behavior
    c. learning
    d. thought
    e. All of the choices are correct

    ANS: E   PTS: 1   REF: The Development of Modern Psychology

16. Modern psychology shares which of the following characteristics with ancient Greek philosophy?
    a. An interest in the same kinds of questions about human nature
    b. The development of common methods of research to answer questions about human nature
    c. A reliance upon biology to help in the understanding of human nature
    d. The denial that humans are composed of a physical body and a spiritual soul
    e. None of the choices are correct

    ANS: A   PTS: 1   REF: The Development of Modern Psychology

17. Modern psychology emerged from philosophy approximately _____ years ago.
    a. 100
    b. 150
    c. 200
    d. 250
    e. 300

    ANS: C   PTS: 1   REF: The Development of Modern Psychology

18. The feature of modern psychology that distinguishes it from its antecedents is its _____.
    a. methodology
    b. focus on learning
    c. focus on motivation
    d. focus on abnormal behavior
    e. use of deductive logic

    ANS: A   PTS: 1   REF: The Development of Modern Psychology

19. Until the last quarter of the 19th century, philosophers studied human nature using which of the following methods?
    a. speculation
    b. intuition
    c. generalizations
    d. All of the choices are correct.
    e. None of the choices are correct.

    ANS: D   PTS: 1   REF: The Development of Modern Psychology

20. The new discipline of psychology was the product of the union of _____.
   a. philosophy and ethics
   b. philosophy and physics
   c. physics and biology
   d. physics and physiology
   e. philosophy and physiology

   ANS: E   PTS: 1   REF: The Development of Modern Psychology

21. The hallmark of psychology's separation from philosophy was its reliance on _____.
   a. physics
   b. biology
   c. experimentation
   d. deduction
   e. psychophysics

   ANS: C   PTS: 1   REF: The Development of Modern Psychology
   MSC: WWW

22. Modern psychology differs from philosophy in which of the following ways?
   a. Modern psychology is concerned with the study of mental processes such as learning, memory, and perception. Philosophy is concerned with the study of human nature.
   b. Modern psychology uses objective methods to study questions. Philosophy depends upon speculation and intuition in order to answer questions.
   c. Modern psychology studies only the brain. Philosophy studies only the mind.
   d. Modern psychology is based upon the use of inductive reasoning. Philosophy is based upon the use of deductive reasoning.
   e. None of the choices are correct.

   ANS: B   PTS: 1   REF: The Development of Modern Psychology

23. Psychology became an independent discipline during the _____.
   a. Renaissance
   b. last quarter of the eighteenth century
   c. last quarter of the nineteenth century
   d. first decade of the nineteenth century
   e. first decade of the twentieth century

   ANS: C   PTS: 1   REF: The Development of Modern Psychology

24. The term *historiography* refers to _____.
   a. historical biography
   b. methods used in psychological autopsy
   c. the techniques, principles, and issues involved in historical research
   d. the scientific study of history
   e. the study of the history of psychology

   ANS: C   PTS: 1
   REF: The Data of History: Reconstructing Psychology's Past

25. In contrast to the events that are studied in science, historical events cannot be _____.
    a. used to predict future outcomes
    b. repeated
    c. discovered
    d. analyzed and explained
    e. understood

    ANS: B   PTS: 1
    REF: The Data of History: Reconstructing Psychology's Past

26. The data of history are most accurately depicted or described as _____.
    a. public records
    b. private records
    c. eyewitness testimony
    d. recollections
    e. data fragments

    ANS: E   PTS: 1
    REF: The Data of History: Reconstructing Psychology's Past

27. The approach of the historian of psychology is similar to the approach taken by _____ in the study of their field.
    a. physicists
    b. archaeologists
    c. chemists
    d. economists
    e. None of the choices are correct.

    ANS: B   PTS: 1
    REF: The Data of History: Reconstructing Psychology's Past

28. Which psychologist burned his/her own letters, manuscripts, and research notes before s/he died?
    a. B. F. Skinner
    b. John Watson
    c. Karen Horney
    d. Sigmund Freud
    e. Margaret Washburn

    ANS: B   PTS: 1
    REF: The Data of History: Reconstructing Psychology's Past

29. At least one of Freud's biographers downplayed the extent of Freud's cocaine use. This is an example of _____.
    a. suppressed data
    b. data distorted by translation
    c. lost data
    d. errors of eyewitnesses
    e. a misrepresentation intended to protect Freud's reputation

    ANS: E   PTS: 1
    REF: The Data of History: Reconstructing Psychology's Past

30. An "autobiography" of Jung was evidently written not by Jung but by an assistant who _____.
    a. slandered him personally
    b. altered and/or deleted some of Jung's writings to present him in a manner suiting his family and followers
    c. exaggerated the degree of the break between Freud and Jung
    d. expanded Jung's theories and attributed the expansion to Jung
    e. None of the choices are correct.

    ANS: B   PTS: 1
    REF: The Data of History: Reconstructing Psychology's Past   MSC: WWW

31. Important personal papers by ____ have been misplaced for decades or more.
    a. Ebbinghaus
    b. Fechner
    c. Darwin
    d. All of the choices are correct.
    e. None of the choices are correct.

    ANS: D   PTS: 1
    REF: The Data of History: Reconstructing Psychology's Past

32. The historical treatment of Freud's impact upon psychology is still incomplete because ____.
    a. he changed his ideas so many times
    b. many of his most important works have not been translated into English
    c. many of his papers and letters will not be publicly available until later in the 21st century
    d. All of the choices are correct.
    e. None of the choices are correct.

    ANS: C   PTS: 1
    REF: The Data of History: Reconstructing Psychology's Past

33. The terms ego and id, which do not precisely represent Freud's ideas, are examples of ____.
    a. suppressed data
    b. data distorted by translation
    c. eyewitness errors
    d. lost data
    e. distortions intended to protect Freud's reputation

    ANS: B   PTS: 1
    REF: The Data of History: Reconstructing Psychology's Past

34. Freud's idea "Einfall" was translated to English into the term ____ which means something other than what Freud implied in the original German.
    a. rationalization
    b. free association
    c. penis envy
    d. dream analysis
    e. fixation

    ANS: B   PTS: 1
    REF: The Data of History: Reconstructing Psychology's Past   MSC: WWW

35. Skinner's self-discipline as a student and Freud's being ignored and rejected early in his career indicated that _____.
    a. biographers disregard the real events in favor of fantasy
    b. data of history are true in their original versions
    c. participants may themselves produce biased accounts
    d. translations errors account for most misinterpretations
    e. All of the choices are correct

    ANS: C   PTS: 1
    REF: The Data of History: Reconstructing Psychology's Past

36. To guard against self-serving data and to assess the truth of a person's recollections and reports of events in the history of psychology, the historian should, whenever possible, _____.
    a. collect data from other observers
    b. learn the language in which the person wrote
    c. read newspaper accounts of the events
    d. read others' research publications of that era
    e. reconstruct the event

    ANS: A   PTS: 1
    REF: The Data of History: Reconstructing Psychology's Past

37. Regardless of how objective a science and its practitioners are alleged to be, that science will be influenced by the _____.
    a. scientists' political beliefs
    b. scientists' religious beliefs
    c. policies of the government that funds that science's research
    d. contextual forces of the time
    e. amount of funding it receives

    ANS: D   PTS: 1   REF: Contextual Forces in Psychology

38. The term "Zeitgeist" refers to _____.
    a. the intellectual and cultural climate of the times
    b. a German dessert
    c. the moment of discovery
    d. the moment of change in scientific revolutions
    e. a blizzard of activity

    ANS: A   PTS: 1   REF: Contextual Forces in Psychology

39. The contextual forces in psychology deal with the _____.
    a. paradigms that exist in modern psychology.
    b. social, economic, and political factors that influenced the field.
    c. great individuals who have developed psychology.
    d. attempt of psychology to separate itself from other disciplines such as physiology.
    e. None of the choices are correct.

    ANS: B   PTS: 1   REF: Contextual Forces in Psychology

40. The three contextual forces in the history of psychology were _____.
    a. economic opportunities, wars, and discrimination
    b. famine, pestilence, and death
    c. theory, research, and application
    d. cognition, motivation, and effect
    e. social, political, and economic

    ANS: A   PTS: 1   REF: Contextual Forces in Psychology

41. A surge in the practice of applied psychology occurred in response to the lack of jobs in academic settings for PhDs. Thus, the development of applied psychology was a direct consequence of the _____.
    a. great number of psychologists Wundt trained
    b. political context of Europe
    c. economic context of the United States
    d. fact that the first generation of American psychologists learned all their courses in German and thus could not practice Wundt's psychology
    e. political context of the United States

    ANS: C   PTS: 1   REF: Contextual Forces in Psychology

42. A wave of employment possibilities in applied psychology in the first two decades of the 20th century was partly due to _____.
    a. 700% increases in public school enrollment
    b. more money being spent on defense than on education
    c. the rise of the Veteran's administration Hospital system
    d. less money being spent on education than on defense and welfare combined
    e. All of the choices are correct

    ANS: A   PTS: 1   REF: Contextual Forces in Psychology

43. Which contextual influence on psychology lead to the growth of psychology in the areas of personnel selection, psychological testing, and engineering psychology?
    a. Demands generated by the world wars
    b. Emigration from Germany of the top psychologists when Hitler took power
    c. Prosperity of the 1920s and 1930s in the United States
    d. Psychological needs of combat pilots
    e. Need to provide education for an unexpected surge in the U.S. population

    ANS: A   PTS: 1   REF: Contextual Forces in Psychology

44. On the basis of the destruction associated with World War I, Freud proposed that _____.
    a. humans have the ability to survive any catastrophe
    b. the defense mechanisms are used by humans to distort reality
    c. humans have an instinct for aggression
    d. the id is stronger than the ego in controlling behavior
    e. None of the choices are correct

    ANS: C   PTS: 1   REF: Contextual Forces in Psychology

45. According to the textbook, psychology as a discipline has _____.
    a. engaged in the discriminatory practices that mark American culture as a whole
    b. been substantially more discriminatory against women than have other sciences
    c. been substantially more discriminatory against minorities than have other sciences
    d. focused on the reduction of discrimination since its beginnings
    e. None of the choices are correct

    ANS: A   PTS: 1   REF: Contextual Forces in Psychology

46. Even when some women were admitted to graduate programs in psychology, they still encountered many barriers to their success, such as _____.
    a. being barred from some laboratory facilities
    b. being prevented from using graduate library facilities
    c. being unable to eat in graduate cafeterias
    d. not being allowed to participate in some seminar topics
    e. All of the choices are correct

    ANS: E   PTS: 1   REF: Contextual Forces in Psychology
    MSC: WWW

47. As recently as the 1960s, why were some universities reluctant to admit women to their graduate programs in psychology?
    a. Their graduate admission scores were not as high as those of male applicants.
    b. Their personal lives, in terms of marriage and becoming pregnant, were viewed as obstacles that reduced the likelihood of completion of graduate school.
    c. In the opinion of some influential psychologists, some women would never amount to anything.
    d. There were too many female applicants.
    e. Their personal lives, in terms of marriage and becoming pregnant, were viewed as obstacles that reduced the likelihood of completion of graduate school and, in the opinion of some influential psychologists, some women would never amount to anything.

    ANS: E   PTS: 1   REF: Contextual Forces in Psychology

48. Julian Rotter, a leading personality theorist was told that "_____ simply could not get academic jobs, regardless of their credentials."
    a. African-Americans
    b. women
    c. graduates above the age of 50
    d. Jews
    e. All of the choices are correct.

    ANS: D   PTS: 1   REF: Contextual Forces in Psychology

49. According to your text, it was so difficult for Jewish psychologists to get a job that some resorted to _____.
    a. only applying to traditionally Jewish colleges and universities
    b. changing their religion
    c. lying about their religion
    d. changing their name to something that didn't seem Jewish
    e. None of the choices are true

    ANS: D   PTS: 1   REF: Contextual Forces in Psychology

50. When _____ enrolled as a graduate student at Clark University, the administration arranged a separate dining table for her/him.
    a. Francis Sumner
    b. Margaret Floy Washburn
    c. Kenneth Clark
    d. Mamie Clark
    e. Maslow

    ANS: A   PTS: 1   REF: Contextual Forces in Psychology

51. Kenneth Clark was rejected by the graduate program in psychology at Cornell because the university _____.
    a. could not tolerate Blacks working closely with Whites
    b. had no dormitory facilities for Blacks
    c. had no dining facilities for Blacks
    d. could not have Black males working with White female graduate students
    e. would not confer the PhD on a Black person even if he or she completed the requisite coursework

    ANS: A   PTS: 1   REF: Contextual Forces in Psychology

52. The first African American president of the APA was _____.
    a. Frances Cecil Sumner
    b. Charles Henry Turner
    c. Kenneth Clark
    d. Mamie Phipps Clark
    e. None of the choices are correct

    ANS: C   PTS: 1   REF: Contextual Forces in Psychology
    MSC: WWW

53. Who conducted a research program on racial identity and self-concept issues for Black children that was cited in the 1954 Supreme Court decision to end racial segregation in public schools?
    a. Francis Sumner
    b. James Bayton
    c. Inez Prosser
    d. Kenneth and Mamie Clark
    e. none of the choices are correct

    ANS: D   PTS: 1   REF: Contextual Forces in Psychology

54. History ignores the work of the majority of _____.
    a. women
    b. African-Americans
    c. Jews
    d. white men
    e. all psychologists

    ANS: E   PTS: 1   REF: Contextual Forces in Psychology

55. The _____ theory would support the claim: "Freud was instrumental in discovering psychoanalysis. If not for Freud, no other psychologist would have been able to undercover the human psyche."

    a. Zeitgeist
    b. personalistic
    c. naturalistic
    d. ortgeist
    e. evolution

    ANS: B   PTS: 1   REF: Conceptions of Scientific History
    MSC: WWW

56. "The man makes the times," reflects which view of history?
    a. panpsychic
    b. personalistic
    c. naturalistic
    d. nativist
    e. regressive

    ANS: B   PTS: 1   REF: Conceptions of Scientific History

57. Which theory suggests that "the times make the person"?
    a. naturalistic
    b. personalistic
    c. nativist
    d. particularistic
    e. panpsychic

    ANS: A   PTS: 1   REF: Conceptions of Scientific History

58. Simultaneous discovery favors which view of history?
    a. dynamic
    b. personalistic
    c. naturalistic
    d. recurrent
    e. syncopated

    ANS: C   PTS: 1   REF: Conceptions of Scientific History

59. Darwin and Wallace developed similar theories of evolution independently; Newton and Leibnitz developed the calculus independently; Twitmyer discovered "Pavlovian" conditioning before Pavlov did. Such independent discoveries are attributed to which theory?
    a. syncopated
    b. personalistic
    c. naturalistic
    d. Ortgeist
    e. evolution

    ANS: C   PTS: 1   REF: Conceptions of Scientific History

60. In the 1970s, the publication of the research of John Garcia was significantly delayed because ____.
   a. his work challenged the cognitive psychology school of thought
   b. his work was regarded as poorly done
   c. his findings challenged the prevailing view in stimulus-response (S-R) learning theory
   d. journal editors tend to accept findings that contradict or oppose current thinking
   e. All of the choices are correct

   ANS: C   PTS: 1   REF: Conceptions of Scientific History
   MSC: WWW

61. The editors and editorial boards of journals in psychology are composed of people eminent in their specialty areas and likely to subscribe to tradition and their own viewpoints. Thus, new knowledge may not be published if it is revolutionary. This situation illustrates which theory?
   a. Zeitgeist
   b. personalistic
   c. naturalistic
   d. Ortgeist
   e. evolution

   ANS: C   PTS: 1   REF: Conceptions of Scientific History

62. In the first years of psychology's emergence as a new discipline, which man determined its direction?
   a. James McKeen Cattell
   b. Edward Bradford Titchener
   c. The Unknown Soldier
   d. Wilhelm Wundt
   e. Thomas Kuhn

   ANS: D   PTS: 1
   REF: Schools of Thought in the Evolution of Modern Psychology

63. A school of thought emerges whenever ____.
   a. a group shares a theoretical orientation and investigates similar problems
   b. some person organizes and markets several compatible themes or practices, as did Wundt and Watson
   c. a group at a particular college or university focuses on a particular problem, such as the "Würzburg school"
   d. a college or university adopts a particular orientation, such as behaviorism at Harvard or the "Chicago school" of functionalism
   e. a college or university adopts a single methodology, such as the experimental psychology program at the University of Illinois

   ANS: A   PTS: 1
   REF: Schools of Thought in the Evolution of Modern Psychology

64. The stage in the development of a science when it is still divided into schools of thought is called ____.
   a. paradigmatic
   b. preparadigmatic
   c. revolutionary
   d. a scientific revolution
   e. messy

   ANS: B   PTS: 1
   REF: Schools of Thought in the Evolution of Modern Psychology

65. Which eminent historian called the process of replacing one paradigm with another a scientific revolution?
   a. E.G. Boring
   b. Gordon Allport
   c. Duane Schultz
   d. Thomas Kuhn
   e. John Garcia

   ANS: D   PTS: 1
   REF: Schools of Thought in the Evolution of Modern Psychology

66. Kuhn (1970) defines a paradigm as ____.
   a. an instance of agreement on theory and methodology by the science's practitioners.
   b. a model that describes a scientific phenomenon.
   c. a model that explains a scientific phenomenon.
   d. the reconciliation of disparate views on the proper subject matter of the field.
   e. the ultimate goal of any science but which is an ideal and will never be realized.

   ANS: A   PTS: 1
   REF: Schools of Thought in the Evolution of Modern Psychology

67. In Kuhn's philosophy of science, when Einstein's theory of relativity replaced Galilean-Newtonian physics, a(n) ____ occurred.
   a. Zeitgeist
   b. Ortgeist
   c. paradigm
   d. scientific revolution
   e. school of thought

   ANS: D   PTS: 1
   REF: Schools of Thought in the Evolution of Modern Psychology
   MSC: WWW

68. Currently, psychology ____.
   a. has reached the paradigmatic stage
   b. has been described as a sequence of failed paradigms
   c. may be more fragmented than at any time in its history
   d. has been described as a sequence of failed paradigms and may be more fragmented than at any time in its history
   e. None of the choices are correct

   ANS: D   PTS: 1
   REF: Schools of Thought in the Evolution of Modern Psychology

69. The various schools of thought in psychology have served well as systems to be opposed. In each case, ____ was the consequence.
   a. a new paradigm
   b. a new school of thought
   c. absorption into the mainstream
   d. a new and unique methodology
   e. a new definition of "mind"

   ANS: B   PTS: 1
   REF: Schools of Thought in the Evolution of Modern Psychology

70. The school of thought that deals with conscious experience as it is dependent on the experiencing person is the _____ school.
    a. structuralist
    b. functionalist
    c. Gestalt
    d. humanistic
    e. cognitive

    ANS: A   PTS: 1   REF: Plan of the Book

71. The school of thought that deals with how the conscious mind enables and facilitates one's adaptation to one's environment is the _____ school.
    a. structuralist
    b. functionalist
    c. Gestalt
    d. humanistic
    e. cognitive

    ANS: B   PTS: 1   REF: Plan of the Book

72. The school of thought that focuses on the processes of knowing and thus represents a return to the study of conscious processes is the _____ school.
    a. structuralist
    b. functionalist
    c. Gestalt
    d. cognitive
    e. humanistic

    ANS: D   PTS: 1   REF: Plan of the Book

73. The school of thought that is distinct in its focus on the role of the unconscious in determining behavior is the _____ school.
    a. functionalist
    b. psychoanalytic
    c. behaviorist
    d. Gestalt
    e. cognitive

    ANS: B   PTS: 1   REF: Plan of the Book

74. The school of thought that focuses on learning and perception and emphasizes the combination of elements to produce new patterns is the _____ school.
    a. structuralist
    b. behaviorist
    c. Gestalt
    d. cognitive
    e. Würzburg

    ANS: C   PTS: 1   REF: Plan of the Book

75. The school of thought that deals solely with observable behaviors that can be described in objective terms is the _____ school.
    a. structuralist
    b. behaviorist
    c. Gestalt
    d. cognitive
    e. humanistic

    ANS: B   PTS: 1   REF: Plan of the Book

76. The school of thought that emphasizes the study of conscious experience and the wholeness of human nature is the _____ school.
    a. structuralist
    b. behaviorist
    c. Gestalt
    d. cognitive
    e. humanistic

    ANS: E   PTS: 1   REF: Plan of the Book

TRUE/FALSE

77. A course in the history of psychology is a typical requirement for only 10% of undergraduate degree programs in psychology.

    ANS: F   PTS: 1   REF: Why Study the History of Psychology?

78. Virtually every modern science includes a course on its history as a part of its curriculum.

    ANS: F   PTS: 1   REF: Why Study the History of Psychology?

79. The authors of your textbook argue that the formal study of the history of psychology is the most systematic way to integrate the areas and issues that constitute modern psychology.

    ANS: T   PTS: 1   REF: Why Study the History of Psychology?
    MSC: WWW

80. Psychology is one of the oldest and one of the newest scholarly disciplines.

    ANS: T   PTS: 1   REF: The Development of Modern Psychology

81. It can be argued that psychology today studies and debates some of the same questions as those that concerned the philosophers of ancient Greece.

    ANS: T   PTS: 1   REF: The Development of Modern Psychology
    MSC: WWW

82. The earliest possible starting point for psychology is approximately 1,000 years ago.

    ANS: F   PTS: 1   REF: The Development of Modern Psychology

83. The distinction between modern psychology and its roots has more to do with the kinds of questions asked than with the methods used.

    ANS: F   PTS: 1   REF: The Development of Modern Psychology

84. Reconstruction refers to the principles, methods, and philosophical issues of historical research.

    ANS: F   PTS: 1
    REF: The Data of History: Reconstructing Psychology's Past

85. The data of history are much like the data of science.

    ANS: F   PTS: 1
    REF: The Data of History: Reconstructing Psychology's Past

86. Although difficult to do, the data of history can be reconstructed or replicated.

    ANS: F   PTS: 1
    REF: The Data of History: Reconstructing Psychology's Past

87. The papers and diaries of Ebbinghaus and Fechner were found more than 70 years after their deaths.

    ANS: T   PTS: 1
    REF: The Data of History: Reconstructing Psychology's Past

88. The written record of Darwin's life and work is now complete.

    ANS: F   PTS: 1
    REF: The Data of History: Reconstructing Psychology's Past

89. Jung wrote his autobiography.

    ANS: F   PTS: 1
    REF: The Data of History: Reconstructing Psychology's Past

90. The terms id, ego, and superego were improperly translated from German.

    ANS: T   PTS: 1
    REF: The Data of History: Reconstructing Psychology's Past   MSC: WWW

91. Freud's original term for free association was Einfall, which means an intrusion or an invasion.

    ANS: T   PTS: 1
    REF: The Data of History: Reconstructing Psychology's Past

92. In his autobiography, Skinner recounts that his graduate days at Harvard were filled with endless work.

    ANS: T   PTS: 1
    REF: The Data of History: Reconstructing Psychology's Past

93. Current evidence demonstrates that Freud's works were ignored or even renounced by intellectuals during his lifetime.

 ANS: F   PTS: 1   REF: Contextual Forces in Psychology

94. The term Zeitgeist refers to the spirit of the times.

 ANS: T   PTS: 1   REF: Contextual Forces in Psychology

95. Three examples of contextual forces in psychology are economic opportunity, war, and prejudice.

 ANS: T   PTS: 1   REF: Contextual Forces in Psychology

96. By 1960, the prejudice against women entering prestigious graduate schools of psychology had ended.

 ANS: F   PTS: 1   REF: Contextual Forces in Psychology

97. The first African American to earn a doctoral degree in psychology was Kenneth Clark.

 ANS: F   PTS: 1   REF: Contextual Forces in Psychology

98. Instances of simultaneous discoveries of theory support the naturalistic concept of scientific history.

 ANS: T   PTS: 1   REF: Conceptions of Scientific History
 MSC: WWW

99. The Zeitgeist is most influential in the naturalistic theory of history.

 ANS: T   PTS: 1   REF: Conceptions of Scientific History

100. The effects of the Zeitgeist in inhibiting or delaying the dissemination and/or acceptance of a discovery operate at a cultural level but also within a science itself.

 ANS: T   PTS: 1   REF: Conceptions of Scientific History

101. In Kuhn's (1970) view, psychology is at the paradigm stage because it has several models from which one might choose.

 ANS: F   PTS: 1
 REF: Schools of Thought in the Evolution of Modern Psychology

102. A new school of thought may overcome its opposition not because the opposing points of view become convinced to accept the new thinking, but because adherents of the old school of thought die off.

 ANS: T   PTS: 1
 REF: Schools of Thought in the Evolution of Modern Psychology
 MSC: WWW

Chapter 2

Philosophical Influences on Psychology

In 1739, a new machine was showcased in France that captured the intellectual spirit, or Zeitgeist, of the seventeenth to nineteenth centuries. The "defecating duck" was revolutionary in that it could quack, rise up on its legs, stretch out its neck, grab and swallow grain, and defecate just like a live duck. This invention is but one example of the new machines that were created for daily living and amusement. Such machines demonstrate mechanism, which is the idea that all natural processes are mechanically determined and can be understood by insight in chemistry and physics. Galileo and Newton started this doctrine with their conceptualization of the clockwork universe, which suggests that every physical effect is derived from a direct cause. Thus, if the cause could be fully understood, one would be able to make predictions. This intellectual atmosphere directly influenced the direction that psychology would eventually take by incorporating new technology into the methods and practice of science. With technology came increased precision. The scientific focus of the time was on observation, experimentation, and measurement.

Another new invention of the seventeenth century was the mechanical clock, which was referred to as the "mother of machines." Clocks brought about regularity, order, and predictability to all levels of social class and economic circumstance. They also ushered in the idea that precision and regularity can apply to the universe. It was believed that a clockwork universe, once set in motion by God, would function with order, regularity, and predictability. This set the tone for determinism, "the doctrine that acts are determined by past events," as well as reductionism, attempting to reduce complex phenomena into simpler components.

Machines built to imitate humans and other animals were called automata. The "defecating duck" was one such machine, and there were many more, such as a five and a half foot tall automaton that looked like a man and could actually play a flute. Philosophers began to incorporate the idea of mechanism and automata in their approach to understanding human nature. Many believed that mechanical laws govern human behavior, and the methods used to investigate the universe can be used to investigate human behavior. The Zeitgeist of the mechanical man that pervaded science and philosophy was echoed in literature, with Mary Shelley's *Frankenstein* and L. Frank Baum's *The Wizard of Oz* books.

Charles Babbage exemplified the intellectual spirit of the time when he invented a "difference calculator" that could imitate human mental actions like playing chess and conducting mathematical calculations. It is the direct forerunner of the modern computer and started the idea of "artificial intelligence". One of Babbage's supporters was Ada Lovelace, who described Babbage's machine and how it worked. She identifies a fundamental difference between a thinking machine and a human, that is, a machine cannot create something new, it can only do what it is programmed to do.

Until the seventeenth century, when empiricism introduced new ideas to be formed through observation, prevailing thought was dictated by the dogmatism of the church. Although many scholars contributed to the introduction of psychology, Rene Descartes is credited as having inaugurated modern psychology. Descartes' approach to philosophy was to discard all that he knew and to build his knowledge from scratch. One of the issues he tackled was the mind-body problem: "the question of the distinction between mental and physical qualities." If the mind and body are different, then how do they interact with each other?

Descartes agreed with previous thought that mind and body are different. Unlike his predecessors who thought that mind controlled body, he believed in a mutual interaction, which means that the body also controls the mind to some extent. This placed more importance on the body's functioning and allowed it to become subject of scientific inquiry.

Being influenced by the automata and machines of his day, Descartes believed that the body could be explained mechanically. For example, he thought that some movements are not governed by the conscious experience but by stimulus outside of the body that elicits an involuntary response, which was later termed the *reflex action theory*. If the body can be described mechanically, then human behavior can be predictable; like with other machines, all movements (effects) happen because of causes and as long as one knows the causes one can predict the effects.

Descartes was a dualist, believing that the mind and body were separate entities. This left him with the problem of how they interact. He looked to the brain, and saw that structures were duplicated in each hemisphere, except for the pineal body. For this reason, he saw this structure as the vehicle through with the mind and body interact. Perhaps his biggest influence on psychology comes through Descartes' *doctrine of ideas*. He believed the mind had two types of ideas; derived ideas, which are "produced by the direct application of an external stimulus" and innate ideas, which "arise from the mind or consciousness, independent of sensory experiences."

Auguste Comte was also influential to modern psychology when he founded positivism (an ideal system based exclusively on facts that are objectively observable and not debatable). Comte believed that while the physical sciences had already reached a positivist stage, the social sciences would have to abandon metaphysical questions and explanations in order to do so. Similarly, the doctrine of materialism believes that "the facts of the universe could be described in physical terms and explained by the properties of matter and energy." On the other hand, the doctrine of empiricism proposed that "all knowledge is derived from sensory experience." Positivism, materialism, and empiricism all provided some of the philosophical basis for psychology, yet empiricism played the major role.

One of the main British empiricists was John Locke. His major influence on psychology is his book *An Essay Concerning Human Understanding*, which "marks the formal beginning of British empiricism." He rejects Descartes' innate ideas, and says that at birth the human mind is a *tabula rasa*, or a blank slate, and we acquire knowledge through our experiences. Locke defines two types of experiences: sensation (direct sensory input), and reflection (interpretations of sensations to form higher-level thinking). These experiences combine to form ideas. The first are simple ideas, which come from both sensation and reflection and can't be broken down further. The second are complex ideas, which are combinations of simple ideas. This sets the ground for *association*, which psychologists later call learning. According to Locke, everything begins with the objects in space and our sensations of them. Such objects have two qualities: primary qualities, which exist in the object whether we perceive them or not (such as size and shape), and secondary qualities, which exist not in the object but in our perception of it ("such as color, odor, sound, and taste"). Locke, like Galileo before him, was making the distinction between what is subjective and what is objective and thus highlighting the importance of human perception.

George Berkeley addressed the question of whether any real differences in stimulus existed. Berkeley believed that there were only secondary qualities, and all knowledge is a function of perception (this position later is called mentalism). With this conception, we can never know the real world in an objective way. However, Berkeley believed that stability exists because God constantly perceives the world. For example, when a tree falls in the forest, it still makes a sound even if no one is around to hear it, because God perceives the sound.

David Hartley, with his work on association, proposed that repetition is necessary to form associations. He believed that ideas occurring simultaneously are associated, and the more frequently those ideas occur together, the stronger the association. He applied the theory of association to explain mental activities, such as memory, reasoning, and emotion, and believed that because of repetition, these mental activities are strengthened in adulthood. He also suggested that nerves were solid (not hollow as Descartes thought) and vibrated to transmit messages.

James Mill applied mechanism to the mind with the aim to prove that the mind was a machine (in contrast to the previous philosophers who stated that the mind was *like* a machine). He believed that the mind simply responds to external stimuli, makes associations passively, and can be studied by reducing it down to elements. His son, John Stuart Mill, said that the mind was not passive but active in associating ideas. He said that complex ideas are more than just the combination of simple ones, because they take on new qualities. This idea is known as *creative synthesis*. His approach applies the laws of chemistry to the mind; "mental chemistry" suggests that simple ideas combine to form complex ideas which are more than just the sum of their parts.

The rise of empiricism lead to a focus on sensation, conscious experience, mental processes, and association of ideas. The methods used to analyze these principles became atomistic, mechanistic, and positivistic.

Outline

I. The Defecating Duck and the Glory of France
   A. In 1739, mechanical duck was a popular marvel, because it:
      1. quacks
      2. rises up on its legs
      3. stretches out its neck
      4. picks up and swallows grain
      5. defecates
   B. Example of the newfound fascination with machines
II. The Spirit of Mechanism
   A. 17th to 19th century Zeitgeist
      1. reflected in the various machines used in daily life
      2. reflected in amusement with mechanical figures that mimicked human action,
      3. fascination with the mechanical clock
      4. considerable advances of technology
      5. reflected in the view of the universe as an enormous machine
      6. reflected in mechanism: all natural processes are mechanically determined and can be explained by the laws of physics and chemistry
      7. originated in physics (then called natural philosophy) with the work of Galileo and Newton (who was trained as a clockmaker)
         a. Galileo: matter is comprised of atoms that affect one another by direct contact
         b. Newton: movement was not by actual physical contact but by forces that attract and repel atoms
      8. implies every physical effect follows from a direct cause, thus it is measurable, predictable, orderly

9. have distinguishing features of science
    a. observation
    b. experimentation
    c. measurement
        (1) describing all phenomena with a numerical value
        (2) measuring devices become more precise
        (3) precise measurements (taken by timepieces) particularly important for observations, navigation, astronomy

III. The Clockwork Universe
  A. Clock as metaphor for mechanism
    1. produced in great quantity and variety
    2. clocks were
      a. available to all levels of society (clocks built into public buildings)
      b. regular
      c. predictable
      d. precise
    3. a model of the universe
      a. Robert Boyle, Johannes Keller, and Rene Descartes believed that the harmony and order of the universe was analogous to the reliability or regularity of the clock
      b. Christian von Wolff: "The universe behaves no differently than a clockwork"
      c. Johann Christophe Gottsched, von Wolff's student, elaborated on this premise
  B. Determinism and reductionism
    1. determinism: acts are caused by past events
    2. explanation for the universe using the model of a clock
      a. its parts function with order and regularity
      b. we can understand its functions and functioning
      c. we can predict changes that will occur from its past and present characteristics
    3. reductionism: phenomena can be explained by reduction to their basic components
      a. reduce a clock to its components such as springs and wheels to understand its functioning
      b. implies that analyzing or reducing the universe to its simplest parts will produce understanding of it
      c. characteristic of every science, including psychology
  C. Automata: mechanical devices built to imitate human and animal movement
    1. similar designs were made by ancient Greeks, Arabs, Chinese
    2. complex machines simulated human/animal behaviors
      a. Examples include: defecating duck, animated flute player, monk, harpsichord player
    3. clockwork technology led to dreams of creating artificial beings
  D. People as machines
    1. model of human beings adopted from the creation of automata: the body as a machine made by God
    2. suggests that human functioning and behavior are governed by mechanical law

PHILOSOPHICAL INFLUENCES ON PSYCHOLOGY   33

3. implies experimental and quantitative methods of physics can be applied to the study of human nature
4. Julien de La Mettrie: the individual as an enlightened machine, like a watch that winds its own string
5. culturally pervasive: in the general population, in literature, in gardens, in clock towers

E. The calculating engine
1. invented by Charles Babbage: British mathematician
2. called "the difference engine," the calculator did basic math, had memory, played games
3. first successful attempt to duplicate human cognitive processes
4. after 10 years, Babbage turned to work on a larger "analytical engine," programmed through punch cards with separate memory and information processing capacity and printed output
5. cost overruns caused the British government to cancel funding
6. Ada Lovelace, age 18 and a math prodigy, published explanations of its functioning, potential uses, philosophical implications, and limitations in terms of originality or creativity.
7. although Babbage thought the significance of his achievements would never be sufficiently acknowledged, the first completely automatic computer was recognized (in 1946) as the realization of Babbage's dream
8. Babbage developed a form of artificial intelligence that was ahead of his time

IV. The Beginnings of Modern Science
A. Empiricism: the pursuit of knowledge through observation and experimentation
1. replaced dogma and church doctrine as ruling forces of inquiry
2. Descartes: symbol of the transition to free scientific inquiry and forerunner of modern psychology

B. René Descartes (1596-1650)
1. born in France
2. inherited wealth allowed him to travel and pursue intellectual and scientific interests
3. attracted to applied research
4. had life-changing dreams
   a. "spirit of truth" convinced him that mathematical principles can be applied to all sciences and produce certainty of knowledge made up his mind to accept as true only those things of which he was completely sure
5. lived a life of solitude, moved frequently, always lived near a Catholic church and a university
6. died in Sweden, tutoring Queen Christina in philosophy
7. 16 years later friends shipped a coffin to return his body to France
   a. coffin too short; head cut off and left in Sweden
   b. finger cut off by French ambassador for a souvenir
   c. ceremonious burial in Paris
   d. skull passed among Swedish collectors for 150 years and eventually buried in France

V. The Contributions of Descartes: Mechanism and the Mind-Body Problem
    A. The mind-body problem
        1. "Are mind and body—the mental world and the material world—distinct from each other?"
        2. pre-Descartes direction of influence: mind influences body, but not vice versa; much like how a puppet (body) and puppeteer (mind) are joined
        3. Descartes: a mutual interaction
        4. functions previously attributed to mind (reproduction, movement) now attributed to body
        5. only function of mind is thought
        6. diverted attention from the soul to the scientific study of mind Descartes shifted the methods of intellectuals: from subjective metaphysical analysis to objective observation and experimentation
    B. The nature of the body
        1. body is matter
            a. has extension and capacity for movement
            b. laws of physics and mechanics account for and explain its movement
        2. body is a machine
            a. nerves are pipes
            b. muscles and tendons are engines and springs
            c. action not voluntary but due to external objects
        3. involuntary movements
            a. undulatio reflexa—movement not determined by conscious will
            b. reflex action theory: external object can bring about an involuntary response (precursor to S-R psychology)
        4. human behavior is predictable if inputs are known
        5. support from physiology
            a. circulation of the blood
            b. muscles work in opposing pairs
            c. sensation and movement depend on the nerves
        6. support of Christian thought
            a. animals do not possess souls, feelings, immortality, thought processes, or free will
            b. animal behavior: explained totally in mechanistic terms
    C. The mind-body interaction
        1. mind
            a. is nonmaterial
            b. is unitary (interacts with body at a single point)
            c. thinks, perceives, wills
            d. provides information about the external world
            e. influences and is influenced by the body
            f. has the brain as its focal point
        2. conarium (pineal gland)
            a. single and unitary
            b. material
            c. the site of the mind-body interaction

3. method of interaction
    a.   movement of animal spirits in nerve tubes impress upon the conarium
    b.   from this impression the mind produces a sensation
    c.   the reverse activity produces mental effects on the body, e.g., voluntary movement

D. The doctrine of ideas
  1. derived ideas
    a.   occur from the immediate application of an external stimulus such as the sound of a bell or sight of a tree
    b.   are products of the experiences of the senses (e.g., the tone, the image)
  2. innate ideas
    a.   develop from within the mind rather than through the senses
    b.   led eventually to the nativistic theory of perception, i.e., perception is innate
    c.   influenced Gestalt psychology
    d.   inspired opposition by Locke, Helmholtz, Wundt

E. Authors' summary of Descartes' contributions to the development of psychology
  1. the mechanistic conception of the body
  2. the theory of reflex action
  3. the mind-body interaction
  4. the localization of mental functions in the brain
  5. the doctrine of innate ideas

VI. Philosophical Foundations of the New Psychology: Positivism, Materialism, Empiricism
  A. European philosophy: foundations of the science of psychology
    1. Comte (1798-1857): positivism
      a.   "The doctrine that recognizes only natural phenomena or facts that are objectively observable."
      b.   in the attempt to review all human knowledge, limited his work to scientific facts refers to the "objects of sense," rather than "nonsense"
    2. materialism: "The doctrine that considers the facts of the universe to be sufficiently explained in physical terms by the existence and nature of matter."
      a.   Consciousness explained in terms of physics and chemistry
      b.   mental processes due to physical properties: brain anatomy and physiology
    3. empiricism: "all knowledge is derived from sensory experience."
      a.   knowledge is from sensory experience
      b.   contrasts with Descartes' nativism (innate knowledge)
      c.   empiricists include John Locke, George Berkeley, David Hartley, James Mill, and John Stuart Mill
    4. positivism, materialism, and empiricism were the philosophical cornerstones of the emerging science of psychology, with empiricism having the greatest   impart

B. John Locke (1632-1704)
   1. life
      a.   at first an indifferent student, amusing himself with dabbling
      b.   became serious when exposed to natural philosophy
      c.   taught Greek, writing, and philosophy and practiced medicine in England
      d.   interested in politics, secretary, confidant, and friend of the Earl of Shaftsbury
      e.   fled to Holland when the Earl, but not he, was in a plot to overthrow King Charles II
      f.   upon return to England, resumed politics, wrote education, religion, and economics books
      g.   particularly concerned with religious freedom and self-government
      h.   advocated government liberalism; influenced the authors of the American Declaration of Independence
      i.   An Essay Concerning Human Understanding (1690)
         (1) represented 20 years of work
         (2) "marks the formal beginning of British empiricism"
   2. How does the mind acquire knowledge?
      a.   rejected existence of innate ideas
      b.   any apparent innateness due to early learning and habit
      c.   all knowledge is empirically derived: mind as a tabula rasa (Aristotle's concept) or blank slate
   3. sensation and reflection: two kinds of experiences
      a.   sensations: input from external physical objects experienced as sense impressions, which operate on the mind
      b.   reflections: mind operates on the sense impressions to produce ideas
      c.   sensations precede reflections
      d.   reflection:
         (1) recollection of past sensory impressions
         (2) combinations yield abstractions and other higher-level ideas
   4. In Their Own Words: Original Source Material on Empiricism from An Essay Concerning Human Understanding (1690)
      a.   illustrates "how...theorists presented their ideas and acquaint you with the explanatory style previous generations of students were required to study."
      b.   all knowledge is founded from experience
      c.   external observation (sense qualities) and internal operations of the mind are the "Fountains of Knowledge" from which all ideas flow
      d.   sense qualities (sensations): "Yellow, White, Heat, cold, Soft, Hard, Bitter, Sweet"
      e.   perceiving the operations of the mind (reflections): "Perception, Thinking, Doubting, Believing, Reasoning, Knowing, Willing, and all the different actings of our own minds...."
      f.   sensation and reflection, "are, to me, the only Originals from whence all our Ideas take their beginnings."

5. simple ideas and complex ideas
    a.   simple
        (1) arise from either sensation or reflection
        (2) "received passively from the mind"
        (3) "cannot be analyzed or reduced to even simpler ideas"
    b.   complex
        (1) creation of new ideas through reflection
        (2) combinations of simple ideas
        (3) can be analyzed and/or reduced

6. theory of association
    a.   association = learning
    b.   linking of simple ideas/elements into complex ones
    c.   laws of association akin to laws of mechanics; mind = machine

7. primary and secondary qualities
    a.   primary qualities: objective, exist independently of being experienced (perceived)
        (1) object size
        (2) object shape
    b.   secondary qualities: subjective, exist in the experience of the object
        (1) color, odor, sound, taste, warmth or coldness
        (2) a feather tickles because of our reaction to it, not the feather itself
    c.   only primary qualities exist apart from the perceiver

C. George Berkeley (1685 – 1753)
  1. perception is the only reality
    a.   primary qualities do not exist if not perceived
    b.   mentalism: "The doctrine that all knowledge is a function of mental phenomena and dependent on the perceiving or experiencing person."
    c.   perception as subjective; experience does not mirror external reality
    d.   physical world is the summation of our sensations
    e.   therefore, we never know physical objects exactly
    f.   apparent independence, stability, and consistency in material objects arises from God, the permanent perceiver
  2. the association of sensations is mechanical
    a.   knowledge is constructed from simple ideas and held together by associations
    b.   depth perception comes from experience of eyes accommodating and converging as we move toward or away from objects

D. David Hartley (1705-1757)
  1. association by contiguity; (Hartley's basic law of association)
    a.   ideas or sensations that occur together, simultaneously or successively, become associated
    b.   contiguity explains memory, reasoning, emotion, voluntary and involuntary actions

2. also law of association by repetition
    a. "The notion that the more frequently two ideas occur together, the more readily they will be associated."
    b. explains why as we reach adulthood, higher systems of thought are developed
3. empiricist, like Locke
    a. developmental approach: adult thinking, judging, and reasoning can be reduced to earlier occurring simple ideas
    b. the first to apply a theory of association to explain all types of mental activity
4. influence of mechanism
    a. applied mechanical principles to physiological processes that underlie psychological processes
    b. vibrations in solid nerves transmit impulses throughout the body
    c. set in motion smaller vibrations in brain which are the physiological counterparts of ideas

E. James Mill (1773-1836)
    1. more radical perspective: the mind is a machine
        a. his goal: to destroy the idea of subjective or psychic activities
        b. like a clock--passive, acted on by external stimuli and operated by "internal physical forces" no place for free will (see Skinner's behaviorism) or spontaneity
        c. mind is to be studied by method of analysis to identify its elements (see Wundt, Titchener)
        d. mental elements: sensations and ideas
        e. extremely mechanistic
        f. complex ideas solely due to contiguity alone; association
            (1) may be simultaneous or successive
            (2) is automatic and passive
        g. the mind has no creative function
        h. agreed with Locke that the mind is a blank slate at birth, upon which experience builds

F. John Stuart Mill (1806 – 1873)
    1. life
        a. treated by his father, James, as a blank slate; unceasingly drilled with hours and hours of facts
        b. by age 3 could read Plato in Greek
        c. was a child prodigy who was clinically depressed by 21
        d. Harriet Taylor was the love of his life
        e. championed women's rights
    2. mental chemistry
        a. complex ideas are more than the sum of simple ideas
        b. creative synthesis: a combination of mental elements always produces some distinct quality
        c. his model: research in chemistry rather than physics
        d. called his approach to the association of ideas "mental chemistry"

3. argued it is possible to study the mind scientifically
4. proposed the field of ethology, "devoted to factors that influence the development of the human personality"

VII. Contributions of Empiricism to Psychology
A. Methods of approach: atomistic, mechanistic, positivistic
B. Emphases of empiricism
1. primary role of sensation
2. analysis of conscious experience into elements
3. synthesis of elements through association
4. focus on conscious processes
C. Mid-19th century: philosophy augmented by the methods of experimental physiology

Lecture prompts/Discussion topics for chapter two

- Ask the class to debate some of the big questions in philosophy, such as: What is the difference between a plant, and animal, and a human? The distinctions seem obvious until the issue is debated. Much of students' thinking will likely reflect the debates in philosophy and psychology, and the animal/human difference will reappear with psychologists' use of animals in research later in the course. Other questions are:
  o Does every event have a cause?
  o Are there types of consciousness?

- How is Babbage's machine the same as and different from human thinking? Again, students' thinking may reflect the discussions that later come up in the course with cognitive psychology (Turing test, Searle's Chinese room).

- Suppose I built a sophisticated automaton that looked very human and could physically replicate human behavior and physiological systems. What could you do (what tests could you perform) to determine if a person you are interacting with is a human being or my automaton? For that matter, what could you do to "prove" that other people have consciousness (what separates people from sophisticated robots)?

Internet Resources for chapter two

The Ancient Philosophy Society
http://www.ancientphilosophysociety.org/
For those interested in learning about the ancient philosophers, this society provides a discussion forum for scholars.

Automata: Automata from the 13th to 19th centuries
http://www.museumstuff.com/learn/topics/automata::sub::Automata_From_The_13th_To_19th_Centuries
Descriptions of automata from the 13th to 19th centuries.

Charles Babbage Institute
http://www.cbi.umn.edu/
This "is an archives and research center dedicated to preserving the history of information technology and promoting and conducting research in the field." It has a very nice page of extensive information about the life and work of Charles Babbage with links for even more information.

The Internet Encyclopedia of philosophy
http://www.iep.utm.edu/
> This site provides a number of articles about philosophy. It is an encyclopedia in the truest sense, in that article titles run from A Priori to Slavoj Zizek

The Society for Philosophy and Psychology
http://www.class.uh.edu/cogsci/spp/spphp.html
> The purpose of this site is "to promote interaction between philosophers, psychologists and other cognitive scientists on issues of common concern."

Potential answers to chapter two discussion questions

1) Why was the defecating duck such a sensation in Paris in 1739? What did it have to do with the development of the new psychology?
The duck could quack, rise up on its legs, stretch out its neck, grab and swallow grain, and defecate. It was but one example of the advances in technology. Replication of such complex actions performed by machines was unheard of at the time. At the same time, new machines were created to assist in daily living and amusement, including the mechanical clock. Such amazing machines captured the spirit and philosophy of mechanism, which is the idea that all natural processes can be explained in terms of the natural laws of physics and chemistry. This provided a way to study human beings using scientific methods.

2) Explain the concept of mechanism. How did it come to be applied to human beings?
Mechanism is the idea that all natural processes can be explained in terms of the natural laws of physics and chemistry. This provided a way to study human beings using scientific methods, because this means that all things can be explained using natural laws, including human behavior.

3) How did the development of clocks and automata relate to the ideas of determinism and reductionism?
Clocks and automata were sensations during seventeenth century Europe, and were built with amazing variety of size and levels of elaborateness. Their popularity represented the Zeitgeist of the time, which was mechanism. Mechanism led to the belief that the precision and regularity of clockworks must also apply to the universe. If true, a clockwork universe, once set in motion by God, would function continuously and seamlessly without any interference. This set the tone for determinism, "the doctrine that acts are determined by past events," as well as reductionism, attempting to reduce complex phenomena into simpler components.

4) Why were clocks considered to be models for the physical universe?
Clocks are the prototypical example of mechanism in the seventeenth century. They become the model for the physical universe because of their "regularity, predictability, and precision." It was believed that the universe operated under the same laws as do clocks, and could be understood, like a clock could, if it was reduced to its basic elements (reductionism). It was also believed that the universe was predictable, as are clockworks where you can see the cause and effect of all actions (determinism).

5) What were the implications of Babbage's calculating engine for the new psychology? Describe the contributions of Ada Lovelace to Babbage's work.

Charles Babbage, who was influenced by the automata and clockworks of his day, invented a mathematical calculator that could also play chess and other games, and had the capacity for an intermediate memory. It is the direct forerunner of the modern computer and the idea of "artificial intelligence." One of Babbage's supporters was Ada Lovelace, a self-educated mathematician (unusual for her day) who published a description of Babbage's machine and how it worked. In this description she also identifies a fundamental difference between a thinking machine and a human, that is, that a machine cannot create something new, it can only do what it is programmed to do.

6) How did Descartes's views on the mind-body issue differ from earlier views?

One of the issues Descartes tackled was the mind-body problem: "the question of the distinction between mental and physical qualities." If the mind and body are different, then how do they interact with each other? Descartes agreed with previous thought that mind and body are different. Unlike his predecessors who though that mind controlled body, he believed that the body also controlled the mind to some extent.

7) How did Descartes explain the functioning and interaction of the human body and the human mind? What is the role of the *conarium*?

Descartes was a dualist, believing that the mind and body were separate entities. This left him with the problem of how they interact. He looked to the brain, and saw that structures were duplicated in each hemisphere, except for the conarium (pineal body). For this reason, he saw this structure as the vehicle through with the mind and body interact. He believed that nerves were hollow tubes through which flowed animal spirits, which "makes an impression on the conarium and from this impression the mind produces a sensation."

8) How did Descartes distinguish between innate ideas and derived ideas?

He believed the mind had two types of ideas; derived ideas, which are "produced by the direct application of an external stimulus" and innate ideas, which "arise from the mind or consciousness, independent of sensory experiences." Descartes identified several ideas that he believed were innate, such as "God, the self, perfection, and infinity." Unlike derived ideas, innate ideas arise without the presence of external stimuli.

9) Define positivism, materialism, and empiricism. What contributions did each viewpoint make to the new psychology?

Positivism is "the doctrine that recognizes only natural phenomena or facts that are objectively observable". Materialism is the belief that "the facts of the universe could be described in physical terms and explained by the properties of matter and energy." Empiricism fit in with prevailing thought in its doctrine that "all knowledge is derived from sensory experience." These three doctrines provided the philosophical basis for psychology. This allows both human behavior and the mind to become the subject of study. With positivism and materialism human behavior becomes observable in an objective way and can be explained using natural science. Empiricism allows the exploration of how the body senses and mind perceives, and how associations are made in the mind.

10) Describe Locke's definition of empiricism. Discuss his concepts of sensation and reflection, and of simple and complex ideas.

Locke rejects Descartes' innate ideas, and says that at birth the human mind is a *tabula rasa*, or a blank slate, and we acquire knowledge through our experiences. Locke defines two types of experiences: sensations from sensory input, and reflections where we recall and combine sensations to form higher-level thinking. Locke also distinguishes two types of ideas. The first are simple ideas, which come from both sensation and reflection and can't be broken down further. The second are complex ideas, which are combinations of simple ideas.

11) What is the mental-chemistry approach to association? How does it relate to the idea that the mind is like a machine?

To John Stuart Mill, the mind was not passive but active in associating ideas. He said that complex ideas are more than just the combination of simple ones, because they take on new qualities. This idea later is known as *creative synthesis* and represents the influence of chemistry. Previous philosophers, including J. S. Mill's father, were influenced by physics and mechanics and applied those disciplines to the mind.

12) How did Berkeley's ideas challenge Locke's distinction between primary and secondary qualities? What did Berkeley mean by the phrase "perception is the only reality"?

George Berkeley believed that there were only secondary qualities, that all knowledge is a function of perception (this position later is called mentalism). Because the world can never be known in an objective way, Berkeley believes that what Locke described as primary qualities (which Locke says exist in the object whether we perceive them or not, such as size or shape) don't exist. Objects in the world have stability, according to Berkeley, because God constantly perceives the world. There is no reality in the world beyond what is perceived.

13) How did Hartley's work exceed the aims of the other empiricists and associationists? How did Hartley explain association?

David Hartley's fundamental law of association is contiguity, and he goes further by contributing the proposition that repetition is necessary to form associations. He is "the first to apply the theory of association to explain all types of mental activity."

14) Compare the explanations of association offered by Hartley, James Mill, and John Stuart Mill.

David Hartley proposes that repetition is necessary to form associations. With James Mill's conception that the mind is a machine, association is mechanical and automatic, and resulting ideas are simply the sum of mental elements. John Stuart Mill said that the mind was not passive but active in associating ideas.

15) Contrast and compare the positions of James Mill and John Stuart Mill on the nature of the mind. Which view had the more lasting impact on psychology?

James Mill applied mechanism to the mind with the aim to prove that the mind was a machine (in contrast to the previous philosophers who stated that the mind was *like* a machine). He believed that the mind simply responds to external stimuli and can be studied by reducing it down to elements. This is reflected in later psychology, such as B. F. Skinner's system. Mill's son, John Stuart Mill, said that the mind was not passive but active in associating ideas. He said that complex ideas are more than just the combination of simple ones, because they take on new qualities.

This idea later is known as *creative synthesis*. John Stuart Mill had a greater impact on psychology, particularly because of his argument that "it was possible to make a scientific study of the mind." John Stuart Mill also proposed the new field "ethology", which would later contribute to the development of personality theory.

Key terms from chapter two

- **Association** The notion that knowledge results from linking or associating simple ideas to form complex ideas. Now commonly known as "learning."
- **Automata** Mechanical devices that mimicked lifelike motion, the building of which exploded in the seventeenth century and gave rise to questions about how humans are different than automata.
- **Calculating Engine** A machine designed by Charles Babbage that could imitate human mental actions.
- **Clockwork universe** The clock in the seventeenth century was a technological sensation. Because of its regularity, predictability, and precision, scientists and philosophers began to think of them as models for the physical universe.
- **Conarium** Also known as the Pineal Body, the structure in the brain that Descartes believed allowed the mind and body to interact.
- **Creative Synthesis** In John Stuart Mill's philosophy, the notion that when complex ideas are formed from simple ones, the combination creates something different and distinct.
- **Determinism** The doctrine that acts are determined by past events.
- **Doctrine of ideas** In Descartes' conception, the mind has two types of ideas
  - Derived: produced by the direct application of an external stimulus (sensory experiences)
  - Innate: arise from consciousness without sensory experience
- **Empiricism** The pursuit of knowledge through the observation of nature and the attribution of all knowledge to experience.
- **Materialism** The doctrine that considers the facts of the universe to be sufficiently explained in physical terms by the existence and nature of matter.
- **Mechanism** The doctrine that natural processes are mechanically determined and capable of explanation by the laws of physics and chemistry.
- **Mentalism** The doctrine that all knowledge is a function of mental phenomena and dependent on the perceiving or experiencing person.
- **Mind-Body problem** The question of the distinction between mental and physical qualities.
- **Positivism** The doctrine that recognizes only natural phenomena or facts that are objectively observable.
- **Primary and Secondary qualities** In Locke's philosophy, objects have two qualities
  - Primary: characteristics (size, shape) that exist in an object whether or not that object is perceived
  - Secondary: characteristics (sweetness, tone) that exist only when they are perceived.
- **Reductionism** The doctrine that explains phenomena on one level (such as complex ideas) in terms of phenomena on another level (such as simple ideas)
- **Reflex action theory** The idea that an external object (a stimulus) can bring about an involuntary response.
- **Repetition** The more frequently two ideas occur together, the more readily they will be associated.

- **Simple and Complex ideas** In Locke's philosophy, there are two types of ideas:
  - o Simple: elemental ideas that arise from sensation and reflection
  - o Complex: compounded from simple ideas and therefore can be broken down into simple ideas

TESTBANK

ESSAY

1. Define mechanism and describe how the idea of mechanism affected and was affected by physics, concepts of God, and the methods and findings of science. How was the concept of mechanism applied to human beings?

   ANS:
   Answer not provided.

   PTS: 1

2. Define determinism and reductionism and describe their relationship to the development of clocks and automata. Why was the mechanical clock the ideal metaphor for the spirit of mechanism?

   ANS:
   Answer not provided.

   PTS: 1

3. Describe Descartes' views of the mind-body problem and his major contributions to the beginnings of modern science, particularly psychology.

   ANS:
   Answer not provided.

   PTS: 1   MSC: WWW

4. Define positivism, materialism, and empiricism and discuss the contributions of each to the emerging science of psychology.

   ANS:
   Answer not provided.

   PTS: 1

5. Describe the general contributions of empiricism to psychology, supporting your selection of each contribution with specific examples from the thought of Locke, Hartley, James Mill, and John Stuart Mill.

   ANS:
   Answer not provided.

   PTS: 1   MSC: WWW

6. The doctrine that natural processes are mechanically determined and capable of explanation by the laws of physics and chemistry is _____.
   a. reductionism
   b. materialism
   c. mechanism
   d. empiricism
   e. positivism

   ANS: C   PTS: 1   REF: The Spirit of Mechanism
   MSC: WWW

7. According to the textbook, the dominant idea of the 17th century was _____.
   a. Zeitgeist
   b. entertainment
   c. water
   d. mechanism
   e. making it to the 18th century

   ANS: D   PTS: 1   REF: The Spirit of Mechanism

8. The Zeitgeist of 17th- to 19th-century Europe and of the United States was marked by _____.
   a. scientific revolution
   b. political revolution
   c. determinism
   d. humanism
   e. mechanism

   ANS: E   PTS: 1   REF: The Spirit of Mechanism

9. The theories of mechanism that invoke the movement of atoms to explain the universe were developed by _____.
   a. Locke and Berkeley
   b. La Mettrie and Condillac
   c. Newton and Hume
   d. Newton and Galileo
   e. Galileo and Copernicus

   ANS: D   PTS: 1   REF: The Spirit of Mechanism

10. Which of the following ideas has psychology borrowed from natural physics?
    a. effects are predictable and measurable
    b. the nature of human beings is basically good, moving toward self-actualization
    c. the paradigm of the source or identity of "cause"
    d. the laws of association
    e. the deductive method of logic

    ANS: A   PTS: 1   REF: The Spirit of Mechanism
    MSC: WWW

11. What invention was considered the perfect metaphor for the "spirit of mechanism"?
   a. automobile
   b. pneumatic pressure
   c. metronome
   d. clock
   e. computer

ANS: D   PTS: 1   REF: The Clockwork Universe

12. The doctrine that acts are determined by past events is ____.
   a. reductionism
   b. determinism
   c. mechanism
   d. materialism
   e. positivism

ANS: B   PTS: 1   REF: The Clockwork Universe

13. The doctrine that explains phenomena on one level (such as complex ideas) in terms of phenomena on another level (such as simple ideas) is ____.
   a. reductionism
   b. determinism
   c. mechanism
   d. positivism
   e. materialism

ANS: A   PTS: 1   REF: The Clockwork Universe

14. Seventeenth century philosophers and scientists argued that like clocks and the universe, ____ are regular, predictable, observable and measurable.
   a. God and/or other deities
   b. nonconscious processes
   c. human beings
   d. cognitive processes
   e. characteristics of self-actualization

ANS: C   PTS: 1   REF: The Clockwork Universe

15. ____ are mechanized figures that could almost perfectly duplicate the movements of living things.
   a. Elements
   b. Automata
   c. Psychomata
   d. Mannequins
   e. Robots

ANS: B   PTS: 1   REF: The Clockwork Universe

16. Philosophers and scientists joined in agreement that ____.
   a. psychology must be an independent science
   b. there is both an unconscious and a nonconscious
   c. human functioning and behavior are governed by mechanical laws
   d. experimental and quantitative methods could be applied to the study of human nature
   e. the dictates of religious figures about human behavior had to be countered and/or refuted

   ANS: D   PTS: 1   REF: The Clockwork Universe
   MSC: WWW

17. ____ was the first successful demonstration of artificial intelligence.
   a. Galileo's telescope
   b. Babbage's calculating machine
   c. La Mettrie's self-winding watch
   d. Descartes's automata
   e. Newton's clocks

   ANS: B   PTS: 1   REF: The Clockwork Universe

18. Contemporary cognitive psychologists' computer model of artificial intelligence is a direct descendant of ____.
   a. Babbage's calculating machine
   b. La Mettrie's self-winding watch
   c. Descartes's automata
   d. Newton's clocks
   e. Bessel's personal equations

   ANS: A   PTS: 1   REF: The Clockwork Universe

19. Who published a clear explanation of how the calculating machine functioned and pointed out its potential use and implications?
   a. Babbage
   b. La Mettrie
   c. Lovelace
   d. Descartes
   e. Locke

   ANS: C   PTS: 1   REF: The Clockwork Universe

20. The pursuit of knowledge through the observation of nature and the attribution of all knowledge to experience is ____.
   a. mentalism
   b. empiricism
   c. positivism
   d. materialism
   e. None of the choices are correct.

   ANS: B   PTS: 1   REF: The Beginnings of Modern Science

21. Empiricism attributes all knowledge to ____.
    a. experience
    b. objectivity in methods
    c. overt behavior
    d. environmental influences
    e. reinforcement schedules

    ANS: A   PTS: 1   REF: The Beginnings of Modern Science
    MSC: WWW

22. Descartes was significant to psychology as a science because he helped liberate ____.
    a. science from the stranglehold of theology
    b. science from the grasp of philosophy
    c. philosophy from the clutches of theology
    d. science from the dictates of government
    e. psychology from the dictates of science

    ANS: A   PTS: 1   REF: The Beginnings of Modern Science

23. Who can be said to have inaugurated the era of modern psychology?
    a. Babbage
    b. Descartes
    c. La Mettrie
    d. Locke
    e. Comte

    ANS: B   PTS: 1   REF: The Beginnings of Modern Science

24. In the 20th century, Carl Jung based important decisions on his dreams. A 17th-century predecessor in this practice was ____.
    a. Newton
    b. Galileo
    c. Freud
    d. Descartes
    e. Spinoza

    ANS: D   PTS: 1   REF: The Beginnings of Modern Science

25. For Descartes, the application of mathematical principles to sciences would produce ____.
    a. theorems of human nature
    b. laws of physics
    c. principles
    d. religious conviction
    e. certainty of knowledge

    ANS: E   PTS: 1   REF: The Beginnings of Modern Science

26. In the 20th century, Hull described and explained behavior by mathematical formulas, axioms, and postulates. Thus, he illustrated whose notion that certainty of knowledge is accomplished by the application of mathematics to science?
    a. Kepler's
    b. Descartes's
    c. Berkeley's
    d. Locke's
    e. John Stuart Mill's

    ANS: B   PTS: 1   REF: The Beginnings of Modern Science
    MSC: WWW

27. The question of the distinction between mental and physical qualities refers to ____.
    a. the bipartisan problem
    b. the freethinking problem
    c. the mind-body problem
    d. positivism
    e. theology

    ANS: C   PTS: 1
    REF: The Contributions of Descartes: Mechanism and the Mind-Body Problem

28. Before Descartes, the accepted point of view was that the interaction between mind and body was essentially unidirectional, that ____.
    a. the body influenced the mind
    b. the mind influenced the body
    c. the soul influenced both the body and mind
    d. the mind and body influenced each other
    e. the vital force influenced both the mind and the body

    ANS: B   PTS: 1
    REF: The Contributions of Descartes: Mechanism and the Mind-Body Problem

29. Descartes's dualism was novel in its emphasis on the ____.
    a. interaction between mind and spirit
    b. influence of the mind on the body
    c. influence of the body on the mind
    d. parallel but non-interacting functioning of the mind and body
    e. predominance of unconscious mental forces

    ANS: C   PTS: 1
    REF: The Contributions of Descartes: Mechanism and the Mind-Body Problem

30. Descartes argued that all processes are functions of the body except ____.
    a. reflexes
    b. will
    c. perception
    d. sensation
    e. thought

    ANS: E   PTS: 1
    REF: The Contributions of Descartes: Mechanism and the Mind-Body Problem
    MSC: WWW

31. Descartes changed the focus from the study of _____ to the study of _____.
    a. conscious processes; the unconscious
    b. the unconscious; conscious processes
    c. the nonconscious; the unconscious
    d. the soul; the mind
    e. science; theology

    ANS: D   PTS: 1
    REF: The Contributions of Descartes: Mechanism and the Mind-Body Problem

32. Descartes makes a case that because the body is matter the laws of _____ apply.
    a. materialism
    b. biology
    c. mechanics
    d. reflexes
    e. mathematics

    ANS: C   PTS: 1
    REF: The Contributions of Descartes: Mechanism and the Mind-Body Problem

33. The body will respond without any internal conscious intent to some external stimulus. This fact illustrates Descartes' principle of _____.
    a. *undulatio reflexa*
    b. *Einfall*
    c. *cogito ergo sum*
    d. *esse est percipi*
    e. spring action

    ANS: A   PTS: 1
    REF: The Contributions of Descartes: Mechanism and the Mind-Body Problem

34. In modern terminology, Descartes would argue that if the inputs are known, the behavioral outputs can be predicted. Thus, he is an intellectual ancestor of _____.
    a. behaviorism
    b. functionalism
    c. structuralism
    d. the French materialists
    e. S-R psychology

    ANS: E   PTS: 1
    REF: The Contributions of Descartes: Mechanism and the Mind-Body Problem

35. The response of salivation following the stimulus of food on the tongue is an illustration of Descartes' _____.
    a. reflex action theory
    b. theory of respondent behavior
    c. theory of operant behavior
    d. *cogito ergo sum* theory
    e. *Einfall* theory

    ANS: A   PTS: 1
    REF: The Contributions of Descartes: Mechanism and the Mind-Body Problem

36. Under Descartes's reflex action theory, an external stimulus can bring about a(n)____ physical response.
    a. theoretical
    b. involuntary
    c. intense
    d. painful
    e. conscious

    ANS: B   PTS: 1
    REF: The Contributions of Descartes: Mechanism and the Mind-Body Problem
    MSC: WWW

37. Which of the following statements best describes Descartes' dualistic theory of human nature?
    a. The mind directs all the activities of the body.
    b. The body directly controls the activities of the mind.
    c. The brain contains derived ideas; the mind contains innate ideas.
    d. The mind and body mutually influence each other's actions.
    e. None of the choices are correct.

    ANS: D   PTS: 1
    REF: The Contributions of Descartes: Mechanism and the Mind-Body Problem

38. Descartes's term for the site of body-mind interaction was the ____, because it is ____.
    a. *conarium*; duplicated in both brain hemispheres
    b. *conarium*; not duplicated in both brain hemispheres
    c. *undulatio reflexa*; duplicated in both brain hemispheres
    d. *undulatio reflexa*; not duplicated in both brain hemispheres
    e. pineal gland; located near the heart

    ANS: B   PTS: 1
    REF: The Contributions of Descartes: Mechanism and the Mind-Body Problem

39. Which of the following is an example of a derived idea?
    a. Solving an algebra equation.
    b. Memorizing a history lesson.
    c. Philosophy.
    d. Playing the guitar.
    e. Seeing a forest.

    ANS: E   PTS: 1
    REF: The Contributions of Descartes: Mechanism and the Mind-Body Problem

40. Descartes posited that the mind-body interaction occurred in the ____.
    a. heart
    b. brain as a whole
    c. pineal body
    d. frontal lobes
    e. corpus callosum

    ANS: C   PTS: 1
    REF: The Contributions of Descartes: Mechanism and the Mind-Body Problem
    MSC: WWW

41. According to Descartes, the pineal gland was the part of the brain ____.
    a. where innate ideas are stored
    b. where derived ideas are stored
    c. that controlled the activities of the mind
    d. where the mind and body interact
    e. where all ideas are stored

    ANS: D   PTS: 1
    REF: The Contributions of Descartes: Mechanism and the Mind-Body Problem

42. Descartes proposed that the mind produces two kinds of ideas, ____ and ____.
    a. derived; innate
    b. body; mind
    c. reasonable; wacky
    d. right; wrong
    e. abstract; pseudo-abstract

    ANS: A   PTS: 1
    REF: The Contributions of Descartes: Mechanism and the Mind-Body Problem

43. Derived ideas ____.
    a. come from God
    b. are part of our genetic makeup when we are born
    c. arise from the direct application of an external stimulus
    d. come into being as a consequence of being socialized into society
    e. are taken from innate ideas

    ANS: C   PTS: 1
    REF: The Contributions of Descartes: Mechanism and the Mind-Body Problem

44. Which of the following is an example of an innate idea?
    a. flowers
    b. sweetness
    c. tone
    d. machines
    e. infinity

    ANS: E   PTS: 1
    REF: The Contributions of Descartes: Mechanism and the Mind-Body Problem

45. Which of the following is a contribution of Rene Descartes to modern psychology?
    a. a mechanistic conception of the body.
    b. the theory of reflex action.
    c. mind-body interaction.
    d. localization of mental function in the brain.
    e. All of the choices are correct.

    ANS: E   PTS: 1
    REF: The Contributions of Descartes: Mechanism and the Mind-Body Problem

46. The idea of a house is an example of Descartes' notion of ____.
    a. innate ideas
    b. *undulatio reflexa*
    c. derived ideas
    d. simple ideas
    e. complex ideas

    ANS: C   PTS: 1
    REF: The Contributions of Descartes: Mechanism and the Mind-Body Problem

47. Descartes theorized that we are born with knowledge of the axioms of geometry. Thus, these axioms are ____ ideas.
    a. innate
    b. derived
    c. synthetic
    d. simple
    e. complex

    ANS: A   PTS: 1
    REF: The Contributions of Descartes: Mechanism and the Mind-Body Problem
    MSC: WWW

48. The doctrine of ____ is important because it stimulated opposition among early empiricists and associationists.
    a. derived ideas
    b. innate ideas
    c. idea principles
    d. simple ideas

    ANS: B   PTS: 1
    REF: The Contributions of Descartes: Mechanism and the Mind-Body Problem

49. Descartes' notion that we are born with certain perceptual processes is also a principle of which modern school of psychology?
    a. behavioristic
    b. psychoanalytic
    c. Gestalt
    d. phenomenological
    e. humanistic

    ANS: C   PTS: 1
    REF: The Contributions of Descartes: Mechanism and the Mind-Body Problem

50. The doctrine that recognizes only natural phenomena or facts that are objectively observable is ____.
    a. materialism
    b. empiricism
    c. positivism
    d. mechanism
    e. reductionism

    ANS: C   PTS: 1
    REF: Philosophical Foundations of the New Psychology: Positivism, Materialism, and Empiricism

51. Both the term and concept of positivism represent the thought of ____.
    a. Descartes
    b. Comte
    c. Locke
    d. Berkeley
    e. Mill

    ANS: B   PTS: 1
    REF: Philosophical Foundations of the New Psychology: Positivism, Materialism, and Empiricism

52. The idea that science should be based totally on objectively observable facts is called ____.
    a. factualism
    b. materialism
    c. absolutism
    d. positivism
    e. observation

    ANS: D   PTS: 1
    REF: Philosophical Foundations of the New Psychology: Positivism, Materialism, and Empiricism

53. In eyewitness testimony, one swears that what one has observed accurately depicts reality. Because this "fact" has not been determined through the methods of science, it does not meet Comtes' strictest application of ____.
    a. positivism
    b. determinism
    c. complex ideas
    d. materialism
    e. mechanism

    ANS: A   PTS: 1
    REF: Philosophical Foundations of the New Psychology: Positivism, Materialism, and Empiricism

54. The doctrine that considers the facts of the universe to be sufficiently explained in physical terms by the existence and nature of matter is ____.
    a. positivism
    b. materialism
    c. mentalism
    d. immaterialism
    e. reductionism

    ANS: B   PTS: 1
    REF: Philosophical Foundations of the New Psychology: Positivism, Materialism, and Empiricism

55. Those who argue today that behavior is no more than the action of chemicals and electrical events in the brain might be labeled "modern ____."
    a. empiricists
    b. positivists
    c. materialists
    d. associationists
    e. determinists

    ANS: C   PTS: 1
    REF: Philosophical Foundations of the New Psychology: Positivism, Materialism, and Empiricism
    MSC: WWW

56. Materialism is the belief that ____.
    a. speculation and inference are acceptable
    b. consciousness exists beyond physics and chemistry
    c. the mental world exists on a plane of its own
    d. all things can be described in physical terms
    e. ideas exist only in Descartes' mind

    ANS: D   PTS: 1
    REF: Philosophical Foundations of the New Psychology: Positivism, Materialism, and Empiricism

57. Locke's ____ marks the formal beginning of British empiricism.
    a. *An Essay Concerning Human Understanding*
    b. *A Treatise Concerning the Principles of Human Knowledge*
    c. *An Essay Toward a New Theory of Vision*
    d. *A Treatise of Human Nature*
    e. *Observations on Man, His Frame, His Duty, and His Expectations*

    ANS: A   PTS: 1
    REF: Philosophical Foundations of the New Psychology: Positivism, Materialism, and Empiricism

58. A fundamental difference between Descartes's psychology and that of Locke was their position about the existence of ____.
    a. innate ideas
    b. derived ideas
    c. idea doctrines
    d. simple ideas
    e. complex ideas

    ANS: A   PTS: 1
    REF: Philosophical Foundations of the New Psychology: Positivism, Materialism, and Empiricism

59. John Locke disagreed with the doctrine of innate ideas. According to Locke, ____.
    a. innate ideas once existed in the human mind, but modern humans do not have them
    b. innate ideas only exist in the most intelligent human beings; most people do not have innate ideas
    c. innate ideas stay in the unconscious mind and never reach the level of consciousness
    d. the mind is a blank slate at birth; therefore, there are no innate ideas
    e. There was no disagreement between Locke and Descartes

    ANS: D   PTS: 1
    REF: Philosophical Foundations of the New Psychology: Positivism, Materialism, and Empiricism

60. Aristotle held that the mind was a wax slate upon which impressions are made. Locke invoked the metaphor of the ____ to illustrate the same phenomenon.
    a. *undulatio reflexa*
    b. *tabula rasa*
    c. cogito
    d. complex idea
    e. reflection

    ANS: B   PTS: 1
    REF: Philosophical Foundations of the New Psychology: Positivism, Materialism, and Empiricism

61. What position did Locke take on the origin of ideas?
    a. Some innate ideas exist, such as self, God, and time.
    b. The only acquired ideas are verbal ideas; all other ideas are innate.
    c. Innate ideas don't change; derived ideas are malleable.
    d. All ideas are innate; experience just makes us aware of their presence.
    e. All ideas are acquired from experience; no ideas are innate.

    ANS: E   PTS: 1
    REF: Philosophical Foundations of the New Psychology: Positivism, Materialism, and Empiricism

62. Locke argued that ideas seem to us to be innate because ____.
    a. they were classically conditioned
    b. they are simple ideas
    c. they are complex ideas
    d. we don't recollect having learned them
    e. we can't identify their component elemental ideas

    ANS: D   PTS: 1
    REF: Philosophical Foundations of the New Psychology: Positivism, Materialism, and Empiricism

63. For Locke, ideas are the result of ____.
    a. reflection and sensations
    b. reasoning about sensations
    c. primary sensations and secondary sensations
    d. experience and cognition
    e. primary qualities and secondary qualities

    ANS: A   PTS: 1
    REF: Philosophical Foundations of the New Psychology: Positivism, Materialism, and Empiricism

64. According to Locke, in human development, what kind of ideas appears first?
    a. sensation
    b. reflection
    c. simple
    d. complex
    e. innate

    ANS: A   PTS: 1
    REF: Philosophical Foundations of the New Psychology: Positivism, Materialism, and Empiricism

65. "Why should I have to read what Locke wrote over 300 years ago? Schultz and Schultz and the instructor get paid to summarize that for me." What answer would the textbook authors give you?
    a. "Full understanding comes from reading the original data of history from the theorists themselves."
    b. "To see how even a good idea can be badly written."
    c. "Because you are expected to do so."
    d. "Don't worry if you do not have time to read the original source material; authors and teachers provide accurate versions."
    e. "Actually, you shouldn't have to."

    ANS: A   PTS: 1
    REF: Philosophical Foundations of the New Psychology: Positivism, Materialism, and Empiricism

66. According to Locke, simple ideas become complex ideas through the process of _____.
    a. association
    b. deductive logic
    c. sensing primary qualities
    d. reflection
    e. recombination

ANS: D   PTS: 1
REF: Philosophical Foundations of the New Psychology: Positivism, Materialism, and Empiricism

67. According to Locke, the idea of an army or a navy would be an example of _____.
    a. a complex idea
    b. an innate idea
    c. a simple idea
    d. a derived idea
    e. a primary quality

ANS: A   PTS: 1
REF: Philosophical Foundations of the New Psychology: Positivism, Materialism, and Empiricism

68. For Locke, the difference between a simple and a complex idea is that a simple idea _____.
    a. contains more premises
    b. is the result of inductive logic
    c. is the result of deductive logic
    d. is contiguous
    e. cannot be reduced

ANS: E   PTS: 1
REF: Philosophical Foundations of the New Psychology: Positivism, Materialism, and Empiricism

69. If a tree falls in the forest and no one is present to hear it, then the fall makes no sound. Using Locke's distinctions, this conclusion assumes that the sound is a(n) _____.
    a. primary quality
    b. secondary quality
    c. association
    d. simple idea
    e. complex idea

ANS: B   PTS: 1
REF: Philosophical Foundations of the New Psychology: Positivism, Materialism, and Empiricism

70. According to Locke, the tickle of a feather would be a(n) _____.
    a. complex idea
    b. primary quality
    c. secondary quality
    d. tertiary quality
    e. essential quality

ANS: C   PTS: 1
REF: Philosophical Foundations of the New Psychology: Positivism, Materialism, and Empiricism

71. The notion of secondary qualities was proposed by Locke to explain ____.
    a. the distinction between the physical world and one's experience of it
    b. the need for objectivity in psychology
    c. the role of positivism in the new science of psychology
    d. Descartes's dualism
    e. the difference between simple ideas and complex ideas

    ANS: A   PTS: 1
    REF: Philosophical Foundations of the New Psychology: Positivism, Materialism, and Empiricism

72. "If a tree falls in the forest and no one is present to hear it, a sound will still occur because God is the permanent perceiver of all objects in the universe." This argument illustrates the position of ____.
    a. Berkeley
    b. Locke
    c. Hume
    d. Hartley
    e. the Mills

    ANS: A   PTS: 1
    REF: Philosophical Foundations of the New Psychology: Positivism, Materialism, and Empiricism

73. Which philosopher believed that the only things that humans know with certainty are those objects that are perceived?
    a. Rene Descartes
    b. John Locke
    c. David Hartley
    d. James Mill
    e. George Berkeley

    ANS: E   PTS: 1
    REF: Philosophical Foundations of the New Psychology: Positivism, Materialism, and Empiricism

74. The doctrine that all knowledge is a function of mental phenomena and is dependent on the perceiving or experiencing person is an illustration of ____.
    a. Locke's associationism
    b. Locke's mentalism
    c. Berkeley's mentalism
    d. Berkeley's associationism
    e. Comte's positivism

    ANS: C   PTS: 1
    REF: Philosophical Foundations of the New Psychology: Positivism, Materialism, and Empiricism

75. Which of the following slogans could be attributed to Berkeley?
    a. I think, therefore I am.
    b. To think is to perceive.
    c. To be is to perceive.
    d. Whatever exists must have a cause of existence.
    e. Go west, young man.

    ANS: C   PTS: 1
    REF: Philosophical Foundations of the New Psychology: Positivism, Materialism, and Empiricism

76. Berkeley's basic difference with Locke was the former's argument that ____.
   a. there are no primary qualities
   b. there is a one-to-one correspondence between physical objects and subjective perceptions
   c. an object is the association of consecutive perceptions
   d. there are only complex ideas
   e. there are only primary qualities

ANS: A   PTS: 1
REF: Philosophical Foundations of the New Psychology: Positivism, Materialism, and Empiricism

77. The phenomenology of the humanistic school focuses on the individual's unique experiences as they define the person's reality. This idea is a direct descendant of ____.
   a. Locke's empiricism
   b. Berkeley's mentalism
   c. Hume's law of resemblance
   d. James Mill's mechanical associationism
   e. J. S. Mill's mental chemistry hypothesis

ANS: B   PTS: 1
REF: Philosophical Foundations of the New Psychology: Positivism, Materialism, and Empiricism

78. For Berkeley, depth perception is the result of ____.
   a. concurrent mechanical associations
   b. innate ideas
   c. the association of primary qualities and complex ideas
   d. the association of ideas that must be learned
   e. contiguity and repetition

ANS: D   PTS: 1
REF: Philosophical Foundations of the New Psychology: Positivism, Materialism, and Empiricism

79. What was the significance of the defecating duck?
   a. It demonstrated the Zeitgeist of the time.
   b. It was widely popular and well-known.
   c. It was described as the "glory of France."
   d. It was one example of the spirit of mechanism.
   e. All of the above.

ANS: E   PTS: 1   REF: The Defecating Duck and the Glory of France

80. Why was the mechanical clock a revolutionary invention?
   a. Clocks brought precision, regularity, and predictability to everyday life, which was later developed into a model for science.
   b. Clocks were used only by the elite to control the masses.
   c. Because of the varying sizes and shapes, clocks helped stimulate the European economy like never before.
   d. Clocks were used for religious practices.
   e. Clocks were built to look like people and animals.

ANS: A   PTS: 1   REF: The Clockwork Universe

81. Which of the following types of automata are NOT described in the book?
    a. A defecating duck
    b. A life-sized animated flute player
    c. A "Lady-Musician" that played the harpsichord
    d. A 16-inch mechanical monk
    e. A singing mouse

    ANS: E   PTS: 1   REF: The Clockwork Universe

82. Which theorist believed that people are similar to machines?
    a. Descartes
    b. Berkeley
    c. Galileo
    d. Locke
    e. Comte

    ANS: A   PTS: 1   REF: The Clockwork Universe

83. What was the basis for Babbage's calculating machine?
    a. The spirit of mechanism
    b. Automata and clocks
    c. The mechanical nature of human mental actions
    d. None of the above
    e. All of the above

    ANS: E   PTS: 1   REF: The Clockwork Universe

84. What was the most influential doctrine to modern psychology?
    a. History
    b. Materialism
    c. Empiricism
    d. Chemistry
    e. Positivism

    ANS: C   PTS: 1
    REF: Philosophical Foundations of the New Psychology: Positivism, Materialism, and Empiricism

85. While Hartley's fundamental law of association was ____, he also proposed that ____ was necessary for associations to be formed.
    a. resemblance; contiguity
    b. contiguity; repetition
    c. resemblance; repetition
    d. temporal contiguity; spatial contiguity
    e. contiguity; similarity

    ANS: B   PTS: 1
    REF: Philosophical Foundations of the New Psychology: Positivism, Materialism, and Empiricism

86. Hartley was the first to apply the theory of association to explain ____.
    a. all mental activity
    b. rote learning
    c. memory
    d. the difference between recall and recognition
    e. the difference between sensations and perceptions

ANS: A   PTS: 1
REF: Philosophical Foundations of the New Psychology: Positivism, Materialism, and Empiricism

87. Hartley argued that the human brain and nervous system transmitted impulses ____.
    a. with electricity
    b. with chemicals
    c. using capillary impulses
    d. with changes in neurochemical intensities
    e. with nerve vibrations

ANS: E   PTS: 1
REF: Philosophical Foundations of the New Psychology: Positivism, Materialism, and Empiricism

88. James Mill demonstrated a radical perspective because he believed that the mind is a(n) ____.
    a. crucible
    b. machine
    c. association
    d. calculator
    e. tool

ANS: B   PTS: 1
REF: Philosophical Foundations of the New Psychology: Positivism, Materialism, and Empiricism

89. ____, the most radically mechanistic of the British empiricists, claimed that the mind is a machine and that there is no freedom of the will, believing instead that the mind is totally a passive entity and all thought can be analyzed in terms of sensations.
    a. John Stuart Mill
    b. David Hume
    c. John Locke
    d. James Mill
    e. George Berkeley

ANS: D   PTS: 1
REF: Philosophical Foundations of the New Psychology: Positivism, Materialism, and Empiricism

90. *Mind is Machine* would be a good book title for ____.
    a. Berkeley
    b. Hume
    c. Hartley
    d. James Mill
    e. J. S. Mill

ANS: D   PTS: 1
REF: Philosophical Foundations of the New Psychology: Positivism, Materialism, and Empiricism

91. James Mill's model says that all knowledge ____.
    a. begins with sensations, and associations create complex ideas
    b. is innate, and combined to form complex ideas
    c. comes from ideas
    d. requires an actively engaged mind
    e. More than one of the choices are correct.

    ANS: A   PTS: 1
    REF: Philosophical Foundations of the New Psychology: Positivism, Materialism, and Empiricism

92. James Mill: ____; John Stuart Mill: ____.
    a. mechanical; chemical
    b. dualistic; monistic
    c. active mind; passive mind
    d. passive mind; active mind
    e. mechanical; chemical and dualistic; monistic

    ANS: A   PTS: 1
    REF: Philosophical Foundations of the New Psychology: Positivism, Materialism, and Empiricism

93. Which British empiricist championed women's rights and condemned the unequal status of women?
    a. David Hartley
    b. John Stuart Mill
    c. James Mill
    d. David Hume
    e. John Locke

    ANS: B   PTS: 1
    REF: Philosophical Foundations of the New Psychology: Positivism, Materialism, and Empiricism

94. The idea that "the whole is greater than the sum of its parts" was the position of ____.
    a. Berkeley
    b. Hume
    c. Hartley
    d. James Mill
    e. John Stuart Mill

    ANS: E   PTS: 1
    REF: Philosophical Foundations of the New Psychology: Positivism, Materialism, and Empiricism

95. John Stuart Mill (JSM) differed from his father's view of the mind by proposing: "Complex ideas emerge from combinations of simple ideas and possess characteristics not found in those elements." JSM was concerned with mental ____.
    a. magic
    b. coordination
    c. mechanics
    d. hospitals
    e. chemistry

    ANS: E   PTS: 1
    REF: Philosophical Foundations of the New Psychology: Positivism, Materialism, and Empiricism

96. Complex ideas formed from simple ideas take on new qualities. This is a definition of ____.
    a. James Mill's creative synthesis
    b. Hartley's creative synthesis
    c. James Mill's active mind theory
    d. Hume's creative synthesis
    e. John Stuart Mill's creative synthesis

    ANS: E   PTS: 1
    REF: Philosophical Foundations of the New Psychology: Positivism, Materialism, and Empiricism

97. John Stuart Mill's metaphor of mental chemistry came to be known as ____.
    a. association
    b. the law of contiguity
    c. classical conditioning
    d. operant conditioning
    e. creative synthesis

    ANS: E   PTS: 1
    REF: Philosophical Foundations of the New Psychology: Positivism, Materialism, and Empiricism

98. Which of the following was not a contribution of British empiricism to the development of psychology?
    a. the role of sensation in consciousness
    b. the analysis of conscious experience into elements
    c. the claim that almost all human knowledge is derived from experience. However, the principles of mathematics are innate ideas.
    d. the focus on conscious experiences
    e. through association, synthesizing elements into complex mental experiences

    ANS: C   PTS: 1   REF: Contributions of Empiricism to Psychology

TRUE/FALSE

99. The idea of mechanism was a result of the initial work of Newton.

    ANS: F   PTS: 1   REF: The Spirit of Mechanism

100. A basic principle of 17th century physics was that every physical effect is predictable and measurable.

    ANS: T   PTS: 1   REF: The Spirit of Mechanism
    MSC: WWW

101. The aspect of technology that 17th century science adopted was precise measurement.

    ANS: T   PTS: 1   REF: The Spirit of Mechanism

102. Determinism is the belief that every act is brought about by past events.

    ANS: T   PTS: 1   REF: The Clockwork Universe

103. Babbage was the first in modern America to create and market software.

    ANS: F   PTS: 1   REF: The Clockwork Universe

104. The doctrine that challenged theological authority as a source of knowledge was determinism.

    ANS: F   PTS: 1   REF: The Clockwork Universe
    MSC: WWW

105. Wundt inaugurated the era of modern psychology.

    ANS: F   PTS: 1   REF: The Beginnings of Modern Science

106. For Descartes, certainty of knowledge was the result of mathematical principles.

    ANS: T   PTS: 1
    REF: The Contributions of Descartes: Mechanism and the Mind-Body Problem

107. A major contribution of Descartes to psychology was to deflect attention from the study of the mind in general to the study of consciousness in particular.

    ANS: F   PTS: 1
    REF: The Contributions of Descartes: Mechanism and the Mind-Body Problem

108. For Descartes, the functions of the body operate according to mechanical principles.

    ANS: T   PTS: 1
    REF: The Contributions of Descartes: Mechanism and the Mind-Body Problem

109. For Descartes, the unique function of the mind is thought.

    ANS: T   PTS: 1
    REF: The Contributions of Descartes: Mechanism and the Mind-Body Problem

110. At the heart of Descartes' notion of the *undulatio reflexa* is the role of the conscious mind in determining behavior

    ANS: F   PTS: 1
    REF: The Contributions of Descartes: Mechanism and the Mind-Body Problem

111. Descartes' contemporaries believed that neither humans nor animals had souls.

    ANS: F   PTS: 1
    REF: The Contributions of Descartes: Mechanism and the Mind-Body Problem
    MSC: WWW

112. Comte's main contribution to psychology was the doctrine of materialism.

    ANS: F   PTS: 1
    REF: Philosophical Foundations of the New Psychology: Positivism, Materialism, and Empiricism
    MSC: WWW

113. Comte would argue that because God perceives the world, objects in it remain constant.

    ANS: F   PTS: 1
    REF: Philosophical Foundations of the New Psychology: Positivism, Materialism, and Empiricism

114. The materialists argued that consciousness could be understood in accordance with the principles of physics and chemistry.

ANS: T   PTS: 1
REF: Philosophical Foundations of the New Psychology: Positivism, Materialism, and Empiricism

115. The nativistic theory of perception holds that certain ideas and mental functions are learned through experience.

ANS: F   PTS: 1
REF: Philosophical Foundations of the New Psychology: Positivism, Materialism, and Empiricism

116. The best-known opponents of nativism were the British empiricists.

ANS: T   PTS: 1
REF: Philosophical Foundations of the New Psychology: Positivism, Materialism, and Empiricism

117. Locke argued that we believe ideas are innate if or when we cannot recall having learned them.

ANS: T   PTS: 1
REF: Philosophical Foundations of the New Psychology: Positivism, Materialism, and Empiricism

118. The first idea of the *tabula rasa* was John Locke's.

ANS: F   PTS: 1
REF: Philosophical Foundations of the New Psychology: Positivism, Materialism, and Empiricism
MSC: WWW

119. "Beauty is in the eye of the beholder," reflects Locke's notion of primary qualities.

ANS: F   PTS: 1
REF: Philosophical Foundations of the New Psychology: Positivism, Materialism, and Empiricism

120. The notion in modern psychology that knowledge depends on the experiencing person is essentially a restatement of Berkeley's position.

ANS: T   PTS: 1
REF: Philosophical Foundations of the New Psychology: Positivism, Materialism, and Empiricism

121. Berkeley used the phenomenon of depth perception to illustrate the presence of innate ideas.

ANS: F   PTS: 1
REF: Philosophical Foundations of the New Psychology: Positivism, Materialism, and Empiricism

122. Locke used simple and complex ideas to describe his theory of association, now commonly known as learning.

ANS: T   PTS: 1
REF: Philosophical Foundations of the New Psychology: Positivism, Materialism, and Empiricism

123. There was little difference between James Mill and son John Stuart Mill in their interpretations of human mental functioning.

ANS: F   PTS: 1
REF: Philosophical Foundations of the New Psychology: Positivism, Materialism, and Empiricism

124. Rote learning has at its core Hartley's law of repetition.

    ANS: T   PTS: 1
    REF: Philosophical Foundations of the New Psychology: Positivism, Materialism, and Empiricism

125. Hartley attempted to explain psychological and physiological processes in terms of mechanical principles.

    ANS: T   PTS: 1
    REF: Philosophical Foundations of the New Psychology: Positivism, Materialism, and Empiricism

126. James Mill denied that people had free will.

    ANS: T   PTS: 1
    REF: Philosophical Foundations of the New Psychology: Positivism, Materialism, and Empiricism

Chapter 3

Physiological Influences on Psychology

David Kinnebrook, an astronomer's assistant at the Royal Observatory in Greenwich, England, was fired from his job in 1795 because the observations he made of the speed of stars differed from his supervisor's (though not by much). Twenty years later, Wilhelm Bessel became interested in how the observations of two individuals can differ. He believed that David's "mistakes" were a function of individual differences that are out of one's control, rather than of intellectual competence. Bessel's work echoed theories of Locke and Berkeley concerning to subjective nature of human perception. His conclusions were twofold. First, astronomers have to take personal characteristics and perceptions into account that influence the reported observations. Second, that *any* science relying on observational methods would have to be wary about individual differences. This caused human perception to become a focus of study.

Physiological research, which was an increasingly experimentally oriented discipline in the 1830's, was first to examine individual difference in perception. For example, Johannes Müller, an advocate of the experimental method, proposed that nerves have specific energies—that stimulating a particular nerve will always lead to a sensation characteristic of that nerve. An optic nerve will only send information about light, even if it is stimulated by pressure, chemicals, or other means, and even in the absence of light.

Other researchers were concerned with trying to map the brain. Marshall Hall observed that decapitated animals would move if their nerve endings were stimulated, and thus located the root of voluntary and involuntary movement in the brain. Pierre Flourens would systematically destroy sections of pigeons' brains to test how it affected their behavior. He in turn deduced that the cerebrum controls higher mental processes, parts of the midbrain control visual and auditory reflexes, the cerebellum controls coordination, and the medulla governs heartbeat, respiration, and other vital functions. Both of these researchers used extirpation (systematically destroying parts of the brain to determine brain function) as a means of mapping brain functioning.

In the mid-1800's, two new experimental methods arose. The clinical method involves examining the human brain postmortem in an attempt to locate damaged areas believed to be responsible for certain behaviors . This began with Paul Broca's work with a man who couldn't speak for many years. After the man died, Broca found that his brain had sustained an injury to an area now known as Broca's area, which is the speech center. Electrical stimulation was also used to observe brain function. This was first promoted by Fritsch and Hitzig, who used weak electrical currents to stimulate the brains of animals and record subsequent motor responses.

When mapping the brain from the inside, Franz Josef Gall learned "the existence of both white and gray matter in the brain, the nerve fibers connecting each side of the brain to the opposite side of the spinal cord, and the fibers connecting both halves of the brain." When he began to look outside the brain for characteristics like size and shape, he developed phrenology, which proposed that personality characteristics and intelligence can be deduced by investigating the shape of one's skull. Phrenology quickly became popular and profitable across Europe and in the United States yet was regarded in the scientific community as quackery. Flourens, for example, discovered that the skull's shape was unrelated to the brain's shape. Another criticism was that as physiologists discovered the functions of areas of the brain, such areas did not match up with Gall's phrenology mapping.

Much work was being done to investigate how the nervous system worked. Luigi Galvani "suggested that nerve impulses were electrical." A Spanish physician, Ramón y Cajal, discovered the "direction of travel for nerve impulses in the brain and spinal cord." Other researchers discovered neurons, and the idea that they somehow connect to each other. This work aligned well with the spirit of mechanism: finding "the mechanisms that underlie mental phenomena."

This set the stage for the advent of experimental psychology, which emerges in Germany (rather than in other countries) for several reasons. First, German scientists favored the inductive approach to science, which involves carefully collecting and cataloging a large number of facts. Germans also defined science to include a wider variety of topics, like biology and physiology, which were not readily accepted in other countries. In the early nineteenth century, German professors and students were allowed the freedom to pursue any topic of study that they wished (a freedom unknown in France and England). At the same time there were far more universities in Germany compared to only two in England, and there were no research universities in the United States until Johns Hopkins was founded in 1876.

Hermann von Helmholtz was one the four German scholars that made a vast contribution to the budding field of psychology. Von Helmholtz took a mechanistic and deterministic approach. The first of his discoveries was measuring the speed of the neural impulse (90 feet per second), which provided evidence that thought and movement were not simultaneous, as was previously believed, but followed each other in distinct quantifiable increments. Following this line of research, reaction-time experiments became fruitful. Von Helmholtz also contributed to the understanding and measurement of psychophysiological processes, like vision and audition, with his work on the Young-Helmholtz theory of color vision as well as research on the perception of tones, harmonies, and discords.

Ernst Weber contributed to psychology with his experiments on cutaneous senses and muscular sensations. Most notably, Weber examined the sense of touch with the *two-point threshold*, "the threshold at which two points of stimulation can be distinguished as such." Weber also explored the point at which a person can tell whether two weights are the same or whether one is heavier, which he termed the *just noticeable difference*. He found that people can detect the difference when the difference was 1:40 of the standard weight. This ratio changed when people lifted the weights vs. when the weights were placed on their hands, and changed for other senses (such as vision). His "research showed that there is not a direct correspondence between a physical stimulus and our perception of it." Both von Helmholtz and Weber provided a useful method to examine the relationship between body and mind, which was perhaps their biggest contribution to psychology.

Gustav Fechner also studied the relationship between mental sensation and material stimuli. While he had lifelong neurotic symptoms, he eventually recovered and developed the idea of the pleasure principle. This theory later influenced Sigmund Freud's psychoanalytic school of thought. Fechner's greatest contribution to psychology was in deducing the relationship between sensation and perception. He believed that changes in the intensity of a stimulus are "relative to the amount of sensation that already exists." This allows the study of not just body, but mind. To pursue such study, he develops the idea of the *absolute threshold*, "the point of sensitivity below which no sensations can be detected and above which sensations can be experienced." He also defined the *differential threshold*, which is the "least amount of change in a stimulus that gives rise to a change in sensation." He found that the relationship between sensation (mind) and stimulus (material object) is captured by the equation $S = K \log R$.

Although some of Fechner's work sounds like Weber's, and although Fechner attended Weber's lectures, Fechner claims to have had the ideas independently. His research is termed *Psychophysics*, which is the "scientific study of the relations between mental and physical processes." Three of the methods he developed are still used today.

One of these is the method of average error (taking the mean of many observations to reduce error). A second method, the method of adjustment, used a stimulus whose intensity was constant while a second set of varying stimuli is compared to it. In the third method, the method of limits, two stimuli are presented, then one stimulus is gradually increased or decreased until a difference is detected. In 1860 Fechner published *Elements of Psychophysics,* which was an important contribution to scientific psychology. Fechner's work, the work of German physiologists, British empiricists, and the Zeitgeist of the time contributed to Wilhelm Wundt's founding of the new science of psychology.

Outline

I. David K. Makes a Mistake: The Importance of the Human Observer
     A. Measurement errors
          1. 1795: Reverend Nevil Maskelyne (1732-1811) was England's royal astronomer
               a.   his assistant, David Kinnebrook, recorded slower observation times than his own for a star to travel from point to point
               b.   fired Kinnebrook
          2. Bessel, a German astronomer, reviewed the above incident 20 years later in addition to other similar incidents
               a.   reasoned that the difference in times was due to individual differences not under personal control
               b.   called these differences among scientists the "personal equation"
               c.   concluded that
                     (1) astronomers must consider the nature of the human observer because recorded data are always affected by personal traits and perceptions
                     (2) this is also an issue in all sciences that use observational methods
     B. Locke and Berkeley
          1. perception is subjective, not objective
          2. cannot assume a one-to-one correspondence between the nature of the physical object and our perception of it
     C. Scientists began to focus on the human sense organs and physiological processes involved in sensing and perceiving
II. Developments in Early Physiology
     A. 1830's physiology
          1. became experimentally oriented
          2. Johannes Müller (1801-1858)
               a.   dominant advocate of experimental method
               b.   1833-1840: Handbook of the Physiology of Mankind
               c.   specific energies of nerves doctrine
                     (1) stimulation of a particular nerve results in a characteristic sensation
                     (2) each sensory nerve has its own specific energy
               d.   consequent research
                     (1) to localize functions within the nervous system
                     (2) to pinpoint peripheral sensory receptor mechanisms
     B. Research on brain functions
          1. Marshall Hall (1790-1857)
               a.   Scottish physician
               b.   stimulated nerve endings of decapitated animals, watched movement of body parts

       c.   concluded different levels of movement depend on different parts of the nervous system

          (1) voluntary movement: cerebrum

          (2) reflex movement: spinal cord

          (3) involuntary movement: direct stimulation of muscles

          (4) respiratory movement: medulla

  2. Pierre Flourens (1794-1867)

       a.   professor of natural history in Paris

       b.   used extirpation: "A technique for determining the function of a given part of an animal's brain by removing it or destroying it and observing the resulting behavior changes."

          (1) higher mental processes: cerebrum

          (2) visual and auditory reflexes: parts of midbrain

          (3) coordination: cerebellum

          (4) heartbeat, respiration, and other vital functions: medulla

  3. Paul Broca (1824-1880)

       a.   the clinical method (1861): "Posthumous examination of brain structures to detect damaged areas assumed to be responsible for behavioral conditions that existed before the person died."

       b.   Broca's area: the speech center in the 3rd frontal convolution of the left hemisphere of the cerebral cortex

  4. Gustav Fritsch and Eduard Hitzig (1870)

          (1) electrical stimulation method: "A technique for exploring the cerebral cortex with weak electric current to observe motor responses."

          (2) stimulation of certain cortical areas results in motor responses such as leg movement

C. Research on brain functions: Mapping from the outside

  1. Franz Josef Gall (1758-1828)

       a.   used the clinical method to map the brain from the inside

          (1) confirmed the existence of brain white and gray matter, nerve fibers from each brain side connecting to the opposite spinal column side, and fibers connecting the two brain hemispheres

       b.   attempted to answer the question, "How does the size and shape of the brain reveal information about brain facilities?" by mapping from the outside

          (1) species with larger brains = more intelligent

          (2) moved to cranioscopy (now known as phrenology),a controversial movement that "proposed that the shape of a person's skull revealed his or her intellectual and emotional characteristics"

          (3) went from a respected scientist to a quack and suspected fraudster

       c.   phrenology was popularized in Europe and the United States by Spurzheim and Combe and the Fowler brothers

          (1) discredited by Flourens ("shape of the skull did not match the contours of the underlying brain tissue")

          (2) demonstration that popularity does not guarantee validity

       d.   Gall's work reinforced the idea that specific brain functions could be localized

D. Research on the nervous system
    1. Luigi Galvani (1737 – 1798)
        a.   suggested nature of nerve impulse is electrical
        b.   by mid 19th century: electrical nature of nerve impulse accepted as fact
        c.   continuing his work, Giovanni Aldini, his nephew, used severed heads of criminals to show muscle movement from electrical stimulation
    2. accepted view: nervous system = conductor of electric impulses; central nervous system is a switching station between sensory and motor nerves
        a.   more sophisticated but conceptually similar to Descartes (nerve tube theory), Hartley (theory of vibrations)
        b.   both older and newer approaches = reflexive
        c.   stimulus → sense organ → nerve impulse → nervous system site → new impulse → motor response
    3. Santiago Ramón y Cajal (1852-1934)
        a.   Spanish physician
        b.   discovered the direction of travel for brain and spinal cord nerve impulses
        c.   won Nobel prize (1906)
        d.   Spanish was not a language of professional journals; others published "new" findings that he had previously demonstrated
        e.   illustrations the disadvantages of not being part of mainstream culture
    4. anatomy of the nervous system defined in the 19th century
        a.   nerve fibers= neurons + synapse (connecting points)
        b.   neurons "bits of matter" that combine to form bigger structures
    5. advances in the anatomy of the nervous system
        a.   supported mechanistic view of human functions
        b.   atomistic structures combined to produce complex structure
    6. the mechanistic spirit
        a.   most pronounced in Germany
        b.   Berlin Physical Society
            (1) formed by former students of Johannes Müller
            (2) principles of physics can explain all phenomena
            (3) wanted to develop a mechanistic physiology linked to physics
            (4) blood oath: "the only forces active within an organism are the common physico-chemical ones"
        c.   union of materialism, mechanism, empiricism, experimentation, and measurement within physiology
        d.   support for the scientific, psychological study of the mind
            (1) British empiricists: sensation as the only source of Knowledge
            (2) Bessel: individual differences in sensation and perception
            (3) Physiologists: mapping structure and function of the senses
        e.   next step = study the mind experimentally and "quantify this doorway to the mind: the subjective, mentalistic experience of sensation"

III. The Beginnings of Experimental Psychology
   A. Four German physiologists directly responsible for initial applications of experimentation to mind: Hermann von Helmholtz, Ernst Weber, Gustav Theodor Fechner, and Wilhelm Wundt
   B. Why Germany?
      1. German approach to science
         a. experimental physiology established and recognized to a unique degree
         b. the German temperament: exactness and precision
         c. use of the inductive method
         d. ready acceptance of biology and physiology as sciences
         e. broad definition of science
      2. reform movement in German universities
         a. principles of academic freedom in research and teaching
         b. encouraged growth of universities and faculty positions
         c. greater opportunities to learn and practice new scientific techniques
         d. great many universities and the most advanced scientific laboratory equipment
         e. one could earn a living as a research scientist
         f. "publish or perish" emphasis
      3. lack of viable research universities outside of Germany
         a. France and England focus on chemistry and physics
         b. other countries skeptical about applying science to the complex human mind
         c. United States had no devoted research institutions until Johns Hopkins University was founded in 1876, after the German model
      4. results
         a. series of important discoveries in the sciences
         b. German university professors directly responsible for growth and development of scientific psychology
IV. Hermann von Helmholtz (1821 – 1894)
   A. Helmholtz's life
      1. born in Potsdam, Germany
      2. delicate health
      3. 1838: enrolled at a Berlin medical institute: free tuition to future army surgeons
      4. seven years as army surgeon
         a. continued to study mathematics and physics
         b. published several articles
         c. mathematically formulated the law of conservation of energy
      5. faculty member in physiology at Universities of Königsberg, Bonn, and Heidelberg; position in physics at Berlin
      6. energetic, multiple scientific interests, on fast track to fame
      7. areas of contribution: physics, physiology, psychology
         a. invented the ophthalmoscope
         b. 1856-1866: Handbook of Physiological Optics
         c. 1863: On the Sensations of Tone (research on acoustics)
         d. also wrote on a diversity of topics including hay fever, glaciers, geometry, Arabian-Persian musical scale, afterimages, color blindness

    e. indirectly contributed to inventions of the wireless telegraph and radio

B. The contributions of Helmholtz: the neural impulse, vision, and audition
  1. first empirical measurement of the rate of conduction of the neural impulse (90 feet/second)
  2. suggested thought and movement are successive, not simultaneous
  3. researched reaction times for sensory nerves in humans
  4. studied mechanism by which internal eye muscles focus the lens
  5. revised and extended a theory (Young-Helmholtz) of color vision
  6. research on audition
    a. perception of tones
    b. nature of harmony and discord
    c. problem of resonance
  7. his study of the senses cultivated the experimental approach to the study of psychological problems
  8. work still cited in psychology texts
  9. recognized importance of applied research
  10. not a psychologist, but a significant contributor to the development of the discipline

V. Ernst Weber (1795 – 1878)
 A. His life
  1. born in Wittenberg, Germany
  2. 1815: PhD at University of Leipzig
  3. 1817 – 1871: taught anatomy and physiology at Leipzig
  4. primary research interest: physiology of sense organs
  5. applied of experimental methods of physiology to problems of psychology
  6. explored new fields--cutaneous and muscular sensations—rather than just vision and hearing

 B. Two-point thresholds: "The threshold at which two points of stimulation can be distinguished as such."
  1. two-points of stimulation on the skin: "the distance between two points that must be spanned before subjects report feeling two distinct sensations"
  2. first systematic experimental demonstration of the concept of threshold

 C. Just noticeable differences
  1. just noticeable difference (jnd) concept: "The smallest difference that can be detected between two physical stimuli."
    a. jnd of two weights = constant ratio of 1:40 (i.e., weight of 41 grams reported as just noticeably different from 40 grams)
  2. contribution of muscle sensations to ability to distinguish between weights: more accurate estimates when weights lifted by subjects versus placed in their hands
  3. discrimination depends on the relative difference between and not on the absolute weights of objects
  4. perception of a stimulus is not directly correlated to the physical stimulus
  5. revealed a way to investigate the mind-body relationship
  6. demonstrated the utility of experimental methods as a means of studying psychological phenomena

VI.   Gustav Theodor Fechner (1801-1887)
A. Lifetime
1. a physiologist for 7 years
2. a physicist for 15 years
3. a psychophysicist for 14 years
4. an experimental estheticist for 11 years
5. a philosopher for 40 years
6. an invalid for 12 years
B. Greatest fame from psychophysics, not his preference for renown
C. Fechner's life
1. born in southeastern Germany
2. 1817: began medical studies at University of Leipzig
3. attended Weber's lectures on physiology
4. protested the mechanism in his scientific training
   a.   as alias Dr. Mises, wrote satirical commentaries on medicine and science
   b.   conflicting sides of his personality: interest in science versus interest in metaphysical
   c.   contrasted his "day view" of regarding the universe from the point of view of consciousness versus the "night view" of mainstream science that both the universe and consciousness consisted only of inert matter
5. turned from medicine to physics and mathematics; 1824 lecturing and conducting research in physics at Leipzig
6. by late 1830's becomes interested in sensation, damages eyes by looking at the sun investigating afterimages
7. 1833: appointed professor was severely depressed for quite a few years
   a.   could not sleep
   b.   starving yet not hungry
   c.   so sensitive to light that he stayed in a dark room painted black
   d.   mother read to him through crack in door
   e.   tried a myriad of cures
   f.   recovered briefly after eating "raw spiced ham marinated in Rhine wine and lemon juice"
   g.   fearing for his sanity, involved himself in routine household chores
   h.   kept eating the ham
   i.   dreamed he would be cured in 77 days and was
8. depression was followed by euphoria and delusions of grandeur
   a.   developed the idea of the pleasure principle
   b.   concept later influenced Freud
9. 1844: officially an invalid, given a pension by University of Leipzig
10. remained at Leipzig in excellent health with continuing important scientific contributions until his death at 86
D. Mind and body: A quantitative relationship
1. October 22,1850: while lying in bed had insight about the law governing the mind-body connection
   a.   a quantitative relationship between a mental sensation and a material stimulus
   b.   the relationship is logarithmic, not a one-to-one increase

      c.   effects of stimulus intensities are relative to the amount of sensation that already exists

      d.   "Fechner crossed the barrier between body [physical stimulation] and mind [mental sensation] by relating one to the other empirically, making it possible to conduct experiments on the mind."

2. Fechner proposed two ways to measure sensation

      a.   presence or absence of a stimulus

      b.   absolute threshold: "The point of sensitivity below which no sensations can be detected and above which sensations can be experienced."

      c.   only the lowest level of a sensation can be determined using method of absolute threshold

3. differential threshold of sensitivity: "The point of sensitivity at which the least amount of change in a stimulus gives rise to a change in sensation."

      a.   the number of differential thresholds can be used as an objective measure of the subjective magnitude of sensation

      b.   measures the stimulus values necessary to create a difference between two sensations

4. Fechner's law: $S = K \log R$

      a.   for each sense, "there is a certain relative increase in stimulus intensity that always produces an observable change in the intensity of the sensation."

      b.   S: magnitude of the sensation [the mind or mental quality]

      c.   K: a constant

      d.   R: magnitude of the stimulus [the body or material (physical) quality]

      e.   log: logarithmic relationship

5. Fechner says his work, though similar to Weber's, was not influenced by him

E. Methods of psychophysics

1. psychophysics: "The scientific study of the relations between mental and physical processes."

2. method of average error (method of adjustment)

      a.   over a number of trials, subject adjusts a variable stimulus until it is perceived to be equal to a standard stimulus

      b.   the average of the obtained differences = error of observation

      c.   used to measure reaction time and visual and auditory discriminations

      d.   calculating the mean is basically drawing on the method of average error

3. method of constant stimuli

      a.   uses two constant stimuli: a standard weight and a comparison weight

      b.   goal is to measure the stimulus difference required to produce a judgment of the second weight as heavier, lighter, or equal to the first weight

4. method of limits (differential threshold)

      a.   two stimuli such as weights presented to the subjects

      b.   experimenter increases or decreases one stimulus until subject detects a difference

      c.   many trials arc used, and differential thresholds are averaged

F. Original source material on psychophysics from Elements of Psychophysics (1860)
   1. psychophysics = "exact theory of the functionally dependent relations of...the physical and psychological worlds"
      a. mental, psychological, soul = understood or abstracted from introspective observation
      b. bodily, corporeal, physical, material = understood or abstracted from observation from the outside
   2. the relationships are lawful
   3. start with the physical because it is measurable; measurement of the psychical is obtained dependently on the physical
   4. "The truly basic empirical evidence for...psychophysics can be sought only in the realm of outer psychophysics [relationship between stimulus and sensation], inasmuch as only is part...is available to immediate experience."
G. In brief, Fechner
   1. countered Kant's insistence that psychology could never be a science because psychological processes not measurable
   2. provided the prerequisites for a science of psychology by making it possible to measure mental experience
   3. provoked Wundt's plan for an experimental psychology
   4. gave psychology precise and elegant techniques of measurement

VII. The Formal Founding of Psychology
A. By the mid 19th century natural science methods being used to study mental phenomena
B. The importance of the senses established by British empiricists and astronomers
C. German physiologists described functioning of the senses Positivistic zeitgeist encouraged melding of philosophy and physiology Final touch provided by Wilhelm Wundt who brought them formally together by founding psychology

Lecture prompts/Discussion topics for chapter three

- What makes phrenology unscientific? (a key point to bring out is the idea of falsifiability) What might be the impact today if Gall's work had not been discredited?

- What are the strengths and weaknesses of each of the three methods outlined by the chapter: extirpation, clinical method, and electrical stimulation?

- The work of these early researchers was an attempt to understand the human nervous system, but a lot of them used animals in their research. Under what conditions would an animal's nervous system be an appropriate avenue to learn about humans, and under what conditions would it be inappropriate?

- Related to the last question: thinking about this early physiological research, was it "worth" the information we gained (particularly the work of Flourens and Aldini)

Internet Resources for chapter three

Ernst Weber Links
http://elvers.us/hop/index.asp?m=3&a=87&key=59
   This is a site that provides a nice photograph of Weber later in life, and a listing of links to other Weber sites.

Hermann Ludwig Ferdinand von Helmholtz
http://www-history.mcs.st-andrews.ac.uk/Mathematicians/Helmholtz.html
> Information about Helmholtz's life and achievements, including several photographs.

The Phrenology Page
http://www.phrenology.org/
> This site is a comprehensive collection of information about the history and current practices of phrenology.

Mind, Brain, and the Experimental Psychology of Consciousness
http://serendip.brynmawr.edu/Mind/Consciousness.html
> This site provides a summary of the experimental work done on consciousness, and focuses on Fechner's contributions.

The Study of Brain Function in the Nineteenth Century
http://www.cerebromente.org.br/n01/frenolog/frenloc.htm
> This site provides a history of the search for cortical localization with nice background information about Flourens, Broca, and a number of other people.

Potential answers to chapter three discussion questions

1. What was David Kinnebrook's role in the development of the new psychology?
David Kinnebrook, an astronomer's assistant at the Royal Observatory in Greenwich, England, was fired from his job in 1795 because the observations he made of the speed of stars differed from his supervisor's (though not by much). Twenty years later, a German astronomer named Bessel became interested in how the observations of two individuals can differ. He believed that David's mistakes (and the mistakes of other astronomers) were a function of individual differences rather than of competence. His conclusions were that astronomers have to take individual differences into account, and also that any science depending on human observation would have to be wary about individual differences. This caused human sensation to become a focus of study.

2. What was the significance of Bessel's work for the new psychology? How did it relate to the work of Locke, Berkeley, and other empirical philosophers?
Bessel found that human observation was subject to individual differences. Furthermore, any science depending on human observation would have to be wary about individual differences. This fit in with what the philosophers Locke and Berkeley promoted: the idea that observations of objects are subjective and may not correspond to the properties of the object.

3. How did developments in early physiology support the mechanistic image of human nature?
The early researchers studying physiology began to investigate the human sense organs. Such an investigation was prompted by the mechanistic Zeitgeist of the time and in turn supports the idea that there are specific mechanisms which govern human physiological processes. Researchers studying physical/physiological process also needed to investigate how these sensations related to mental perceptions. Thus, early physiological research made the connection between mind and body using the mechanistic premise that humans function in the same measurable ways as machines.

4. Discuss the methods that scientists developed to map brain functions.
There were three general approaches to mapping brain functions. With extirpation, parts of the brain are systematically destroyed to observe the subsequent behavior (Marshall Hall and Pierre Fourens). In the clinical method, the researcher looks at the brains of people after they died who exhibited odd behavior in life (Paul Broca). Finally, electrical stimulation of the brain and body was used to observe the muscle twitches (Fritsch and Hitzig).

5. Describe Gall's cranioscopy method and the popular movement that derived from it. How were they discredited?
Gall was concerned with mapping brain functions from both inside and outside. When looking at the brain from the outside, he developed cranioscopy, later known as phrenology, which proposes that the shape of one's skull reveals intellectual or emotional characteristics. Phrenology quickly became popular and profitable across Europe and in the United States. Physiologists, however, were critical of phrenology. Flourens, for example, proved that the skull's shape was unrelated to the brain's shape. In addition, physiologists located the functions of areas of the brain using other methods and subsequently discovered that those functions did not match up with Gall's phrenology mapping.

6. What was the ultimate goal of the Berlin Physical Society?
This group, founded in the 1840's, was made up largely of the former students of Johannes Müller. Their believed that all phenomena could be accounted for by the principles of physics. Four of them declared that "the only forces active within an organism are the common physio-chemical ones." What they hoped to do was connect physiology with physics, that is, to develop a physiology in the framework of mechanism.

7. Explain how developments in physiology combined with British empiricism to produce the new psychology.
British empiricists argued that sensation was the only source of knowledge. This was the basis for physiologists' investigations of the connection between mind and body, as well as research into the mechanisms used by the human body.
Bessel's contribution was to show these new scientific fields that individual differences can greatly affect sciences whose methods use human observation. These methods and scientific frameworks all coalesced to form early psychology, as the focus of investigation shifted onto the mind and body connection.

8. For what reasons did experimental psychology emerge in Germany and not elsewhere?
First, German scientists favored the inductive approach to science, which involves carefully collecting and cataloging a large number of facts. Germans also defined science to include a wider variety of topics. Thus, Germans were more readily accepting of new sciences like biology and physiology. In the early nineteenth century, German professors and students were allowed the freedom to pursue any topic of study that they wished (a freedom unknown in France and England). German universities were also more research focused, whereas France and England were both lacking in research funding. At the same time there were far more universities in Germany compared to only two in England, and there were no research universities in the United States until Johns Hopkins was founded in 1876.

9. What is the significance of Helmholtz's research on the speed of the neural impulse?
Before Helmholtz's research, it was thought that neural transmission was instantaneous. He discovered that neural impulses are delayed from the time of stimulation, and that neural impulses

travel at 90 feet/second. The implication of this is "that thought and movement follow each other at a measurable interval and do not occur simultaneously."

10. Describe Weber's research on two-point thresholds and on just noticeable differences. What was the importance of these ideas for psychology?
Ernst Weber explored the sense of touch with the *two-point threshold*, "the threshold at which two points of stimulation can be distinguished as such." Weber also explored the point at which a person can tell whether two weights are the same or whether one is heavier, which he termed the *just noticeable difference*. He found that people can detect the difference when the difference was 1:40 of the standard weight. This ratio changed when people lifted the weights vs. when the weights were placed on their hands, and changed for other senses (such as vision). His "research showed that there is not a direct correspondence between a physical stimulus and our perception of it."

11. What was Fechner's insight on October 22, 1850? How did Fechner measure sensations?
His insight on October 22, 1850, was that there could be a "quantitative relationship between a mental sensation and a material stimulus" and that perceived changes in the intensity of a stimulus are "relative to the amount of sensation that already exists."
This allows the study of not just body, but mind. He measured sensations using several methods. First, have someone determine the presence or absence of a stimulus. Second, have someone report the intensity at which they first sense the stimulus (absolute threshold). Third, have someone determine when they notice that the intensity of a stimulus has changed (differential threshold).

12. What is the relationship between the intensity of the stimulus and the intensity of the sensation, as represented by the equation $S = K \log R$?
S represents the magnitude of the sensation and R represents the magnitude of the stimulus. With the logarithmic function, one of these variables changes arithmetically and the other geometrically. Specifically, as the intensity of a stimulus increases, the changes have to be bigger for us to notice the change.

13. What psychophysical methods did Fechner use? How did psychophysics influence the development of psychology?
Fechner developed three methods that are still used today. One of these is the method of average error (taking the mean of many observations to reduce error). A second method used a stimulus whose intensity was constant while a second set of varying stimuli is compared to it. In the third method, "the method of limits, two stimuli...are presented to the subjects" and one stimulus is increased or decreased until a difference is detected. Fechner's work provided the methods to measure mental/conscious/psychological phenomena.

14. Do you think experimental psychology would have developed when it did without Fechner's work? Without Weber's work? Why?
I doubt it, particularly if both are absent from the historical record—these are people doing systematic and scientific study of conscious processes, something thought to be impossible (see Immanuel Kant). Some of Fechner's ideas are similar to Weber's, and it is possible that the Zeitgeist would have forced the discoveries out if one of these men was missing, but not both. Of the two, Fechner's work is of greater importance. His methodology was innovative but valid, so much so that it is still used today.

15. What is the difference between inner psychophysics and outer psychophysics? Which was Fechner forced to focus on? Why?

"Inner psychophysics refers to the relationship between the sensation and the accompanying brain and nerve excitation." Outer psychophysics was the "relationship between the stimulus and the subjective intensity of the sensation, as measured by his" methods. Because the technology was not present to engage in inner psychophysics (as it is now), he concentrated on outer psychophysics.

Key terms from chapter three

- **Absolute threshold** Found by Fechner, "the point of sensitivity below which no sensations can be detected and above which sensation can be experienced."
- **Broca's area** An area of the brain that controls speech, found by Broca using the clinical method.
- **Clinical method** One of three techniques to find out what a particular brain part controls in the body, the brain of a patient with unusual symptoms in life is recovered after the patient dies and examined to assess brain damage.
- **Cranioscopy** Developed by Franz Josef Gall and later known as phrenology, the belief (since discredited) that bumps on the exterior of the skull revealed "intellectual and emotional characteristics."
- **Differential threshold** Found by Fechner, "the point of sensitivity at which the least amount of change in a stimulus gives rise to a change in sensation."
- **Electrical stimulation** One of three techniques to find out what a particular brain part controls in the body, electrical current is used to stimulate the nervous system to see what motor responses ensue.
- **Extirpation** One of three techniques to find out what a particular brain part controls in the body, brain parts are systematically destroyed and the animal is subsequently observed.
- **Just noticeable difference** Found by Ernst Weber, "the smallest difference that can be detected between two physical stimuli."
- **Neural impulse speed** Found by Hermann von Helmholtz to be 90 feet/second.
- **Personal equation** Discovered by Friedrich Bessel, the idea that differences in measurement between astronomers was expected, and later comes to be known as "individual differences."
- **Phrenology** Developed by Franz Josef Gall and first known as cranioscopy, the belief (since discredited) that bumps on the exterior of the skull revealed "intellectual and emotional characteristics."
- **Psychophysics** Research that involves "the relationship between the mental...and material...world" and was founded by Fechner.
- **Two-point threshold** Found by Ernst Weber, "the threshold at which two points of stimulation can be distinguished as such."

ESSAY

1. Describe the circumstances under which Bessel discovered the importance of the human observer. To what two conclusions did his findings lead? What were the consequences of his work in terms of subsequent developments in early physiology?

   ANS:
   Answer not provided.

   PTS: 1   MSC: WWW

2. Describe Müller's doctrine of the specific energies of nerves. Why was it so important to the early years of modern psychology?

   ANS:
   Answer not provided.

   PTS: 1

3. Identify the early physiologists who made substantial contributions to the mapping of brain functions and describe the methods and findings of each.

   ANS:
   Answer not provided.

   PTS: 1

4. Why did experimental psychology begin in Germany rather than in other European countries?

   ANS:
   Answer not provided.

   PTS: 1   MSC: WWW

5. What contributions led to the description of Helmholtz as "one of the greatest scientists of the 19th century"?

   ANS:
   Answer not provided.

   PTS: 1

6. Describe the research and findings of Ernst Weber. What was the importance of his work on later physiologists? What was its importance to the new psychology?

   ANS:
   Answer not provided.

   PTS: 1

CHAPTER 3

7. Discuss why Fechner's work may have been the necessary precondition for the founding of psychology as a separate discipline.

ANS:
Answer not provided.

PTS: 1

MULTIPLE CHOICE

8. Why was David Kinnebrook fired?
   a. He dated, but did not marry, the daughter of his boss.
   b. His observations differed from the observations of his boss.
   c. He was incompetent.
   d. He was never able to learn to use the equipment correctly.
   e. None of the choices are correct.

   ANS: B   PTS: 1
   REF: David K. Makes a Mistake: The Importance of the Human Observer

9. Bessel began the study of individual differences in perception by noting that _____.
   a. humans differ in the speed with which they react to a loud sound
   b. animals, such as dogs, have a wider range for hearing sounds than do humans
   c. time space must be measured in relative units
   d. astronomers differed in their time estimates in measuring the transit of a star
   e. None of the choices are correct.

   ANS: D   PTS: 1
   REF: David K. Makes a Mistake: The Importance of the Human Observer

10. Whose research would support the argument that there is no such thing as objective observation?
    a. Maskelyne's
    b. Bessel's
    c. Locke's
    d. Muller's
    e. Wundt's

    ANS: B   PTS: 1
    REF: David K. Makes a Mistake: The Importance of the Human Observer

11. Bessel's discovery had an impact on which of the following sciences?
    a. Psychology
    b. Physiology
    c. Biology
    d. Astronomy
    e. All of the above

    ANS: E   PTS: 1
    REF: David K. Makes a Mistake: The Importance of the Human Observer

12. Until the work of _____, experimentation was not the preferred method in physiology.
    a. Galileo
    b. Newton
    c. J. Müller
    d. Broca
    e. Wundt

    ANS: C   PTS: 1   REF: Developments in Early Physiology
    MSC: WWW

13. Johannes Müller found that nerves only give information characteristic of the sense associated with it. This means that when an auditory nerve is stimulated, it will result in someone hearing a sound, even when no noise is present. Müller called this _____.
    a. the doctrine of the specific energies of nerves
    b. specificity
    c. neuronal tubule clarity
    d. the postmortem method
    e. the experimental method in physiology

    ANS: A   PTS: 1   REF: Developments in Early Physiology

14. Johannes Müller's most influential publications was _____.
    a. *The Nervous system of Animals*
    b. *The Senses*
    c. *The Handbook of the Physiology of Mankind*
    d. *Experimental Methods*
    e. *Interpretation of Dreams*

    ANS: C   PTS: 1   REF: Developments in Early Physiology

15. The practice of psychosurgery such as prefrontal lobotomies, has its roots in the _____.
    a. implementation of the experimental method in physiology
    b. doctrine of the specific energies of nerves
    c. electrical stimulation method
    d. postmortem method
    e. extirpation method

    ANS: E   PTS: 1   REF: Developments in Early Physiology

16. _____ was a pioneer in research on reflex behavior showing that reflexes could occur in the absence of brain involvement.
    a. Hall
    b. Broca
    c. Flourens
    d. Galvani
    e. Gall

    ANS: A   PTS: 1   REF: Developments in Early Physiology

17. In his research, Flourens localized specific functions to how many brain areas?
    a. 2
    b. 3
    c. 4
    d. 5
    e. 6

    ANS: C   PTS: 1   REF: Developments in Early Physiology
    MSC: WWW

18. "Acts like a chicken with its head cut off" is a description of behavior that has its roots in ____ research.
    a. Hall's
    b. Flouren's
    c. Broca's
    d. Fritsch's
    e. Helmholtz's

    ANS: A   PTS: 1   REF: Developments in Early Physiology

19. In modern medicine, the cause of a person's dementia typically cannot be determined until autopsy. Thus, ____ clinical research method continues to be of significance in medicine and psychology.
    a. Marshall's
    b. Flouren's
    c. Broca's
    d. Fritsch's
    e. Helmhotz's

    ANS: C   PTS: 1   REF: Developments in Early Physiology

20. The ____ method is described as a type of posthumous extirpation.
    a. experimental
    b. clinical
    c. scientific
    d. electrical stimulation
    e. introspection

    ANS: B   PTS: 1   REF: Developments in Early Physiology

21. Electrical stimulation as a method of mapping the cerebral cortex was introduced by ____.
    a. Galvani and Aldini
    b. Flourens and Hall
    c. Gall and Spurzheim
    d. Broca and Kinnebrook
    e. Fritsch and Hitzig

    ANS: E   PTS: 1   REF: Developments in Early Physiology

22. ____ produced the theory of cranioscopy.
    a. Flourens
    b. Broca
    c. Spurzheim
    d. Gall
    e. Hall

    ANS: D   PTS: 1   REF: Developments in Early Physiology
    MSC: WWW

23. ____ discovered, among other things, that the brain had both white and gray matter, and that fiber connect the two halves of the brain.
    a. Gall
    b. Spurzheim
    c. Broca
    d. Hall
    e. Flourens

    ANS: A   PTS: 1   REF: Developments in Early Physiology

24. ____ created phrenology, which proposed that the topography of a person's skull revealed his or her intellectual and emotional characteristics.
    a. Flourens
    b. Gall
    c. Spurzheim
    d. Broca
    e. Hall

    ANS: B   PTS: 1   REF: Developments in Early Physiology

25. Although he did not develop the theory called phrenology, ____ served as its popularizer.
    a. Gall
    b. Spurzheim
    c. Galvani
    d. Fritsch
    e. Hall

    ANS: B   PTS: 1   REF: Developments in Early Physiology

26. In the Unites States, the ____ brothers had a profitable and extensive business selling phrenology readings.
    a. Ringling
    b. Fowler
    c. Barnum
    d. Smithson
    e. James

    ANS: B   PTS: 1   REF: Developments in Early Physiology

27. The most effective criticisms of phrenology came from whom?
    a. Broca
    b. Hall
    c. Spurzheim
    d. Fechner
    e. Flourens

    ANS: E   PTS: 1   REF: Developments in Early Physiology

28. ____ systematically destroyed parts of the brain using extirpation.
    a. Broca
    b. Gall
    c. Spurzheim
    d. Flourens
    e. Fowler

    ANS: D   PTS: 1   REF: Developments in Early Physiology

29. The researcher credited with the finding or conclusion that nerve impulses are electrical within the neuron is ____.
    a. Flourens
    b. Galvani
    c. Helmholtz
    d. Müller
    e. Sherrington

    ANS: B   PTS: 1   REF: Developments in Early Physiology
    MSC: WWW

30. The representation of the nervous system as a complex switching system reveals the 19th-century reliance on ____.
    a. mechanism
    b. determinism
    c. experimentation
    d. materialism
    e. mentalism

    ANS: A   PTS: 1   REF: Developments in Early Physiology

31. Who discovered the direction of travel of nerve impulses in the brain and spinal cord?
    a. Flourens
    b. Fechner
    c. Helmholtz
    d. Cajal
    e. Gall

    ANS: D   PTS: 1   REF: Developments in Early Physiology

32. The method of logic that characterizes psychology and that was favored in Germany of the 19th century was ____.
    a. the deductive method
    b. the inductive method
    c. the experimental method
    d. the hypothetico-deductive method
    e. structural equation modeling

    ANS: B   PTS: 1   REF: The Beginnings of Experimental Psychology

33. In the 19th century, the British and French defined science as including ____.
    a. only physics
    b. physiology and medicine only
    c. physics and chemistry only
    d. all fields that used the experimental method
    e. all areas that took a positivistic approach

    ANS: C   PTS: 1   REF: The Beginnings of Experimental Psychology

34. German universities were especially fertile ground for scientific advances because ____.
    a. there were only two of them, so each received only the most talented faculty and students
    b. there was academic freedom for students and faculty alike
    c. the British and the French were using unscientific methods to research the mind
    d. anyone with independent income could be a gentleman-scientist
    e. None of the answers are correct.

    ANS: B   PTS: 1   REF: The Beginnings of Experimental Psychology

PHYSIOLOGICAL INFLUENCES ON PSYCHOLOGY   87

35. The "publish or perish" ethic, which is a hallmark of the most prestigious U.S. research universities and colleges, is a direct descendant of the 19th-century _____ universities.
    a. British
    b. French
    c. German
    d. Austrian
    e. Russian

    ANS: C   PTS: 1   REF: The Beginnings of Experimental Psychology

36. Helmholtz emphasized a(n) _____ approach.
    a. materialistic and mechanistic
    b. deterministic and mentalistic
    c. experimental and mentalistic
    d. mechanistic and deterministic
    e. materialistic and experimental

    ANS: D   PTS: 1   REF: Hermann von Helmholtz (1821-1894)

37. Who invented the ophthalmoscope?
    a. Weber
    b. Fechner
    c. Helmholtz
    d. Cajal
    e. Wundt

    ANS: C   PTS: 1   REF: Hermann von Helmholtz (1821-1894)

38. Which of the following was NOT one of the research areas of Helmholtz?
    a. theory of color vision
    b. perception of combination and individual tones
    c. resonance theory of hearing
    d. speed of neural impulse
    e. All of the choices were research areas of Helmholtz.

    ANS: E   PTS: 1   REF: Hermann von Helmholtz (1821-1894)

39. One of Helmholtz's particular contributions to psychology was his work on _____.
    a. vision
    b. the skin senses
    c. the conservation of energy
    d. geometric axioms
    e. mental telegraphy

    ANS: A   PTS: 1   REF: Hermann von Helmholtz (1821-1894)

40. Why did Helmholtz abandon his research into human reaction times?
    a. He found differences from one individual to the next.
    b. He found differences in the same individual.
    c. He never did any such research on human subjects.
    d. He did not abandon this research.
    e. He found differences from one individual to the next and he found differences in the same individual.

    ANS: E   PTS: 1   REF: Hermann von Helmholtz (1821-1894)

41. Who devised a theory of color vision as well as conducted research on audition?
    a. Cajal
    b. Fechner
    c. Wundt
    d. Helmholtz
    e. Weber

    ANS: D   PTS: 1   REF: Hermann von Helmholtz (1821-1894)
    MSC: WWW

42. With regard to the speed of the nerve impulse, perhaps the most important conclusion of Helmholtz's research for psychology was the determination ____.
    a. that the nerve impulse's speed is 900 feet/second
    b. that thought and movement are not simultaneous
    c. of the specific energies of nerves
    d. of the nature of harmony
    e. of the problem of resonance

    ANS: B   PTS: 1   REF: Hermann von Helmholtz (1821-1894)

43. The modern notion of subliminal perception rests on the idea that the threshold of perception or consciousness can be determined. The first experimental illustration of psychological threshold was demonstrated by ____.
    a. Helmholtz
    b. Weber
    c. Fechner
    d. Wundt
    e. Freud

    ANS: B   PTS: 1   REF: Ernst Weber (1795-1878)

44. Weber's Law, the formulation of how much change in a stimulus is required for a subject to detect it, rests on the measurement of the ____.
    a. threshold of consciousness
    b. just noticeable difference
    c. cognizant awareness
    d. limen of consciousness
    e. method of average error

    ANS: B   PTS: 1   REF: Ernst Weber (1795-1878)

45. Who developed both the two-point threshold and the concept of the just noticeable difference?
    a. Weber
    b. Helmholtz
    c. Fechner
    d. Wundt
    e. Cajal

    ANS: A   PTS: 1   REF: Ernst Weber (1795-1878)
    MSC: WWW

46. Whose major contributions to the new psychology involved the two-point threshold and the just noticeable difference?
    a. Hermann von Helmholtz
    b. Gustav Fechner
    c. Friedrich Bessel
    d. Wilhelm Wundt
    e. Ernst Weber

    ANS: E   PTS: 1   REF: Ernst Weber (1795-1878)

47. What is the smallest detectable difference between two stimuli?
    a. absolute threshold
    b. doctrine of specific nerve energies
    c. decision threshold
    d. just noticeable difference
    e. threshold of consciousness

    ANS: D   PTS: 1   REF: Ernst Weber (1795-1878)

48. What was the ratio of a weight to its just noticeable difference weight when they were lifted? What was the ratio of a weight to its just noticeable difference weight when the weights were placed in the subject's hands?
    a. 1:40; 1:30
    b. 1:30; 1:40
    c. 1:40; 1:25
    d. 1:25; 1:50
    e. None of the choices are correct.

    ANS: A   PTS: 1   REF: Ernst Weber (1795-1878)

49. Weber suggested that discrimination among sensations depended on ____.
    a. audition
    b. vision
    c. a constant ratio that would be consistent for all of the senses
    d. the absolute difference between two weights
    e. the relative difference or ratio between two weights

    ANS: E   PTS: 1   REF: Ernst Weber (1795-1878)

50. Weber's experiments led to two important contributions: (a) further research and (b) the focus of attention of later physiologists and the new psychology on the development of ____.
    a. experimental methods for studying mind-body relationships
    b. the method of introspection
    c. the application of experimentation to physiological events
    d. the field he called "psychophysics"
    e. cranioscopy

    ANS: A   PTS: 1   REF: Ernst Weber (1795-1878)

51. Which of the following is true of Fechner?
    a. He taught at Leipzig.
    b. He developed the notion of the pleasure principle.
    c. He seriously damaged his eyes by looking at the sun through colored glasses.
    d. He was "cured" of some symptoms by eating spiced raw ham soaked in Rhine wine and lemon juice.
    e. All of the choices are correct.

    ANS: E   PTS: 1   REF: Gustav Theodor Fechner (1801-1887)

52. Fechner wrote satirical essays ridiculing medicine and science under the pen name ____.
    a. Dr. Weber
    b. Dr. Mises
    c. Mr. Misfortune
    d. Dr. Kopf
    e. Dr. Misfortune

    ANS: B   PTS: 1   REF: Gustav Theodor Fechner (1801-1887)

53. After Fechner obtained the very important appointment of professor at the University of Leipzig, he ____.
    a. became depressed
    b. married his fiancé
    c. became angry
    d. was "cured" of depression
    e. celebrated in an inappropriate manner

    ANS: A   PTS: 1   REF: Gustav Theodor Fechner (1801-1887)

54. As a form of occupational therapy, Fechner ____.
    a. chopped carrots and turnips
    b. made strings and bandages
    c. grinded a sugarloaf into powdered sugar
    d. dipped candles
    e. All of the choices are correct.

    ANS: E   PTS: 1   REF: Gustav Theodor Fechner (1801-1887)

55. While euphoric and suffering from delusions of grandeur, Fechner ____.
    a. had to be hospitalized
    b. developed the idea of the pleasure principle
    c. stumbled on the notion of free association
    d. ate ham soaked in Rhine wine
    e. declared he was Napoleon

    ANS: B   PTS: 1   REF: Gustav Theodor Fechner (1801-1887)
    MSC: WWW

56. Fechner's flash of insight about the mind-body connection was that there is a(n) ____ relationship between a mental sensation and a material stimulus.
    a. null
    b. quantitative
    c. one-to-one
    d. qualitative
    e. unobservable

    ANS: B   PTS: 1   REF: Gustav Theodor Fechner (1801-1887)

57. According to Fechner, the effects of stimulus intensities are not ____ but are ____ to the amount of sensation that already exists.
   a. equal; related
   b. relative; absolute
   c. noticeable; relevant
   d. related; equal
   e. absolute; relative

   ANS: E   PTS: 1   REF: Gustav Theodor Fechner (1801-1887)

58. Fechner's most important contribution to psychology was the ____.
   a. quantification of the mind-body relationship
   b. determination that the effect of a stimulus intensity change is relative to the intensity that already exists
   c. determination of the pleasure principle
   d. qualitative relationship between a physical stimulus and the mental sensation of it
   e. study of the differential threshold

   ANS: A   PTS: 1   REF: Gustav Theodor Fechner (1801-1887)

59. Fechner proposed two ways to measure the lowest level of a sensation. One was the point of stimulus intensity below which no sensation is reported and above which subjects do experience a sensation; the other was ____.
   a. whether or not a stimulus is present or absent, sensed or not sensed
   b. the point of sensitivity at which the least change in a stimulus results in a change of sensation
   c. the level at which two points of stimulation can be distinguished
   d. the smallest difference that can be detected between two physical stimuli
   e. None of the choices are correct.

   ANS: A   PTS: 1   REF: Gustav Theodor Fechner (1801-1887)
   MSC: WWW

60. The point of sensitivity at which the least amount of change in a stimulus gives rise to a change in a sensation is a definition of ____.
   a. the just noticeable difference
   b. the absolute threshold
   c. Weber's Law
   d. the differential threshold
   e. the stimulus change threshold

   ANS: D   PTS: 1   REF: Gustav Theodor Fechner (1801-1887)

61. The point of sensitivity below which no sensation can be detected and above which sensation can be experienced is a definition of the ____.
   a. just noticeable difference
   b. absolute just noticeable difference
   c. differential threshold
   d. differential just noticeable difference
   e. absolute threshold

   ANS: E   PTS: 1   REF: Gustav Theodor Fechner (1801-1887)

62. ____ discovered the law, $S = K \log R$.
   a. Müller
   b. Weber
   c. Helmholtz
   d. Fechner
   e. Wundt

   ANS: D   PTS: 1   REF: Gustav Theodor Fechner (1801-1887)

63. The scientific study of the relations between mental and physical processes is a definition of ____.
   a. psychophysics
   b. Wundt's psychology
   c. Weber's Law
   d. Fechner's Law
   e. cranioscopy

   ANS: A   PTS: 1   REF: Gustav Theodor Fechner (1801-1887)

64. In Fechner's Law as one variable increases arithmetically, the other variable increases ____.
   a. arithmetically
   b. geometrically
   c. metaphysically
   d. mathematically
   e. psychophysically

   ANS: B   PTS: 1   REF: Gustav Theodor Fechner (1801-1887)
   MSC: WWW

65. In Fechner's law, S is the ____.
   a. magnitude of the stimulus
   b. duration of the stimulus
   c. intensity of the stimulus
   d. magnitude of the sensation
   e. duration of the sensation

   ANS: D   PTS: 1   REF: Gustav Theodor Fechner (1801-1887)

66. Late in his career, Fechner noted that the idea for describing the mind-body relationship ____.
   a. came in a vision
   b. was essentially what Weber's work had shown
   c. had not been suggested to him by Weber's work
   d. was inspired by Helmholtz
   e. would not have come to him if he hadn't eaten wine-soaked ham

   ANS: C   PTS: 1   REF: Gustav Theodor Fechner (1801-1887)

67. The calculation of the mean of a group of scores is the same as Fechner's ____.
   a. method of limits
   b. differential threshold
   c. method of constant stimuli
   d. method of average error
   e. differential average

   ANS: D   PTS: 1   REF: Gustav Theodor Fechner (1801-1887)

68. The original source material on Fechner reproduced in your textbook was taken from the book ____.
    a. *Physics and Medicine*
    b. *The Connection between Mind and Body*
    c. *Dealing with Depression*
    d. *Physics, Physiology, and Psychophysics*
    e. *Elements of Psychophysics*

    ANS: E   PTS: 1   REF: Gustav Theodor Fechner (1801-1887)

69. According to Fechner in the original source material, "Psychophysics should be understood as an exact theory of the functionally dependent relations of..." ____ and ____.
    a. soul; body
    b. physical world; psychological world
    c. the material; the mental
    d. All of the choices are correct.
    e. None of the choices are correct.

    ANS: D   PTS: 1   REF: Gustav Theodor Fechner (1801-1887)

70. In the original source material from one of his books, Fechner states that, "____ depends on ____".
    a. an outer part; an inner part
    b. an inner part; an outer part
    c. empirical; metaphysical
    d. stimulation; sensation
    e. sensation; stimulation

    ANS: E   PTS: 1   REF: Gustav Theodor Fechner (1801-1887)
    MSC: WWW

71. How did the British empiricists (BritE) and the German physiologists (GerP) differ in their approach to the study of the senses?
    a. The BritE developed more precise experiments than the GerP to study the senses.
    b. The BritE applied mathematics to the study of the senses whereas the Germans did not.
    c. The BritE concentrated on the study of vision and the GerP studied hearing.
    d. The BritE studied the senses from the viewpoint of philosophy. The GerP used scientific methods to study the senses.
    e. They did not differ.

    ANS: D   PTS: 1   REF: The Formal Founding of Psychology

72. Fechner's work had proved Immanuel Kant wrong when Kant said that ____.
    a. nothing good ever comes out of Leipzig
    b. psychology could never be a science
    c. the brain would never be mapped
    d. mental phenomena do not exist
    e. sensations reliably reflect the object in the material world

    ANS: B   PTS: 1   REF: Gustav Theodor Fechner (1801-1887)

73. Psychology was founded by ____.
    a. Helmholtz
    b. Weber
    c. Fechner
    d. Wundt
    e. James

    ANS: D   PTS: 1   REF: The Formal Founding of Psychology

TRUE/FALSE

74. The royal astronomer of England, Nevil Maskelyne, discovered the phenomenon that is known as the personal equation.

   ANS: F   PTS: 1
   REF: David K. Makes a Mistake: The Importance of the Human Observer
   MSC: WWW

75. The personal equation is a formula that describes the precise role that each of a person's voluntary behaviors contributes to his or her personality (behavioral style).

   ANS: F   PTS: 1
   REF: David K. Makes a Mistake: The Importance of the Human Observer

76. Physiology did not adopt the experimental method until the 1830s.

   ANS: T   PTS: 1   REF: Developments in Early Physiology

77. The theory of the specific energies of nerves was the work of Johannes Müller.

   ANS: T   PTS: 1   REF: Developments in Early Physiology
   MSC: WWW

78. Flourens is known for the systematic nature of his extirpation research.

   ANS: T   PTS: 1   REF: Developments in Early Physiology

79. Both Hall and Flourens studied localization of function using the method of electrical stimulation.

   ANS: F   PTS: 1   REF: Developments in Early Physiology

80. Broca's area was discovered using the extirpation method.

   ANS: F   PTS: 1   REF: Developments in Early Physiology

81. Today, a differential diagnosis of Alzheimer's or Pick's disease can be made only by autopsy. Thus, the extirpation method continues to be invaluable to research in psychology.

   ANS: F   PTS: 1   REF: Developments in Early Physiology

82. Hall and Flourens found that stimulating particular cortical areas in animals caused motor responses.

   ANS: F   PTS: 1   REF: Developments in Early Physiology

83. Gall's work on phrenology has been strongly supported by subsequent research.

   ANS: F   PTS: 1   REF: Developments in Early Physiology

84. Gall's ideas reinforced the growing belief among scientists that it was possible to localize specific brain functions.

   ANS: T   PTS: 1   REF: Developments in Early Physiology
   MSC: WWW

85. The electrical nature of the nerve impulse was one of the most important discoveries in physiology concurrent with the founding of psychology in the late 1800s.

    ANS: T   PTS: 1   REF: Developments in Early Physiology

86. The major principle of the Berlin Physical Society was that all phenomena could be accounted for by the principles of physics.

    ANS: T   PTS: 1   REF: Developments in Early Physiology

87. The work of Helmholtz along with that of Fechner and Wundt was instrumental in starting the new discipline of psychology.

    ANS: T   PTS: 1   REF: The Beginnings of Experimental Psychology

88. Biology was very rapidly accepted as a science in England and France.

    ANS: F   PTS: 1   REF: The Beginnings of Experimental Psychology

89. Unlike Cambridge University, Oxford University facilitated and supported scientific research in the 19th century.

    ANS: F   PTS: 1   REF: The Beginnings of Experimental Psychology

90. In 19th-century England, the sole means of pursuing a career in science was as a gentleman-scientist.

    ANS: T   PTS: 1   REF: The Beginnings of Experimental Psychology

91. U.S. universities' principle of "publish or perish" can be traced directly to the ideology of the 19th-century German university system.

    ANS: T   PTS: 1   REF: The Beginnings of Experimental Psychology

92. Even though he made contributions to the emerging discipline of psychology, Helmholtz was a minor figure in 19th century science.

    ANS: F   PTS: 1   REF: Hermann von Helmholtz (1821-1894)

93. The first empirical measurement of the rate of conduction of the nerve impulse was by Galvani.

    ANS: F   PTS: 1   REF: Hermann von Helmholtz (1821-1894)

94. Helmholtz produced the first empirical evidence that thought and movement are successive and not concurrent.

    ANS: T   PTS: 1   REF: Hermann von Helmholtz (1821-1894)
    MSC: WWW

95. The work of Helmholtz served to strengthen the experimental approach to the study of psychological questions.

    ANS: T   PTS: 1   REF: Hermann von Helmholtz (1821-1894)

96. Helmholtz's work included the first systematic experimental demonstration of the sensory threshold.

ANS: F   PTS: 1   REF: Hermann von Helmholtz (1821-1894)

97. Fechner discovered the two-point threshold.

ANS: F   PTS: 1   REF: Ernst Weber (1795-1878)

98. The essence of Weber's Law is that the just noticeable difference depends on the relative difference between two intensities of stimulation.

ANS: T   PTS: 1   REF: Ernst Weber (1795-1878)

99. Helmholtz's work was more important than Weber's in demonstrating the utility of experimentation to assess psychological events.

ANS: F   PTS: 1   REF: Ernst Weber (1795-1878)

100. Fechner wanted to be remembered for his work on psychophysics.

ANS: F   PTS: 1   REF: Gustav Theodor Fechner (1801-1887)

101. Fechner began his medical studies and ended his career at the University of Leipzig.

ANS: T   PTS: 1   REF: Gustav Theodor Fechner (1801-1887)

102. Fechner seriously injured his eyes in the chemistry lab.

ANS: F   PTS: 1   REF: Gustav Theodor Fechner (1801-1887)

103. Fechner found that an increase in the intensity of a stimulus produces a one-to-one increase in the intensity of the resultant sensation.

ANS: F   PTS: 1   REF: Gustav Theodor Fechner (1801-1887)

104. Fechner's most important contribution to psychology was his work in physiology.

ANS: F   PTS: 1   REF: Gustav Theodor Fechner (1801-1887)

105. The unique aspect of Weber's Law was the discovery of the logarithmic relationship between the stimulus and the experience.

ANS: F   PTS: 1   REF: Gustav Theodor Fechner (1801-1887)
MSC: WWW

106. The originator of psychophysics was Gustav Fechner.

ANS: T   PTS: 1   REF: Gustav Theodor Fechner (1801-1887)

107. Gustav Fechner founded the independent discipline of psychology.

ANS: F   PTS: 1   REF: Gustav Theodor Fechner (1801-1887)

Chapter 4

The New Psychology

Wilhelm Wundt began his career as a physiological researcher and part-time lecturer in Germany. After reading of Frederick Bessel's research on the "personal equation," Wundt was interested in the idea of multitasking and aimed to identify whether or not one could attune to two stimuli simultaneously. Bessel's work determined that "it was impossible for an observer to focus his attention on both objects at the same time." Going off of this earlier work, Wundt created a thought meter, or Gedankenmesser, to see whether he could attune to both visual and auditory stimuli simultaneously. He determined that it took one-eighth of a second to register both stimuli sequentially. Similar to Bessel, Wundt concluded that it is impossible for one to perceive two stimuli at the same time.

Wundt is widely regarded as the founder of psychology because "he established the first laboratory, edited the first journal, and began experimental psychology as a science." Although much of Wundt's work would not have been possible without the original ideas of Fechner, his predecessor, Wundt is credited as founder because he deliberately and vigorously promoted the idea of systematic experimentation. Without Wundt's "selling" psychology as a new discipline, the scientific community may have overlooked the unique contributions of those before him.

As a boy, Wundt was more preoccupied with daydreaming than with his studies, and it seemed as if he was not to attain the scholarship that was prevalent in his family line. He eventually earned admittance to university studies. After having some training to become a physician, he changed his mind and focused on physiology. He studied under Johannes Müller, and later was a laboratory assistant to Helmholtz. He began to see psychology as its own discipline and published this idea in his book *Contributions to the Theory of Sensory Perception* (published across 1858-1862) in which he used the phrase "experimental psychology" for the first time. He taught a course on physiological psychology, which was at the time synonymous with experimental psychology. Lectures from this course were published in 1873-1874 in an important book called Principles of Physiological Psychology, which has been published in "six editions over 37 years."

In 1875 Wundt became a professor at the University of Leipzig where he stayed for 45 years. There, he began a laboratory and in 1881 established the first psychology journal *Philosophical Studies*, later renamed *Psychological Studies*. His reputation and work drew students from all around the world (i.e., United States, Italy, Russia, Japan). On returning to their own countries, many of these students became pioneers in their own right, using the research methods they learned in Wundt's lab. "Wundt was a popular lecturer. At one time, the enrollment in his Leipzig courses exceeded 600 students."

Wundt believed that simple mental functions like sensation and perception could be studied with experimental methods. However, higher mental processes like memory and learning would need to employ nonexperimental methods similar to those used in sociology and anthropology. He thoroughly investigated the various stages of human mental development as manifested in language, art, myths, social customs, law, and morals. He termed this study cultural psychology. Between 1900 and 1920, his multi-volume work *Cultural Psychology* was published, the content of which was overshadowed by the implications. This publication divided the field into two branches: social psychology (a descendant of Wundt's cultural psychology) and experimental psychology (influenced by physiological foundations).

For Wundt, psychology meant the study of the conscious experience. He named his system of psychology *voluntarism* which reflected his belief in the mind willing itself to organize into higher cognitive processes. Unlike the British empiricists, Wundt was not interested in the elements of consciousness per se, but instead on "the process of actively organizing...those elements." Wundt differentiated two types of experiences: *mediate experiences*, which are affected by interpretations, and *immediate experiences*, which are "unbiased or untainted by any personal interpretation." These immediate experiences, for Wundt, form the mental elements that the mind organizes. His method to observe conscious experience was introspection, which involves "examination of one's own mind to inspect and report on personal thoughts or feelings." His efforts to make introspection as experimentally controlled as possible are reflected in his requirement that introspective observers complete 10,000 observations in training before they could "supply meaningful data."

Some of the things introspective observers might report on were *sensations* (when a sense organ is stimulated) and their "intensity, duration, and sense modality." Besides sensations, observers might report on their *feelings* which are subjective and do not arise from a sense organ. Wundt believed that feelings have three dimensions (his *tridimensional theory of feelings*): pleasure/displeasure, tension/relaxation, and excitement/depression. This conception has not received empirical support.

Although he sought to discover the elements of conscious experience, Wundt recognized that people may actively organize the elements of experiences into a cohesive whole. The book authors use an example of a tree: we see a whole tree, not the individual pieces that make it up. Wundt calls this automatic synthesizing of the elements *apperception*. The authors include an excerpt from Wundt's *Outline of Psychology* (1896).

Because Wundt's psychology, with its focus on elements of consciousness, had little practical application to real-world problems, governmental officials did not see any reason to separate psychology as a distinct field from philosophy. Thus, Wundt's psychology remained small and failed to develop as its own discipline. Meanwhile, branches of psychology grew quickly in the United States as an applied discipline that solved real-world problems in education and business.

There were substantial criticisms of Wundtian psychology. First, there were individual differences in the reports of introspective observers. Second, his nationalistic defense of Germany in World War I caused many U.S. psychologists to turn from his system. Third, other schools of thought rose in Germany, Austria, and the U.S. that eclipsed his system. Last, because of the economic ruin of Germany after World War I, many universities (including those that supported Wundt's work) suffered from a lack of funding. Despite the fact that his scientific findings have for the most part not survived, Wundt's legacy is that he purposefully founded a new science, created a laboratory which was designed to add new knowledge to psychology, developed new techniques unique to experimental psychology, created the first psychology journal, and taught hundreds of students (many of whom founded their own labs).

Other researchers in Germany were working on psychology problems at about the same time as Wundt. One of these was Hermann Ebbinghaus, who applied experimental techniques to learn about higher mental processes (something Wundt said could not be done). He generated lists of nonsense syllables, then tested memory using methods like counting the number of repetitions it took to learn a list, determining how long it took to forget items from the list (his forgetting curve), and counting the number of repetitions it took to re-learn a forgotten list. He also compared the speed at which he learned a list of nonsense syllables versus meaningful words. Many of these findings are still valid today because of his carefully controlled of experimental conditions as well as his quantitative analysis of learning time.

Franz Brentano's work rose in opposition to Wundt's system. He is a precursor to two schools of psychology: Gestalt and humanism. Whereas Wundt's system was experimental, Brentano's work was empirical (based in observation). Brentano argued that psychology should not "study the content of conscious experience," as Wundt proposed, but should study the actions of consciousness (which he termed Act psychology). In Act psychology, acts "are not accessible through introspection." Such acts could only be studied through memory and/or imagination.

Carl Stumpf, a student of Brentano's, incorporated his lifelong passion for music into a psychological study of music. He "argued that the primary data for psychology are phenomena" and named his system *Phenomenology*. He used introspection, but not to break down conscious experiences into elements as Wundt did (he saw this as artificial and its results not reflective of real life), but rather to report on "experience just as it occurs." Wundt and Stumpf argued vigorously about their opposing views. Two of the three founders of Gestalt psychology were students of Stumpf.

Oswald Külpe was trained by and originally agreed with Wundt. He accepted a professorship at the university of Würzburg (where Brentano had been for some time and where Stumpf was trained) and established a lab there. Külpe believed that the higher mental process "thought" could be scientifically studied (as opposed to Wundt's view). Külpe developed *systematic experimental introspection*, which involved having subjects perform a complex task then retrospectively report on the process (Wundt only studied processes as they occurred). Külpe discovered that sometimes "thought can occur without any sensory or imaginal content," a finding called *imageless thought*. This finding also directly opposed Wundt's system because Wundt believed that all experiences are composed of sensation and images. Other experiments at Würzburg supported the idea that some mental processes happen outside of conscious awareness. Despite the divisions within the burgeoning field of psychology, early psychologists were united in their goal of developing psychology as a formal discipline.

Outline

I.   No Multitasking Allowed
    A. multitasking was not a widely known or researched experience
    B. in 1861, a 29-year-old Wilhem Wundt is conducting research in his home
        1. influenced by Bessel's writing on the "personal equation" (individual differences in observations)
        2. he developed a clock that gave both auditory and visual stimulus (Gedankenmesser, or thought meter)
        3. he, as the only subject, concluded that the stimuli are registered sequentially rather than simultaneously
        4. determined that it took 1/8th of a second to register both auditory and visual stimuli sequentially
    C. recent research supports Wundt's earlier work, suggesting that multi-tasking is ineffective because humans cannot attune to more than one stimulus at a time

II.   The Founding Father of Modern Psychology
    A. started the first laboratory and the first journal in experimental psychology
    B. viewed Fechner's work as the first experimental psychology
    C. Fechner was the originator of psychology; Wundt, as the agent and promoter, was the founder
        1. founding is deliberate and intentional
        2. founding is different from making brilliant scientific contributions
        3. founding requires integration of prior knowledge
        4. founding involves promotion of the newly integrated material
        5. founding requires selling an idea to the scientific community

6. Wundt did all of the above plus promoted systematic experimentation as the essential method of psychology
  D. Preface to Principles of Physiological Psychology (1873-1874)
    1. announced his goal to establish a new discipline
    2. supported by Zeitgeist
III. Wilhelm Wundt (1832-1820)
  A. Wundt's life
    1. reared as an only child, a poor student, always disliked school
    2. did not get along with classmates, ridiculed by teachers
    3. early life goal: MD – work in science and make a living
    4. upon entering university study: disliked medicine, switched to physiology
        a. student of Johannes Müller
        b. lab assistant to Helmholtz
    5. while working in physiology, conceived of independent, experimental science of psychology
    6. 1858 – 1862: Contributions to the Theory of Sensory Perception
        a. original experiments in home laboratory
        b. offered proper methods for psychology
        c. term *experimental psychology* first used
    7. 1863: Lectures on the Mind of Men and Animals
        a. discussed problems that were the focus of psychology research for years
        b. examples include reaction time and psychophysics
    8. taught 1st psychology course at University of Heidelberg: physiological psychology
        a. "physiological" = "experimental"
        b. first time such a course offered anywhere in the world
        c. wrote Principles of Physiological Psychology (1873–1874) based on his lectures
          (1) his masterpiece
          (2) established psychology as an independent laboratory science with
            (a) its own problems
            (b) its own methods of experimentation
          (3) became the record of psychology research: six editions
  B. The Leipzig years
    1. professor of philosophy at Leipzig: 1875 – 1920
    2. first psychology laboratory: model for psychology laboratories everywhere
    3. first journal for psychology research
        a. 1881: Journal of Philosophical Studies
        b. 1906: new title = Journal of Psychological Studies
    4. drew hundreds of students worldwide (including Americans)
    5. trained first generation of experimental psychologists
    6. significantly influenced the foundational ideas of modern psychology
    7. work was reproduced in Italy, Russia, and Japan; laboratory replicated in Russia and Japan
    8. popular lecturer
    9. workdays had regimented schedule
  C. Cultural psychology
    1. 1880 – 1891: wrote on ethics, logic, systematic philosophy

THE NEW PSYCHOLOGY 101

2. 1900: *Cultural Psychology*, 10 volumes
   a. is not "folk psychology"
   b. dealt with stages of human mental development
   c. manifestations: language, art, myths, customs, law, morals
3. divided psychology in two parts: experimental and social
4. argued higher mental processes such as learning and memory
   a. cannot be studied experimentally
   b. are conditioned by language and culture
   c. can be studied using nonexperimental methods of sociology, anthropology, and social psychology
5. cultural psychology was satisfying for Wundt; had little influence on the field for several reasons
   a. timing was bad (1900-1920)
   b. United States developed their own form of psychology and paid little attention to European ideas

D. The study of conscious experience
   1. Zeitgeist in philosophy and physiology
   2. subject matter of psychology: consciousness
      a. relation to empiricism and associationism
      b. reduction to its elements
      c. active in organizing its contents
      d. elements of consciousness are not static
   3. voluntarism: Wundt's name for his system
      a. from "volition" = will
      b. is power of the will to organize mental contents into higher-level thought processes
      c. emphasized the activity, not the elements
   4. mediate experience: mediated by past experience, involved interpretation
   5. immediate experience: unbiased by interpretation
      a. forms the states of consciousness/mental elements that the mind then organizes
      b. Wundt may have wanted to develop a periodic table of the mind
   6. example: mediate experience=description of event (i.e., "I have a toothache"; immediate experience=description of your experience of the event (i.e., describing discomfort from a toothache)

E. The method of introspection
   1. method requires observation of conscious experience; observer reports on their own conscious experiences
   2. is the examination of one's own mental state, "internal perception"
   3. did not originate with Wundt
   4. Wundt added precise experimental control over the conditions
   5. its use is derived from physics
   6. Wundt's four rules
      a. observers must know when the procedure will begin
      b. observers must be "in a state of readiness or strained attention"
      c. the observation must be repeatable numerous times
      d. the experimental conditions must be varied in terms of control over stimulus manipulation
   7. stringent conditions make observations more controlled and replicable

8. rigorously trained observers logged 10,000 introspective observations before they are able to provide data
9. mechanical, automatic observations; no time for reflection
10. required quantitative judgments, not qualitative
11. used sophisticated equipment for objective measurements

F. Elements of conscious experience
   1. Wundt's three goals for psychology
      a. "analyze conscious processes into their basic elements"
      b. "discover how these elements are synthesized or organized, and"
      c. " determine the laws of connection governing the organization of the elements"
   2. suggested two elementary forms of experience
      a. sensations
         (1) stimulation of a sense organ leads to impulses that reach the brain
         (2) classified by intensity, duration, and sense modality
         (3) not different from images
      b. feelings
         (1) along with sensations are "simultaneous aspects of immediate experience"
         (2) subjective complements of sensations
         (3) "do not arise directly from a sense organ"
         (4) tridimensional theory of feelings
            (a) pleasure/displeasure, tension/relaxation, and excitement/depression
            (b) stimulated research
            (c) not supported today
         (5) emotions = compounds of elementary feeling elements

G. Organizing the elements of conscious experience
   1. doctrine of apperception (law of psychic resultants): "The process by which mental elements are organized"
      a. leads to emergent qualities not merely the sum of the mental elements (creative synthesis)
      b. active process
         (1) similar to Gestalt idea that the whole is different from the sum of its parts
         (2) opposite of the passive, mechanical associationism of most of the other British empiricists
   2. Original source material on the law of psychic resultants and the principle of creative synthesis from Outline of Psychology (1896)
      a. law of psychical resultants: "...every psychical compound shows attributes which may ...be understood from the attributes of its elements...but which are by no means to be looked upon as the mere sum of the attributes of these elements....the aggregate...is a new psychical content that was made possible...by these elements, but was by no means contained in them."
         (1) the new content expresses the principle of creative synthesis
         (2) creative synthesis is not contrary to laws of the natural world
            (a) physical measurements deal with objective masses, forces, and energies

(b) psychical measurements deal with subjective values and ends

(i) "...its purpose may be different and higher than [objective components] without any change in the masses, forces, and energies concerned."

H. The fate of Wundt's psychology in Germany
1. spread rapidly
2. did not transform nature of academic psychology within the country
3. remained a subspecialty of philosophy for 20 years
   a. academic reasons
   b. political reasons
   c. financial reasons
4. practicality of the discipline was doubted
5. in contrast, psychology in the United States grew more rapidly
   a. departures from Wundt's model
   b. addressed practical problems using applied psychology
   c. dealt with issues in education and business

I. Criticisms of Wundtian psychology
1. disapproval of method of introspection
   a. differences in results obtained by different observers; who is correct?
   b. introspection as a private experience and difficult to make objective
   c. cannot settle disagreements through replication
2. Wundt's personal political views
   a. blamed England for starting WWI
   b. viewed the German invasion of Belgium as self-defense
3. after WWI two schools of thought in Europe challenged and outshined Wundt's views (Gestalt in Germany, psychoanalysis in Austria)
4. in the United States, functionalism and behaviorism overshadowed Wundtian psychology
5. economic and political contextual forces also played a part
   a. economic collapse of Germany after World War I
   b. financial ruin of German universities
   c. destruction of Wundt's laboratory during World II bombing
6. "...the nature, content, form, and even home of Wundtian psychology" lost

J. Wundt's legacy
1. rejection of nonscientific thinking
2. severing of ties between psychology and non-modern philosophy
3. avoiding discussions of the soul by stressing conscious experience and empirical methods
4. publishing extensively
5. training the first generation of psychologists
6. considered by many as the "most important psychologist of all time"
7. served well in provoking rebellions

IV. Other Developments in German Psychology
A. Common enterprise: the expansion of psychology as a science
1. Wundt monopoly short-lived
2. Several influential developers made Germany the center of the new discipline but their viewpoints were sometimes different

B. Psychology took a different course in England and exerted more influence in America than did Wundt's work
C. American psychologists trained under Wundt transformed is system to a distinctively American psychology
D. Psychology divided into factions; Wundt's version one of many

V. Hermann Ebbinghaus (1850 – 1909)
A. In general:
   1. Wundt claimed it was impossible to study higher mental processes
   2. First to investigate learning and memory experimentally (proved Wundt wrong)
   3. Changed the way association (aka learning) can be studied
B. Ebbinghaus's life
   1. studied at the University of Bonn, then at Halle and Berlin
   2. interests shifted from history and literature to philosophy
   3. military service in Franco-Prussian War
   4. seven years of independent study in England and France, leading to science interests
   5. influenced by Fechner's mathematical approach to psychological phenomena
   6. wanted to apply Fechner's rigid and systematic measurement to higher mental processes
C. Research on learning
   1. novelty: made study of associations objective
      a. study of formation of associations as they occur, not post hoc
      b. control the conditions of acquisitions and recall
   2. his work revealed original genius
   3. first undertaking outside physiology with a completely psychological problem
   4. basic learning measure: equation of recall with frequency of associations by associationists led to counting the number of repetitions needed to reproduce material completely
   5. used non-identical but similar lists of syllables
   6. obtained averages
   7. controlled for extraneous variables by keeping daily routines and time of day constant
   8. thereby provided quantification of learning, memory, recall, forgetting
D. Research with nonsense syllables
   1. nonsense syllables
      a. Ebbinghaus: "meaningless series of syllables"
      b. mistranslation: 'series of nonsense syllables"
      c. usually consonant – vowel – consonant
      d. meaningless material is nine times harder to learn than meaningful material
      e. found longer material requires more repetitions
   2. methodology
      a. careful control of the experimental conditions
      b. quantitative analysis of the data
      c. found that time to learn is a function of the number of syllables
   3. also examined the effects of:
      a. over learning
      b. associations between lists
      c. reviewing the material
      d. time between learning and recall

THE NEW PSYCHOLOGY 105

        4.   the forgetting curve

    E. Ebbinghaus's other contributions to psychology

        1.   with Arthur König founded a new journal: Journal of Psychology and Physiology of the Sense Organs (1885)

        2.   emphasized relationship between psychology and physiology

        3.   research findings still relevant, so more influential than Wundt

VI.   Franz Brentano (1838 – 1917)

    A. In general

        1.   students included Stumpf, von Ehrenfels, Freud

        2.   precursor of Gestalt and humanistic psychology

        3.   shared Wundt's goal: psychology as a science

        4.   1874: Psychology From an Empirical Standpoint, was in direct opposition to Wundt's view

        5.   was empirical, not experimental

        6.   method was observation, not experimentation

        7.   did not reject experimentation

        8.   data are from observation and individual experience

    B. The study of mental acts

        1.   rejected study of the content of conscious experience

        2.   proper subject matter is mental activity

        3.   experience as structure distinct from experience as activity

        4.   termed his system of psychology: Act Psychology

        5.   requires new methods

            a.   acts are not accessible through introspection

            b.   study of mental acts requires empirical observation

        6.   relied on systematic observation

        7.   two methods: memory and imagination

VII.   Carl Stumpf (1848 – 1936)

    A. In general

        1.   accomplished musician

        2.   studied with Brentano

        3.   Wundt's major rival

        4.   trained two psychologists who later founded Gestalt psychology

        5.   early in career about perception of space

        6.   most influential work is: Psychology of Tone (1883, 1890)

            a.   second only to Helmholtz in work on acoustics

            b.   pioneer in psychological study of music

    B. Phenomenology

        1.   argued primary data of psychology are phenomena

        2.   phenomenology = examination of the unbiased experience

        3.   analysis of experience into elements rendered it artificial

        4.   bitter debate with Wundt re: credibility of introspection of tones. Wundt's highly trained lab observers vs. Stumpf's expert musicians

    C. Other works

        1.   founded Berlin Association for Child Psychology

        2.   published theory of emotion that attempted to reduce feelings to sensations (influenced modern cognitive psychology)

        3.   established center for primitive music collection from around the world

VIII. Oswald Külpe (1862 – 1915)
    A. In general
        1. initially a follower of Wundt
        2. later led a protest against the limitations of Wundtian psychology
        3. worked on problems that Wundt ignored
        4. 1893: Outline of Psychology
            a. dedicated to Wundt
            b. psychology is the science of facts of experience
            c. psychology as dependent on the experiencing person
        5. established laboratory at Würzburg
        6. students included Angell (who later helped develop functionalism)
    B. Külpe's differences with Wundt
        1. thought processes should be studied experimentally
        2. developed systematic experimental introspection
            a. involved performance of a complex task
            b. subjects gave retrospective report of the cognitive processes experienced during the task
            c. emphasized subjective, qualitative, and detailed reports
            d. aim: identifying what was going on in the subject's mind during a conscious experience
        3. goals:
            a. to include higher mental processes in psychology
            b. to refine the method of introspection
        4. Imageless thought: "thought can occur without any sensory or imaginal content"
    C. Research topics at the Würzburg laboratory
        1. Marbe: sensations and images play no part in the process of the judgments of weights
        2. Watt: word-association task: conscious experience cannot be reduced solely to sensations and images
            a. unconscious set (determining tendency)
            b. tendency of Watt's subjects to respond in the desired manner
IX. Comment
    A. Psychology fraught with divisions and controversies from the beginning
    B. Germany did not remain the center of psychology
    C. Titchener brought his own version of Wundt's psychology to the United States

Lecture prompts/Discussion topics for chapter four

- Make a case that each of the following could have been the founder of psychology: Fechner, Ebbinghaus, Külpe, Stumpf.
- Have students introspect with a metronome, as Wundt's research participants had to do. Vary the timing of the beats, and stop the metronome unexpectedly after it has run for a while. Then have students report on whether any of Wundt's three dimensional of feelings seemed to apply. If you don't have a metronome, there is one online at www.metronomeonline.com

Wilhelm Wundt Biographical Information
http://web.lemoyne.edu/~hevern/narpsych/nr-theorists/wundt_wilhelm.html
> This is a site that provides a ton of information about Wundt's life and work, including links to related Internet sources.

Human Intelligence Project: Hermann Ebbinghaus
http://www.indiana.edu/%7Eintell/ebbinghaus.shtml
> This site has Information about Ebbinghaus's life and achievements.

Franz Brentano's Ontology
http://www.formalontology.it/brentanof.htm
> This site is a description of Brentano's life and work, with excerpts from some of his writings.

Classics in the History of Psychology website, James Cattell describes Wundt's lab
http://psychclassics.yorku.ca/Cattell/earlylabs.htm
> This article provides an interesting glimpse into the day-to-day workings of Wundt's laboratory as reported by one of his students (who rose to his own eminence in psychology).

Psyography: Biographies on Psychologists
http://faculty.frostburg.edu/mbradley/psyography/stumpf.html
> This page gives some extra information about the life and work of Carl Stumpf, it is a page from a series at Frostburg State University.

Potential answers to chapter four discussion questions

1. On what basis did Wundt conclude that a person cannot engage in more than one mental activity at precisely the same moment in time?
When Wilhelm Wundt was around 29, he began his investigations into what could be labeled psychology. He was interested in the "personal equation" errors identified by Frederick Bessel. In these early studies he was trying to determine if he could pay attention to two things at once. He designed a piece of equipment (a modified pendulum clock) that would provide "both an auditory and a visual stimulus." Using himself as the participant, he conducted an experiment to gage whether he could attune to both auditory and visual stimuli at the same time, as measured by response times. He concluded that he could not attend to both at the same time, and gathered that it is impossible to attend to more than one stimulus at a given time.

2. Why is Wundt, and not Fechner, considered the founder of the new psychology?
For many reasons, Wundt is the designated founder of psychology. "He established the first laboratory, edited the first journal, and began experimental psychology as a science." Although Fechner's scientific work came earlier and has been more enduring, Wundt deliberately set out to found the discipline and promoted the idea of systematic experimentation. In addition, Wundt promoted the idea of experimental psychology as a unique discipline—separate from philosophy—to the scientific community thereby extending psychology's reach and influence. If not for Wundt's "selling" of psychology, the influential contributions of his predecessors may have gone unnoticed.

3. Describe the differences between "founding" and "originating" in science.

"Founding is a deliberate and intentional act. It involves personal abilities and characteristics that differ from those necessary for brilliant scientific contributions. Founding requires the integration of prior knowledge and the publication and promotion of the newly organized material." Originating in science has more to do with how the knowledge base in the field is built. Originating a science is more reflective of the scientific work itself, rather than its promotion/marketing.

4. Describe Wundt's cultural psychology. How did it lead to division within psychology?

Wundt believed that while simpler psychological functions like sensation and perception could be measured experimentally, more complex functions like memory and learning could not. Thus he made the theoretical distinction between what is now referred to as social and experimental psychology. After choosing to focus on what he termed cultural psychology, he explores the roles of such things as language, arts, customs in society using nonexperimental methods that were common in sociology and anthropology. For Wundt, this was the way to study higher mental processes. This work divided "the new science of psychology into two major parts: the experimental and the social."

5. Why did cultural psychology have little impact on American psychology?

It had little impact because of, for the most part, the timing of its publication which was between 1900 and 1920. Because Wundt's psychology, with its focus on elements of consciousness, had little practical application to real-world problems, governmental officials did not see any reason to separate psychology as a distinct field from philosophy. Thus Wundt's cultural psychology remained small and failed to develop as its own discipline. Meanwhile in the U.S. psychology grew quickly, but as an applied discipline that solved real-world problems in education and business. Other schools of psychology were formed and overshadowed cultural psychology.

6. How was Wundt's psychology influenced by the work of the German physiologists and the British empiricists? Describe the concept of voluntarism.

Wundt was heavily influenced by the experimental methods and techniques used by the physiologists. He was also influenced by the British empiricists because of their emphasis on "the method of analysis or reduction." For Wundt, psychology meant the study of consciousness. He named his system of psychology *voluntarism* which reflected his belief in the mind willing itself to organize into higher cognitive processes.

7. What are elements of consciousness? What is their role in mental life?

Wundt defined two elements of consciousness: sensations and feelings. Sensations are when a sense organ is stimulated and introspective observers could report on the "intensity, duration, and sense modality" of these sensations. Feelings are subjective and do not arise from a sense organ. These elements would combine in the process of apperception, and new properties would emerge as a result of this combination.

8. Distinguish between mediate and immediate experience.

Wundt differentiated two types of experiences: *mediate experiences*, which are affected by interpretations, and *immediate experiences*, which are "unbiased or untainted by any personal interpretation." These immediate experiences, for Wundt, form the mental elements that the mind organizes.

9. Describe Wundt's methodology and his rules for introspection. Did he favor quantitative or qualitative introspection? Why?

Wundt's methodology was introspection: "the examination of one's own mental state", and he required a rigorous training for introspective observers. He had four rules for introspection, taken from page 98 of the text:

- Observers must be able to determine when the process is to be introduced.
- Observers must be in a state of readiness or strained attention.
- It must be possible to repeat the observation several times.
- It must be possible to vary the experimental conditions in terms of the controlled manipulation of the stimuli.

The type of report that he favored was quantitative: "judgments about the size, intensity, and duration of various physical stimuli." Wundt preferred quantitative to qualitative reports (on the nature of the inner experiences) because they were easier to replicate and control, and were more objective than subjective.

10. Distinguish between internal and external perception. What is the purpose of apperception?

Internal perception is what Wundt called introspection: examining one's own mental processes. With external perception the "focus of observation is outside of the observer." Apperception is the idea that people organize and combine the elements of experiences "which creates new properties."

11. How did apperception relate to the work of James Mill and John Stuart Mill?

James Mill believed that the mind can be studied by reducing it down to elements. His son, John Stuart Mill, said that complex ideas are more than just the combination of simple ones, because they take on new qualities. This is *creative synthesis*. His approach applies the laws of chemistry to the mind, which is why it is called "mental chemistry."

Wundt's work can be seen as a product of these earlier ideas. Apperception is the idea that people organize and combine the elements of experiences "which creates new properties" in *creative synthesis*.

12. Trace the fate of Wundtian psychology in Germany. On what grounds was Wundt's system criticized?

His system spread rapidly, but did not transform the field in Germany because of a variety of contextual events. Government officials did not see the value of psychology so did not fund them as separate departments from philosophy. Wundt's system was criticized because of the lack of reliability in introspective reports. Also, Wundt's avid German nationalism caused psychologists in the U.S. and England to turn away from his system. In addition, Wundt's system focused on consciousness, which could not readily be applied to solving real-world problems and thus not viewed as particularly a useful system.

13. Describe Ebbinghaus's research on learning and memory. How was it influenced by the work of Fechner?

Ebbinghaus was inspired by Fechner's careful experimental methods and Ebbinghaus strove to quantify and study some higher mental processes. He generated lists of nonsense syllables, then tested such things as number of repetitions it took to learn a list, how long it took to forget items from the list (his forgetting curve), and number of repetitions it took to re-learn a forgotten list, and comparing the speed at which he learned a list of nonsense syllables vs. meaningful words. Many of these findings are still valid today.

14. How does Brentano's act psychology differ from Wundtian psychology?

Franz Brentano's work rose in opposition to Wundt's system. Brentano argued that psychology should not "study the content of conscious experience" as Wundt proposed, but rather should study the actions of consciousness (his system is called Act psychology to reflect this stance). Act psychology makes introspection useless because acts "are not accessible through introspection." Such acts could only be studied through recalling mental processes and/or imagining them.

15. How did Stumpf differ with Wundt on introspection and on the reduction of experience to elements?

Stumpf used introspection, but not to break down conscious experiences into elements as Wundt did (he saw this as artificial and its results not reflective of real life), but rather to report on "experience just as it occurs." Wundt and Stumpf argued vigorously about their opposing views.

16. What did Külpe mean by systematic experimental introspection? How did Külpe's approach differ from Wundt's?

Külpe believed that the higher mental process "thought" could be scientifically studied (as opposed to Wundt's view). Külpe developed *systematic experimental introspection*, which involved having subjects perform a complex task then retrospectively recall the process (Wundt only studied processes as they occurred).

17. How did the idea of imageless thought challenge Wundt's conception of conscious experience?

Külpe discovered that sometimes "thought can occur without any sensory or imaginal content," a finding called *imageless thought*. This finding directly opposed Wundt's system because Wundt believed that all experiences are composed of sensation and images.

18. Despite their many differences, what did the works of Wundt, Ebbinghaus, Brentano, and Stumpf have in common?

"For all their differences…the early psychologists were united in the goal of developing an independent science of psychology." Psychology no longer involved studying the soul, but focused on conscious experiences.

Key terms from chapter four

- **Act psychology** Brentano's system, so named because of his focus on mental activities rather than mental elements.
- **Apperception** "The process by which mental elements are organized."
- **Creative synthesis** In Wundt's system also known as the law of psychic resultants, in which new properties emerge when one combines mental elements.
- **Cultural Psychology** A 10-volume work by Wundt in which he discusses "language, art, myths, social customs, law, and morals"
- **Feelings** For Wundt, one of two elementary forms of experience (the other is Sensations). "Feelings are the subjective complements of sensations but do not arise directly from a sense organ."
- **Forgetting curve** The curve plotted by Ebbinghaus to describe the pattern of how nonsense syllables are forgotten over time.

- **Imageless thought** Kulpe's finding that some thought occurs "without any sensory or imaginal content", which goes against Wundt's belief that all experiences are "composed of sensations and images."
- **Immediate experience** Information reported by an introspective observer that is not influenced by interpretation.
- **Internal perception** Wundt's term for introspection
- **Introspection** the "examination of one's own mental state."
- **Law of psychic resultants** In Wundt's system also known as creative synthesis, in which new properties emerge when one combines mental elements.
- **Mediate experience** Information reported by an introspective observer that is influenced by interpretation.
- **Nonsense syllables** The material generated by Ebbinghaus to study the mental processes of learning and forgetting.
- **Phenomenology** Stumpf's system, in which he used introspection differently than did Wundt: he attempted to describe experiences as they occurred naturally.
- **Sensations** For Wundt, one of two elementary forms of experience (the other is Feelings). "Sensations are aroused whenever a sense organ is stimulated."
- **Systematic experimental introspection** Külpe's method of introspection that had subjects engage in a complex task and then retrospectively report on these activities.
- **Tridimensional theory of feelings** Wundt's theory that feelings fall on 3 dimensions: pleasure/displeasure, tension/relaxation, and excitement/depression.
- **Voluntarism** Wundt's label for his own system, which emphasizes the active role played by the mind in organizing mental contents into higher processes.

TESTBANK

ESSAY

1. Describe the process of founding a school of thought. Using the criteria involved in this process, explain why Wundt, not Fechner, is judged to be the "founding father of modern psychology."

ANS:
Answer not provided.

PTS: 1

2. Toward the end of his career, Wundt wrote a 10- volume work, *Cultural Psychology*. What did cultural psychology include? What implications did it have for psychology in terms of areas of study? Why was American psychology so little affected by Wundt's visions for the field of cultural psychology?

ANS:
Answer not provided.

PTS: 1

3. What was the subject matter of Wundt's psychology? Why did he label his system "voluntarism"? How did this approach differ from that of most British empiricists in terms of the elements of consciousness?

ANS:
Answer not provided.

PTS: 1   MSC: WWW

4. How did Wundt define and differentiate between mediate and immediate experience? Which did he view as forming the elements of the mind? Describe Wundt's method of introspection, including his rationale and rules for using it and his differentiation between internal and external perception.

ANS:
Answer not provided.

PTS: 1

5. What were Wundt's three goals for psychology? Describe and give examples of the experimental conditions he used in his research related to the first goal.

ANS:
Answer not provided.

PTS: 1

6. Define apperception and briefly describe the process of apperception (also called the law of psychic resultants). Expand your discussion by drawing upon Wundt's explanation in the *Original Source Material on the Law of Psychic Resultants and the Principle of Creative Synthesis*.

ANS:
Answer not provided.

PTS: 1   MSC: WWW

7. Describe how Wundt was able to exclude philosophical questions about the soul from his new, experimental psychology.

ANS:
Answer not provided.

PTS: 1

8. Some of Ebbinghaus's findings, such as the fact that it takes more time to learn long as opposed by short pieces of material, were not new. What, then, was the significance of his research, both at the time he completed it and now?

ANS:
Answer not provided.

PTS: 1

9. Describe Brentano's act psychology. What are the similarities and differences between it and Wundt's psychology?

ANS:
Answer not provided.

PTS: 1

10. Discuss the differences between Wundt and Külpe, and describe some ramifications of those differences on contemporary psychology.

ANS:
Answer not provided.

PTS: 1

MULTIPLE CHOICE

11. In his early work when he was his own experimental subject, the 29-year-old Wilhelm Wundt found that he could ____.
    a. pay attention to two things at once
    b. not pay attention to two things at once
    c. pay attention to two things at once, but not three
    d. pay attention to three things at once, but not four
    e. sustain his attention on one thing for a little less than 12 minutes at a time

    ANS: B   PTS: 1   REF: No Multitasking Allowed

12. Wilhelm Wundt is the ____ of psychology as a discipline.
    a. originator
    b. antecedent
    c. forerunner
    d. founder
    e. originator and founder

    ANS: D   PTS: 1   REF: The Founding Father of Modern Psychology

13. What book marks the "literary birth" of the new science of psychology?
    a. Müller's *Handbook of Physiology of Mankind* (1833-1840)
    b. Helmholtz's *Handbook of Physiological Optics* (1856-1866)
    c. Fechner's *Elements of Psychophysics* (1860)
    d. Wundt's *Contributions to the Theory of Sensory Perception* (1858-1862)
    e. Fechner's *Elements of Psychophysics* (1860) **and** Wundt's *Contributions to the Theory of Sensory Perception* (1858-1862)

    ANS: E   PTS: 1   REF: Wilhelm Wundt (1832-1920)

14. In 1867, Wundt offered the first course ever given in ____.
    a. psychophysics
    b. physiological psychology
    c. social psychology
    d. volkerpsychologie
    e. introspection

    ANS: B   PTS: 1   REF: Wilhelm Wundt (1832-1920)
    MSC: WWW

15. Wundt's system is most accurately called ____.
    a. structural psychology
    b. experimental psychology
    c. physiological psychology
    d. psychophysics
    e. reductionism

    ANS: B   PTS: 1   REF: Wilhelm Wundt (1832-1920)

16. Wundt established psychology as distinct from philosophy primarily in terms of its ____.
    a. subject matter
    b. emphasis on physiology
    c. use of the experimental method
    d. use of the deduction and induction
    e. focus on behavior

    ANS: C   PTS: 1   REF: Wilhelm Wundt (1832-1920)

17. Wundt's influence was so widely felt that, as a tribute, his lab was later replicated in ____.
    a. the United States and Sweden
    b. Italy and Japan
    c. Russia and the United States
    d. Sweden and Italy
    e. Japan and Russia

    ANS: E   PTS: 1   REF: Wilhelm Wundt (1832-1920)

18. Which of the following statements is true of Wundt's cultural psychology?
    a. It was the same thing as folk psychology.
    b. It became the discipline known as anthropology.
    c. It was never published, although some lectures and articles remain.
    d. It was the study of socioeconomic strata in society.
    e. It dealt with various stages of human mental development.

    ANS: E   PTS: 1   REF: Wilhelm Wundt (1832-1920)

19. The cultural psychology of Wundt examined evidence from ____.
    a. studies of children and their thinking
    b. examination of language, myths, customs, law, and morals
    c. philosophy
    d. experimentation
    e. a content analysis of contemporary newspapers

    ANS: B   PTS: 1   REF: Wilhelm Wundt (1832-1920)

20. Wundt argued that cognitive processes such as learning and memory could **not** be studied by experimental methods because ____.
    a. they were influenced by language and aspects thereof
    b. he considered them to be lower lever cognitive processes
    c. one cannot control the relevant factors
    d. one cannot objectively observe the behavioral manifestations of these phenomena
    e. they are not the proper subject matter of psychology, regardless of the methodology one uses

    ANS: A   PTS: 1   REF: Wilhelm Wundt (1832-1920)

21. Wundt's productivity as a writer can be quantified by his output, which averaged ____.
    a. 5 pages a day for over 50 years
    b. 2.2 pages a day for over 50 years
    c. 1.5 pages a day for approximately 25 years
    d. 4.7 pages a day for approximately 15 years
    e. just about 1 page a day for his working life

    ANS: B   PTS: 1   REF: Wilhelm Wundt (1832-1920)
    MSC: WWW

22. For Wundt, the subject matter of psychology was ____.
    a. sensations
    b. perceptions
    c. consciousness
    d. associations
    e. introspection

    ANS: C   PTS: 1   REF: Wilhelm Wundt (1832-1920)

23. The first system or school of thought in psychology was called ____.
    a. cultural psychology by Wundt
    b. voluntarism by Wundt
    c. structuralism by Wundt's student, Titchener
    d. structuralism in Germany and functionalism in the United States
    e. volkerpsychologie by Wundt

    ANS: B   PTS: 1   REF: Wilhelm Wundt (1832-1920)

24. Wundt's term *voluntarism* reflects his emphasis on the ____.
    a. elements of consciousness
    b. individual's choice to apply his/her knowledge base to a situation
    c. idea that a stimulus in the environment can force us to pay attention
    d. power of the will to organize the contents of the mind
    e. ability of the individual to "make the nonconscious conscious"

    ANS: D   PTS: 1   REF: Wilhelm Wundt (1832-1920)

25. In Wundt's laboratory, introspection was used to assess ____.
    a. immediate experience
    b. mediate experience
    c. sensations
    d. feelings
    e. stimulus intensities

    ANS: A   PTS: 1   REF: Wilhelm Wundt (1832-1920)

26. According to Wundt, psychology should be concerned with the study of ____.
    a. mediate experience
    b. the time required for sensory organs to transmit impulses to consciousness
    c. conscious experience
    d. the different stages of childhood development
    e. immediate experience

    ANS: E   PTS: 1   REF: Wilhelm Wundt (1832-1920)

27. If you look at a rose and observe, "The rose is red," you are observing the ____.
    a. mediate experience
    b. immediate experience
    c. basic human experience
    d. stimulus error
    e. elements of experience

    ANS: A   PTS: 1   REF: Wilhelm Wundt (1832-1920)

28. Introspection as used by Wundt is also called ____.
    a. internal perception
    b. internal observation
    c. retrospection
    d. the method of limits
    e. the method of constant stimuli

    ANS: A   PTS: 1   REF: Wilhelm Wundt (1832-1920)

29. Wundt's modification of introspection was the ____.
    a. use of experimental controls
    b. quantification of the sensations in accord with Fechner's Law
    c. analysis of mediate experience into immediate experience and its confounds
    d. use of children as observers (subjects)
    e. comparison of normal subjects' reports of elements of consciousness with reports. of hallucinations by psychiatric patients and by those using drugs such as cocaine

    ANS: A   PTS: 1   REF: Wilhelm Wundt (1832-1920)

30. Which of the following is NOT one of Wundt's experimental conditions?
    a. Observers must be able to describe the qualitative aspects of their experiences.
    b. Observers must be able to determine when the process is to begin.
    c. Observers must be in a state of readiness.
    d. The observations must be repeatable.
    e. It must be possible to control and manipulate the stimuli.

    ANS: A   PTS: 1   REF: Wilhelm Wundt (1832-1920)

31. Wundt's observers used introspection to report ____.
    a. judgments about the size and intensity of physical stimuli
    b. their reaction times
    c. the processes of sensing and perceiving
    d. retrospective accounts of their experiences
    e. All of the above choices are correct

    ANS: A   PTS: 1   REF: Wilhelm Wundt (1832-1920)
    MSC: WWW

THE NEW PSYCHOLOGY   117

32. Which of the following is NOT one of Wundt's goals for his psychology?
    a. To analyze conscious processes
    b. To identify the basic elements of consciousness
    c. To determine how the elements of consciousness are synthesized
    d. To determine the principles of the linking that occurs in the organization of the elements
    e. To identify the principles that govern the synthesis of those elements into higher cognitive processes such as learning

    ANS: E   PTS: 1   REF: Wilhelm Wundt (1832-1920)

33. According to Wundt, the stimulation of a sense organ sufficiently to have the nerve impulse reach the brain defines a(n) _____.
    a. reflex
    b. afferent response
    c. sensation
    d. perception
    e. cognition

    ANS: C   PTS: 1   REF: Wilhelm Wundt (1832-1920)

34. Wundt classified sensations according to which characteristics?
    a. intensity and extensity
    b. intensity, duration, and sense modality
    c. clearness, quality, and duration
    d. sense modality, clearness, and quality
    e. reaction time and intensity

    ANS: B   PTS: 1   REF: Wilhelm Wundt (1832-1920)

35. For Wundt, the difference between sensations and images was _____.
    a. nonexistent
    b. that images are weaker than sensations
    c. that images have a longer duration than sensations
    d. that images are what today we call perceptions
    e. that sensations last for microseconds, whereas images can be retained in memory for indeterminate periods of time

    ANS: A   PTS: 1   REF: Wilhelm Wundt (1832-1920)

36. According to Wundt, there were two elementary forms of experience, namely _____.
    a. sensation and perception
    b. sensation and feelings
    c. images and feelings
    d. sensation and images
    e. immediate experience and mediate experience

    ANS: B   PTS: 1   REF: Wilhelm Wundt (1832-1920)
    MSC: WWW

37. For Wundt, feelings are _____.
    a. the same as sensations
    b. based on three dimensions including pleasure/displeasure
    c. derived directly from a sense organ
    d. complex compounds of elementary emotions
    e. a complex idea

    ANS: B   PTS: 1   REF: Wilhelm Wundt (1832-1920)

38. Wundt's theory of feelings was based on _____.
    a. Weber's earlier work on emotions
    b. retrospective reports of trained observers
    c. his own introspections
    d. Fechner's discovery of the pleasure principle
    e. Fechner's Law ($S = k \log R$)

    ANS: C   PTS: 1   REF: Wilhelm Wundt (1832-1920)

39. Which of the following are the three dimensions of Wundt's tridimensional theory of feelings?
    a. pleasure/displeasure; tension/relaxation; excitement/depression.
    b. clarity/opaqueness; tension/relaxation; excitement/depression.
    c. tension/ relaxation; pleasure/depression; clarity/opaqueness.
    d. pleasure/pain; tension/relief; mania/depression.
    e. intensity/extensity; immediacy/delay; pleasure/displeasure.

    ANS: A   PTS: 1   REF: Wilhelm Wundt (1832-1920)

40. Wundt's doctrine of apperception refers to _____.
    a. the breaking down of mental elements
    b. perception
    c. the process of training introspective observers over 10,000 observations
    d. the process of organizing mental elements into a whole
    e. None of the choices are correct

    ANS: D   PTS: 1   REF: Wilhelm Wundt (1832-1920)
    MSC: WWW

41. Wundt's doctrine of apperception was also known as the _____.
    a. principle of creative synthesis
    b. law of psychic resultants
    c. principle of psychic compounding
    d. law of Gestalt resultants
    e. law of creative resultants

    ANS: B   PTS: 1   REF: Wilhelm Wundt (1832-1920)

42. The law of psychic resultants governs _____.
    a. the organization of mental elements
    b. perception
    c. the production of images and their retention
    d. the mechanical linking (association) of mental elements into simple ideas
    e. the mechanical linking (association) of mental elements into complex ideas

    ANS: A   PTS: 1   REF: Wilhelm Wundt (1832-1920)

43. The Gestalt psychologists' best-known tenet is that the whole is greater than the sum of its parts. This same tenet was alleged in Wundt's principle of _____.
    a. sensations
    b. feelings
    c. emotions
    d. the tridimensional theory of feelings
    e. apperception

    ANS: E   PTS: 1   REF: Wilhelm Wundt (1832-1920)

THE NEW PSYCHOLOGY

44. As Wundt stated in the Original Source Material on the Law of Psychic Resultants and the Principle of Creative Synthesis from the *Outline of Psychology (1896)*, the _____ *"finds its expression in the fact that every psychical compound shows attributes which may...be understood from the attributes of its elements...but which are by no means to be looked upon as the mere sum of the attributes of these elements.*
   a. principle of creative synthesis
   b. use of physical measurements
   c. use of psychic measurement
   d. concept of habit
   e. law of psychic resultants

   ANS: E   PTS: 1   REF: Wilhelm Wundt (1832-1920)

45. Which statement best describes the basic content of the Original Source Material by Wundt?
   a. Psychology studies how the mind comes to have innate knowledge.
   b. Psychology is concerned with the study of how the brain controls mental processes.
   c. Psychology studies how the conscious mind uses mental elements to conceal unconsciousness processes.
   d. Psychology is concerned with the complete listing of mental elements and how these mental elements combine according to the principles of association to form states of consciousness.
   e. Psychology is concerned with how the active powers of the mind synthesize mental elements into states of consciousness.

   ANS: E   PTS: 1   REF: Wilhelm Wundt (1832-1920)

46. In the Original Source Material from the *Outline of Psychology*, Wundt states "The law of psychical resultants...expresses a principle which we may designate, in view of its results as a _____."
   a. periodic chart of the elements of the mind
   b. principle of creative synthesis
   c. tridimensional theory of feelings
   d. catalog of all possible sensations and feelings
   e. None of the choices are correct.

   ANS: B   PTS: 1   REF: Wilhelm Wundt (1832-1920)

47. According to Wundt, _____ has/have "to do with objective masses, forces, and energies" while _____ has/have "to do with subjective values and ends."
   a. psychical measurements; physical measurements
   b. creative synthesis; the law of psychic resultants
   c. the law of psychic resultants; creative synthesis
   d. physical measurements; psychical measurements
   e. None of the choices are correct.

   ANS: D   PTS: 1   REF: Wilhelm Wundt (1832-1920)

48. Wundtian psychology in Germany was slow to develop because _____.
   a. Germans were resistant to introspection
   b. experimentation was not valued
   c. it was not seen as having practical value
   d. there were not enough journals and textbooks
   e. Wundt could not adequately distinguish between feelings and sensations

   ANS: C   PTS: 1   REF: Wilhelm Wundt (1832-1920)
   MSC: WWW

49. Which of the following is **not** a reason for decline of Wundt's approach to psychology?
   a. Wundt's approach represented a pure science of psychology with little opportunity for practical application.
   b. German universities did not have the economic resources to support scientific psychology.
   c. Wundt's theories were difficult to understand. Therefore, he attracted very few students to his work.
   d. Wundt's approach was overshadowed by the development of Gestalt psychology in Germany and psychoanalysis in Austria.
   e. The pragmatic culture of the United States precluded Wundt's system.

   ANS: C   PTS: 1   REF: Wilhelm Wundt (1832-1920)

50. The ultimate fate of Wundt's laboratory at Leipzig was that it ____.
   a. was destroyed by the Gestapo in World War II
   b. is still in existence but serves solely as a historical attraction
   c. is still a productive research facility
   d. was destroyed by allied bombing raids in World War II
   e. was destroyed in World War II but rebuilt as a historical museum

   ANS: D   PTS: 1   REF: Wilhelm Wundt (1832-1920)

51. Research suggests that many psychology historians consider ____ to be the most important psychologist of all time.
   a. Wundt
   b. Freud
   c. Fechner
   d. Titchener
   e. Ebbinghaus

   ANS: A   PTS: 1   REF: Wilhelm Wundt (1832-1920)

52. Wundt's most important contribution to psychology was ____.
   a. "selling" psychology to the scientific community
   b. describing psychology as an experimental science
   c. beginning the first psychological journal
   d. his publications, which are still widely read today
   e. All of the above

   ANS: E   PTS: 1   REF: Wilhelm Wundt (1832-1920)

53. While Wundt had argued that learning and memory could not be studied experimentally, who soon proved him wrong?
   a. Titchener
   b. Ebbinghaus
   c. Külpe
   d. Brentano
   e. Galton

   ANS: B   PTS: 1   REF: Hermann Ebbinghaus (1850-1909)
   MSC: WWW

54. Ebbinghaus is important for the history of psychology because he ____.
    a. used reaction times to measure the speed of recalling information from memory
    b. wrote the first definitive work on child psychology
    c. successfully challenged Wundt's claim that higher mental processes, such as learning and memory, could not be studied in the laboratory
    d. united with Gestalt psychology to oppose the spread of Wundt's psychology in Germany
    e. taught Freud and influenced humanism and Gestalt psychology

    ANS: C   PTS: 1   REF: Hermann Ebbinghaus (1850-1909)

55. This person was influenced by Fechner's rigid and systematic use of measurement in developing his own methods for researching higher level cognitive processes.
    a. Georg Elias Müller
    b. Hermann von Helmholtz
    c. Carl Stumpf
    d. Hermann Ebbinghaus
    e. Oswald Külpe

    ANS: D   PTS: 1   REF: Hermann Ebbinghaus (1850-1909)

56. Ebbinghaus's focus of study was on the ____.
    a. examination of associations that were already formed
    b. initial formation of associations
    c. work of Helmholtz
    d. nature of the mind/body problem
    e. evolutionary theory as it applied to the mind

    ANS: B   PTS: 1   REF: Hermann Ebbinghaus (1850-1909)

57. ____ work on ____ was the first "venture into a truly psychological problem area" rather than on physiology.
    a. Wundt's; sensation
    b. Ebbinghaus'; learning
    c. Fechner's; psychophysics
    d. Brentano's; mental activity
    e. none of the other choices

    ANS: B   PTS: 1   REF: Hermann Ebbinghaus (1850-1909)

58. While conducting his research, Ebbinghaus used ____.
    a. a single subject
    b. fewer than 10 subjects at a time
    c. a method to "erase" memories
    d. over 1,000 subjects
    e. a laboratory to systematically test 20 subjects at a time

    ANS: A   PTS: 1   REF: Hermann Ebbinghaus (1850-1909)

59. As his measure of learning, Ebbinghaus adapted a method from ____.
    a. the psychophysicists
    b. Wundt's lab
    c. the early mentalists
    d. the Cartesian dualists
    e. the associationists

    ANS: E   PTS: 1   REF: Hermann Ebbinghaus (1850-1909)

60. Ebbinghaus measured the rate of human learning by _____.
   a. counting associations that had already been formed
   b. using an *a priori* method
   c. looking at the relationship between a behavior and its consequence
   d. making it more objective
   e. counting the number of repetitions needed for one perfect reproduction of the material

   ANS: E   PTS: 1   REF: Hermann Ebbinghaus (1850-1909)
   MSC: WWW

61. Titchener noted that the first significant advance in the study of learning since Aristotle was _____.
   a. Wundt's experimental methods
   b. the use of introspection
   c. the influence of the basic elements of sensation and feeling on the rate of learning
   d. the development of the nonsense syllable
   e. the conceptualization of imageless thought

   ANS: D   PTS: 1   REF: Hermann Ebbinghaus (1850-1909)

62. The fundamental purpose of creating nonsense syllables is to _____.
   a. control for previous learning
   b. be able to replicate the research in all languages that use the same alphabet
   c. assess word associations that are not influenced by unconscious material
   d. offset the influence of past reinforcements and punishments that one may associate with certain words
   e. control for apperception

   ANS: A   PTS: 1   REF: Hermann Ebbinghaus (1850-1909)

63. What was "meaningless" for Ebbinghaus?
   a. The use of introspection
   b. A mathematical approach to psychological phenomena
   c. Each syllable created for his research
   d. Each series of syllables created for his research
   e. Having a specific criterion to identify when learning had occurred

   ANS: D   PTS: 1   REF: Hermann Ebbinghaus (1850-1909)

64. When Ebbinghaus compared the speed of memorizing lists of nonsense syllables versus stanzas of a poem he found that _____.
   a. meaningless material is nine times harder to learn than meaningful material
   b. Byron's poem, "Don Juan," was so uninteresting that stanzas from took longer to learn than did lists of syllables
   c. each stanza had 80 syllables, requiring 80 repetitions while it required 9 readings to memorize 80 syllables from the meaningless list
   d. it is possible to construct an association-free syllable
   e. it is not possible to construct an association-free syllable

   ANS: A   PTS: 1   REF: Hermann Ebbinghaus (1850-1909)

THE NEW PSYCHOLOGY   123

65. What may be "the most brilliant single investigation in the history of experimental psychology"?
   a. Ebbinghaus's *On Memory*
   b. Titchener's *On Memory*
   c. Wundt's *On Forgetting*
   d. Ebbinghaus's *On Forgetting*
   e. Titchener's *A Summary of Psychology*

   ANS: A   PTS: 1   REF: Hermann Ebbinghaus (1850-1909)

66. The significance of Ebbinghaus's work is in his ____.
   a. finding that longer material takes more time to learn
   b. rigorous use of experimental control and his quantitative analysis of data
   c. tolerance for boredom
   d. use of large numbers of subjects to replicate his experiments
   e. ability to further the approach and findings of Wundt

   ANS: B   PTS: 1   REF: Hermann Ebbinghaus (1850-1909)

67. Ebbinghaus' curve of forgetting shows that ____.
   a. material is forgotten slowly in the first hours after learning and then the forgetting speeds up
   b. the decay theory of forgetting is essentially correct
   c. material learned first is forgotten last
   d. material is forgotten rapidly in the first hours after learning and then the forgetting slows down
   e. forgetting occurs at a gradual, even rate across time

   ANS: D   PTS: 1   REF: Hermann Ebbinghaus (1850-1909)

68. Ebbinghaus and König argued that psychology and physiology ____.
   a. must be separated if the new science was to flourish
   b. are inseparable halves of a new great double science
   c. must each address classic problems from philosophy
   d. must remain parallel and together but not intersect while studying the mind-body problem
   e. must unite to remove introspection and replace it with experimentation in the new science

   ANS: B   PTS: 1   REF: Hermann Ebbinghaus (1850-1909)

69. Ebbinghaus developed a(n) ____ considered by some to be the first successful test of higher mental process and used today, in modified form, in cognitive ability tests.
   a. problem-solving template
   b. ability test of memorization
   c. sentence-completion exercise
   d. tolerance of boredom
   e. memory and retention exercise

   ANS: C   PTS: 1   REF: Hermann Ebbinghaus (1850-1909)

70. Ebbinghaus dedicated *The Principles of Psychology* to ____.
   a. Titchener
   b. Wundt
   c. Fechner
   d. Brentano
   e. Külpe

   ANS: C   PTS: 1   REF: Hermann Ebbinghaus (1850-1909)

71. Given that many of his research findings remain valid today, _____ can be seen as more influential than
_____.
   a. Ebbinghaus; Wundt
   b. Wundt; Ebbinghaus
   c. König; Brentano
   d. Wundt; Brentano
   e. Brentano; König

   ANS: A   PTS: 1   REF: Hermann Ebbinghaus (1850-1909)

72. *Psychology from an Empirical Standpoint* (1874) was the major contribution to psychology from _____.
   a. Wundt
   b. Brentano
   c. Ebbinghaus
   d. Titchener
   e. Stumpf

   ANS: B   PTS: 1   REF: Franz Brentano (1838-1917)

73. This popular lecturer at the University of Vienna influenced many students including von Ehrenfels and
Freud and was the intellectual antecedent of Gestalt psychology and humanistic psychology.
   a. Edward Titchener
   b. Hermann Ebbinghaus
   c. Franz Brentano
   d. Oswald Külpe
   e. Carl Stumpf

   ANS: C   PTS: 1   REF: Franz Brentano (1838-1917)

74. For Brentano, the primary research method was _____.
   a. experimentation
   b. observation
   c. factor analysis
   d. functional analysis
   e. psychoanalysis

   ANS: B   PTS: 1   REF: Franz Brentano (1838-1917)

75. The subject matter of psychology is the act of experiencing, according to _____.
   a. Wundt
   b. Ebbinhaus
   c. Brentano
   d. Stumpf
   e. Titchener

   ANS: C   PTS: 1   REF: Franz Brentano (1838-1917)

76. Brentano's system of psychology was called _____ psychology.
   a. Act
   b. Cognitive
   c. Sense
   d. Content
   e. Memory

   ANS: A   PTS: 1   REF: Franz Brentano (1838-1917)

77. Act psychology, in contrast to Wundt's approach, claimed that psychology should _____.
    a. try to analyze consciousness into discrete mental states called "moments"
    b. actively fight for its place in the academic world
    c. be concerned with the development of rigorous methods of scientific research in the laboratory
    d. incorporate the study of music into laboratory research
    e. study mental processes or functions and not mental structure

    ANS: E   PTS: 1   REF: Franz Brentano (1838-1917)

78. Act psychologists argued that the two ways of systematically studying mental acts were _____.
    a. introspection and retrospection
    b. learning and memory
    c. learning and imagination
    d. memory and imagination
    e. experimentation and empiricism

    ANS: D   PTS: 1   REF: Franz Brentano (1838-1917)

79. Other than Stumpf's research, his greatest influence on psychology may have been _____.
    a. educating the founders of Gestalt psychology
    b. the legitimization of music as a therapy for mentally ill and developmentally disabled persons
    c. the legitimization of introspection as an experimental technique
    d. the legitimization of *un*trained observers to do introspection in experimental research
    e. the discovery of imageless thought and the ensuing debate with Wundt

    ANS: A   PTS: 1   REF: Carl Stumpf (1848-1936)
    MSC: WWW

80. The psychological study of music was pioneered by _____.
    a. Helmholtz
    b. Fechner
    c. Wundt
    d. Stumpf
    e. Külpe

    ANS: D   PTS: 1   REF: Carl Stumpf (1848-1936)

81. Stumpf's method of observation was _____.
    a. phenomenology
    b. retrospection
    c. introspection
    d. systematic experimental introspection
    e. insight

    ANS: A   PTS: 1   REF: Carl Stumpf (1848-1936)

82. Which of the following methods is defined as "the examination of experience as it occurred without any attempt to reduce experience to elementary components."
    a. Epiphenomenology
    b. Phenomenology
    c. Voluntarism
    d. Introspection
    e. Imageless thought

    ANS: B   PTS: 1   REF: Carl Stumpf (1848-1936)

83. Stumpf and Wundt engaged in a bitter fight over the topic of ____.
    a. phenomenology
    b. the introspection of tones
    c. music as mediate experience
    d. imageless thought
    e. classical music

    ANS: B   PTS: 1   REF: Carl Stumpf (1848-1936)

84. "Psychology is the science of the facts of experience as dependent on the experiencing person," according to whom?
    a. Wundt
    b. Brentano
    c. Stumpf
    d. Külpe
    e. Ebbinghaus

    ANS: D   PTS: 1   REF: Oswald Külpe (1862-1915)

85. Systematic experimental introspection involves ____.
    a. retrospection
    b. introspection
    c. the presentation of sensory stimuli
    d. the performance of a complex task
    e. retrospection and the performance of a complex task

    ANS: E   PTS: 1   REF: Oswald Külpe (1862-1915)
    MSC: WWW

86. Külpe's method emphasized all of the following **except** ____.
    a. subjective reports
    b. qualitative reports
    c. after-the-fact questions to direct observers' attention
    d. investigating unconscious processes
    e. having subjects perform a complex task

    ANS: D   PTS: 1   REF: Oswald Külpe (1862-1915)

87. Külpe's identification of nonsensory aspects or contents of consciousness refuted Wundt's ____.
    a. contention that the sole mental elements were sensations or images
    b. contention that emotions are composed of simple feelings and can be reduced to them
    c. contention that feelings are the subjective complements of sensations
    d. research on sensations
    e. findings on voluntarism

    ANS: A   PTS: 1   REF: Oswald Külpe (1862-1915)

88. Külpe opposed Wundt by claiming that conscious thought processes can be carried out without the presence of sensations or feelings. Külpe's view is known as ____.
    a. intentionality
    b. act psychology
    c. imageless thought
    d. retrospection
    e. systematic experimental realism

    ANS: C   PTS: 1   REF: Oswald Külpe (1862-1915)

THE NEW PSYCHOLOGY   127

89. Marbe and Watt extended the work and influence of the Würzburg school with their ____.
   a. discovery of imageless thought
   b. discovery of the influence of the unconscious mind
   c. reduction of imageless thoughts to nonconscious memories of sensations
   d. identification of a method to retrieve unconscious material
   e. experimental work on nonconscious learning (subliminal perception)

   ANS: B   PTS: 1   REF: Oswald Külpe (1862-1915)

TRUE/FALSE

90. Fechner is the founder of psychology as a formal discipline.

   ANS: F   PTS: 1   REF: The Founding Father of Modern Psychology

91. Fechner's Elements of Psychophysics was the "first conquest" of experimental psychology.

   ANS: T   PTS: 1   REF: The Founding Father of Modern Psychology

92. Psychology was established as an independent discipline with Wundt's *Principles of Physiological Psychology*.

   ANS: T   PTS: 1   REF: The Founding Father of Modern Psychology

93. Wilhelm Wundt started the first journal of experimental psychology, *Philosophical Studies*.

   ANS: T   PTS: 1   REF: Wilhelm Wundt (1832-1920)
   MSC: WWW

94. Wundt's Cultural Psychology was an attempt to investigate the effects of group membership on decision making.

   ANS: F   PTS: 1   REF: Wilhelm Wundt (1832-1920)

95. For Wundt, the subject matter of experimental psychology was consciousness.

   ANS: T   PTS: 1   REF: Wilhelm Wundt (1832-1920)

96. If you look at a rose and report "The rose is red" then you are describing immediate experience.

   ANS: T   PTS: 1   REF: Wilhelm Wundt (1832-1920)
   MSC: WWW

97. Among Wundt's rules for introspection was that the subject/observer was not to be forewarned because a preparatory set (expectation) would interfere with the immediate experience.

   ANS: F   PTS: 1   REF: Wilhelm Wundt (1832-1920)

98. Wundt's data were objective measures.

   ANS: T   PTS: 1   REF: Wilhelm Wundt (1832-1920)

99. For Wundt, the elements of the mind are sensations and feelings.

ANS: T   PTS: 1   REF: Wilhelm Wundt (1832-1920)

100. The components of the tridimensional theory are pleasantness, brightness, and contrast.

ANS: F   PTS: 1   REF: Wilhelm Wundt (1832-1920)

101. In the Original Source Material, Wundt states that ,"the law of psychical resultants expresses a principle that is the opposite of the principle of creative synthesis".

ANS: F   PTS: 1   REF: Wilhelm Wundt (1832-1920)
MSC: WWW

102. For Wundt, as stated in the Original Source Material, physical measurements and psychical measurements essentially have to do with the same thing.

ANS: F   PTS: 1   REF: Wilhelm Wundt (1832-1920)

103. Wilhelm Wundt's psychology immediately and completely transformed the nature of academic psychology in Germany.

ANS: F   PTS: 1   REF: Wilhelm Wundt (1832-1920)

104. Wundt's cultural psychology gained acclaim by distinguishing itself from philosophy.

ANS: F   PTS: 1   REF: Wilhelm Wundt (1832-1920)
MSC: WWW

105. Paramount among the factors that contributed to the demise of Wundtian psychology was World War I and the economic crisis that followed it.

ANS: T   PTS: 1   REF: Wilhelm Wundt (1832-1920)

106. Wundt debated questions about "soul," vehemently arguing that such was the subject matter of philosophy and religion.

ANS: F   PTS: 1   REF: Wilhelm Wundt (1832-1920)

107. In terms of the Zeitgeist of 19th-century German universities, the time was right for Wundtian psychology.

ANS: T   PTS: 1   REF: Wilhelm Wundt (1832-1920)
MSC: WWW

108. Wundt is regarded by many modern psychology historians as the most important psychologist of all time.

ANS: T   PTS: 1   REF: Wilhelm Wundt (1832-1920)

109. Schultz and Schultz compare Ebbinghaus's conception of memory with the process of association espoused by the British empiricists.

ANS: T   PTS: 1   REF: Hermann Ebbinghaus (1850-1909)

110. Ebbinghaus's work on learning and forgetting has been judged one of the great instances of original genius in experimental psychology.

   ANS: T   PTS: 1   REF: Hermann Ebbinghaus (1850-1909)

111. The book, *Psychology from an Empirical Standpoint*, was a defining work for the British laws of association.

   ANS: F   PTS: 1   REF: Franz Brentano (1838-1917)

112. The basic distinction between Wundt's and Brentano's systems was that the former's was experimental and the latter's was empirical.

   ANS: T   PTS: 1   REF: Franz Brentano (1838-1917)

113. Brentano argued that mental acts could be studied by memory and imagination.

   ANS: T   PTS: 1   REF: Franz Brentano (1838-1917)

114. Phenomenology was the type of observation of experience preferred by Stumpf.

   ANS: T   PTS: 1   REF: Carl Stumpf (1848-1936)

115. The method of systematic experimental introspection was developed by Wundt.

   ANS: F   PTS: 1   REF: Oswald Külpe (1862-1915)

116. Külpe emphasized qualitative reports from his observers.

   ANS: T   PTS: 1   REF: Oswald Külpe (1862-1915)

117. Watt's work was important for its identification of unconscious determining tendencies that subjects manifested.

   ANS: T   PTS: 1   REF: Oswald Külpe (1862-1915)

Chapter 5

Structuralism

In the beginning of the 20th century, Edward Bradford Titchener, a professor at Cornell University, was conducting controversial experiments using his graduate students as subjects in order to collect data for his burgeoning system of psychology. Many of these experiments used introspection as the experimental method. One example is the stomach tube experiment, which was used to study the sensitivity of students' internal organs. During the experiment, students would swallow a rubber tube and subsequently have hot and cold water poured down the tube. The tube often remained in the body for the entire day, during which students were asked to report on the sensations they experienced. Another study asked students to reports on their feelings and sensations during urination and defecation. A third study asked married students to record their feelings and sensations during sexual intercourse.

Titchener presented himself as a representative of Wilhelm Wundt's experimental psychology when he introduced it in the United States. The truth was just the opposite. Titchener changed Wundtian psychology so radically that his branch of psychology was labeled "structuralism." As such, structuralism was the first American school of thought and lasted approximately 20 years. Whereas Wundt's central concern was with apperception (the active synthesis of conscious elements into the higher-level mental processes), Titchener instead emphasized association (focus on mental elements and their mechanical linking). In this way, the goal of Titchener's psychology was to discover the nature of elementary conscious experiences.

Titchener's persona was a stereotype of Germanic imperiousness, as was demonstrated by the authoritative and formal lecture style he adopted from Wundt. Despite his demeanor, Titchener drew large audiences to his grand lectures and was respected by students and faculty alike. During his career, Titchener supervised over 50 doctoral candidates whose dissertations and later work reflected many of Titchener's own interests and ideas. He published over 60 scholarly articles and spent a significant amount of time translating Wundt's work into English.

One confounding aspect of Titchener's career was his treatment of women. "Although he did not relent about permitting women to attend meetings of the Titchener Experimentalists, he did work to open doors to women that were kept firmly closed by most other male psychologists." Titchener was one of the few male psychologists at the time to welcome women into graduate programs, and he was one of the few prominent psychologists to support women in faculty appointments. In 1929, two years after Titchener's death, Titchener's Experimentalists became the Society for Experimental Psychologists and welcomed women members.

Titchener's most important book was Experimental Psychology: *A Manual of Laboratory Practice* (1901-1905) as it prompted the growth of psychology laboratories and was the training manual for the first generation of American experimental psychologists. He insisted that conscious experience is the only appropriate subject matter for the science of psychology. Original source material written by Titchener discusses the difference between dependent and independent experience. His method was rigorous experimentation, and his technique was introspection. Titchener cautioned against the stimulus error (confusing mental processes with the stimulus or object being observed), because when one focuses on the stimulus/object instead of the conscious content, they neglect what has been learned in the past about the object. In this way, he distinguished between consciousness (the sum of our experiences at a given time) and mind (the sum of our experiences over a lifetime).

Titchener was adamant that the only appropriate subject pool was normal adult humans. The study of any other subject population simply was not psychology. In addition, the practice of applied psychology was anathema to him. He believed that psychology's purpose was to discover the structures of the mind. He was unconcerned with the application of such knowledge and opposed branches that dealt with practical issues, such as child or animal psychology.

Titchener's work focused on the first of three tasks he defined for the new science, namely, the reduction of consciousness to its elements. He proposed three states of consciousness: sensations, images, and affective states. He argued that elements of sensation could be assessed and grouped not solely on the basis of quality and intensity, as Wundt had proposed, but on the basis of duration and clearness. He rejected Wundt's tridimensional theory, arguing that feelings have but one dimension: pleasure/displeasure.

In his last years, Titchener discarded the notion of mental elements and proposed that the focus of psychology should be on processes of mental life. He questioned the term structural, replacing it with the term existential. He also began to favor the phenomenological approach instead of the introspection method because it examines experiences as they occur.

Titchener continued to hold firm in his ideas about what psychology should be about while psychology moved beyond him. When he died of a brain tumor in 1927, the era of structuralism died with him. The strongest criticisms of structuralism are argued against its primary research method: introspection. A century before Titchener, philosophers questioned the possibility of the mind studying itself. Titchener himself could not clearly define what introspection was and how it should be done. In practice, there was low reliability between observers. Other critics said that introspection was more retrospection because of the time lag between experience and report. On the other hand, Titchener did clearly define conscious experience, and used the most rigorous scientific methods. Today introspection (defined as self-report) is used in a variety of fields. Titchener's structuralism also served well as a target of criticism that developing movements in psychology could push against as these new movements were defined.

Outline

I.   Swallow the rubber tube – A college prank?

    A. Titchener conducted research at Cornell to collect data for the psychological system he was developing

        1. method: introspection

    B. Titchener asked his students to do a variety of outrageous things

        1. swallow a rubber tube, leave in for a day, return to lab to have hot water poured down, then have cold water poured down

            a. to study organ sensitivity

            b. many vomited before keeping tubes down

            c. when water poured down, they reported the sensations

        2. students carried notebooks to record feelings while urinating or defecating

        3. married students were asked to report on sensations during sex

II.   Edward Bradford Titchener (1867 – 1927)

    A. Wundt's experimental psychology was introduced in America by Titchener

        1. although Titchener claimed to represent Wundt's ideas, in fact he radically altered them

        2. the label "structuralism" can only be applied to Titchener's work

B. Wundt: experimental psychology
   1. acknowledged the elements of consciousness
   2. emphasis on apperception: the active organization or synthesis of elements
   3. organization of mental elements voluntary, not mechanical
C. Titchener: structuralism
   1. emphasis on elements of consciousness
   2. association (mental linking of elements) is mechanical
   3. discarded Wundt's apperception
   4. central task of psychology: discover the nature of elementary conscious experiences
D. Titchener's career
   1. most of his career was spent at Cornell University
   2. like Wundt, made every lecture a dramatic presentation
   3. often mistaken for being German because of authoritative style and formal manner
   4. as he grew older became more intolerant of dissent
E. Titchener's life
   1. Oxford
      a. philosophy and the classics
      b. research assistant in physiology
      c. colleagues skeptical of scientific approach to psychological issues
      d. seen as a brilliant student with a flair for languages
   2. Ph.D. with Wundt: 1892
   3. Cornell University
      a. 1893 – 1900: established laboratories, did research, wrote
      b. from 1900
         (1) directed students' research
         (2) that research produced his system
         (3) translated Wundt's books
   4. Dies of a brain tumor at age 60
   5. his books
      c. 1896: An Outline of Psychology
      d. 1898: Primer of Psychology
      e. 1901 – 1905: Experimental Psychology: A Manual of Laboratory Practice
         (1) one of the most important books in history of psychology
         (2) stimulated growth of laboratory work in psychology in the United States
         (3) influenced a generation of experimental psychologists
         (4) popular text, translated into 5 languages
   6. his personal style and life
      a. praised as an outstanding teacher
      b. had a variety of hobbies
         (1) conducted a weekly musical ensemble
         (2) coin collecting
         (3) learned Chinese and Arabic
      c. was autocratic toward students, though kind as long as they were deferential
      d. Titchener was concerned and involved with his students even after they left Cornell

F. Titchener's Experimentalists: No women allowed!
1. beginning in 1904 a group named Titchener's Experimentalists held regular meetings to discuss research observations in experimental psychology
2. Titchener's rule: no women
    a. desire for active discussion and interaction in a "smoke-filled room"
    b. women "too pure to smoke"
    c. refused Christine Ladd-Franklin's request to present her research
    d. Ladd actively protested Titchener's rule
3. Titchener actively worked to advance women in psychology
    a. accepted women in his graduate programs
    b. 1/3 of the 56 doctorates awarded by him were to women
    c. more female doctorates than any other contemporary psychologist
    d. hired female faculty
    e. Margaret Floy Washburn 1st women to earn doctorate in psychology and Titchener's 1st doctoral student
        (1) wrote Animal Mind, major comparative psychology book
        (2) 1st female psychologist elected to National Academy of Sciences
        (3) president of APA
4. firmly adhered to "no women" rule for Titchener experimentalists yet backed female psychologists
G. The content of conscious experience
1. subject matter of psychology: conscious experience
2. dependent on the experiencing person; other sciences independent of experiencing persons
    a. Original source material on structuralism from A Textbook of Psychology (1909)
    b. Titchener discusses his dependent/independent distinction
3. warned against stimulus error: "Confusing the mental process under study with the stimulus or object being observed"
4. consciousness: the sum of our experiences existing at a given time
5. mind: the sum of our experiences accumulated over a lifetime
6. Titchener sees structural psychology as a pure science
    a. only legitimate purpose: to discover the facts (structure) of the mind
    b. no applied aspects; objected to branches that dealt with applied issues
    c. subjects: only normal adult humans
H. Introspection: describe the elements of conscious state rather than report the observed stimulus by its familiar name
1. self -observation
2. trained observers
3. adopted Külpe's label, "systematic experimental introspection"
    a. used detailed, qualitative, subjective reports of mental activities during the act of introspecting
4. opposed Wundt's approach (focus on objective quantitative measurements)
5. goal in line with empiricists and associationists: to discover the atoms of the mind
6. mechanist: subjects were "reagents": impartial, detached, mechanical recording instruments

7. mechanistic viewpoint: observers as machines
8. Titchener's experimental approach
    a.   experiment = an observation "that can be repeated, isolated, varied"
        (1) frequent repetition
        (2) strict isolation (control)
        (3) vary observations widely
    b.   reagents (subjects)
        (1) introspected on variety of stimuli
        (2) gave long, detailed reports of elements observed
        (3) for example, a chord is struck on a piano
            (a) chord consisted of three individual notes
            (b) subjects report on how many tones, mental
            characteristics of the sounds, any other elements

I. Elements of consciousness
1. defined three essential problems for psychology (the bulk of his work)
    a.   reduce conscious processes to simplest components
    b.   determine laws by which elements associated
    c.   connect the elements with their physiological conditions
2. aims same as those of the natural sciences
    a.   decide the area of study
    b.   discover its elements (stage that Titchener was working on)
    c.   demonstrate how those elements form complex phenomena
    d.   formulate laws governing those phenomena
3. proposed three elementary states of consciousness
    a.   sensations: "...basic elements of perception and occur in the sounds, sights, smells, and other experiences evoked by physical objects in our environment."
    b.   Images: "...elements of ideas...not actually present in the moment," e.g., "memory of a past experience."
    c.   affective states: "elements of emotions"
4. characteristics of mental elements
    a.   discovered 44,500 basic and irreducible elements of sensation
        (1) each is conscious
        (2) each is distinct from all others
        (3) each could combine with others to form perceptions and ideas
    b.   each element could be categorized according to characteristics basic to all sensations (Titchener added duration and clearness to Wundt's quality and intensity)
        (1) quality: attribute differentiating each element from the other, e.g., "cold," "red"
        (2) intensity: strength, weakness, loudness, or brightness of sensation
        (3) duration: sensation's path over time
        (4) clearness: the role of attention in conscious processing
    c.   sensations and images have all four
    d.   affective states lack clearness because focusing on an element of emotion makes it disappear
    e.   some sensory processes have extensity (they take up space)

     5. rejected Wundt's tridimensional theory; proposed affections have only one dimension: pleasure/displeasure

     6. 1918:
        a. dropped concept of mental elements
        b. suggested study of dimensions (quality, etc.)

     7. early 1920s
        a. questioned term structural psychology
        b. called it "existential psychology"
        c. considered replacement of introspection with phenomenological approach (experience as it occurs, without analysis)

III. Criticisms of Structuralism
  A. Titchener stood firm as psychology moved beyond him
  B. he thought he was establishing a foundation for psychology, but he was only one phase in its history
  C. Structuralism collapses when he dies

IV. Criticisms of Introspection
  A. Titchener and Külpe's approaches were subject to criticism because they were qualitative; Wundt's approach not as criticized because more objective
  B. introspection had been attacked for a century or more
     1. Kant
     2. Comte
     3. Maudsley
  C. one direct criticism: Titchener's approach more precise yet not defined well
  D. a second direct criticism: precise task of trained observer is unclear/unknown
     1. unreliability within and between subjects
     2. special introspective language never created
  E. a third direct criticism: introspection is retrospection
  F. additional criticisms of Titchener
     1. artificiality and sterility
     2. the structuralist definition of psychology is too narrow

V. Contributions of Structuralism
  A. Subject matter (conscious experience) clearly defined
  B. Research methods: good science
  C. Introspection remains a viable method
  D. Impact on cognitive psychology
  E. Strong base against which others could rebel

Lecture prompts/Discussion topics for chapter five

- Is it possible for the mind to observe itself? Is there any other way one could observe a mind?
- How is Titchener's style different from/similar to the professors you have had? What about his personal style would have benefited the discipline? What would have been disadvantageous?
- Provide several stimuli and ask students to become introspectionists by reporting, as best they can, on their <u>sensations</u>, <u>images</u> (a memory that is recalled), and <u>affective</u> states (emotions). Probably the easiest for them to report will be the affective states, especially if you choose vivid stimuli (such as an image of war or triumph, or a noxious or pleasant

odor or taste). Probably the most difficult will be the sensations, but you can cue them with Titchener's 4 aspects of sensations. <u>Quality</u> is a characteristic like "cold" or "red". <u>Intensity</u> is the strength or weakness of the sensation. <u>Duration</u> is the course of the sensation over time. <u>Clearness</u> is if our attention is easily drawn to the stimulus.

- One of the criticisms the book brings up is that "The structuralist movement was accused of artificiality and sterility for attempting to analyze conscious processes into elements." To some extent, can the same criticism be leveled at pure laboratory experiments in Psychology? Is it fair to criticize Titchener for one of the strengths of his position (his rigorous scientific methods)?

Internet Resources for chapter five

Society of experimental psychologists
http://www.sepsych.org/
> This is the organization founded by Titchener with a link to a narrative description of its history as well as photographs of some earlier meetings.

Guide to the Edward Bradford Titchener Papers, Cornell University Library
http://rmc.library.cornell.edu/EAD/htmldocs/RMA00545.html
> This is a listing of Titchener's correspondence and manuscripts that the Cornell University Library holds, which shows the vigorous levels of communication between these early psychologists. The list of senders/recipients reads like a "who's who" of early psychology.

Human Intelligence project: Edward Bradford Titchener
http://www.indiana.edu/~intell/titchener.shtml
> This site provides additional information about Titchener's life and work. Particularly interesting are the connections the site makes of the intellectual influences of a number of people (including Titchener).

Titchener Illusion
http://mathworld.wolfram.com/TitchenerIllusion.html
> This is a website that contains a nice graphic of an illusion discovered by Titchener relating to how the size of a circle is perceived to be different depending on its context.

Titchener's photo album, Max Planck Institute
http://vlp.mpiwg-berlin.mpg.de/essays/data/art11/
> This site contains a brief biography followed by images of Titchener's personal photo album. These are his collected images and drawings for instruments he wished to use for his psychological research. Such instruments give great information about the types of research he performed.

Potential answers to chapter five discussion questions

1. Why did some of Titchener's graduate students swallow rubber tubes, take notebooks to the bathroom, and record their feelings during intercourse?

This was data collection. Titchener asked his students to introspect while engaging in these activities.

2. Contrast and compare Titchener's and Wundt's approaches to psychology.

Titchener virtually ignored Wundt's central concern with the active synthesis of conscious elements into the higher-level mental processes (what Wundt called apperception). Rather, Titchener emphasized the elements of consciousness and focused instead on determining the structure of the mind.

3. Describe the paradoxical views of Titchener regarding the place of women in psychology. Did he act to assist them in their careers or discriminate against them?

Titchener founded the Experimentalists, and intentionally excluded women from membership. At the same time, however, he welcomed women into graduate programs (about a third of his Ph.D. students were women, and he taught the first woman to receive a Ph.D. in Psychology, Margaret Floy Washburn) and welcomed them as faculty colleagues as well. Thus, he both assisted and impeded the careers of women.

4. According to Titchener, what is the proper subject matter for psychology? How does it differ from the subject matter of other sciences?

"Other sciences are independent of experiencing persons. Titchener offered, from physics, the example of temperature. The temperature in a room may be measured at, let us say, 85° Fahrenheit, whether or not anyone is in the room to experience it. When observers are present in that room and report that they feel uncomfortably warm, however, that feeling—that experience of warmth—is dependent on the experiencing individuals, the people in the room.
To Titchener, this type of conscious experience was the only proper focus for psychological research."

5. What is the stimulus error? Give an example. How, in Titchener's view, could the stimulus error be avoided?

The stimulus error happens when an introspective observer confuses the mental process under study with the stimulus or object being observed. The example given in the book is about looking at an apple. Upon seeing an apple, an observer would commit the stimulus error if he or she reported seeing an "apple" instead of reporting the elements of color, brightness, shape, intensity of the apple, etc. This error could be avoided, Titchener believed, if a new language was created free from previous associations and interpretations that could be used to report on introspection experiences.

6. What distinction did Titchener draw between consciousness and mind?

For Titchener, consciousness is the sum of our experiences as they exist at a given moment in time, while mind is the sum of our experiences accumulated over a lifetime.

7. Describe Titchener's method of introspection. How did it differ from Wundt's?
The methods were quite different. With Titchener, introspective reports were more "detailed, qualitative, subjective reports of his subjects' mental activities". With Wundt, introspective reports were brief, and had a "focus on objective, quantitative measurements."

8. Describe the difference between experience as *independent* of the experiencing person and experience as *dependent* on the experiencing person. Give examples. According to Titchener, which type provides the data for psychology?
Independent experiences occur without having to be perceived by an observer. Dependent experience separates psychology from other sciences, because observation of the conscious mind is necessarily dependent on the observer. The example given by Titchener is about temperature. To measure temperature, one can place a thermometer in a room whether or not there is someone there to experience the temperature (independent experience). With psychology, an individual must sense and perceive the temperature, and in fact the same temperature may be reported as being "warm" by one person and "cool" by another (dependent experience).

9. What did Titchener's use of the term *reagent* indicate about his views of human subjects and of people in general?
Reagent is a term adopted from chemistry. In chemistry, reagents are "substances that, because of their capacity for certain reactions, are used to detect, examine, or measure other substances. A reagent is usually passive, an agent used to elicit or prompt responses from some other substance." With Titchener choosing this term to refer to his introspective observers, we see that he views his subjects (and people in general) as mechanistic (materialist) instruments that passively record events.

10. Describe Titchener's three elementary states of consciousness and the four attributes of mental elements.
The three elementary states of consciousness were sensations (the "basic elements of perception"), images (the "elements of ideas" that "are not actually present at the moment, such as a memory of a past experience"), and affective states (the "elements of emotion"). The four attributes of mental elements are Quality (the distinguishing characteristic of an element), Intensity (the "sensation's strength"), Duration (how long a sensation lasts), and Clearness (whether or not we are focusing attention).

11. In what ways did Titchener begin to alter his system late in his career?
He began to not use the term 'structural psychology' to label his system, but preferred the term 'existential psychology'. This marks a dramatic shift in his search to no longer look for the elements of conscious experience but rather look at conscious experience in a more natural setting. He also considered replacement of introspection with the phenomenological approach.

12. What criticisms had been made of the method of introspection before the work of Titchener?
Introspection had been criticized about 100 years before Titchener adopted its use by philosophers (Kant, Comte) who questioned the mind's ability to objectively observe itself.

13. On what grounds was Titchener's approach to introspection criticized? How did he answer his critics?
Titchener's approach was criticized because it was unclear what the introspective reporters were trained to do. Ordinary words were full of meaning that would cloud their reports. To counteract this, Titchener attempted to create an introspectionist language free from previously learned associations/interpretations. However, this language was never actually created.

14. How did Titchener distinguish between inspection and introspection?
For Titchener, introspection is the method of observation used in psychology, while inspection, which he defined as "observation and experiment" is used in the natural sciences.

15. What was the role of *retrospection* in psychological research, according to Titchener?
Because there was often a time lapse between an event and Titchener's introspectionists' reports of the event, critics called it retrospection instead of introspection. Titchener answered this criticism by having "observers work with the briefest time intervals, and, second, by proposing the existence of a primary mental image that was alleged to maintain the experience for the observers until it could be reported."

16. What additional criticisms have been made of Titchener's structuralism? What contributions has Titchener's structuralism made to psychology?
Introspection, the primary methodology of Titchener's structuralism, was the target of many criticisms. Outside of these criticisms, structuralism was criticized because of "artificiality and sterility" and the insistence that looking at elements cannot capture the wholeness of an experience. Titchener's exclusion of any application of psychology findings to real-world problems also was criticized. Contributions of structuralism are the clear definition of consciousness it provided, its use of good scientific controls, and the fact that forms of introspection are still used by some modern psychologists to study conscious experiences (such as cognitive psychologists).

Key terms from chapter five

- **Consciousness vs. Mind** Titchener defines consciousness as the sum of our experiences as they exist at a given moment in time, while mind is the sum of our experiences accumulated over a lifetime.
- **Cornell University** The University where Titchener worked from 1893-1927. It was at Cornell where he defined structuralism and trained graduate students.
- **Dependent vs. Independent experience** Dependent experience separates psychology from other sciences, because observation of the conscious mind is necessarily dependent on the observer.
  - Example: To measure temperature, one can place a thermometer in a room whether or not there is someone there to experience the temperature (independent experience). With psychology, an individual must sense and perceive the temperature, and in fact the same temperature may be reported as being "warm" by one person and "cool" by another (dependent experience).
- **Elementary States of consciousness** Titchener defines three: sensations, images, and affective states. Sensations are the basic elements of perception (such as sights, sounds, smells, etc.). Images are the elements of ideas not present in the moment (such as memories). Affective states are the elements of emotion (what the observer feels).

- **Existential Psychology** Toward the end of his career, Titchener favored this term above "Structuralism". This demonstrates his move away from examining the elements of experience toward experiences as they occur in whole.
- **Experimental Psychology: A Manual of Laboratory Practice** (1901-1905) Titchener's most important book, which stimulated the growth of laboratory work in psychology in the United States and influenced a generation of experimental psychologists.
- **Introspection** The sole technique used by Titchener, a form of self-observation that relied on observers being rigorously trained. Observers were required to report on the elements of their conscious state (experience).
- **Reagents** The term Titchener used to describe his introspective observers. "Reagent" is a term chemists use to describe a substance that is used solely to detect other substances. Using this term demonstrates Titchener's mechanistic leanings.
- **Stimulus error** Confusing the mental process under study with the stimulus or object being observed.
    o Example: Upon seeing an apple, an observer would commit the stimulus error if he or she reported seeing an "apple" instead of reporting the elements of color, brightness, shape, intensity of the apple, etc.
- **Structuralism** For most of his career, the term used by Titchener to describe his psychology. It reflects his efforts to discover the elements of and structures underlying conscious experience.
- **Titchener and women** Although Titchener chose to exclude women from the Experimentalist Society, he supported their professional work in Psychology. More women received their Ph.D. under Titchener than from anyone else in his time, and he advocated hiring female faculty despite the protest of colleagues.
- **Pleasure/Displeasure** Titchener rejects Wundt's tridimensional theory of feelings, suggesting only one, pleasure and displeasure.

ESSAY

1. Compare and contrast Titchener's and Wundt's systems of psychology, including their goals, methodology, and theories. Why is it important to stress that Wundt's system is *not* structuralism?

   ANS:
   Answer not provided.

   PTS: 1

2. For Titchener, what is the subject matter of psychology? How is psychology similar to and different from other sciences?

   ANS:
   Answer not provided.

   PTS: 1

3. In terms of studying conscious experience, what is the stimulus error as discussed by Titchener? How does it relate to Wundt's distinction between immediate and mediate experience? Describe Titchener's differentiation between consciousness and mind. What was his vision for structural psychology?

   ANS:
   Answer not provided.

   PTS: 1   MSC: WWW

4. Describe Titchener's form of introspection. What are the similarities and differences between his approach and that of Wundt? What was Titchener's experimental approach, particularly with regard to the concept and role of reagents?

   ANS:
   Answer not provided.

   PTS: 1

5. Name and define the three basic states (types) of conscious as identified by Titchener? Each state is composed of elements, which are irreducible and groupable according to their characteristics. Name and describe the characteristics of mental elements that Titchener used to categorize (group) them. Are these characteristics fundamental to each of the three states of consciousness? Explain your answer.

   ANS:
   Answer not provided.

   PTS: 1   MSC: WWW

6. Titchener's behavior toward women in Psychology was contradictory, in that he sometimes supported and sometimes impeded their professional growth. Please discuss this contradiction using examples.

   ANS:
   Answer not provided.

   PTS: 1

7. Discuss and give examples of the central criticisms of structuralism. What contributions has structuralism made to psychology?

ANS:
Answer not provided.

PTS: 1

MULTIPLE CHOICE

8. Subjects in Titchener's laboratory were asked to ____.
   a. swallow a stomach tube
   b. record their sensations and feelings during urination and defecation
   c. make notes of their sensations and feelings during sexual intercourse
   d. attach measuring devices to their bodies to record their physiological responses during sexual intercourse
   e. All of the choices are correct

   ANS: E   PTS: 1   REF: Swallow the Rubber Tube-A College Prank?

9. The school of structuralism includes the work and/or systems of which of the following?
   a. Wundt
   b. Külpe
   c. Titchener
   d. both Wundt and Külpe
   e. both Wundt and Titchener

   ANS: C   PTS: 1   REF: Edward Bradford Titchener (1867-1927)

10. Wundt's focus was on ____, whereas Titchener's was on ____.
    a. introspection; inspection
    b. elements of consciousness; synthesis of elements
    c. apperception; perception
    d. synthesis; apperception
    e. synthesis of elements; analysis of elements

    ANS: E   PTS: 1   REF: Edward Bradford Titchener (1867-1927)

11. Titchener discarded aspects of Wundt's system, including ____.
    a. his focus on consciousness
    b. introspection
    c. apperception
    d. elements of consciousness
    e. none of the choices are correct; Titchener retained virtually all of Wundt's system

    ANS: C   PTS: 1   REF: Edward Bradford Titchener (1867-1927)
    MSC: WWW

12. Titchener spent most of his career at ____.
    a. Cornell University
    b. Harvard University
    c. Cambridge University
    d. University of London
    e. Oxford University

    ANS: A   PTS: 1   REF: Edward Bradford Titchener (1867-1927)

13. Titchener's manner with his students during lectures was one of ____.
   a. formality
   b. concern
   c. humility
   d. good humor
   e. All of the choices are correct

   ANS: A   PTS: 1   REF: Edward Bradford Titchener (1867-1927)

14. Titchener's relationship with Wundt and his family was one of ____.
   a. distance
   b. formality
   c. closeness
   d. false cordiality
   e. None of the choices are correct

   ANS: C   PTS: 1   REF: Edward Bradford Titchener (1867-1927)

15. When Titchener returned to Oxford with his doctorate from Wundt, his colleagues ____.
   a. quickly followed in his footsteps
   b. incorporated his new ideas into their own approaches
   c. tried their best to convince him to stay in England and add the new approaches he had learned to the department of philosophy
   d. were skeptical of the use of scientific approaches to philosophical questions
   e. None of the choices are correct

   ANS: D   PTS: 1   REF: Edward Bradford Titchener (1867-1927)

16. As more and more students became drawn to Titchener's lectures at Cornell, he ____.
   a. had more active involvement in all aspects of laboratory research.
   b. did not allow these students to do his research.
   c. became a popularizer.
   d. allowed these students to choose their own dissertation topics.
   e. became less actively engaged in laboratory research.

   ANS: E   PTS: 1   REF: Edward Bradford Titchener (1867-1927)

17. One of the main reasons that Titchener's thought was believed to closely parallel that of Wundt was that Titchener ____.
   a. did not depart from Wundtian ideas in any significant manner
   b. took great care to scrupulously present all of Wundt's ideas, whether he agreed with them or not
   c. did not, himself, have any creative ideas
   d. translated Wundt's books from German into English
   e. was Wundt's cousin

   ANS: D   PTS: 1   REF: Edward Bradford Titchener (1867-1927)

18. One of Titchener's most profound influences on the development of experimentation in psychology was his publication _____.
    a. *Principles of Physiological Psychology* (1873, 1874)
    b. *Principles of Psychology* (1890)
    c. *An Outline of Psychology* (1896)
    d. *Primer of Psychology* (1898)
    e. *Experimental Psychology: A Manual of Laboratory Practice* (1901-1905)

    ANS: E   PTS: 1   REF: Edward Bradford Titchener (1867-1927)
    MSC: WWW

19. For many of his early years at Cornell, Titchener was known as "the professor in charge of _____."
    a. music
    b. philosophy
    c. coin collecting
    d. correspondence
    e. everything

    ANS: A   PTS: 1   REF: Edward Bradford Titchener (1867-1927)

20. Provided that students and colleagues were properly respectful, Titchener was _____ to them.
    a. distant but cordial
    b. kind and helpful
    c. condescending
    d. dismissing
    e. None of the choices are correct.

    ANS: B   PTS: 1   REF: Edward Bradford Titchener (1867-1927)

21. Titchener excluded women from the meetings of the Titchener Experimentalists because women:
    a. were not admitted to graduate programs in psychology.
    b. were believed unable to grasp the pure research methods of experimentation.
    c. psychologists were almost exclusively engaged in applied research.
    d. could not be admitted without their husbands, and none had married experimental psychologists.
    e. were too pure to smoke.

    ANS: E   PTS: 1   REF: Edward Bradford Titchener (1867-1927)

22. Who scolded Titchener for still practicing "a very old fashioned standpoint" in excluding women from psychology meetings?
    a. Ladd-Franklin
    b. Washburn
    c. Comte
    d. Friedline
    e. Dallenbach

    ANS: A   PTS: 1   REF: Edward Bradford Titchener (1867-1927)
    MSC: WWW

23. ____ was the first American woman to receive a Ph.D. degree in psychology.
   a. Karen Horney
   b. Cora Friedline
   c. Margaret Mead
   d. Christine Ladd-Franklin
   e. Margaret Floy Washburn

   ANS: E   PTS: 1   REF: Edward Bradford Titchener (1867-1927)

24. Of the 56 doctoral degrees Titchener conferred, what percentage were given to women?
   a. about 2%
   b. about 10%
   c. more than a third
   d. over half
   e. three of every four

   ANS: C   PTS: 1   REF: Edward Bradford Titchener (1867-1927)

25. Who was Titchener's first doctoral student?
   a. Ladd-Franklin
   b. Washburn
   c. Comte
   d. Friedline
   e. Dallenbach

   ANS: B   PTS: 1   REF: Edward Bradford Titchener (1867-1927)
   MSC: WWW

26. Who was the first female psychologist elected to the National Academy of Sciences?
   a. Ladd-Franklin
   b. Friedline
   c. Washburn
   d. Boring
   e. Dallenbach

   ANS: C   PTS: 1   REF: Edward Bradford Titchener (1867-1927)

27. Titchener's definition of the appropriate subject matter of psychology is ____.
   a. conscious experience
   b. behavioral events
   c. mental and behavioral events
   d. both conscious and unconscious experiences
   e. anything that could be observed scientifically

   ANS: A   PTS: 1   REF: Edward Bradford Titchener (1867-1927)

28. Titchener argued that psychology is unique among the sciences because ____.
   a. psychology alone is dependent on experiencing persons
   b. only psychology studies brain-behavior relationships
   c. only psychology uses introspection
   d. only psychology depends on human observers
   e. None of the choices are correct; he believed psychology was virtually identical to the natural sciences

   ANS: A   PTS: 1   REF: Edward Bradford Titchener (1867-1927)

29. Who defined the subject matter of psychology as being a conscious experience as that experience is dependent on the person who is actually experiencing it?
    a. Wundt
    b. Külpe
    c. Titchener
    d. Washburn
    e. Comte

    ANS: C   PTS: 1   REF: Edward Bradford Titchener (1867-1927)

30. In the Original Source Material from *A Textbook of Psychology*, Titchener described the difference between ____.
    a. independent and dependent experience
    b. immediate and mediate experience
    c. structuralism and Wundtian psychology
    d. truth and fiction
    e. inspection and introspection

    ANS: A   PTS: 1   REF: Edward Bradford Titchener (1867-1927)

31. Titchener vigorously cautioned experimental psychologists about the stimulus error, that is, about ____.
    a. assuming a one-to-one correspondence between the stimulus and its perception
    b. assuming a logarithmic relationship between the strength of the objective stimulus and the intensity of the psychological experience of the stimulus
    c. describing the observed object rather than the experience of it
    d. describing feelings instead of sensations
    e. describing qualities of the stimulus instead of quantities

    ANS: C   PTS: 1   REF: Edward Bradford Titchener (1867-1927)

32. To confuse the mental process under study with the stimulus or object being observed was to commit

    ____.
    a. introspective error
    b. retrospective error
    c. stimulus error
    d. inspection rather than introspection
    e. retrospection rather than introspection

    ANS: C   PTS: 1   REF: Edward Bradford Titchener (1867-1927)

33. If you described the test you are now taking as being on paper, you would not be giving a true introspective report of your conscious experience according to Titchener. In introspection, to use everyday words such as "paper" is to ____.
    a. deny reality
    b. commit the stimulus error
    c. reason illogically
    d. use abbreviated syntax
    e. be a rational human being

    ANS: B   PTS: 1   REF: Edward Bradford Titchener (1867-1927)

34. Titchener opposed the development of areas such as child psychology and animal psychology because
____.
   a. these areas did not focus on discovering the structures of mind
   b. these areas were more subject to the stimulus error
   c. he supported applying psychological knowledge
   d. psychology should instead be interested in curing sick minds
   e. None of these answers is correct

   ANS: A   PTS: 1   REF: Edward Bradford Titchener (1867-1927)

35. The sum of our experiences as they exist at a particular moment is Titchener's definition of ____.
   a. mind
   b. conscious experience
   c. consciousness
   d. perception
   e. apperception

   ANS: C   PTS: 1   REF: Edward Bradford Titchener (1867-1927)

36. The sum of our experiences accumulated over a lifetime is Titchener's definition of ____.
   a. mind
   b. consciousness
   c. memory
   d. apperception
   e. learning

   ANS: A   PTS: 1   REF: Edward Bradford Titchener (1867-1927)

37. Who said psychology was NOT in the business of curing sick minds?
   a. Wundt
   b. Külpe
   c. Titchener
   d. James
   e. Comte

   ANS: C   PTS: 1   REF: Edward Bradford Titchener (1867-1927)

38. Titchener's introspection method was most like ____ method.
   a. Wundt's
   b. Brentano's
   c. Stumpf's
   d. Külpe's
   e. Fechner's

   ANS: D   PTS: 1   REF: Edward Bradford Titchener (1867-1927)

39. While Wundt emphasized ____ and ____ reports during introspection, Titchener used ____ and ____ introspective reports.
   a. subjective, quantitative; objective; qualitative
   b. objective, quantitative; subjective, qualitative
   c. subjective, qualitative; objective, quantitative
   d. objective, qualitative; subjective, quantitative
   e. perceptive, brief; sensation, extended

   ANS: B   PTS: 1   REF: Edward Bradford Titchener (1867-1927)

40. Titchener's opinion about how introspection should be used probably became formed ____.
   a. before he went to Leipzig
   b. while working with Wundt in Leipzig
   c. when he returned to Oxford after leaving Leipzig
   d. when he was at Cornell
   e. during a visit to Clark University, in a discussion with Freud

   ANS: A   PTS: 1   REF: Edward Bradford Titchener (1867-1927)

41. The influence of mechanism on Titchener is exemplified in his ____.
   a. atomism
   b. elementism
   c. determinism
   d. use of the dehumanizing term *subjects* rather than *observers*
   e. use of the chemistry term *reagents* instead of *observers*

   ANS: E   PTS: 1   REF: Edward Bradford Titchener (1867-1927)

42. In his introspection experiments, Titchener wanted his subjects (observers) to ____.
   a. try to create new images in consciousness from the presented stimuli
   b. search for their inner self
   c. have their galvanic skin response recorded while they gave their introspective reports
   d. be passive recorders of the experiences registering on the conscious mind
   e. remember their childhood experiences

   ANS: D   PTS: 1   REF: Edward Bradford Titchener (1867-1927)

43. Which of the following is NOT one of the three essential problems for psychology, according to Titchener?
   a. to reduce conscious processes to their simplest components
   b. to study how these components were synthesized into higher-level processes
   c. to determine laws by which these elements of consciousness were associated
   d. to connect these elements with their physiological correlates
   e. None of the answers is correct.

   ANS: B   PTS: 1   REF: Edward Bradford Titchener (1867-1927)

44. Which of the following was a topic to be explored by Titchener's psychology?
   a. the reduction of conscious processes
   b. the determination of the laws of association of elements of consciousness
   c. to identify the physiological correlates of the elements
   d. All the choices are correct.
   e. None of the answers is correct.

   ANS: D   PTS: 1   REF: Edward Bradford Titchener (1867-1927)
   MSC: WWW

45. Titchener's research identified three elements of consciousness: sensations, affective states, and ____.
   a. subliminal perception
   b. perception
   c. images
   d. behavioral intention
   e. elements of emotion

   ANS: C   PTS: 1   REF: Edward Bradford Titchener (1867-1927)

46. By 1896, Titchener had identified approximately how many elements of sensation?
    a. 1
    b. 4
    c. 5
    d. 11,600
    e. more than 44,000

    ANS: E   PTS: 1   REF: Edward Bradford Titchener (1867-1927)

47. For Titchener, distinct sensations combined with others to form ____.
    a. emotions
    b. apperceptions
    c. beliefs
    d. affective states
    e. perceptions and ideas

    ANS: E   PTS: 1   REF: Edward Bradford Titchener (1867-1927)

48. Titchener's descriptors of sensations did NOT include which of the following?
    a. quality
    b. intensity
    c. duration
    d. clearness
    e. propensity

    ANS: E   PTS: 1   REF: Edward Bradford Titchener (1867-1927)

49. Which of Titchener's basic elements of consciousness does not possess clearness?
    a. perceptions
    b. apperceptions
    c. ideas
    d. affective states
    e. limens

    ANS: D   PTS: 1   REF: Edward Bradford Titchener (1867-1927)

50. Feelings or emotions lack clearness because ____.
    a. if we focus on them to determine clearness, the feeling or emotion disappears.
    b. if we focus on them to determine clearness, the feeling or emotion becomes more intense.
    c. duration, not clearness, is the essence of emotion.
    d. quality and intensity are sufficient to explain emotion.
    e. None of the choices are correct.

    ANS: A   PTS: 1   REF: Edward Bradford Titchener (1867-1927)

51. Titchener's research led him to conclude that affective states had only ____ dimension(s); namely ____.
    a. two; pleasure/displeasure and tension/ relaxation
    b. one; tension/relaxation
    c. one; pleasure/displeasure
    d. one; excitement/depression
    e. two; pleasure/displeasure and excitement/depression

    ANS: C   PTS: 1   REF: Edward Bradford Titchener (1867-1927)

52. Toward the end of Titchener's career, he came to favor the ____ method instead of the ____ method.
    a. psychophysiological; psychological
    b. psychoanalytic; structuralist
    c. introspective; Wundtian
    d. behavioristic; mentalistic
    e. phenomenological; introspective

    ANS: E   PTS: 1   REF: Edward Bradford Titchener (1867-1927)

53. By the 1920s the term used by Titchener for his system of psychology was ____.
    a. functionalism
    b. voluntarism
    c. existential
    d. behaviorism
    e. introspection

    ANS: C   PTS: 1   REF: Edward Bradford Titchener (1867-1927)
    MSC: WWW

54. In their evaluation of Titchener's theoretical viewpoint toward the end of his career, Schultz and Schultz conclude that he was ____.
    a. too rigid and dogmatic to ever change
    b. a minor figure in the history of modern psychology
    c. too tied to Wundtian thought to make any original contributions of his own
    d. as flexible and open to change as scientists are supposed to be
    e. None of the choices are correct

    ANS: D   PTS: 1   REF: Edward Bradford Titchener (1867-1927)

55. When Titchener died, the era of structuralism ____.
    a. was turned over to the Chicago school of thought
    b. collapsed
    c. reverted to Wundtian psychology
    d. was taken over by his student, E. B. Boring
    e. continued vigorously for another decade

    ANS: B   PTS: 1   REF: Edward Bradford Titchener (1867-1927)

56. The criticisms directed at the method of introspection are more relevant to the kind of introspection practiced by ____ than by ____.
    a. Wundt; Külpe
    b. Külpe; Titchener
    c. Wundt; Locke
    d. Wundt; Titchener and Külpe
    e. Titchener and Külpe; Wundt

    ANS: E   PTS: 1   REF: Criticisms of Structuralism

57. A century before Titchener's work the philosopher ____ wrote that the act of introspection itself altered the conscious experience being studied.
    a. Hume
    b. Locke
    c. Mill
    d. Kant
    e. Descartes

    ANS: D   PTS: 1   REF: Criticisms of Structuralism

58. Who argued that the mind may observe all phenomena but its own?
    a. Mill
    b. Comte
    c. Hume
    d. Titchener
    e. Ebbinghaus

    ANS: B   PTS: 1   REF: Criticisms of Structuralism

59. The English physician _____ wrote "due to the extent of the pathology of mind, self-report is hardly to be trusted."
    a. Turner
    b. Maudsley
    c. Mill
    d. Berkeley
    e. Gray

    ANS: B   PTS: 1   REF: Criticisms of Structuralism

60. Substantial doubts about and attacks on introspection _____.
    a. began when Titchener started using it as a method of study
    b. were unknown before the work of Titchener
    c. began when Titchener started using it as a method of study and were unknown before the work of Titchener
    d. existed long before Titchener used the method
    e. None of the choices are correct

    ANS: D   PTS: 1   REF: Criticisms of Structuralism
    MSC: WWW

61. In terms of describing the method of introspection, Titchener _____.
    a. defined it with the precision of an Oxford scholar
    b. had difficulty defining exactly what he meant
    c. used inspection and retrospection
    d. relied on Wundt's definition
    e. used Comte's operational definition

    ANS: B   PTS: 1   REF: Criticisms of Structuralism

62. If one of Titchener's introspectionists reported seeing a table, this report would not be accepted because _____.
    a. this would be stimulus error
    b. this would involve using a meaning word
    c. a table would be an objective, quantitative report
    d. this would be a stimulus error **and** involve using a meaning word
    e. a table would be a subjective, qualitative report

    ANS: D   PTS: 1   REF: Criticisms of Structuralism

63. Titchener's graduate student observers were instructed to ignore certain classes of words called _____ words.
    a. stimulus
    b. error
    c. meaning
    d. distractor
    e. reagent

    ANS: C   PTS: 1   REF: Criticisms of Structuralism

64. Ordinary words such as "table" were not to be used by Titchener's introspectionists. Therefore, it became a goal to _____.
    a. less carefully control external experimental conditions
    b. develop a working vocabulary free of meaning
    c. use languages other than English as a control measure
    d. use inspection rather than introspection
    e. specify the use of obscure terms

    ANS: B   PTS: 1   REF: Criticisms of Structuralism
    MSC: WWW

65. The idea of developing an introspective language was _____.
    a. carefully controlled
    b. not of interest to Titchener
    c. really a form of inspection
    d. never realized
    e. an idea whose time had come

    ANS: D   PTS: 1   REF: Criticisms of Structuralism

66. Because some time elapsed between the experience and the reporting of it, critics charged that introspection was really a form of _____.
    a. inspection
    b. illusion
    c. retrospection
    d. delusion
    e. error

    ANS: C   PTS: 1   REF: Criticisms of Structuralism
    MSC: WWW

67. In his treatment of women, Titchener _____.
    a. provided unwavering support of the advancement of women
    b. demonstrated both support of and obstruction of women in psychology
    c. gave no notable contribution
    d. showed unflagging protest to women in academic appointments
    e. wanted nothing more than a male dominated profession

    ANS: B   PTS: 1   REF: Edward Bradford Titchener (1867-1927)

68. In addition to introspection, another criticism of Titchener's system was its ____.
    a. practicality
    b. artificiality and sterility
    c. difficulty of use
    d. ease of use
    e. genuineness and productiveness

    ANS: B   PTS: 1   REF: Criticisms of Structuralism

69. Titchener's view of the field of psychology was ____.
    a. breathtakingly broad
    b. one of his most lasting contributions
    c. too limited to embrace new work and dimensions
    d. more encompassing than most critics then and now realized
    e. not shared by others but widely respected nonetheless

    ANS: C   PTS: 1   REF: Criticisms of Structuralism

70. The two most important contributions of Titchener's system to modern psychology are ____.
    a. his version of introspection and the experimental method
    b. his experimental method and a strong position to protest
    c. the delineation of a single dimension of affect and the identification of three (not two)
       elements of consciousness
    d. facilitating the transition from a focus on self-report to a focus on the objective
       observation of behavior and insisting on pure research
    e. the insistence on pure research and the focus on normal individuals as subjects

    ANS: B   PTS: 1   REF: Contributions of Structuralism
    MSC: WWW

71. Which of the following statements is true about the status of the introspective method in modern
    psychology?
    a. The introspective method has been abandoned in all fields of modern psychology.
    b. The cognitive field of research is still debating whether introspection is a legitimate
       research method.
    c. Psychophysics in the only area of modern research that still continues to use introspection.
    d. Several areas of modern psychology, such as clinical and industrial/organizational, use the
       introspective method.
    e. None of the choices are correct.

    ANS: D   PTS: 1   REF: Contributions of Structuralism

72. According to the textbook, a significant contribution of structuralism was ____.
    a. its adherence to Wundt's original paradigm
    b. development of interest in brain research
    c. incorporation of varied research methods into the examination of consciousness
    d. its service as a stimulus for psychoanalysis
    e. its service as a target for criticism

    ANS: E   PTS: 1   REF: Contributions of Structuralism

73. With Titchener's structuralism as an idea to oppose, psychology _____.
    a. moved far beyond his initial boundaries
    b. made few advances in the United States
    c. became even more mysterious
    d. went from an emphasis on applied research to an emphasis on basic research
    e. None of the choices are correct

    ANS: A   PTS: 1   REF: Contributions of Structuralism

TRUE/FALSE

74. Titchener's focus was on the synthesis of elements of consciousness into higher-order cognitive processes.

    ANS: F   PTS: 1   REF: Edward Bradford Titchener (1867-1927)

75. Experimental laboratory work in psychology in the United States was most influenced by Wundt's *Principles*.

    ANS: F   PTS: 1   REF: Edward Bradford Titchener (1867-1927)

76. The Titchener Experimentalists would admit women to their meetings on the condition that they could smoke an entire cigar.

    ANS: F   PTS: 1   REF: Edward Bradford Titchener (1867-1927)
    MSC: WWW

77. The first woman to earn a PhD in psychology was Margaret Washburn.

    ANS: T   PTS: 1   REF: Edward Bradford Titchener (1867-1927)

78. Among Titchener's most influential works on the direction of the new psychology in the United States was *The Animal Mind*.

    ANS: F   PTS: 1   REF: Edward Bradford Titchener (1867-1927)

79. Titchener could be regarded as somewhat open-minded in his attitudes toward the rights of women.

    ANS: T   PTS: 1   REF: Edward Bradford Titchener (1867-1927)
    MSC: WWW

80. More women completed doctoral degrees with Titchener than with any other psychologist of that period.

    ANS: T   PTS: 1   REF: Edward Bradford Titchener (1867-1927)

81. While Titchener would accept women as graduate students, he was firmly opposed to women being hired as faculty.

    ANS: F   PTS: 1   REF: Edward Bradford Titchener (1867-1927)

82. One of Titchener's more influential books was *Elements of Psychophysics*.

    ANS: F   PTS: 1   REF: Edward Bradford Titchener (1867-1927)

83. "Conscious experience as it is dependent upon the experiencing person" was Titchener's definition of the topic of study for psychology.

ANS: T   PTS: 1   REF: Edward Bradford Titchener (1867-1927)

84. Titchener distinguished consciousness, which is momentary, from mind, which is a lifelong accumulation of experiences.

ANS: T   PTS: 1   REF: Edward Bradford Titchener (1867-1927)
MSC: WWW

85. Titchener's introspection methods were similar in some respects to Külpe's.

ANS: T   PTS: 1   REF: Edward Bradford Titchener (1867-1927)

86. Titchener adopted Külpe's term for introspection, "systematic experimental introspection."

ANS: T   PTS: 1   REF: Edward Bradford Titchener (1867-1927)

87. Titchener abandoned Wundt's notion of voluntarism but retained the concept of apperception.

ANS: F   PTS: 1   REF: Edward Bradford Titchener (1867-1927)

88. Titchener's system was marked by mechanism.

ANS: T   PTS: 1   REF: Edward Bradford Titchener (1867-1927)
MSC: WWW

89. To Wundt's two basic elements of consciousness, Titchener added extensity.

ANS: F   PTS: 1   REF: Edward Bradford Titchener (1867-1927)

90. Later in his career, Titchener adopted the designation "existential psychology" for his system.

ANS: T   PTS: 1   REF: Edward Bradford Titchener (1867-1927)

91. Throughout his professional life, Titchener remained consistent in his views of structural psychology.

ANS: F   PTS: 1   REF: Edward Bradford Titchener (1867-1927)

92. When Titchener died, the era of structuralism collapsed.

ANS: T   PTS: 1   REF: Edward Bradford Titchener (1867-1927)

93. The criticisms directed at the method of introspection were more relevant to Titchener's method of observation than they were to Wundt's method.

ANS: T   PTS: 1   REF: Criticisms of Structuralism
MSC: WWW

94. Kant had attacked the method of introspection a century before Titchener's work.

ANS: T   PTS: 1   REF: Criticisms of Structuralism

95. In his criticism of introspection Comte wrote, "The mind may observe all phenomena but its own."

ANS: T   PTS: 1   REF: Criticisms of Structuralism

96. Titchener defined exactly what he meant by the introspective method.

ANS: F   PTS: 1   REF: Criticisms of Structuralism

97. Titchener's introspective observers agreed quite closely when reporting on the same stimulus.

ANS: F   PTS: 1   REF: Criticisms of Structuralism

98. By Titchener's later years, psychology was moving quickly beyond his views.

ANS: T   PTS: 1   REF: Edward Bradford Titchener (1867-1927)

Chapter 6

Functionalism: Antecedent Influences

The chapter begins with the story of Jenny, an orangutan on display at the London Zoo in 1838. Jenny bore an amazing resemblance to a two-year old human child in both appearance and mannerisms. She could understand commands, take direction, and mimic human behaviors. She also exhibited emotions, like shame. One of the many visitors that were captivated by Jenny was Charles Darwin, whose theory of evolution would inspire functionalist psychology. Functionalism is concerned with answering the questions "what does the mind do and how does it do it?" A natural consequence of functionalism, which began and grew in the U.S., was the application of psychological findings to real-life problems, which is now known as applied psychology.

Charles Darwin created little new thought with his theory, in that many of the ideas postulated in his theory had been around for some time. One of his predecessors was his grandfather, Erasmus Darwin. Erasmus believed that God put life on the planet and then that life changed over time without God's intervention. Jean-Baptiste Lamarck also developed a theory of evolution where species change over time, and suggested that acquired traits could be passed to offspring. Charles Lyell brought "the notion of evolution into geological theory," by describing the evolution of plant and animal life. In this way, centuries of belief in creationism were called into question in order to explain the newly discovered species of animals that were constantly being found.

In the 1830's primates were exhibited in zoos, and people were astonished to see the similarities between them and humans, while at the same time individuals strove to own fossils of long extinct animals. The Zeitgeist of the time, having been influenced by changes in science and industry, called for a theoretical change, which Darwin's book *On the Origin of Species* provided.

As a boy, Darwin was prone to playing pranks rather than being a good student. He enjoyed collecting things such as "coins, shells, and minerals" and later beetles. In the midst of his studies at Cambridge University, one of his professors recommended him to be the naturalist for the ship *HMS Beagle*. This allowed him to collect a large amount of data and specimens. When he returned to England he was "a dedicated scientist with a single passion: to develop a theory of evolution."

Darwin married and moved to the country after 3 years so that he could concentrate on his work. Unfortunately, he developed neurotic health symptoms that plagued him under instances of stress or disruptions to his daily life. He worked steadily on his theory of evolution yet was afraid to present it to the public for fear of scrutiny. Thus he "waited 22 years before presenting his ideas." In 1858, Darwin received a letter from Alfred Russel Wallace in which Wallace outlined a similar evolutionary theory, though with little supporting evidence. In the interest of fair play, Darwin proposed that both Wallace's paper and parts of his own book be read at a meeting of the Linnaean Society.

The crux of Darwin's theory of evolution begins with natural selection. He believed that all species have spontaneous variability, which allows some members to be equipped to survive in their given environment. Over time, this results in "the survival of those organisms best suited for their environment and the elimination of those not fit." Darwin developed the idea of "survival of the fittest" after reading work by Thomas Malthus detailing human adaptability and survival. Using the Malthusian principle, Darwin postulated that: "those life forms that survive the struggle and reach maturity tend to transmit to their offspring the skills or advantages that enabled them to thrive."

Darwin's evolutionary theory raised much controversy. Although he was reticent to personally engage his critics, he had defenders like the charismatic Thomas Huxley. Darwin's other works are also influential, including his second major book *The Descent of Man* (1871), which draws comparisons between human and animal mental processes. He also made early contributions to child psychology with his journal *Mind*, which chronicles the development of his son and proposes that child developmental stages parallel human evolutionary stages.

To follow up on Darwin's work, researchers recently investigated the beaks of finches on the Galapagos islands for over 30 years starting in 1973. These researchers found that the changing environment (drought followed by rains) changed the thickness of finch beaks in as little as one generation.

Darwin's work influenced psychology in four ways: 1) a focus on animal psychology, 2) an emphasis on functionalism (the functions of consciousness), 3) incorporating methods and data from diverse fields, and 4) focus on measurement of individual differences. The authors provide source material from Darwin's autobiography in which he provides an opportunity to observe how he saw himself—and from this reading he seems modest and gracious.

Shortly after Darwin published his theory of evolution, Francis Galton, his cousin, was captivated by the biological and social implications of the theory. Galton focused on the idea of individual differences, which was not new given that Huarte published a book in the 1500's analyzing individual differences in students. However, Galton was the first to apply the idea of individual differences to psychology. During his life, Galton did work in a wide variety of areas, such as "fingerprints, …fashions, the geographical distribution of beauty, weightlifting, and the effectiveness of prayer." It was evident when he was only 12 months old that he was intellectually gifted, and came from a family of wealth and prominence. He received training in medicine and mathematics, then spent considerable time traveling.

Galton's first important book was *Hereditary Genius* (1869) in which he demonstrated that eminent individuals produce eminent offspring. Using statistical analyses of 997 famous contemporary men, Galton showed that "greatness…occurred within families far too often to be explained solely by environmental influences." With this evidence, he postulated that the human race would improve if society rewarded gifted individuals for bearing children. He founded the science of "eugenics" because he wished to encourage higher birth rate among the eminent. In original source material, Galton elaborates on his idea that although a person can improve his (or her) state, genes place limits on how far one can go (he uses examples of physical prowess as an analogy to intelligence).

One of Galton's main contributions to the science of psychology comes from his groundbreaking work with statistical analyses. Early work from Belgian mathematician Quetelet applied the statistical normal curve to human variability. Galton then applied the logic to his study of mental characteristics, arguing that most individuals hover near the average and fewer people are found at either extreme. Thus, the most valuable information about the distribution of human variability lies in the arithmetic mean and the standard deviation. Galton then developed the correlation to measure relationships between variables, upon which modern methods of validity, reliability, and factor-analysis have stemmed. Galton was also the first to introduce the idea of regression to the mean, which shows that human traits will become more "average" over time. To calculate correlations, Karl Pearson (a student of Galton's) developed the Pearson *r* value used today.

Galton began mental testing because he believed that intelligent individuals had keener senses compared to the less intelligent. As opposed to intelligence testing, which measures higher level mental processes, mental tests measured motor skills and sensory capacities. To do so, Galton invented a number of devices used to measure physiological sensitivity and responses. He created the anthropometric lab, which used his inventions to collect and catalogue data from 9,000 people. The data are useful to examine physical and developmental benchmarks for late 19-century England.

Galton also worked on how ideas become associated, specifically on two problems: "1) the diversity of associations of ideas; and 2) reaction time, the time required to produce associations." He proposed that many associations are linked to childhood experiences and unconscious events. He then wrote an article in which he discusses the unconscious, which may have influenced Freud. To investigate mental imagery, Galton used, for the first time, a questionnaire to collect data. He concluded that the qualities of mental imagery are distributed on the normal curve. Other areas of interest include trying to understand paranoia by role playing it, investigating the power of prayer, attempting to count everything by smell instead of numbers.

One result of Darwin's work was the study of animal psychology. Darwin's theory introduced "no sharp distinction….between human minds and animals minds." Thus, the animal mind became an appropriate focus for psychologists. One of these psychologists was George Romanes, who wrote the first comparative psychology book *Animal Intelligence* (1883). He examined the similarity in mental functioning between humans and a very wide variety of animals. He created the "mental ladder" which ranks the mental functioning of animals using the anecdotal method (the use of observational reports of animal behavior). Using these stories, Romanes engaged in "introspection by analogy," which assumes that the human observer and the animal share the same mental processes. He believed that animals were capable of engaging in the highest forms of mental functioning.

Romanes' work was criticized by C. Lloyd Morgan, who proposed a law of parsimony: "animal behavior must not be attributed to a higher mental process when it can be explained in terms of a lower mental process." "He believed that most animal behavior resulted from learning or association based on sensory experience." Both comparative and animal psychology stemmed from Darwin's theory of evolution, and served as a turning point within psychology that introduced functionalism.

Outline

I. Scientist Captivated by Childlike Jenny
   A. An orangutan on display in Europe in 1838
   B. Looks and acts like a two-year old human child
   C. Human qualities
      1. used spoon, plate, teacup
      2. would throw tantrums
      3. would obey handler but also be disobedient
      4. asked for permission to do things
      5. demonstrated shame if she did something wrong
      6. one visitor was Charles Darwin, who was impressed
II. The Functionalist Protest
   A. Functionalists' central interest: how the organism uses the mind to adapt to the environment
   B. First uniquely American system of psychology

C. Deliberate protest against Wundt's and Titchener's systems

D. Interest in applying psychology to real world

E. Forerunners of Functionalism
   1. Darwin's On the Origin of Species by Means of Natural Selection (1859)
   2. Fechner's Elements of Psychophysics (1860)
   3. Galton's work measuring individual differences (1869)
   4. Wundt's Principles of Physiological Psychology (1873-1874)
   5. Animal psychology experiments (1880s)

III. The Evolution Revolution: Charles Darwin (1809-1882)

A. On the Origin of Species by Means of Natural Selection (1859): contained nothing new

B. The idea of living things changing with time dates to 5th century B.C.

C. Darwin's grandfather, Erasmus Darwin: all mammals evolved from a single strand made alive by God

D. Lamarck (1809): modification of animal's bodily form
   1. through efforts to adapt to environment
   2. inherited by succeeding generations

E. Lyell (mid-1800s): evolution of geology of earth

F. Movement from acceptance of biblical creation story to curiosity about other species
   1. many new species discovered: how could they all fit in Noah's ark? (Amerigo Vespucci)
   2. chimpanzees and orangutans available for viewing: intelligent, humanlike behavior
   3. skeleton of gorilla and human strikingly similar
   4. fossils and bones of extinct species found
   5. Zeitgeist: constant change in science and industry affects everyday life
   6. industrial revolution causing migration to urban areas
   7. growing domination of science
   8. Darwin's theory was appropriate for the Zeitgeist

G. Darwin's life
   1. early academic problems
   2. journey on HMS Beagle as a naturalist motivated theory of evolution
   3. problems with physical health upon return to England
   4. worked on his theory of evolution for 22 years
   5. Alfred Russel Wallace: wrote Darwin about a theory of evolution similar to Darwin's that Wallace developed in 3 days→ ethical dilemma for Darwin
   6. Darwin took friends' suggestion to have Wallace's paper and portion of his forthcoming book presented at the meeting of the Linnaean Society
   7. 1st printing of On the Origin of Species sold out on first day
   8. Wallace not bitter over Darwin's fame; instead was happy to have unintentionally spurred Darwin to complete his book

H. On the Origin of Species by Means of Natural Selection (1859)
   1. spontaneous variability among members of a species is inheritable
   2. natural selection: over time, organisms that adapt to the environment survive while those that do not are eliminated
   3. provided the data to support the idea of evolution
   4. there is a variation among members of a species
   5. survival of the fittest: "...species that cannot adapt do not survive."

6. influenced by Thomas Malthus, Essay on the Principle of Population (1789)
    a. food supply increases arithmetically
    b. human population increases geometrically
    c. result = many humans live in near-starvation state
    d. only the most aggressive, intelligent, and flexible survive
7. generalized from Malthus' observations and principles to all living beings to develop theory of natural selection
8. organisms that live to reproduce transmit to offspring characteristics that led to their own survival
9. failure to adapt results in failure to survive
10. offspring show variation among themselves some offspring have advantageous qualities to higher degree than parents
11. over generations, changes occur
12. also accepted Lamarck's doctrine that changes in form due to experiences are inheritable
13. Thomas Henry Huxley (1825-1895) and the evolution controversy
    a. striving biologist; leader among England's scientists
    b. champion of Darwin's theory
    c. debate on theory of evolution at Oxford: Huxley versus Bishop Samuel Wilberforce who defended the bible
    d. Robert Fitzroy, captain of HMS Beagle, attended in support of the Bible
    e. Fitzroy blamed self for giving Darwin chance to collect data, committed suicide 5 years later

I. Darwin's other work
  1. 1871: The Descent of Man
    a. evidence for human evolution from lower forms of life
    b. emphasized similarity between animal and human mental processes
  2. 1872: The Expression of the Emotions in Man and Animals
    a. interprets emotional expression in evolutionary terms
    b. emotional expressions once served a function and only the useful ones are still used
    c. facial expressions and body language are "uncontrollable manifestations of internal emotional states
    d. example: smile=pleasure; grimace=pain
  3. 1877: Mind: A Biographical Sketch of an Infant
    a. journal that chronicles his son's childhood development
    b. proposed that children's developmental stages parallel human evolutionary stages
    c. early contribution to child psychology literature

J. The finches' beaks: evolution at work
  1. Galápagos Islands: evidence of differential adaptation to the environment among animals of same species
  2. Peter and Rosemary Grant: visited islands in 1973 to observe modifications in several generations of 13 finch species
    a. study lasted more than 20 years
    b. finches' evolution occurred quicker than Darwin predicted
    c. severe drought: food supply = large, "tough spiky seeds"

        d.   only the 15% of finches with thickest beak could open seeds; many with slender beaks couldn't and died

        e.   thicker beaks = tool for adaptation

        f.   offspring inherited that characteristic; 4-5% thicker beaks

        g.   adaptation in one generation

        h.   rain and floods: large seeds swept away; only small ones left

        i.   same cycle but reverse outcome as above: slender beaks a survival advantage

        j.   only the most fit in a given environment lived

K. Darwin's influence on psychology

   1. hypothesis: continuity in mental functioning between humans and lower animals

   2. studying animal behavior vital to understanding human behavior

   3. evolutionary theory changed: subject matter of psychology from elements to functions of consciousness

   4. goal became how organism functioned in adapting

   5. methods and techniques were broadened in scope

   6. increased focus on individual differences and their measurement

L. Original source material from The Autobiography of Charles Darwin (1878)

   1. goal: "...analyze the mental qualities and conditions on which my success has depended."

        a.   not clever

        b.   poor critic: admired work upon 1st reading; only after reflection perceived deficits

        c.   limited ability to follow abstract thought

        d.   memory "extensive, yet hazy"

        e.   careful, astute, industrious observer and collector of facts

        f.   love of natural science

        g.   motivation to explain the observed; group facts under general laws

        h.   hypothesis generation: free mind open to modification

        i.   distrust of deductive reasoning

        j.   methodical habits

        k.   ample leisure; no need to earn income

        l.   success in science: determined by "complex and diversified mental qualities and conditions"

        m.   most important qualities: "love of science, unbounding patience..., industry...and a fair share of invention as well as of common sense."

        n.   "With such moderate abilities...surprising that I should have influenced...the belief of scientific men..."

IV. Individual Differences: Francis Galton (1822-1911)

A. Individual differences

   1. Juan Huarte in 1500's investigated individual differences in students for the purpose of identifying the individual course of study that best suits the person

   2. the topic was considered inappropriate for psychology

   3. individual difference had been reported but not investigated scientifically by Weber, Fechner, Helmholtz

B. Galton's life

   1. estimated IQ = 200

   2. diverse, novel ideas and inventions

3. youngest of 9 children
4. wealthy family
5. pressured by father to study medicine; didn't like it
6. entered Cambridge University to study mathematics under Newton
7. traveled extensively; wrote popular book, The Art of Travel
8. cousin Charles Darwin published On the Origin of Species: Galton fascinated by biological and social implications of evolution

C. Mental inheritance
   1. *Hereditary Genius* (1869)
      a. eminent men have eminent sons
      b. specific forms of genius inherited (e.g., scientists breed scientist sons)
      c. eugenics: the science of improving inherited human traits through artificial selection
      d. applied statistical concepts to heredity problems
      e. eminence not a function of opportunity
   2. *English Men of Science* (1874)
   3. *Natural Inheritance* (1889)
   4. 1901 founded journal, Biometrika
   5. established Eugenics Laboratory at University College, London
   6. original source material from Hereditary Genius: An Inquiry Into Its Laws and Consequences (18699)
      a. objects to "pretensions of natural equality"
      b. acknowledges the role of social influences/opportunities
      c. limit to muscular and intellectual powers of individuals

D. Statistical methods
   1. Quetelet
      a. first to apply statistical methods and normal curve to biological and social data
      b. idea of "the average man": most physical measurements cluster around the average
   2. Galton
      a. assumed similar results true of mental characteristics
      b. highlighted the importance of mean and standard deviation in describing the distribution of a population, regardless of the variable measured
      c. produced correlation measure
         (1) modern derivatives: methods for validity, reliability, factor analysis
         (2) his student Karl Pearson developed product-moment coefficient of correlation (Pearson's r)
      d. discovery of regression toward the mean

E. Mental tests
   1. originated by Galton, but term from Cattell
   2. mental tests: intelligence can be measured in terms of motor skills and sensory capacities (different from intelligence tests that measure complex mental abilities)
   3. developed his own instruments and tests that were prototypes for standard psychology lab equipment
      a. whistle: test human and animal capacity for sound frequency

        b.   photometer: measure precision for matching two color spots

        c.   calibrated pendulum: reaction speed for light and sound

        d.   weights: kinesthetic and muscle sensitivity

    4. 1884: established Anthropometric Laboratory

        a.   aim: the definition of the range of human capacities of the entire British population

        b.   to determine its collective mental resources

    5. his data

        a.   statistically reliable (1985)

        b.   provided information on developmental trends

F. The association of ideas

    1. two problems in association

        a.   diversity of association of ideas

        b.   reaction time: time required to produce associations

    2. Galton found

        a.   40% of associations traced to events in childhood and adolescence

        b.   The unconscious influenced thought processes

        c.   word-association test: first experiment attempt to examine associations

        d.   wrote an article on the unconscious; influenced Freud

    3. experimental method: technique adapted by Wundt, elaborated by Jung

G. Mental imagery

    1. Galton: first extensive use of psychological questionnaire

    2. determined imagery distributed normally in the population

    3. found similar images more likely to occur between siblings than between unrelated persons

H. Arithmetic by smell and other topics

    1. tested self-induced paranoia through imagination

    2. questioned validity of religious beliefs; determined that the power of prayer provided nothing substantial (e.g., better health, longer life)

    3. hoped to provide a new set of beliefs structured in terms of science

    4. yawns and coughs as a measure of boredom

    5. arithmetic by smell: dispelled idea of numbers and counted in smells

I. Comment

    1. breadth topics researched

    2. greater impact than Wundt

V.   Animal Psychology and the Development of Functionalism

A. Before Darwin: animals considered automata

B. With Darwin's *The Expression of the Emotions in Man and Animals* (1872)

    1. continuity between humans and animals

    2. evidence of intelligence in animals

    3. human emotional behavior: inheritance of behavior once useful to animals (e.g., human sneer similar to animals bearing teeth)

    4. Wundt argued

        a.   possession of minimal sensory capacities implies possession of judgment and conscious inference

        b.   "inferior" animals had less education and training rather than necessarily lesser abilities

C. Studies of animal intelligence
  1. George John Romanes (1848-1894)
     a. British physiologist
     b. formalized and systematized study of animal intelligence
     c. selected by Darwin to apply theory of evolution to the mind
     d. *Animal Intelligence* (1883)
        (1) first book on comparative psychology
        (2) purposes
            (a) demonstrate high level of animal intelligence
            (b) show similarity of animal intelligence to human intellectual functioning
            (c) show continuity in mental development in evolutionary terms
     e. anecdotal method: "the use of observational, often causal, reports or narratives about animal behavior"
     f. introspection by analogy: "A technique for studying animal behavior by assuming that the same mental processes that occur in the observer's mind also occur in the animal's mind"
     g. criticisms:
        (1) short on scientific rigor
        (2) line between fact and subjective interpretation in his data not clear
  2. Conway Lloyd Morgan (1852-1936)
     a. Romanes's designated successor
     b. proposed a law of parsimony: "The notion that animal behavior must not be attributed to a higher mental process when it can be explained in terms of lower mental processes"
        (1) also called Lloyd Morgan's Canon (1894)
        (2) suggested by Wundt (1892)
     c. goal: give comparative psychology a more scientific basis
     d. believed most animal behavior due to learning based on sensory experience
     e. first to conduct large-scale experimental studies in animal psychology
  3. legacy of Darwin, Galton, Romanes, and Morgan
     a. regard each anatomical structure as a utilitarian element in a total living adaptive system
     b. functional psychology

Lecture prompts/Discussion topics for chapter six

- Galton believed that all things can be counted. Do you believe this to be true? Are there things that cannot be counted?
- What are the checks to balance human population? Should governments intercede into and influence natural evolution to either a) promote the fittest individuals to procreate? b) prevent the unfit from procreating? and/or c) provide financial support to the unfit so that they may survive? What are the results and implications of the answers to these questions?

Internet Resources for chapter six

The Complete Work of Charles Darwin Online
http://darwin-online.org.uk/
> The title of the page is self-explanatory, this page houses Darwin's full publications, images of his handwritten manuscripts, and links to his letters.

American Eugenics Movement
http://www.eugenicsarchive.org/eugenics/list3.pl
> This is an amazing collection of information relating to the history of the Eugenics movement, with a large number of photographs and information about the involuntary sterilization movement.

Sir Francis Galton
http://galton.org/
> This site houses all of Galton's published work, including books, letters, and other artifacts, including images of some of his handwritten notes.

George Romanes
http://www.muskingum.edu/~psych/psycweb/history/romanes.htm
> On these Web pages, you can find more information about Romanes' life and work, and the page includes links to other Romanes pages.

Autobiography of C. Lloyd Morgan
http://psychclassics.yorku.ca/Morgan/murchison.htm
> This Web site reproduces Morgan's autobiography which first appeared in Carl Murchison's *History of Psychology in Autobiography* (1930).

Potential answers to chapter six discussion questions

1. Why did some people find it such a disturbing experience to see Jenny the Orangutan in the London Zoo? How did her behavior affect Charles Darwin?
Before such primates were on display, animals were seen as distinctly different than humans. Jenny's human-like qualities, and the human-like behaviors of other primates as well, were disturbing because the distinction between animals and humans began to blur. Darwin, after seeing such displays, suggested that humans are not special in their higher level mental processes. He was later motivated to write his theory of evolution, which went on to influence functionalism.

2. What aspects of consciousness did the functionalists deal with?
The functionalists were interested in determining what the function of consciousness was. This is in stark contrast to contemporary schools of thought (Titchener's and Wundt's systems) that were trying to determine the elements or structure of consciousness.

3. On what grounds did the functionalists protest against Wundt's psychology and Titchener's structuralism?
The functionalists believed that Wundt's and Titchener's psychological systems were too restrictive. "These early schools of thought could not answer the questions the functionalists were

asking: What does the mind do? And how does it do it?" Later, the functionalists become interested in applying psychology to solve real-life problems.

4. Why did it seem inevitable that a theory of evolution would be proposed and accepted by the middle of the nineteenth century? How did the Zeitgeist influence the success of Darwin's ideas?

There was a confluence of events and ways of thinking that made the time right for Darwin's theory. First, others scientists had previously developed theories that laid the groundwork for Darwin's theory (including his grandfather, Erasmus Darwin). In the 1830's primates were exhibited in zoos, and people were astonished to see the similarities between them and humans, while at the same time individuals strove to own fossils of long extinct animals. The industrial revolution was changing everyday life and causing migration from rural to urban areas, and a respect for science was in the air. The Zeitgeist was right to accept Darwin's theory. His book *On the Origin of Species* was well written and well supported, which further guaranteed success.

5. Explain the approaches to evolution taken by Erasmus Darwin and Jean-Baptiste Lamarck.

Erasmus Darwin believed that "all warm-blooded animals had evolved from a single living filament and were given animation by God". Furthermore he said, animal species changed over time in reaction to their environment. Lamarck also believed that species changed over time, but thought that evolutionary characteristics could be passed on to offspring.

6. How did increasing travel and exploration, and the public fascination with fossils, influence attitudes toward the idea of evolution?

With increasing travel, people were able to see the many forms of life, which gave rise to skepticism about how all animals could fit on Noah's ark. Fossils were discovered that did not match with any living creatures. This meant that there is not constancy to living things: species can become extinct. The natural next step is to determine the process by which some species live while others do not.

7. Explain how the study of bird beaks supports evolutionary theory.

In their study over a 30-year time period starting in 1973, the Grants looked at the shape of finch beaks on the Galapagos islands and found that with one generation the beaks change in response to the changing environment. When there was a drought, a thicker beak was more useful to crack larger seeds, thereafter thicker beaks became more prominent. When the heavy rain washed away the larger seeds, smaller beaks that could obtain tiny seeds became more prominent.

8. What did Darwin mean when he referred to himself as the "devil's chaplain" and said that his work was like confessing to murder?

"Darwin referred to himself as the devil's chaplain, telling a friend that working on a theory of evolution was like confessing to murder." He meant that because the creationist theory had been the dominant theory at the time, his work would bring immense resistance from those that believed in the Bible. An argument was that the devil had sent him to bring doubt to Bible followers. "Darwin knew that when he finally published his book, he would be damned as a heretic."

9. How was Darwin's concept of natural selection influenced by Malthus's doctrine of population and food supply?

Thomas Malthus wrote about the difference in growth of the human food supply (which grows arithmetically) and human population (which grows geometrically). Because of the pressures of the different growth curves, "Only the most forceful, cunning, and adaptable will survive."

10. Describe the role of Thomas Henry Huxley in promoting Darwin's theory.

Darwin's theory raised much controversy. Although he was reticent to engage critics, he had his defenders, one of which was the charismatic Thomas Huxley. A debate was scheduled at Oxford University, but shortly before it was to be held Darwin fell ill so Huxley took his place to debate Bishop Wilberforce.

11. In what ways did Darwin's data and ideas alter the subject matter and methods of psychology?

Darwin's work influenced psychology in four ways: 1) animals become appropriate research subjects (their minds are similar to ours if we share heritage), 2) "an emphasis on the functions rather than the structure of consciousness", 3) incorporating methods and data from diverse fields (not relying solely on the psychophysics methods of Fechner and Wundt), and 4) individual differences.

12. Describe the work of Juan Huarte in anticipating the contributions of Galton.

Huarte wrote a book that was published in the 1500's, called *The Examination of Talented Individuals* in which he discussed "individual differences in human capacities." Furthermore, he discussed tailoring a child's education depending on the child's talents. This foreshadows aptitude testing and Galton's work in Eugenics, where he argues in favor of childbearing by talented individuals.

13. How was Galton's work on mental tests influenced by Locke's empiricist view?

Locke said that "all knowledge comes through the senses." If true, it would make sense that the more intelligent among us would have more sensitive senses (wider range, etc.), so Galton applied this to testing. His anthropometric lab, purportedly designed to measure intelligence, actually measured a variety of physical and sense acuity characteristics.

14. What statistical tools did Galton develop to measure human characteristics? Describe Galton's research on hereditary genius.

Galton applied the normal distribution to mental characteristics for the first time, and advocated using the mean and standard deviation to describe distributions. He also developed the correlation (refined later by his student Karl Pearson). In his book *Hereditary Genius*, Galton argued that greatness occurred in families far more often than can be explained by environmental influences.

15. How did Galton study the association of ideas? How did he test for intelligence?

Galton worked on two problems related to association of ideas: "1) the diversity of associations of ideas; and 2) reaction time (the time required to produce associations)." In one method, he walked down a busy street and focused on objects until an associated idea emerged. In another method, he wrote down 75 words then later viewed them and timed how long it took for two associations to emerge. To test for intelligence in his anthropometric lab, he measured a variety of physical and sense acuity characteristics.

16. How did Darwin's evolutionary theory stimulate the development of animal psychology? What was Wundt's initial reaction to this development?

With Darwin's theory there is "no sharp distinction...between human minds and animals minds." Thus, animal minds became an appropriate focus of attention for psychologists. Wundt's initial reaction was to believe that if an animal had even a simple sense system, it could have consciousness.

17. Describe the anecdotal method and introspection by analogy. What was Romanes's mental ladder?

Romanes used the anecdotal method which is collecting the narrative stories people told about what they saw animals do. With these stories he engaged in "introspection by analogy" which assumes that the human observer and the animal share the same mental processes. He believed that animals were engaging in the highest forms of mental functioning. He also created the "mental ladder" which ranks the mental functioning of animals.

18. How did Morgan limit the use of introspection by analogy? Which of the following techniques did Morgan use to study the animal mind: (a) collecting anecdotes, (b) experimental studies, (c) the method of extirpation, (d) electrical stimulation?

Romanes work was roundly criticized by C. Lloyd Morgan, who proposed a law of parsimony: "animal behavior must not be attributed to a higher mental process when it can be explained in terms of a lower mental process." Morgan, like Romanes, engaged in explaining an animal's behavior "through an introspective examination of his own mental processes" but did explain the animal's processes using the lowest level processing possible, using (a) anecdotes minimally.

Key terms from chapter six

- **Anecdotal method** Romanes' research methodology by which he collected narrative reports from people about the animals they saw.
- **Anthropometric laboratory** This was the laboratory created by Galton to measure the mental acuity of people, although the tests largely measured physical and developmental characteristics.
- **Correlation** The statistical measure of the relationship between two variables, invented by Galton and refined by his student Karl Pearson.
- **Eugenics** A new science founded by Galton, its aim was to improve the stock of the human race by encouraging those with "noble qualities" to reproduce.
- **Evolution** Darwin's theory which explains how species change over time, it has three components: individuals vary in characteristics, some characteristics are inherited, and some of these characteristics are more suited to the environment than others.
- **HMS Beagle** Name of the ship carrying Darwin on his 5 year voyage around the world
- **Introspection by analogy** "A technique for studying animal behavior by assuming that the same mental processes that occur in the observer's mind also occur in the animal's mind.", used by Romanes
- **Law of parsimony** "The notion that animal behavior must not be attributed to a higher mental process when it can be explained in terms of a lower mental process," and is also called Morgan's Canon.
- **Mental test** A phrase coined by James Cattell, although the idea of the mental test was created by Galton. These are tests whose aim is to measure mental qualities.

- **Morgan's Canon** "The notion that animal behavior must not be attributed to a higher mental process when it can be explained in terms of a lower mental process," and is also called the law of parsimony.
- *On the Origin of Species* (1859) The famous book in which Darwin outlines the theory of evolution supported by overwhelming evidence.
- **Thomas Malthus** Economist whose work on the growth of food vs. populations inspired Darwin's thinking.

<u>TESTBANK</u>

ESSAY

1. Describe the functionalist protest, including the definition of functionalism and the bases on which the functionalists objected to Wundt's psychology and Titchener's structuralism.

   ANS:
   Answer not provided.

   PTS: 1   MSC: WWW

2. Making specific reference to material contained in your textbook, defend the following statement: "The suggestion that living things change with time, which is the fundamental notion of evolution, did not originate with Darwin."

   ANS:
   Answer not provided.

   PTS: 1

3. Explain evolutionary theory using the study of finches' beaks.

   ANS:
   Answer not provided.

   PTS: 1

4. In what specific ways did Darwin's data and theory influence psychology in terms of both subject matter and methods?

   ANS:
   Answer not provided.

   PTS: 1   MSC: WWW

5. Summarize Galton's contributions to psychology. Describe five examples of his influence that are familiar in contemporary psychology.

   ANS:
   Answer not provided.

   PTS: 1

6. Describe/explain the role of Darwin's work in the development of comparative psychology.

    ANS:
    Answer not provided.

    PTS: 1

7. What were the major contributions of George Romanes and C. Lloyd Morgan to animal psychology and the development of functionalism?

    ANS:
    Answer not provided.

    PTS: 1

MULTIPLE CHOICE

8. The _____ ask, "What's the mind made of?" whereas the _____ demand, "What does it do?"
    a. experimentalists; structuralists
    b. structuralists; functionalists
    c. functionalists; behaviorists
    d. functionalists; structuralists
    e. Gestalt psychologists; functionalists

    ANS: B   PTS: 1   REF: The Functionalist Protest

9. Which of the of the following statements best summarizes the protest of functional psychology against Wundt and Titchener?
    a. Functional psychology proposed that more mental elements exist than allowed by Wundt and Titchener.
    b. Functional psychology emphasized that Wundt's and Titchener's approaches to psychology were too broad and included too many topics of study.
    c. Functional psychology claimed that Wundt's and Titchener's approaches were too restrictive because they did not study the practical value of mental processes.
    d. In contrast to Wundt and Titchener, functional psychology said that consciousness could not be studied scientifically.
    e. None of the choices are correct.

    ANS: C   PTS: 1   REF: The Functionalist Protest

10. Functionalism was an intentional protest of the limitations of _____.
    a. Wundt's structuralism
    b. Wundt's experimentalism
    c. Titchener's structuralism
    d. James's pragmatism
    e. Wundt's experimentalism and Titchener's structuralism

    ANS: E   PTS: 1   REF: The Functionalist Protest

11. The most important consequence of functionalism was ____.
    a. the introduction of evolution
    b. the replacement of experimentalism
    c. the status it gave to pragmatism
    d. the development of applied psychology
    e. the development of clinical psychology

    ANS: D   PTS: 1   REF: The Functionalist Protest

12. Which of the following works were most influential in the development of functionalism?
    a. Weber's and Fechner's work in psychophysics
    b. Quetelet's and Galton's work in statistics
    c. Wundt's and Titchener's systems
    d. The comparative research of physiologists and Darwin's work
    e. The work of Darwin and Galton and comparative research

    ANS: E   PTS: 1   REF: The Functionalist Protest
    MSC: WWW

13. ____, a predecessor of Darwin, speculated that all mammals had evolved from a single filament and given movement by God.
    a. Anaximander
    b. Plato
    c. Isaac Newton
    d. Erasmus Darwin
    e. Jean-Baptiste Lamarck

    ANS: D   PTS: 1
    REF: The Evolution Revolution: Charles Darwin (1809-1882)

14. ____ argued that our bodies adapt to the environment and those adaptations will be heritable.
    a. La Mettrie
    b. René Descartes
    c. Charles Lyell
    d. Erasmus Darwin
    e. Jean-Baptiste Lamarck

    ANS: E   PTS: 1
    REF: The Evolution Revolution: Charles Darwin (1809-1882)

15. ____ was an early evolutionary theorist who argued that acquired characteristics could be inherited.
    a. Erasmus Darwin
    b. Charles Darwin
    c. Jean-Baptiste Lamarck
    d. Bain
    e. Charles Lyell

    ANS: C   PTS: 1
    REF: The Evolution Revolution: Charles Darwin (1809-1882)

16. _____ was a confidant of Darwin who introduced the concept of evolution into geological theory.
    a. Wilberforce
    b. Huxley
    c. Butler
    d. Lyell
    e. Galton

    ANS: D   PTS: 1
    REF: The Evolution Revolution: Charles Darwin (1809-1882)

17. Why, after many centuries of accepting biblical stories, did scholars question the one about Noah's ark?
    a. No inland body of water would hold such a vessel.
    b. Because the attitude of positivism allowed for no supernatural explanations.
    c. The giraffe's neck had become too long after generations of having to reach for higher and higher branches to find food.
    d. Galton's work in statistics showed that it was mathematically impossible.
    e. There were too many identified species to fit two of each into a boat.

    ANS: E   PTS: 1
    REF: The Evolution Revolution: Charles Darwin (1809-1882)   MSC: WWW

18. What event(s) led common people to question whether humans were really unique creatures, totally unlike other species?
    a. Many took cruises to South America and other places where they were exposed to species of apes very similar to human beings.
    b. The tenet of natural selection became widely known and popular.
    c. Displays of orangutans and chimpanzees became common in zoos, as well as fossil comparisons of gorilla and human skeletons.
    d. Helmholtz's and Fechner's research findings made such questioning inevitable.
    e. None of the choices are correct.

    ANS: C   PTS: 1
    REF: The Evolution Revolution: Charles Darwin (1809-1882)

19. Darwin's ideas of evolution were not new. What *was* new about Darwin's work was his _____.
    a. hard data to support such a theory
    b. focus on lower animals
    c. work on emotions
    d. idea of natural selection
    e. idea of survival of the fittest

    ANS: A   PTS: 1
    REF: The Evolution Revolution: Charles Darwin (1809-1882)

20. When in England, Darwin displayed a wide variety of physical symptoms. These symptoms were probably _____.
    a. caused by the muscular disorder he later died from
    b. psychosomatic-neurotic in origin
    c. faked
    d. caused by over-exposure to lead in his drinking water
    e. None of the choices are correct.

    ANS: B   PTS: 1
    REF: The Evolution Revolution: Charles Darwin (1809-1882)

21. How many years did Darwin wait to present his theory publicly?
    a. 2
    b. 11
    c. 17
    d. 22
    e. 34

    ANS: D   PTS: 1
    REF: The Evolution Revolution: Charles Darwin (1809-1882)

22. A theory of evolution based on natural selection was developed independently by ____.
    a. Charles Darwin and Alfred Wallace
    b. Charles Darwin and Charles Lyell
    c. Joseph Hooker and Charles Darwin
    d. Erasmus Darwin and Charles Darwin
    e. Jean Lamarck and Charles Darwin

    ANS: A   PTS: 1
    REF: The Evolution Revolution: Charles Darwin (1809-1882)

23. The essential difference between Wallace's theory of evolution and Darwin's was that the work of the former ____.
    a. was a restatement of Lamarck's ideas
    b. was a restatement of Spencer's ideas
    c. did not have empirical data to support it
    d. included the heritability of acquired traits
    e. was suppressed by Darwin

    ANS: C   PTS: 1
    REF: The Evolution Revolution: Charles Darwin (1809-1882)

24. ____ is the preeminent book of Darwin's theory of evolution, which details the evolution of humans from lower forms of life.
    a. *On the Origin of Species*
    b. *The Descent of Man*
    c. *The Expression of the Emotions in Man and Animals*
    d. *Hereditary Genius*
    e. *Natural Inheritance*

    ANS: A   PTS: 1
    REF: The Evolution Revolution: Charles Darwin (1809-1882)

25. The most fundamental point of Darwin's theses was the ____.
    a. fact of variation among members of the species
    b. heritability of variations
    c. process of natural selection
    d. tenet of survival of the fittest
    e. normal distribution of traits in a population

    ANS: A   PTS: 1
    REF: The Evolution Revolution: Charles Darwin (1809-1882)   MSC: WWW

26. Who predicted that humans in the future will live on the edge of starvation because the population of humans increases geometrically while the supply of food increases arithmetically?
    a. Lamarck
    b. Lyell
    c. Huxley
    d. Malthus
    e. Hooker

    ANS: D   PTS: 1
    REF: The Evolution Revolution: Charles Darwin (1809-1882)

27. Darwin's position on Lamarck's idea that changes due to experiences can be inherited was the ____ of Lamarck's ____.
    a. acceptance; doctrine
    b. replacement; doctrine with the variability hypothesis
    c. total rejection; doctrine
    d. replacement; doctrine with the doctrine of social Darwinism
    e. synthesis; ideas with Galton's theory of the normal distribution

    ANS: A   PTS: 1
    REF: The Evolution Revolution: Charles Darwin (1809-1882)

28. Who could be described as the driving force of England's scientific establishment?
    a. Lyell
    b. Huxley
    c. Hooker
    d. Darwin
    e. Wilberforce

    ANS: B   PTS: 1
    REF: The Evolution Revolution: Charles Darwin (1809-1882)

29. Today, scientists are sometimes portrayed as offering science as a new religion or as being enemies of religion. This stance could be traced to ____.
    a. Huxley
    b. Hooker
    c. Darwin
    d. Lyell
    e. Wilberforce

    ANS: A   PTS: 1
    REF: The Evolution Revolution: Charles Darwin (1809-1882)

30. In a public debate on evolution, ____ refuted the points made against evolution by ____.
    a. Huxley; Hooker
    b. Huxley; Lyell
    c. Darwin; Fitzroy
    d. Huxley; Wilberforce
    e. Wilberforce; Huxley

    ANS: D   PTS: 1
    REF: The Evolution Revolution: Charles Darwin (1809-1882)

31. In his book ____, Darwin emphasized the similarity between human and animal mental processes.
    a. *The Expression of the Emotions in Man and Animals*
    b. *The Ascent of Man*
    c. *The Descent of Man*
    d. *On the Origin of Species*
    e. *The Phylogeny of Thought*

    ANS: C   PTS: 1
    REF: The Evolution Revolution: Charles Darwin (1809-1882)

32. In his book ____, Darwin explained human emotional gestures, postures, and other aspects of body language that convey emotion as remnants of adaptive movements by animals.
    a. *The Descent of Man*
    b. *The Ascent of Man*
    c. *The Expression of Emotions in Man and Animals*
    d. *A Biography of Emotions*
    e. *Physiological Psychology*

    ANS: C   PTS: 1
    REF: The Evolution Revolution: Charles Darwin (1809-1882)

33. One of the early sources of modern child psychology was an article in 1877 by ____.
    a. E. Darwin
    b. C. Darwin
    c. F. Galton
    d. K. Pearson
    e. J. M. Cattell

    ANS: B   PTS: 1
    REF: The Evolution Revolution: Charles Darwin (1809-1882)

34. In the study of finches' beaks, the biologists Peter and Rosemary Grant found that ____.
    a. Darwin had underestimated the power of natural selection
    b. under drought conditions, more thick-than thin-beaked birds survived and reproduced
    c. in only one generation, natural selection produced a better-adapted species
    d. when heavy rains became common, birds with slender beaks flourished
    e. All of the choices are correct.

    ANS: E   PTS: 1
    REF: The Evolution Revolution: Charles Darwin (1809-1882)   MSC: WWW

35. In his journal *Mind*, Darwin describes ____.
    a. the developmental stages of his son in relation to human evolution
    b. an ape whose mental processes are analyzed
    c. early theory that has since been the foundation of cognitive psychology
    d. simple stimuli that elicit the same responses in humans and animals
    e. the evolution of human mental functions

    ANS: A   PTS: 1
    REF: The Evolution Revolution: Charles Darwin (1809-1882)

36. The influence of Darwin's work can be seen most directly in ____.
    a. comparative psychology
    b. functionalism
    c. animal psychology
    d. All of the above.
    e. None of the above.

ANS: A   PTS: 1
REF: The Evolution Revolution: Charles Darwin (1809-1882)   MSC: WWW

37. A consequence of Darwin's work for psychology was ____.
    a. the legitimization of analog introspection in the study of animals
    b. the legitimization of nonexperimental descriptive methods
    c. the theory of eugenics
    d. the use of the tenets of selective breeding for determining U.S. immigration quotas
    e. acknowledgment of the necessity of statistical analysis in psychological research

ANS: B   PTS: 1
REF: The Evolution Revolution: Charles Darwin (1809-1882)

38. A consequence of Darwin's work for psychology was ____.
    a. the legitimization of the collective unconscious
    b. work in comparative physiology
    c. the theory of eugenics
    d. a focus on individual differences
    e. statistical analyses

ANS: D   PTS: 1
REF: The Evolution Revolution: Charles Darwin (1809-1882)

39. In the Original Source Material from his autobiography, Charles Darwin described himself as ____.
    a. having "no great quickness of apprehension or wit"
    b. "a poor critic"
    c. "moderate abilities"
    d. possessing a "love of natural science [which] has been steady and ardent"
    e. All of the choices are correct.

ANS: E   PTS: 1
REF: The Evolution Revolution: Charles Darwin (1809-1882)

40. Today, our acceptance that the study of individual differences is appropriate subject matter for psychology is due to whose work?
    a. Quetelet
    b. Helmholtz
    c. Galton
    d. Pearson
    e. Spencer

ANS: C   PTS: 1
REF: Individual Differences: Francis Galton (1822-1911)

41. Who wrote a 16th-century book on individual differences and argued that children's education should be individualized to recognize such differences?
    a. Butler
    b. Huarte
    c. Galton
    d. Quetelet
    e. Wundt

    ANS: B   PTS: 1
    REF: Individual Differences: Francis Galton (1822-1911)

42. Who wrote *Hereditary Genius*?
    a. Galton
    b. Darwin
    c. Cattell
    d. Quetelet
    e. Helmholtz

    ANS: A   PTS: 1
    REF: Individual Differences: Francis Galton (1822-1911)

43. Galton's *Hereditary Genius* was mainly concerned with ____.
    a. exploring his lineage and the eminent men in his family
    b. a statistical analysis of the concept of eminent men producing eminent offspring
    c. isolating the gene responsible for making geniuses
    d. None of the above.
    e. All of the above.

    ANS: B   PTS: 1
    REF: Individual Differences: Francis Galton (1822-1911)

44. When Galton founded the science of eugenics, he ____.
    a. was following in the footsteps of Huxley
    b. invented the term "eugenics"
    c. studied the incidence of behaviors in northern Europeans versus southern Europeans
    d. became personally involved in aiding blood transfusions between Jews and Gentiles and between Africans and Caucasians
    e. denounced the study of blood transfusions between rabbits

    ANS: B   PTS: 1
    REF: Individual Differences: Francis Galton (1822-1911)

45. The early 20th-century American government policy of sterilizing mentally retarded females is an example of ____.
    a. artificial selection
    b. eugenics
    c. product-moment correlations
    d. Darwin's theory of evolution
    e. natural selection

    ANS: B   PTS: 1
    REF: Individual Differences: Francis Galton (1822-1911)   MSC: WWW

46. Galton argued that what proportion of eminence could be reliably attributed to environmental influences?
    a. 0%
    b. 15%
    c. 25%
    d. 50%
    e. 82%

    ANS: A   PTS: 1
    REF: Individual Differences: Francis Galton (1822-1911)

47. Which of the following did Galton not endorse in the material from *Hereditary Genius?*
    a. the idea of natural equality
    b. definite limits to muscular and intellectual powers
    c. limiting one's undertakings to matters within one's reach
    d. babies are born alike
    e. None of the choices was endorsed by Galton.

    ANS: A   PTS: 1
    REF: Individual Differences: Francis Galton (1822-1911)

48. Who first highlighted the importance of central tendency?
    a. Quetelet
    b. Darwin
    c. Galton
    d. Pearson
    e. Cattell

    ANS: A   PTS: 1
    REF: Individual Differences: Francis Galton (1822-1911)

49. Who was the first to show that biological and social data were normally distributed?
    a. Galton
    b. Quetelet
    c. Pearson
    d. Huarte
    e. Moyen

    ANS: B   PTS: 1
    REF: Individual Differences: Francis Galton (1822-1911)

50. Who arrived at the concept of the "average man" to describe findings from a large group of subjects?
    a. Pearson
    b. Quetelet
    c. Huarte
    d. Galton
    e. Cattell

    ANS: B   PTS: 1
    REF: Individual Differences: Francis Galton (1822-1911)

51. The idea of measures clustering around the of center or average of a distribution should be attributed to
____.
   a. Quetelet
   b. Darwin
   c. Newton
   d. Pearson
   e. Cattell

   ANS: A   PTS: 1
   REF: Individual Differences: Francis Galton (1822-1911)

52. Who was the first to show that human mental characteristics followed a normal distribution?
   a. Pearson
   b. Quetelet
   c. Huarte
   d. Galton
   e. Cattell

   ANS: D   PTS: 1
   REF: Individual Differences: Francis Galton (1822-1911)   MSC: WWW

53. Galton proposed that measurement of human traits could be defined and summarized by two numbers,
which are ____.
   a. the mean and the median
   b. the variance and the standard deviation
   c. the median and the mode
   d. the mean and the standard deviation
   e. the mean and the mode

   ANS: D   PTS: 1
   REF: Individual Differences: Francis Galton (1822-1911)

54. The formula currently used for calculating the correlation coefficient was developed by ____.
   a. Galton
   b. Thorndike
   c. Cattell
   d. Binet
   e. Pearson

   ANS: E   PTS: 1
   REF: Individual Differences: Francis Galton (1822-1911)

55. The term *mental tests* was coined by ____, but ____ originated this concept.
   a. Galton; Cattell
   b. Cattell; Galton
   c. Quetelet; Galton
   d. Galton; Quetelet
   e. Huarte; Quetelet

   ANS: B   PTS: 1
   REF: Individual Differences: Francis Galton (1822-1911)

56. Mental tests were originated by ____.
   a. Binet
   b. Simon
   c. Morgan
   d. Galton
   e. Romanes

   ANS: D   PTS: 1
   REF: Individual Differences: Francis Galton (1822-1911)

57. Galton's measures of intellectual functioning assumed correlation between intelligence and ____.
   a. acuteness of the senses
   b. reaction times to stimuli
   c. Fechner's Law
   d. average error in psychophysics tasks
   e. just noticeable differences

   ANS: A   PTS: 1
   REF: Individual Differences: Francis Galton (1822-1911)

58. What had the greatest impact upon Galton's view on the measurement of intelligence?
   a. Descartes' theory of innate ideas
   b. Herbart's argument that a threshold separates the conscious and unconscious mind
   c. Wundt's doctrine of creative synthesis
   d. Berkeley's mentalism
   e. Locke's theory that all knowledge comes through the senses

   ANS: E   PTS: 1
   REF: Individual Differences: Francis Galton (1822-1911)

59. The aim of the research at the Anthropometric Laboratory was to assess ____.
   a. developmental trends over the lifespan
   b. the sensory capacities of humans
   c. the collective mental resources of the British people
   d. the correlates of intelligence among eminent men
   e. eugenics policy development

   ANS: C   PTS: 1
   REF: Individual Differences: Francis Galton (1822-1911)

60. What additional interest(s) did Galton research?
   a. Arithmetic by smell
   b. Paranoid disorders
   c. The power of prayer
   d. All of the above.
   e. None of the above.

   ANS: D   PTS: 1
   REF: Individual Differences: Francis Galton (1822-1911)

61. Which of the following are influenced by Galton's work?
    a. child development
    b. heredity
    c. statistical techniques
    d. testing methods
    e. All of the above.

    ANS: E   PTS: 1
    REF: Individual Differences: Francis Galton (1822-1911)

62. Galton found that a substantial proportion of word associations were evidence of ____.
    a. rationalism as purported by Berkeley, Kant, and Descartes
    b. empiricism as purported by Locke and Mill
    c. Müller's interference theory of memory
    d. Ebbinghaus's decay theory of memory
    e. the effects of childhood experiences on the adult

    ANS: E   PTS: 1
    REF: Individual Differences: Francis Galton (1822-1911)   MSC: WWW

63. The first experimental attempt to study word associations was by ____.
    a. Ebbinghaus
    b. Galton
    c. Wundt
    d. Freud
    e. Jung

    ANS: B   PTS: 1
    REF: Individual Differences: Francis Galton (1822-1911)

64. To study mental imagery, Galton used which self-report method?
    a. introspection
    b. retrospection
    c. the questionnaire
    d. projective tests
    e. dream analysis

    ANS: C   PTS: 1
    REF: Individual Differences: Francis Galton (1822-1911)

65. Galton studied paranoid disorders by ____.
    a. visiting insane asylums
    b. reading every book and article about it on which he could get his hands
    c. imaging that every person or thing he saw was spying on him
    d. inviting people suffering from paranoid disorders to the Anthropometric Laboratory
    e. All of the choices are correct.

    ANS: C   PTS: 1
    REF: Individual Differences: Francis Galton (1822-1911)

66. In comparing evolutionary theory to theology, Galton's concluded that ____.
    a. there was insufficient evidence to support religious beliefs
    b. there was insufficient evidence to support evolutionary theory
    c. they were both correct
    d. religious beliefs facilitated adaptation to environmental demands
    e. there was insufficient evidence to support neither theology nor evolution

    ANS: A   PTS: 1
    REF: Individual Differences: Francis Galton (1822-1911)

67. According to ____, animals have no soul and thus are automata.
    a. Descartes
    b. Darwin
    c. Galton
    d. Romanes
    e. Morgan

    ANS: A   PTS: 1
    REF: Animal Psychology and the Development of Functionalism
    MSC: WWW

68. The notion that there is a continuity of consciousness and cognitive processes between animals and humans was suggested and/or demonstrated by ____.
    a. Darwin's evidence
    b. Galton's selective breeding notions
    c. the structuralists
    d. the functionalists
    e. the behaviorists

    ANS: A   PTS: 1
    REF: Animal Psychology and the Development of Functionalism

69. According to Darwin, human emotional expressions reflect ____.
    a. a similarity of nervous systems between people and animals
    b. a correspondence of the "fight or flight" responses in humans and animals
    c. the inheritance of animal responses that may not be adaptive for humans
    d. evidence of animal intelligence
    e. evidence of instincts in humans

    ANS: C   PTS: 1
    REF: Animal Psychology and the Development of Functionalism

70. Wundt's early position on animal intelligence was that ____.
    a. any sensory capacity at all allowed for judgment and drawing of conscious inferences
    b. animals and humans differ only in the range of stimuli that they can detect
    c. human's erect stature makes smell and taste much less necessary than vision and audition for human adaptation to environments
    d. people have language; animals do not
    e. humans simply have more education than animals

    ANS: A   PTS: 1
    REF: Animal Psychology and the Development of Functionalism

71. The first systematic study of animal intelligence was by _____.
    a. Galvani
    b. Huarte
    c. Sherrington
    d. Romanes
    e. Morgan

    ANS: D   PTS: 1
    REF: Animal Psychology and the Development of Functionalism

72. The work of Romanes was especially flawed because of his _____.
    a. assumption of a continuity of intelligence between animals and people
    b. use of anthropometric methods
    c. use of the anecdotal method
    d. use of psychophysics methods
    e. reliance on reaction times to sensory stimuli in humans and animals

    ANS: C   PTS: 1
    REF: Animal Psychology and the Development of Functionalism

73. Whenever we think we "know what's on someone's mind," we are using which technique?
    a. projection
    b. the anecdotal method
    c. introspection
    d. introspection by analogy
    e. identification

    ANS: D   PTS: 1
    REF: Animal Psychology and the Development of Functionalism

74. Despite Romanes's deficiencies in methodology, he is respected by scientists for his _____.
    a. reliance on experimentation
    b. subjective interpretations
    c. critical thinking regarding the inner workings of the animal mind
    d. stimulation of the development of comparative psychology
    e. phenomenological psychology

    ANS: D   PTS: 1
    REF: Animal Psychology and the Development of Functionalism
    MSC: WWW

75. The intent of Lloyd Morgan's canon was to _____.
    a. exclude anthropological findings from the natural sciences
    b. make comparative psychology more scientific
    c. make comparative psychology more behavioral
    d. rid psychology of all traces of the technique of introspection
    e. impose a criterion for a distinction between instincts and thinking in both animals and humans

    ANS: B   PTS: 1
    REF: Animal Psychology and the Development of Functionalism

76. The first person(s) to engage in large studies of experimental comparative psychology was/were _____.
    a. Conway
    b. Romanes
    c. Morgan
    d. the functionalists
    e. the behaviorists

    ANS: C   PTS: 1
    REF: Animal Psychology and the Development of Functionalism

TRUE/FALSE

77. Structuralism asked, "What does the mind do?" whereas functionalism asked, "How does it do it?"

    ANS: F   PTS: 1   REF: The Functionalist Protest
    MSC: WWW

78. The most important legacy of functionalism is applied psychology.

    ANS: T   PTS: 1   REF: The Functionalist Protest

79. A sturdy root of functional psychology is animal behavior research.

    ANS: T   PTS: 1   REF: The Functionalist Protest

80. The intellectual Zeitgeist of the 19th century was ready for Darwin's theory, although the social Zeitgeist was not.

    ANS: F   PTS: 1
    REF: The Evolution Revolution: Charles Darwin (1809-1882)   MSC: WWW

81. A fundamental thesis of Darwin's *Origin* was the principle of survival of the strongest.

    ANS: F   PTS: 1
    REF: The Evolution Revolution: Charles Darwin (1809-1882)

82. Observations made over the course of two decades in the Galapagos Islands indicate that evolutionary changes occur much faster than Darwin previously thought.

    ANS: T   PTS: 1
    REF: The Evolution Revolution: Charles Darwin (1809-1882)

83. Drastic environmental changes can drive evolutionary changes in animal forms to occur over decades rather than over millennia.

    ANS: T   PTS: 1
    REF: The Evolution Revolution: Charles Darwin (1809-1882)

84. Other than his theory of evolution, Darwin made no significant contributions to the field of psychology.

ANS: F   PTS: 1
REF: The Evolution Revolution: Charles Darwin (1809-1882)   MSC: WWW

85. Ironically, Darwin's theory of evolution brought both consciousness and the study of animal behavior to the forefront of psychology.

ANS: T   PTS: 1
REF: The Evolution Revolution: Charles Darwin (1809-1882)

86. While expanding the scope of the subject matter of psychology, Darwin's theory added emphasis to the notion that experimentation is the only method proper to the science of psychology.

ANS: F   PTS: 1
REF: The Evolution Revolution: Charles Darwin (1809-1882)

87. Quetelet was the first to apply statistical methods to the examination of individual differences.

ANS: T   PTS: 1
REF: Individual Differences: Francis Galton (1822-1911)

88. Galton gave us the correlational coefficient measure.

ANS: T   PTS: 1
REF: Individual Differences: Francis Galton (1822-1911)   MSC: WWW

89. Galton created the term "mental tests".

ANS: F   PTS: 1
REF: Individual Differences: Francis Galton (1822-1911)

90. Galton's basic assumption was that one's sensory abilities directly reflect one's intelligence.

ANS: T   PTS: 1
REF: Individual Differences: Francis Galton (1822-1911)

91. The quality of Galton's research is verified by its reliability, as assessed as recently as 1985.

ANS: T   PTS: 1
REF: Individual Differences: Francis Galton (1822-1911)   MSC: WWW

92. The first experimental examination of associations was by Wundt and Ebbinghaus.

ANS: F   PTS: 1
REF: Individual Differences: Francis Galton (1822-1911)

93. Wundt argued that if an animal has any sensory ability, then it can make judgments and conscious inferences.

ANS: T   PTS: 1
REF: Animal Psychology and the Development of Functionalism

94. Darwin selected G. J. Romanes to investigate the evolution of the mind.

   ANS: T   PTS: 1
   REF: Animal Psychology and the Development of Functionalism

95. The first book on comparative psychology was *Animal Intelligence* by Romanes.

   ANS: T   PTS: 1
   REF: Animal Psychology and the Development of Functionalism

96. Romanes's anecdotal method used observational reports about animal behavior.

   ANS: T   PTS: 1
   REF: Animal Psychology and the Development of Functionalism

97. When you say, " I know what my dog is thinking," you are practicing introspection by analogy.

   ANS: T   PTS: 1
   REF: Animal Psychology and the Development of Functionalism

98. Lloyd Morgan's Canon was an attempt to limit the tendency to attribute human cognitive processes and abilities to animals.

   ANS: T   PTS: 1
   REF: Animal Psychology and the Development of Functionalism

99. Romanes was the first scientist to conduct large-scale experimental studies in animal psychology.

   ANS: F   PTS: 1
   REF: Animal Psychology and the Development of Functionalism

100. The initial work in comparative psychology was carried out in England and the leadership in the field stayed there for more than a decade.

   ANS: F   PTS: 1
   REF: Animal Psychology and the Development of Functionalism

101. When psychologists began to examine mental processes in a completely different way than biologists studied anatomy, they laid the groundwork for functional psychology.

   ANS: F   PTS: 1
   REF: Animal Psychology and the Development of Functionalism

Chapter 7

Functionalism: Development and Founding

The chapter opens with a description of the odd and perhaps neurotic behaviors of Herbert Spencer. Spencer, a British philosopher, argued that Darwin's theory of evolution applied to all aspects of the universe, including the mind and human behavior. Spenser coined the term "social Darwinism." He suggested that if a society was free to develop on its own and was left alone by government interference, then stronger, more fit people and organizations would thrive while the weaker and less adequate would go extinct. His beliefs were widely accepted in the U.S. because they fit with the individualistic laissez-faire economic system in place. Spencer named his system synthetic philosophy, which suggests that knowledge and experience can be explained in terms of evolutionary principles.

Other thinkers extended Darwin's ideas as well. Samuel Butler wondered if machines could evolve to a higher form, as animals do, and wrote that he believed evolution was already happening for machines. He also believed that machines had already surpassed animal evolution in terms of speed, and one day machines would simulate human thought. Towards that end, Henry Hollerith developed punch-card processing in order to compute the 1890 census, which astonished Americans because of the computational power. These and other individuals served as predecessors to William James, a leading figure in the field of psychology.

James was born into a very wealthy family and received schooling in both Europe and the U.S., yet suffered from poor health. Eventually he enrolled in Harvard, then changed his studies from chemistry to medicine, dabbled in zoology/biology, then returned to medicine. He suffered from "neurasthenia", which appeared to be neurotic in origin and was an epidemic at the time. Eventually, James began to develop his own philosophy and came to believe in free will. He also became interested in "mind-altering chemicals." The idea that body states would affect conscious experience was fascinating to him. He accepted a teaching position at Harvard in 1872 and three years later taught a course in Psychology, the first such course ever taught in the United States. He published *The Principles of Psychology* in 1890, which became one of the most influential books in psychology. After its publication, however, James left the field to become a philosopher and put Hugo Münsterberg in charge of the psychology lab at Harvard.

"In The Principles of Psychology, James presents what eventually became the central tenet of American functionalism—that the goal of psychology is…the study of living people as they adapt to their environment." He highlights the importance of nonrational processes like emotion and passion. This is in direct opposition to Wundt's and Titchener's elementalism. He asserts that consciousness must be studied in a more natural setting, with consideration to the relationship between physical states and the mind. He sees conscious experience as "a continuous flow" that is ever-changing and coins the phrase "stream of consciousness" to describe this. James believes consciousness must be cumulative (a culmination of experiences over one's lifetime) and not recurrent (constant over time). In addition, he states that consciousness must serve some biological purpose or it would not have survived over time. The text authors provide original source material from James' *Psychology (Briefer Course)* in which he discusses and elaborates on these ideas about consciousness.

Despite his differences with Wundt and Titchener, James did espouse introspection as a method for psychology, but he also advocated experimental methods as well as the use of a wide variety of research subjects (e.g., children, animals, disturbed). He believed that psychology should be pragmatic (have practical application). James developed a theory of emotions which subsequently generated much research and interest.

He also developed a theory of personality (the three-part self) whereby the self is made up of the material ("our body, family, home, or style of dress"), the social ("recognition we get from others"), and the spiritual (the "inner subjective being"). Finally, James discussed the idea of habit, whereby actions that are repeated require less and less attention from us and become more difficult to change.

One of James' graduate students was Mary Whiton Calkins. Despite her brilliant work as a student, and despite the protests of James, Harvard refused to confer her a Ph.D. because she was a woman. It was accepted as fact by most institutions and scientists that women were intellectually and physically inferior to men. This was derived from the variability hypothesis, which was the belief that males are more variable in physical and mental characteristics than females, with females clustered closer to the mean. This led to the conclusion that there are far fewer women of superior intelligence compared to men, and the belief that educating women would cause them physical and emotional damage and decrease "the maternal urge."

Two women challenged the variability hypothesis using empirical research methods: Helen Bradford Thompson Woolley and Leta Stetter Hollingworth. Woolley was born into a family that supported the education of women. She received her Ph.D. from the University of Chicago, and her dissertation was the first experimental test of the variability hypothesis. The results showed no significant differences between men and women in physical responses. Small yet insignificant differences were seen in intelligence, which she attributed to social and environmental factors. Hollingworth came from humble beginnings to earn her Ph.D. from Columbia University. Her research also tested the variability hypothesis, and found no sex differences in intelligence. Her research also spanned areas such as clinical, child, and school psychology. The findings of both women, as well as the objectivity of the researchers, were criticized, yet their contributions are deemed vastly significant today. One of the most vocal critics was G. Stanley Hall.

Hall was an influential early psychologist, and "compiled an outstanding record of firsts in American psychology." He had a pious upbringing, and attended seminary for a while but then decided that he was not cut out to be a minister, mainly because of his interest in evolution. He went to Germany to pursue a number of disciplines but returned to the U.S. when his parents stopped financially supporting him. He completed seminary and preached for only 10 weeks. He tutored for a while, read a book by Wundt, came to Harvard, and earned the first Ph.D. in psychology in the U.S. As a post-doctoral candidate, he went to Wundt's laboratory and worked there for 2 years, came back to the U.S. and began to advocate for the psychological study of children. This landed him a position at Johns Hopkins University, where he founded the first psychology laboratory in the U.S. "In 1887, Hall founded the American Journal of Psychology," in "the following year, Hall became the first president of Clark University in Worcester, Massachusetts" and then became the first president of the APA in 1892. Because of his growing interest in psychoanalysis, Hall invited Freud to speak at Clark's 20th anniversary. Despite his resistance to co-education, women (as well as Jews and African Americans) were admitted to Clark. The first African American to earn a Ph.D. in psychology was Cecil Sumner, which he earned under Hall at Clark.

Hall thoroughly incorporated the theory of evolution into his system of psychology, which focused on the study of childhood. To do his research Hall used the questionnaire technique, which was new to American psychology (it had originated with Galton). His most influential work is *Adolescence* (1904) in which he elaborates on his recapitulation theory. This is the idea that "children in their personal development repeat the life history of the human race." Critics said that the book focused too much and too frankly on sex. Later in life, Hall published *Senescence* (1922), which is the first psychological focus on old age.

Functionalism was not purposefully founded by its proponents; none were interested in the promotion and development of a school of thought. Instead, they shared a common vision to study "the functions of consciousness."

Their legacy is the rapid development of applied psychology. Titchener may have inadvertently formalized the school when he wrote an article articulating the differences between what he called structuralism and functionalism.

The two individuals who can be considered founders of functionalism are John Dewey and James Rowland Angell, both from the University of Chicago. Dewey received his Ph.D. from Johns Hopkins in 1884. He published the first American textbook *Psychology* in 1886 and it was the standard until James' *Principles of Psychology* was published. He spent 10 years at University of Chicago, then went to Columbia. Dewey published "The Reflex Arc Concept in Psychology," which became popular and influential. In the article, "Dewey attacked the psychological molecularism, elementism, and reductionism of the reflex arc." He argues that the reflex of a child reaching for and being burned by a flame cannot be reduced to elements, because the child's interpretation of the flame changes with the interaction. Thus, the shape of the arc is more circular than previously believed. "Dewey concluded that the proper subject matter for psychology had to be the study of the total organism as it functions in its environment."

James Rowland Angell was born into an academic family. He received his Master's degree under James at Harvard then went to study in Europe. Although he completed much of his doctoral work, he ran out of money and never received his Ph.D. Eventually he received an appointment to teach at the University of Chicago, where he stayed for 25 years. It is there where functionalism becomes as formalized as it will ever be, much of this through Angell's work. His text *Psychology* (1904) is heavily influenced by functionalism. In his 1906 address as the new APA president, he outlines functionalism as: 1) "the psychology of mental functions", 2) determining the "utilities of consciousness", and 3) the declaration of "no real distinction between mind and body." Functionalism becomes so linked to the University of Chicago that it becomes known as the "Chicago school."

Harvey Carr followed in the footsteps of his predecessors at the University of Chicago and refined functionalism. Carr received his Ph.D. at Chicago working under Angell and with John Watson. Later, Carr chairs the psychology department at U. of Chicago where functionalism "reaches its peak as a formal system." Two major points from his textbook *Psychology* (1925) are that psychology should study mental activity, and that the "function of mental activity is to....evaluate experiences," which will determine one's actions.

Functionalism also emerged at Columbia University, largely under Robert Sessions Woodworth, who received his Ph.D. under Cattell. He was a popular lecturer and reportedly beloved by students. He introduced what he called dynamic psychology, which focused on motivations and the physiology of behavior.

Functionalism presented the first divide within psychology: between functionalists and structuralists, but it was not perfect. There was no consensus regarding how to define the term "functionalism." Titchener argued that functionalism was not psychology at all, because structuralism defined psychology. Another criticism from some was on the functionalist focus on practical applicability to real world problems. Although there is no modern-day school of functionalism, its imprint can be seen in contemporary psychological thought: inclusion of animals as well as "infants, children, and people with mental disabilities" as research subjects, a broadening of accepted research methods, and the field of applied psychology.

Outline

I.   Evolution's Neurotic Philosopher: Herbert Spencer (1820-1903)

    A. A famous man who engaged in odd behavior

        1. provoked by unwanted people and disturbances

        2. wore earmuffs to insulate himself from noise

        3. had neurotic physical symptoms

    B. He comes from Britain to America; in U.S. he and his ideas are celebrated

    C. Despite the praise, he suffers from neurotic illnesses

II.   Evolution comes to America

    a. Spencer extends Darwin's theory of evolution

    b. Social Darwinism: application of the "theory of evolution to human nature and society"

        i.   evolutionary development of all aspects of universe

        ii.   principle of "survival of the fittest" (coined the phrase)

        iii.   utopian view: human perfection inevitable if nothing interferes with the natural order

        iv.   promoted individualism and a laissez-faire economic system; opposed government interference (e.g., welfare programs)

        v.   individuals and institutions that fail to adapt should be allowed to perish

        vi.   well-suited to America's individualist spirit

        vii. U.S. as living example

        viii. nation of productive, enterprising, self-sufficient people with a pragmatic outlook

        ix.   functional psychology and theory of evolution well-suited to the American temperament

        x.   consequence: Spencer's views permeated every field

    c. Synthetic philosophy: "Spencer's idea that knowledge and experience can be explained in terms of evolutionary principles"

        i.   application of evolutionary principles to all human knowledge and experience

        ii.   1860-1897: ideas published in sequence of 10 volumes

        iii.   The Principles of Psychology: the two synthetic philosophy volumes

            1.   used by James as textbook for psychology course at Harvard

            2.   mind exists in present form due to past and continuing efforts to adapt to environments

        iv.   human processes: adaptable

        v.   increasing complexity of experiences/behavior: normal evolution

        vi.   organism survival depends on adaptation to the environment

   B. The continuing evolution of machines

    a. Do machines evolve the way animals do?

    b. Samuel Butler (1835-1902)

        i.   wrote "Darwin among the machines" and extended theory of evolution to machines

        ii.   processes: natural selection and struggle for existence

        iii.   machines evolve faster than animals

        iv.   predicted machines would become self-regulating and self-acting

        v.   predicted machines would be capable of simulating human intelligence

c. Machines more complex than Babbage's calculating engine were needed
    i. anticipated complexity of 1890 U.S. census
    ii. 1880 census: 1,500 clerks took seven years to hand-tally data reported in 21,000 page document
d. Henry Hollerith and the punched cards
    i. engineer Hollerith (1859-1929) invented information-processing method
    ii. census data for individuals punched on paper or cards as a pattern of holes
    iii. machines used to count holes and tabulate results
    iv. 62 million participated
    v. card capacity: 36 eight-bit bytes of information
    vi. census completed in two years
    vii. cost savings: $5 million
    viii. Hollerith started own company, Tabulating Machine Company, which eventually turned into the IBM Corporation

C. William James (1842-1910): Anticipator of Functional Psychology
  a. General paradox
    i. major American precursor of functional psychology
    ii. pioneer of new scientific psychology in the United States
    iii. viewed by some colleagues as negative force re: scientific psychology
      1. espoused mentalistic and psychical phenomena
      2. not an experimentalist in attitude or deed
      3. later in life, viewed psychology as:
        a. that "nasty little science"
        b. "an elaboration of the obvious"
    iv. did not found functional psychology
    v. did influence the movement
  b. James's life
    i. wealthy family
    ii. early schooling: international
    iii. frequent journeys to Europe, particularly when ill
    iv. early interest in chemistry; created mishaps with chemistry sets, etc.
    v. age 18: failed artist
    vi. enrolled at Harvard: Lawrence Scientific School
    vii. decline in health and self-esteem: became lifelong neurotic
    viii. abandoned chemistry: lab work too demanding
    ix. medicine: cynical view of it
    x. rejected biology after a zoological trip on Amazon River: intolerant of methodological precision and arduous field work
    xi. returned to medical studies; frequently ill
    xii. depressed, he departed for a German spa
    xiii. attended lectures at University of Berlin
    xiv. speculated: time for psychology to be a science
    xv. expressed interest in learning from Helmholtz and Wundt
    xvi. 1869: earned M.D. from Harvard
    xvii. considered suicide
    xviii. intensely fearful; institutionalized himself
    xix. an epidemic of neurasthenia
      1. George Beard 1st used term to refer to a peculiarly American nervousness; James called it "Americanitis"

        a.   insomnia, hypochondria, nervous symptoms and the like

        b.   most typically afflicted: educated, self-aware people

        c.   often led to career postponement

2.   Rexall drug company: Americanitis Elixir

3.   Prescription

        a.   women: 6 week bed rest+ weight gain

        b.   men: travel, adventure, exercise

xx. discovering psychology

1.   1869: started building a philosophy of life after months of depression

2.   after reading about free will decided 1st act of free will would be to believe in it

3.   1872: taught physiology at Harvard

4.   interested in mind-altering chemicals; experimented with them

5.   academic year 1875-1876: taught his first course in psychology

6. 1st time experimental psychology taught in United States

7. 1st psych lecture James attended was his own

8.   1878

        a.   married wife of his father's choice

        b.   publishing contract with Henry Hold

        c.   started 1st book on honeymoon; finished it 12 years later

9.   compulsive traveler

10.   birth of children: made him nervous and jealous; traveled and flirted

11.   1885: professor of philosophy

12.   1889: title changed to professor of psychology

13.   1890: Principles of Psychology published

        a.   12–year effort

        b.   two volumes

        c.   great success

        d.   influential

14.   criticized by Wundt and Titchener

15.   panned by James, who thought it was two things:

        a.   proved "there is no such thing as a science of psychology"

        b.   "[James] is an incapable"

16.   decided he had nothing more to say about psychology

17.   not an experimentalist

        a.   no longer interested in the laboratory: hired Münsterberg

        b.   never convinced of the value of lab work

18.   1890's America's leading philosopher

19.   began educational psychology with *Talks to Teachers* (1899)

20.   *The Varieties of Religious Experience* (1902)

c. *The Principles of Psychology* (1890)

    i. James: perhaps greatest American Psychologist

      1.   wrote with a clarity rare in science

      2.   opposed Wundt re: goal of psychology

      3.   offered alternative view of mind

    ii. The Principles presents the central tenet of American functionalism

      1.   goal of psychology: study of people as they adapt

      2.   function of consciousness: survival

3. treats psychology as a biological science
4. emphasizes nonrational aspects of human nature: emotion & passion
5. intellect operates under physiological influences of the body
6. beliefs are determined by emotional factors
7. reason and concept formation affected by human wants and needs

iii. The subject matter of psychology: A new look at consciousness
   1. "Psychology is the Science of Mental Life, both of its phenomena and their conditions."
      a. phenomena: the subject matter is immediate experience
      b. conditions: the importance of the body, especially the brain
      c. physical substructures of consciousness: a basic part of psychology
      d. unique to James: awareness of biology and brain's effect on consciousness
   2. rebelled against artificiality and narrowness of the Wundtian position
   3. introspection does not show elements exist outside of the laboratory: to think otherwise = psychologists' fallacy
   4. simple sensations are inferred, they do not exist in consciousness experiences
   5. mental life is a unity
   6. consciousness is
      a. a continuous flow: stream of consciousness
      b. always changing
      c. not recurrent (the same every time)
      d. cumulative (culmination of experiences over lifetime)
   7. consciousness is selective: criterion is relevance
   8. consciousness is purposive
      a. has some biological utility
      b. enables one to adapt to one's environment by allowing one to choose
   9. conscious choice vs. habit (which is involuntary and unconscious)
   10. original source material on consciousness from Psychology (Briefer Course) (1892)
      a. "Consciousness is in constant change."
         i. has duration but not repeatable once a given state is gone
         ii. "...there is no proof than an incoming current ever gives us just the same bodily sensation twice."
         iii. instead, get a repeat of the same object
         iv. want to detect the "sameness of things"
      b. reports of subjective character of different sensations = virtually worthless as proof of fact
      c. cannot tell if two separate sense impressions are exactly alike
      d. attend to ratio rather than absolute quality
      e. feel things differently according to circumstances or mental state

       f.   nonetheless, believe we are experiencing the same world

       g.   state of our mind: never exactly the same

  d. The methods of psychology

      i.   introspection is a basic tool, albeit less than perfect

      ii.   experimental method

        1.   did not use it much

        2.   acknowledged its use as means to psychological knowledge, especially for psychophysics experimentation

     iii.   supplemented with comparative method: comparing consciousness of wide variety of subjects (including animals, children, emotionally disturbed, etc.)

     iv.   eclectic approach: implied functional psychology is not restricted to a single technique

  e. Pragmatism

      i.   James emphasized the value of pragmatism

      ii.   validity of an idea is its practical utility

     iii.   anything is true if it works

     iv.   advanced by C.S. Peirce (1870s mathematician and philosopher)

      v.   1907: Pragmatism: formalized the doctrine as a philosophical movement

  f. The theory of emotions

      i.   the then-current theory: emotion precedes physical arousal/response

      ii.   James: physical arousal/response precedes emotion

        1.   bodily change is the emotion

        2.   if not bodily change, then no emotion

     iii.   simultaneous discovery: Carl Lange (Denmark)

  g. The three-part self

        1.   self is three components: material (anything that is your own), social (recognition from other people), spiritual (inner, subjective being)

        2.   clothing is an example of all three selves being expressed

        3.   James starting dressing peculiar (i.e., polka dot ties and checkered pants)

  h. Habit

      i.   living creatures are "bundles of habits"

      ii.   habit involves the nervous system

        1.   repetitive action increases plasticity of neural matter

        2.   repetitions become easier to perform

        3.   repetitions require less conscious attention

        4.   become difficult to change

     iii.   enormous social implications

D. The functional inequality of women

  a. Mary Whiton Calkins (1863-1930)

      i.   James facilitated her graduate education; helped her overcome prejudice and discrimination

      ii.   later in career

        1.   developed paired associate technique for memory research

        2.   1st woman president of APA

        3.   1906: ranked 12th among 50 most important psychologists

     iii.   not allowed to formally enroll at Harvard

     iv.   James invited her to his classes and urged Harvard to grant her a doctoral degree

     v.   James though Calkins's Ph.D. examination "brilliant"
    vi.   denied Ph.D. from Harvard University
   vii.   later Professor of Psychology at Wellesley
1. starting program of research on memory
2. Harvard offered her a degree from Radcliffe College (their undergrad college for women)
3. she refused
4. was discriminated against solely because she was a woman
5. made repeated requests for her earned degree
6. awarded honorary degree from Columbia University

b. Calkin's experience = example of discrimination of women in higher ed continuing into the 20th century
c. Generations previous to Calkins: not admitted to universities at all at any level
d. No women accepted by any colleges until 1830s
e. First 20 years of psychology: no women allowed to contribute
f. Widespread belief in the so-called natural intellectual superiority of men
g. Currently: women = majority of psychology undergrad and grad students
h. History of psychology dominated by men
i. Myth of male superiority
     i.   derivative of variability hypothesis based on Darwinian ideas
    ii.   variability hypothesis: "The notion that men show a wider range and variation of physical and mental development than women; the abilities of women are seen as more average."
   iii.   therefore, it was argued, women
1. are less likely to benefit from education
2. are less likely to achieve intellectually
3. had less evolved brains than men
4. showed a smaller range of talents than men
5. are inferior to men physically and mentally
   iv.   common acceptance of functional inequality between sexes
j. Belief that exposure to education would damage women physically and emotionally
k. Helen Bradford Thompson Woolley and Leta Stetter Hollingworth: empirically demonstrated women not inferior
     i.   Helen Bradford Thompson Woolley (1874-1947)
1. parents supported educating women
2. University of Chicago
   a. 1897: undergraduate degree
   b. 1900: Ph.D.
   c. mentors = Angell and Dewey
   d. Dewey: she was one of his most brilliant students
3. married Paul Woolley, a physician
4. research on child labor
5. studied child development and mental abilities at Merrill-Palmer
6. Director of Institute of Child Welfare Research, Columbia University
7. doctoral dissertation: 1st experimental test of male superiority
   a. administered battery of motor, sensory, intellectual, and personality tests to males and females

        b.   found no sex difference in emotional functioning; nonsignificant differences in intellectual functioning

        c.   attributed any differences to social and environmental childrearing factors; different expectations for girls and boys

        d.   wrote results in a book

        e.   accused by male psychologists of feminist bias

        f.   retired prematurely because of bad health and a traumatic divorce

    ii. Leta Stetter Hollingworth (1886-1939)

       1.   University of Nebraska: graduated in 1906, Phi Beta Kappa

       2.   taught high school for 2 years

       3.   married psychologist Harry Hollingworth in 1908

       4.   Harry taught at Barnard College in New York; law prohibited married women to teach in public schools

       5.   wrote fiction; unable to publish

       6.   she and husband saved money for her to pursue graduate education

       7.   1916: PhD. from Columbia University

       8.   studied with Edward Thorndike

       9.   civil service psychology for New York City

      10.   cited in American Men of Science for contributions to the psychology of women

      11.   conducted extensive research on variability hypothesis

          a.   1913-16: focused on physical, sensorimotor and intellectual functioning of wide range of subjects

          b.   data refuted variability hypothesis and so-called female inferiority

      12.   challenged notion of innate motherhood instinct

      13.   supported women's work outside of marriage and family as healthy

      14.   social and cultural attitudes, not biology, responsible for keeping women behind men in contributions

      15.   women should not be restrict aspirations to socially acceptable fields

      16.   significant contributions to clinical, educational and school psychology

      17.   noted for work with "gifted children" (coined term)

      18.   never able to receive grant support for her research

      19.   active in woman's suffrage and rights movements

E. Granville Stanley Hall (1844-1924)

    a. Growth of psychology 1875-1900 due to Hall as well as James

    b. Large number of firsts

        i. received first American doctoral degree in psychology

       ii. started first psychology lab in U.S.

      iii. started first American psychology journal

      iv. first president of Clark University

       v. organized and was first president of APA

      vi. one of the first applied psychologists

    c. His life

        i. born on Massachusetts farm

       ii. mother pious and kind, father stern and demanding

iii. father hit Hall sometimes
iv. intensely ambitious boy
v. 1863 enters Williams College
    1. Graduated with honors
    2. Voted smartest man
    3. Developed enthusiasm for evolutionary theory
vi. after graduation, enrolls in seminary
    1. no strong commitment to the ministry
    2. interest in evolution not helpful
    3. Hall gives a trial sermon, seminary president prays for his soul
vii. leaves seminary, goes to Germany
    1. studies philosophy and theology
    2. later adds physiology and physics
    3. also goes to beer gardens and theaters, very daring for him
    4. he reports having romantic interludes
    5. passionate affairs "made life seem richer"
viii. returns to U.S. in 1871 (parents revoke support)
    1. has no degree
    2. is heavily in debt
ix. completes seminary studies
    1. is not ordained
    2. preaches in a country church
    3. leaves after 10 weeks
x. gets teaching job at Antioch College in Ohio
xi. reads Wundt's book Physiological Psychology (1874)
    1. becomes interested in psychology
    2. becomes uncertain of his career
xii. goes to Harvard, acts as tutor of English and takes graduate classes
xiii. gets first doctoral degree in psychology in the U.S. (1878)
xiv. leaves for Europe
    1. studies physiology in Berlin
    2. becomes Wundt's student
    3. lives next door to Fechner
    4. he dutifully attends Wundt's lectures and serves as research subject
    5. conducts his own physiological research
    6. Wundt has little influence on his later work
xv. Hall returns to U.S.
    1. no job
    2. within 10 years, becomes nationally important figure
xvi. decides to apply psychology to education
    1. 1882 : gives talk to National Educational Association, urging psychological study of children
    2. repeats this message whenever/wherever he can
    3. president of Harvard invites him for lecture series
        a. speeches brought him publicity
        b. speeches bring him invitation to teach part time at Johns Hopkins

FUNCTIONALISM: DEVELOPMENT AND FOUNDING

xvii. eventually offered a professorship at Johns Hopkins
1. 1883 establishes first American lab there, his "laboratory of psychophysiology"
2. teaches students who later become famous
   a. John Dewey
   b. James McKeen Cattell

xviii. 1887 Hall founds American Journal of Psychology
1. first American psych. journal
2. still considered important today
3. provides a platform for theory and experiment
4. Hall printed too many copies of first issue, takes him 5 years to pay back costs

xix. 1888 Hall becomes first president of Clark University
1. before takes job, takes a tour of Europe to "study"
2. one historian calls it a "paid vacation"
3. Hall hopes to model Clark on Johns Hopkins and German universities
4. emphasis on research, not teaching
5. Hall is both president and faculty member

xx. Hall establishes journal: Pedagogical Seminary (now Journal of Genetic Psychology)
1. outlet for child study
2. outlet for educational psychology

xxi. 1915 establishes Journal of Applied Psychology (the 16th American journal)

xxii. American Psychological Association
1. organized by Hall 1892
2. about 12 psychologists meet in his home
3. elect Hall first president
4. by 1900 had 127 members

xxiii. one of first American psychologists interested in Freud
1. largely responsible for early U.S. interest in Freud
2. 1909 20th anniversary of Clark
   a. Hall invites Freud and Jung
   b. courageous because psychoanalysis viewed with suspicion
3. initially invited Wundt, who declined
   a. too old
   b. scheduled to speak at Leipzig's 500th anniversary

xxiv. psychology prospers at Clark under Hall (36 years there)
1. 81 doctorates in psychology
2. students recall exhausting but exhilarating seminars in Hall's home
3. after meetings, all shared in tub of ice cream
4. Terman recalls that Hall's comments could be devastating
5. nurtured students well, as long as they were deferential
6. Hall was generous and supportive
7. at one time, the majority of American psychologists had worked with him at Clark or Johns Hopkins

        8. one third of his doctoral students followed him into college administration

    xxv. makes Clark receptive to women and minorities, despite his opposition to coeducation

        1. admitted female graduate students and faculty; opposed equal undergraduate education

        2. encouraged Japanese students to enroll

        3. refused to restrict hiring Jewish faculty

        4. encouraged Black graduate students

            a. first African American to earn Ph.D. was Cecil Sumner at Clark

                i. studied under Hall

                ii. later chairs psych department at Howard U.

                iii. creates strong psychology program at Howard

                iv. translates thousands of "articles from German, French, and Spanish journals"

    xxvi. Hall retires in 1920, continues to write

    xxvii. Hall dies four years later during second term as APA president

    xxviii. Hall admired by psychology colleagues

        1. survey of APA members: 99 out of 120 ranked him in top 10 psychologists

        2. teaching abilities praised

        3. ability to promote field

        4. defiance of orthodoxy

    xxix. personal characteristics

        1. "Difficult, untrustworthy, unscrupulous, devious, and aggressively self-promoting"

        2. James said Hall was mix of "bigness and pettiness"

d. Evolution and the recapitulation theory of development

    i. unitary theme to Hall's work: evolution

    ii. belief that growth of mind follows evolutionary stages

    iii. Hall often called genetic psychologist

        1. concern with human and animal development

        2. problems with adaptation

    iv. leads him to study of childhood

        1. calls for such study at 1892 world's fair speech

        2. intended to how child functions in real world

        3. child becomes "Hall's laboratory"

    v. uses questionnaires

        1. method learned in Germany

        2. he and students gave 194 covering wide variety of topics

        3. method became associated with Hall in America

        4. originated with Francis Galton

        5. early approaches generate enthusiasm, not much for results

            a. inadequate samples

            b. unsound questionnaires

            c. untrained data collectors

            d. poor analysis

      6. despite setbacks, child study movement picked up steam
- vi. Hall's influential book *Adolescence* (1904)
  1. two volumes, 1300 pages
  2. develops recapitulation theory: "children in their personal development repeat the life history of the human race"
  3. controversial because of excessive focus on sex
     a. Hall accused of having prurient interest
     b. Thorndike: Hall's book is "chock full of errors, masturbation, and Jesus"
     c. lectures on sex at Clark cancelled
- vii. at age 78 publishes *Senescence* (1922), first survey of old age issues
- viii. two autobiographies: *Recreations of a Psychologist* (1920) and *The Life and confessions of a Psychologists* (1923)

F. The Founding of Functionalism
  a. No formal founders, none interested in promotion of the school
  b. There were differences, but interested in studying functions of consciousness
  c. Formalized by Titchener
     i. 1898: "Postulates of a Structural Psychology"
        1. used "structural" as distinct from "functional"
        2. argued structuralism the only proper study for psychology

G. The Chicago School
  a. Central in the founding of functional psychology
  b. Dewey and Angell from the University of Chicago; James named the "Chicago school"

H. John Dewey (1859-1952)
  a. Life
     i. showed little intellectual promise until junior year at University of Vermont
     ii. taught high school, studied philosophy on his own, wrote scholarly articles
     iii. 1884: received Ph.D. from Johns Hopkins
     iv. progressive parenting: practiced nudity at home
  b. Career
     i. 1886: *Psychology* (first American textbook in psychology)
     ii. established a laboratory school
     iii. 1904: Columbia, to work on application of psychology to educational and philosophical problems
     iv. brilliant researcher, not a good teacher
  c. 1896: "The Reflex Arc Concept in Psychology"
     i. reflex arc= connection between sensory stimuli and motor responses
     ii. attacked molecularism, elementism, and reductionism of reflex arc
     iii. suggested reflex is a circle rather than an arc
     iv. behavior cannot be reduced to sensorimotor elements
     v. consciousness cannot be meaningfully analyzed into elements
     vi. artificial analysis removes all meaning, leaves a construct
     vii. behavior should be treated in terms of its significance to the organism as it functions in its environment
     viii. proper subject for psychology: study of the total organism as it functions in its environment
     ix. consciousness results in appropriate responses for survival
     x. functional psychology: study of the organism in use

   xi. argued structure and function cannot be meaningfully separated

   xii. influenced development of the philosophical framework for functionalism

I. James Rowland Angell (1869 –1949)

  a. Life

    i. academic family; father and grandfather both presidents of Universities

    ii. undergraduate work at Michigan, under Dewey

    iii. influenced by James's Principles of Psychology

    iv. 1892: Masters from Harvard, studied under James

    v. graduate studies in Halle; studied under Helmholtz and Ebbinghaus

    vi. never finished Ph.D. requirements because it was contingent on being re-written in German

    vii. accepted appointment at University of Minnesota to earn a living

    viii. one year later, went to University of Chicago for the next 25 years

  b. Career

    i. made functionalism into a working school

    ii. made the University of Chicago the most influential

    iii. at the University of Michigan, studied under Dewey, read James

    iv. worked with James for one year

    v. no PhD; 23 honorary degrees

    vi. president of Yale University; helped develop the Institute of Human Relations

    vii. served on the board of the National Broadcasting Company (NBC)

  c. The province of functional psychology

    i. *Psychology* (1904)

     1. function of consciousness: to improve the organism's adaptive abilities

     2. goal of psychology: to study how the mind assists the adjustment of the organism to its environment

    ii. 1906 APA presidential address: "The Province of Functional Psychology"

     1. drew the battle lines

     2. argued structural psychology was the aberration

    iii. identified three themes: functionalism is:

     1. the psychology of mental operations

      a. how a mental process operates

      b. what it accomplishes

      c. under what conditions it occurs

     2. the psychology of the fundamental utilities of consciousness

      a. mediates needs of organism and demands of the environment it has survived

      b. must be essential

      c. must identify how it serves

     3. the psychology of psychological relations

      a. no distinction between mind and body

      b. total relation of organism to its environment

      c. shaped functional psychology into prominent enterprise

    iv. gave functionalism necessary focus and stature

J. Harvey A. Carr (1873-1954)
  a. Career
      i. mathematics major, switched to psychology
      ii. first course in experimental psychology taught by Angell
      iii. lab assistant to J.B. Watson
      iv. introduced to animal psychology by Watson
      v. PhD at Chicago (1905)
      vi. chair at Chicago: 1919-1938; 150 PhDs conferred
      vii. eventually succeeded Angell as head of Department of Psychology of University of Chicago
K. Functionalism: The Final Form
  a. Peaked under Carr
      i. *the* American psychology
      ii. other viewpoints added nothing to psychology
      iii. Psychology (1925)
          1. the finished form of functionalism
          2. the subject matter is mental activity/processes, including memory, perception, feeling, imagination, judgment, will
          3. function of mental activity
              a. to acquire, fixate, retain, organize, and evaluate experiences
              b. to use these experiences to determine one's actions
          4. adaptive behavior: the specific form of action in which mental activities appear
      iv. was the mainstream
      v. accepted data from introspection and experiments
      vi. emphasis on objectivity
      vii. accepted both animal and human data
      viii. Carr believed study of cultural creations provided information about the mental activities that produced them (like Wundt's Völkerpsychologie)
      ix. Chicago school bridged move from study of subjective mind to study of objective behavior
L. Functionalism at Columbia University
  a. There was not a single form of functional psychology
  b. In addition to the major base of functionalism at University of Chicago, Robert Woodworth developed another approach at Columbia University
  c. Columbia also the academic home of two other functionally oriented psychologists
      i. Cattell (memory tests)
      ii. E. L. Thorndike (animal learning)
M. Robert Sessions Woodworth (1869-1962)
  a. Not a formal member of school of functionalism; would be too confining
  b. But his work reflected the functionalist spirit
  c. Added an important perspective
  d. Woodworth's life
      i. heard Hall and read James; had to become a psychologist
      ii. 1899: Ph.D. from Columbia with Cattell
      iii. taught physiology three years, studied with Sherrington for one
      iv. 1903-1945: Columbia (retired a second time in 1958)
          1. popular teacher
          2. taught large lectures until 2nd retirement at 89

3. Gardner Murphy deemed Woodworth the best teacher he ever had
    v. *Dynamic Psychology* (1918)
    vi. *Psychology* (1921) (best selling introductory text)
    vii. *Dynamics of Behavior (1958)*
    viii. *Experimental Psychology* (1938, 1954) deemed a classic
    ix. given APA's first Gold Medal Award

e. Dynamic psychology
    i. psychological knowledge
        1. begin with investigation of nature of the stimulus and the response (external, objective)
        2. most important part: the living organism
            a. stimulus not the single cause of a response
            b. organism also acts to determine the response
            c. "Psychology must consider the organism as interpolated between the stimulus and response."
    ii. subject matter: consciousness and behavior
    iii. introspection necessary to know what occurs inside the organism
    iv. observational and experimental methods also necessary
    v. dynamic psychology: "Woodworth's system of psychology; concerned with the causal factors and motivations in feelings and behavior."
        1. elaborated on Dewey and James
        2. dynamic psychology concerned with motivation
        3. Woodworth wanted to develop "motivology"
    vi. emphasized physiological events underlying behavior
    vii. focused on cause-and-effect relationships, drive, and motive
    viii. psychology's goal: determine why people behave as they do
    ix. viewpoint not a protest; was an extension, elaboration, synthesis

N. Criticisms of Functionalism
a. "Functionalism" not well defined
    i. an activity versus the use of an activity
    ii. Carr: the two definitions are not inconsistent
b. Titchener's structuralists: functionalism is not psychology
c. Applied aspects
    i. Carr: for both pure and applied psychology
        1. scientific rigor can occur in each
        2. valid research can be accomplished in each
        3. it is the method, not the subject matter, that counts
    ii. applied aspects: functionalism's legacy

O. Contributions of Functionalism
a. Opposition to structuralism
b. Legitimacy of research on animal behavior
c. Inclusion of humans other than "normal adults" as subjects
d. Development and inclusion of methods beyond introspection

Lecture prompts/Discussion topics for chapter seven

- Samuel Butler believed that machine evolution would eventually cause people to become so dependent on technology that the human race would not be able to survive without technology. What would happen today if technology suddenly went away. Is Butler correct?

- There is an interesting quote from the text: "Identical education of the sexes is a crime before God and humanity." This may seem unbelievably simple-minded, arrogant, and wrong-thinking to us today. How can we know, however, that our current ways of thinking about a variety of topics aren't suffering from the same arrogance?

- William James believed that clothing communicated much about the self. In what ways do the clothing on your campus communicate? What sorts of messages are communicated by professor clothing? student clothing? administrative staff?

Internet Resources for chapter seven

Herbert Spencer: Internet Encyclopedia of Philosophy
http://www.iep.utm.edu/s/spencer.htm
> This page gives a lot more detail about the life and work of Spencer.

William James
http://www.des.emory.edu/mfp/james.html
> This is an amazing collection of information relating to William James, including full text articles he wrote, photographs, links to other sites, and commentary on his life and work.

Human Intelligence: Leta Stetter Hollingworth
http://www.indiana.edu/~intell/lhollingworth.shtml
> Hollingworth's life and work, including references to interesting publications.

Leta Stetter Hollingworth
http://www.webster.edu/~woolflm/letahollingsworth.html
> More information about Hollingworth's life and work, including the connections between her work and the work of other intellectuals.

History of Clark University
http://www.clarku.edu/aboutclark/timeline/
> This is Clark University's history timeline, which puts much of Hall's early work in the context of his university presidency

The Clark University Archives re: G. Stanley Hall
http://www.clarku.edu/research/archives/hall/
> Information about the archive collection of materials relevant to G. Stanley Hall. The pages lead to a brief biography of Hall as well as a description of the archive contents.

Center for Dewey studies
http://www.siu.edu/~deweyctr/
> This is a very large website dedicated to the archived collection of materials relevant to John Dewey.

1. Describe Spencer's notion of social Darwinism.
Spencer, a British philosopher, argued that Darwin's theory of evolution applied to all aspects of the universe, including the mind and human behavior. His beliefs were widely accepted in the U.S. The term social Darwinism was coined to suggest that if society was left free and unrestricted by government sanctions then it would eventually evolve into a better society because the weaker companies and individuals would be allowed to perish.

2. Why was the United States so receptive to Spencer's ideas about social Darwinism?
The message of social Darwinism "was compatible with America's individualistic spirit, and the phrases 'survival of the fittest' and 'the struggle for existence' quickly became part of the national consciousness." In the "late nineteenth century...the United States was a living embodiment of Spencer's ideas."

3. Who extended Darwin's ideas on evolution to machines? Describe this person's position on mechanical evolution.
Samuel Butler wondered if machines could evolve to a higher form as animals do, and wrote that he believed such evolution was already happening for machines. He also believed that one day machines would simulate human thought.

4. Why was the type of calculating machine developed by Babbage in the mid-nineteenth century no longer appropriate by the end of that century?
Babbage's system was not efficient for processing information, especially in large quantities. Computing the 1880 census by hand took over seven years, and officials realized that the next census would take longer than 10 years to compute using the same methods. Henry Hollerith developed punch-card processing in order to compute the 1890 census, which astonished Americans. The new system was fast, efficient, and drastically reduced the cost of census taking compared to the manual approach.

5. Describe Hollerith's approach to processing information by machine.
Henry Hollerith developed punch-card processing in order to compute the 1890 census, which astonished Americans because of the computational power.

6. What is neurasthenia? What segment of nineteenth-century American society was most likely to be afflicted with neurasthenia?
Neurasthenia appears to be neurotic in origin, and affected wealthy Americans. Symptoms included "insomnia, hypochondria, headache, skin rash, nervous exhaustion, and something called brain collapse."

7. How did the prescribed cures for neurasthenia differ for men and for women?
Women were told to "spend 6 weeks or more in bed without any work, reading, or social life, and to gain large amounts of weight on a high-fat diet." Men were told to engage in "travel, adventure, [and] vigorous physical exercise."

8. Why was James considered to be the most important American psychologist? Describe his attitude toward laboratory work.

He published *The Principles of Psychology* in 1890, which became one of the most influential books in psychology. In it "James presents what eventually became the central tenet of American functionalism—that the goal of psychology is…the study of living people as they adapt to their environment." He detested doing laboratory work, but seemed to respect its results.

9. How did James's view of consciousness differ from Wundt's view? According to James, what was the purpose of consciousness?

He sees conscious experience as "a continuous flow" that is ever-changing and coins the phrase "stream of consciousness" to describe this. He asserts that consciousness must be studied in a more natural setting, with consideration to the relationship between physical states and the mind. This is in direct opposition to Wundt's and Titchener's elementalism and their approach to reduce conscious experience into elements.

10. What methods did James consider appropriate for the study of consciousness? What was the value of pragmatism for the new psychology?

Despite his differences with Wundt and Titchener, James did espouse introspection as a method for psychology, but he also advocated experimental methods as well as the use of a wide variety of research subjects (i.e., children, animals, disturbed). He believed that psychology should be pragmatic (have practical application).

11. According to James, what are the components of a person's sense of self? What role does clothing seem to play in our sense of self, in James's view?

He developed a theory of personality whereby the self is made up of the material ("our body, family, home, or style of dress"), the social ("recognition we get from others"), and the spiritual (the "inner subjective being"). James thought that what one chooses to wear is very important, in that clothes communicate much about how we see ourselves. Clothes also reflect all three aspects of the self, in that they are telling about social influences.

12. Describe the variability hypothesis and its influence on the idea of male superiority. How did research by Woolley and Hollingworth refute these ideas?

The variability hypothesis was the belief that males are more variable in physical and mental characteristics than females, with females clustered close to the mean. This leads to the conclusion that there are far fewer women of superior intelligence compared to men, and the belief that educating women would cause them physical and emotional damage and decrease "the maternal urge." Woolley and Hollingworth empirically tested the hypothesis, and found no support for the hypothesis. In contrast, they both found they there was little difference between men and women on measures of physical acuity and mental intelligence, except for slight (yet insignificant) differences produced by limited education of women and differential child-rearing practices.

13. How was the work of G. Stanley Hall influenced by Darwin's evolutionary theory? Describe Hall's recapitulation theory of development.

Hall incorporated evolution into his system of psychology, which focused on childhood. To do his research Hall used the questionnaire technique, which was new to American psychology (it had originated with Galton). His most influential work is *Adolescence* (1904) in which he elaborates on his recapitulation theory. This is the idea that "children in their personal development repeat the life history of the human race." This same idea was espoused by Darwin's early works, especially the journal *Mind*, which describes the developmental milestones of his son.

14. What "firsts" in American psychology can be attributed to Hall? Why was he called a genetic psychologist?

He earned the first Ph.D. in psychology in the U.S., founded the first psychology laboratory in the U.S. at Johns Hopkins, "In 1887, Hall founded the American Journal of Psychology," in "the following year, Hall became the first president of Clark University in Worcester, Massachusetts" and the first president of the APA in 1892. "Hall is often called a genetic psychologist because of his concern with human and animal development and the related problems of adaptation."

15. In what ways did Titchener and Dewey contribute to the founding of functional psychology? Why was there no single form of functionalism as there was a single structuralism?

Functionalism was not purposefully founded by its proponents; none were interested in the promotion and development of a school of thought. Instead, they shared a common vision to study "the functions of consciousness." Titchener may have inadvertently formalized the school when he wrote an article articulating the differences between what he called structuralism and functionalism. Dewey published "The Reflex Arc Concept in Psychology", which became popular and influential. In the article, "Dewey attacked the psychological molecularism, elementism, and reductionism of the reflex arc." He argues that the reflex of a child reaching for and being burned by a flame cannot be reduced to elements, because the child's interpretation of the flame changes with the interaction. "Dewey concluded that the proper subject matter for psychology had to be the study of the total organism as it functions in its environment." There was no single form to functionalism because the functions of organisms are so multifaceted, whereas structuralism reduced consciousness to basic elements and was better able to identify the components they were interested in studying.

16. According to Angell, what were functionalism's three major themes? What research methods did Carr consider appropriate for functional psychology?

In his 1906 address as the new APA president, he outlines functionalism as: 1) "the psychology of mental functions", 2) determining the "utilities of consciousness", and 3) the declaration of "no real distinction between mind and body." Carr believed both introspection and experimentation to be appropriate methods for psychology.

17. Describe Woodworth's dynamic psychology and his views on introspection. Did Woodworth consider himself to be a functional psychologist? Why or why not?

Woodworth introduced what he called dynamic psychology, which focused on the motivations and physiology which cause behavior. He did not consider himself to be a functionalist because "he disliked the constraints imposed by membership in any school of thought."

18. Compare functionalism's contributions to psychology with the contributions of structuralism.

Although there is no modern-day school of functionalism, its imprint can be seen in contemporary psychological thought: inclusion of animals as well as "infants, children, and people with mental disabilities" as research subjects, a broadening of accepted research methods, and the application of psychology to solve real-life problems. It is difficult to see the imprint of structuralism on modern-day psychology beyond the experimental methods practiced by the structuralists as well as their predecessors.

19. Why did applied psychology develop under functionalism and not under structuralism?
"The structuralists disdained any application of psychological knowledge to real-world problems, whereas the functionalists had no stake in maintaining psychology as a pure science and never apologized for their practical interests." In addition, the Zeitgeist of the United States was ready to accept functionalism as the dominant school of thought. Thus, the advocates of functionalism were able to thrive.

Key terms from chapter seven

- **Chicago school** The nickname for Functionalism, so named because so much of functionalism was shaped by individuals at or from the University of Chicago.
- **Dynamic psychology** Introduced by Robert Sessions Woodworth, it focused on the motivations and physiology which cause behavior.
- **Habit** Defined by James and includes physiological influences on behavior.
- **Neurasthenia** A pandemic of neurotic symptoms that afflicted the wealthy and well educated in the late 1800's.
- **Pragmatism** The idea, supported by James, that "the validity of ideas is measured by their practical consequences."
- **The Principles of Psychology** Probably the one book that influenced most the direction of early psychology and inspired many American psychologists, published by William James in 1890.
- **Recapitulation theory** G. Stanley Hall's idea that "children in their personal development repeat the life history of the human race."
- **Reflex arc** "The connection between sensory stimuli and motor responses," and discussed in Dewey's article that criticizes structuralism.
- **Self** James' conception of self is made up of 1) the material ("our body, family, home, or style of dress"), 2) the social ("recognition we get from others"), and 3) the spiritual (the "inner subjective being").
- **Social Darwinism** The belief, created by Herbert Spencer, that Darwin's theory of evolution applied to all aspects of the universe, including the mind and human behavior.
- **Stream of consciousness** "James' idea that consciousness is a continuous flowing process and any attempt to reduce it to elements will distort it.
- **Survival of the fittest** Phrase associated with Darwin's theory of evolution, coined by Herbert Spencer.
- **Synthetic philosophy** "Spencer's idea that knowledge and experience can be explained in terms of evolutionary principles."
- **Variability hypothesis** "The notion that men show a wider range and variation of physical and mental development than women."

ESSAY

1. Describe Spencer's adaptations and extensions of the theory of evolution. Why was his philosophy, particularly his concept of social Darwinism, so popular in the United States?

    ANS:
    Answer not provided.

    PTS: 1

2. According to Schultz and Schultz, "Much is paradoxical about William James and his role in American psychology." Discuss this paradox, describing the arguments for and against viewing James as one of psychology's most important figures.

    ANS:
    Answer not provided.

    PTS: 1   MSC: WWW

3. Describe James's early life and his days as a student. What are the symptoms of neurasthenia and what was the "epidemic of neurasthenia" in the United States? Why are these relevant to a discussion of James's life?

    ANS:
    Answer not provided.

    PTS: 1

4. Describe and compare James's new look at consciousness with the views of Wundt.

    ANS:
    Answer not provided.

    PTS: 1

5. What is the major theme or central thesis of the Original Source Material on Consciousness from *Psychology (Briefer Course)* (1892) by William James? What arguments does he use to support his thesis?

    ANS:
    Answer not provided.

    PTS: 1

6. Describe James's approach to methodology. What methods of studying consciousness did he find appropriate? What are the possible relationships between James's views of methods and his philosophy of pragmatism?

    ANS:
    Answer not provided.

    PTS: 1

7. Describe the variability hypothesis, its influence on the notion of male superiority, and the research of Woolley and Hollingworth in refuting this position.

    ANS:
    Answer not provided.

    PTS: 1

8. What achievements are noteworthy in G. Stanley Hall's life? Describe his work in developmental psychology, including his theory of psychological development.

    ANS:
    Answer not provided.

    PTS: 1

9. Describe the founding of functionalism. In what ways was its founding different from that of Titchener's structuralism? What were the contributions of Titchener and Dewey to functionalism as an emerging school of thought?

    ANS:
    Answer not provided.

    PTS: 1

10. What did Angell consider to be the three major themes of functionalism? What were Carr's major points? Distinguish between Angell's and Carr's contributions to psychology.

    ANS:
    Answer not provided.

    PTS: 1   MSC: WWW

11. Describe at least three contributions of Robert Sessions Woodworth to psychology.

    ANS:
    Answer not provided.

    PTS: 1

12. Discuss the several ways in which functionalism expanded the field and/or practice of psychology.

    ANS:
    Answer not provided.

    PTS: 1

13. Defend the proposition that functionalism was a transitory bridge from the study of the subjective mind and consciousness to the objective study of overt behavior.

    ANS:
    Answer not provided.

    PTS: 1

14. Who did Darwin call "our philosopher"?
    a. Spencer
    b. James
    c. Dewey
    d. Hollerith
    e. Cattell

    ANS: A   PTS: 1   REF: Evolution's Neurotic Philosopher
    MSC: WWW

15. Perhaps the most important factor that enabled functionalist psychology to flourish in the United States was the ____.
    a. social Zeitgeist
    b. political Zeitgeist
    c. economic Zeitgeist
    d. American temperament as a whole
    e. fruition of Darwin's theory in the United States

    ANS: D   PTS: 1
    REF: Evolution Comes to America: Herbert Spencer (1820-1903)

16. Spencer's philosophy was ____.
    a. Darwinism
    b. natural selection
    c. survival of the fittest
    d. eugenics
    e. pragmatism

    ANS: A   PTS: 1
    REF: Evolution Comes to America: Herbert Spencer (1820-1903)

17. Who coined the phrase "survival of the fittest"?
    a. James
    b. Galton
    c. Dewey
    d. Spencer
    e. Darwin

    ANS: D   PTS: 1
    REF: Evolution Comes to America: Herbert Spencer (1820-1903)

18. Who originated the idea of social Darwinism?
    a. James
    b. Darwin
    c. Spencer
    d. Galton
    e. Hollerith

    ANS: C   PTS: 1
    REF: Evolution Comes to America: Herbert Spencer (1820-1903)

19. According to Spencer, the universe operates in accord with ____.
    a. mathematical principles
    b. what we call "chaos theory"
    c. principles of pragmatism
    d. principles of functionalism
    e. the principle of the survival of the fittest

    ANS: E   PTS: 1
    REF: Evolution Comes to America: Herbert Spencer (1820-1903)

20. Which of the following statements is <u>NOT</u> part of social Darwinism?
    a. Nations of the world are in competition for survival analogous to competition among species for survival.
    b. Governments should not try to restrict the activities of business.
    c. Governments should not impede the rich by heavy taxes because the rich are needed for economic growth.
    d. Each nation should have a social welfare program that supports the poor.
    e. All of the choices are a part of social Darwinism.

    ANS: D   PTS: 1
    REF: Evolution Comes to America: Herbert Spencer (1820-1903)

21. The most appealing aspect of Spencer's philosophy for Americans was the notion of ____.
    a. evolution of the human character
    b. evolution of social institutions
    c. natural selection
    d. survival of the fittest
    e. pragmatism

    ANS: D   PTS: 1
    REF: Evolution Comes to America: Herbert Spencer (1820-1903)

22. Spencer developed synthetic philosophy, which was an attempt to ____.
    a. bring together the works of Darwin and Wundt to form a new school of psychology
    b. ban the use of animal experimentation in psychology
    c. use evolutionary theory as a way to understand any process that undergoes change and development
    d. argue that consciousness had no use since it did not aid survival. therefore, psychology should give up the study of consciousness
    e. introduce the idea that evolution should be guided by governmental programs to "synthetically" direct evolution in a particular direction

    ANS: C   PTS: 1
    REF: Evolution Comes to America: Herbert Spencer (1820-1903)

23. Synthetic as used in the name "synthetic philosophy" refers to ____.
    a. the artificial nature of the physical universe
    b. unnatural circumstances
    c. the superiority of polyester over cotton
    d. combining or synthesizing
    e. the artificial nature of the physical universe and unnatural circumstances

    ANS: D   PTS: 1
    REF: Evolution Comes to America: Herbert Spencer (1820-1903)

24. Who was the earliest to argue that the mind exists in its present form because of past and present efforts to adapt to various environments?
    a. Spencer
    b. James
    c. Darwin
    d. Hollerith
    e. Dewey

    ANS: A   PTS: 1
    REF: Evolution Comes to America: Herbert Spencer (1820-1903)

25. Spencer's (1855) *The Principles of Psychology* was based on ____.
    a. the work of the British empiricists
    b. James's pragmatic philosophy
    c. Darwin's theory of the evolution of nonhuman species
    d. his synthetic philosophy
    e. Galton's work

    ANS: D   PTS: 1
    REF: Evolution Comes to America: Herbert Spencer (1820-1903)

26. The first person who applied evolution to machines was ____.
    a. Butler
    b. Hollerith
    c. James
    d. Spencer
    e. Babbage

    ANS: A   PTS: 1   REF: The Continuing Evolution of Machines

27. Who pioneered an innovative method of information processing?
    a. Spencer
    b. Hollerith
    c. Dewey
    d. Babbage
    e. James

    ANS: B   PTS: 1   REF: The Continuing Evolution of Machines

28. The fear in the 1960s that we would all be reduced to punched cards may not have happened without the work of ____.
    a. Babbage
    b. Hollerith
    c. Hollingworth
    d. Lovelace
    e. James

    ANS: B   PTS: 1   REF: The Continuing Evolution of Machines

29. Who had an interest in mystical events or what we call parapsychology?
    a. Hollerith
    b. James
    c. Dewey
    d. Hollingworth
    e. Spencer

    ANS: B   PTS: 1
    REF: William James (1842-1910): Anticipator of Functional Psychology

30. The major antecedent of functionalism in the United States was the work of ____.
    a. Titchener
    b. Pierce
    c. Galton
    d. Jung
    e. James

    ANS: E   PTS: 1
    REF: William James (1842-1910): Anticipator of Functional Psychology

31. James was vocally criticized by other early psychologists because he ____.
    a. criticized the use of the experimental method
    b. loathed laboratory work and refused to do it
    c. hired Münsterberg, thus imposing Wundt's psychology and its limitations on the new American psychology
    d. was a "gentleman scientist" rather than a traditional academic
    e. studied psychic phenomena and moved away from scientific psychology

    ANS: E   PTS: 1
    REF: William James (1842-1910): Anticipator of Functional Psychology
    MSC: WWW

32. "That nasty little science" was James's label for ____.
    a. medicine
    b. physiology
    c. psychology
    d. phenomenology
    e. structuralism

    ANS: C   PTS: 1
    REF: William James (1842-1910): Anticipator of Functional Psychology

33. "An elaboration of the obvious" was James's description of ____.
    a. structuralist
    b. the introspective method
    c. functionalism
    d. psychoanalysis
    e. psychology

    ANS: E   PTS: 1
    REF: William James (1842-1910): Anticipator of Functional Psychology

34. This person was born into a wealthy American family. He eventually received a medical degree and taught psychology at Harvard University.
    a. John Dewey
    b. James Angell
    c. Edward Bradford Titchener
    d. Herbert Spencer
    e. William James

    ANS: E   PTS: 1
    REF: William James (1842-1910): Anticipator of Functional Psychology

35. James became familiar with the work of Wundt ____.
    a. because of Titchener establishing a psychology department at Cornell University
    b. because of Spencer's *The Principles of Psychology*
    c. in the late 1860s, before Wundt founded the Leipzig psychology laboratory
    d. as a result of using Fechner's books for his first lectures in psychology in 1890
    e. as a result of his first teaching position at Harvard, in physiology

    ANS: C   PTS: 1
    REF: William James (1842-1910): Anticipator of Functional Psychology

36. While today people might suffer from chronic fatigue syndrome, in James's day a very fashionable disorder to suffer from was ____.
    a. syphilis
    b. neurasthenia
    c. suicidal depression
    d. opium or heroin addiction
    e. phrenology

    ANS: B   PTS: 1
    REF: William James (1842-1910): Anticipator of Functional Psychology

37. James's term for his debilitating disorder was ____.
    a. neurasthenia
    b. neuritis
    c. Americanitis
    d. psychitis
    e. neurasthenitis

    ANS: C   PTS: 1
    REF: William James (1842-1910): Anticipator of Functional Psychology

38. James's position on determinism versus free will can be characterized by which of the following?
    a. Free will is an illusion to me.
    b. My first act of free will shall be to believe in free will.
    c. This ego is not master of its fate.
    d. We are slaves to our biology.
    e. If one believes in free will, one is free to so believe.

    ANS: B   PTS: 1
    REF: William James (1842-1910): Anticipator of Functional Psychology

39. James believed that his bout of depression was relieved when he ____.
    a. stopped believing in free will and accepted determinism
    b. chose to believe in free will
    c. completed *The Varieties of Religious Experiences*
    d. talked to the dead in séances
    e. got married

    ANS: B   PTS: 1
    REF: William James (1842-1910): Anticipator of Functional Psychology

40. James's experiments with mind-altering chemicals interested him because they ____.
    a. relieved his neurasthenia
    b. cured him of depression
    c. allowed him a form of escape from reality
    d. fascinated him because of the way bodily changes influenced consciousness
    e. felt good and relieved his symptoms

    ANS: D   PTS: 1
    REF: William James (1842-1910): Anticipator of Functional Psychology

41. The lecturer in James's first course in psychology was ____.
    a. Münsterberg
    b. Wundt
    c. James
    d. Titchener
    e. Cattell

    ANS: C   PTS: 1
    REF: William James (1842-1910): Anticipator of Functional Psychology

42. Although it took twelve years to complete, ____'s great book on psychology represented a commitment to evolutionary principles and a rejection of Wundt's approach to psychology.
    a. John Dewey
    b. Herbert Spencer
    c. Edward Bradford Titchener
    d. James Angell
    e. William James

    ANS: E   PTS: 1
    REF: William James (1842-1910): Anticipator of Functional Psychology
    MSC: WWW

43. James described the manuscript of his book, *The Principles of Psychology*, as testimony to the fact that ____.
    a. Wundt's experimentation was the sole method to be used in the new science
    b. structuralism's focus on the elements of consciousness needed to be the focus of functionalism
    c. religious experiences were inseparable from psychological experiences
    d. religious experiences might be studied with experimental introspection
    e. a "science of psychology" did not exist

    ANS: E   PTS: 1
    REF: William James (1842-1910): Anticipator of Functional Psychology

44. ____ is often called America's greatest philosopher.
    a. John Dewey
    b. Herbert Spencer
    c. Edward Bradford Titchener
    d. William James
    e. James Angell

    ANS: D   PTS: 1
    REF: William James (1842-1910): Anticipator of Functional Psychology

45. Educational psychology as a discipline began with the work of ____.
    a. Cattell
    b. James
    c. Binet
    d. Thorndike
    e. Dewey

    ANS: B   PTS: 1
    REF: William James (1842-1910): Anticipator of Functional Psychology

46. "The study of living people as they adapt to their environment" is the central tenet of ____.
    a. Darwin's theory of the evolution of humans and their emotional expressions
    b. Spencer's systematic philosophy
    c. James's philosophy of pragmatism
    d. James's psychology
    e. Butler's evolution theory

    ANS: D   PTS: 1
    REF: William James (1842-1910): Anticipator of Functional Psychology

47. William James ____.
    a. founded functional psychology
    b. established an environment favorable for functionalism with his *Principles of Psychology*
    c. wrested psychology away from synthetic philosophy
    d. used pragmatism to recombine psychology and philosophy
    e. effectively nullified the influence of Wundt on American psychologists

    ANS: B   PTS: 1
    REF: William James (1842-1910): Anticipator of Functional Psychology

48. For James, what was most essential to human evolution?
    a. natural selection
    b. natural variations of a species
    c. survival of the fittest
    d. regression to the mean
    e. consciousness

    ANS: E   PTS: 1
    REF: William James (1842-1910): Anticipator of Functional Psychology

49. For James, the "conditions" of mental life are the influences of ____.
    a. consciousness
    b. the body
    c. the central nervous system
    d. the irrational
    e. the environment we have adapted to

    ANS: B   PTS: 1
    REF: William James (1842-1910): Anticipator of Functional Psychology

50. The idea of "objective experience" would be ____.
    a. consistent with James's position
    b. contrary to James's position
    c. congruent with the idea of immediate experience
    d. consistent with James's definition of consciousness
    e. consistent with James's synthetic philosophy

    ANS: B   PTS: 1
    REF: William James (1842-1910): Anticipator of Functional Psychology

51. The notion of analysis of consciousness is, in James's view, the ____.
    a. psychologists' fallacy
    b. strength of experimentation
    c. difference between immediate and mediate experience
    d. basic difference between structuralism and functionalism
    e. difference between religion and spirituality

    ANS: A   PTS: 1
    REF: William James (1842-1910): Anticipator of Functional Psychology

52. William James used the term "stream of consciousness" to indicate ____.
    a. that the analysis of consciousness into mental elements is difficult but possible
    b. that the use of introspection to study consciousness is possible
    c. that consciousness is not as important as the unconscious in controlling behavior since consciousness is always changing
    d. that the changing nature of consciousness prevents its analysis into mental elements
    e. that unconscious thoughts can be accessed through free association

    ANS: D   PTS: 1
    REF: William James (1842-1910): Anticipator of Functional Psychology
    MSC: WWW

53. For James, one's stream of consciousness ____.
    a. can be reduced to sensations by introspection
    b. can be reduced to components by experimental methods without introspection
    c. is distorted when analyzed into distinct elements
    d. reflects the continuous movement of material from nonconscious to conscious
    e. reflects the continuous synthesis of elements through the principles of association

    ANS: C   PTS: 1
    REF: William James (1842-1910): Anticipator of Functional Psychology

54. In the Original Source Material on Consciousness from *Psychology (Briefer Course)* (1892) James said, "*Consciousness is in constant ____.*"
    a. motion
    b. evolution
    c. jeopardy
    d. agitation
    e. change

    ANS: E   PTS: 1
    REF: William James (1842-1910): Anticipator of Functional Psychology

55. For James, choice and habit are different in that ____.
    a. choice is a fallacy, and habit is real
    b. habit is a fallacy, and choice is real
    c. habit is nonconscious
    d. the purpose of habit is human adaptation to the environment
    e. choice is antithetical to pragmatism

    ANS: C   PTS: 1
    REF: William James (1842-1910): Anticipator of Functional Psychology

56. James's position on Wundt's methodology was to ____.
    a. accept both introspection and experimentation
    b. accept introspection but reject experimentation
    c. reject introspection but accept experimentation
    d. reject both introspection and experimentation
    e. replace both with the comparative method

    ANS: A   PTS: 1
    REF: William James (1842-1910): Anticipator of Functional Psychology

57. James's position on psychophysics was to ____.
    a. reject it because it is a field of physiology, not psychology
    b. reject Fechner's methods
    c. reject Weber's Law and Fechner's Law
    d. accept it as a component of psychology to be studied by experimentation
    e. incorporate it into his subsequent research on phenomena such as séances

    ANS: D   PTS: 1
    REF: William James (1842-1910): Anticipator of Functional Psychology

58. James recommended the ____ method to supplement introspection and experimentation.
    a. Wundtian
    b. observational
    c. cumulative
    d. comparative
    e. structural

    ANS: D   PTS: 1
    REF: William James (1842-1910): Anticipator of Functional Psychology

59. The basic tenet of ____ is that the validity of an idea or conception must be tested by its practical consequences.
    a. empiricism
    b. rationalism
    c. scientism
    d. pragmatism
    e. cynicism

ANS: D   PTS: 1
REF: William James (1842-1910): Anticipator of Functional Psychology

60. Peirce's role in American psychology was to ____.
    a. act as a sounding board for Herbert Spencer
    b. introduce the new psychology of Fechner and Wundt to U.S. scholars
    c. found functionalism
    d. posit synthetic philosophy
    e. synthesize pragmatism and evolutionary theory

ANS: B   PTS: 1
REF: William James (1842-1910): Anticipator of Functional Psychology

61. According to James, the value or worth of beliefs can be evaluated in terms of ____.
    a. the spiritual basis for a belief
    b. the habitual nature of a belief
    c. whether it works or not
    d. its adaptive value
    e. its effect on emotions

ANS: C   PTS: 1
REF: William James (1842-1910): Anticipator of Functional Psychology

62. Which of the following statement expresses the James-Lange theory of emotions?
    a. Emotion results from the activation of certain neural centers in the brain.
    b. Emotion results from how an individual perceives a situation, with or without physiological arousal.
    c. Emotion is completely a psychological state. There are no physiological equivalents to the emotions.
    d. Physiological arousal precedes the experience of an emotion.
    e. The emotion is experienced first, which is followed by physiological arousal.

ANS: D   PTS: 1
REF: William James (1842-1910): Anticipator of Functional Psychology

63. James believed that a person has three components that make up their self. Which of the following elements were included in James's theory of self?
    a. feelings, actions, and conscious experience
    b. feelings, free will, and actions
    c. materials, social, and actions
    d. spiritual, material, and conscious experience
    e. materials, social, and spiritual

ANS: E   PTS: 1
REF: William James (1842-1910): Anticipator of Functional Psychology

64. James's description of habit indicates that it is ____.
   a. a repetitive action
   b. a component of the preconscious
   c. an intervening variable
   d. evidence of latent learning
   e. a classically conditioned response

   ANS: A   PTS: 1
   REF: William James (1842-1910): Anticipator of Functional Psychology

65. For James, ____ "is what keeps us all within the bounds of ordinance."
   a. consciousness
   b. emotions
   c. learning
   d. habit
   e. religion

   ANS: D   PTS: 1
   REF: William James (1842-1910): Anticipator of Functional Psychology

66. James argued that habitual actions would ____ the plasticity of ____.
   a. increase; character
   b. decrease; character
   c. increase; neural matter
   d. decrease; neural matter
   e. increase; habits

   ANS: C   PTS: 1
   REF: William James (1842-1910): Anticipator of Functional Psychology

67. Whose Ph.D. work was described as the "most brilliant examination for the PhD that we have ever had at Harvard"?
   a. Woolley
   b. Calkins
   c. Hollingworth
   d. Dewey
   e. Washburn

   ANS: B   PTS: 1   REF: The Functional Inequality of Women

68. In contemporary measures of memory, a common task is to assess one's learning of paired associates. This technique was developed by ____.
   a. Titchener
   b. James
   c. Calkins
   d. Dewey
   e. Woolley

   ANS: C   PTS: 1   REF: The Functional Inequality of Women
   MSC: WWW

69. The "myth of male intellectual superiority" is derived from which of Darwin's ideas?
    a. natural selection
    b. variability hypothesis
    c. the survival of the fittest
    d. sexual selection
    e. emotional expression

    ANS: B   PTS: 1   REF: The Functional Inequality of Women

70. The idea that men show a wider range of variations in physical and mental development than women and that the abilities of women are more clustered about the average is a definition of the ____.
    a. selection variability hypothesis
    b. variability hypothesis
    c. sexual selection hypothesis
    d. male superiority hypothesis
    e. female evolution hypothesis

    ANS: B   PTS: 1   REF: The Functional Inequality of Women

71. Early 20th-century research on the effects of child labor was conducted by ____.
    a. Calkins
    b. Woolley
    c. Hollingworth
    d. Anastasi
    e. Radcliffe

    ANS: B   PTS: 1   REF: The Functional Inequality of Women

72. Woolley's research on sex differences and alleged male superiority was ____.
    a. refuted by contemporary research
    b. the first experimental test of the variability hypothesis of male superiority
    c. supported by contemporary research
    d. attributed to genetic differences
    e. challenged by the "men's issues" movement

    ANS: B   PTS: 1   REF: The Functional Inequality of Women

73. Consistent with contemporary research on sex differences, Woolley found that ____.
    a. there were no sex differences in mental intelligence
    b. men are more prone than women to anger and violence
    c. men are more susceptible to sexually provocative material
    d. women are more susceptible than men to depression and histrionic psychosis
    e. men are more prone than women to anger and violence and women are more susceptible than men to depression and histrionic psychosis

    ANS: A   PTS: 1   REF: The Functional Inequality of Women

74. A unique aspect of Woolley's dissertation research was the ____.
    a. inclusion of faculty women in her sample
    b. attribution of sex differences to genetic factors
    c. attribution of sex differences to social and environmental factors
    d. inclusion of women faculty on her dissertation committee
    e. endorsement of G. Stanley Hall

    ANS: C   PTS: 1   REF: The Functional Inequality of Women

75. The results of Woolley's sex differences research were attributed by some to _____.
   a. her skills as a researcher
   b. the fact that she was a woman and therefore biased in interpreting her results
   c. poor methodology
   d. the influence of her professors, Dewey and Angell
   e. the fact that she was a woman and therefore not as intelligent as men

   ANS: B   PTS: 1   REF: The Functional Inequality of Women

76. Hollingworth's research refuted _____.
   a. the variability hypothesis
   b. Woolley's finding that women are more emotional and less rational during menses
   c. the belief that "maternal behaviors" decline during menses
   d. Fechner's Law
   e. None of the choices are correct.

   ANS: A   PTS: 1   REF: The Functional Inequality of Women
   MSC: WWW

77. The notion of a "motherhood instinct" was _____.
   a. supported by Woolley's research
   b. refuted by Woolley's research
   c. supported by Hollingworth's research
   d. refuted by Hollingworth's research
   e. supported by Woolley's research on the maternal behaviors displayed by mothers of gifted children

   ANS: D   PTS: 1   REF: The Functional Inequality of Women

78. The term *gifted children* was coined by _____.
   a. Woolley
   b. Calkins
   c. Hollingworth
   d. Galton
   e. Binet

   ANS: C   PTS: 1   REF: The Functional Inequality of Women

79. The first American Ph.D. in psychology was earned by _____.
   a. Titchener
   b. James
   c. Hall
   d. Cattell
   e. Yerkes

   ANS: C   PTS: 1   REF: Granville Stanley Hall (1844-1924)

80. What is often considered to be the first psychology laboratory in the United States was established by _____.
   a. Titchener
   b. James
   c. Cattell
   d. Angell
   e. Hall

   ANS: E   PTS: 1   REF: Granville Stanley Hall (1844-1924)

81. Hall may be the best representative of the earliest roots of modern psychology in that his education included ____.
   a. philosophy
   b. physiology
   c. physics
   d. All of the choices are correct.
   e. None of the choices are correct.

   ANS: D   PTS: 1   REF: Granville Stanley Hall (1844-1924)

82. Who said, "I think I must have been hypnotized by the word 'evolution,' which was music to my ear?"
   a. Cattell
   b. Hall
   c. Yerkes
   d. Witmer
   e. Münsterberg

   ANS: B   PTS: 1   REF: Granville Stanley Hall (1844-1924)

83. Hall's interest in the new science of psychology was aroused when he ____.
   a. read Wundt's *Physiological Psychology*
   b. attended James's lectures in psychology at Harvard
   c. read James's *Principles of Psychology*
   d. read Spencer's *Principles of Psychology*
   e. read Angell's "The Province of Functional Psychology"

   ANS: A   PTS: 1   REF: Granville Stanley Hall (1844-1924)

84. Who was one of the most outspoken critics of Woolley and Hollingworth?
   a. J.M. Catell
   b. John Dewey
   c. G.S. Hall
   d. Harry Hollingworth
   e. M.W. Calkins

   ANS: C   PTS: 1   REF: The Functional Inequality of Women

85. ____ was one major area that G.S. Hall was interested in, as evidenced by his research in his doctoral dissertation.

   a. Introspection of tones
   b. Touch thresholds
   c. Space perception
   d. Gender roles
   e. Adult physiology

   ANS: C   PTS: 1   REF: Granville Stanley Hall (1844-1924)

86. Hall referred to his laboratory as a ____.
   a. laboratory of evolution
   b. laboratory of psychophysics
   c. laboratory of psychophysiology
   d. laboratory of mental evolution
   e. center for the study of children

   ANS: C   PTS: 1   REF: Granville Stanley Hall (1844-1924)

87. Hall's *Pedagogical Seminary* reflected his early interest in _____.
    a. evolutionary theory
    b. eugenics
    c. child development
    d. heritability
    e. physiological psychology

ANS: C   PTS: 1   REF: Granville Stanley Hall (1844-1924)
MSC: WWW

88. Hall had an interest in _____.
    a. psychic phenomena
    b. music and tones
    c. religion
    d. emotions
    e. the education of women

ANS: C   PTS: 1   REF: Granville Stanley Hall (1844-1924)

89. _____ has been described as "difficult, untrustworthy, unscrupulous, devious, and aggressively self-promoting."
    a. Hall
    b. Cattell
    c. Witmer
    d. Goddard
    e. Münsterberg

ANS: A   PTS: 1   REF: Granville Stanley Hall (1844-1924)

90. Hall was one of the first American psychologists to become interested in _____.
    a. equal political opportunity for women
    b. sexual equality
    c. physiological psychology
    d. psychoanalysis
    e. behaviorism

ANS: D   PTS: 1   REF: Granville Stanley Hall (1844-1924)

91. Who arranged for Freud and Jung to visit and lecture in America?
    a. Cattell
    b. Hall
    c. Witmer
    d. Münsterberg
    e. Scott

ANS: B   PTS: 1   REF: Granville Stanley Hall (1844-1924)

92. Who was the founder and first president of the American Psychological Association?
    a. James
    b. Hall
    c. Wundt
    d. Jung
    e. Freud

ANS: B   PTS: 1   REF: Granville Stanley Hall (1844-1924)

93. The introduction of psychoanalysis to the American public was accomplished by ____.
    a. James
    b. Angell
    c. Dewey
    d. Witmer
    e. Hall

    ANS: E   PTS: 1   REF: Granville Stanley Hall (1844-1924)

94. The force behind Howard University's becoming a leading institution for the education of African American psychologists was ____.
    a. Carver
    b. Bond
    c. Sumner
    d. Clark
    e. Hall

    ANS: C   PTS: 1   REF: Granville Stanley Hall (1844-1924)

95. The first African American to earn a Ph.D. in psychology was ____.
    a. Bond
    b. DuBois
    c. Clark
    d. Sumner
    e. Howard

    ANS: D   PTS: 1   REF: Granville Stanley Hall (1844-1924)

96. Hall's framework for human development was ____.
    a. physiological psychology
    b. evolutionary theory
    c. functionalism
    d. life-span psychology
    e. animal psychology

    ANS: B   PTS: 1   REF: Granville Stanley Hall (1844-1924)

97. A method long attributed to Hall, albeit erroneously, is ____.
    a. genetic engineering
    b. the laboratory school
    c. the use of questionnaires
    d. introspection by recapitulation
    e. retrospection with children and adolescents

    ANS: C   PTS: 1   REF: Granville Stanley Hall (1844-1924)

98. The child study movement was based on the work of ____.
    a. Hall
    b. Freud
    c. Witmer
    d. Münsterberg
    e. Binet

    ANS: A   PTS: 1   REF: Granville Stanley Hall (1844-1924)

99. Important books on adolescence and old age were written by _____.
   a. James
   b. Freud
   c. Binet
   d. Hall
   e. Thorndike

   ANS: D   PTS: 1   REF: Granville Stanley Hall (1844-1924)

100. The notion that children's development reflects the history of the human race is the _____.
   a. child study movement
   b. primary law of evolution
   c. collective unconscious
   d. theoretical basis for Binet's tests
   e. recapitulation theory

   ANS: E   PTS: 1   REF: Granville Stanley Hall (1844-1924)
   MSC: WWW

101. The theory that the psychological development of children repeats the history of the human race is known
   as the _____ theory, proposed by _____.
   a. mental evolution; Hall
   b. recapitulation; Hall
   c. mental phylogeny; Cattell
   d. mental phylogeny; James
   e. psychical phylogeny; Münsterberg

   ANS: B   PTS: 1   REF: Granville Stanley Hall (1844-1924)

102. Lifespan developmental psychology is reflected in whose work?
   a. Cattell
   b. Scott
   c. Münsterberg
   d. Yerkes
   e. Hall

   ANS: E   PTS: 1   REF: Granville Stanley Hall (1844-1924)

103. Hall's writings on *Adolescence* were criticized for _____.
   a. placing too much emphasis on sex
   b. applying evolutionary theory to human development
   c. being too "Freudian"
   d. being too unscientific
   e. ignoring research on animals

   ANS: A   PTS: 1   REF: Granville Stanley Hall (1844-1924)

104. The first large-scale study of aging from a psychological point of view was _____.
   a. James's *Enjoy Old Age*
   b. Hall's *Life Span Evolution*
   c. Hall's *Life Span Development*
   d. Hall's *Senescence*
   e. James's *Senescence*

   ANS: D   PTS: 1   REF: Granville Stanley Hall (1844-1924)

FUNCTIONALISM: DEVELOPMENT AND FOUNDING

105. Functionalism is said to have been indirectly founded by _____.
    a. Titchener
    b. James
    c. Dewey
    d. Angell
    e. Calkins

    ANS: A   PTS: 1   REF: The Founding of Functionalism

106. The first American psychology textbook was published by _____.
    a. Titchener
    b. James
    c. Dewey
    d. Angell
    e. Woodworth

    ANS: C   PTS: 1   REF: John Dewey (1859-1952)

107. Who established a "laboratory school" to study innovations in educational practices?
    a. Hollingworth
    b. Dewey
    c. Woolley
    d. Carr
    e. Angell

    ANS: B   PTS: 1   REF: John Dewey (1859-1952)

108. Dewey's analysis of _____ was the work that most keenly protested structuralism.
    a. educational psychology
    b. applied psychology
    c. respondent behavior
    d. operant behavior
    e. the reflex arc

    ANS: E   PTS: 1   REF: John Dewey (1859-1952)

109. John Dewey is credited with initiating the early development of functional psychology in his paper
    entitled, "The Reflex Arc Concept in Psychology." What was the major point that Dewey made in this
    paper?
    a. Psychology should try to analyze behavior into stimulus-response units only.
    b. Psychology should try to become a biological science and attempt to explain mental
       processes in terms of brain activity.
    c. Psychology should only apply the evolutionary doctrine to the development of organisms.
       The evolutionary doctrine should not be used to analyze society.
    d. Behavior cannot be properly understood or analyzed into simple stimulus-response units.
       Behavior must be understood in terms of its result and the adaptive significance of the
       behavior to the organism.
    e. Psychology should be concerned with behavior only.

    ANS: D   PTS: 1   REF: John Dewey (1859-1952)
    MSC: WWW

110. The study of the total organism as it functions in its environment was the focus of the system posited by
_____.
   a. James
   b. Dewey
   c. Angell
   d. Darwin
   e. Woodworth

   ANS: B   PTS: 1   REF: John Dewey (1859-1952)

111. Dewey's position was that _____.
   a. structure and function cannot be meaningfully separated
   b. form follows function
   c. function follows form
   d. reflexes travel in a straight line
   e. None of the choices are correct.

   ANS: A   PTS: 1   REF: John Dewey (1859-1952)

112. The functionalist advocate _____ never completed a Ph.D. in psychology, yet went on to greatly influence
the Chicago school.
   a. James
   b. Dewey
   c. Carr
   d. Thorndike
   e. Angell

   ANS: E   PTS: 1   REF: James Rowland Angell (1869-1949)

113. According to _____, the goal of psychology is to study how the mind enables and facilitates the adaptation
of the organism to its environment.
   a. Darwin
   b. Galton
   c. Angell
   d. Watson
   e. Titchener

   ANS: C   PTS: 1   REF: James Rowland Angell (1869-1949)

114. In his presidential address to the American Psychological Association, Angell presented the goals of
functional psychology. Which of the following statements represents the main concern of functionalism
according to Angell?
   a. Functionalism tries to explain consciousness in terms of neural activity.
   b. Functionalism tried to understand the instinctive behavior of humans.
   c. Functionalism tries to analyze behavior into stimulus-response units.
   d. Functionalism tries to answer why mental processes exist and how they aid survival.
   e. None of the choices are correct.

   ANS: D   PTS: 1   REF: James Rowland Angell (1869-1949)

FUNCTIONALISM: DEVELOPMENT AND FOUNDING   231

115. Who guided functionalism into becoming a formal school by giving it the focus and stature to earn respect in the scientific community?
    a. James
    b. Dewey
    c. Angell
    d. Carr
    e. Thorndike

    ANS: C   PTS: 1   REF: James Rowland Angell (1869-1949)

116. Angell described functional psychology as the psychology of _____.
    a. stimulus and response
    b. mental operations
    c. mind-body relations
    d. immediate experiences of adaptation
    e. the development of adaptive habits

    ANS: B   PTS: 1   REF: James Rowland Angell (1869-1949)

117. For Angell, functionalism was to study the adaptive utility of _____.
    a. consciousness
    b. immediate experiences
    c. mediate experiences
    d. consciousness and behavior
    e. behavior

    ANS: A   PTS: 1   REF: James Rowland Angell (1869-1949)

118. For Angell, the fact that consciousness exists demonstrates that it is _____.
    a. the appropriate subject matter of psychology
    b. adaptive and essential for an organism's survival
    c. the cause of its adaptation to the environment
    d. not a reason for it to be studied
    e. the function, not the structure, of the animal that is important

    ANS: B   PTS: 1   REF: James Rowland Angell (1869-1949)
    MSC: WWW

119. Carr's contribution to psychology was _____.
    a. the legitimization of animal psychology
    b. the extension and elaboration of Angell's system
    c. to actively pursue the demise of structuralism
    d. to establish Chicago as the base for applied psychology
    e. indirect, through his mentoring of John B. Watson

    ANS: B   PTS: 1   REF: Harvey A. Carr (1873-1954)

120. _____ maintained that functional psychology was *the* American psychology.
    a. Dewey
    b. Hollingworth
    c. Angell
    d. Woodworth
    e. Carr

    ANS: E   PTS: 1   REF: Harvey A. Carr (1873-1954)

121. Who stated that the subject matter of psychology was mental activity?
    a. Watson
    b. Carr
    c. Thorndike
    d. Titchener
    e. Hollingworth

    ANS: B   PTS: 1   REF: Harvey A. Carr (1873-1954)

122. Who succeeded Angell as head of the University of Chicago's department of psychology, under which functionalism at Chicago reached its peak?
    a. Calkins
    b. Dewey
    c. Carr
    d. Hall
    e. Jung

    ANS: C   PTS: 1   REF: Harvey A. Carr (1873-1954)

123. _____ at Columbia University believed that introspection was a useful tool for psychology.
    a. Cattell
    b. Carr
    c. Woodworth
    d. James
    e. Hall

    ANS: C   PTS: 1   REF: Robert Sessions Woodworth (1869-1962)

124. Carr defined the subject matter of psychology as mental activity. Which of the following are examples of what Carr described?
    a. memory
    b. perception
    c. imagination
    d. All of the above.
    e. None of the above.

    ANS: C   PTS: 1   REF: Functionalism: The Final Form

125. Which of the following best describes Carr's view of functionalism?
    a. Functionalism is concerned with mental activity. Mental processes control behavior that is conducive to survival.
    b. Functionalism studies how mental elements found in consciousness through introspection can be used to understand how humans adapt to environments.
    c. Functionalism should give up the study of the mind and concentrate on the study of behavior.
    d. Functionalism should try to perfect Titchener's introspective method in order to make it more reliable in the analysis of consciousness.
    e. None of the choices are correct.

    ANS: A   PTS: 1   REF: Functionalism: The Final Form

126. Although the primary development and founding of the functionalist school of thought occurred at the University of Chicago, another approach was shaped at ____.
   a. Columbia University
   b. University of Chicago, Lakeside
   c. Harvard University
   d. Clark University
   e. Yale University

   ANS: A   PTS: 1   REF: Functionalism at Columbia University

127. Who disliked the constraints imposed by membership in any school of thought?
   a. Dewey
   b. Woodworth
   c. Angell
   d. Carr
   e. Wundt

   ANS: B   PTS: 1   REF: Robert Sessions Woodworth (1869-1962)

128. Woodworth decided to become a psychologist after hearing ____ and reading ____.
   a. William James; John Dewey
   b. E. L. Thorndike; James McKeen Cattell
   c. James McKeen Cattell; E. L. Thorndike
   d. William James; G. Stanley Hall
   e. G. Stanley Hall; William James

   ANS: E   PTS: 1   REF: Robert Sessions Woodworth (1869-1962)

129. In contrast to Dewey, Woodworth was ____.
   a. a good teacher
   b. well known for his philosophy
   c. a strong proponent of introspection
   d. more structural than functional
   e. None of the choices are correct.

   ANS: A   PTS: 1   REF: Robert Sessions Woodworth (1869-1962)

130. According to Woodworth, psychological knowledge must *begin* with ____.
   a. the stimulus and response
   b. animal psychology and then move to human psychology
   c. nonexperimental observation
   d. the living organism
   e. introspection

   ANS: A   PTS: 1   REF: Robert Sessions Woodworth (1869-1962)

131. In Woodworth's view, what occurs inside the organism ____.
   a. is known only by God
   b. is irrelevant for psychology
   c. can be known only through introspection
   d. can be known objectivity
   e. is independent of all other matters

   ANS: C   PTS: 1   REF: Robert Sessions Woodworth (1869-1962)

132. Woodworth's system of psychology, concerned with causal factors and motivations in feelings and behavior, was known as ____.
    a. pragmatism
    b. motivational psychology
    c. synthetic psychology
    d. dynamic psychology
    e. act psychology

    ANS: D   PTS: 1   REF: Robert Sessions Woodworth (1869-1962)

133. The hallmark of Woodworth's psychology was his ____.
    a. focus on motivation
    b. focus on the dynamics of conscious experience
    c. focus on intervening variables
    d. refusal to ascribe to a particular system or school of thought
    e. protest against functionalism

    ANS: A   PTS: 1   REF: Robert Sessions Woodworth (1869-1962)

134. Woodworth's psychology was distinct from the Chicago school in his ____
    a. emphasis on the physiological correlates of behavior
    b. rejection of introspection
    c. acceptance of introspection
    d. acceptance of observation but rejection of experimentation as artificial
    e. emphasis on overt observable behavior of the organism

    ANS: A   PTS: 1   REF: Robert Sessions Woodworth (1869-1962)

135. Functionalism was most loudly criticized by the ____.
    a. structuralists
    b. behaviorists
    c. Gestalt psychologists
    d. humanistic psychologists
    e. Darwinians

    ANS: A   PTS: 1   REF: Robert Sessions Woodworth (1869-1962)

TRUE/FALSE

136. Spencer's particular contribution was the application of the survival of the fittest hypothesis to human nature and society.

    ANS: T   PTS: 1
    REF: Evolution Comes to America: Herbert Spencer (1820-1903)

137. Social Darwinism flourished in the United States primarily as a result of the American character and propensities.

    ANS: T   PTS: 1
    REF: Evolution Comes to America: Herbert Spencer (1820-1903)
    MSC: WWW

138. Spencer would find the U.S. welfare, affirmative action, and social security programs to be antithetical (opposing) to social Darwinism.

ANS: T   PTS: 1
REF: Evolution Comes to America: Herbert Spencer (1820-1903)

139. Spencer's pragmatism was extended and elaborated by William James into synthetic philosophy.

ANS: F   PTS: 1
REF: Evolution Comes to America: Herbert Spencer (1820-1903)

140. Spencer found psychology to be a "nasty little science."

ANS: F   PTS: 1
REF: William James (1842-1910): Anticipator of Functional Psychology

141. A medicinal product called *Americanitis Elixir* was marketed for the treatment of Americanitis.

ANS: T   PTS: 1
REF: William James (1842-1910): Anticipator of Functional Psychology
MSC: WWW

142. James would probably advocate belief in the ability to will oneself back to good health.

ANS: T   PTS: 1
REF: William James (1842-1910): Anticipator of Functional Psychology

143. James said that "there is no such thing as a science of psychology."

ANS: T   PTS: 1
REF: William James (1842-1910): Anticipator of Functional Psychology

144. Spencer's *The Principles of Psychology* became the most influential book ever written in psychology.

ANS: F   PTS: 1
REF: William James (1842-1910): Anticipator of Functional Psychology

145. James wrote the first textbook on, and thereby initiated, educational psychology.

ANS: T   PTS: 1
REF: William James (1842-1910): Anticipator of Functional Psychology

146. James hypothesized that one's reasoning abilities and belief systems are strongly influenced by one's emotions and desires.

ANS: T   PTS: 1
REF: William James (1842-1910): Anticipator of Functional Psychology

147. James's *Principles* treated psychology as a biological science.

ANS: T   PTS: 1
REF: William James (1842-1910): Anticipator of Functional Psychology

148. One of his rare points of agreement with Wundt was James's position that simple sensations exist in conscious experience, but are nearly impossible to identify.

ANS: F   PTS: 1
REF: William James (1842-1910): Anticipator of Functional Psychology

149. James borrowed the term *stream of consciousness* from Brentano.

ANS: F   PTS: 1
REF: William James (1842-1910): Anticipator of Functional Psychology

150. James proposed that the factor that determined whether an object or event would be apperceived was contiguity.

ANS: F   PTS: 1
REF: William James (1842-1910): Anticipator of Functional Psychology

151. According to James's *Principles*, consciousness is always selectively changing.

ANS: T   PTS: 1
REF: William James (1842-1910): Anticipator of Functional Psychology

152. It was significant to the development of behaviorism by later functionalists that James rejected introspection as a method.

ANS: F   PTS: 1
REF: William James (1842-1910): Anticipator of Functional Psychology

153. James's pragmatism included the argument that even if a research topic does not work now, it may work later and be true or valid.

ANS: F   PTS: 1
REF: William James (1842-1910): Anticipator of Functional Psychology

154. The core of James's theory of emotion is that physiological events are perceived first, then subsequently one identifies an emotion.

ANS: T   PTS: 1
REF: William James (1842-1910): Anticipator of Functional Psychology

155. James was interested in the physiological influences on behavior.

ANS: T   PTS: 1
REF: William James (1842-1910): Anticipator of Functional Psychology

156. James is often criticized for his theory of emotions, which he developed with Carl Lange.

ANS: F   PTS: 1
REF: William James (1842-1910): Anticipator of Functional Psychology

157. Calkins invented the paired associates technique to study memory and also was denied her Ph.D. by Harvard University.

ANS: T   PTS: 1   REF: The Functional Inequality of Women

158. Mary Calkins attended graduate classes under the supervision of Dewey.

ANS: F   PTS: 1   REF: The Functional Inequality of Women

159. Although Woolley's and Hollingworth's research refuted the notion of male superiority, it did not disconfirm the variability hypothesis.

ANS: F   PTS: 1   REF: The Functional Inequality of Women

160. Hall established the first American psychology laboratory at Johns Hopkins University.

ANS: T   PTS: 1   REF: Granville Stanley Hall (1844-1924)

161. After his book *Adolescence* was published, Hall was criticized as being "obsessed with sex."

ANS: T   PTS: 1   REF: Granville Stanley Hall (1844-1924)
MSC: WWW

162. Titchener indirectly founded functional psychology.

ANS: T   PTS: 1   REF: The Founding of Functionalism
MSC: WWW

163. The first American textbook in psychology was Dewey's *Psychology*.

ANS: T   PTS: 1   REF: John Dewey (1859-1952)

164. Woodworth's "Dynamic Psychology" was the first defining work of functionalism.

ANS: F   PTS: 1   REF: John Dewey (1859-1952)

165. In his most significant work in psychology, Dewey rejected the reductionism of the natural sciences and of the European philosophies.

ANS: T   PTS: 1   REF: John Dewey (1859-1952)

166. Pragmatism was defined by Dewey as the study of the organism in use.

ANS: F   PTS: 1   REF: John Dewey (1859-1952)

167. Angell argued that the goal of psychology was to study how the mind serves the adaptation of the organism to its environment.

ANS: T   PTS: 1   REF: James Rowland Angell (1869-1949)

168. Angell argued that functional psychology is concerned with psychophysical associations.

ANS: T   PTS: 1   REF: James Rowland Angell (1869-1949)

169. Carr described adaptive behavior as the manifestation of mental activities.

ANS: T   PTS: 1   REF: Harvey A. Carr (1873-1954)
MSC: WWW

170. The Chicago school was important in the evolution of psychology in that it advanced the movement from the study of the mind to the study of behavior.

ANS: T   PTS: 1   REF: Functionalism: The Final Form

171. The founder of dynamic psychology was R. S. Woodworth.

ANS: T   PTS: 1   REF: Robert Sessions Woodworth (1869-1962)

172. In Woodworth's motivology, introspection was a method to be used to investigate what occurs inside the organism.

ANS: T   PTS: 1   REF: Robert Sessions Woodworth (1869-1962)
MSC: WWW

Chapter 8

Applied Psychology: The Legacy of Functionalism

One of the precipitating events in applied psychology was the Coca-Cola trial. Coke contained caffeine, which was restricted by FDA regulations because of its purportedly addictive nature. Thus, the company was prosecuted by the Federal government. Coke hired Harry Hollingworth to test the effects of caffeine on a number of physical and mental tasks. No negative effects were found and Coke won the initial court battle. This case proved that private companies can fund psychological research without biasing the results, and highlighted the practical use of experimental psychology outside of the academic setting.

Psychology in America was rapidly growing, and the work of Darwin, Galton, and Spencer was increasingly more influential than that of Wundt, despite the fact that Wundt trained many American psychologists. This was partly due to the American Zeitgeist, which valued practicality. Applied psychology blossomed in the early 20th century because it solved real world problems. For example, from 1880 to 1900, 41 psychology laboratories, 3 journals, and 40 doctoral programs developed where few previously existed.

Part of psychology's popularity resulted from economic forces. During this time, the number of people with a Ph.D. in psychology rose and there were not enough academic positions to employ them. In addition, psychology programs were not respected and underfunded. Meanwhile, an emerging societal problem was a dramatic increase in public school enrollment, which caused government funding to be directed towards education research. This opened doors for many psychologists. Thus, applied psychology has expanded into many industries, including mental health clinics, criminal justice, and psychological testing.

One of the early influences on the mental testing movement was James McKeen Cattell. Cattell studied philosophy and began his interest in psychology when he experimented with drugs like tobacco, opium, and caffeine. Early in his career, he studied under Hall and Wundt, yet was most influenced by Galton's work on individual differences. Under Galton, Cattell's use of quantification emerged and blossomed (Wundt did not use statistical analyses). Statistical analysis allowed the comparison of large data sets and "opened new research possibilities." Graphic displays of data were used by "Galton, Ebbinghaus, Hall, and…Thorndike" and Karl Pearson refined the correlation as well as devised the chi-square test. Meanwhile, "a psychologist at Stanford University was apparently the first to advocate the use of experimental and control groups."

In working with Galton, Cattell also became interested in Eugenics and argued for sterilization of delinquents and deficit persons. Eventually, he obtained a teaching position at Columbia University. Cattell started the journal *Psychological Review*, acquired *Science*, and wrote a series of reference books. He also helped found the AAUP faculty union. However, he had strained relations with the administration at Columbia, which eventually forced him to resign.

Cattell went on to found the Psychological Corporation, which sold (and still sells) psychological tests. In addition, he coined the term "mental test" in an 1890 article and began large scale testing in his research. His tests looked much like Galton's, which measure psychomotor rather than cognitive abilities. After many years of collecting data, he correlated mental test scores with academic performance and concluded that his tests were poor measures of intelligence (because he yielded low correlations). Cattell's influence on psychology was mainly as an organizer, executive, and administrator.

The first true test of mental ability came from the work of Alfred Binet, a French psychologist who had a variety of research interests. He disagreed with Galton and Cattell in their approach to mental testing. Using observations of his own young daughters, Binet developed true cognitive tests based on memory, attention, imagination, and comprehension.

With Théodore Simon, he developed a test of 30 problems arranged in ascending difficulty to be used to help schoolchildren. The tests were later revised to measure mental age, the age at which children of average ability could perform tasks. In 1916, Lewis Terman developed the test further, renaming it the Stanford-Binet, and adopted the term intelligence quotient (IQ). This test continues to be revised and is widely used today.

World War I highlighted the need for psychologists to aid in the war effort. The Stanford-Binet was not practical to use because it was administered individually and required thorough training to administer. To solve this problem, Yerkes developed the first group-administered intelligence tests: Army Alpha and Army Beta (for those illiterate in English). More than a million recruits were tested. This spurred the visibility and acceptance of psychological testing, and other types of testing began being developed (i.e., personality). By "the early 1920's up to 4 million intelligence tests were being purchased every year, mostly for use in public schools." There was "an epidemic of testing" in the U.S., including a substantial number of invalid tests which removed some of the luster of testing in the eyes of the public. To bolster the reputation of testing Psychologists used metaphors from medicine and engineering.

Unfortunately, mental testing was also used to enhance unethical social programs. Henry Goddard, who had translated Binet's test, visited Ellis island because he believed that mentally retarded and other "feeble-minded" immigrants were being allowed to enter the country. He proposed using the Stanford-Binet to identify such immigrants, despite their unfamiliarity with American culture and the English language. Goddard concluded that at least 80% of the immigrants coming to Ellis Island tested as "feeble-minded." These results were used to create restrictive immigration laws. Later, the results of Army Alpha and Beta were publically released and showed that there were ethnic differences in IQ scores, specifically that Blacks and immigrants scored lower than whites. Combined, these racial differences led to the misleading conclusion that there were biological difference in intelligence. A vocal critic of this conclusion was Horace Mann Bond who argued that differences in scores were due to environment, as evidenced by the fact that White southerners scored lower than Black northerners on IQ tests.

Because academic positions were not generally open to women, many found work in applied fields. Florence Goodenough developed the Draw-A-Man test, a version of which is still used today. Maude Merrill James worked with Terman on the Stanford-Binet, and Thelma Thurstone worked with her husband on the Primary Mental Abilities test. Psyche Cattell extended the Stanford-Binet to be used with babies as young as 3 months. Anne Anastasi became an authority on psychological testing, writing over 150 articles and a testing textbook. Although these women were successful, careers outside of academia tended to be invisible with regard to enduring professional reputation.

Lightner Witmer (1867-1956), another student of Wundt's and Cattell, "opened the world's first psychology clinic" in 1896. He did not practice psychotherapy, but instead assessed and treated learning and behavioral problems of children. He received his undergraduate degree at U. of Penn., and earned his Ph.D. from Wundt in 1892. In 1896, Witmer was teaching a course when someone approached him about a troubled child. Shortly thereafter, he prepared courses on methods for treating mentally challenged children. He presented a paper at an "APA meeting, using the term 'clinical psychology' for the first time" and in 1907 he founded the journal Psychological Clinic.

Because Witmer was the first clinical psychologist, he had to devise his own methods. The children who came to his clinic faced a wide variety of problems. His confidence, and his clinic and staff, grew with time. Part of his assessment was medical, recognizing that physical issues could impact on cognition and behavior. He came to see the importance of environment on children's well-being.

By 1914 there were 20 psychology clinics in the U.S. patterned after Witmer's. His work influenced special education, and spread to vocational counseling through his student Morris Viteles. Other influences on the growth of clinical psychology included books by Clifford Beers and Hugo Münsterberg. Later, Freud's influence led to the inclusion of psychotherapy into the realm of clinical psychology. Despite these developments, the field grew slowly until World War II, when a large number of clinical psychologists were needed to treat emotionally disturbed draftees. After the war, the need increased because of the large number of veterans being assisted by the Veteran's Association. Today the VA is the largest employer of psychologists in the U.S. Clinical psychology today is a firmly established area of education and employment.

Industrial and organizational psychology is an area that arose because of the functionalist movement. Walter Dill Scott, a former student of Wundt, applied psychology to advertising and business operations. He was born on his family's farm and earned his own way to college, with intentions of becoming a missionary to China. A course in psychology interested him, and he went to Leipzig for his graduate work. After earning his Ph.D. he secured a teaching job at Northwestern University. "A few years later, his interests changed when an advertising executive sought him out and asked him to attempt to apply psychology to make advertisements more effective." He wrote the first book applying psychology to advertising, *The Theory and Practice of Advertising* (1903), and his reputation quickly grew. When World War I began, he "offered his skills to...help select military personnel", for which he later earned the army's Distinguished Medal of Honor. After the war he started a consulting company and became president of Northwestern University.

The work he is most known for is his advertising work, in which he suggested that emotions would increase suggestibility. He advised clients to use direct language (*Use Pears Soap*), and promoted the idea of return coupons as a means of promoting consumer action. Scott also created rating scales to be used in employee selection, which were used to compare the results of successful employees with the results of potential employees. He also designed group-administered tests, like tests for applied intelligence, which measured quickness, accuracy, and judgment. World War II created another spurt in growth, particularly in recruit classification and human factors engineering as well (human-machine interface design), both of which are broadly used today.

The expansion of industrial psychology happened, in part, because of the Hawthorne Studies. From 1927 into the 1930's, these studies set out to determine "the effects of the physical work environment" on productivity. Instead, the researchers discovered that the social and emotional environment has an even greater impact on productivity. "The Hawthorne studies led psychologists to explore the social-psychological work climate, including the behavior of leaders, informal work groups, employee attitudes, communication patterns between workers and managers, and other factors capable of influencing motivation, productivity, and satisfaction." In doing so, these experiments set the tone for the field of industrial and organizational psychology.

As a field, industrial and organizational psychology has been mostly receptive to the contributions of women, yet not without some setbacks. Lillian Gilbreth was the first to receive a Ph.D. in industrial and organizational psychology. She pioneered the time-and-motion analysis technique, along with her husband Frank. However, publishers refused to put her name on books she wrote for fear that executives would not purchase the books. Despite these setbacks she had a long and prosperous career.

Hugo Münsterberg was another psychologist who made his living in applied psychology. He highly successful and well-known, as he wrote hundreds of articles (both academic and popular), and "almost two dozen books." For some time, he was honored as a professor, had been president of APA and the American Philosophical Association. When he died, however, he was regarded by some as "one of the most hated individuals in America."

Münsterberg obtained his Ph.D. under Wundt and an M.D. two years later. He obtained a professorship in Germany and set up a lab in his own home, began to do research and started to attract students and attention. In 1892 William James asked Münsterberg to come to Harvard to direct the lab, and he accepted. At first Münsterberg was critical of applied work, but he soon wrote a book *American Traits* (1902) in which he analyzed characteristics of American society. It received instant applause from the general public and Münsterberg loved the attention. He then wrote a large number of popular articles on a variety of applied topics, such as courtroom trials, mental health, vocational counseling, etc. He even made some films. He inserted himself in the center of some controversial events, like on sensational murder trial and the prohibition debate, which cost him some of his good reputation. His views on women were paradoxical. He supported some women in the Harvard program. However, he generally believed that "graduate work was too demanding," and that women should stay at home, should not teach in schools, and should not serve on juries because "they were incapable of rational deliberation." At the outbreak of World War I, Münsterberg defended Germany, which caused his ostracism. He died towards the end of the war from a massive stroke while giving a lecture.

Münsterberg's work was varied. He published *On the Witness Stand* (1908) in which he discussed such things as false confessions and the reliability of eyewitness testimony. He wrote *Psychotherapy* (1909), and believed that because of his perceived authority he could create mental good health through suggestion. He also promoted industrial psychology beginning with an article he wrote in 1909, consulted with organizations, and in his book *Psychology and Industrial Efficiency* (1913) promotes the use of mental/psychological testing for job applicants.

By the time World War I ended, applied psychology was fully entrenched and valued in America. The number of psychologists and graduate programs boomed. However, in 1919, the APA created changes that effectively banned applied psychologists from membership. Still, applied psychology kept growing until the economic decline in the 1930's, when applied psychology became somewhat of a scapegoat, and its reputation declined until World War II. About "25% of American psychologists were directly involved in the war effort", and psychology has generally been well-regarded ever since. The majority of contemporary psychologists are applied rather than university-based.

Outline

I.   FDA Raid: Target Coca-Cola
  A. Federal agents stop a truck full of Coke syrup
       1. syrup contains caffeine, a drug restricted under the new FDA regulations
       2. FDA claims caffeine is poisonous and habit-forming
  B. Coca-Cola had no research about the effects of caffeine, sought psychologists to test caffeine
       1. they ask James McKeen Cattell, who says no
       2. they ask several others who say no
       3. Harry Hollingworth says yes
            a.   He needed the money
                 (1) His teaching job at Barnard College had a low salary
                 (2) His wife Leta Stetter couldn't find teaching work because she was married
                 (3) She couldn't sell her short stories

(4) She had hoped to go to graduate school but they could not afford to

(5) She is appointed assistant director of the project

(6) They earned enough for her to go to graduate school

    b.   Harry insists on high standards

        (1) Did not want to be accused of fudging results

        (2) Coke allowed him to publish results, even if damaging to the company

        (3) Coke agreed that findings could not be used in advertising

4. 40-day research program

    a.   Rigorous and sophisticated

    b.   Involved 64,000 individual measurements

    c.   Data on motor and mental functions

    d.   Variety of caffeine levels

    e.   No harmful effects found

5. Coke wins court case, though verdict overturned by Supreme Court

C. Psychology wins: psychologists can apply research without sacrificing integrity

D. Toward a practical psychology

1. Evolution took rapid hold in U.S.

2. American psychology guided by Darwin, Galton, and Spencer rather than Wundt

    a.   Even though Wundt had trained many of them, American psychology bore little resemblance to Wundt

    b.   They didn't bring his ideas home

    c.   Psychology adapted to new environment

3. Wundt and Titchener's work incompatible with American Zeitgeist

    a.   Could not be applied to everyday problems

    b.   America oriented to practical application

    c.   Hall: "We need a psychology that is usable"

4. Americans transform psychology

    a.   Study not what mind is but what it does

    b.   James, Angell, Carr developing functionalism in academic settings

    c.   Others are outside universities

    d.   Thus, practical psychology evolves at the same time as functionalism

5. applied psychologists take psychology to real world

    a.   schools, factories, advertising, courthouses, child and mental health clinics

    b.   have greater effect on psychology than functionalists

    c.   impact seen in professional literature

        (1) by 1900, 25% of articles in America are applied

        (2) at same time, only 3% involved introspection

    d.   even Titchener acknowledges the great wave of applied psychology

E. The Growth of American Psychology

1. Psychology grew tremendously from 1880-1900

    a.   1880: no U.S. labs, 1900: 41, the majority worldwide

    b.   1880: no U.S. psych. journals, 1895: 3

    c.   1880: Americans had to go to Germany to study, 1900: most entered grad school in U.S. in one of 40 doctoral programs

  d. 1892-1904: 100 Ph.D.s conferred in U.S., more than all other sciences but 3

  e. 1910: 50% of articles were in German, 1933: 52% in English and only 14% German

  f. British Who's Who in Science (1913) names the U.S. as predominant in psychology

 2. About 20 years after its founding in Europe, U.S. assumes undisputed leadership

  a. Cattell's 1895 APA presidential address reflects this

   (1) Cattell: growth without precedent

   (2) Psychology now required in undergrad curricula

   (3) Attracts students

  b. General public is interested as well

   (1) Public introduced at 1893 Chicago world's fair

    (a) Exhibit similar to Galton's anthropometric lab

    (b) Testing laboratory for fairgoers to be tested for a fee

    (c) Enthusiastically received

   (2) Another extensive exhibition at the 1904 Louisiana Purchase Exposition in St. Louis, speakers included Titchener, Morgan, Janet, Hall, and Watson

  c. Such public interest not fostered in Germany with Wundt

F. Economic influences on applied psychology

 1. Contextual forces also compel applied psychology

  a. There are more Ph.D.s than academic position/labs to employ them

  b. Psychologists need to work, look outside universities

   (1) Found practical work challenging and stimulating

   (2) Human behavior can be studied outside lab

   (3) Was a lucrative outlet

  c. Even some within universities receive pressure

   (1) Less endowed universities in West and Midwest

   (2) Need to prove psychology's worth to administrators, legislators

    (a) Survey shows administrators regard psychology with low worth

    (b) Courses and labs under-funded, poorly equipped

   (3) Push to prove worth by solving problems

  d. Opportunity calls: increase in public school enrollments

   (1) 1870-1915 rose from 7 to 20 million

   (2) Government spending for education grows from $63 to $605 million

   (3) Hall calls for applied psychology in education

   (4) James publishes *Talks to Teachers* (1899)

   (5) By 1910, the majority of psychologists working on education issues

   (6) Four psychologists (trained by Wundt) extend psychology

    (a) Industry

    (b) Psychological testing

    (c) Criminal justice

    (d) Mental health

II.   Mental Testing
       A. James McKeen Cattell (1860-1944)
           1. born in Easton PA
           2. earned bachelor's at Lafayette College (father was its president) in 1880
           3. went to Europe: Göttingen then Liepzig (studied with Wundt)
           4. won fellowship to Johns Hopkins in 1882
           5. interest in philosophy
           6. no psychology courses at Hopkins at the time
           7. drug dabbling leads to psychology interest
                   a.   experiments with hashish, morphine, opium, caffeine, tobacco, and
                         chocolate
                   b.   he notes that hashish reduced his depression
                   c.   wrote of his drug experiences in a journal
                   d.   thorough observation of self under influence
           8. 2nd semester at Hopkins, Hall offers psychology course
                   a.   Cattell enrolls
                         (1) does reaction time experiments
                         (2) reinforces his interest in psychology
           9. returns to Wundt in Germany in 1883
                   a.   According to legend,
                         (1) Cattell boldly announces to Wundt that he will be Wundt's
                         assistant
                         (2) Cattell insists on doing his own individual difference research
                         (3) Wundt calls Cattell "typically American"
                         (4) Cattell gives Wundt his first typewriter
                               (a) On which many books are written
                               (b) Cattell is teased by colleagues for enabling Wundt "to
                               write twice as many books"
                   b.   The truth, according to evidence (letters and journals)
                         (1) Difference in the story when comparing Cattell's letters and
                         journals
                         (2) Wundt did think highly of Cattell, appointed him lab assistant in
                         1886
                         (3) No evidence of Cattell's interest in individual difference
                         research
                         (4) Cattell showed Wundt how to use a typewriter but did not give
                         him one
                   c.   Cattell was confident in Wundt's lab, in a letter home he writes of
                         his own "phenomenal genius"
                   d.   Obtains Ph.D. in 1886
           10. returns home, teaches psychology at Bryn Mawr and U. Penn.
           11. lectures in England at Cambridge, meets Galton
                   a.   both interested in individual differences
                   b.   Galton at peak of career
                   c.   Galton interested in measuring "psychological differences between
                         people"
           12. Influenced by Galton, Cattell stresses quantification, ranking, and ratings
                   a.   Although personally "mathematically illiterate", made simple
                         computation errors

b.   Developed order-of-merit ranking method
c.   First American to teach statistical analysis on experimental results (Galton's influence)
d.   Wundt hadn't favored statistics; used individual subjects instead

13. Emphasis on statistics characterizes new American psychology
   a.   Focus on large groups, comparisons of them
   b.   Statistics opened new research opportunities
   c.   New opportunities pushed need for new analyses
   d.   Graphic displays of data: Galton, Ebbinghaus, Hall, Thorndike
   e.   Karl Pearson (who refined correlation formula) "devised the chi-square test," both techniques used more by Americans than anyone else
   f.   1907, John Cover from Stanford advocates using experimental and control groups

14. Cattell also interested in Galton's Eugenics
   a.   Argued for sterilizing "delinquents and so-called defective persons"
   b.   Promoted offering incentives to the "healthy and intelligent" who intermarry
   c.   Promised his own children $1000 if they married professor offspring

15. 1888 Cattell becomes professor of psychology at University of Pennsylvania
   a.   Appointment is arranged by his father
   b.   Father was old friend of U. Penn. provost
   c.   Father urged Cattell to
        (1) publish more
        (2) travel to Leipzig to secure letter from Wundt
   d.   Father told provost that family had money so Cattell's salary could be low
   e.   Cattell later claims inaccurately that this was world's first psychology professorship (was really philosophy)
   f.   Stays 3 years

16. Goes to Columbia University as psychology professor and department chair, Stays 26 years
   a.   Begins Psychological Review with Baldwin in 1894
   b.   Purchases weekly journal Science
        (1) Purchased from Alexander Graham Bell
        (2) About to run out of money
        (3) 5 years later becomes official journal of American Association for the Advancement of Science (AAAS)
   c.   Institutes reference books in 1906
        (1) American Men of Science
        (2) Leaders in Education
   d.   Bought Popular Science Monthly in 1900
        (1) Sells name in 1915
        (2) Continues to publish as Scientific Monthly
   e.   Started weekly School and Society in 1915
   f.   Organizing and editing these take time from research productivity which is thin at Columbia

g. More doctorates given at Columbia under Cattell than from any other American grad program
  (1) Cattell advocated independent work
  (2) Gave students freedom
  (3) Believed professor should have distance
    (a) lived 40 miles from campus
    (b) Had lab and editorial office at home
    (c) Visited campus only a few days a week

h. Aloofness strained relations between Cattell and Columbia's administration
  (1) Cattell urged faculty governance
  (2) Helped found American Association of University Professors (AAUP)
  (3) Seen as not tactful in dealings with administration
  (4) Described as "ungentlemanly, irretrievably nasty, and lacking in decency" when dealing with administration
  (5) Between 1910 and 1917 university trustees considered asking for his resignation
  (6) Cattell writes two letters protesting sending draftees into combat in World War I
  (7) He is dismissed in 1917, charged with disloyalty to the U.S.
  (8) He sues for libel, wins $40,000 but not reinstated
  (9) He becomes isolated, writes satirical pamphlets about administration

17. Never returns to academia
18. Devotes life to publications and professional societies
19. 1921 founds the Psychological Corporation
  a. Stock purchased by APA members
  b. Provides psychological services to community
  c. Initially is a failure, very low profit first 2 years
  d. By 1969, $5 million in sales, bought by Harcourt Brace
  e. 10 years later $30 million

20. Mental Tests: tests of motor skills and mental capacities
  a. Coins phrase in article published in 1890
  b. Administers series of tests to students at University of Penn, continues to collect data from students at Columbia
  c. Tests look more like Galton's anthropometric lab, less like cognitive or intelligence tests (which are more complex)
  d. Cattell correlates test scores with academic performance, which are "disappointingly low"
  e. Similar results from Titchener's lab
  f. Concludes that these types of tests were not valid for measuring intelligence.

21. Cattell's influence on American psychology
  a. Organizer, executive, and administrator
  b. Link between psychology and greater scientific community
  c. Ambassador of psychology with lectures, editing, promotion
  d. Developed order-of-merit ranking, used to rank American Men of Science (which did include women)
  e. Through his students: two were Woodworth and Thorndike

III. The psychological testing movement
  A. Binet, Terman, and the IQ test
    1. first true test of mental ability is Alfred Binet's (1857-1911)
        a. Independently wealthy, self-taught French psychologist
        b. Published over 200 articles and books, 4 plays
        c. Used more complex methods than Cattell and initiated the era of intelligence testing
        d. Contributed to developmental, experimental, education, and social psychology
        e. Disagreed with Galton, Cattell (sensorimotor approach)
        f. Should assess memory, attention, imagination, comprehension
        g. Discovered this by watching his 2 young daughters
            (1) at first, used sensorimotor tests with them
            (2) they performed as well as adults
            (3) switched to cognitive tasks, then found differences with adults
        h. 1904 opportunity knocks
            (1) French ministry of education appoints commission
                (a) Learn about children having learning difficulties
                (b) Binet and Théodore Simon (psychiatrist) appointed
            (2) Investigated intellectual tasks across age groups
            (3) Created 30-problem test
                (a) Ordered by ascending difficulty
                (b) Measured 3 functions: judgment, comprehension, reasoning
        i. 3 years later
            (1) revises and expands test
            (2) introduces mental age: "age at which children of average ability can perform certain tasks"
        j. 1911 3rd revision, after Binet's death
        k. Test development moves to U.S.
            (1) Translated by Henry Goddard (student of Hall)
                (a) Works with mentally disabled children in New Jersey
                (b) Goddard translates as "Binet-Simon Measuring Scale for Intelligence"
                (c) Introduces the term 'moron' (Greek for 'slow')
            (2) 1916 Lewis Terman develops version that becomes standard
                (a) The Stanford-Binet (he works at Stanford U.)
                (b) Adopts the concept Intelligence Quotient (IQ)
                    (i) ratio of mental to chronological age
  B. World War I and Group Testing
    1. Titchener's Experimentalists meet on day WWI erupts
        a. Yerkes is there, urges group to consider how to help war effort
        b. Titchener leaves, claiming because he is British
    2. U.S. army is mobilizing, how to assess/classify the recruits?
        a. Stanford-Binet not appropriate, designed for individual administration, too much training to do
        b. Yerkes, with 40 psychologists, develops group intelligence test
            (1) Review large number of available tests
            (2) Model based on Arthur Otis' test which uses multiple choice

        c.   Army Alpha and Army Beta (for non-English speaking and illiterates) created

        d.   Over 1 million tested, though too late for army to use

    3. These created publicity and sparked testing movement

        a.   Tests for other concepts developed (i.e., personality)

           (1) Previous personality tests not sufficient (Kraepelin, Jung's word association tests)

        b.   Woodworth's Personnel Data Sheet measured neuroticism

        c.   Testing now widely accepted in variety of settings (employment, schoolchildren, college applicants)

        d.   Early 1920's 4 million intelligence tests purchased per year

        e.   Public education "reorganized around the concept..IQ"

        f.   Babe Ruth was tested to see why he was a great baseball player

        g.   Poor tests also created; Contributed to a loss of faith in testing

C. Terminology borrowed from medicine and engineering

    1. Subjects tested were "patients"

    2. Tests were "thermometers", required training

    3. Tests promoted as X-ray machines into the mind

    4. Schools became "education factories"

    5. Test measured "factory products"

    6. Society as bridge, tests used to find "weakest elements": the feeble-minded to be removed

D. Racial differences in intelligence

    1. Testing movement creates controversy

    2. Henry Goddard

        a.   1912 visits Ellis Island

        b.   Believed that physicians there only identified 10% of feeble-minded

        c.   Proposed psychologists conduct tests, using Binet test

        d.   During his visit, he tests a young man

           (1) Tests and diagnoses him as feeble-minded

           (2) Interpreter said when he was newly arrived he would have failed as well, said test unfair to those unfamiliar with American culture and English language

        e.   Later testing on immigrants with limited English skills shows majority as feeble-minded, mental age less than 12

           (1) 87% of Russians

           (2) 83% of Jews

           (3) 80% of Hungarians

           (4) 79% of Italians

         f.   1921: Additional evidence for racial differences in IQ

           (1) World War I testing of army recruits made public

           (2) Blacks and immigrants from Mediterranean and Latin American countries had lower measured IQs than Whites

           (3) Only northern European immigrants had IQs equal to those measured for Whites

        g.   Evidence used to create restrictive immigration laws

    3. Vocal critic was Horace Mann Bond

        a.   African-American scholar, president of Lincoln University in PA

        b.   Ph.D. in education from University of Chicago

        c.   Published many books and articles arguing that environment not genes caused differences in test scores: Blacks from north scored higher IQs than Whites from south
    4. Many responded that tests were biased, controversy faded
    5. 1994 *The Bell Curve* by Herrnstein and Murray
        a.   Argued that Blacks are inferior in intelligence to Whites
    6. Evidence now shows that soundly researched intelligence tests have no cultural bias

E. Contributions of Women to the testing movement
    1. Women often barred from academic positions
    2. Many found applied employment instead
        a.   Florence Goodenough, Ph.D. from Stanford
             (1) created Draw-A-Man test, a version of which still used
             (2) worked for 20 years at Institute of Child Development at U. of Minnesota
        b.   Maude Merrill James, wrote Stanford-Binet revision with Terman
        c.   Thelma Thurstone, helped develop Primary Mental Abilities test with her husband
        d.   Psyche Cattell (daughter of James McKeen Cattell) extended age for Stanford-Binet test to 3-month-old infants
        e.   Anne Anastasi
             (1) An authority on testing
             (2) Earned Ph.D. at 21
             (3) Wrote more than 150 articles and books
             (4) One was popular testing textbook
             (5) APA president, 1971
             (6) Many honors (e.g., National Medal of Science)
             (7) Retired from Fordham
             (8) Unable to have children; felt "free to concentrate on her career without guilt or conflict"
    3. Such applied work is disadvantageous to attaining prominence
        a.   Little time, support, no grad students to do publishable research
        b.   In an organization, good work not recognized outside
        c.   Their good work largely invisible
        d.   Applied work denigrated by some as "women's work"
        e.   No woman elected president of American Association for Applied Psychology although 1/3 of membership were women by 1941

IV.   The Clinical Psychology Movement
    A. Lightner Witmer (1867-1956)
        1. Taught psychology at U. of Penn., filled Cattell's position when he left for Columbia U.
        2. "Described as contentious, antisocial, and conceited"
        3. 1896: opened world's first psychology clinic
        4. His clinical psychology is not psychotherapy
        5. Practiced assessing and treating learning and behavioral problems; more closely "school psychology"
        6. Offered first college course in clinical psychology
        7. Started and edits (for 29 years) first clinical journal: Psychological Clinic

8. Life
   a. Born in Philadelphia; son of pharmacist who valued education
   b. Undergraduate degree from U. of Penn. in 1884
   c. Taught history and English at a private school
   d. Returns to U. of Penn. for law, switches to psychology
      (1) Needed money, secured paid assistantship under Cattell
      (2) Begins to study individual differences in reaction time
      (3) Cattell chooses Witmer as his successor at U. of Penn.
      (4) Cattell has Witmer finish Ph.D. under Wundt in Leipzig
         (a) Studies under Wundt and Külpe
         (b) Titchener was classmate
         (c) Witmer unimpressed with Wundt's methods: slovenly
         (d) Witmer's reaction times too fast, Wundt questions validity
         (e) Comes to doubt introspection method
         (f) Later said got nothing out of Leipzig except degree
   e. Returns to U. of Penn. again as professor in 1892
      (1) Same year Titchener earns degree and goes to Cornell
      (2) Same year Münsterberg is brought to Harvard by James
      (3) Same year Hall started APA (Witmer was charter member)
   f. First two years: experimental psychologist working on individual differences and psychology of pain
   g. Searching for opportunity to apply psychology to abnormal behavior
   h. March 1896: opportunity knocks
      (1) Many state education boards required teachers to take classes
      (2) Influx of students into psychology departments, which offered many such courses
      (3) Witmer taught some, a teacher brought a problem
         (a) 14-year old student
         (b) He couldn't spell, progressed in other areas
         (c) Creates makeshift clinic to help him
   i. Within months, Witmer is teaching methods for treating the mentally challenged
   j. Publishes article in Pediatrics "recommending that psychology be applied to practical affairs"
   k. Presents paper on topic at APA, using "clinical psychology" for the first time
   l. 1907: founds journal Psychological Clinic
   m. 1908: establishes boarding school for retarded/disturbed children
   n. 1909: expands university clinic
   o. Retires from U. of Penn. in 1937
9. Clinics for Child Evaluation
   a. He develops his own "diagnostic and treatment approaches"
   b. Referred children had broad range of problems (e.g., hyperactivity, learning disabilities, poor speech, motor development)
   c. He developed standard assessments and treatments
   d. Added physicians, social workers, psychologists to staff

   e. Assessments involved physical examinations
     (1) Witmer recognized the influence of physical deficits on emotional and cognitive functions
     (2) Tested for malnutrition, visual and hearing deficits
   f. At first, Witmer believed genetics played key role, later realized the importance of environmental factors
     (1) Saw need for a variety of sensory experiences early in life
     (2) Believed in having families, schools involved in treatment
  10. Witmer's Contribution
   a. Set an example: by 1914, 20 psychology clinics opened
   b. Trained students and spread his approach to clinical work
   c. Contributed to special education
   d. Student Morris Viteles extended Witmer's work by establishing a vocational guidance clinic
   e. Work extended to adult populations later on

B. The profession of clinical psychology
  1. Two books provide impetus to field
   a. Clifford Beers (1908), a former mental patient, on the need to deal humanely with the mentally ill
   b. Hugo Münsterberg (1909), describing treatments for mental disorders
  2. First child guidance clinic 1909, aim to treat child disorders early, used Witmer's team approach (used physicians, psychologists, psychiatrists, etc.)
  3. Sigmund Freud, whose ideas broadened the definition of clinical psychology to include psychotherapy
  4. Still, clinical psychology grew slowly
   a. As late as 1918 no graduate programs in clinical
   b. By 1940, clinical psychology still minor
     (1) Few treatment facilities for disturbed adults
     (2) Few job opportunities
   c. Training limited
   d. Jobs limited to doing test administrations
  5. Situation changes during World War II
   a. Draftees have problems with anxiety, depression, antisocial behavior, uncontrollable anger, etc.--> 2 million men rejected for service because of psychological problems
   b. Army establishes training programs for several hundred clinical psychologists
   c. Needed to treat emotionally disturbed soldiers
  6. After WWII need for clinicians even greater
   a. Veteran's Administration (VA) responsible for over 40,000 psychiatric patients (veterans)
   b. Three million other veterans needed vocational/personal counseling
   c. Over 300,000 needed help adjusting to physical disabilities
   d. VA funded graduate programs, paid tuition for those willing to work for VA
  7. This changes clinical psychology
   a. Before war, dealt mostly with children
   b. After war, adults with severe emotional problems

8. The VA is still the largest employer of psychologists in U.S.
9. Today, clinical is largest area of psychology, in a variety of settings

V. The Industrial-Organizational Psychology Movement
   A. Walter Dill Scott (1869-1955)
      1. Student of Wundt
      2. Applied psychology to advertising and business
      3. Historian notes: Scott's writings reflect his shift from Germanic theorizing to describing how to influence others (e.g., consumers, audiences, workers)
      4. Several "firsts"
         a. first to apply psychology to personnel management and advertising
         b. first author of book in the field
         c. first to have title: Professor of Applied Pscyhology
         d. founded first psychological consulting company
         e. first psychologist to receive Distinguished Service Medal from U.S. army
      5. His life
         a. born on family farm near Normal, Illinois
         b. discovered need for efficiency by working on the farm; reading books while horses rested between plow lines in the field
         c. picked up odd jobs to earn college tuition
         d. won scholarship to Northwestern, took tutoring jobs for extra money
         e. met woman who would become his wife
         f. decided to be a missionary to China
         g. after graduating seminary, no more spots in China
         h. took up psychology because had a class
         i. read article about Wundt's lab, went to Germany with new bride
         j. he and wife earn Ph.D. (his: psychology, hers: literature)
         k. joins faculty at Northwestern
         l. executive approaches him about applying psychology to advertising
         m. later writes *The Theory and Practice of Advertising* (1903)
         n. reputation grows, becomes in demand
         o. World War I, offers skills to Army to help select military personnel
            (1) at first, not well received
            (2) takes skeptical army general to lunch, wins him over
            (3) later is given Distinguished Service Medal
         p. created The Scott Company (consulting firm)
         q. president of Northwestern 1920-1939
      6. Advertising and human suggestibility
         a. writes about the sense organs as "windows of the soul", how advertising must "awaken in the reader as many different kinds of images as the object itself can excite"
         b. consumers often not rational, so can be influenced easily
         c. should use "emotion, sympathy, and sentimentality"
         d. believed women more suggestible than men
         e. recommends using direct commands; example "Use Pears Soap"
         f. promoted using return coupons to make consumer actively engaged

7. Employee selection
  a. devised rating scales, group tests (first measure characteristics of people already successful, then use those results to screen applicants)
    (1) interviewed army officers and business managers
    (2) they ranked subordinates on several variables
    (3) then he ranked job applicants on the same variables
    (4) compared applicants' test scores to those of successful employees
  b. created tests that could be administered to groups, not individuals, for maximum efficiency
  c. other psychological tests, such as for intelligence, interested not in just general intelligence, but in how person applies their intelligence (e.g., judgment, quickness, accuracy)
8. Scott often barely mentioned in history of psychology
  a. because of applied work; little experimental research
  b. applied work often traditionally derogated by academicians; little publishing in mainstream journals
  c. Scott and other applied psychologists believed their work outside of the academic setting brought recognition to the importance of psychology and afforded it the esteem it received
B. The impact of the World Wars
  1. WWI broadened "scope, popularity, and growth of I/O psychology"
    a. Scott had tested 3 million soldiers
    b. after war, industry seeks I/O practitioners
  2. WWII also creates big boom
    a. by 1941 German military employed 500 psychologists
    b. for Americans, equipment more complex, required higher skills, training
    c. spurred human factors engineering, active today in a large variety of fields
    d. engineering psychologists used to supply info about human capacities and limitations
C. The Hawthorne Studies and Organizational Issues
  1. primary focus of I/O psychologists in 1920's was selection
  2. 1927, start of multi-year research program at the Western Electric plant in Hawthorne, IL
  3. extends field to human relations, motivation, morale
  4. research begins by seeking effects of physical environment on productivity
  5. psychologists found that more profound effects on productivity came from the social-psychological factors
  6. for example, being watched and interviewed by the researchers increased production, made workers feel like employers care about them personally
  7. leads to study of "behavior of leaders, informal work groups, employee attitudes, communication patterns...and other factors"
  8. causes APA Division of Industrial Psychology to be renamed "Industrial and Organizational Psychology"

D. Contributions of Women to I/O
    1. historically has provided careers to women
    2. first person to get Ph.D. in I/O is Lillian Gilbreth, from Brown University
        a.   with husband Frank Gilbreth, promote time-and-motion studies
        b.   they both write a book, but publisher won't put Lillian's name on it, says "no one will buy it"
        c.   her own book published under: L. M. Gilbreth
        d.   she overcomes these and other barriers, has successful career
        e.   has likeness on postage stamp
        f.   gave birth 13 times at 15 month intervals; was also efficient in organizing the home
        g.   designed the shelves on the inside of refrigerators for maximum efficiency
    3. today, over half of Ph.D. I/O candidates are women

VI.   Hugo Münsterberg (1863-1916)
A. for a time, enjoyed phenomenal success, popularity
    1. influence in applied areas like clinical, industrial, and forensic psychology
    2. wrote hundreds of articles, dozens of books
    3. most directed to popular, not academic, audience
    4. frequent guest to White House, acquainted with variety of powerful, famous, and influential people
    5. an honored professor at Harvard
    6. founder of applied psychology in U.S. and Europe
    7. a flair for promotion, sensationalism
    8. described as self-centered, egotistical
B. toward end of life, subject of scorn and caricature, "most hated individual in America"
C. his life
    1. goes to Leipzig, takes psychology course, is hooked
    2. gets Ph.D. under Wundt: 1885
    3. two years later gets M.D.
    4. accepts teaching position at University of Freiburg
        a.   sets up lab in own house, own expense
        b.   wrote articles in psychophysics
        c.   attracts followers, students
    5. receives and accepts invitation from William James to head lab at Harvard: 1892
    6. at first, disapproves of applied psychology
        a.   attacks applied colleagues work in article
        b.   criticizes those who wrote for general public, gave paid lectures, provide service for fee
    7. wrote *American Traits* (1902) analysis of American culture
        a.   dictated this 400-page book in less than a month
        b.   James: Münsterberg's brain never tires
        c.   book enthusiastically received
    8. soon writing other popular articles/books on wide variety of topics: courtroom trials, advertising, mental health, vocational guidance, education, business issues, etc.
    9. never shies from controversy
        a.   during sensational murder trial
             (1) he gives mental tests to confessed killer

     (2) Münsterberg announces that the confession implicating the
      labor leader is true
     (3) jury acquits labor leader
     (4) Münsterberg's credibility damaged
   b.   Prohibition
     (1) he argues against it, says alcohol in moderation beneficial
     (2) German-American brewers give Münsterberg large amounts of
      cash for his foundation
     (3) "coincidence" of donation suspicious to the public
   c.   beliefs about women
     (1) supportive of the women grad students at Harvard
     (2) thought graduate work too demanding for women
     (3) should get no career training, takes them from home
     (4) should not teach, not good role model for boys
     (5) should not serve on juries because "incapable of rational
      deliberation"
  10. Harvard president displeased, strained relationship, advised him to not respond
   to reporter's questions
  11. Münsterberg defends Germany at WWI outbreak
   a.   American public opinion anti-German
   b.   Münsterberg still German citizen
   c.   Newspapers: Münsterberg is a spy, force him to resign from
     Harvard
   d.   Harvard alumnus: will bequeath $10 million if you fire Münsterberg
     snubbed and ostracized by colleagues and public, gets death threats
  12. Dies of a stroke while giving a lecture.
 D. Forensic psychology
  1. psychology and law: writes articles on crime prevention, using hypnosis,
   giving mental tests, reliability of eyewitness testimony
  2. does research on eyewitness testimony; finds it to be fallible/unreliable
  3. writes *On the Witness Stand* (1908); discusses psychological factors in jury
   trials
   a.   false confessions
   b.   power of suggestion in cross-examination
   c.   use of physiological measurement to detect emotional arousal
 E. *Psychotherapy* (1909)
  1. treated patients in his lab
  2. did not charge a fee
  3. believed power of suggestion could cure
  4. believed mental illness was "behavioral maladjustment problem", not
   unconscious conflicts as Freud said
   a.   Münsterberg: "there is no subconscious"
   b.   when Freud comes to Clark in 1909, Münsterberg leaves country to
     avoid conflict, returns when Freud has left country
  5. brings clinical psychology to public, but Witmer displeased
   a.   Witmer never sought fame
   b.   Witmer: Münsterberg has 'cheapened' the profession, calls him a
     faith healer

F. Industrial psychology promoter
    1. 1909 article: "Psychology and the Market", which applies psychology to "vocational guidance, advertising, personnel management, mental testing, employee motivation, and the effects of fatigue and monotony on job performance."
    2. works as consultant
    3. publishes *Psychology and Industrial Efficiency* (1913), becomes best-seller
       a.   argues that selection is best way to improve productivity, etc.
       b.   select using psychological tests on job applicants
    4. conducts research on variety of occupations: "ship captain, streetcar driver, telephone operator, and salesperson"
    5. showed that talking while working reduces productivity. Solution: put workstations/physical barriers between workers

VII. Applied Psychology in the United States: A National Mania
  A. World War I put psychologists "on the map"
  B. Some experimental journals stopped publication during war, others (Journal of Applied Psychology) thrive
  C. At war's end, applied psychology fully entrenched
  D. Support spills over to university positions: new buildings, labs, programs, and better funding
  E. APA membership increases threefold
  F. APA controlled by academicians who derogate applied work
  G. 1919: APA rule requires published experimental work for entry, in turn prohibiting membership for applied psychologists
  H. Still, applied psychology skyrockets in popularity with the public
    1. people thought psychologists could "fix anything"
    2. new magazines: "The Modern Psychologist" and "Psychology: Health, Happiness, Success"
    3. New York Times editorial: psychology "always proves its value"
  I. Psychologists drawn away from academia to applied work
  J. 1921 American Men of Science: 75% of listed psychologists doing applied work, up from 50% in 1910
  K. Economic depression of the 1930's, psychology under attack
    1. psychologists perceived as failing
    2. psychologists blamed for "corporate ills"
    3. Grace Adams (student of Titchener): psychology had "forsaken its scientific roots"
    4. New York Times: psychologists had overstated their abilities
  L. Public interest in psychology declines; disenchantment with applied psychology
  M. World War II revives interest
    1. 25% of American psychologists involved directly in war effort (although female psychologists largely excluded)
  N. Since then, psychology enjoys respect from general public
  O. Applied psychology bigger than academic
  P. Shift in power in APA, to clinical work
  Q. 1988: new professional organization: American Psychological Society

Lecture prompts/Discussion topics for chapter eight

- What was Münsterberg's influence on psychology? Who was more important to I/O psychology, Munsterberg, the Gilbreths, or Walter Dill Scott? Who should be the designated "parent" of industrial and organization psychology?
- Can there be a psychology without tests and measures of mental characteristics? If so, what might that psychology look like? Would it still be a science?

Internet Resources for chapter eight

History of Psychology at the University of Pennsylvania

http://www.psych.upenn.edu/history/history.htm

> This nifty website includes many of the people discussed in this chapter and throughout the text. For example there are links from the page listed above to more extensive information about Cattell and Witmer.

Human Intelligence Project: Robert Mearns Yerkes

http://www.indiana.edu/~intell/yerkes.shtml

> This site gives more information about Yerkes, including a photograph of his commission that created the Army Alpha and Army Beta tests.

Internet Archive: The Films of Frank Gilbreth

http://www.archive.org/search.php?query=gilbreth

> This site is a repository of a variety of materials. Two films that may be of interest are the ones on the page above made by Frank Gilbreth, showing the improvement in work performance using his and Lillian's time and motion studies.

Society for Industrial and Organizational Psychology

www.siop.org

> This is the professional society for Industrial and Organizational psychology, and has extensive information about the discipline, its history, and the types of work performed by its practitioners.

The Vineland Training School: History

http://www.vineland.org/history/trainingschool/history/eugenics.htm

> This is the organization that Henry Goddard directed. This website gives more detailed information about Goddard's beliefs and work, particularly in reference to the Eugenics movement.

Potential answers to chapter eight discussion questions

1. What was the significance for psychology of the Coca-Cola trial and Hollingworth's research?

One of the first precipitating (and visible) events in applied psychology was the Coca-Cola trial. Because Coke contained caffeine, the company was restricted by FDA regulations and thus pursued by the Federal government. In preparing for the trial, Coke hired Harry Hollingworth to test the effects of caffeine on a number of outcomes. Hollingworth who found no ill effects and Coke won the initial court battle. This case demonstrated the applicability of psychology to real world problems, using strict experimental methods.

2. Why did the approaches to psychology pursued by Wundt and by Titchener fail to survive in the United States?

Oddly enough, even though Wundt had trained many of the first American psychologists, his ideas had little influence on their work. The work of "Darwin, Galton, and Spencer" was much more influential. This was partly due to the American Zeitgeist, which valued practicality. There were contextual forces as well at work in America to foster the growth of applied psychology. The number of people with a Ph.D. in psychology rose and there were not enough academic positions to employ them, and when one attained a teaching job many administrations did not value (or fund) psychology programs. An emerging societal problem was a dramatic increase in public school enrollment, which opened doors for some psychologists.

3. In what ways did psychology grow and prosper in the U.S. in the period from 1880 to 1900? Give specific examples.

During this 20-year period in America 41 psychology laboratories, 3 journals, and 40 doctoral programs appeared where there were none before. At the same time applied psychology blossomed.

4. How did economic forces influence the development of applied psychology? Do you think applied psychology would have developed when it did without these forces?

The number of people with a Ph.D. in psychology rose and there were not enough academic positions to employ them, and when one attained a teaching job many administrations did not value (or fund) psychology programs. An emerging societal problem was a dramatic increase in public school enrollment, which opened doors for some psychologists. Without this pull, applied psychology would not have developed when it did. In addition, many psychologists, like Hollingworth, had few opportunities for economic advancement and so took contracts from corporations. The economic condition of psychologists at the time made it more plausible for the shift into business and industry.

5. How did Cattell's work alter the nature of American psychology? How did he promote psychology to the public?

One of the early influences on the mental testing movement was James McKeen Cattell. While working under Galton, Cattell's use of quantification emerges and blossoms. Such statistical analysis later allows the comparison of large data sets and "opened new research possibilities." He also promoted psychology to the general publish through his popular science magazines.

6. Compare the approaches of Cattell and Binet to the development of mental tests.
Cattell coins the term "mental test" in an 1890 article and begins large scale testing in his research. His tests looked much like Galton's, psychomotor rather than cognitive tests. The first true test of mental ability came from the work of Alfred Binet, a French psychologist. He disagreed with Galton and Cattell in their approach to mental testing, and using observations of his own young daughters developed true cognitive tests based on memory, attention, imagination, and comprehension. With Théodore Simon, he developed a test of 30 problems arranged in ascending difficulty to be used to help schoolchildren. The tests were later revised to measure mental age, the age at which children of average ability could perform tasks.

7. Describe the impact of World War I on the testing movement.
The day World War I began, there was a meeting of Titchener's Experimentalists. At the meeting "Robert Yerkes urged the group to consider how psychology could aid the war effort." One problem was the classification of the large number of recruits in the army. The Stanford-Binet was not practical to use (it was administered individually and required training to administer). Yerkes received a commission from the army for which he developed intelligence tests that could be administered in groups: Army Alpha and Army Beta (for those illiterate in English). More than a million recruits were tested.

8. Define the concepts of *mental age* and *IQ*. How are they calculated?
Mental age "is the age at which children of average ability can perform certain tasks." IQ was created by William Stern, and is the ratio of one's mental age to one's chronological age (multiplying mental age by 100 and dividing by chronological age). IQ is measured by intelligence tests, which measure more complex mental processes. IQ is also standardized according to the bell curve, and thus a more accurate measure of distribution.

9. Why did some organizations abandon the use of psychological tests in the 1920s despite their popularity?
"An epidemic of testing swept the United States, but in the haste to answer the urgent call of business and education, it was inevitable that some poorly designed and inadequately researched tests would be promoted, leading to disappointing results. As a result, many organizations abandoned their use of psychological tests for a time."

10. How were analogies with medicine and engineering used to lend scientific authority to intelligence testing?
Psychologists used metaphors from medicine and engineering to bolster the reputation of testing. Subjects became labeled "patients", tests were "thermometers" that required training to administer correctly, and were promoted as X-ray machines into one's mind. Schools were called "education factories" and educational tests measured "factory products."

11. How were tests used in the United States to support the notion of racial differences in intelligence and the alleged inferiority of immigrants?
Henry Goddard, who had translated Binet's test, visited Ellis island because he believed that mentally retarded and other "feeble-minded" immigrants were being allowed to enter the country. He proposed using the Stanford-Binet to identify such immigrants, despite their unfamiliarity with American culture and the English language. It was not a surprise that Goddard concluded at least 80% of the immigrants coming to Ellis Island were "feeble-minded." These results were used later to create restrictive immigration laws. Combining these results with the results of Army

Alpha and Beta led to the inaccurate conclusion that there were biological differences in intelligence attributable to race.

12. In your opinion, are intelligence tests biased against members of minority groups? Defend your answer.

This is an opinion question. Support for the "Yes" response: There is a long history showing differences in intelligence between racial groups. These differences either reflect: a) actual differences, or b) problems with the tests. Scores can be affected by such things as socioeconomic status, which is related to racial groupings. Results from Bond's studies suggest that White southerners score lower than Black northern on measures of IQ, thus the test has an environmental bias. Support for the "No" response: Although older tests of intelligence did have a built in racial and cultural biases, modern tests that are more well-researched have removed those biases. By giving the tests in a variety of languages and testing skills rather than knowledge, many modern intelligence tests are much improved.

13. Discuss the role of women in the testing movement. Why was their work at a professional disadvantage?

Because many academic positions were not open to women, many found work in applied fields. Florence Goodenough developed the Draw-A-Man test, a version of which is still used today. Maude Merrill James worked with Terman on the Stanford-Binet, and Thelma Thurstone worked with her husband on the Primary Mental Abilities test. Psyche Cattell extended the Stanford-Binet to be used with babies as young as 3 months. Anne Anastasi became an authority on psychological testing, writing over 150 articles and a testing textbook. Although these women were successful, careers outside of academia tend to be invisible with regard to enduring professional reputation, because the opportunities and motivations to publish are slim.

14. How did the work of Witmer and Münsterberg influence the growth of clinical psychology?

Lightner Witmer (1867-1956) opened the world's first psychology clinic in 1896. He did not practice psychotherapy, instead he assessed and treated learning and behavioral problems in children. Later he created the first clinical psychology journal, and is acknowledged as the world's first clinical psychologist although he shied away from popular attention. Münsterberg wrote popular articles and books on a variety of issues, including a book called *Psychotherapy* (1908). He believed that the power of suggestion can cure mental ill health, and believed there is no subconscious, rather mental illness was a "behavioral maladjustment problem." These two psychologists shifted the attention from what is normal behavior to what is abnormal and suggested that abnormal behavior requires remedy, whereby emphasizing individual differences.

15. How did Witmer and Münsterberg differ in their views of clinical psychology?

Witmer did not practice psychotherapy, instead he assessed and treated learning and behavioral problems in children. Because he was the first clinical psychologist, Witmer had to devise his own methods. The children who came to his clinic faced a wide variety of problems. His confidence, and his clinic and staff, grew with time. He created a team approach, including staff from a variety of health fields. For example, part of his assessment was medical, recognizing that physical issues could impact on cognition and behavior. He came to see the importance of environment on children's well-being. In contrast, Münsterberg believed that he could heal mental illness using suggestibility as treatment, and because of his strong reputation he believed he could command patients to good mental health.

16. Discuss the roles of Scott and Münsterberg in the origin of industrial-organizational psychology.

Walter Dill Scott, a former student of Wundt, applied psychology to advertising and to business operations. The work he is most known for is his advertising work, in which he suggested that emotions would increase suggestibility and advised his clients to use direct commands to sell products. He promoted the idea of the return coupon to promote consumer action. Scott also created rating scales to be used in employee selection, although they were group-administered tests. Münsterberg promoted industrial psychology beginning with an article he wrote in 1909, consulted with organizations, and in his book *Psychology and Industrial Efficiency* (1913) promotes the use of mental/psychological testing for job applicants.

17. How was industrial-organizational psychology affected by the Hawthorne studies and the wars?

Another broadening of industrial psychology happened because of the Hawthorne Studies. This set of studies, lasting from 1927 into the 1930's, set out to determine "the effects of the physical work environment" on productivity. Instead, the researchers discovered that the workplace is a complex social environment, which lead to the human relations movement and the expansion of Industrial Psychology into Industrial/Organizational Psychology.

18. What role did women play in the development of industrial/organizational psychology?

Women were welcome into industrial and organizational psychology, yet not without some setbacks. "The first person to receive a Ph.D. in the field was Lillian Gilbreth" (who shared a field with husband, Frank Gilbreth). Publishers refused to put her name on books she wrote for fear that executives would not purchase the books. However, she had a long and prosperous career. Today nearly 50% of I/O psychologists are women.

19. Describe Münsterberg's contributions to forensic psychology.

Münsterberg published *On the Witness Stand* (1908) in which he discusses such things as false confessions and the reliability of eyewitness testimony. He also wrote a series of popular articles about psychological issues in the courtroom.

20. Why were Münsterberg's outspoken views often unpopular with other psychologists? How did he come to be a despised figure among the general public?

He inserted himself in the center of some controversial events, which cost him some of his good reputation from both the public and from other psychologists. His views on women, for example, were paradoxical—he supported some in the Harvard program but believed generally that "graduate work was too demanding," and that women should stay at home, should not teach in schools, and should not serve on juries because "they were incapable of rational deliberation." At the outbreak of World War I, Münsterberg defended Germany, which caused his ostracism. Witmer berated Münsterberg for making sham promises in clinical work, and labeled him as a "faith healer."

21. Compare the growth and popularity of applied psychology in the 1920s, the 1930s, and the period since the end of World War II.

By the time World War I ends, applied psychology was fully entrenched and valued in America. The number of psychologists and graduate programs boomed. As a result, in 1919 the APA created changes that effectively banned applied psychologists from membership. Still, applied psychology kept growing until the economic decline in the 1930's, when applied psychology became somewhat of a scapegoat, and its reputation declined until World War II. About "25% of

American psychologists were directly involved in the war effort", and psychology has generally been well-regarded ever since. The majority of contemporary psychologists are applied rather than university-based.

Key terms from chapter eight

- **Army Alpha and Army Beta** Tests developed by psychologists to help classify soldiers in World War I (Beta was used for those without English proficiency or literacy).
- **Caffeine** A drug according to the newly-formed FDA, which caused the Federal government to take Coca Cola to court.
- **Clinical psychology** Field created by Lightener Witmer to assist children who had educational difficulties.
- **Hawthorne studies** Multi-year study with intention to study physical environment on productivity, the real finding is the effect of the social environment on productivity and psychological variables.
- **Industrial and Organizational Psychology** Field created by Walter Scott that applies psychology to advertising and business.
- **Intelligence Quotient** A concept originating with William Stern, the ratio of mental to chronological age.
- **Mental age** "The age at which children of average ability can perform certain tasks", and is developed by Binet and Simon.
- **Mental test** Term coined by James McKeen Cattell in an article he published in 1890, although his mental tests look more like tests of sensorimotor abilities than cognitive ability.
- **Personal Data Sheet** A test developed by Robert Sessions Woodworth that was used to identify neurotic recruits in World War I.

TESTBANK

ESSAY

1. Essentially, the first generation of American psychologists was educated by Wundt yet he had less influence on American psychology than did Darwin and Galton. Discuss the reasons for this paradox.

   ANS:
   Answer not provided.

   PTS: 1

2. Describe the economic forces that influenced the growth of applied psychology in America.

   ANS:
   Answer not provided.

   PTS: 1

3. Describe Cattell's contributions to psychology. How did these contributions alter the character of American psychology? How did he make psychology known to the public?

ANS:
Answer not provided.

PTS: 1   MSC: WWW

4. Describe, compare, and contrast the approaches to mental and intelligence testing taken by Cattell and Binet.

ANS:
Answer not provided.

PTS: 1

5. Discuss and provide supporting evidence for your analysis of the statement that "Intelligence testing has been both psychology's greatest contribution to society and its biggest source of shame."

ANS:
Answer not provided.

PTS: 1

6. Describe, compare, and contrast the applied psychology of Lightner Witmer and Walter Dill Scott.

ANS:
Answer not provided.

PTS: 1

7. Discuss Münsterberg's contributions to I/O psychology, psychotherapy, and forensic psychology.

ANS:
Answer not provided.

PTS: 1

8. Discuss the role of women in at least two different areas of applied psychology. Why was it difficult for them to make the kinds of professional contributions made by men?

ANS:
Answer not provided.

PTS: 1   MSC: WWW

9. Why did the FDA take Coca Cola to court in 1911?
   a. Because one of Coke's ingredients was cocaine.
   b. Because one of Coke's ingredients was caffeine.
   c. Because of illegal hiring practices.
   d. Because of irregularities in the pricing of their stock.
   e. Because they made unsupported claims in advertising.

   ANS: B   PTS: 1   REF: FDA Raid: Target Coca-Cola

10. Who was hired by Coca Cola to perform research in their 1911 court case?
    a. James McKeen Cattell
    b. Hugo Munsterberg
    c. Walter Dill Scott
    d. Robert Yerkes
    e. Harry Hollingworth

    ANS: E   PTS: 1   REF: FDA Raid: Target Coca-Cola

11. The main reason Wundt's and Titchener's systems did not survive in the United States was that they _____.
    a. were German psychologies
    b. were not pragmatic
    c. were not fruitful
    d. were opposed to the behavioristic bent of Americans
    e. relied on introspection

    ANS: B   PTS: 1   REF: Toward a Practical Psychology

12. According to Cattell, by 1895 psychology was _____.
    a. a required subject for an undergraduate degree
    b. being irreparably damaged by the Structuralist-functionalist quarreling
    c. still synonymous with metaphysics for most Americans
    d. most vigorously opposed by the traditional natural sciences
    e. relatively unpopular in those few colleges that offered courses in it

    ANS: A   PTS: 1   REF: Toward a Practical Psychology

13. In 1900, the American public's response to the new science of psychology was _____.
    a. concern about psychologists' ability to read people's minds
    b. to reject it until World War I and the development of intelligence tests
    c. to embrace it
    d. to reject functionalism but accept structuralism
    e. to reject structuralism but accept functionalism

    ANS: C   PTS: 1   REF: Toward a Practical Psychology
    MSC: WWW

14. At the end of the 19th century, the field of ____ demanded the application of psychological principles to practical problems with rise in private school education.
    a. physiology
    b. military science
    c. education
    d. social casework
    e. criminal justice

    ANS: C   PTS: 1   REF: Toward a Practical Psychology

15. What persuaded psychologists to apply their expertise to problems in education?
    a. World War I and immigration
    b. An increase in public school enrollment
    c. Intelligence testing
    d. The popular appeal and status of psychology
    e. James's *Talks to Teachers* and the need to test and educate newly arrived immigrants

    ANS: B   PTS: 1   REF: Toward a Practical Psychology

16. Cattell's work was novel in its focus on ____.
    a. conscious content
    b. conscious process
    c. human abilities
    d. personality
    e. reaction time studies

    ANS: C   PTS: 1   REF: Mental Testing

17. Cattell's interest in psychology was provoked by ____.
    a. Fechner's book on psychophysics
    b. Wundt's book on experimental psychology
    c. James's *Principles*
    d. Freud's papers on cocaine
    e. his own use of drugs

    ANS: E   PTS: 1   REF: James McKeen Cattell (1860-1944)

18. Cattell wrote that he found himself "making brilliant discoveries in science and philosophy" when ____.
    a. with Wundt at Leipzig
    b. with Hall at Johns Hopkins
    c. with James at Harvard
    d. using drugs
    e. studying psychophysics

    ANS: D   PTS: 1   REF: James McKeen Cattell (1860-1944)

19. Cattell's Ph.D. was earned with ____.
    a. Wundt at Leipzig
    b. James at Harvard
    c. Titchener at Cornell
    d. Angell at Chicago
    e. Hall at Johns Hopkins

    ANS: A   PTS: 1   REF: James McKeen Cattell (1860-1944)

20. Cattell's interest in mental tests probably was aroused most by _____.
    a. his work on reaction times in Wundt's laboratory
    b. Freud's development of projective tests
    c. Hall's use of questionnaires
    d. his meeting with Galton while at Cambridge University
    e. Hall's child study movement

    ANS: D   PTS: 1   REF: James McKeen Cattell (1860-1944)
    MSC: WWW

21. Which of the following methods did Cattell develop?
    a. the chi-square test
    b. the order-of-merit ranking method
    c. correlational methods
    d. the eugenics formula
    e. the standard deviation formula

    ANS: B   PTS: 1   REF: James McKeen Cattell (1860-1944)

22. Galton's influence on Cattell led to _____.
    a. Cattell promoting the use of experimental and control groups
    b. Cattell's method of average error
    c. Cattell's work on the army Alpha and army Beta tests
    d. Witmer's work with dyslexic children
    e. the study of large groups rather than single subjects

    ANS: E   PTS: 1   REF: James McKeen Cattell (1860-1944)

23. Which of the following techniques became more widely applied in American psychology than in England?
    a. graphic display of data
    b. correlation coefficient
    c. chi-square test
    d. anthropometric techniques
    e. correlation coefficient and chi-square test

    ANS: E   PTS: 1   REF: James McKeen Cattell (1860-1944)

24. Cattell was a strong proponent of _____.
    a. eugenics
    b. the single-subject design
    c. Watson's behaviorism
    d. social Darwinism
    e. United States involvement in World War I

    ANS: A   PTS: 1   REF: James McKeen Cattell (1860-1944)

25. Who argued for the sterilization of mental defectives and delinquents and cash incentives for the best and the brightest to marry and have children?
    a. Scott
    b. Hall
    c. Yerkes
    d. Münsterberg
    e. Cattell

    ANS: E   PTS: 1   REF: James McKeen Cattell (1860-1944)

26. Which early psychologist "rescued" the journal *Science*?
    a. Scott
    b. Hall
    c. Yerkes
    d. Münsterberg
    e. Cattell

    ANS: E   PTS: 1   REF: James McKeen Cattell (1860-1944)

27. Unlike Titchener, Cattell believed graduate students should ____.
    a. study the contents of consciousness
    b. adopt Carr's final form of functionalism
    c. study children as well as adults
    d. study animals as well as humans
    e. study whatever they liked

    ANS: E   PTS: 1   REF: James McKeen Cattell (1860-1944)
    MSC: WWW

28. The original purpose for the founding of The Psychological Corporation was to ____.
    a. bolster the public image of psychologists after Cattell's public dalliance with the occult
    b. bolster the public image of psychologists after Cattell's termination for disloyalty to the United States in World War I
    c. deliver applied psychological services
    d. create a corporation that would publish Cattell's many books and journals
    e. take revenge on G. Stanley Hall, who Cattell detested

    ANS: C   PTS: 1   REF: James McKeen Cattell (1860-1944)

29. The results of Cattell's research on mental tests with students at Columbia University indicated that his measures ____.
    a. were valid predictors of college achievement but not of intelligence
    b. were valid predictors of intelligence but not of college grades
    c. predicted students' grades in psychology courses but not in courses in the natural sciences
    d. were unreliable because of personal equations
    e. None of the choices are correct.

    ANS: E   PTS: 1   REF: James McKeen Cattell (1860-1944)

30. The largest "family" of second-generation psychologists was fostered by ____.
    a. Titchener
    b. James
    c. Binet
    d. Cattell
    e. Watson

    ANS: D   PTS: 1   REF: James McKeen Cattell (1860-1944)

31. The first effective tests of mental faculties were developed by ____.
    a. Hall
    b. Cattell
    c. Binet
    d. Terman
    e. Wechsler

    ANS: C   PTS: 1   REF: The Psychological Testing Movement
    MSC: WWW

32. Binet and Simon's test differed from those of Galton and Cattell in its ____.
    a. emphasis on the relationship of higher cognitive processes to intelligence
    b. emphasis on the evolution of children's mental abilities
    c. emphasis on the recapitulation of childhood abilities in adolescence
    d. emphasis on using sensorimotor tests to assess mental abilities
    e. inclusion of Hall's questionnaires as a device for assessing mental abilities

    ANS: A   PTS: 1   REF: The Psychological Testing Movement

33. Binet based his conclusion about appropriate measure of intelligence based on research conducted with
    ____.
    a. French school children
    b. Cattell's students
    c. G. Stanley Hall
    d. his daughters
    e. Lewis Terman

    ANS: D   PTS: 1   REF: The Psychological Testing Movement

34. If a 10-year-old can perform the same tasks as the average 15-year-old, then the child's ____ is 15 and
    ____ is 150.
    a. mental age; IQ score
    b. IQ score; mental age
    c. mental age; developmental quotient.
    d. developmental quotient; IQ score
    e. developmental quotient; mental age

    ANS: A   PTS: 1   REF: The Psychological Testing Movement

35. Who translated and introduced the Binet intelligence test to American psychologists?
    a. Cattell
    b. Scott
    c. Simon
    d. James
    e. Goddard

    ANS: E   PTS: 1   REF: The Psychological Testing Movement

36. Who revised the Binet intelligence test into what is known as the Stanford-Binet test?
    a. Terman
    b. Goddard
    c. Cattell
    d. Witmer
    e. Yerkes

    ANS: A   PTS: 1   REF: The Psychological Testing Movement

37. The construct called "IQ" was developed by ____.
    a. Binet
    b. Simon
    c. Pearson
    d. Cattell
    e. Stern

    ANS: E   PTS: 1   REF: The Psychological Testing Movement

38. The fundamental difference between the Binet tests and the army Alpha and Beta tests was that _____.
    a. Binet's tests were in French; the army tests were in English
    b. the army tests included sensorimotor skills and reaction times
    c. Binet's tests were individually administered; the army tests were for groups
    d. the army tests could not assess mental ages lower than 17
    e. Binet's tests required literate subjects; the army tests did not

    ANS: C   PTS: 1   REF: The Psychological Testing Movement

39. The results of testing by the Yerkes research group _____.
    a. precluded retarded men from serving in World War I
    b. established the criterion for admission to Officer Candidate School
    c. separated the less intelligent into the infantry because they were considered more expendable
    d. showed that testing could be used successfully in criterion development
    e. had no impact on recruitment and selection or the war effort as a whole

    ANS: E   PTS: 1   REF: The Psychological Testing Movement

40. Woodworth's Personal Data Sheet was designed to _____.
    a. separate White from not-White recruits in World War I
    b. separate the literate from the illiterate in World War I
    c. separate the neurotic from the average recruit
    d. assess personality complexes of combat pilots
    e. separate the psychotic from the neurotic recruits

    ANS: C   PTS: 1   REF: The Psychological Testing Movement
    MSC: WWW

41. The effect of World War I on the evolution of psychological testing was to _____.
    a. establish a hospitable environment for such endeavors
    b. identify the need for "culture fair" tests
    c. establish a baseline of racial differences in IQs in the United States
    d. refute the assumption that illiterates are mentally retarded
    e. pave the way for aptitude tests for high-school students

    ANS: A   PTS: 1   REF: The Psychological Testing Movement

42. One consequence of the adoption of the Stanford-Binet test in the United States is that _____.
    a. public education has revolved around the IQ construct ever since
    b. special education courses were established by 1919
    c. Terman used it to study genius among cross-sections of ethnic groups
    d. gifted programs were established by 1923
    e. the campaign to identify learning disabilities was firmly established by 1920

    ANS: A   PTS: 1   REF: The Psychological Testing Movement

43. Unlike _____, who used sensorimotor tests, _____ assessed cognitive functions to measure intelligence.
    a. Darwin; Galton and Cattell
    b. Cattell; Witmer
    c. Galton and Cattell; Binet
    d. Binet; Terman
    e. Goddard; Binet

    ANS: C   PTS: 1   REF: The Psychological Testing Movement

44. The intelligence test, first developed by ____, is the basis for those still used today.
    a. Cattell
    b. Edison
    c. Witmer
    d. Goddard
    e. Binet

    ANS: E   PTS: 1   REF: The Psychological Testing Movement
    MSC: WWW

45. The purpose of adopting metaphors from medical and engineering terminology was to ____.
    a. liken psychology to the established sciences
    b. reduce the stigma attached to seeking psychological help by adopting the terms "doctor"
       and "patient"
    c. show that psychology was scientific
    d. establish psychology as a legitimate profession in medical and industrial settings
    e. refocus the public's attention on the experimental and statistical methods of psychology

    ANS: A   PTS: 1   REF: The Psychological Testing Movement

46. ____ used the Binet test at Ellis Island to restrict the entry of immigrants to the United States.
    a. Simon
    b. Terman
    c. Thorndike
    d. Goddard
    e. Herrnstein

    ANS: D   PTS: 1   REF: The Psychological Testing Movement

47. According to the intelligence testing of U.S. army recruits, which group scored higher on average?
    a. Black Americans
    b. White Americans
    c. Latin American immigrants
    d. Mediterranean immigrants
    e. southern European immigrants

    ANS: B   PTS: 1   REF: The Psychological Testing Movement

48. With regard to racial differences in IQs, the work of African American ____ demonstrated the strong
    effects of environment.
    a. Herrnstein
    b. Goddard
    c. Terman
    d. Bond
    e. Murray

    ANS: D   PTS: 1   REF: The Psychological Testing Movement

49. With regard to racial differences in IQs, the work of ____ revealed that southern Whites test as less
    intelligent than northern Blacks.
    a. Goddard
    b. Thorndike
    c. Herrnstein
    d. Terman
    e. Bond

    ANS: E   PTS: 1   REF: The Psychological Testing Movement

50. Who developed the *Draw-A-Man Test*, a widely used nonverbal intelligence test for children?
    a. Bond
    b. Thurstone
    c. Goodenough
    d. Anastasi
    e. Cattell

    ANS: C   PTS: 1   REF: The Psychological Testing Movement
    MSC: WWW

51. Who extended the age range of the Stanford-Binet downward?
    a. James Cattell
    b. Psyche Cattell
    c. Florence Goodenough
    d. Thelma Thurstone
    e. Anne Anastasi

    ANS: B   PTS: 1   REF: The Psychological Testing Movement

52. The assessment and treatment of abnormal behavior in children was established in American psychology by ____.
    a. Münsterberg
    b. Freud
    c. Goddard
    d. Healey
    e. Witmer

    ANS: E   PTS: 1   REF: Lightner Witmer (1867-1956)

53. Witmer's "clinical psychology" is today known as ____.
    a. the child guidance movement
    b. the child study movement
    c. educational psychology
    d. school psychology
    e. genetic psychology

    ANS: D   PTS: 1   REF: Lightner Witmer (1867-1956)

54. Cattell agreed to employ Witmer at the University of Pennsylvania if he would ____.
    a. study with Freud
    b. study with James at Harvard
    c. earn his Ph.D. with Hall at Clark
    d. earn his Ph.D. at Columbia
    e. earn his Ph.D. with Wundt at Leipzig

    ANS: E   PTS: 1   REF: Lightner Witmer (1867-1956)

55. Witmer's methods of assessment and diagnosis ____.
    a. were constructed as he needed them
    b. were subject to stringent experimental study in laboratories
    c. were subject to stringent experimental study in the field
    d. were tailored to the individual child and thus were not standardized
    e. relied heavily on systems theory for their framework

    ANS: A   PTS: 1   REF: Lightner Witmer (1867-1956)

56. To whom did Witmer turn for his diagnostic and treatment approaches?
    a. Freud
    b. Münsterberg
    c. Cattell
    d. himself
    e. Wundt

    ANS: D   PTS: 1   REF: Lightner Witmer (1867-1956)

57. Behavioral and cognitive disorders would be attributed most heavily to ____ by Witmer.
    a. genetic factors
    b. environmental factors
    c. race
    d. inbreeding
    e. cultural differences

    ANS: B   PTS: 1   REF: Lightner Witmer (1867-1956)

58. The team approach to the assessment and treatment of mental disorders was introduced by ____.
    a. Healey
    b. Münsterberg
    c. Witmer
    d. Beers
    e. Anna Freud

    ANS: C   PTS: 1   REF: Lightner Witmer (1867-1956)

59. Who wrote *Psychotherapy*?
    a. Münsterberg
    b. Viteles
    c. Scott
    d. Beers
    e. Healey

    ANS: A   PTS: 1   REF: Hugo Münsterberg (1863-1916)
    MSC: WWW

60. The first techniques of psychological therapy to be used in America were developed by ____.
    a. Witmer
    b. Münsterberg
    c. Healey
    d. Bleuler
    e. Freud

    ANS: A   PTS: 1   REF: Lightner Witmer (1867-1956)

61. The two most profound influences on the growth of clinical psychology as a specialty were ____.
    a. World War I and World War II
    b. World War II and the VA hospital system
    c. the works of Binet and Freud
    d. Witmer's work and the world wars
    e. the influx of German psychologists in the 1930s and the VA hospital system

    ANS: B   PTS: 1   REF: Lightner Witmer (1867-1956)

62. The first to apply psychology to personnel selection was ____.
    a. Yerkes
    b. Münsterberg
    c. Scott
    d. Witmer
    e. Hawthorne

    ANS: C   PTS: 1   REF: Walter Dill Scott (1869-1955)

63. The first Ph.D. recipient to apply psychological principles to advertising was ____.
    a. Scott
    b. Watson
    c. Hall
    d. Cattell
    e. Münsterberg

    ANS: A   PTS: 1   REF: Walter Dill Scott (1869-1955)

64. Who wrote *The Theory and Practice of Advertising*, the first book on the psychology of advertising?
    a. Münsterberg
    b. Beers
    c. Goodenough
    d. Healey
    e. Scott

    ANS: E   PTS: 1   REF: Walter Dill Scott (1869-1955)

65. Scott argued that the most effective advertisement consisted of ____.
    a. a multiple-media approach
    b. bright colors (such as McDonald's golden arches)
    c. a sudden change in volume (such as television ads)
    d. subliminal erotic components
    e. a big picture accompanied by the fewest possible words (such as the Nike logo)

    ANS: A   PTS: 1   REF: Walter Dill Scott (1869-1955)

66. Scott argued that consumers ____.
    a. are more influenced by the mystical than by the practical
    b. will purchase whatever assists their adaptation to their habitats
    c. will respond to whatever interrupts the stream of consciousness
    d. are not rational beings
    e. label their emotional responses to a stimulus only after they respond to it

    ANS: D   PTS: 1   REF: Walter Dill Scott (1869-1955)

67. Scott's hypothesis that consumers will do what they are told is called the ____.
    a. law of suggestibility
    b. "tea and sympathy" approach to advertising
    c. contraliminal perception principle
    d. law of least effort
    e. "trial and accidental success" method

    ANS: A   PTS: 1   REF: Walter Dill Scott (1869-1955)

68. The technique of telling consumers to "Use Brand X!" is traceable to ____ law of ____.
    a. Münsterberg's; suggestibility
    b. Scott's; direct pitch
    c. Scott's; suggestibility
    d. Witmer's; suggestion
    e. Scott's; direct action

    ANS: C   PTS: 1   REF: Walter Dill Scott (1869-1955)

69. Organizational psychology was initiated with ____.
    a. Walter Scott's work
    b. the demands of the VA hospital system after World War II
    c. the Hawthorne studies
    d. the Zeigarnik effect research
    e. Lewin's work on social conflict

    ANS: A   PTS: 1   REF: Walter Dill Scott (1869-1955)

70. The first person to earn a PhD in industrial/organizational psychology was ____.
    a. Walter Scott
    b. Lightener Witmer
    c. Frank Gilbreth
    d. Lillian Gilbreth
    e. Anna Berliner

    ANS: D   PTS: 1   REF: Walter Dill Scott (1869-1955)
    MSC: WWW

71. Münsterberg was best known ____.
    a. through his publications in the popular press on applied psychology
    b. through his scholarly publications in applied psychology
    c. for his research in psychophysics and his disputes with Wundt
    d. for his research on animal learning
    e. for his feminist sentiments

    ANS: A   PTS: 1   REF: Hugo Münsterberg (1863-1916)

72. Forensic psychology was established with the work of ____.
    a. Scott
    b. Hall
    c. Münsterberg
    d. Healey
    e. Witmer

    ANS: C   PTS: 1   REF: Hugo Münsterberg (1863-1916)

73. Which American psychologist is noteworthy for writing in industrial/organizational psychology, psychotherapy, and forensic psychology?
    a. Scott
    b. Münsterberg
    c. Berliner
    d. Frank Gilbreth
    e. Lillian Gilbreth

    ANS: B   PTS: 1   REF: Hugo Münsterberg (1863-1916)

74. The use of physiological responses to assess a person's truthfulness was proposed by ____.
   a. Titchener
   b. Cattell
   c. Scott
   d. Münsterberg
   e. Lange

   ANS: D   PTS: 1   REF: Hugo Münsterberg (1863-1916)

75. Who said, "There is no subconscious?"
   a. Scott
   b. Münsterberg
   c. Berliner
   d. Witmer
   e. Gilbreth

   ANS: B   PTS: 1   REF: Hugo Münsterberg (1863-1916)

76. Whose therapeutic technique might be described as "therapist-centered?"
   a. Witmer's
   b. Münsterberg's
   c. Hall's
   d. Freud's
   e. Scott's

   ANS: B   PTS: 1   REF: Hugo Münsterberg (1863-1916)
   MSC: WWW

77. In 1919 the APA, controlled by academic psychologists, did which of the following?
   a. changed membership requirements to increase the number of applied psychologists
   b. changed membership requirements to decrease the number of applied psychologists
   c. made the APA an "official" scientific organization (distinct from philosophy)
   d. created the first wartime commission
   e. officially declared Behaviorism as the "only psychology"

   ANS: A   PTS: 1
   REF: Applied Psychology in the United States: A National Mania

TRUE/FALSE

78. American psychology was influenced more by the works of Wundt and Titchener than by the work of Darwin and Galton.

ANS: F   PTS: 1   REF: Toward a Practical Psychology
MSC: WWW

79. The first major alternative market for PhDs in psychology was the field of education.

ANS: T   PTS: 1   REF: Toward a Practical Psychology

80. Galton's most important influence on Cattell was on reaction time studies.

ANS: F   PTS: 1   REF: James McKeen Cattell (1860-1944)

81. Unlike Galton's eugenics, Cattell's position on that subject was that data on individual differences should be used to develop programs to teach people to adapt more successfully to their environments.

ANS: F   PTS: 1   REF: James McKeen Cattell (1860-1944)
MSC: WWW

82. Cattell learned about and gained his interest in statistical analysis from Wundt's analysis techniques.

ANS: F   PTS: 1   REF: James McKeen Cattell (1860-1944)

83. Anticipating Binet's work on intelligence testing, Cattell replaced Galton's sensorimotor measures of human abilities with assessments of cognitive abilities.

ANS: F   PTS: 1   REF: James McKeen Cattell (1860-1944)

84. Cattell's mental tests, like those of Galton, dealt primarily with sensorimotor measures.

ANS: T   PTS: 1   REF: James McKeen Cattell (1860-1944)

85. During his years at Columbia, Münsterberg trained more graduate students in psychology than anyone else in the United States.

ANS: F   PTS: 1   REF: Hugo Münsterberg (1863-1916)

86. The first Binet-Simon test focused on learning, thinking, and memory.

ANS: F   PTS: 1   REF: The Psychological Testing Movement

87. Binet's test was introduced to the United States by Terman.

ANS: F   PTS: 1   REF: The Psychological Testing Movement

88. The concept of the IQ was developed by Stern.

ANS: T   PTS: 1   REF: The Psychological Testing Movement

89. The army Alpha and army Beta tests were essential in separating the literate recruits from the illiterate in World War I.

    ANS: F   PTS: 1   REF: The Psychological Testing Movement

90. Attempts by psychologists during World War I to develop group tests of personality characteristics were a dismal and embarrassing failure.

    ANS: F   PTS: 1   REF: The Psychological Testing Movement

91. The testing movement even spread to ways to identify potential baseball players.

    ANS: T   PTS: 1   REF: The Psychological Testing Movement

92. The psychologist responsible for using mental tests to assess whether immigrants were mentally defective was Goddard.

    ANS: T   PTS: 1   REF: The Psychological Testing Movement

93. The intelligence test data from World War I recruits indicated that whites scored higher than all other groups.

    ANS: T   PTS: 1   REF: The Psychological Testing Movement

94. H. M. Bond was perhaps the most vocal in arguing that White versus non-White differences in IQ scores reflect nature, not nurture.

    ANS: F   PTS: 1   REF: The Psychological Testing Movement

95. It is the prevailing and undisputed opinion that intelligence tests are culturally biased.

    ANS: F   PTS: 1   REF: The Psychological Testing Movement

96. Witmer was the father of clinical psychology and school psychology.

    ANS: T   PTS: 1   REF: Lightner Witmer (1867-1956)

97. Witmer's Ph.D. training with Wundt was a key part of his knowledge base in clinical psychology.

    ANS: F   PTS: 1   REF: Lightner Witmer (1867-1956)

98. A significant finding by Witmer was that behavior disorders and cognitive deficits are substantially influenced by a child's environment.

    ANS: T   PTS: 1   REF: Lightner Witmer (1867-1956)
    MSC: WWW

99. Clinical psychologists' initial psychological methods of therapy were those developed by Freud.

    ANS: T   PTS: 1   REF: Lightner Witmer (1867-1956)

100. The first person to apply psychology to advertising was Watson.

    ANS: F   PTS: 1   REF: Walter Dill Scott (1869-1955)

101. Scott wrote that the sense organs are the "windows of the soul."

ANS: T PTS: 1 REF: Walter Dill Scott (1869-1955)

102. Scott developed the "direct commands" approach to advertising.

ANS: T PTS: 1 REF: Walter Dill Scott (1869-1955)

103. The law of suggestibility argues that advertisers must sway consumers' cognitions and not underestimate their reasoning abilities.

ANS: F PTS: 1 REF: Walter Dill Scott (1869-1955)

104. Scott's approach to personnel selection was to assess the traits of those successful in an occupation, rather than to define necessary traits ahead of time.

ANS: T PTS: 1 REF: Walter Dill Scott (1869-1955)
MSC: WWW

105. Scott's approach to the assessment of intelligence was novel in that he examined how people use their cognitive abilities rather than only how much of a particular ability they have.

ANS: T PTS: 1 REF: Walter Dill Scott (1869-1955)

106. The Hawthorne studies were crucial in exposing the importance of the conditions of the psychological work environment.

ANS: T PTS: 1 REF: Walter Dill Scott (1869-1955)

107. The first doctoral-level I/O psychologist was Lillian Gilbreth.

ANS: T PTS: 1 REF: Walter Dill Scott (1869-1955)

108. Münsterberg stated that women should not serve on juries because they are too irrational.

ANS: T PTS: 1 REF: Hugo Münsterberg (1863-1916)

109. Münsterberg made direct suggestions to his patients about how he believed they could be cured.

ANS: T PTS: 1 REF: Hugo Münsterberg (1863-1916)
MSC: WWW

Chapter 9

Behaviorism: Antecedent Influences

In the early 1900's, Clever Hans the wonder horse was famous worldwide. Clever Hans purportedly had the numerical reasoning ability of a 14-year-old boy: he could add, subtract, spell, and recognize and identify a number of objects as well as answer questions on a variety of topics. The horse's owner, William Von Osten, was a retired math teacher and never accepted money to exhibit Clever Hans. The horse was a mystery; the puzzle was eventually solved by a psychologist.

When psychology moved from its beginnings to functionalism and then to applied psychology, the movement was not deliberate or directed—rather was more of an evolution. This is not the case with Behaviorism, which formally began with "a declaration of war" published by John Watson in 1913 in which he declares that psychology should study only overt behavior, rejecting any ideas regarding consciousness and/or mind. The foundation of Watson's behaviorism was not new—its precursors were the philosophical school of positivism, animal psychology, and functionalism. Positivism was founded by Comte, and it "emphasized positive knowledge (facts), the truth of which was not debatable."

Although Romanes and Morgan had begun the animal psychology movement, they both were interested in the animal mind. Jacques Loeb's approach was different, in that he built on the concept of tropism ("involuntary forced movement") wherein he "believed that an animal's reaction to a stimulus is direct and automatic." Even so, he did discuss "animal consciousness" with the idea of associative memory in animals, which is the cognitive mechanism for animals to learn the connection between stimulus and response. Loeb taught for a time at the U. of Chicago and had John Watson as a student.

In the early 1900's there were a number of breakthroughs in animal psychology. Robert Yerkes used a variety of animals, Willard Small (Clark U.) used a rat maze for the first time, comparative psychology labs were being set up (8 by 1910), and Washburn published *Animal Mind* (1908). Up until Washburn's book it was common to discuss animal consciousness, but her book demarcates the acceptability of such anthropomorphizing. Subsequent literature dealt with animal behavior rather than animal mind. During this time, it was difficult to be a comparative psychologist because the field was seen as not practical. Universities were unlikely to support the required labs and equipment (and faculty).

In 1906, a lecture by Pavlov was printed in Science, more of his work was published in English in 1909, and by 1911 the *Journal of Animal Behavior* began being published. The field was slowly becoming established and objective. In 1904 the German government established a committee to investigate Clever Hans, with Carl Stumpf as a member. He appointed Oskar Pfungst to investigate, who found that Hans' owner and onlookers would unwittingly give subtle visual cues as to how to respond. In essence, there was no evidence of Hans having extraordinary cognitive abilities, rather only evidence of Hans learning how to respond to people's tiny head movements. Thus, comparative psychology proved itself to be useful.

Edward Lee Thorndike "fashioned a mechanistic, objective learning theory that focused on overt behavior." He received all of his education in the United States, which was unusual at the time. He became interested in psychology after reading William James' *The Principles of Psychology* and went to Harvard for graduate work. While there, he devised mazes for learning and studied chicks (because children were controversial). Believing he was rejected by a woman, he left the Boston area and completed his Ph.D. under Cattell at Columbia University. While there, he devised the puzzle boxes to work with cats and dogs.

After this line of research, he secured a teaching job at Columbia and "worked with human subjects on problems of learning, adapting his animal research techniques for children and young people." He became vastly successful, as evidenced by his becoming president of APA and by his high yearly income of $70,000.

Thorndike called his approach connectionism: the idea that situations and responses become connected over time, and that an individual contains a large collection of these connections. Although there is "a mentalistic tinge to Thorndike's work," particularly when he discusses "satisfaction, annoyance, and discomfort," his work is mechanistic, arguing that behavior can be reduced to stimulus and response.

In the puzzle boxes Thorndike made, hungry cats had to learn to escape the box using levers to get to food. The first time they escape, Thorndike said, it is an accident. In repeated trials, the response gets "stamped in" with trial-and-error learning. Thorndike named his discoveries the "law of effect," where a favorable consequence is associated with a particular situation, and the "law of exercise," where the more frequently an animal responds in a particular way, the more the response is associated with a particular situation. Thorndike has been hailed as "one of psychology's most productive and influential figures."

As an example of independent simultaneous discovery, another key figure was conducting research on the same issues in Russia. Ivan Pavlov's work brought responses to the physiological level: "glandular secretions and muscular movements." Pavlov is the eldest of 11 children and intended to enter the seminary, but after reading Darwin's theory he changed his mind. He received his degree in St. Petersburg, where he began his "fanatic devotion to pure science and to experimental research." He spent much of his life in poverty and seemed uninterested in money. On one occasion his students collected money on his behalf under the pretext of paying for lectures. II then spent the money on dogs and lab supplies. He was famous for his tirades and tempers, although once this rage was expressed he moved on. "He tried to be as humane as possible with the dogs," particularly given that they had to undergo surgical procedures. He was one of the few Russian scientists that allowed both women and Jews to work in his lab. He was critical of the 1917 Russian revolution and of Stalin, although he continued to receive financial support from the government, and was allowed to conduct his research without government interference.

Pavlov's most relevant work to psychology is on conditioned reflexes. He was working on problems of digestion by collecting dogs' saliva. He then noticed that they began to salivate before food was placed in their mouths. At first he tried to explain the phenomenon by "imagining the subjective state of the animal," which proved fruitless. He then began his objective experimentation to investigate the phenomenon. He found that dogs salivate when food is in their mouth, which is a reflex and not learned behavior; Pavlov called this the unconditioned reflex. Salivating at the sight of food is learned through association between food and sight: he calls this the conditional reflex (which was mistranslated as "conditioned"). He and his assistants discovered that a variety of stimuli can be conditioned to cause salivation without food being present in the mouth (e.g., light, whistle, buzzer). Because Pavlov was so concerned about having pristine experimental conditions, he eventually builds a "three-story research building, known as the 'tower of silence.'" The text authors include an excerpt from Pavlov's *Conditioned Reflexes* (1927) in which he discusses the conditioning process.

Pavlov's discovery about conditioned reflexes had been found independently on two other occasions. In the U.S., Edwin Burket Twitmyer presented a paper at the 1904 APA conference about conditioning the knee-jerk reflex, but because it received no interest from conference-goers he abandoned the idea.

Much earlier, in 1896, an Austrian named Alois Kreidl noted that goldfish "learned to anticipate feedings from the stimuli associated with the laboratory attendant walking toward their tank." In any case, Pavlov's work had a great impact on psychology in its search to become more objective and mechanistic.

Another contributor to animal psychology was Vladimir Bekhterev, another Russian physiologist. Like Pavlov he was critical of the politics in Russia, and like Pavlov he accepted women and Jews as students in his lab. He received some, but not all, of his training under Wundt. He and Pavlov were sworn enemies and apparently could not be at the same place without exchanging insults. Unfortunately, Bekhterev was summoned by Stalin to give a medical diagnosis. After giving a diagnosis of paranoia, Bekhterev was suspiciously found dead that day. Stalin then made sure his work was suppressed. Bekhterev contributed to animal psychology with research on motor responses, whose conditioning he called associated reflexes. He found that reflexes (like drawing back one's finger after an electric shock) could be elicited by the original stimuli (electric shock) and *also* by an associated stimuli (light, sound, etc.). In addition, "Bekhterev argued for a completely objective approach to psychological phenomena and against the use of mentalistic terms and concepts."

With the contributions of the aforementioned researchers, animal psychology became the foundation for Behaviorism. In addition, Cattell and other functionalists, with their emphasis on behavior and objectivity, helped shape the methods and study of Behaviorism. This new trend in psychology marks a distinct move away for introspection and the study of consciousness, and towards a science of behavior.

Outline

I.   Hans the Wonder Horse—Math Genius?
    A. Early 1900's, Hans was world famous
    B. Lived in Berlin, Germany
    C. Advertisers used his likeness to sell products
    D. He "inspired songs, magazine articles, and books"
    E. Judged to have numeric reasoning of 14-year-old boy
    F. Purportedly did a variety of cognitive tasks
        1. add and subtract
        2. use fractions and decimals
        3. read
        4. identify coins
        5. play card games
        6. spell
        7. recognize objects and colors
        8. perform feats of memory
    G. answered questions by tapping hoof, swaying head
    H. Owner is Willhelm von Osten, retired schoolteacher
        1. taught Hans, had been unsuccessful with a cat and bear
        2. never took fee for exhibitions
        3. wanted to prove Darwin correct: humans and animals have similar mind
        4. believed animals had insufficient education
    I. There were skeptics, a psychologist "finally solved the puzzle"

II.   Toward a Science of Behavior
        A. Background
                1. 2nd decade of 20th Century: disagreement within psychology
                        a.   on value of introspection
                        b.   on existence of mental elements
                        c.   on the need to remain a pure science
                2. functionalism movement: evolutionary, not revolutionary
                3. 1913: behaviorism declares war (Watson)
                        a.   protest against both structuralism and functionalism
                        b.   deliberately abrupt
                        c.   designed to shatter the two dominant schools
                4. Behaviorism
                        a.   rejects consciousness and introspection
                        b.   scientific
                        c.   dealt solely with observable behavioral acts
                        d.   objective descriptions of the data
                        e.   rejection of mentalistic concepts and terms
                        f.   consciousness comparable to soul, introspection irrelevant
                5. Watson not the originator; organized and promoted already existing ideas
                        a.   philosophical tradition of objectivism and mechanism
                        b.   animal psychology
                        c.   functional psychology
                6. appreciation of the need for objectivity had lengthy history
                        a.   Descartes (mechanistic description of the body)
                        b.   Comte (positivism; emphasis on undebatable facts)
                        c.   positivism became part of the Zeitgeist in science
                7. resulting science of behavior viewed human beings as machines
III.   The Influence of Animal Psychology on Behaviorism
        A. Background
                1. Watson: "Behaviorism is a direct outgrowth of studies in animal behavior...."
                2. animal psychology product of evolutionary theory
                3. the most important antecedent of behaviorism
                4. influenced by Romanes (anecdotal method) and Morgan (law of parsimony; experimental method)
        B. Jacques Loeb (1859-1924)
                1. significant step toward objectivity in animal psychology
                2. tropism ("involuntary forced movement") as basis for theory of animal behavior: consciousness not necessary
                3. completely mechanistic approach to behavior
                4. did not totally reject consciousness for more evolved species (i.e., humans)
                5. consciousness revealed by associative memory (an association between stimulus and response, taken to indicate evidence of consciousness)
                6. taught Watson at Chicago
        C. Rats, ants, and the animal mind
                1. Yerkes: strengthened comparative psychology
                2. Willard Small
                        a.   1900: introduced the rat maze to study learning
                        b.   used mentalistic terms (rat's ideas and images)

3. John Watson
   a.   early career: also interested in mental concepts
   b.   1903 dissertation: "Animal Education: The *Psychical* Development of the White Rat"
   c.   1907: discussed conscious experience of sensation in rats
4. Charles Henry Turner: 1906 paper on ant behavior
   a.   article favorably reviewed by Watson in Psychological Bulletin
   b.   1st time Watson used term behavior
   c.   Turner
      (1) African American
      (2) 1907: Ph.D. magna cum laude, University of Chicago, zoology
      (3) some claimed him as psychologist
      (4) teaching opportunities limited by discrimination
      (5) despite being a high school science teacher, made important discoveries in insect learning and behavior
5. 1910: 8 comparative labs in U.S.; many departments offered courses
6. Margaret Floy Washburn
   a.   Titchener's first doctoral student
   b.   taught animal psychology at Cornell
   c.   1908: *The Animal Mind*
      (1) 1st comparative psychology book published in U.S.
      (2) attribution of consciousness to animals
      (3) method of introspection by analogy
7. textbooks after Washburn's were behavioristic, focused on learning
D. On becoming an animal psychologist
   1. lack of funding for comparative psychologists
      a.   Harvard president: "no future in Yerkes's...comparative psychology"
      b.   Yerkes advised to take up educational psychology
      c.   his students took up applied jobs when none available in comparative
      d.   in academia, first to be fired were comparative psychologists
      e.   result: very few comparative psychologists
      f.   Watson: no place to keep animals and no funding
      g.   1908: only 6 animal studies had been published in journals (4% of the research that year)
      h.   meeting of all animal psychologists in 1909: only 9
      i.   1910: 6/218 psychologists active in animal research
   2. 1911: Journal of Animal Behavior (later Journal of Comparative Psychology) published
   3. 1906: Pavlov lecture reprinted in Science
   4. 1909: description of Pavlov's work published by Yerkes and Morgulis in Psychological Bulletin
   5. objective psychology and Watson's research supported by Pavlov's work
   6. conscious experience disappearing from animal psychology
E. Was Hans really clever?
   1. trend continues with investigation of Clever Hans
      a.   government investigation headed by Stumpf; found no fraud or deceit

BEHAVIORISM: ANTECEDENT INFLUENCES   285

       b.   Stumpf asked his student Pfungst to investigate further

       c.   used experimental approach

          (1) two groups of questioners

             (a) Group 1 knew the answers

             (b) Group 2 did not know the answers

             (c) Hans only answered correctly when questioners knew the answers

       d.   conclusion: Hans receiving some type of information from questioners

       e.   further experiments showed that Hans would tap hoof upon downward movement of von Osten's (or anyone else's) head; when he looked up after correct number of taps, Hans stopped tapping

       f.   Pfungst discovered Han's partial reinforcement schedule

   2.   case demonstrated value of experimental approach to animal behavior

   3.   Watson reviews results from study in Journal of Comparative Neurology and Psychology

   4.   conclusions influence Watson: promote a psychology that only deals with behavior, not consciousness

IV.   Edward Lee Thorndike (1874–1949)

  A. In general

     1.   objective, mechanistic theory of learning

     2.   focus on overt behavior

     3.   did allow some reference to consciousness and mental processes

     4.   simultaneous discovery: Thorndike and Pavlov

  B. Thorndike's life

     1.   read James's Principles, later studied with James

     2.   planned research with children but prohibited

     3.   inspired by Morgan, used chicks to study learning, created mazes for them

     4.   1898: Ph.D. from Columbia University with Cattell

       a.   used cats and dogs

       b.   "Animal Intelligence: An Experimental Study of the Associative Processes in Animals"

     5.   turned to research with other species; uninterested in animal research

     6.   research at Columbia

       a.   joined faculty in 1899

       b.   problems in human learning

       c.   foci: educational psychology and mental testing

       d.   wrote several textbooks

       e.   1910: founded *Journal of Educational Psychology*

       f.   1912: president of APA

       g.   1924: earned $70,000/year

       h.   50 years at Columbia; retired 1939

  C. Connectionism

     1.   Thorndike's experimental approach to the study of association

     2.   learning = connections between stimuli and responses

     3.   influence of Romanes and Morgan: mentalistic concepts (subjective judgements about animal's conscious experience)

     4.   like Loeb, did not give high levels of consciousness to animals

     5. after Thorndike

        a.   decreased role of consciousness

        b.   increased focus on experimental method

     6. mechanism: behavior reduced to S-R elements

D. The puzzle box

     1. built puzzle boxes to measure rate of learning in animals

        a.   example: put food deprived cat in box

        b.   food left outside of box as reward for escaping

        c.   cat needs to pull lever/chain; some boxes involved many actions to escape

        d.   first trial: cat displays random behaviors (i.e., scratching, sniffing) until correct behavior unlatches box

        e.   on subsequent trials: less random behaviors

        f.   when learning complete, cat exhibits correct behavior as soon as in the box

     2. quantitative measures of learning

        a.   number of wrong behaviors (i.e., those that do not lead to escape)

        b.   time lapse

     3. stamping in/out: a response tendency dictated by favorable or unfavorable consequence

     4. trial and error or "trial and accidental success" learning: learning based on repetition of response tendencies that lead to success

E. Laws of learning

     1. law of effect: "Acts that produce satisfaction in a given situation become associated with that situation; when the situation recurs, the act is likely to recur."

     2. law of exercise or law of use and disuse: "The more an act or response is used in a given situation, the more strongly the act becomes associated with that situation."

     3. Thorndike's research: reward more effective than mere repetition; punishment does not always have comparable negative effect as reward

F. Comment

     1. beginning of the ascension of learning theory

     2. his objectivism influenced behaviorism

     3. 1998: American Psychologist honored Thorndike's work

V.   Ivan Petrovitch Pavlov (1849-1936)

A. In general

     1. his work helped shift of associationism from subjective ideas to objective physiological responses

     2. provided Watson with a new method

B. Pavlov's life

     1. intended to study for the priesthood

     2. read Darwin, chose to study animal physiology

     3. born into peasantry; worked hard to become member of Russian (and Soviet) intelligentsia

     4. total dedication to research; wife took care of everything else

     5. family lived in poverty until he was 41

     6. his students felt bad for his financial situation and gave him money on pretext of paying for lectures; spent all the money on dogs for his lab

7. 1890: professor of pharmacology at St. Petersburg, Russia
8. famous temper that would quickly flare up and die down
9. overriding interest: lab work; did not conduct research himself but oversaw 150 students in his career
10. allowed women and Jewish students to work in his laboratory
11. openly critical of Soviet government
12. received support from government; allowed to conduct research free from interference

C. Conditioned reflexes: "Reflexes that are conditional or dependent on the formation of an association or connection between stimulus and response."

1. Pavlov's three research areas
    a. function of coronary nerves
    b. primary digestive glands (1904 Nobel Prize for work on digestion)
    c. conditioned reflexes (most relevant to psychology)
2. serendipitous finding when studying natural reflex of salivation
    a. to study digestive glands in dogs, Pavlov surgically diverted gland so salvia could be collected outside dog's cheek
    b. dogs salivated when food placed in mouth
    c. noticed that dogs soon salivated at sight of food or sound of feeder's footsteps
    d. unlearned salivation reflex now conditioned (connected) to stimuli associated with food delivery
    e. Pavlov turned his attention to studying how this comes about
3. psychic reflexes
    a. Zeitgeist: focus on mentalistic experiences of laboratory animals
    b. animals' mental events: described in subjective, human terms
    c. such conceptions not fruitful; Pavlov instituted objective methodology
4. gave Descartes credit for concept of nervous reflex
5. first simple experiments
    a. show dog bread in hand
    b. bread in dog's mouth
    c. dog salivates
    d. dog eats
    e. soon, dog salivates to sight of bread alone
6. salivating to the food in mouth is innate: unconditional reflex
7. salivating to the sight of food is learned: conditional reflex (dog must form an association for this to happen)
8. a translator, Gantt, changed "conditional" to "conditioned; latter is now the accepted term
9. many stimuli can elicit "conditional" reflex (i.e., light, whistle, buzzer)
10. painstaking research
    a. sophisticated equipment used to collect saliva to measure drops of saliva
    b. standardized experimental conditions
    c. rigorous controls
    d. elimination of sources of error
11. The tower of silence
    a. Pavlov concerned about outside influences affecting his results

b.   controlled for such influences by designing special cubicles for dog and for experimenter

c.   dog could not see experimenter

d.   still concerned about issues of experimental control Pavlov designed a research building

     (1) three stories

     (2) known as "Tower of Silence"

     (3) extra thick windows

     (4) double steel, airtight doors

     (5) supported by steel girders set in sand

     (6) surrounded by straw-filled moat

     (7) eliminated temperature changes, vibrations, extraneous noises, etc.

e.   the tower effectively eliminated the outside influences on the experimental animals that Pavlov had worried about

12. A conditioning experiment

a.   present a conditioned stimulus, e.g., a light

b.   immediately present the unconditioned stimulus, e.g., food

c.   dog salivates

d.   after several pairings of conditional and unconditional stimuli, dog salivates to the light

e.   dog has formed an association between the light and food

f.   must pair light and food multiple times

g.   reinforcement (being fed) necessary for learning

h.   demonstrated extinction, spontaneous recover, generalization, discrimination, higher-order conditioning

i.   most extensive research program since Wundt's

13. In their own words Original source material from Conditioned Reflexes (1927)

a.   starting point is Descartes' concept of the nervous reflex

b.   stimulus > nervous receptor > nervous impulse > transmitted along incoming nerve fibers > central nervous system > nervous impulse > transmitted along outgoing nerve fibers to active organ > leads to activity of cellular structures

c.   thus, stimulus > response; cause > effect

d.   reflexes as elemental units, stemming from "the original organization of the nervous system

e.   reflexes as "driving-belts" of human-designed machines

f.   beginning of research: experimenter the source of so many different stimuli that experiments were invalid

g.   even when experimenter outside of dog's room in another room, outside sounds, vibrations, changes in light, etc., disturb the experiment

h.   solution: special laboratory at the Petrograd Institute of Experimental Medicine

i.   funds provided by Moscow businessman

j.   primary task: "the protection of the dogs from uncontrolled extraneous stimuli"

k.   isolating trench around building, isolated floors, isolated rooms, soundproof and separate compartments for animal and researcher.

    l. responses transmitted electrically or pneumatically

    m. now possible to stabilize environmental conditions and conduct successful experiments

  D. A note on E.B. Twitmyer (1873-1943)

    1. American

    2. 1902: dissertation on knee-jerk reflexes

    3. 1904: presentation at APA

      a. topic: knee-jerk reflex

      b. findings: knee-jerk elicited by other stimuli present when the original stimulus (tap of hammer just below knee)

      c. suggested this as topic worthy of further research

      d. no one in audience expressed interest

      e. findings ignored

      f. due to Zeitgeist, Twitmyer's inexperience, inability to continue his work, scheduling of his talk just before lunch, James' failure to allow time for comments, or some combination of these reasons, Twitmyer missed out on making one of the most significant findings in the history of psychology

    4. Another unknown person, Alois Kreidl

      a. Austrian physiologist

      b. demonstrated conditioning in 1896

      c. found that goldfish anticipate feedings through cues that precede feeding

  E. Comment on Pavlov

    1. demonstrated study of higher mental processes in physiological terms

    2. broad practical applicability

    3. continued the tradition of mechanism and atomism

    4. provided psychology with a basic element of behavior

    5. behavior could be reduced to elements and studied in experimental laboratory

    6. agreed with James that psychology still not a science

      a. excluded psychology from his work

      b. much later self-identified as an experimental psychologist

VI. Vladimir M. Bekhterev (1857-1927)

  A. In general

    1. helped lead psychology away from subjective ideas

    2. pioneer in several research areas

    3. accepted women and Jews as students and colleagues

    4. 1881: MD, then study with Wundt

    5. 1893: chair of mental and nervous diseases at St. Petersburg, Russia

    6. 1907: founded the Psychoneurological Institute

    7. Pavlov published negative review of a Bekhterev book: became enemies for life

    8. may have been assassinated at Stalin's request; Stalin suppressed his work after his death

  B. Associated reflexes: "Reflexes that can be elicited not only by unconditioned stimuli but also by stimuli that have become associated with the unconditioned stimuli."

    1. interested in the motor conditioning response whereas Pavlov concentrated on conditioning glandular responses

    2. his basic discoveries: associated reflexes

3. higher-level and complex behaviors explained in the same way
4. thought processes
    a. depend on inner actions of speech muscles
    b. notion adopted by Watson
5. 1907: Objective Psychology

VII. The Influence of Functional Psychology on Behaviorism
  A. Some functionalists
    1. more objective than previous schools
    2. called for an objective psychology
    3. called for focus on behavior instead of consciousness
  B. 1904: Cattell emphasized behavior and objectivity and criticized introspection
  C. 1911: Walter Pillsbury, student of Titchener, defined psychology as the "science of behavior" in his textbook
  D. 1910: Angell
    1. depicted psychology as prepared for greater objectivity
    2. by 1930 said it would be advantageous to forget consciousness and describe the behavior of humans and animals objectively
  E. Watson: the agent of the inevitable
    1. not the first to propose a science of behavior but saw the need clearly
    2. boldly called for a revolution that was already started

Lecture prompts/Discussion topics for chapter nine

- Do you believe animals "think"? How do you know? Can their behavior be explained without using mentalist concepts? Can ours? What is it, if anything, that separates animals from us?
- Why should results found with animals answer any questions about humans? Is it really relevant to us that a chick can escape from a maze or a cat from a box?

Internet Resources for chapter nine

The Alex Foundation
http://www.alexfoundation.org/index2.html
    This is a link to Dr. Irene Pepperberg's research, in which she investigates the cognitive abilities of an African Grey Parrot. It includes a link to a video clip showing some of the research. Is this Clever Hans all over again or better research?

Ivan Pavlov Biography
http://nobelprize.org/nobel_prizes/medicine/laureates/1904/pavlov-bio.html
    This is the biography of Pavlov provided by the Nobel Prize Foundation.

Jacques Loeb
http://www.brynmawr.edu/Acads/Psych/rwozniak/loeb.html
    This site offers an extensively footnoted biography of Jacques Loeb, who provided an early and heavy influence on John Watson's thinking.

Key Theorists in Psychology: Thorndike
http://www.muskingum.edu/~psych/psycweb/history/thorndike.htm
> You can find more information here about Thorndike, including links to some full text of some of his articles.

The Skeptic's Dictionary: Clever Hans
http://skepdic.com/cleverhans.html
> This site gives a more detailed description of Clever Hans and Oskar Pfungst, and includes links to related sites.

Potential answers to chapter nine discussion questions

1. Why was Clever Hans considered such a sensation throughout the Western world?
Clever Hans purportedly had the numerical reasoning ability of a 14-year-old boy: he could add, subtract, spell, and recognize and identify a number or objects as well as answer questions on a variety of topics.

2. In what ways had psychology changed by the second decade of the twentieth century?
When psychology moved from its beginnings to functionalism and then to applied psychology, the movement was not deliberate or directed—rather it seemed more like events pulled psychologists along. This is not the case with Behaviorism, which formally began with "a declaration of war" published by John Watson in 1913 in which he declared that psychology should study only overt behavior, rejecting all study of consciousness and/or mind.

3. Describe the basic tenets of Watson's behaviorism and show how they differed from the positions of Wundt and Titchener.
The primary research method of Wundt and Titchener, introspection, was used to study what, for both, was psychology: conscious experience. Watson "called for a scientific psychology that dealt only with observable behavioral acts that could be described objectively in terms such as 'stimulus' and 'response'. Further, Watson's psychology rejected all mentalistic concepts" because they were "meaningless for a science of behavior."

4. Why was Watson so opposed to the study of consciousness and the method of introspection?
"He believed that consciousness had absolutely no value for behavioral psychology. Further, he said that consciousness had 'never been seen, touched, smelled, tasted, or moved" and it was an impossible-to-prove assumption along the lines of the concept "soul."

5. What were the three major forces Watson brought together to form his new psychology?
The ideas behind Watson's behaviorism were not new—its precursors were the philosophical school of positivism, animal psychology, and functionalism. Positivism was founded by Comte, and it "emphasized positive knowledge (facts), the truth of which was not debatable." The animal movement allowed animals to be a legitimate research subject whose results would apply to humans. Functionalism and many of the functional psychologists did work that could serve as precursory to behaviorism as well, in discussing the need for objective observation. This sets the stage for Watson's crystallization of behaviorism.

6. What role did positivism play in the scientific Zeitgeist of the twentieth century?
Positivism was founded by Comte, and it "emphasized positive knowledge (facts), the truth of which was not debatable."

7. Describe the development of animal psychology since the work of Romanes and Morgan. Why was it difficult to be an animal psychologist?
Romanes and Morgan began the animal psychology movement, but both were interested in the animal mind. Jacques Loeb's approach was different, in that he built on the concept of tropism ("involuntary forced movement") wherein he "believed that an animal's reaction to a stimulus is direct and automatic." In the early 1900's there were a number of breakthroughs in animal psychology. Robert Yerkes used a variety of animals, Willard Small (Clark U.) used a rat maze for the first time, comparative psychology labs were being set up (8 by 1910), and Washburn published *Animal Mind* (1908). It was difficult to be a comparative psychologist then because the field was seen as not practical, so universities were unlikely to support the required labs and equipment (and faculty).

8. In what ways did Loeb, Washburn, Small, and Turner influence the new animal psychology?
Watson said that "Behaviorism is a direct outgrowth of studies in animal behavior during the first decade of the twentieth century." The work of these four individuals moved animal psychology away from the introspection-by-analogy methods of Romanes and Morgan, and toward a more objective study. In addition, these theorists avoided the mentalistic descriptions used by Romanes and Morgan.

9. Discuss the impact of the Clever Hans incident on animal psychology. What did Pfungst's experiments demonstrate?
In 1904 the German government established a committee to investigate Clever Hans, with Carl Stumpf as a member. He appointed Oskar Pfungst to investigate, who found that Hans' owner and onlookers would unwittingly give subtle visual cues as to how to respond. In essence, there was no evidence of Hans having extraordinary cognitive abilities, rather only evidence of Hans learning how to respond to people's tiny head movements. Hans helped animal psychology establish that it was a legitimate psychological field that could address real world problems.

10. Relate Thorndike's connectionism to the older philosophical notion of association.
Thorndike called his approach connectionism: the idea that situations and responses become connected over time, and that an individual contains a large collection of these connections. Although there is "a mentalistic tinge to Thorndike's work", particularly when he discusses "satisfaction, annoyance, and discomfort", his work is mechanistic, arguing that behavior can be reduced to stimulus and response. This idea of connectionism is almost the same concept as the philosophical idea of association, except association deals with ideas while connectionism deals with behaviors. Both concepts are designed to describe the process of learning.

11. Describe Thorndike's puzzle-box research and the laws of learning suggested by the results.
In the puzzle boxes Thorndike made, hungry cats had to learn to escape the box using levers to get to food. The first time they escape, Thorndike says, it is an accident. Over trials, the response gets "stamped in" with trial-and-error learning. Thorndike named his discoveries the "law of effect", where a favorable consequence is associated with a particular situation, and the "law of

exercise", where the more frequently an animal response in a particular way, the more the response is associated with a particular situation.

12. Discuss the overall significance for the development of behaviorism of Thorndike's research on human and animal learning.

Thorndike called his approach connectionism: the idea that situations and responses become connected over time, and that an individual contains a large collection of these connections. Although there is "a mentalisitc tinge to Thorndike's work", particularly when he discusses "satisfaction, annoyance, and discomfort", his work is mechanistic, arguing that behavior can be reduced to stimulus and response. This mechanism became amplified later with Watson.

13. Describe Pavlov's initial focus on mentalistic experiences and his attempts to control outside influences on his research.

Initially Pavlov called his conditioned reflex the "psychic reflex" and tried to explain it with such things as "animals' desires, judgment, and will." Eventually he drops these mentalistic terms. In his attempts to control outside influences, Pavlov built the "Tower of Silence" which separated his lab and experiments from stimuli from outside. To do this, a building was built with "extra-thick glass," "double steel doors," and "steel girders embedded in sand", finished with a "straw-filled moat"

14. How would you design an experiment to condition a rabbit to salivate to the ringing of a cell phone?

You would do the following: make a cell phone ring and follow that immediately with food in the rabbit's mouth. Repeat this several times, making sure to reinforce with food until learning is complete. Eventually, when the cell phone rings, the rabbit will salivate with no food in its mouth.

15. How did Pavlov's work influence Watson's behaviorism?

Pavlov described higher mental processes (learning) with physiological terms. Additionally, to Pavlov all animals are machines, something Watson agreed with. Pavlov's work set high standards for the carefully controlled experiments that will become characteristic of behaviorism. In addition, Pavlov's use of stimulus, response, and control variables are all influential to behaviorism.

16. Compare Pavlov's concept of conditioned reflex with Bekhterev's associated reflex.

Pavlov conditioned glandular secretions, while Bekhterev conditioned motor (muscular) responses. Beyond this difference, the work of the two is very similar.

17. Why is Twitmyer's experience of interest to historians of psychology?

Interestingly, Pavlov's discovery about conditioned reflexes had been found before. In the U.S, Edwin Burket Twitmyer presented a paper at the 1904 APA conference about conditioning the knee jerk reflex, but because it received no interest from conference-goers he abandoned the research. This illustrates the tenuousness of fame in the history of psychology. Perhaps had he received encouragement, Twitmyer may have become an important figure in the history of psychology, rather than the footnote he is (at best) given.

18. Discuss the Zeitgeist in American psychology in the second decade of the twentieth century with reference to ideas promoted by the structuralists and functionalists.
In this time period, there was movement to concentrate on behavior only and move away from any study of the mind. For example, "In 1911, Walter Pillsbury...defined psychology in his textbook as the science of behavior." Books were written about "human behavior", and Knight Dunlap proposed banning introspection from psychology.

19. How did the functionalist school influence Watson's behaviorism?
Functionalism "did represent greater objectivity than did its predecessors. Cattell and other functionalists emphasized behavior and objectivity and expressed dissatisfaction with introspection."

Key terms from chapter nine

- **Associated reflexes** From the work of Vladimir Bekhterev, these are "Reflexes that can be elicited not only by unconditioned stimuli but also by stimuli that have become associated with the unconditioned stimuli."
- **Associative memory** To Jacques Loeb, the fact that there is an association between stimulus and response indicates the presence of consciousness.
- **Clever Hans** A horse promoted as being able to answer complex problems, do math, spell, etc. He was tested by a psychologist who discovered that the horse was responding to subtle head movements of the people around him.
- **Conditioned reflexes** Pavlov's "Reflexes that are conditional or dependent on the formation of an association or connection between stimulus and response."
- **Connectionism** Thorndike named his approach to learning "connectionism" because it is "based on connections between situations and responses."
- **Law of effect** "Acts that produce satisfaction in a given situation become associated with that situation; when the situation recurs, the act is likely to recur."
- **Law of exercise** Also called the "Law of use and disuse", this is "the more an act or response is used in a given situation, the more strongly the act becomes associated with that situation."
- **Psychic reflexes** Pavlov's original name for conditioned reflexes, and represents his early attempts to include animal consciousness in his research findings.
- **The Puzzle box** Constructed by Thorndike, the famous mechanism from which cats had to learn to escape by activating a lever.
- **Rat maze** The standard method to study learning, introduced by Willard Small from Clark U.
- **Reinforcement** "Something that increases the likelihood of a response."
- **The Tower of Silence** Pavlov's attempt to block all outside stimuli from entering his lab and fouling his research. The building was built in an elaborate way to insulate the lab from the world.
- **Trial-and-error learning** Thorndike believed animals to learn in this way, through simple trial and error which either "stamps in" or "stamps out" a response.
- **Tropism** The concept that animals have "involuntary forced movements" which drove the thinking of Jacques Loeb.

ESSAY

1. What were the central tenets of behaviorism as set forth by Watson? How did they differ from the principles and approaches of Wundt and Titchener? Why was the method of introspection unacceptable to Watson?

   ANS:
   Answer not provided.

   PTS: 1

2. Identify and describe the three major forces that formed Watson's system of behavioral psychology. What was Watson's position and that of his contemporaries on positivism?

   ANS:
   Answer not provided.

   PTS: 1   MSC: WWW

3. Describe the evolution of animal psychology from Romanes and Morgan to Pavlov and Bekhterev. Why was it difficult to be an animal psychologist in the United States before behaviorism was well established?

   ANS:
   Answer not provided.

   PTS: 1

4. What were the specific contributions of Loeb, Washburn, Small, and Turner to animal psychology?

   ANS:
   Answer not provided.

   PTS: 1

5. Tell the story of Clever Hans, the clever horse. Who are the main characters and what are their roles? Explain how experimentation was used to determine the source of Hans' cleverness. Who served as the experimenter and what were his/her conclusions?

   ANS:
   Answer not provided.

   PTS: 1

6. Describe Thorndike's work with cats in the puzzle box, including the nature of the box, what he observed, and the link between the results and his laws of learning.

   ANS:
   Answer not provided.

   PTS: 1

7. Compare and contrast Thorndike's law of effect and Pavlov's law of reinforcement.

ANS:
Answer not provided.

PTS: 1   MSC: WWW

8. What was Twitmyer's contribution to modern psychology? Why is his work so often overlooked?

ANS:
Answer not provided.

PTS: 1

9. Describe Pavlov's work on conditioning, including his experimental method and the extent to which he attempted to control irrelevant variables.

ANS:
Answer not provided.

PTS: 1

10. Compare and contrast the work of Pavlov on conditioned reflexes and that of Bekhterev on associated reflexes. How did their work influence Watsonian behaviorism?

ANS:
Answer not provided.

PTS: 1

11. Discuss the ways in which functional psychology influenced behaviorism.

ANS:
Answer not provided.

PTS: 1

MULTIPLE CHOICE

12. By the second decade of the 20th century, psychologists agreed on the _____.
    a. value of introspection
    b. existence of mental elements
    c. need for psychology to be a pure science
    d. replacement of structuralism by functionalism
    e. None of the choices are correct.

    ANS: E   PTS: 1   REF: Toward a Science of Behavior

13. Watson's approach to structuralism and functionalism was ____.
   a. conciliatory
   b. to reject structuralism but retain aspects of functionalism
   c. to demand a return to pure science
   d. an overreaction to the quick popularity of psychoanalysis
   e. a revolt

   ANS: E   PTS: 1   REF: Toward a Science of Behavior
   MSC: WWW

14. Which of the following terms should be banned from psychology according to behaviorism?
   a. image
   b. mind
   c. consciousness
   d. All of the choices are correct.
   e. None of the choices are correct.

   ANS: D   PTS: 1   REF: Toward a Science of Behavior

15. For Watson, such subject matter as mind, consciousness, and images was ____.
   a. meaningless for a science of psychology
   b. necessary for human thought
   c. best dealt with by psychoanalysis
   d. the necessary starting point for the study of behavior
   e. regulated by Pavlov's law of reinforcement

   ANS: A   PTS: 1   REF: Toward a Science of Behavior

16. Who argued that consciousness, as a concept, was as unprovable as the concept of the soul?
   a. Loeb
   b. Watson
   c. Pavlov
   d. Thorndike
   e. Angell

   ANS: B   PTS: 1   REF: Toward a Science of Behavior

17. For Watson, introspection was ____.
   a. irrelevant
   b. appropriate only for research with normal humans
   c. acceptable as used by Wundt, i.e., with systematic observation, controls, and replication
   d. acceptable only if performed by exceptionally well-trained observers
   e. necessary to the understanding of behavior

   ANS: A   PTS: 1   REF: Toward a Science of Behavior

18. For Comte, valid knowledge is that which is ____.
   a. objectively observable
   b. social in nature
   c. reliable
   d. truthful, as defined by internal observation
   e. objectively observable and social in nature

   ANS: E   PTS: 1   REF: Toward a Science of Behavior

19. The early 20th-century Zeitgeist in science was marked by _____.
    a. behaviorism
    b. positivism
    c. functionalism
    d. experimentation
    e. nihilism

    ANS: B   PTS: 1   REF: Toward a Science of Behavior

20. The most important antecedent of Watson's behaviorism was _____.
    a. evolutionary theory
    b. functionalism
    c. positivism
    d. animal psychology
    e. the anecdotal method

    ANS: D   PTS: 1
    REF: The Influence of Animal Psychology on Behaviorism

21. Who had a theory of tropisms?
    a. Bekhterev
    b. Watson
    c. Loeb
    d. Morgan
    e. Twitmyer

    ANS: C   PTS: 1
    REF: The Influence of Animal Psychology on Behaviorism   MSC: WWW

22. For Loeb, a tropism is a(n) _____.
    a. involuntary forced movement
    b. reflex arc
    c. indication of consciousness
    d. reflex
    e. toucan

    ANS: A   PTS: 1
    REF: The Influence of Animal Psychology on Behaviorism

23. For Loeb, if an animal's response is forced by a stimulus, the _____.
    a. behavior does not need explanation
    b. behavior is positivist
    c. behavior requires no inferences about consciousness
    d. animal is unable to perceive and discriminate between objects
    e. animal is unable to display purposive behavior

    ANS: C   PTS: 1
    REF: The Influence of Animal Psychology on Behaviorism

24. The white rat and the rat maze became staples of research in psychology in 1900 with the work of _____.
    a. Jacques Loeb
    b. C. Lloyd Morgan
    c. Willard S. Small
    d. Carl Lashley
    e. John B. Watson

    ANS: C   PTS: 1
    REF: The Influence of Animal Psychology on Behaviorism

25. Watson's dissertation was on _____.
    a. the conscious experience of rats
    b. the conscious experience of toddlers
    c. the latent learning of rats
    d. fear conditioning in rats
    e. fear conditioning in toddlers

    ANS: A   PTS: 1
    REF: The Influence of Animal Psychology on Behaviorism

26. An early African American researcher in comparative psychology was _____.
    a. Loeb
    b. Bond
    c. Turner
    d. James
    e. Twitmyer

    ANS: C   PTS: 1
    REF: The Influence of Animal Psychology on Behaviorism

27. *The Animal Mind*, the first textbook on comparative psychology, was written by _____.
    a. Mary Calkins
    b. Margaret Washburn
    c. Mary Cover Jones
    d. Rosalie Rayner
    e. Maude Merrill

    ANS: B   PTS: 1
    REF: The Influence of Animal Psychology on Behaviorism

28. Who wrote a paper on ant behavior that was highly praised by Watson?
    a. Turner
    b. Loeb
    c. Washburn
    d. Twitmyer
    e. Yerkes

    ANS: A   PTS: 1
    REF: The Influence of Animal Psychology on Behaviorism

29. The "last stand" of mentalistic interpretations of animal behavior was the text _____ written by _____.
    a. *Animal Intelligence*; Thorndike
    b. *The Animal Mind*; Yerkes
    c. *The Animal Mind*; Washburn
    d. *Animal Education*; Turner
    e. *Objective Psychology*; Bekhterev

    ANS: C   PTS: 1
    REF: The Influence of Animal Psychology on Behaviorism

30. After *The Animal Mind*, textbooks on comparative psychology focused on _____.
    a. reflex behavior
    b. respondent conditioning
    c. operant conditioning
    d. learning
    e. physiology

    ANS: D   PTS: 1
    REF: The Influence of Animal Psychology on Behaviorism   MSC: WWW

31. Which of the following statements best describes the change that took place in animal psychology following the work of Romanes and Morgan?
    a. The field became more subjective as methods to study animal consciousness were perfected.
    b. The field became more objective as mentalistic terms were dropped from the descriptions of behavior.
    c. The field stopped growing after Angell's 1906 presidential address describing functionalism.
    d. The field was growing in popularity in Russia but was never a major part of psychology in the United States.
    e. There was no change, the methods of Romanes and Morgan are still widely used today.

    ANS: B   PTS: 1
    REF: The Influence of Animal Psychology on Behaviorism

32. According to Schultz and Schultz, *"Whether dealing with mind or with behavior, it was not easy to be _____."*
    a. *a functionalist*
    b. *an experimentalist*
    c. *a beginning psychologist*
    d. *an animal psychologist*
    e. *a mechanist*

    ANS: D   PTS: 1
    REF: The Influence of Animal Psychology on Behaviorism

33. The particular contribution of Pavlov's work to Watson's behaviorism was Pavlov's _____.
    a. objective methodology
    b. evidence of the feasibility of an objective psychology
    c. refutation of Dewey's criticisms of the reflex arc concept
    d. refutation of the laboratory animal
    e. refutation of Thorndike's law of effect

    ANS: A   PTS: 1
    REF: The Influence of Animal Psychology on Behaviorism

34. Pfungst demonstrated that the apparent thinking ability of the horse Clever Hans was really due to the animal's ability to respond to ____.
    a. voice commands
    b. head movements
    c. touches
    d. odors
    e. None of the choices are correct.

    ANS: B   PTS: 1
    REF: The Influence of Animal Psychology on Behaviorism   MSC: WWW

35. The case of Clever Hans served to ____.
    a. illustrate the importance of objective, experimental study of animal behavior with proper control conditions
    b. demonstrate transference between animals and humans
    c. refute Lashley's equipotentiality principle
    d. focus public attention on introspection by analogy
    e. demonstrate the importance of studying both human and animal subjects

    ANS: A   PTS: 1
    REF: The Influence of Animal Psychology on Behaviorism

36. Thorndike's (1898) law of effect is similar to ____.
    a. Pavlov's law of reinforcement
    b. Tolman's purposive behaviorism
    c. Guthrie's one-trial learning
    d. Jones's behavior modification
    e. Wundt's tridimensional feelings

    ANS: A   PTS: 1   REF: Edward Lee Thorndike (1874-1949)

37. The first doctoral dissertation in psychology to use animal subjects was that of ____.
    a. Washburn
    b. Turner
    c. Watson
    d. Thorndike
    e. Yerkes

    ANS: D   PTS: 1   REF: Edward Lee Thorndike (1874-1949)

38. In Thorndike's early research, he worked with all of the following *except* ____.
    a. chicks
    b. cats
    c. dogs
    d. children
    e. None of the above.

    ANS: D   PTS: 1   REF: Edward Lee Thorndike (1874-1949)

39. Thorndike earned his Ph.D. in 1898 and after 1899 studied ____.
    a. human learning
    b. mental testing
    c. educational psychology
    d. All of the choices are correct.
    e. human learning **and** mental testing **only**

    ANS: D   PTS: 1   REF: p. 277

40. An approach to learning termed _____ was developed by Thorndike.
    a. associationism
    b. reflexology
    c. instrumental conditioning
    d. connectionism
    e. reinforcement

    ANS: D   PTS: 1   REF: Edward Lee Thorndike (1874-1949)

41. For Thorndike, learning is _____.
    a. simple associations
    b. complex associations
    c. making connections
    d. a stimulus-response unit
    e. "satisfaction"

    ANS: C   PTS: 1   REF: Edward Lee Thorndike (1874-1949)

42. The influence of Romanes and Morgan on Thorndike was shown in Thorndike's _____.
    a. use of mentalistic processes
    b. freely granting high levels of consciousness to animals
    c. use of introspection as an additional methodology
    d. All of the choices are correct.
    e. None of the choices are correct.

    ANS: A   PTS: 1   REF: Edward Lee Thorndike (1874-1949)

43. Thorndike's approach was similar to that of structuralism in his focus on _____.
    a. mechanism
    b. introspection
    c. mentalism
    d. positivism
    e. phenomenalism

    ANS: A   PTS: 1   REF: Edward Lee Thorndike (1874-1949)

44. Who used puzzle boxes to study animal behavior?
    a. Washburn
    b. Turner
    c. Watson
    d. Thorndike
    e. Yerkes

    ANS: D   PTS: 1   REF: Edward Lee Thorndike (1874-1949)
    MSC: WWW

45. The puzzle box is traditionally associated with the work of _____.
    a. Thorndike
    b. Watson
    c. Skinner
    d. Köhler
    e. Tolman

    ANS: A   PTS: 1   REF: Edward Lee Thorndike (1874-1949)

46. Thorndike used _____ measures of learning to record his data.
    a. qualitative
    b. quantitative
    c. qualitative as well as quantitative
    d. no
    e. outdated

    ANS: B   PTS: 1   REF: Edward Lee Thorndike (1874-1949)

47. Thorndike's "trial and accidental success" learning is more commonly known as _____ learning.
    a. respondent
    b. stamping in
    c. trial-and-error
    d. one-trial
    e. latent

    ANS: C   PTS: 1   REF: Edward Lee Thorndike (1874-1949)

48. Habit strength is a function of repetition. This is an instance of _____.
    a. Thorndike's law of effect
    b. Thorndike's law of exercise
    c. Pavlov's law of reinforcement
    d. Skinner's principle of the extinction of competing responses
    e. vicarious learning

    ANS: B   PTS: 1   REF: Edward Lee Thorndike (1874-1949)

49. Thorndike's ideas about the stamping in or stamping out of a response tendency led to his statement of _____.
    a. the S-R connection
    b. reinforcement
    c. the law of satisfaction
    d. the law of exercise
    e. the law of effect

    ANS: E   PTS: 1   REF: Edward Lee Thorndike (1874-1949)

50. Who first demonstrated that reward had a stronger effect than punishment?
    a. Pavlov
    b. Watson
    c. Thorndike
    d. Tolman
    e. Skinner

    ANS: C   PTS: 1   REF: Edward Lee Thorndike (1874-1949)

51. Thorndike's revision of his law of effect stated that _____.
    a. rewards are unrelated to the strength of connection between stimuli and responses
    b. stimuli that satisfy physiological needs are most effective as rewards
    c. punishing a response weakened a connection but not to the same degree that rewards strengthened a connection
    d. the law of exercise was unrelated to it
    e. All of the choices are correct.

    ANS: C   PTS: 1   REF: Edward Lee Thorndike (1874-1949)

52. The "original" law of effect states that ____.
    a. punishment always weakens a response
    b. reward strengthens a response, but punishment does not always weaken a response
    c. any act that produces satisfaction is more likely to occur again; any act that produces discomfort is less likely to occur again
    d. any act that produces reward will always be extinguished
    e. rewards stamp in connections, and punishments stamp out connections

    ANS: C   PTS: 1   REF: Edward Lee Thorndike (1874-1949)
    MSC: WWW

53. Thorndike's particular contribution to behaviorism was his focus on ____.
    a. animal research
    b. objective observation
    c. the experimental method
    d. principles of association
    e. S-R units

    ANS: C   PTS: 1   REF: Edward Lee Thorndike (1874-1949)

54. Pavlov's work effected a change in focus from ____ to observable physiological events.
    a. introspection
    b. subjective speculation about associationism
    c. connectionism
    d. determinism
    e. mechanism

    ANS: B   PTS: 1   REF: Ivan Petrovitch Pavlov (1849-1936)

55. Whose work has been described as "a shift from speculation to experimentation?"
    a. Pavlov
    b. Thorndike
    c. Bekhterev
    d. Watson
    e. Yerkes

    ANS: A   PTS: 1   REF: Ivan Petrovitch Pavlov (1849-1936)

56. What led Pavlov to shift from a study of theology to that of animal psychology?
    a. becoming familiar with the psychology of Wundt
    b. the work of Thorndike
    c. Darwin's theory
    d. the case of Clever Hans
    e. the writings of Fechner

    ANS: C   PTS: 1   REF: Ivan Petrovitch Pavlov (1849-1936)

57. Who could be described as an absent-minded genius?
    a. Bekhterev
    b. Thorndike
    c. Pavlov
    d. Watson
    e. Twitmyer

    ANS: C   PTS: 1   REF: Ivan Petrovitch Pavlov (1849-1936)

BEHAVIORISM: ANTECEDENT INFLUENCES   305

58. The term *psychic reflexes* reflects _____.
    a. Pavlov's early inclination to use mentalistic terms
    b. Pavlov's familiarity with Watson's dissertation on the psychic development of the white rat
    c. the distortion of the data of history by an error in translation
    d. Pavlov's training as a neurologist
    e. Pavlov's early identification with the new science of psychology

    ANS: A   PTS: 1   REF: Ivan Petrovitch Pavlov (1849-1936)

59. Pavlov's conditioned reflexes require _____ for learning to occur.
    a. reinforcement
    b. knowledge
    c. two or more unconditioned responses
    d. S-R connections
    e. reinforcements and S-R connections

    ANS: E   PTS: 1   REF: Ivan Petrovitch Pavlov (1849-1936)

60. More than any other researcher in psychology before him, Pavlov attempted to _____.
    a. eliminate sources of error from his studies.
    b. implement the experimental method.
    c. reject all responses that were not objectively observable.
    d. analyze S-R units into their component elements.
    e. eliminate sources of error from his studies **and** implement the experimental method.

    ANS: E   PTS: 1   REF: Ivan Petrovitch Pavlov (1849-1936)

61. In the typical conditioning experiment done by Pavlov, the <u>food</u> placed in the dog's mouth is called the
    _____.
    a. conditioned stimulus
    b. unconditioned stimulus
    c. conditioned response
    d. unconditioned response
    e. conditional response

    ANS: B   PTS: 1   REF: Ivan Petrovitch Pavlov (1849-1936)

62. For Pavlov, _____ is necessary for learning to take place.
    a. punishment
    b. reinforcement
    c. emission of a voluntary behavior
    d. clean dogs
    e. None of the choices are correct.

    ANS: B   PTS: 1   REF: Ivan Petrovitch Pavlov (1849-1936)
    MSC: WWW

63. Pavlov conducted research on _____.
    a. reinforcement
    b. extinction
    c. generalization
    d. discrimination
    e. All of the choices are correct.

    ANS: E   PTS: 1   REF: Ivan Petrovitch Pavlov (1849-1936)

64. According to Pavlov in the original Source Material from *Conditioned Reflexes* (1927), his starting point in research was ____.
    a. his previous work in physiology
    b. careful observation of dogs salivating
    c. Darwin's theory of evolution
    d. Washburn's book on the animal mind
    e. Descartes idea of the nervous reflex

    ANS: E   PTS: 1   REF: Ivan Petrovitch Pavlov (1849-1936)

65. In the last half of the original Source Material from *Conditioned Reflexes* (1927), Pavlov discussed ____.
    a. his work on higher order conditioning
    b. many of his experimental variations
    c. Darwin's theory of evolution
    d. Washburn's book on the animal mind
    e. the building of what became known as the "Tower of Silence"

    ANS: E   PTS: 1   REF: Ivan Petrovitch Pavlov (1849-1936)

66. While Pavlov was exploring conditioning in Russia, an American named ____ also discovered the existence of conditioned reflexes.
    a. Walter Pillsbury
    b. John Watson
    c. Edward Thorndike
    d. Edwin Burket Twitmyer
    e. Willard Small

    ANS: D   PTS: 1   REF: Ivan Petrovitch Pavlov (1849-1936)
    MSC: WWW

67. If the 1904 APA attendees been more attentive, we might today speak of ____.
    a. canine introspection
    b. Twitmyer's dogs
    c. Bekhterev's knees
    d. Twitmyerian conditioning
    e. Bekhterev's dogs

    ANS: D   PTS: 1   REF: Ivan Petrovitch Pavlov (1849-1936)

68. Which of the following is (are) true?
    a. Pavlov argued that higher mental processes in animals could be described in physiological terms.
    b. Pavlovian methods have had practical applications.
    c. Pavlov published extensively with his lifelong friend Bekhterev.
    d. Both a and b.
    e. None of the above are true.

    ANS: D   PTS: 1   REF: Ivan Petrovitch Pavlov (1849-1936)

69. Pavlov's work illustrated the study of higher mental processes in ____.
    a. psychical terms
    b. physical terms
    c. physiological terms
    d. reinforcement
    e. associations

    ANS: C   PTS: 1   REF: Ivan Petrovitch Pavlov (1849-1936)

70. For Pavlov, humans and animals were ____.
    a. machines
    b. allies
    c. enemies
    d. incompatible
    e. essentially different, needing different research methods

    ANS: A   PTS: 1   REF: Ivan Petrovitch Pavlov (1849-1936)

71. Consistent with James's views, Pavlov argued that ____.
    a. psychology was not yet a science
    b. psychology was in the preparadigmatic phase
    c. classical conditioning was the paradigm needed for psychology to become a science
    d. psychology was a mentalistic interpretation of physiology
    e. psychology was still in the realm of philosophy

    ANS: A   PTS: 1   REF: Ivan Petrovitch Pavlov (1849-1936)

72. Pavlov's view of psychology was ____.
    a. initially favorable, then somewhat negative
    b. always negative
    c. always favorable
    d. initially negative, then somewhat favorable
    e. uncertain; he never said one way or the other

    ANS: D   PTS: 1   REF: Ivan Petrovitch Pavlov (1849-1936)

73. Which of the following statements is **not** true regarding Bekhterev?
    a. Bekhterev was a physiologist, neurologist, and psychiatrist.
    b. Bekhterev had a cordial relationship with Pavlov.
    c. Bekhterev hypothesized that high-level behaviors were compounded from simpler
       reflexive behaviors.
    d. Bekhterev argued for a completely objective approach for psychology.
    e. Bekhterev was probably assassinated by Stalin

    ANS: B   PTS: 1   REF: Vladimir M. Bekhterev (1857-1927)

74. Bekhterev discovered ____.
    a. the associated reflexes
    b. the reflex arc
    c. the knee-jerk response
    d. one-trial learning
    e. that punishment is not effective

    ANS: A   PTS: 1   REF: Vladimir M. Bekhterev (1857-1927)

75. Bekhterev ____.
    a. never used reinforcement for his conditioning
    b. applied Pavlovian principles to the muscles
    c. was a close friend of Pavlov
    d. had a research program that blossomed when he emigrated to the U.S.
    e. None of the choices are correct.

    ANS: B   PTS: 1   REF: Vladimir M. Bekhterev (1857-1927)

76. *Objective Psychology* was authored by ____.
    a. Thorndike
    b. Comte
    c. Watson
    d. Pavlov
    e. Bekhterev

    ANS: E   PTS: 1   REF: Vladimir M. Bekhterev (1857-1927)
    MSC: WWW

77. Bekhterev ___.
    a. argued that thought processes depended upon muscle responses of the speech
    b. did work on glandular conditioning
    c. influenced Freud
    d. All of the choices are correct.
    e. None of the choices are correct.

    ANS: A   PTS: 1   REF: Vladimir M. Bekhterev (1857-1927)

78. Watson was not the first to demand an objective psychology and, according to one historian, ____ is
    considered the grandfather of Watson's behaviorism.
    a. Fechner
    b. Cattell
    c. Thorndike
    d. Pavlov
    e. Bekhterev

    ANS: B   PTS: 1
    REF: The Influence of Functional Psychology on Behaviorism   MSC: WWW

79. Who first defined psychology as the study of behavior?
    a. Watson
    b. Cattell
    c. Pillsbury
    d. Pavlov
    e. Washburn

    ANS: C   PTS: 1
    REF: The Influence of Functional Psychology on Behaviorism

80. Angell proposed that the term *consciousness* had about the same life expectancy in psychology as the term
    ____.
    a. *mind*
    b. *psychic*
    c. *soul*
    d. *respondent*
    e. *mental element*

    ANS: C   PTS: 1
    REF: The Influence of Functional Psychology on Behaviorism

TRUE/FALSE

81. Behaviorism was a protest against structuralism, not functionalism.

    ANS: F   PTS: 1   REF: Toward a Science of Behavior

82. The founder of positivism was Comte.

    ANS: T   PTS: 1   REF: Toward a Science of Behavior
    MSC: WWW

83. One criterion of positivism is that knowledge must be private in nature.

    ANS: F   PTS: 1   REF: Toward a Science of Behavior

84. According to positivism, introspective knowledge cannot be considered valid knowledge.

    ANS: T   PTS: 1   REF: Toward a Science of Behavior

85. Animal psychology was an outcome of evolutionary theory.

    ANS: T   PTS: 1
    REF: The Influence of Animal Psychology on Behaviorism

86. The notion that single-celled organisms engage in purposive behavior was given by Wundt.

    ANS: F   PTS: 1
    REF: The Influence of Animal Psychology on Behaviorism

87. The advantage of Loeb's concept of tropism was that consciousness was irrelevant.

    ANS: T   PTS: 1
    REF: The Influence of Animal Psychology on Behaviorism

88. For Loeb, if an S-R association is formed, then the organism has consciousness.

    ANS: T   PTS: 1
    REF: The Influence of Animal Psychology on Behaviorism   MSC: WWW

89. The rat maze was introduced in the research of Willard S. Small.

    ANS: T   PTS: 1
    REF: The Influence of Animal Psychology on Behaviorism

90. The author of "Animal Education: The Psychical Development of the White Rat" was Washburn.

    ANS: F   PTS: 1
    REF: The Influence of Animal Psychology on Behaviorism

91. The first text on comparative psychology was by Margaret Washburn.

    ANS: T   PTS: 1
    REF: The Influence of Animal Psychology on Behaviorism

92. In the early years, animal psychology was discouraged because it appeared to lack pragmatic value.

ANS: T   PTS: 1
REF: The Influence of Animal Psychology on Behaviorism

93. The work of Skinner on intermittent reinforcement was anticipated by the conditioning of Clever Hans.

ANS: T   PTS: 1
REF: The Influence of Animal Psychology on Behaviorism

94. Thorndike argued that psychology should study behavior as well as conscious experience.

ANS: F   PTS: 1   REF: Edward Lee Thorndike (1874-1949)

95. Most of Thorndike's career was concerned with animal learning.

ANS: F   PTS: 1   REF: Edward Lee Thorndike (1874-1949)

96. Thorndike posited that "The mind is man's connection-system."

ANS: T   PTS: 1   REF: Edward Lee Thorndike (1874-1949)

97. Thorndike used the phrase "trial and accidental success."

ANS: T   PTS: 1   REF: Edward Lee Thorndike (1874-1949)

98. In his mechanistic approach to psychology, Thorndike discarded concepts of satisfaction and discomfort.

ANS: F   PTS: 1   REF: Edward Lee Thorndike (1874-1949)

99. In anticipation of Skinner's work on reinforcement schedules, Thorndike concluded that reward is as important as repetition of a response.

ANS: F   PTS: 1   REF: Edward Lee Thorndike (1874-1949)

100. Pavlov was constantly conducting experiments as he insisted on his own hands-on involvement.

ANS: F   PTS: 1   REF: Ivan Petrovitch Pavlov (1849-1936)

101. A revolution with fighting in the streets was no excuse for being late if you were one of Pavlov's lab assistants.

ANS: T   PTS: 1   REF: Ivan Petrovitch Pavlov (1849-1936)

102. Pavlov's Nobel Prize was for his work on conditioning.

ANS: F   PTS: 1   REF: Ivan Petrovitch Pavlov (1849-1936)

103. Pavlov's original term for learned responses was "psychic reflexes."

ANS: T   PTS: 1   REF: Ivan Petrovitch Pavlov (1849-1936)
MSC: WWW

104. In Pavlov's terms, the conditional reflex is dependent on the formation of an association.

ANS: T   PTS: 1   REF: Ivan Petrovitch Pavlov (1849-1936)

105. Pavlov changed his terminology for a learned response from "psychic reflex" to "conditioned reflex."

ANS: F   PTS: 1   REF: Ivan Petrovitch Pavlov (1849-1936)

106. While the cartoon character Superman had his Tower of Silence, Pavlov had his laboratory called the Fortress of Solitude.

ANS: F   PTS: 1   REF: Ivan Petrovitch Pavlov (1849-1936)

107. In Pavlovian conditioning, reinforcement is *not* essential.

ANS: F   PTS: 1   REF: Ivan Petrovitch Pavlov (1849-1936)

108. E. B. Twitmyer was the first to describe classical conditioning.

ANS: F   PTS: 1   REF: Ivan Petrovitch Pavlov (1849-1936)

109. The crux of Pavlov's work on conditioning was that higher mental processes could be studied in physiological terms.

ANS: T   PTS: 1   REF: Ivan Petrovitch Pavlov (1849-1936)
MSC: WWW

110. The element of Pavlov's work most readily appropriated by Watson was the conditioned reflex.

ANS: T   PTS: 1   REF: Ivan Petrovitch Pavlov (1849-1936)

111. Bekhterev's work is distinct from Pavlov's in the former's focus on voluntary motor responses.

ANS: F   PTS: 1   REF: Vladimir M. Bekhterev (1857-1927)

112. Bekhterev's discoveries concerned associated reflexes.

ANS: T   PTS: 1   REF: Vladimir M. Bekhterev (1857-1927)

113. V. M. Bekhterev wrote *Objective Psychology*.

ANS: T   PTS: 1   REF: Vladimir M. Bekhterev (1857-1927)

114. Watson was the sole proponent of a "science of behavior" prior to his 1913 paper on the subject.

ANS: F   PTS: 1
REF: The Influence of Functional Psychology on Behaviorism

115. By 1910, it was expected that mind would soon become as irrelevant to psychology as the concept of soul.

ANS: T   PTS: 1
REF: The Influence of Functional Psychology on Behaviorism   MSC: WWW

Chapter 10

Behaviorism: The Beginnings

The chapter begins with an in-depth look at the Little Albert study, in which an 8-month old child was conditioned to fear objects that did not previously evoke fear. To begin, John Watson used a previously neutral stimuli (white rat) and paired it with a unconditioned stimuli that elicited fear (hammer noise). After several pairings, Little Albert was conditioned to fear the white rat, even in the absence of the hammer noise. The fear response was generalized to other furry white things, such as a dog and fur coat. Watson deduced that all adult fears are a product of similar conditioning in infancy and childhood. Although similar studies were conducted with animals, Watson's major contribution was to crystallize previous thought and deliberately found a new school based on the ideas already emerging in psychology.

Watson came from humble beginnings and as a young man he tended to behave aggressively and get into trouble with the law. Not surprisingly, he was not a good student. Because of a promise he made his mother, he went to college with intentions of becoming a minister. His mother died, and he went to the University of Chicago to study philosophy. There, he was "attracted to psychology" by Angell. He stayed there, earned his Ph.D., began working with white rats, became an instructor, and met his future wife Mary Ickes.

In 1908 Watson accepted a position at Johns Hopkins in Baltimore that was offered by James Baldwin. Soon after Watson's arrival Baldwin was asked to resign because of a sex scandal, which was a boon to Watson's career; he became the chair of the psychology department at Hopkins and the editor of *Psychological Review*. In 1913 he published his famous article, which started Behaviorism. In his further work he advocated the use of animals as research subjects and strove for behaviorism to have "practical value". To that end, he applied it to such areas as advertising and industrial psychology. During World War I he helped develop selection tests for pilots. He continued to refine behaviorism, for example writing *Psychology from the Standpoint of a Behaviorist* (1919).

Although his professional life was thriving, his personal life was falling apart. He tended to womanize, and had an affair with Rosalie Raynor, his graduate student (who co-ran and co-wrote the Little Albert study). He was forced to resign from Hopkins and was never able to obtain an academic job again. He moved to New York City, divorced his wife, married Rosalie, and began a prosperous job in advertising. Watson began to give lectures and write magazine articles and books whose audience was the general public. In doing so, Watson brought public attention to psychology, particularly the burgeoning field of behaviorism. He published *Behaviorism* in 1925 and *Psychological Care of the Infant and Child* in 1928, both of which sold well. The 1928 book changed the way children were raised in America, although his advice was unusual, such as not giving your children hugs or kisses, rather a "pat on the head" at most. Watson's sons by Rosalie, William and James, "both suffered from serious depression" and led to suicide attempts. Rosalie publically disagreed with his childrearing practices.

Rosalie died in 1935, which devastated Watson. He became "a recluse", and when the APA awarded him with a citation in 1957, at the last moment he could not enter the ceremony and sent in his son to accept it in his place. He died a year later. The authors include an excerpt from Watson's famous 1913 article, *Psychology as the Behaviorist Views It*, in which Watson advocates banning mental concepts from psychology.

Watson's vision was not accepted immediately, and it wasn't until his "1919 book…did the movement begin to have significant impact." Watson had many critics. For example, Mary Whiton Calkins believed introspection to be the only way to study "certain processes."

Watson proposed that, to make psychology more like a natural science, psychologists should focus only on objectively studying behavior through observation. The only methods to be used, he said, were these four: 1) observation, 2) tests (what others might call 'mental tests') 3) verbal report (for which he was criticized for including because it sounds too much like introspection), and 4) conditioned reflex. With this change in focus and methods, subjects no longer contribute to observations (as they did with introspection). These new methods promoted a mechanistic stance, as the subjects were no longer involved in the observation process.

Behavior became the focus in Watson's system, and he reduced all behavior to basic stimulus-response units. Responses can be explicit (overtly observable) or implicit (such things as glandular secretions, not overtly observable). Stimuli can be simple or complex. The text authors then focus on three topics that Watson concentrated on, "instincts, emotions, and thoughts." Although originally Watson believed that instincts existed; he later claimed that there were none—that all behavior is learned, nothing is inherited. This optimistic stance took out the role of genetics and attributed all behavior to nurture. It also proposes that behaviors can be unlearned, and manipulated, through psychology.

For Watson, "emotions were…physiological responses to specific stimuli," and believed that we are born with three: "fear, rage, and love." These three act in conditioning to create other emotions. Watson used the fear response in the Little Albert experiment to condition the baby to fear new objects. Interestingly, the Little Albert study has never been successfully replicated, although it was a landmark study. Albert was never conditioned to eliminate his fears, but Mary Cover Jones became interested in using conditioning to rid people of fears. Her subject was a 3-year old boy named Peter, who was afraid of rabbits. Jones was able to condition Peter's fear response away.

Watson also attempted to address and explain thoughts in behavioral terms. He believed it to be related to unspoken speech which relies on the same muscle movements as speech. He tried to measure "tongue and larynx movements during thought" with little success. Watson's behaviorism became popular because he promoted the idea of creating a society based on behavioral principles. Perhaps most influential was the idea that, with Watson's vision, it is possible for anyone to become anything, unfettered by inherited characteristics. Furthermore, with behaviorism came the idea that all behavior can be shaped by conditioning, even "adult disturbances." This caused psychology to be seen as a way to "health, happiness, and prosperity." It also began the practice of behavioral therapy.

Behaviorism's popular appeal comes somewhat from Watson's utopian vision. In describing his new psychology, Watson outlines a program that can be used to raise successful children, fix unwanted adult behaviors, and improve society. Such a program provided hope in a society that was disenchanted with traditional doctrines. Behaviorism introduced the idea that nature has an overestimated role in behaviors and brought a new hope that could not be found in religion.

A number of other individuals helped to popularize behavioral psychology. Joseph Jastrow, a psychologist, published a great number of popular articles and had a newspaper column called "Keeping Mentally Fit." Albert Wiggam was not a psychologist, but wrote a column called "Exploring your Mind." These figures helped psychology transition from strictly being used on college campuses to its vast appeal in mass media and everyday life.

Despite its wide acceptance, behaviorism had its critics as well. Karl Lashley studied the brain and found that the "brain plays a more active role in learning than Watson could accept." One of Watson's more forceful critics, however, was William McDougall. McDougall developed his own theory that "human behavior derives from innate tendencies to thought and action." They also differed in their belief in free will. McDougall and Watson met to debate their viewpoints in 1924, which was well attended by the general public as well as psychologists. McDougall was judged to win the debate. However, Watson's impact on psychology is stunning, considering his short career in psychology (less than 20 years). This speaks to his strength and charisma, as well as his effectiveness as a popularizer.

Outline

I. The Psychologist, the Baby, and the Hammer: Description of Little Albert study
    A. Watson and Rosalie Raynor (graduate student) attempt to condition the fear response
    B. Albert had been chosen because he was "emotionally stable," and not easily excited
    C. Steel rod hung behind Albert's head
    D. John Watson struck the rod with a hammer, creating a noise
    E. Baby reacted fearfully and cried (Fear=Unconditioned response)
    F. Watson then paired the noise with other previously neutral stimuli (i.e., white rat), which were the conditioned stimuli
    G. After seven pairings, child cried at the site of rat, even when no sound followed
    H. Produced conditioned emotional response: crying at the site of the rat
    I. Prior to the conditioning, Albert showed little fear response to a variety of objects (including the white rat)
    J. After the conditioning, Albert shows fear in reaction to the rat
    K. Fear generalized to other furry white things: rabbit, god, fur coat, Santa mask
    L. Watson and Raynor show that fears can be conditioned
    M. Deduce that adults' fears are result of conditioning in infancy and childhood
    N. Nothing is known about what happened to Albert later in life

II. John B. Watson (1878-1958)
    A. Overview
       1. Watson credited the work of others as originators of behaviorism
       2. saw himself as bringing together the emergent ideas
       3. deliberate goal: to found a new school
    B. Watson's life
       1. Born on a farm in South Carolina
          a. mother: religious; father: heavy drinker, violent, had affairs, couldn't hold a job
          b. family lived on edge of poverty
          c. Watson's father ran off with another women when the boy was 13
          d. Watson never forgives him, even after he becomes successful and father visits him
       2. delinquent behavior in youth
          a. bad grades
          b. fistfights
          c. arrested for shooting a gun in city limits
       3. determined to be a minister to fulfill mother's wish
          a. enrolled at Furman University: studied philosophy, math, Latin, Greek
          b. 1899: intended entry into Princeton Theological Seminary
          c. 1900: earned master's degree at Furman and mother died

4. 1900: enrolled at the University of Chicago
   a. academically ambitious and status concerned but insecure because of little means and lack of socially sophistication
   b. planned to pursue graduate degree in philosophy with Dewey, but found him hard to understand
   c. attracted to psychology through work with Angell
   d. studied biology and physiology with Loeb
   e. 1903: at age 25, youngest person to earn PhD from University of Chicago
   f. worked odd jobs: waiter, rat caretaker, janitor
   g. began having neurotic symptoms: anxiety attacks, sleeplessness
   h. feelings of inferiority when Dewey and Angell said dissertation wasn't as good as another student
5. Married a student: Mary Ickes, from wealth family

C. Academic career
   1. dissertation published
      a. neurological and psychological maturation of the white rat
      b. not successful at introspection
   2. 1903: considered a more objective approach to psychology
   3. 1908: expressed such ideas in lectures at Yale and in a paper
   4. 1908: offered professorship at Johns Hopkins University
      a. reluctant to leave University of Chicago
      b. new job offered promotion, salary raise, and opportunity to direct the psychology laboratory
   5. James Mark Baldwin (1861-1934)
      a. offered the John Hopkins's job to Watson
      b. a founder with Cattell of Psychological Review
      c. 1909: forced by the university president to resign after caught in a police raid on a brothel
      d. 11 years later Watson forced to resign by the same president after he had affair with graduate student that led to a scandal
   6. 1909: chair of psychology department
   7. 1909: editor of Psychological Review
   8. 1912: presented ideas for a more objective psychology in lectures at Columbia
   9. 1913: "Psychology as the Behaviorist Views It" (launched behaviorism)
   10. 1914 published: "Behavior: An Introduction to Comparative Psychology"
       a. argued for acceptance of animal psychology
       b. described advantages of animal subjects
       c. discussed importance of ridding psychology of the remnants of philosophy
   11. president of APA
   12. desired practical applications: valued applied psychology, trained students in industrial psychology
   13. World War I: Served in army as a major
       a. developed perceptual and motor ability tests
       b. research on how oxygen reduction affects performance
       c. established Industrial Service Corporation: provide personnel selection and management consulting services

14. 1919: Psychology From the Standpoint of a Behaviorist
    a.   most complete account of behaviorism to date
    b.   argued methods and principles of animal research are appropriate for study of humans
15. 1920: forced resignation from Johns Hopkins University
    a.   marriage deteriorated and led to divorce due to his infidelities
    b.   fell in love with Rosalie Rayner, graduate assistant
        (1) half his age
        (2) from family of wealthy donors to the university
    c.   wife found his passionate but rather scientific love letters to Rosalie
    d.   excerpts published in Baltimore Sun
    e.   astonished when forced to resign
    f.   married Rosalie but still banished from academia
    g.   Titchener one of the few academics who reached out to comfort him
16. 1921 began second career: applied psychology to advertising
    a.   joined advertising agency, became vice president within three years
    b.   mechanistic view of humans
    c.   proposed experimental (lab) study of consumer behavior
17. publicity for psychology in the popular media by publishing in newspapers and magazines
18. 1925 published "Behaviorism"; introduced plan to perfect the social order
19. 1928: Psychological Care of the Infant and Child
    a.   strong environmentalist position
    b.   recommended perfect objectivity in child-rearing practices; little emotional/physical attention
    c.   had the greatest impact of all his work
    d.   wife, Rosalie, publically disagrees with his childrearing practices
    e.   one of Watson's sons attempted suicide unsuccessfully; another had suicidal thoughts; daughter had several suicide attempts
20. described as "unresponsive, emotionally uncommunicative, unable to express and cope with any feelings or emotions of his own"
21. 1935: his wife died; he became a recluse
22. 1957: at age 79 awarded APA citation for his vital and fruitful work
    a.   refused to go inside to receive award
    b.   Watson afraid that he would show his emotions and cry
    c.   son accepted it in his place
23. burned all of his papers prior to his death

D. Original Source Material: from "Psychology as the Behaviorist Views It" (1913)
    1. the definition and goal of behaviorism
    2. criticisms of structuralism and functionalism
    3. the role of heredity and habit in adaptation
    4. applied psychology is truly scientific
    5. importance of standardized or uniform experimental procedures

III.   The Reaction to Watson's Program
    A. His major points
        1. the science of behavior
        2. a purely objective experimental branch of natural science
        3. both animal and human behavior are studied
        4. discard all mentalistic concepts

5. use only behavior concepts
6. goal: prediction and control of behavior
B. Initial reactions
1. behaviorism was not embraced
2. his 1919 book *Psychology from the Standpoint of a Behaviorist* hastened the movement's impact
3. Calkins: disputed Watson; adhered to introspection as the sole method for studying some processes
4. Washburn: called Watson an enemy of psychology
C. 1920's
1. university courses in behaviorism
2. the word "behaviorist" appeared in journals
3. McDougall: issued a public warning against behaviorism
4. Titchener: complained of its force and extent
5. other forms of behaviorism emerging

IV. The Methods of Behaviorism
A. Adoption of the methods of the natural sciences
B. Only accepted objective methods
1. observation, with and without instruments
2. testing methods
3. verbal report method
4. conditioned reflex method
C. Observation is the basis for all methods
D. Test results are samples of behavior, not indices of mental qualities
E. Verbal reports
1. legitimate in psychophysics
2. speech reactions are objectively observable
3. thinking is speaking covertly
4. admitted the lack of precision and limitations
5. limited it to situations where it could be verified
6. came under attack (sounded like introspection)
F. Conditioned reflex method
1. adopted in 1915
2. Watson responsible for its widespread use in U.S. research
3. Influenced by Bekhterev and Pavlov
4. conditioning is stimulus substitution
5. selected because it is an objective method of behavior analysis
6. reflected reductionism and mechanism, reduced everything to stimulus/response bonds
7. human subject: the observed rather than the observer
a. designation changed from "observer" to "subject"
b. experimenter became the observer
c. focus shifted; humans merely actors/machines: demoted in status

V. The Subject Matter of Behaviorism
A. Subject matter of behavioral psychology: muscular movements and glandular secretions
B. Items or elements of behavior
1. goal: understand overall behavior of the total organism

2. acts versus responses
    a.   act: complex behaviors
    b.   response act accomplishes some result
    c.   capable of being reduced to simple, lower-level motor or glandular responses
3. explicit versus implicit responses
    a.   explicit is overtly observable
    b.   implicit happen inside organism (ex., glandular secretions)
        (1) must be potentially observable
        (2) must be observable through the use of instruments
4. simple versus complex stimuli
    a.   complex stimulus situation can be reduced to simple, component stimuli
    b.   example of simple stimuli: light waves striking retina
5. specific laws of behavior
    a.   identified through analysis of S-R complexes
    b.   must find elementary S-R units
6. major topics: instinct, emotion, thought
7. all areas of behavior: must use objective S-R terms

C. Instincts
1. 1914: Watson described 11 instincts
2. 1925: eliminated the concept of instinct
    a.   an extreme environmentalist
    b.   denied inherited capacities, temperaments, talents
    c.   children can become anything one desires
    d.   a factor in his popularity with the American lay public
3. seemingly instinctive behavior is actually a socially conditioned response
4. optimistic position: no genetic limitations, only nurture influences outcomes
5. psychology can be applied to modify behavior

D. Emotions
1. defined as bodily responses to specific stimuli
2. denied conscious perception of emotion or sensations from internal stimuli
3. each emotion = specific configuration of physiological changes
4. a form of implicit behavior: internal responses are evident in overt physical signs such as blushing
5. critical of James' more complex position involving conscious perception and a feeling state
6. emotions completely described by three things
    a.   objective stimulus situation
    b.   overt bodily response
    c.   internal physiological changes
7. fear, love, and rage are not learned emotional response patterns to stimuli
    a.   loud noises or sudden lack of support lead to fear
    b.   restriction of bodily movements leads to rage
    c.   caressing, rocking, patting lead to love

E. Albert, Peter, and the rabbits
1. Albert study demonstrated conditioned (learned) emotional responses
2. Watson: adult fears are learned, do not arise from Freud's unconscious conflicts

        3. Mary Cover Jones
            a.   worked with 3-year Peter who came to her with a rabbit phobia
            b.   treatment method
                (1) involve Peter in eating
                (2) bring in rabbit at a distance that does not produce crying
                (3) each day, decrease the distance
                (4) after a few months, Peter could touch the rabbit without exhibiting fear
                (5) this approach is a forerunner of behavior therapy
            c.   generalized fear responses also eliminated
            d.   1968: Jones given G. Stanley Hall award for her outstanding work in developmental psychology
   F. Thought processes
        1. traditional view:
            a.   thinking occurs in the absence of muscle movements
            b.   not accessible to observation and experimentation
        2. Watson's view:
            a.   thinking is implicit motor behavior
            b.   type of sensorimotor behavior
            c.   involves implicit speech reactions or movements
            d.   reduced it to subvocal talking
            e.   Watson made experimental attempts to record tongue and larynx movements during thought; results reveal slight movements during thinking
            f.   same muscular habits as used for overt speech
            g.   others warn us not to talk aloud to ourselves, so we become unaware of the muscular habits used while thinking
            h.   thinking = silent talking to oneself
VI.   Behaviorism's Popular Appeal
   A. Watson called for a society based on scientifically shaped and controlled behavior
        1. free of myths, customs, and convention
        2. The Religion Called Behaviorism (Berman, 1927): read by Skinner
   B. Emphasis on childhood environment and minimization of heredity
   C. Conditioned reflex experiments
        1. implied emotional disturbances in adulthood due to conditioned responses during earlier years
        2. implies proper childhood conditioning precludes adult disorders
   D. Experimental ethics
        1. based on behaviorism
        2. part of a plan to improve society
        3. a framework for research
        4. elaborated by Skinner
VII.   Behaviorism's Popular Appeal
   A. Behaviorism as religion
        1. Watson called for a society based on scientifically shaped, controlled behavior
        2. Zeitgeist: disenchantment with old ideas, open to accepting new doctrine
        3. Berman writes The Religion Called Behaviorism, influences Skinner
   B. Nurturing in childhood
        1. Watson proposed any child (regardless of race and ancestry) could be molded to go into any profession and excel

2. "adult disturbances are a function of faulty childhood conditioning"
3. necessity of control over childhood behavior

C. Watson plans to replace religion-based ethics with experimental-based ethics (never actually carried out)

VIII. An Outbreak of Psychology
A. Product of a public already attentive to and receptive of psychology and Watson's considerable charm and vision of hope for behavioral change and the betterment of society
B. Exemplified by
1. psychological advice columns
2. Joseph Jastrow's popularization of psychology through magazine articles, newspaper column "Keeping Mentally Fit," radio program, and pop psychology book, *Piloting Your life: the Psychologist as Helmsman*
3. Albert Wiggam's column "Exploring Your Mind"
4. psychology moves from only college campuses to everywhere else

IX. Criticisms of Watson's Behaviorism
A. Omitted sensory and perceptual processes
B. Karl Lashley (1890-1958)
1. student of Watson at Johns Hopkins
2. a physiological psychologist
3. 1929: Brain Mechanisms and Intelligence
   a. law of mass action: "The efficiency of learning is a function of the total mass of cortical tissue."
   b. principle of equipotentiality: "The idea that one part of the cerebral cortex is essentially equal to another in its contribution to learning."
4. challenged Watson's notion of a point-to-point connection in reflexes
   a. brain more active in learning than Watson accepted
   b. disputed the notion that behavior is a mechanical compounding of conditioned reflexes
5. confirmed the value of objective methods in psychology research; did not weaken behaviorist school
C. William McDougall (1871-1938)
1. English psychologist, affiliated with Harvard and Duke
2. noted for his instinct theory of behavior
   a. human behavior results from innate tendencies to thought and action
3. noteworthy book on social psychology spurred that field
4. supported free will, Nordic superiority, psychic research
5. 1924: debate with Watson
   a. defended introspection and consciousness
   b. agreed data of behavior are a proper focus for psychology
   c. argued data of consciousness also necessary
   d. questioned Watson's tenet that human behavior is fully determined
   e. critical of Watson's use of the verbal report method

X. Contributions of Watson's Behaviorism
A. Made psychology more objective in methods and terminology
B. Stimulated a great deal of research
C. Surmounted earlier positions and schools
D. Objective methods and language became part of the mainstream

Lecture prompts/Discussion topics for chapter ten

- What were the implications for Watson's behaviorism, with consideration to the Eugenics movement which was mushrooming at about the same time in the United States? What, do you think, was Watson's stance on Eugenics?
- Is behaviorism psychology? Can there be a psychology without the mind? Recall that psyche = mind.
- Do you think behaviorism makes psychology more like a natural science?
- Debate the presence of free will: do we have free will? What are the implications in terms of responsibility for one's own actions?

Internet Resources for chapter ten

John B. Watson at Furman
http://facweb.furman.edu/~einstein/watson/watson1.htm
> These Web pages are housed at Furman University, where Watson received his college education. There are some details of his life, including some photographs of Watson and his family.

John Watson: A Science Odyssey
http://www.pbs.org/wgbh/aso/databank/entries/bhwats.html
> Information from the PBS series A Science Odyssey about Watson and Behaviorism.

Conditioned Emotional Reactions
http://psychclassics.yorku.ca/Watson/emotion.htm
> This is a full text version of the Little Albert paper by Watson and Raynor. Of particular interest to bring to your students' attention is the second-to-last paragraph of the paper, where they speculate a future where Albert seeks psychoanalysis.

A Laboratory study of fear: The case of Peter
http://psychclassics.yorku.ca/Jones/
> This is a full text version of the article by Mary Cover Jones of her experiment with Peter. Jones' description of her intervention is thorough, well-written, and fun to read.

The Watson and McDougall Debate
http://psychclassics.yorku.ca/Watson/Battle/
> This is the full text of the published debate between Watson and McDougall.

Potential answers to chapter ten discussion questions

1. What ethical and moral considerations do you think were involved in the Little Albert study?
Probably the most salient ethical consideration is the fact that a child was used in the psychological conditioning of a fear response. No effort was made to remove Albert's fears, although Watson later attempted to contact the family without avail. Nobody knows what happened to Albert, but conceivably he may have lived his life as a frightened man, even though he was originally chosen because of his emotional stability.

2. How did Watson establish a conditioned emotional response in Albert? Did that response generalize to other stimuli? If so, to what kind of stimuli?

To begin, John Watson used a previously neutral stimuli (white rat) and paired it with a unconditioned stimuli that elicited fear (hammer noise). After several pairings, Little Albert was conditioned to fear the white rat, even in the absence of the hammer noise. The fear response was generalized to other furry white things, such as a dog and fur coat.

3. Was Watson concerned about the practical value of behaviorism? If your answer is yes, to what areas of everyday life did he apply his findings?

"He wanted his new behaviorism to be of practical value; his ideas were not only for the laboratory but for the real world as well. He promoted psychology's applied specialties and became a personnel consultant for a large insurance company. He also offered a course for business students at Hopkins on the psychology of advertising and started a program to train graduate students to work in industrial psychology." During World War I he developed selection tests for pilots.

4. Describe Watson's approach to childrearing. What were the results of that approach within his family?

Watson wrote *Psychological Care of the Infant and Child* (1928) which sold well. This book changed the way children were raised in America, although his advice was unusual, such as not giving your children hugs or kisses, rather a "pat on the head" at most. Watson's sons by Rosalie, William and James, "both suffered from serious depression".

5. In Watson's 1913 article, what criticisms did he make of structuralism and functionalism? On what basis did he argue that applied psychology could be called scientific?

The main criticism he voices is the method that both schools employed: introspection. A second criticism is that the subject of both schools is consciousness. Watson argues that applied psychology is scientific because it controls human behavior.

6. How were Watson's ideas received by the younger generation of psychologists?

The younger generation of psychologists tended to be more accepting of and excited by Watson's behaviorism. Mary Cover Jones, for example, is quoted in the text as saying that Watson's behaviorism "pointed the way from armchair psychology to action and reform and was therefore hailed as a panacea."

7. What research methods did Watson accept for a scientific psychology?

Watson proposed that, to make psychology more like a natural science, psychologists should focus only on objectively studying behavior. The only methods to be used, he said, were these four: 1) observation, 2) tests (what others might call 'mental tests' 3) verbal report (for which he was criticized for including because it sounds too much like introspection), and 4) conditioned reflex.

8. Why was Watson's use of verbal reports considered to be controversial?

The method "verbal report" sounded too much like introspection, which was a method that Watson was heavily critical of. Critics said that Watson was "playing word games", but Watson restricted their use to instances when they could be verified (more like the psychophysics research).

9. How did the behaviorists' view of the role and task of human subjects differ from that of the introspectionists?

For the introspectionists, the experimenter and the observer are the same and therefore the subject plays the central role in research. With the abolition of introspection, subjects no longer contribute to observations, instead they are simply behaving. This is a more mechanistic method, which sees the subject are just an actor.

10. Discuss how Watson's subject matter and methodology continued the atomistic, mechanistic, empiricistic tradition.

"Because all behavior could be reduced to [stimulus-response] elements, the conditioned reflex method permitted psychologists to conduct laboratory investigations of complex human behaviors. Thus, Watson was continuing in the atomistic and mechanistic tradition established by the British empiricists and adopted by the structural psychologists. He intended to study human behavior in the same way the physical scientists were studying the universe, by breaking it down into its component parts, into its atoms and elements."

11. How did Watson distinguish between responses and acts? Between explicit and implicit responses?

A response can be as simple as a knee jerk, but it can also be more complex. "Watson called these more complex responses "acts." He considered response acts to include such events as eating, writing, dancing, or constructing a house. In other words, an act involves the organism's movement in space." Explicit responses were those that were overtly observable. Implicit responses occurred inside the person, and included such things as glandular secretions.

12. Describe Watson's views on instinct and thought processes.

Although originally Watson believed that there were instincts, he later claimed that there were none—that all behavior is learned, nothing is inherited. Watson also attempted to address and explain thoughts in behavioral terms. He believed it to be related to unspoken speech which relies on the same muscle movements as speech. He tried to measure "tongue and larynx movements during thought" with small success.

13. How do the studies of Albert and Peter support Watson's ideas on the role of learning in emotion?

With both studies, emotional responses change because of conditioning. Albert learned to fear a variety of objects, and Peter learned to no longer fear rabbits.

14. Discuss the reasons for behaviorism's popular appeal.

Watson's behaviorism became popular because he promoted the idea of creating a utopian society based on behavioral principles. Perhaps most influential was the idea that, with Watson's vision, it is possible for anyone to become anything, unfettered by inherited characteristics. Furthermore, with behaviorism came the idea that all behavior can be shaped by conditioning, even "adult disturbances." This caused psychology to be seen as a way to "health, happiness, and prosperity."

15. Describe Lashley's law of mass action and principle of equipotentiality.

Lashley's law of mass action states that "the more cortical tissues available, the better the learning". The principle of equipotenciality states that "one part of the cortex is essentially equal to another in terms of its contribution to learning." These laws attribute processes like thinking and learning to physical characteristics.

16. In what way did Lashley's research results discredit a portion of Watson's system?
Karl Lashley studied the brain and found that the "brain plays a more active role in learning than Watson could accept." Thus, Lashley countered Watson's idea that learning is solely a product of conditioning and environment.

17. Do you think Watson's behaviorism would have become so popular without the earlier work of the functional psychologists? Explain your answer.
Perhaps not. The functionalists laid the way for applied psychology, which was embraced by the American public. The applied psychology movement not only made psychology more valued (because of its practicality) but more visible as well. Both the practicality and visibility were important components of Watson's psychology.

18. On what grounds did McDougall criticize Watson's form of behaviorism?
McDougall developed his own theory that "human behavior derives from innate tendencies to thought and action." They also differed in their belief in free will. McDougall and Watson met to debate their viewpoints in 1924, which was well attended by the general public as well as psychologists. McDougall was judged to win the debate.

Key terms from chapter ten

- **Emotions** According to Watson, humans are born with only three: fear, rage, and love. All other emotions are learned.
- **Explicit responses** Those responses that can be overtly seen
- **Free will** One of the points of contention between Watson and McDougall: McDougall believed humans have free will, Watson did not.
- **Implicit responses** Those responses that cannot be overtly seen and that take place within the organism, such as glandular secretions.
- **Law of mass action** In Lashley's system, the idea that learning is related to the amount of cortical tissue available.
- **Little Albert** Probably the most famous baby in psychology, Watson and Raynor purportedly conditioned Albert to fear objects he did not previously fear.
- **Principle of equipotentiality** In Lashley's system, the idea that "one part of the cortex is essentially equal to another in terms of its contribution to learning.

ESSAY

1. Using Watson's arguments in the Original Source Material from *Psychology as the Behaviorist Views It*, describe why he thought that psychology had failed to become a natural science and what it needed to do to become one.

   ANS:
   Answer not provided.

   PTS: 1   MSC: WWW

2. Describe the four objective methods of study that Watson found acceptable. What are the strengths and flaws of each?

   ANS:
   Answer not provided.

   PTS: 1

3. How did Watson describe the conditioned reflex method? Why did he find it indispensable from a behaviorist perspective? Describe how Watson and Raynor used this method to condition an emotional response.

   ANS:
   Answer not provided.

   PTS: 1

4. Describe Watson's treatment of instincts between 1910 and 1925.

   ANS:
   Answer not provided.

   PTS: 1

5. What was Watson's plan for the improvement of society? Describe what were seen as its strengths and weakness? How well was it accepted within psychology and by the general public?

   ANS:
   Answer not provided.

   PTS: 1   MSC: WWW

6. Describe Lashley's contributions to behaviorism.

   ANS:
   Answer not provided.

   PTS: 1

7. Like many of the first generation of psychologists, Watson's first graduate school area of study was ____.
   a. Physiology
   b. Positivism
   c. Philosophy
   d. Psychophysics
   e. Physics

   ANS: C   PTS: 1   REF: John B. Watson (1878-1958)

8. Watson's introduction to mechanism was through his association with ____.
   a. Dewey
   b. Angell
   c. Loeb
   d. Carr
   e. Baldwin

   ANS: C   PTS: 1   REF: John B. Watson (1878-1958)

9. Watson was attracted to psychology through his association with ____.
   a. Dewey
   b. Angell
   c. Loeb
   d. Carr
   e. Baldwin

   ANS: B   PTS: 1   REF: John B. Watson (1878-1958)

10. John B. Watson was quite dismayed to learn that his dissertation was less brilliant in the eyes of Dewey and Angell than that of ____.
    a. Mary Baldwin
    b. Mary Calkins
    c. Helen Woolley
    d. Rosalie Rayner
    e. Mary Cover Jones

    ANS: C   PTS: 1   REF: John B. Watson (1878-1958)

11. Watson chose to pursue research with white rats, he said, because he ____.
    a. wanted to maintain a close association with biology
    b. wanted to dissociate himself from philosophy
    c. wanted to dissociate himself from his original pursuits in theology
    d. could not learn to do introspection
    e. found rats to be more cooperative than human subjects

    ANS: A   PTS: 1   REF: John B. Watson (1878-1958)
    MSC: WWW

12.   _____ at John Hopkins University hired Watson and one year later was forced to resign because of a scandal.
      a.   B. F. Skinner
      b.   Robert Yerkes
      c.   William McDougall
      d.   James Mark Baldwin
      e.   James McKeen Cattell

      ANS: D   PTS: 1   REF: John B. Watson (1878-1958)

13.   Watson's work has been involved with which of the following divisions of psychology?
      a.   animal psychology
      b.   industrial/organizational psychology
      c.   behaviorism
      d.   developmental psychology
      e.   All of the above.

      ANS: E   PTS: 1   REF: John B. Watson (1878-1958)

14.   Behaviorism was officially established in _____.
      a.   1904, at the St. Louis Exposition
      b.   1907, with Bekhterev's *Objective Psychology*
      c.   1908, with Watson's lectures at Yale
      d.   1911, with McDougall's *Psychology: The Study of Behavior*
      e.   1913, with Watson's "Psychology as the Behaviorist Views It"

      ANS: E   PTS: 1   REF: John B. Watson (1878-1958)

15.   In his 1914 book, *Behavior: An Introduction to Comparative Psychology*, Watson argued _____.
      a.   for positivism in psychology
      b.   for the acceptance of animal psychology
      c.   that mental concepts are "valueless to science"
      d.   for a functional and pragmatic approach to psychology
      e.   for experimental research on human infants

      ANS: B   PTS: 1   REF: John B. Watson (1878-1958)

16.   Watson has been criticized for which of the following?
      a.   methods of behaviorism
      b.   his childrearing beliefs
      c.   his personality
      d.   A and B only
      e.   All of the above.

      ANS: E   PTS: 1   REF: John B. Watson (1878-1958)
      MSC: WWW

17.   Watson's second career was in _____.
      a.   pediatric psychology
      b.   behavior modification
      c.   advertising
      d.   personnel selection
      e.   developmental psychology

      ANS: C   PTS: 1   REF: John B. Watson (1878-1958)

18. Watson believed that the behavior of people as consumers of goods and services could be predicted and controlled, just like the behavior of ____.
    a. machines
    b. rats
    c. animals
    d. viruses
    e. organisms

    ANS: A   PTS: 1   REF: John B. Watson (1878-1958)

19. Watson argued that consumer behavior was ____.
    a. under the control of fundamental or conditioned emotional stimuli
    b. controlled according to the law of suggestibility
    c. immune to aversive conditioning
    d. vulnerable to the law of exercise
    e. controlled by the law of resemblance

    ANS: A   PTS: 1   REF: John B. Watson (1878-1958)

20. Watson proposed that consumer behavior ____.
    a. was unpredictable
    b. could not be controlled
    c. should be studied in the lab
    d. was driven by emotionless pleas
    e. was driven by the message in an ad, rather than the style in the ad

    ANS: C   PTS: 1   REF: John B. Watson (1878-1958)

21. Watson's view of consumers' responses was much like ____.
    a. Descartes's view of automata
    b. Wundt's view of feelings
    c. James's view of emotion
    d. Pavlov's view of cats
    e. Dewey's view of reflexes

    ANS: A   PTS: 1   REF: John B. Watson (1878-1958)
    MSC: WWW

22. After his dismissal from Johns Hopkins, Watson ____.
    a. abandoned his research on behavioral psychology
    b. published in scholarly journals under a pseudonym
    c. published for the American public through popular media
    d. joined the army to conduct research on personnel selection
    e. lectured at universities throughout Europe

    ANS: C   PTS: 1   REF: John B. Watson (1878-1958)

23. Watson's position on childrearing was ____.
    a. that of a strong environmentalist
    b. to "spare the rod, spoil the child"
    c. to use affection and social reinforcements exclusively
    d. to follow Thorndike's law of effect
    e. to follow Pavlov's law of reinforcement

    ANS: A   PTS: 1   REF: John B. Watson (1878-1958)

24. The most significant public impact of Watson's varied undertakings was to ____.
    a. introduce pop psychology as a new field
    b. prepare the way for Skinner
    c. transform childrearing practices
    d. eliminate all remains of functionalism from the science of psychology
    e. reverse the trend toward applied psychology in the United States

    ANS: C   PTS: 1   REF: John B. Watson (1878-1958)

25. Watson's behaviorism was mechanistic. His own behavior might also be called mechanistic with regard to his relationship with ____.
    a. his wife, Rosalie
    b. his children
    c. women in general
    d. his male buddies
    e. his dogs

    ANS: B   PTS: 1   REF: John B. Watson (1878-1958)

26. Although ____ publicly disagreed with her husband's childrearing practices and occasionally wanted to break his rules, their son did not recall that happening.
    a. Margaret Floy Washburn
    b. Mary Ickes
    c. Mamie Phipps Clark
    d. Rosalie Raynor Watson
    e. Christine Ladd-Franklin

    ANS: D   PTS: 1   REF: John B. Watson (1878-1958)

27. In *Psychology as the Behaviorist Views It*, Watson argues that psychology is ____.
    a. a purely experimental branch of natural science
    b. a radical environmentalism
    c. in Kuhn's terms, a "paradigm"
    d. a return to Descartes's dualism
    e. big enough to include both mental and behavioral phenomena

    ANS: A   PTS: 1   REF: John B. Watson (1878-1958)
    MSC: WWW

28. For Watson, the goal of psychology is ____.
    a. a utopia based on operant conditioning principles
    b. the prediction and control of behavior
    c. the expansion of Pavlovian conditioning to voluntary behaviors
    d. the reduction of cognitive processes to their biological correlates
    e. a unitary scheme of animal responses

    ANS: B   PTS: 1   REF: John B. Watson (1878-1958)

29. For Watson, the distinction between humans and animals is ____.
    a. an explanatory fiction
    b. at the point where language is observed
    c. arbitrary
    d. explained by one's efficiency in adapting to the environment
    e. necessary if psychology is to be a natural science of behavior

    ANS: C   PTS: 1   REF: John B. Watson (1878-1958)

30. Watson argued that the failure of psychology as a natural science was due to ____.
   a. the fact that data of introspection cannot be replicated
   b. blaming the observer rather than the method for failure to replicate in introspection
   c. the failure to operationally define terms in common use by psychologists
   d. the use of mechanistic terms
   e. All of the choices are correct.

   ANS: B   PTS: 1   REF: John B. Watson (1878-1958)

31. Watson argued that areas of applied psychology can be considered scientific because they ____.
   a. are obviously so by their very nature
   b. were considered to be so even by Wundt
   c. were consistent with the theory of evolution
   d. seek general laws for the prediction and control of behavior
   e. None of the choices are correct.

   ANS: D   PTS: 1   REF: John B. Watson (1878-1958)

32. Watson's position on the use of the term *consciousness* was to ____.
   a. eliminate it entirely from psychological research because it is not an objective method
   b. examine its relevance to overt behaviors
   c. infer the elements of consciousness from overt behaviors
   d. infer the elements of consciousness from observable physiological substrates
   e. infer its processes from its measurable blood metabolites

   ANS: A   PTS: 1   REF: John B. Watson (1878-1958)

33. Watson's 1913 paper *Psychology as the Behaviorist Views It* ____.
   a. engendered much attention in the professional literature
   b. was wholeheartedly embraced by the general public
   c. engendered a firestorm of protest from both the functionalists and the structuralists
   d. was eclipsed by the attention given to Freud's new theories
   e. was relatively ignored by the professional journals

   ANS: E   PTS: 1   REF: John B. Watson (1878-1958)

34. This person said, in criticizing Watson, that introspection had to be used to study certain psychological processes.
   a. Calkins
   b. Lashley
   c. Washburn
   d. Thorndike
   e. Hall

   ANS: A   PTS: 1   REF: The Reaction to Watson's Program

35. Which of the following was NOT one of Watson's methods?
   a. observation with instruments
   b. observation without the use of instruments
   c. the verbal report method
   d. the conditioned reflex method
   e. All of the choices were acceptable to Watson.

   ANS: E   PTS: 1   REF: The Methods of Behaviorism

36. Watson's contribution to the method of objective testing was _____.
    a. to qualify the results
    b. to create a measure of reliability
    c. to argue that the subjects' responses were under the stimulus control of the test items
    d. to advocate for its widespread use
    e. to create a series of tests which are still used today

    ANS: C   PTS: 1   REF: The Methods of Behaviorism
    MSC: WWW

37. Watson's position on verbal reports was _____.
    a. to redefine them as motor responses
    b. to redefine thinking as speaking to oneself
    c. to limit their use to situations in which they could be verified
    d. All of the choices are correct.
    e. None of the choices are correct.

    ANS: D   PTS: 1   REF: The Methods of Behaviorism

38. The most important research method of the behaviorists was _____.
    a. observation with the use of instruments
    b. observation without the use of instruments
    c. the verbal report method
    d. the conditioned reflex method
    e. testing methods

    ANS: D   PTS: 1   REF: The Methods of Behaviorism

39. Watson described conditioning in terms of _____.
    a. symptom substitution
    b. stimulus substitution
    c. respondent substitution
    d. response substitution
    e. associated reflexes

    ANS: B   PTS: 1   REF: The Methods of Behaviorism

40. All of Watson's methods are based on the concept of _____.
    a. observation
    b. animal psychology
    c. functionalism
    d. structuralism
    e. physiology

    ANS: A   PTS: 1   REF: The Methods of Behaviorism

41. Watson adopted the conditioned reflex method of research established by _____.
    a. James and Peirce
    b. Pavlov and Bekhterev
    c. Angell and Carr
    d. Woodworth and Cattell
    e. Wundt and Titchener

    ANS: B   PTS: 1   REF: The Methods of Behaviorism

42. According to Watson, the elements of behavior are ____.
    a. associations among S-R connections
    b. the body's muscular movement and glandular responses
    c. an exchange of ideas between the conscious and the unconscious mind
    d. a synthesis of mental elements involving sensations, images, and feelings
    e. a series of actions

    ANS: B   PTS: 1   REF: The Subject Matter of Behaviorism

43. For Watson, a response or behavioral "act" ____.
    a. is always overtly observable with the naked eye
    b. involves a response through movement in space
    c. cannot be reduced further
    d. should be reported by the subject and by the experimenter
    e. None of the choices are correct.

    ANS: B   PTS: 1   REF: The Subject Matter of Behaviorism
    MSC: WWW

44. In Watson's system, implicit responses are those that are ____.
    a. irreducible
    b. reducible
    c. potentially observable
    d. responses to verbal test items
    e. indicative of higher cognitive processes

    ANS: C   PTS: 1   REF: The Subject Matter of Behaviorism

45. For Watson, stimuli ____.
    a. are always simple elements
    b. are always complex and reducible to simpler elements
    c. may be simple or complex
    d. are irreducible
    e. occur after responses

    ANS: C   PTS: 1   REF: The Subject Matter of Behaviorism

46. Watson predicted that the laws of behavior would be identified when ____.
    a. behaviors were reduced to their basic S-R units
    b. the stimulus elements could be perfectly controlled
    c. the smallest elements of responses were discovered
    d. the response elements could be perfectly predicted
    e. Both B and D are correct.

    ANS: A   PTS: 1   REF: The Subject Matter of Behaviorism

47. Watson listed how many instincts in his 1914 book on comparative psychology?
    a. 0
    b. 3
    c. 11
    d. 15
    e. over 100

    ANS: C   PTS: 1   REF: The Subject Matter of Behaviorism

48. In Watson's final system, instincts _____.
   a. exist, but there are only three
   b. do not exist
   c. exist at birth and are limited, but more are learned
   d. do not exist at birth, but can be learned
   e. are what drive most behaviors

   ANS: B   PTS: 1   REF: The Subject Matter of Behaviorism

49. Which of the following statements would Watson endorse?
   a. The human has no conscious perception of his or her emotions.
   b. All emotions are learned.
   c. Emotions are implicit.
   d. Emotions are equal to internal physiological changes.
   e. All of the choices are correct.

   ANS: D   PTS: 1   REF: The Subject Matter of Behaviorism

50. How many fundamental emotions were seen in infants, according to Watson?
   a. 2
   b. 3
   c. 4
   d. 5
   e. 6

   ANS: B   PTS: 1   REF: The Subject Matter of Behaviorism

51. According to Watson, the three fundamental emotions displayed by infants were _____.
   a. fear, sadness, and love
   b. fear, rage, and sadness
   c. fear, rage, and love
   d. fear, loneliness, and rage
   e. loneliness, rage, and love

   ANS: C   PTS: 1   REF: The Subject Matter of Behaviorism

52. For Watson, emotions are explained by the _____.
   a. James-Lange theory of emotion
   b. perception of the individual's environment
   c. internal physiological responses to a stimulus
   d. individual's analysis and labeling of his or her physiological responses
   e. None of the choices are correct.

   ANS: C   PTS: 1   REF: The Subject Matter of Behaviorism

53. In Watson's system, fear, rage, and love are _____.
   a. meaningless labels people have adopted
   b. unconditioned responses
   c. conditioned responses
   d. associated reflexes
   e. precognitions

   ANS: B   PTS: 1   REF: The Subject Matter of Behaviorism
   MSC: WWW

54. Watson rejected the whole notion of the unconscious because _____.
    x a. it , like the rest of psychoanalysis, was voodooism
    b. it called for use of the method of introspection
    c. it could not be objectively observed
    d. it, like the rest of psychoanalysis, was voodooism and it could not be objectively observed
    e. None of the choices are correct.

    ANS: D   PTS: 1   REF: The Subject Matter of Behaviorism

55. The Little Albert study _____.
    a. was a prototype for the modern learned helplessness paradigm
    b. was replicated by Mary Cover Jones
    c. showed that fears could not be conditioned
    d. demonstrated the value of punishment
    e. has never been replicated

    ANS: E   PTS: 1   REF: The Subject Matter of Behaviorism

56. The first person to de-condition a learned fear was _____.
    a. Rayner
    b. Watson
    c. Jones
    d. Lashley
    e. McDougall

    ANS: C   PTS: 1   REF: The Subject Matter of Behaviorism

57. Mary Cover Jones's study of Peter _____.
    x a. was a forerunner of behavior therapy
    b. showed that fears are instinctive
    c. predates the Little Albert study
    d. supports the notion of one-trial learning
    e. has never been replicated

    ANS: A   PTS: 1   REF: The Subject Matter of Behaviorism

58. For Watson, the mentalistic term *thinking* could be _____.
    a. redefined as the behavior of subvocal talking
    b. measured by its behavior correlates (gestures)
    c. observed in measures of movements of the vocal apparatus
    d. All of the choices are correct.
    e. None of the choices are correct.

    ANS: D   PTS: 1   REF: The Subject Matter of Behaviorism

59. Watson proposed that society as a whole could be improved by _____.
    a. electing psychologists to political office
    b. enforcing tough crime laws
    c. replacing religion-based ethics with experimental ethics
    d. forming a colony and living a communal life
    e. None of the choices are correct.

    ANS: C   PTS: 1   REF: Behaviorism's Popular Appeal

60. An early popularizer of psychology was ____.
    a. Jones
    b. Jastrow
    c. Dewey
    d. Wiggam
    e. both Jastrow and Wiggam

    ANS: E   PTS: 1   REF: An Outbreak of Psychology

61. A major criticism of Watson's system is that it discounts ____.
    a. sensation and perception
    b. thought processes
    c. emotions
    d. social relationships
    e. extrasensory perception

    ANS: A   PTS: 1   REF: Criticisms of Watson's Behaviorism

62. One criticism of Watson was that his strict objectivity ____.
    a. was hard to achieve
    b. was good for the discipline
    c. needed to be discarded
    d. was second to the introspection method
    e. None of the above.

    ANS: A   PTS: 1   REF: Criticisms of Watson's Behaviorism

63. One part of the cerebral cortex is essentially equal to another in its contribution to learning; this is ____ principle of ____.
    a. Watson's; equipotentiality
    b. Lashley's; equipotentiality
    c. Lashley's; mass action
    d. Jastrow's; cortical substitution
    e. Jastrow's; mass action

    ANS: B   PTS: 1   REF: Criticisms of Watson's Behaviorism

64. The efficiency of learning is a function of the total amount of brain tissue; this is ____ law of ____.
    a. Watson's; equipotentiality
    b. Lashley's; equipotentiality
    c. Lashley's; mass action
    d. Jastrow's; cortical substitution
    e. Jastrow's; mass action

    ANS: C   PTS: 1   REF: Criticisms of Watson's Behaviorism

65. Some argue that humans should learn more readily than lower animals because of humans' greater amount of gray matter. Such a belief is variation of ____.
    a. Watson's purposive behaviorism
    b. Watson's concept of internal drives
    c. Lashley's law of mass action
    d. Lashley's principle of equipotentiality
    e. Watson's paradigm of evolution from animals to humans

    ANS: C   PTS: 1   REF: Criticisms of Watson's Behaviorism

66. McDougall believed that human behavior ____.
    a. derives from innate tendencies
    b. could not be studied
    c. was a function of God's will
    d. could not be predicted or controlled
    e. was solely determined by the environment

    ANS: A   PTS: 1   REF: Criticisms of Watson's Behaviorism
    MSC: WWW

67. McDougall's arguments against Watson included that ____.
    a. humans had free will
    b. data pertaining to consciousness were valuable
    c. an appeal to God as the director of human behavior
    d. free will made prediction and control unlikely
    e. humans had free will **and** data pertaining to consciousness were valuable

    ANS: E   PTS: 1   REF: Criticisms of Watson's Behaviorism
    MSC: WWW

68. McDougall's argument that the data of consciousness are an appropriate focus of research was later upheld by the ____.
    a. physiologists
    b. humanistic school
    c. social learning theorists
    d. structuralists
    e. humanistic school **and** social learning theorists

    ANS: E   PTS: 1   REF: Criticisms of Watson's Behaviorism

69. McDougall was especially critical of Watson's ____.
    a. reductionism
    b. determinism
    c. positivism
    d. mechanism
    e. All of the choices are correct.

    ANS: B   PTS: 1   REF: Criticisms of Watson's Behaviorism

70. According to the text, Watson's primary contribution to psychology was ____.
    a. the rejection of consciousness
    b. his advocacy of a science of behavior that was objective in methods and language
    c. his rejection of the instinct theory
    d. his acceptance of social Darwinism
    e. openness to different viewpoints

    ANS: B   PTS: 1   REF: Contributions of Watson's Behaviorism
    MSC: WWW

71. In the long run, Watson's behaviorism _____.
    a. supplanted structuralism, pragmatism, and functionalism
    b. supplanted structuralism but has continued to evolve alongside functionalism
    c. has continually interacted with functionalism, borrowing some concepts while criticizing others
    d. supplanted structuralism and absorbed pragmatism and functionalism
    e. was absorbed into the mainstream of psychology and thereby lost its distinctiveness and revolutionary spirit and initiative

    ANS: E   PTS: 1   REF: Contributions of Watson's Behaviorism

TRUE/FALSE

72. Like many of psychology's forebears, Watson intended to pursue a PhD in physiology.

    ANS: F   PTS: 1   REF: John B. Watson (1878-1958)
    MSC: WWW

73. It has been speculated that Watson rejected introspection because he could not do it.

    ANS: T   PTS: 1   REF: John B. Watson (1878-1958)

74. Controversy regarding Watson's childrearing practices is evidenced by his own children's attempts at suicide.

    ANS: T   PTS: 1   REF: John B. Watson (1878-1958)
    MSC: WWW

75. In his 1913 paper "Psychology as the Behaviorist Views it, " Watson argued for the application of the methods of animal psychology to the study of humans.

    ANS: F   PTS: 1   REF: John B. Watson (1878-1958)

76. Before leaving academia for the advertising world, Watson taught a course on the psychology of advertising.

    ANS: T   PTS: 1   REF: John B. Watson (1878-1958)

77. Watson's approach to advertising was filled with the doctrine of mechanism.

    ANS: T   PTS: 1   REF: John B. Watson (1878-1958)

78. Watson's *Psychological Care of the Infant and Child* takes a clear-cut environmental stance.

    ANS: T   PTS: 1   REF: John B. Watson (1878-1958)

79. Watson's most profound public impact was on American educational practices.

    ANS: F   PTS: 1   REF: John B. Watson (1878-1958)
    MSC: WWW

80. Consistent with the Darwinian notion that there is a continuum between animals and humans, Watson argued that there is no dividing line between humans and other animals in the application of experimental methods.

   ANS: T   PTS: 1   REF: The Methods of Behaviorism

81. It was not until after Watson's death that the goal of behaviorism was defined as the prediction and control of behavior.

   ANS: F   PTS: 1   REF: John B. Watson (1878-1958)

82. In *Psychology as the Behaviorist Views It*, Watson stated that psychology is a natural science because it relies on the experimental method.

   ANS: T   PTS: 1   REF: The Methods of Behaviorism
   MSC: WWW

83. Watson argued that unless psychology discarded the introspective method, the debates of his time would still be raging unresolved 200 years in the future.

   ANS: T   PTS: 1   REF: The Methods of Behaviorism

84. In *Psychology as the Behaviorist Views It*, Watson found encouraging calls for a science of behavior but *not* for a science of mental behavior.

   ANS: F   PTS: 1   REF: John B. Watson (1878-1958)

85. In *Psychology as the Behaviorist Views It*, Watson pointed out the importance of keeping all results on an entirely objective level.

   ANS: T   PTS: 1   REF: John B. Watson (1878-1958)

86. Watson described conditioning in terms of cortical excitation.

   ANS: F   PTS: 1   REF: The Methods of Behaviorism

87. In behaviorism, subjects were both "observer" and "observed."

   ANS: F   PTS: 1   REF: The Methods of Behaviorism

88. For Watson, the only elements of behavior were muscle movements.

   ANS: F   PTS: 1   REF: The Subject Matter of Behaviorism
   MSC: WWW

89. For Watson, a behavioral act was goal-oriented.

   ANS: T   PTS: 1   REF: The Subject Matter of Behaviorism

90. Watson's analysis of behavior was reductionistic.

   ANS: T   PTS: 1   REF: The Subject Matter of Behaviorism

91. The "Little Albert" study has been successfully replicated.

ANS: F   PTS: 1   REF: The Subject Matter of Behaviorism

92. Watson proposed that thinking could be observed in subvocal speech and gestures.

ANS: T   PTS: 1   REF: The Subject Matter of Behaviorism

93. Watson planned to replace religion-based ethics with his experimental ethics based on behaviorism.

ANS: T   PTS: 1   REF: Behaviorism's Popular Appeal

94. Part of behaviorism's popularity is attributed to Watson's charismatic promotion of it as a science that helps men and women understand the principles of their own behavior.

ANS: T   PTS: 1   REF: Behaviorism's Popular Appeal

95. Lashley's findings on the role of the brain in learning perfectly supported Watson's theories, thereby solidifying behaviorism.

ANS: F   PTS: 1   REF: Criticisms of Watson's Behaviorism

96. Watson defended his hypotheses in the debate with McDougall and was declared the winner.

ANS: F   PTS: 1   REF: Criticisms of Watson's Behaviorism

Chapter 11

Behaviorism: After the Founding

The chapter begins with a description of the IQ Zoo (now closed), which housed animals that had been trained to do a wide variety of amazing tasks, like clean a room, play tick tack toe, and tap dance. Psychologists Keller and Marian Breland trained the animals to perform these tasks using Skinner's operant conditioning, an evolved form of behaviorism.

By the 1920's Watson's behaviorism was well entrenched. Because of its popularity, the field quickly evolved through three distinct stages, beginning with Watson's behaviorism. 1930 demarcates the beginning of the second stage, neobehaviorism, which lasted until about 1960. The "neobehaviorists agreed on several points: 1) the core of psychology is the study of learning, 2) Most behavior, no matter how complex, can be accounted for by the laws of conditioning, and 3) Psychology must adopt the principle of operationism." The third stage of behaviorism (neo-neobehaviorism or sociobehaviorism) began in 1960 and lasted until 1990.

Operationism refers to the idea of making language and terms more "objective and precise," and discarding from study any object that cannot be objectively studied. For psychology, this means discarding "the concept of individual or private conscious experience." Operationism was first adopted by physicists, and psychology soon followed this model. As a result, the new generation of neobehaviorists were heavily influenced by operationism.

Edward Tolman was one of the first "converts to behaviorism," and received his psychology training from Harvard and in Germany under Kurt Koffka. He taught at Northwestern University and then at Berkeley, where "he became dissatisfied with Watson's form of behaviorism." He developed "purposive behaviorism" because he saw all behavior as purpose-driven or goal-directed. He believed there were 5 variables that cause behavior: "environmental stimuli, physiological drives, heredity, previous training, and age." For Tolman, the S-R of Watson must include the organism, S-O-R. Unlike Thorndike, Tolman believed that a reward is not what drives learning. Instead, the organism develops expectations (what he called "sign Gestalts") as it learns. For example, when a rat is learning a maze it creates a "cognitive map" to help it negotiate the maze. Tolman's work foreshadows modern cognitive psychology.

Another neobehaviorist was Clark Hull, who "dominated American psychology from the 1940's until the 1960's." Early in his career, Hull dabbled in a variety of research interests, all of which demonstrated his preference for objective methods. He went to Yale in 1929 and began his work in learning theory and conditioning. Hull believed that behaviorists should view people as machines, and that human behavior could be reduced to "the language of physics." Hull sought to describe behavior with a large set of mathematical equations. Hull believed that "motivation was a state of bodily need that arose from a deviation from optimal biological conditions." This need was expressed in terms of primary drives (innate needs, like hunger) and secondary drives (learned needs, such as opening a refrigerator). Hull also discussed the idea of secondary reinforcement, which is a neutral stimulus that has been paired with a primary reinforcer and becomes reinforcing in itself. With Hull, learning requires reinforcement because the drive must be reduced. This is a difference between Hull and Tolman.

The most influential of the neobehaviorists is B. F. Skinner, whose work was the predominant view of psychology at the time, and whose ideas charmed the American public. Skinner graduated from Hamilton College in English and intended to become a writer, but then decided he had "nothing to say."
He read about the work of Watson and Pavlov and went to Harvard where he received his Ph.D. His first book, *The Behavior of Organisms* (1938) outlines his system, but had disappointing sales

at first. Fifty years later it was judged to have "changed the face of psychology." He remained productive right up until his death from leukemia in 1990.

Skinner's system is in many ways similar to Watson's. Unlike Hull, who attempted to build a theory on mathematics, Skinner was atheoretical and descriptive in nature; his focus was on applying behaviorism to real-world problems. Thus his brand of behaviorism was applicable to clinical, education, and applied psychology branches. Skinner did not include any "internal entities" such as drives, which is why his approach is sometimes called the "empty organism" approach. Skinner did not deny the presence of internal states, but he did deny their usefulness as a focus of scientific study. Instead, he highlighted observable behaviors as the focus of his studies. Skinner also used single-subject designs rather than representative samples, because his intention was to predict behavior—something that could not be done based on measurements of the "average" person. The authors include source material from *Science and Human Behavior* (1953) in which Skinner discusses the evolution of machines and compares moving machines to people.

Skinner studied operant conditioning (the conditioning of "voluntary" behavior) in contrast to the respondent conditioning (the conditioning of "reflexive" behavior) studied by Pavlov. For Skinner, operant behavior requires that the organism is active in his or her environment. For example, a food-deprived rat placed in a "Skinner box" will eventually press a lever that will provide food. In this example, the food acts as a reinforcer to increase the chances that the behavior (pressing the lever) occurs again. This lead to Skinner's Law of acquisition: "the strength of an operant behavior increases when it is followed by" a reinforcer. Reinforcements do not need to be presented every time in order to condition the behavior. Skinner used different schedules to test the effectiveness of intermittent reinforcement, where the reinforcer is presented after a specific time period (interval) or after a specific number of responses (ratio). Skinner developed the technique called "successive approximation" to shape more complex behaviors (such as those exhibited at the IQ Zoo) and suggested that this process also shapes complex human behavior.

Skinner was involved in a variety of projects that applied his system, some of which gave him notoriety. For example, he invented the aircrib (and marketed it with little success) which was intended to provide an optimal environment for babies. He developed the teaching machine to help improve students' learning. During World War II Skinner attempted to create a pigeon-guided missile for the military, who was not convinced of its usefulness. Skinner also wrote a novel, *Walden Two* (1948), which was a description of a utopian commune built using Skinner's behaviorism. The application of Skinner's system, called "behavior modification" is still used widely today in just about every setting (prisons, at home, at work, in hospitals) and includes only reinforcement, not punishment, to shape and modify behavior.

Criticisms of Skinner's work target his lack of theory and his insistence that all behavior is learned. The Brelands, who were trained by Skinner and who created the IQ Zoo, wrote an article that addressed "instinctive drift". This is the idea that some behaviors are exhibited by animals (innately driven) even though the behaviors may interfere with reinforcement. Finally, Skinner's belief that language is shaped through his principles was successfully challenged by Noam Chomsky, who believed that there is some inherited characteristic that guides language acquisition. Skinner's work was influential and widespread and he is acknowledged to be one of the most important psychologists in the history of psychology.

The third stage of behaviorism (sociobehaviorism) incorporates cognitive processes into the study of overt behaviors, which is in stark contrast to Skinner's system. Albert Bandura received his Ph.D. in 1952 and went on to teach at Stanford University. Bandura considered himself a behaviorist in that he "emphasized the importance of rewards…in acquiring and modifying behavior." However, he incorporated cognition as a key component of his work. He developed the idea of "vicarious reinforcement," where an individual's behavior can be influenced by watching others' behaviors and the consequences they receive. Thus, cognition becomes

342   CHAPTER 11

important because the person sees others receive consequences, imagines their own behaviors in that context, and makes a judgment about whether they desire the consequence. For Bandura, the schedule of reinforcement is not as important as is the person's belief about what the schedule is.

One major contribution was Bandura's work on self-efficacy (our estimates of our own competence), which has received much empirical support. Higher self-efficacy indicates that one expects to overcome obstacles, seek challenges, persevere, and maintain a high level of confidence, whereas low self-efficacy is indicative of hopelessness, helplessness, and have little chance to affect the situations they confront. This body of literature suggests that self-efficacy (one's self-esteem and competence in dealing with life's problems) has significant implications was one's success and mental/physical health.

For Bandura, modeling techniques are useful to help change behavior. This technique involves using a model to demonstrate appropriate or desirable behavior. His work on modeling has been used for solving practical problem (i.e., "controlling the spread of AIDS, promoting literacy"). Although criticized by Skinnerian psychologists for including cognition, Bandura's work has been widely praised and applied.

Another sociobehaviorist is Julian Rotter, who was "the first psychologist to use the term 'social learning theory'." Rotter believed that individuals must be studied in the context of their social environment, and that behavior is not only controlled by environmental consequences, but also by: 1) our subjective expectations of outcomes, 2) our estimated likelihood of receiving a consequence if we behave a certain way, 3) the value we place on consequences, and 4) the fact that each of us values the same consequences differently. Rotter developed the idea of locus of control, which is the extent to which we feel competent in our environments. He studied the difference between people who have an internal locus of control (i.e., believe we control our own consequences) or an external locus of control (i.e., others or the environment control our consequences). Similar to Bandura's work, Rotter found that those with an internal locus of control are vastly more successful in work and academic setting. In addition, internal locus of control people have lower scores of depression and anxiety, report better coping skills, and have better social relationships.

Behaviorism is still a strong force in contemporary psychology. However, the type of behaviorism that is most accepted in modern psychology is the *methodological* behaviorism of Bandura and Rotter, because they take cognitive processes into account. Skinner's radical behaviorism "peaked in the 1980's and declined after Skinner's death in 1990."

Outline

I.   The IQ Zoo: Animal House?
   A. Was in Arkansas, no longer open
   B. animals trained to do amazing tricks
   C. Priscilla the pig who switched on a radio, picked up dirty clothes, vacuumed, etc.
   D. Birdbrain, a chicken who played tic tac toe and never lost, not even to Skinner
   E. Zoo started by Keller and Marion Breland, who had been students of Skinner and made their living training animals
   F. Peak of success=140 animal shows at major tourist attractions
   G. Also trained animals for movies, TV, and commercials
II.   Three Stages of Behaviorism
   A. Overview
      1. 1924: Titchener conceded that Watsonian behaviorism had engulfed the United States
      2. 1930: other varieties of behaviorism emerged

B. The Stages
1. Stage 1: 1913-1930: Watsonian bchaviorism
2. Stage 2: 1930-1960: Neobehaviorism
    a. Tolman, Hull, Skinner
    b. core of psychology is the study of learning
    c. most behavior can be accounted for by the laws of conditioning
    d. psychology must adopt the principle of operationism
3. Stage 3: 1960-1990: sociobehaviorism and the return to cognitive processes
    a. Bandura, Rotter
    b. focus on observing overt behavior

III. Operationism
A. Purpose and definition
1. a key feature of neobehaviorism
2. purpose:
    a. to render the language and terminology of science more objective and precise
    b. to rid science of pseudo-problems
3. definition: "the doctrine that a physical concept can be defined in precise terms relating to the set of operations or procedures by which it is determined"
4. basic principle: " the validity of a finding or construct depends on the validity of the operations used to achieve that finding
5. can be traced to the British empiricists
B. Bridgman: The Logic of Modern Physics (1927)
1. called for the precise definition of all physical concepts; concepts lacking physical referents must be discarded
2. a concept is the same as the procedures by which it is determined
    a. example of length
    b. contemporary use of operational definitions
3. if a concept cannot be measured and manipulated under controlled conditions, it is a pseudo-problem and should be discarded
4. thus, consciousness and soul is NOT relevant in scientific psychology
C. Physics continued to be the paradigm for psychology, so Bridgman's views had a tremendous impact
D. Psychologists felt they needed to follow this model: neobehaviorists heavily influenced by operationism

IV. Edward Chace Tolman (1886-1959)
A. Career
1. studied engineering at MIT
2. Harvard PhD in 1915
3. 1912: studied Gestalt psychology with Kurt Koffka
4. graduate school
    a. trained as Titchenerian structuralist
    b. questioned scientific utility of introspection
    c. became acquainted with Watsonian behaviorism
5. professional experience
    a. instructor at Northwestern University
    b. 1918 hired by the University of California at Berkeley
        (1) taught comparative psychology
        (2) conducted research on learning in rats

344   CHAPTER 11

(3) formed his own form of behaviorism after becoming dissatisfied with Watson's
    c.   during WWII was the Office of Strategic Services (OSS), which later became the Central Intelligence Agency (CIA)
    d.   in the early 1950's, was a Berkeley faculty leader of opposition to the state loyalty oath

B. Purposive behaviorism
    1. Tolman argues all actions are goal directed
    2. 1932: Purposive Behavior in Animals and Men
        a.   rejected introspection
        b.   had no interest in any presumed internal experiences unless accessible to objective observation
        c.   purposiveness
            (1) defined in objective behavioral terms
            (2) all behavior is directed toward some goal
        d.   the fact of learning is objective evidence of purpose
    3. the attribution of purpose to behavior was criticized by Watsonian behaviorists because it implied the existence of conscious processes
    4. Tolman responded that whether or not presence or degree of organisms were conscious was not relevant to him or did it affect behavioral responses
    5. measurements: changes in response behavior as a function of learning
    6. central focus was overt responses

C. Intervening variables
    1. the initiating causes as well as the results of behavior must be observable and operationally defined
    2. causes are independent variables
        a.   environmental stimuli
        b.   psychological drives
        c.   heredity
        d.   previous training
        e.   age

    3. resultant behaviors
        a.   a function of the five causes (independent variables)
        b.   relationship expressed in a mathematical formula
    4. intervening variables
        a.   the actual determinants of behavior
        b.   connect the stimulus situation with the observed response
            (1) S-O-R
            (2) not S-R
        c.   hunger as the classic example
        d.   cannot be objectively observed
        e.   useful only if clearly related to both the observable independent variable and the observable behavior
            (1) allowed Tolman to operationally define unobservable, internal states
        f.   initially called this approach "operational behaviorism"

D. Learning theory
    1. learning was central in Tolman's purposive behaviorism.

2. rejected Thondike's law of effect
   a. reward has little influence on learning
   b. proposed a cognitive explanation of learning in its place
3. repeated performance of a task strengthens the learned relationship between environmental cues and the organism's expectations
   a. called these relationships "sign Gestalts"
      (1) are learned
      (2) cue expectancy associated with a particular choice point either leads or does not lead to reinforcement
      (3) built up by the continued performance of a task
4. cognitive map
   a. a pattern of sign Gestalts
   b. animal learns a cognitive map, not just a set of motor habits (place versus response learning)

E. Comment
   1. a forerunner of the cognitive movement
   2. intervening variables
      a. engendered scientific respect for operationally defining internal states
   3. the rat as an important research subject
      a. 1930's-1960's primary subject for neobehaviorists
      b. assumption that one could generalize from rats to other animals and humans
      c. simple, easy to study, readily available

V. Clark Leonard Hull (1884-1952)
   A. Hull's life
      1. Early challenges
         a. ill health
         b. poor eyesight
         c. nearly died of typhoid→ memory impaired
         d. polio at age 24 → one leg permanently disabled
         e. poor family; took teaching jobs to earn money instead of going to school
         f. meet challenges with persistence and resolve
         g. intense motivation to achieve
      2. University of Wisconsin: studied mining engineering before psychology
      3. 1918: Ph.D. from Wisconsin; remained on faculty for 10 years
      4. early work revealed continued interest in using objective methods and developing useable laws
         a. concept formation
         b. effects of tobacco on behavioral efficiency
         c. tests and measurements
         d. applied area: Aptitude Testing (1928)
         e. practical methods of statistical analysis
         f. invented a machine for calculating correlations
         g. hypnosis and suggestibility: 10 years, 32 papers, 1 book
      5. 1929: research professor at Yale

6. interested in developing a theory of behavior based on Pavlov's laws of conditioning
   a. 1927: read Pavlov
   b. 1930's articles about basic conditioning and its usefulness in understanding complex higher-order behaviors
7. 1943: Principles of Behavior, an ambitious theoretical attempt to account for all behavior
   a. 1940's: Hull is most frequently cited psychologist
8. 1952: A Behavior System, the final form of Hull's theory

B. The spirit of mechanism
1. omitted mentalistic terms, including consciousness and purpose
2. used mechanistic terms
3. human behavior
   a. mechanistic, robotic
   b. automatic
   c. reducible to the language of physics
4. machines could be constructed that would display human cognitive functions

C. Objective methodology and quantification
1. objective, experimental methods
2. quantitative
3. laws of behavior expressed in the precise language of mathematics
   a. equations
   b. empirical constants
   c. theorems and corollaries
4. objective definitions
5. rigorous deduction
6. four methods
   a. simple observation
   b. systematic controlled observation
   c. experimental testing of hypotheses
   d. the hypothetico-deductive method
      (1) deductions from a set of formulations that are *a priori*
      (2) establish postulates that can deduce experimentally testable hypotheses
      (3) submit them to experimental test
      (4) is the method necessary for psychology to be a science

D. Drives
1. motivation
   a. a state of bodily need
   b. arises from a deviation from optimal biological conditions
2. drive
   a. an intervening variable
   b. defined as a "stimulus arising from a state of tissue need that arouses or activates behavior"
   c. drive reduction is the only basis of reinforcement
   d. drive strength is empirically determined using key characteristics of the environment or of the resulting behavior
      (1) length of deprivation
      (2) intensity, strength, and energy expenditure of the behavior

(3) Hull emphasized the latter measure of response strength
3. reinforcement: reduction or satisfaction of a drive
4. primary drives
   a. arise from a state of physical need
   b. are vital to the organism's survival
   c. food, air, water, defecation, sleep, activity
5. secondary drives
   a. are learned
   b. are situations or environmental stimuli associated with the reduction of primary drives
   c. as a result of the association with primary drives, become drives themselves

E. Learning
   1. has a key role in Hull's system
   2. focuses on principle of reinforcement (Thorndike's law of effect)
   3. law of primary reinforcement: "When a stimulus-response relationship is followed by a reduction in a bodily need, the probability increases that on subsequent occasions the same stimulus will evoke the same response"
      a. reinforcement defined in terms of the reduction of a primary need
      b. primary reinforcement (reduction of a primary drive) is the basis for learning
      c. secondary reinforcement (reduction of a secondary drive)
   4. habit strength: the strength of the S-R connection
      a. a function of the number of reinforcements that have occurred
      b. refers to the persistence of the conditioning
   5. learning cannot occur without reinforcement
      a. reinforcement necessary for drive reduction
      b. Hull's system as ultimately based on need-reduction is contrasted with Tolman's cognitive approach

F. Comment
   1. experienced the same type of attacks as those directed at Watson and other behaviorists
   2. Hull's system faulted for its lack of generalizability
   3. pronounced effect on psychology through
      a. the amount of research generated and provoked
      b. the achievements of his students and followers
      c. defending, extending, and expounding objective behaviorism
   4. called a "theoretical genius"

VI. B.F. Skinner (1904-1990)
A. one of the most influential psychologists in the 20th Century
   1. beginning in 1950's, the major embodiment of behaviorism
   2. large and loyal group of followers
   3. developed and wrote about subjects that had considerable impact
      a. behavioral control
      b. behavior modification
      c. utopian society (Walden Two)

4. pop culture appeal
   a. created automated crib for infants
   b. 1971: Beyond Freedom and Dignity, a national bestseller
5. became a celebrity in his own right

B. Skinner's life
   1. recalled early childhood environment as affectionate and stable
   2. same small community and school as attended by parents
   3. built things as a child; worked with and observed animals
   4. used his early life experiences as a base for his system of psychology
      a. a product of past reinforcements
      b. seemingly predetermined, lawful, and orderly
      c. his experiences traceable to environmental stimuli
   5. unhappy undergraduate career at Hamilton College (NY)
   6. 1925: Hamilton College (NY): degree in English, no courses in psychology, Phi Beta Kappa
   7. worked at writing for two years after favorable feedback from Robert Frost
   8. depressed by lack of success as a writer and in romance
   9. read about Pavlov's and Watson's experimental work
   10. 1931: PhD from Harvard
   11. dissertation: a reflex is a correlation between stimulus and response
   12. 1938: The Behavior of Organisms; covered basic points of his system
      a. sold few copies at first (500 in first 8 years)
      b. largely negative reviews
      c. fifty years later: "one of the handful of books that changed the face of modern psychology"
      d. later success attributed to its application to applied areas
      e. Skinner had interest in solving real-world problems
   13. 1953: Science and Human Behavior; basic textbook for his system
   14. controlled Skinner box built in his basement
      a. lived in a yellow plastic tank large enough for a mattress, bookshelves, and television
      b. went to bed at 10pm, slept for three hours, worked for an hour, slept for three more hours, woke up at 5am to work for three more hours
      c. reinforced himself by listening to music every afternoon
   15. later in life
      a. enjoyed writing-a source of positive reinforcement
      b. published an article "Intellectual Self-Management in Old Age"
      c. described his feelings of dying with leukemia in a radio interview
      d. 1990: vigorously attacked the growth of cognitive psychology in a paper delivered at the Boston meeting of the American Psychological Association eight
      e. 1990 (final article): "Can Psychology Be a Science of Mind?"
   16. died in 1990 at the age of 86

C. Skinner's behaviorism
   1. in some ways a regeneration of Watsonian Behaviorism
   2. although as rigorous as Hull, important contrasts exist
      a. Hull emphasized the importance of theory
      b. Skinner advocated an empirical system with no theoretical framework

BEHAVIORISM: AFTER THE FOUNDING   349

3. devoted to the study of responses
4. concerned with describing behavior rather than explaining it
5. dealt only with observable behavior
6. the task of scientific inquiry: to establish functional relationships between experimenter-controlled stimulus and the organism's response
7. the "empty organism" approach
    a. no presumptions about internal entities
    b. internal physiological and mental events exist but not useful to science
8. single-subject design
    a. large numbers of subjects not necessary
    b. statistical comparisons of group means not necessary
    c. a single subject provides valid and replicable results
        (1) cannot predict behavior of a particular individual from knowledge of the average individual
        (2) Journal of the Experimental Analysis of Behavior established because mainstream journals did not accept an n of one.
D. Original Source Material: from Science of Human Behavior (1953)
    1. behavior as the "primary characteristic of living things"
    2. influence of work of Descartes and the 17th Century automata on Skinner's approach to behavior
    3. evolution of machines in becoming more lifelike
E. Operant Conditioning
    1. contrasted with respondent (Pavlovian) conditioning, which is elicited by a specific observable stimulus
    2. operant behavior
        a. occurs without an observable external stimulus; response appears spontaneous
        b. operates on the organism's environment (respondent conditioning does not)
        c. the behavior is instrumental in securing a stimulus such as food
        d. more representative of everyday learning
        e. most effective approach to science of behavior: the study of the conditioning and extinction of operant behaviors
    3. studied bar pressing in the Plexiglas "Skinner box" with rats
        a. measured the rate of response
        b. rat's behaviors are random at first
        c. when rat presses bar and is reinforced with food then the behavior is rapidly conditioned
        d. Skinner Box eliminates extraneous stimuli
    4. law of acquisition: "the strength of an operant behavior increases when it is followed by the presentation of a reinforcing stimulus"
        a. key variable: reinforcement
        b. practice provides opportunities for additional reinforcement
        c. differs from Thorndike's and Hull's positions
            (1) Thorndike and Hull: explanatory
            (2) Skinner: strictly descriptive
            (3) Hull: internal drives, Skinner: empty organism

F. Schedules of reinforcement: Conditions involving various rates and times of reinforcement
    1. in real life, reinforcements are intermittent and hardly ever continuous (i.e., salary; gambling)
    2. reinforcement is necessary in operant behavior
    3. reinforcement schedules
        a. continuous
        b. intermittent
            (1) fixed or variable time of delivery or rate
            (2) ratio (of responses)
    4. schedules discovered accidentally because of food pellet shortage
    5. "the shorter the time interval between reinforcers, the more rapidly the animals responded; as the interval between reinforcers lengthened, the response rate declined"
    6. intermittent schedules take longer to extinguish

G. Successive Approximation (AKA shaping)
    1. lever pressing is simple behavior, most operant behavior more complex
    2. see examples from IQ Zoo at chapter's beginning
    3. with shaping, behaviors that come closer and closer to the target operant behavior are reinforced; reinforcement at each step
    4. Skinner says that is how children learn language

H. Aircribs, teaching machines, and pigeon-guided missiles
    1. 1945: aircrib
        a. brought Skinner public notoriety
        b. mechanized environment invented to relieve menial labor (air conditioned, automated sheet changing)
        c. not commercially successful
        d. daughter reared in it with no ill effects
    2. teaching machine
        a. invented in the 1920's by Pressey, not enthusiastically received
            (1) surplus of teachers
            (2) no public pressure to improve learning
        b. resurgence of interest in 1950's when Skinner promoted similar device
            (1) excess of students
            (2) public pressure to improve education so U.S. could compete with Soviet Union in space exploration
        c. 1968: *The Technology of Teaching*: Skinner summarized his work in this field
        d. was replaced in the 1960s when computer-assisted instructional methods became dominant
    3. pigeon-guided missiles
        a. developed by Skinner during WWII
            (1) guidance system to steer bombs from warplanes to ground targets
            (2) pigeons housed in missile nose-cones
                (a) trained through prior conditioning to peck at target image
                (b) pecking affected angles of missile's fins
                (c) resultant adjustments kept missile on target

(d) pigeons very accurate

(e) military not impressed and did not use in combat

I. Walden Two (1948)—a behaviorist society
   1. program of behavioral control
   2. a technology of behavior
   3. application of laboratory findings to society at large
   4. novel of a 1,000-member rural community
   5. behavioral control through positive reinforcement
   6. outgrowth of Skinner's midlife depression, expressing his own conflicts and despair
   7. reflected mechanism of Galileo, Newton, and the empiricists→ based on idea that human nature is machinelike

J. Behavior modification
   1. uses positive reinforcement to control or modify the behaviors of people
   2. applied in a variety of settings (mostly clinical or I/O)
   3. works with people in same manner as with animals, by reinforcing desired behavior and extinguishing undesired behavior
   4. focus exclusively on overt behaviors, not what is causing those behaviors
   5. modern research: behavior modification successful only within the organizations they are carried out in (effects not applied outside of that setting)
   6. punishment was never included in Skinner's behavior modification program; believed that punishment much less effective than reinforcement

K. Criticisms of Skinner's behaviorism
   1. his extreme positivism
   2. his opposition to theory
   3. his willingness to extrapolate beyond the data (e.g., utopian society he proposed)
   4. the narrow range of behavior studied
   5. his position that all behaviors are learned
      a. problem of instinctive drift: tendency "to substitute instinctive behaviors for behaviors that had been reinforced"
         (1) introduced by the work of the Brelands
         (2) innate behaviors stronger than learned behaviors, even when latter delayed access to food
   6. his position on verbal behavior, successfully challenged by Noam Chomsky

L. Contributions of Skinner's behaviorism
   1. shaped American psychology for 30 years
   2. his goal: the improvement of society
   3. strength and ramifications of his radical behaviorism

VII. Sociobehaviorism: The Cognitive Challenge
A. social learning or sociobehaviorist approach
   1. Bandura & Rotter: primarily behaviorists
   2. reflected the broader cognitive revolution in psychology
   3. marks the third stage of behaviorism

VIII. Albert Bandura (1925-   )
A. Background
   1. experience with the psychopathology of ordinary life
   2. 1952: PhD from the University of Iowa
   3. 1981: APA Distinguished Scientific Contribution Award

B. Social cognitive theory
    1. behavioristic
        a.   less extreme than Skinner's behaviorism
        b.   reflects Zeitgeist: interest in cognitive variables
    2. research focus: observation of the behavior of humans in interaction
    3. emphasizes the role of reinforcement in learning and behavior modification
    4. cognitive aspect: stresses the influence of thought processes on external reinforcement schedules
    5. reactions to stimuli are self-activated, person-initiated rather than automatic
    6. reinforcer effective if:
        a.   person is consciously aware of what is being reinforced
        b.   person anticipates the same reinforcer if the behavior is repeated
    7. vicarious reinforcement: learning "by observing how other people behave and seeing the consequences of their behavior" rather than direct experience
        a.   assumes human capacity to anticipate and appreciate those outcomes
        b.   one can regulate one's behavior by
            (1) imagining those consequences, and
            (2) making a conscious selection of the behavior to manifest
        c.   is like the S-O-R model, with O being equal to cognitive processes
    8. cognitive processes distinguish Bandura's views from Skinner's
        a.   actual schedule of reinforcement less important that what the person believes it is
        b.   who controls behavior
            (1) Skinner: whoever controls reinforcers
            (2) Bandura: whoever controls the models in a society
    9. modeling
        a.   observing people and patterning our behavior on theirs
        b.   salient characteristics of influential models
            (1) same age and sex as self
            (2) peers with similar problems
            (3) high in status and prestige
            (4) exhibit simple behaviors
            (5) display hostile and aggressive behaviors
            (6) example: "research conducted in several countries has consistently found that children who watch a great deal of violence on television and in movies, or who spend time playing action-packed video games, display far more violent and aggressive behavior as adolescents and young adults than do children who are exposed to less violence"
   10. a social learning theory
        a.   behavior as formed and modified in social situations
        b.   criticisms of Skinner's work
            (1) use of single subjects
            (2) did not study humans interacting (because few people live in isolation)
C. Self-efficacy: "our sense of self-esteem or self-worth, our feeling of adequacy, efficiency, and competence in dealing with problems"
    1. high versus efficacy persons
        a.   believe they can cope with diverse problems

b. expect to overcome obstacles

c. seek challenges

d. persevere

e. confident of ability to succeed

f. exert control over their life

2. low self-efficacy persons

    a. feel helpless or hopeless about coping

    b. do not expect to overcome or even affect obstacles or situations

    c. give up when initial attempts fail

    d. believe nothing they can do will make a difference

    e. believe they have little or no control over their fate

3. wide range of effects of self-efficacy beliefs

    a. research shows that high self-efficacy persons experience positive outcomes in most aspects of life

    b. high efficacy= better

        (1) higher grades, more career possibilities, greater job success, higher personal goals, better physical and mental health,

        (2) "are less bothered by stress, more tolerant of physical pain, and likely to recover more quickly from illness or surgery"

        (3) "employees high in self-efficacy have been found to be more satisfied with their work, committed to their organization, and motivated to perform well on the job and in training programs than are employees low in self-efficacy"

        (4) feel confident about social interaction and new friendships

        (5) "They score high on measures of emotional well-being and are less likely to become addicted to Internet use than are those who score low in social self-efficacy"

    c. men generally higher than women in self-efficacy

    d. self-efficacy peaks in middle age and declines at about age 60

4. diverse groups develop collective high efficacy levels

    a. "the stronger the perceived collective efficacy, the higher the group's aspirations and motivational investment in their undertakings, the stronger their staying power in the face of impediments and setbacks, the higher their morale and resilience to stressors, and the greater their performance accomplishments"

D. Behavior modification

1. Bandura's goal: change or modify socially undesirable behavior

2. focus: external aspects of abnormality, i.e., behavior

3. example of the use of modeling: the model does something that the patient is fearful of and shows that the feared object is non-threatening

4. Bandura's form of behavior therapy is widely used in diverse settings and has strong research support

    a. preventing unwanted pregnancies

    b. controlling the spread of AIDS

    c. promoting literacy

    d. raising the status of women

    e. adopting family planning strategies

E. Comment

1. criticized by traditional behaviorists who maintain that cognitive processes do not cause behavior
2. positive aspects of Bandura's theory
    a. consistent with the functionalism of American psychology
    b. objective
    c. amenable to precise laboratory methods
    d. responsive to the current cognitive Zeitgeist
    e. applicable to practical problems
3. widely accepted by peers
    a. Bandura president of APA (1974)
    b. receives APA Distinguished Scientific Contribution Award (1980)
    c. APA's Outstanding Contribution to Psychology Award (2004)
    d. American Psychological Foundation's Gold Medal Award for Life Achievement in the Science of Psychology (2006)

IX. Julian Rotter (1916-   )
A. Background
    1. grew up comfortably in Brooklyn
    2. father lost his business in 1929 crash
        a. turning point for the 13-year-old
        b. triggered life-long concern for social justice
        c. lesson on the effects of situational conditions on personality and behavior
    3. read Freud and Adler in high school
    4. learned that jobs scarce in psychology
    5. majored in chemistry at Brooklyn College
    6. met Adler and switched to psychology
    7. 1941: PhD from Indiana University
    8. dissuaded from academic jobs due to prejudice against Jews
    9. worked at Connecticut state mental hospital
    10. WWII: psychologist in U.S. Army
    11. taught at Ohio State University then at University of Connecticut
    12. received APA Distinguished Scientific Contribution Award
B. Cognitive processes
    1. 1947: the first to use the term "social learning theory"
    2. cognitive approach to behaviorism
    3. invokes the existence of subjective experiences
    4. criticized Skinner's study of single subjects in isolation
    5. relies on rigorous, well-controlled laboratory research
    6. studies only human subjects in social interaction
    7. deals with cognitive processes more extensively than Bandura
        a. both external stimuli and the reinforcement they provide affect behavior
        b. cognitive factors mediate the nature and extent of that influence
    8. four cognitive principles determine behaviors
        a. expectation of amount and kind of reinforcement
        b. estimation of probability the behavior will lead to a particular reinforcement
        c. differential values of reinforcers and assessment of their relative worth

d.　　different people place different values on the same reinforcer

C. Locus of control: "beliefs about the source of our reinforcers"
　　1. beliefs about the source of one's reinforcements
　　2. internal locus of control: belief that reinforcement depends on one's own behavior
　　3. external locus of control: belief that "reinforcement depends on outside forces such as fate, luck, or the actions of other people"
　　4. results:
　　　　a.　　internal locus of control: expect to be in charge of their lives and behave accordingly; physically and mentally healthier; lower blood pressure, fewer heart attacks, lower levels of depression and anxiety, better able to cope with stress; better grades; greater freedom of choice; more popular, socially skilled; higher self-esteem
　　　　b.　　external locus of control: one's own abilities and behaviors make little difference, powerless with respect to outside forces, minimal attempts to change or improve situation
　　5. is learned in childhood from the ways one is treated
　　　　a.　　parents of internal locus of control adults: supportive, generous with praise for achievement, consistent with discipline, not authoritarian in attitude
　　6. Rotter's 23 item forced-choice test
　　7. product of a chance discovery
　　　　a.　　told participants they were being tested on ESP abilities
　　　　b.　　afterwards, subjects asked to guess how successful they would be at the second task
　　　　c.　　many said they would do worse; attributed prior success to luck
　　　　d.　　others suggested they would do better because they believed they may have ESP abilities

D. Comment
　　1. Rotter's theory attracts followers who
　　　　a.　　are experimentally oriented
　　　　b.　　think cognitive variables influence behavior
　　2. a great many studies support his theory, particularly regarding internal and external locus of control

X.　The Fate of Behaviorism
A. Cognitive challenge to behaviorism from within modified the behaviorist movement
B. Sociobehaviorists still consider themselves behaviorists
　　1. are called *methodological* behaviorists because they employ internal cognitive processes
　　2. are contrasted with radical behaviorists like Watson and Skinner who do not deal with presumed internal states
　　　　a.　　Skinnerian behaviorism peaked in the 1980s
　　　　b.　　declined after Skinner's death in 1990
C. Today's behaviorism, particularly in applied psychology, is different from forms it took from 1913 (Watson) to 1990 (Skinner)
D. In an evolutionary sense, the spirit of behaviorism still lives

Lecture prompts/Discussion topics for chapter eleven

356　　　　　　　　　　　　　　CHAPTER 11

- Of the variables that Tolman believed caused behavior (environment, physiological drives, heredity, previous training, and age) which ones do you think Watson would agree with? Hull? Skinner? Bandura and Rotter?
- Here is a quote from a contemporary philosopher, John Searle, from page 52-53 of "*Mind: A Brief Introduction*", Oxford University Press (2004). Ask your students for their reactions to this quote, and if his is a fair and/or accurate criticism of behaviorism.

"By the middle decades of the twentieth century, the difficulties of behaviorism had led to its general weakening and eventual rejection. It was going nowhere as a methodological project in psychology, and indeed was under quite effective attack, especially from the linguist Noam Chomsky. Chomsky claimed that the idea that when we study psychology we are studying behavior is as unintelligent as the idea that when we study physics we are studying meter readings. Of course we use behavior as evidence in psychology, just as we use meter readings as evidence in physics, but it is a mistake to confuse the evidence that we have about a subject matter for the subject matter itself.
The subject matter of psychology is the human mind, and human behavior is evidence for the existence and features of the mind, but is not itself the mind"

Internet Resources for chapter eleven

Albert Bandura Biographical Sketch
http://www.des.emory.edu/mfp/bandurabio.html
This webpage was clearly created with the blessing of Bandura, as it contains both personal and professional information (ex., photographs of his grandchildren). There are many active links to gain more information about his life and work.

B.F. Skinner Foundation
http://www.bfskinner.org/
You can find out a lot of information about Skinner's life and work, particularly how it is being carried on after his death.

Edward Chace Tolman bookplate
http://www.gslis.utexas.edu/~landc/bookplates/30_3_Tolman.htm
This page gives some interesting information about Tolman and includes the custom-made bookplates he used for his books. The design is a white rat superimposed on a maze.

IQ Zoo—Encyclopedia of Arkansas
http://encyclopediaofarkansas.net/encyclopedia/entry-detail.aspx?entryID=2538
This page gives some nifty information about the IQ Zoo, including photographs of the Brelands and some of the zoo's star attractions.

Twin Oaks
http://www.twinoaks.org/
This is a communal society that was originally based on the one Skinner proposed in Walden Two. Although it no longer operates as did Walden Two, it retains many of Skinner's principles. There is much information on the site about Skinner and Walden Two.

Potential answers to chapter eleven discussion questions

1. What does Priscilla the Fastidious Pig have to do with the history of psychology? By what techniques was this animal trained?
Priscilla could perform an amazing collection of tasks: "she switched on a radio, then ate breakfast at a table, picked up an array of dirty clothes, stowed them in a hamper, and ran a vacuum cleaner around her room." She was one of several animals in the IQ Zoo (now closed), which housed animals that had been trained to do a wide variety of amazing tasks. They were trained by applying Skinner's operant conditioning. This demonstrates a point in the history of psychology where behaviorism was widely accepted and praised for its ability to alter behavior—even that of animals.

2. Describe the three stages in the evolution of the behaviorist school of thought.
Stage one began with Watson's behaviorism, which thrived up until 1930. Stage two began in 1930, and was termed neobehaviorism, which lasted until about 1960. This was marked by Skinnerian behaviorism. Stage three, neo-neobehaviorism or sociobehaviorism, began in 1960 and lasted until 1990. Leading figures in sociobehaviorism were Bandura and Rotter, who incorporate a cognitive approach to the study of behavior.

3. Which psychologists can be classified as neobehaviorists? On what major points did they agree?
Neobehaviorists covered in the chapter include Edward Tolman, Clark Hull, and B. F. Skinner. The "neobehaviorists agreed on several points: 1) the core of psychology is the study of learning, 2) Most behavior, no matter how complex, can be accounted for by the laws of conditioning, and 3) Psychology must adopt the principle of operationism."

4. What was operationism and how did it influence the neobehaviorists of the 1920s and 1930s?
Operationism is the idea of making the language and terms of scientific study more "objective and precise," and discarding from study anything that cannot be objectively studied. It also calls for agreement on the areas of study and types of measurements that are appropriate. For psychology, this means discarding "the concept of individual or private conscious experience," and defining variables in terms of how they will be measured.

5. What are pseudo-problems? Why was the notion of pseudoproblems so appealing to behaviorists?
Pseudoproblems are "problems that are not actually observable or physically demonstrable." The "insistence on discarding pseudoproblems—those questions that defy answer by any known objective test—was particularly appealing to behavioral psychologists." This made the study of personal and private consciousness a pseudoproblem. It was appealing to behaviorists because they focused on objective behaviors; pseudoproblems gave them reason to discard previously accepted notions of consciousness and soul.

6. Give an example of an intervening variable. Describe how it can be defined operationally.
"The intervening variable is whatever is going on within...the organism that brings about the behavioral response to a given stimulus situation." An example is hunger. Hunger itself cannot be measured, but we can measure hunger by measuring the last time the organism ate, or by measuring the amount of food eaten.

7. What did Tolman mean by purposive behaviorism?

To Tolman, all behavior as purpose-driven or goal-directed He named his system "purposive behaviorism" to reflect this. This suggests that organism do not just react or behave without an end-goal in mind. It suggests that consciousness, thought, and mind exist.

8. How did Hull's behaviorism differ from the views of Watson and Tolman?

Hull believed Watson's behaviorism to be "too simple and crude." Unlike Watson, Hull included inner drives as motivators of behaviors. A difference between Hull and Tolman is that with Hull, learning requires reinforcement because the drive must be reduced, where Tolman said that a reinforcement is not necessary for the organism to learn.

9. What role did the spirit of mechanism play in Hull's approach to behaviorism?

Mechanism played the central role in Hull's approach. In fact, he even wrote that "It has struck me many times that the human organism is one of the most extraordinary machines—and yet a machine."

10. Define Hull's concepts of primary and secondary drives, and primary and secondary reinforcement.

Primary drives are innate (such as hunger) and secondary drives are learned (such as opening a refrigerator). Secondary drives are also derivatives of primary drives which, over time, became drives in and of themselves. Hull also discussed the idea of secondary reinforcement, which is a neutral stimulus that has been paired with a primary reinforcer (innately rewarding) and becomes reinforcing in itself.

11. What is the hypothetico-deductive method? List some criticisms of Hull's system.

The hypothetico-deductive method "uses deduction from a set of formulations that are determined a priori. This method involves establishing postulates from which experimentally testable conclusions can be deduced." Some problems with Hull's system is that it lacked generalizability—sometimes postulates were formed based on results from a single experiment.

12. Describe Skinner's views on theorizing, the mechanistic spirit, intervening variables, and the use of statistics.

Skinner was atheoretical (descriptive) and his focus was on applying his ideas to real life. Skinner did not include any "internal entities" such as drives, which is why his approach is sometimes called the "empty organism" approach. Skinner did not deny the presence of internal states, but he did deny their usefulness as a focus of scientific study. Skinner also used single-subject designs rather than samples, so statistics were not used to analyze his research. Skinner's mechanistic spirit can be seen in the excerpted source material from *Science and Human Behavior* in which he discusses and compares animated machines to humans.

13. Distinguish between operant and respondent conditioning. How is operant conditioning used to modify behavior?

Skinner studied operant conditioning (the conditioning of "voluntary" behavior) in contrast to the respondent conditioning (the conditioning of "reflexive" behavior) studied by Pavlov. For Skinner, operant behavior requires that the organism is active in his or her environment. For example, a food-deprived rat placed in a Skinner box will eventually depress a lever that will allow access to food. This lead to Skinner's Law of acquisition: "the strength of an operant behavior increases when it is followed by" a reinforcer. Consequences, like reinforcement, then act to shape more behaviors.

14. What is Skinner's law of acquisition? How did it differ from Thorndike's and Hull's positions on learning?

Skinner's law of acquisition is the idea that "the strength of an operant behavior increases when it is followed by" a reinforcer. "Skinner did not deal with any pleasure/pain or satisfaction/dissatisfaction consequences of reinforcement as did Thorndike. Nor did Skinner make any attempt to interpret reinforcement in terms of reducing drives as did Hull."

15. What is the difference between fixed-interval and fixed-ratio reinforcement schedules? Give a few examples of each.

With a fixed-interval schedule an organism receives reinforcement when the target response is given after a specific time period. An example is a weekly or monthly paycheck not tied to commission. With a fixed-ratio schedule an organism receives reinforcement after a specific number of target responses. Examples are a slot machine, scratch lottery tickets, and a paycheck determined by commission or personal production.

16. How would you apply the method of successive approximation to train a dog to walk in a circle?

You could reinforce the following behaviors: the first time the dog stands, the first time the dog begins to walk, the first time the dog turns its head while it walks, the first time it turns its body while walking, and finally as it begins to walk in a circle. In this way, you should reinforce each behavior independently while the next behaviors builds on the last.

17. On what grounds has Skinner's system been criticized?

Criticisms of Skinner's work target his lack of theory and his insistence that all behavior is learned. The Brelands, who were trained by Skinner and who created the IQ Zoo, wrote an article that addressed "instinctive drift." This is the idea that some behaviors are exhibited by animals (innately driven) even though the behaviors may interfere with reinforcement. Finally, Skinner's belief that language is shaped through his principles was successfully challenged by Noam Chomsky, who believed that there is some inherited characteristic that guides language acquisition.

18. How do Bandura's and Rotter's views on cognitive factors differ from Skinner's views?

Bandura and Rotter "question [Skinner's] total disavowal of mental or cognitive processes and propose instead a social learning or sociobehavioral approach, a reflection of the broader cognitive movement in psychology as a whole."

19. How is modeling used to change behavior? Give an example.

Modeling techniques are used to change behavior by having subjects observe a model in a situation that usually causes them some anxiety. For example, children who are afraid of dogs watch a child their age approach and touch a dog. Observing from a safe distance, the fearful children see the model make progressively closer and bolder movements toward the dog. The model pets the dog through the bars of a playpen, then enters the pen to play with the dog. As a result of this observational learning situation, the children's fear of dogs can be reduced.

20. How do people high in self-efficacy differ from people low in self-efficacy?

People who are high in self-efficacy believe they can cope with diverse problems, expect to overcome obstacles, seek challenges, persevere, are confident of their own ability to succeed, and exert control over their life. People low in self-efficacy feel helpless or hopeless about coping, do not expect to overcome or even affect obstacles or situations, give up if their initial attempts fail, believe nothing they can do will make a difference, and believe they have little or no control over their fate.

21. Distinguish between self-efficacy and locus of control in terms of their effects on behavior.

The terms are very related when one looks at the effect on behavior. Those high in self-efficacy probably have an internal locus of control, and those low in self-efficacy probably have an external locus of control. People who have an internal locus of control "tend to be physically and mentally healthier than those with an external locus of control. In general, internals have lower blood pressure, fewer heart attacks, less anxiety and depression, and are better able to cope with stress. They receive better grades in school and believe they have greater freedom of choice. They are more popular and socially skilled and rank higher in self-esteem." Whereas self-efficacy refers to one's believes about their competence, locus of control refers to whether or not one attributes success internally (to their own merit) or externally (to luck). Self-efficacy does not take the attribution into consideration—only the concept of ability—and vice versa.

Key terms from chapter eleven

- **Behavior modification** In Skinner's system, "The use of positive reinforcement to control or modify the behavior of individuals or groups."
- **Drive** In Hull's system, drive is an intervening variable defined as "a state of tissue need that arouses or activates behavior."
- **Habit strength** In Hull's system, "the strength of the S-R connection."
- **Hypothetico-deductive method** Hull's method to build and test his theory, predictions are made ahead of time and tested. The results either support the theory or cause the theory to be changed.
- **Intervening variables** In Tolman's system, unobservable factors that nonetheless determine behavior, they are internal to the organism.
- **IQ Zoo** Zoo, created by the Brelands, which contained animals who had been trained using Skinner's techniques, and who could perform amazing and complex behaviors.
- **Law of acquisition** In Skinner's system, "the strength of an operant behavior increases when it is followed by the presentation of a reinforcing stimulus."
- **Law of primary reinforcement** In Hull's system "when a stimulus-response relationship is followed by a reduction in need, the probability increases that on subsequent occasions the same stimulus will evoke the same response."
- **Locus of control** In Rotter's system, the "perceived source of reinforcement," either internal or external
- **Methodological behaviorism** The label attached to behaviorists who include internal states in their systems (Hull, Tolman, Bandura, Rotter)
- **Operant conditioning** In Skinner's system, the conditioning of behaviors we think of as being 'voluntary'.
- **Operationism** The idea, promoted by physicist Percy Bridgman, that variables should be defined by how they can be measured.
- **Primary drives** In Hull's system, innate biological need states
- **Purposive behavior** In Tolman's system, he believed behavior to be goal-driven and named his system to reflect this belief.

- **Radical behaviorism** The label attached to Skinner and Watson's vision of a behaviorism free from all internal states.
- **Reinforcement schedule** In Skinner's system, "conditions involving various rates and times of reinforcement."
- **Secondary drives** In Hull's system, these are learned and associated with reducing primary drives.
- **Self-efficacy** In Bandura's system, "One's sense of self-esteem and competence in dealing with life's problems."
- **Sign Gestalts** In Tolman's system, these are learned relationships between the "environmental cues and the organism's expectations."
- **Successive approximation** In Skinner's system (also known as Shaping), complex behaviors are reinforced as they approximate the target behavior.
- **Vicarious reinforcement** In Bandura's system, the idea that a person's behavior can change when they see someone else receive behavior consequences.

TESTBANK

ESSAY

1. Describe, compare, and contrast the three stages of behaviorism.

   ANS:
   Answer not provided.

   PTS: 1

2. Describe the points of agreement among the neobehaviorists. What are the major differences between the neobehaviorists as a group and Watsononian behaviorism?

   ANS:
   Answer not provided.

   PTS: 1   MSC: WWW

3. Describe what Tolman meant by the name "purposive behaviorism," how it is manifested in his learning theory, and the classic experiment that supports his theory.

   ANS:
   Answer not provided.

   PTS: 1

4. Describe Tolman's five "causes" of behavior. What were Hull's positions on each of these factors?

   ANS:
   Answer not provided.

   PTS: 1

5. What is an intervening variable? Explain how they are operationally defined and used by the neobehaviorists, describing in detail at least one intervening variable used by Tolman and one used by Hull.

ANS:
Answer not provided.

PTS: 1   MSC: WWW

6. What role did mechanism and mathematics play in Hull's theory? Describe the four methods he considered useful for scientific research, identifying and explaining the method that was unique to him.

ANS:
Answer not provided.

PTS: 1

7. What were Skinner's opinions about theory, mechanism, intervening variables, statistics, and large sample sizes?

ANS:
Answer not provided.

PTS: 1

8. What are the central differences between respondent and operant conditioning? How did Skinner propose using operant conditioning to modify behavior and to improve society?

ANS:
Answer not provided.

PTS: 1

9. Describe Bandura's social cognitive theory, focusing in detail on his conceptualizations regarding reinforcement as well as behavior modification.

ANS:
Answer not provided.

PTS: 1

10. What is Rotter's approach to cognitive processes? Describe his concept of locus of control including the difference between internal and external.

ANS:
Answer not provided.

PTS: 1

11. Skinner's former students demonstrated which of the following with the advent of the IQ Zoo?
    a. Operant conditioning can be taken out of the lab and applied to the real world.
    b. Behaviorism is a very lucrative business after receiving a Ph.D. from Skinner.
    c. Animals, like humans, are intelligent and have vastly complex minds.
    d. Behaviorism is useless to solving real-world problems.
    e. There are many hardships associated with animal psychology.

    ANS: A   PTS: 1   REF: The IQ Zoo

12. Watson's behaviorism ____.
    a. transformed psychology overnight
    b. was the first stage in the evolution of the behavioral school of thought
    c. was essentially the same as neobehaviorism
    d. lead directly to the cognitive revolution
    e. eventually was abandoned by psychology

    ANS: B   PTS: 1   REF: Three Stages of Behaviorism

13. The era of neobehaviorism consisted of the years ____.
    a. 1913-1958
    b. 1925-1938
    c. 1930-1960
    d. 1930-1990
    e. 1904-1990

    ANS: C   PTS: 1   REF: Three Stages of Behaviorism
    MSC: WWW

14. The dominant area of study for the neobehaviorists was ____.
    a. perception
    b. the neurophysiology of the brain
    c. learning
    d. unconscious mental processes
    e. None of the choices are correct.

    ANS: C   PTS: 1   REF: Three Stages of Behaviorism

15. A point on which the neobehaviorists agreed AND to which they gave much more emphasis than did Watson was ____.
    a. the importance of human subjects
    b. learning and conditioning as the crux of the science of psychology
    c. operationism
    d. positivism
    e. the rejection of the concept of consciousness

    ANS: C   PTS: 1   REF: Operationism

16. Operationism was ____.
    a. a major characteristic of neobehaviorism
    b. intended to rid psychology of pseudo-problems
    c. intended to make the language of science more objective and precise
    d. All of the choices are correct.
    e. None of the choices are correct.

    ANS: D   PTS: 1   REF: Operationism

17. Operationism was formulated by ____.
    a. John B. Watson
    b. B.F. Skinner
    c. Percy Bridgman
    d. Edward Tolman
    e. Clark Hull

    ANS: C   PTS: 1   REF: Operationism

18. Operationism means that a concept ____.
    a. must be defined in logical terms
    b. is synonymous with its methods of measurement
    c. must be mathematical
    d. operates to control human mental processes
    e. All of the choices are correct.

    ANS: B   PTS: 1   REF: Operationism
    MSC: WWW

19. The idea that a concept is the same as the corresponding set of procedures to measure it is called ____.
    a. positivism
    b. science
    c. operationism
    d. mechanism
    e. determinism

    ANS: C   PTS: 1   REF: Operationism

20. If we define consciousness in terms of EEG output, then the construct of consciousness is ____.
    a. acceptable to materialists
    b. acceptable to operationists
    c. still a metaphysical construct
    d. still lacks epistemological meaningfulness
    e. inappropriate

    ANS: B   PTS: 1   REF: Operationism

21. For Bridgman, a construct was acceptable if and only if it ____.
    a. could be objectively measured
    b. was detectable by the instruments used in physics
    c. was observable by humans *and* simultaneously detectable by instruments used in physics
    d. was confined to the domain of human experiences (animal psychology was unacceptable)
    e. could be measured qualitatively as well as quantitatively

    ANS: A   PTS: 1   REF: Operationism

22. Bridgman argued that a construct must be ____.
    a. measurable
    b. able to be manipulated under controlled laboratory conditions
    c. measurable in terms of its effects on behavior
    d. invisible to experimenters
    e. All of the choices are correct.

    ANS: A   PTS: 1   REF: Operationism

23. The concept of operationism can be directly traced to the theories of ____.
    a. Descartes
    b. Comte
    c. Mach
    d. the British empiricists
    e. the French materialists

    ANS: D   PTS: 1   REF: Operationism

24. A primary reason psychology so quickly embraced operationism was that it ____.
    a. was first adopted by physics
    b. validated their desire for greater consistency in the science of psychology
    c. validated the use of rats to determine basic laws of *human* behavior
    d. facilitated a new relationship with research endeavors in medicine
    e. was easy to apply to experiments

    ANS: A   PTS: 1   REF: Operationism
    MSC: WWW

25. Tolman's graduate training was in ____, as is reflected in his later work.
    a. philosophy
    b. structuralism
    c. Gestalt psychology
    d. behaviorism
    e. Both B and C

    ANS: E   PTS: 1   REF: Edward Chace Tolman (1886-1959)

26. Tolman's concept of cognitive maps, i.e., that the animal learns the "whole," might be traced to his work
    ____.
    a. with Koffka on Gestalt psychology during graduate school
    b. with Lewin and Lewin's system of the "life space"
    c. with Lewin and Lewin's use of topology and geometry to explain behavior
    d. in engineering at Harvard
    e. with the OSS in World War II

    ANS: A   PTS: 1   REF: Edward Chace Tolman (1886-1959)

27. Edward C. Tolman's system combining the objective study of behavior with the consideration of goal-
    orientation in behavior is called ____.
    a. molar behavior
    b. stimulus-response associations
    c. intervening behaviorism
    d. purposive behaviorism
    e. goal setting theory

    ANS: D   PTS: 1   REF: Edward Chace Tolman (1886-1959)

28. For Tolman, the obvious and objective behavioral evidence of purpose was ____.
    a. that the rat readily leaves the start box of a maze
    b. that the rat behaves so as to obtain food
    c. that the animal changes its speed of running when the reward size is altered
    d. learning
    e. sign Gestalts

    ANS: D   PTS: 1   REF: Edward Chace Tolman (1886-1959)
    MSC: WWW

29. Tolman described the conscious experience of the animal as _____.
    a. having no influence on the animal's overt behavior
    b. defined by intervening variables
    c. necessary for learning to take place
    d. being the animal's private business and therefore of no interest to him
    e. important but unobservable by any means

    ANS: A   PTS: 1   REF: Edward Chace Tolman (1886-1959)

30. Which of the following did Tolman *not* consider to be a cause of behavior?
    a. environmental stimuli
    b. physiological drives
    c. heredity
    d. motivation
    e. age

    ANS: D   PTS: 1   REF: Edward Chace Tolman (1886-1959)

31. Tolman specified that the independent variables (stimuli) affect processes within the organism. These processes then control the occurrence of behavior (response). These internal processes are known as _____.
    a. operational variables
    b. mental sets
    c. cognitive variables
    d. intervening variables
    e. concrete variables

    ANS: D   PTS: 1   REF: Edward Chace Tolman (1886-1959)

32. In Tolman's system, intervening variables were _____.
    a. observable
    b. dependent variables
    c. the determinants of behavior
    d. independent variables
    e. as useful as the notion of consciousness

    ANS: C   PTS: 1   REF: Edward Chace Tolman (1886-1959)

33. The term *intervening variable* refers to _____.
    a. irrelevant stimuli in the conditioning setting
    b. cognitive factors that may either interfere with or facilitate conditioning
    c. internal processes that "connect" the stimulus with a response
    d. an explanation for insight learning
    e. preventive conditioning

    ANS: C   PTS: 1   REF: Edward Chace Tolman (1886-1959)

34. Tolman's position on Thorndike's law of effect was to _____.
    a. accept it
    b. accept it as long as reward or reinforcement was omitted from the law
    c. reject it
    d. incorporate it into his own purposive behavior theory
    e. None of the choices are correct.

    ANS: C   PTS: 1   REF: Edward Chace Tolman (1886-1959)

35. For Tolman, each experience with a task strengthens the relationship between cues in the environment and the organism's ____.
    a. learned responses
    b. learned associations
    c. expectations
    d. response cues
    e. habit strength

    ANS: C   PTS: 1   REF: Edward Chace Tolman (1886-1959)

36. In Tolman's system, the repetition of an act leads to ____.
    a. no change in the habit strength
    b. sign Gestalts
    c. knowledge of environment cues
    d. cognitive awareness of the environment cues
    e. the combination of movements into acts

    ANS: B   PTS: 1   REF: Edward Chace Tolman (1886-1959)

37. For Tolman, a cognitive map is ____.
    a. the same as consciousness
    b. a pattern of sign Gestalts
    c. a set of S-R cues
    d. a set of motor habits
    e. None of the choices are correct.

    ANS: B   PTS: 1   REF: Edward Chace Tolman (1886-1959)

38. According to Tolman's learning theory, as a rat learns all of the sign-Gestalt relationships in a maze, the rat has acquired a ____.
    a. Habit
    b. Drive
    c. Tropism
    d. cognitive map
    e. good habit

    ANS: D   PTS: 1   REF: Edward Chace Tolman (1886-1959)

39. What is the primary difference between locus of control and self-efficacy?
    a. The former emphasizes success and failure whereas the latter emphasizes mental state.
    b. The former emphasizes internal versus external attribution of success while the latter ignores it.
    c. The latter emphasizes internal versus external attribution of success while the former ignores it.
    d. The latter is not a useful construct whereas the former is.
    e. The latter is the basis of sociobehaviorism whereas the former is an elaboration of it.

    ANS: B   PTS: 1   REF: Julian Rotter (1916-)
    MSC: WWW

40. Whose system was a forerunner of contemporary cognitive psychology?
    a. Tolman's
    b. Guthrie's
    c. Lewin's
    d. Wertheimer's
    e. Köhler's

    ANS: A   PTS: 1   REF: Edward Chace Tolman (1886-1959)

41. The pragmatic value of intervening variables is that they _____.
    a. obscure the consciousness versus behaviorist distinction
    b. are positivist
    c. are observable
    d. are essential for dealing with hypothetical constructs
    e. have been reified

    ANS: D   PTS: 1   REF: Edward Chace Tolman (1886-1959)

42. Tolman described _____ as alternatively "creepy" and "delightful."
    a. Watson's ideas
    b. operational definitions
    c. intervening variables
    d. white laboratory rats
    e. the laboratories in which he worked

    ANS: D   PTS: 1   REF: Edward Chace Tolman (1886-1959)

43. From 1930 until the 1960s, the _____ was the primary research subject for the neobehaviorists and learning theorists.
    a. human being
    b. white man
    c. white bunny
    d. white rat
    e. cat

    ANS: D   PTS: 1   REF: Edward Chace Tolman (1886-1959)
    MSC: WWW

44. It was assumed by Tolman and others that research on white rats would _____.
    a. demonstrate the role of reinforcement in learning
    b. provide the basic foundation from which other studies could be devised in order to replicate the results with other species
    c. provide insights into the basic processes underlying the behavior of humans and other animals
    d. yield basic information on motivation and motivation
    e. serve as an intervening variable between higher and lower species

    ANS: C   PTS: 1   REF: Edward Chace Tolman (1886-1959)

45. According to Schultz and Schultz, "perhaps no other psychologist was so devoted to the problems of the scientific method" than was ____.
    a. Watson
    b. Tolman
    c. Hull
    d. Holt
    e. Skinner

    ANS: C   PTS: 1   REF: Clark Leonard Hull (1884-1952)

46. Hull had an immense knowledge of ____ and ____.
    a. biology and chemistry
    b. formal logic and mathematics
    c. mathematics and operationism
    d. behavior and thought processes
    e. psychology and the occult

    ANS: B   PTS: 1   REF: Clark Leonard Hull (1884-1952)

47. Hull's form of behaviorism was ____ than ____.
    a. much freer of intervening variables; Tolman's
    b. much less free of intervening variables; Tolman's
    c. less sophisticated and complex; Watson's
    d. more sophisticated and complex; Watson's
    e. more organismic; Tolman's

    ANS: D   PTS: 1   REF: Clark Leonard Hull (1884-1952)

48. Throughout his life, Hull ____.
    a. remained one of the wealthiest psychologists
    b. kept himself in top physical condition
    c. was able to run races faster than most of his contemporaries
    d. had inadequate laboratory facilities
    e. suffered from poor health and eyesight

    ANS: E   PTS: 1   REF: Clark Leonard Hull (1884-1952)

49. According to Schultz and Schultz, Hull's "greatest asset was ____."
    a. an intense motivation to succeed
    b. an intellect greater than that of his contemporaries
    c. the quiet perseverance learned from his father
    d. his inherited wealth
    e. the social connections he made

    ANS: A   PTS: 1   REF: Clark Leonard Hull (1884-1952)

50. The learning theorist ____ persevered in the face of numerous obstacles to success.
    a. Tolman
    b. Hull
    c. Skinner
    d. Bandura
    e. Rotter

    ANS: B   PTS: 1   REF: Clark Leonard Hull (1884-1952)

51. Hull's work contributed to which of the following?
    a. the hypothetico-deductive method
    b. learning theory
    c. drive reduction theory
    d. increasing generalizability
    e. A, B, and C

    ANS: E   PTS: 1   REF: Clark Leonard Hull (1884-1952)

52. Throughout his professional career, Hull emphasized ____.
    a. objective methods and functional laws
    b. the importance of being open-minded
    c. that psychology must, above all, stress the basic
    d. the importance of schedules of reinforcement
    e. None of the choices are correct.

    ANS: A   PTS: 1   REF: Clark Leonard Hull (1884-1952)

53. From the 1940s to the 1960s, who dominated American psychology?
    a. Tolman's students and disciples
    b. functional theorists
    c. Hullians
    d. radical behaviorists
    e. Skinnerians

    ANS: C   PTS: 1   REF: Clark Leonard Hull (1884-1952)
    MSC: WWW

54. Who authored an early study of the effects of tobacco on behavioral efficiency?
    a. Hull
    b. Spence
    c. Miller
    d. Mowrer
    e. Brown and Farber

    ANS: A   PTS: 1   REF: Clark Leonard Hull (1884-1952)

55. Hull's background in mathematics and engineering was demonstrated in ____.
    a. his development of statistical analysis methods
    b. his invention of a machine to calculate correlations
    c. the use of postulates and axioms in his system
    d. his description and explanation of behavior in mathematical equations
    e. All of the choices are correct.

    ANS: E   PTS: 1   REF: Clark Leonard Hull (1884-1952)

56. Which of the following men devoted 10 years to the experimental investigation of hypnotic suggestibility?
    a. Dollard
    b. Tolman
    c. Pavlov
    d. Hull
    e. Miller

    ANS: D   PTS: 1   REF: Clark Leonard Hull (1884-1952)

57. Hull's primary research focus was grounded in ____.
    a. Pavlov's laws of conditioning
    b. respondent behavior
    c. Watson's behaviorism
    d. Estes's stimulus-sampling hypothesis
    e. None of the choices are correct.

    ANS: A   PTS: 1   REF: Clark Leonard Hull (1884-1952)

58. Hull's system sought to describe and explain ____.
    a. respondent behavior
    b. operant behavior
    c. intervening variables
    d. referents of consciousness
    e. all behavior

    ANS: E   PTS: 1   REF: Clark Leonard Hull (1884-1952)

59. Of all the neobehaviorists, the one who most obviously espoused mechanism was ____.
    a. Tolman
    b. Rotter
    c. Hull
    d. Skinner
    e. Bridgman

    ANS: C   PTS: 1   REF: Clark Leonard Hull (1884-1952)

60. Hull intended to express the laws of behavior in the language of ____.
    a. field theory
    b. vectors (response directions and strengths)
    c. valences (reward values)
    d. mathematics
    e. behavior

    ANS: D   PTS: 1   REF: Clark Leonard Hull (1884-1952)

61. Hull's training in engineering was manifest in his belief that all behavior could be reduced to the language of ____.
    a. mathematics
    b. vectors (response directions and strengths)
    c. valences (reward values)
    d. field theory
    e. biology

    ANS: A   PTS: 1   REF: Clark Leonard Hull (1884-1952)

62. Hull's experiments were directed by ____.
    a. deduced theorems and corollaries
    b. equations
    c. objective definitions
    d. the limitations of the rat and maze method
    e. and limited to respondent conditioning

    ANS: A   PTS: 1   REF: Clark Leonard Hull (1884-1952)

63. Contemporary path analysis techniques let us test theoretical propositions. Such an approach appears similar to whose research method?
    a. Newton's
    b. Tolman's
    c. Guthrie's
    d. Hull's
    e. Wundt's

    ANS: D   PTS: 1   REF: Clark Leonard Hull (1884-1952)
    MSC: WWW

64. The technique that Hull added to the then-accepted battery of experimental methods was ____.
    a. simple observation
    b. systematic controlled observation
    c. experimental testing of hypotheses
    d. the hypothetico-deductive method
    e. one-trial learning

    ANS: D   PTS: 1   REF: Clark Leonard Hull (1884-1952)

65. Hull proposed that to achieve a paradigm (in Kuhn's sense of the term) in psychology, one would have to implement which method?
    a. simple observation
    b. systematic controlled observation
    c. experimental testing of hypotheses
    d. operant conditioning
    e. the hypothetico-deductive method

    ANS: E   PTS: 1   REF: Clark Leonard Hull (1884-1952)

66. Hull proposed the hypothetico-deductive method as the means to develop learning theory. Which of the following statements is the best explanation of Hull's method?
    a. Psychology should try to develop strictly empirical principles of behavior. Theory should only include statements as to how reinforcement controls behavior.
    b. From a set of theoretical postulates, deductions are made. These deductions become hypotheses that are tested experimentally. The experimental results are then used to confirm the postulates or change them if necessary.
    c. Data from experiments are used to produce theories of learning. Once the theory is formed, there is no need to test the theory, since theory is more important than data.
    d. Any of the choices might be correct, depending on the circumstances.
    e. None of the choices are correct.

    ANS: B   PTS: 1   REF: Clark Leonard Hull (1884-1952)
    MSC: WWW

67. "A state of tissue need that arouses or activates behavior" is a definition of ____.
    a. drive
    b. habit strength
    c. magnitude of conditioning
    d. reflex reserve
    e. magnitude of a respondent

    ANS: A   PTS: 1   REF: Clark Leonard Hull (1884-1952)

BEHAVIORISM: AFTER THE FOUNDING   373

68. For Hull, drive reduction is ____.
    a. an intervening variable
    b. the sole basis for reinforcement
    c. an independent variable
    d. a dependent variable
    e. a vector

    ANS: B   PTS: 1   REF: Clark Leonard Hull (1884-1952)

69. Hull's concept of motivation is grounded in the doctrine of ____.
    a. biology
    b. drive reduction
    c. the hypothetico-deductive method
    d. induction
    e. the variability hypothesis

    ANS: A   PTS: 1   REF: Clark Leonard Hull (1884-1952)

70. In Hull's system, a drive is a(n) ____.
    a. intervening variable
    b. stimulus
    c. response
    d. intervening variable and stimulus
    e. All of the choices are correct.

    ANS: E   PTS: 1   REF: Clark Leonard Hull (1884-1952)

71. Which of the following is NOT an example of a primary drive?
    a. hunger
    b. defecation
    c. sleep
    d. pain relief
    e. exercise

    ANS: E   PTS: 1   REF: Clark Leonard Hull (1884-1952)

72. In Hull's system, drive ____.
    a. is a specific consequence of a specific state manipulated by the experimenter
    b. directs behavior toward a specific goal
    c. energizes behavior
    d. is always learned
    e. is a respondent

    ANS: C   PTS: 1   REF: Clark Leonard Hull (1884-1952)

73. In Hull's system, the reduction or satisfaction of a drive is the sole basis of ____.
    a. purposive behavior
    b. intervening variables
    c. the length of deprivation of a physiological need
    d. the degree of satisfaction the organism expects
    e. reinforcement

    ANS: E   PTS: 1   REF: Clark Leonard Hull (1884-1952)

74. Secondary drives are ____.
    a. those less vital than primary drives
    b. learned drives
    c. those not included in the categories of food, liquid, or warmth
    d. those not associated with food, water, or warmth
    e. those that occur in uncontrolled (nonexperimental) situations such as "real life"

    ANS: B   PTS: 1   REF: Clark Leonard Hull (1884-1952)

75. Hull's law of primary reinforcement is a restatement of ____.
    a. Hartley's law of contiguity
    b. Rotter's locus of control
    c. Thorndike's law of effect
    d. Thorndike's law of exercise
    e. Skinner's continuous reinforcement principle

    ANS: C   PTS: 1   REF: Clark Leonard Hull (1884-1952)

76. Thorndike and Hull agreed that, in order for learning to occur, the organism must ____.
    a. form cognitive maps of the situation
    b. represent the environment in terms of mental elements
    c. have a need state
    d. experience reinforcement occurring after a response
    e. None of the choices are correct.

    ANS: D   PTS: 1   REF: Clark Leonard Hull (1884-1952)

77. Secondary drives are ____.
    a. innate drives
    b. biologically driven
    c. a result of pairing with a primary drive
    d. only used to reduce pain responses
    e. reinforced only when primary drives are satisfied

    ANS: C   PTS: 1   REF: Clark Leonard Hull (1884-1952)

78. If seeing McDonald's golden arches decreases your hunger, then the arches are ____.
    a. primary reinforcement
    b. secondary reinforcement
    c. habits
    d. organismic variables
    e. dependent variables

    ANS: B   PTS: 1   REF: Clark Leonard Hull (1884-1952)

79. In Hull's system, habit strength is ____.
    a. the strength of the S-R connection
    b. evidence of latent learning
    c. a function of the number of reinforcements
    d. a function of the size of the drive
    e. a function of the size of the reward (incentive)

    ANS: A   PTS: 1   REF: Clark Leonard Hull (1884-1952)

80. This person claimed that his own life was "predetermined, lawful, and orderly" just as his system would predict.
    a. Pavlov
    b. Watson
    c. Tolman
    d. Hull
    e. Skinner

    ANS: E   PTS: 1   REF: B. F. Skinner (1904-1990)
    MSC: WWW

81. Skinner pursued graduate work in psychology at Harvard ____.
    a. because he was inspired by William James
    b. because he was awed by the work of Watson and Pavlov
    c. after reading Bridgman's work on operationism
    d. after reading Berman's (1927) *The Religion Called Behaviorism*
    e. because a woman he was interested in also went there

    ANS: B   PTS: 1   REF: B. F. Skinner (1904-1990)

82. Skinner defined a reflex as a(n) ____.
    a. objectively observable product of the autonomic nervous system
    b. intervening variable
    c. respondent
    d. S-R connection
    e. S-R correlation and nothing more

    ANS: E   PTS: 1   REF: B. F. Skinner (1904-1990)

83. The author of *The Behavior of Organisms* was ____, who did not receive acclaim for the text until 50 years later.
    a. Skinner
    b. Washburn
    c. Tolman
    d. Hull
    e. Frost

    ANS: A   PTS: 1   REF: B. F. Skinner (1904-1990)

84. The success of Skinner's book *The Behavior of Organisms* can be attributed to ____.
    a. how clearly it was written
    b. the Zeitgeist, demonstrated by its immediate success
    c. the publicity about and popularity of the air crib
    d. the utopia he described in *Walden Two* and the book's popularity among college students in the 1950s
    e. the application of his principles in education and clinical psychology

    ANS: E   PTS: 1   REF: B. F. Skinner (1904-1990)

85. To the end of his life, Skinner questioned whether psychology could be a science if it ____.
   a. ignored biological factors
   b. was a science of the mind
   c. could not explain cognition
   d. did not adapt to the changing world
   e. was not a natural science in its methods

   ANS: B   PTS: 1   REF: B. F. Skinner (1904-1990)

86. Skinner was the complete opposite of Hull with regard to the ____.
   a. importance of contiguity
   b. importance of reinforcement
   c. focus on operants rather than on respondents
   d. quantification of responses
   e. lack of theoretical framework

   ANS: E   PTS: 1   REF: B. F. Skinner (1904-1990)

87. Skinner's research was unique among that of the major neobehaviorists in his ____.
   a. use of the single-subject design
   b. relative lack of a theoretical framework
   c. concern with describing rather than explaining behavior
   d. rejection of variables inside the organism
   e. All of the choices are correct.

   ANS: E   PTS: 1   REF: B. F. Skinner (1904-1990)

88. For Skinner, what is the primary characteristic of living things?
   a. oxygen
   b. life on earth
   c. behavior
   d. stimuli
   e. All of the choices are correct.

   ANS: C   PTS: 1   REF: B. F. Skinner (1904-1990)

89. Which of the following philosophers is discussed by Skinner in the "In Their Own Words" section of the text?
   a. Nietzsche
   b. John Stuart Mill
   c. Descartes
   d. Berkeley
   e. James Mill

   ANS: C   PTS: 1   REF: B. F. Skinner (1904-1990)

90. Who first distinguished between respondent and operant behavior?
   a. Skinner
   b. Hull
   c. Watson
   d. Tolman
   e. Bandura

   ANS: A   PTS: 1   REF: B. F. Skinner (1904-1990)

91. Who drew a distinction between operant behavior and respondent behavior?
    a. Pavlov
    b. Hull
    c. Watson
    d. Tolman
    e. Skinner

    ANS: E   PTS: 1   REF: B. F. Skinner (1904-1990)

92. Skinner claimed that he studied ____ while Pavlov studied ____.
    a. free behavior; reflexive behavior
    b. acquired behavior; reflexive behavior
    c. elicited behavior; emitted behavior
    d. explanations; descriptions
    e. operant behavior; respondent behavior

    ANS: E   PTS: 1   REF: B. F. Skinner (1904-1990)

93. For Skinner, the dependent variable is the ____.
    a. rate of response
    b. force of the response
    c. velocity of the response
    d. number of trials to criterion
    e. number of reinforced trials

    ANS: A   PTS: 1   REF: B. F. Skinner (1904-1990)

94. The law of acquisition states that the key variable in learning is ____.
    a. practice
    b. repetition
    c. reinforcement
    d. the operant
    e. stimulus control

    ANS: C   PTS: 1   REF: B. F. Skinner (1904-1990)

95. The central difference between Skinner's law of acquisition and Thorndike and Hull's position on learning is that ____.
    a. Skinner thought that all behavior is controlled by reinforcement whereas Thorndike and Hull did not think reinforcement was necessary for learning to occur
    b. There is none because all were interested in acquisition, not learning
    c. For Thorndike and Hull human behavior is purposive and controlled by free will whereas Skinner was a strict determinist
    d. Thorndike and Hull were concerned with description; Skinner was concerned with explanation
    e. Skinner's law is strictly descriptive while Thorndike and Hull's positions are explanatory

    ANS: E   PTS: 1   REF: B. F. Skinner (1904-1990)

96. A schedule of reinforcement ____.
    a. lists which behaviors can be conditioned
    b. depicts the steps necessary to establish an operant response
    c. is not used by operant researchers
    d. depicts the steps necessary to establish a respondent
    e. determines when reinforcement occurs

    ANS: E   PTS: 1   REF: B. F. Skinner (1904-1990)

97. Parents and employers must determine when and under what conditions children will be rewarded and employees will be paid. In both cases, they must select ____.
    a. applied psychology principles
    b. schedules of reinforcement
    c. rates of responding
    d. only continuous schedules
    e. extinction schedules

    ANS: B   PTS: 1   REF: B. F. Skinner (1904-1990)

98. Skinner raised his daughter in an "air crib" with the result that she ____.
    a. is a behaviorally disturbed individual
    b. was not adversely affected
    c. took longer to be cared for than children raised by traditional methods
    d. refused to look at people as an adult
    e. was unable to sleep in a regular bed

    ANS: B   PTS: 1   REF: B. F. Skinner (1904-1990)

99. The use of positive reinforcement to control the behavior of individuals and groups is called ____.
    a. behavior modification
    b. chaining
    c. trial-and-learning
    d. omission training
    e. sneaky

    ANS: A   PTS: 1   REF: B. F. Skinner (1904-1990)

100. A criticism of Skinner's work is his ____.
    a. use of the hypothetico-deductive method
    b. emphasis on positive reinforcement and rejection of punishment
    c. willingness to extrapolate from the data, especially with regard to human behavior
    d. work on instinctive behavior
    e. unassailable adherence to operationism

    ANS: C   PTS: 1   REF: B. F. Skinner (1904-1990)

101. Animals tend to substitute instinctive behaviors for behaviors that have been reinforced. This tendency is called ____.
    a. contrariness
    b. reinforcement drift
    c. reinforcement flow
    d. instinctual drift
    e. reward flow

    ANS: D   PTS: 1   REF: B. F. Skinner (1904-1990)

102. From the 1950s to the 1980's, American Psychology was shaped more by the work of ____ than by the work of any other psychologist.
    a. Tolman
    b. Hull
    c. Skinner
    d. Tolman.
    e. Mowrer

    ANS: C   PTS: 1   REF: B. F. Skinner (1904-1990)

103. The "third stage" of behaviorism refers to ____.
    a. the advent of humanism
    b. sociobehaviorism
    c. the reframing of psychoanalytic concepts in behavioristic terms
    d. the implementation of behaviorism's laws of learning in clinical psychology
    e. the return to Watsonian thought

    ANS: B   PTS: 1   REF: Sociobehaviorism: The Cognitive Challenge

104. Bandura proposed that reactions to stimuli ____.
    a. are self-activated
    b. require observable S-R contiguity
    c. require reinforcement for acquisition
    d. occur in one trial
    e. are often overlooked because of the focus on acts rather than movements

    ANS: A   PTS: 1   REF: Albert Bandura (1925-)

105. A type of reinforcement identified by Bandura is ____.
    a. fixed interval
    b. variable interval
    c. fixed ratio
    d. variable ratio
    e. vicarious

    ANS: E   PTS: 1   REF: Albert Bandura (1925-)

106. Bandura argues that what changes a person's behavior is ____.
    a. what the organism thinks the schedule of reinforcement is
    b. the actual schedule of reinforcement
    c. their free will
    d. the result of his or her intelligence
    e. None of the choices are correct.

    ANS: A   PTS: 1   REF: Albert Bandura (1925-)

107. For Bandura, the agent who controls the ____ controls behavior.
    a. reinforcers
    b. punishers
    c. models
    d. stimuli
    e. expectancies

    ANS: C   PTS: 1   REF: Albert Bandura (1925-)

108. A concept of Bandura that reflects one's beliefs about one's own adequacy is ____.
   a. striving for superiority
   b. self-esteem
   c. self-concept
   d. feelings of inferiority
   e. self-efficacy

   ANS: E   PTS: 1   REF: Albert Bandura (1925-)

109. Whereas a concern of Skinner was the improvement of society through his technology of behavior, Bandura's is more specific, namely the ____.
   a. alleviation of abnormal behavior
   b. reduction of media violence
   c. identification of the characteristics that are most potent
   d. identification of factors that influence locus of control
   e. identification of the observable referents of self-efficacy

   ANS: A   PTS: 1   REF: Albert Bandura (1925-)

110. The main criticism of Bandura's system is ____.
   a. the notion that cognitive processes cause behavior
   b. that cognitive processes are as mystical as consciousness
   c. that cognitive processes have no physiological or physical referents
   d. the importance he attributes to modeling
   e. the importance he attributes to the construct of self-efficacy

   ANS: A   PTS: 1   REF: Albert Bandura (1925-)

111. The term *social learning* theory was coined by ____.
   a. Tolman
   b. Bandura
   c. Rotter
   d. Neisser
   e. Skinner

   ANS: C   PTS: 1   REF: Julian Rotter (1916-)

112. People who believe reinforcement depends on their own behavior have ____.
   a. a tendency toward depression
   b. an external locus of control
   c. an internal locus of control
   d. a subjective expectations and experiences
   e. a low locus of control

   ANS: C   PTS: 1   REF: Julian Rotter (1916-)

113. Rotter has suggested that locus of control ____.
   a. is acquired in infancy, much like Horney's basic anxiety
   b. is acquired in childhood
   c. is acquired in adolescence, much like Erikson's ego identity
   d. is acquired over the life span, much like Erikson's ego integrity
   e. fluctuates in accord with one's self-efficacy

   ANS: B   PTS: 1   REF: Julian Rotter (1916-)

BEHAVIORISM: AFTER THE FOUNDING   381

TRUE/FALSE

114. The neobehaviorists agreed that the essence of psychology is learning.

    ANS: T   PTS: 1   REF: Three Stages of Behaviorism

115. Bridgman argued that a construct is the same as its corresponding set of operations.

    ANS: T   PTS: 1   REF: Operationism

116. If a concept can be measured and manipulated under controlled conditions to determine its effects on behavior, then it is *not* a pseudo-problem.

    ANS: T   PTS: 1   REF: Operationism

117. For Tolman, the sheer fact of learning was evidence of purpose in animals.

    ANS: T   PTS: 1   REF: Edward Chace Tolman (1886-1959)

118. Tolman proposed ten causes of behavior in addition to environmental stimuli.

    ANS: F   PTS: 1   REF: Edward Chace Tolman (1886-1959)

119. Tolman argued that factors within the organism are the actual causes of behavior.

    ANS: T   PTS: 1   REF: Edward Chace Tolman (1886-1959)

120. In Tolman's system, learned relationships are sign Gestalts.

    ANS: T   PTS: 1   REF: Edward Chace Tolman (1886-1959)

121. In experiments that tested the presence of rats' cognitive maps, Tolman found that rats "learned to turn right" rather than learning the location of food.

    ANS: F   PTS: 1   REF: Edward Chace Tolman (1886-1959)

122. Tolman is recognized as the forerunner of contemporary applied psychology.

    ANS: F   PTS: 1   REF: Edward Chace Tolman (1886-1959)
    MSC: WWW

123. Tolman's intervening variables were not accepted by mainstream psychology because they could not be operationally defined.

    ANS: F   PTS: 1   REF: Edward Chace Tolman (1886-1959)

124. Tolman hated rats throughout his entire career.

    ANS: F   PTS: 1   REF: Edward Chace Tolman (1886-1959)

125. Tolman recognized that research on rats could not uncover basic processes of human behavior.

    ANS: F   PTS: 1   REF: Edward Chace Tolman (1886-1959)

126. Hull's behaviorist approach to psychology dominated American Psychology from the 1940s to the 1960s.

   ANS: T   PTS: 1   REF: Clark Leonard Hull (1884-1952)

127. Hull was interested in developing a theory of behavior based on Pavlov's laws of conditioning.

   ANS: T   PTS: 1   REF: Clark Leonard Hull (1884-1952)

128. For Hull, behavior could be reduced to the language of physiology.

   ANS: F   PTS: 1   REF: Clark Leonard Hull (1884-1952)

129. Hull's system is exemplary in the degree to which it is quantifiable.

   ANS: T   PTS: 1   REF: Clark Leonard Hull (1884-1952)

130. The method least unique to Hull's system of psychology is the hypothetico-inductive method.

   ANS: F   PTS: 1   REF: Clark Leonard Hull (1884-1952)

131. In Hull's theory, primary reinforcement results in drive reduction.

   ANS: T   PTS: 1   REF: Clark Leonard Hull (1884-1952)

132. In Hull's system, the strength of a drive can be empirically determined.

   ANS: T   PTS: 1   REF: Clark Leonard Hull (1884-1952)

133. For Hull, habit strength is wholly dependent on the number and size of the reinforcements.

   ANS: F   PTS: 1   REF: Clark Leonard Hull (1884-1952)

134. Skinner defined a reflex as a correlation between a stimulus and a response.

   ANS: T   PTS: 1   REF: B. F. Skinner (1904-1990)
   MSC: WWW

135. Skinner's behaviorism is devoted to the study of responses.

   ANS: T   PTS: 1   REF: B. F. Skinner (1904-1990)

136. Skinner borrowed the term *empty organism approach* from Descartes's concept of the *undulatio reflexa*.

   ANS: F   PTS: 1   REF: B. F. Skinner (1904-1990)

137. Skinner stressed the importance of individual differences.

   ANS: T   PTS: 1   REF: B. F. Skinner (1904-1990)

138. For Skinner, the dependent variable is the rate of response.

   ANS: T   PTS: 1   REF: B. F. Skinner (1904-1990)

139. The key variable in Skinner's system is vicarious reinforcement.

ANS: F   PTS: 1   REF: B. F. Skinner (1904-1990)
MSC: WWW

140. A key aspect of Skinner's behavior modification is a reliance on punishment.

ANS: F   PTS: 1   REF: B. F. Skinner (1904-1990)

141. In vicarious reinforcement, learning can occur in the absence of personal reinforcement.

ANS: T   PTS: 1   REF: Albert Bandura (1925-)

142. Bandura suggested that there is not a direct link between stimulus and response.

ANS: T   PTS: 1   REF: Albert Bandura (1925-)

143. In Bandura's system, social interaction is a critical factor in human learning.

ANS: T   PTS: 1   REF: Albert Bandura (1925-)

144. Self-efficacy is defined by Bandura as a sense of self-esteem and competence in dealing with life's problems.

ANS: T   PTS: 1   REF: Albert Bandura (1925-)
MSC: WWW

145. Bandura believed that using modeling techniques was ineffective to change behavior.

ANS: F   PTS: 1   REF: Albert Bandura (1925-)

146. The term *social learning theory* was coined by Bandura.

ANS: F   PTS: 1   REF: Julian Rotter (1916-)

147. In Rotter's system, our subjective expectations and values are not important.

ANS: F   PTS: 1   REF: Julian Rotter (1916-)

148. Locus of control is variable and changes for everyone daily.

ANS: F   PTS: 1   REF: Julian Rotter (1916-)

149. A major cognitive variable in Bandura's system is locus of control.

ANS: F   PTS: 1   REF: Julian Rotter (1916-)
MSC: WWW

Chapter 12

Gestalt Psychology

Wolfgang Köhler studied apes on the island of Tenerife in order to test theories on animal behavior. Unlike the animal experiments of the behaviorists, the apes Köhler studied did not change their behavior as a result of trial-and-error learning. Instead, the apes demonstrated purposeful behavior by using tools to obtain food. There were no random behaviors, as was observed by Thorndike and Skinner. Instead, the behaviors Köhler observed were goal-oriented and deliberate. This way of learning was new.

Similar to behaviorism—and during the same time period, Gestalt psychology was rising in Germany as a revolt against Wundtian thought (opposing Wundt's elementalism). However, there are vast differences between Gestalt psychology and behaviorism, mainly that the former insists that consciousness was valuable to the study of psychology. Gestalt psychologists emphasized the wholeness of the conscious experience and criticized behaviorism and Wundtian psychology for its reductionist approach. In summary, the Gestalt psychologists believed "the whole is different from the sum of its parts."

Gestalt thought began with the philosopher Immanuel Kant who discussed the idea that the mind actively organizes perceptions. Franz Brentano thought that psychology should "study the act of experiencing." Ernst Mach discussed how the shapes of objects may appear to change (as we move around a table, for example), but we perceive them as constants. Mach's work was extended by Christian von Ehrenfels (who taught Max Wertheimer, one of Gestalt's founders). William James discussed that "people see objects as wholes, not as bundles of sensations." Another precursor was the philosophical movement "Phenomenology," which was the study of experiences as they happen. The Zeitgeist of the time also contributed to the development of Gestalt psychology. As physics was "becoming less atomistic" and concentrating on "fields of force," the scientific focus shifted to an analyses of wholes rather than parts. Köhler, one of the founders of the Gestalt movement, made the connection between the fields of force movement in physics and the Gestalt movement in psychology, suggesting that both were progressive movements whereas the behaviorist school was a return to elementism.

Gestalt began with Max Wertheimer who was struck with an idea while he was on a train; he wished to study instances where people see motion when there is actually no motion occurring. Wertheimer later named this the phi phenomenon, which occurs when two lights are presented side-by-side and appeared to create movement. It significantly contradicted Wundtian thought because the phenomenon could not be reduced to its individual elements. Even the most thoroughly trained observer would not report two individual lights, as Wundt had suggested. Thus, the whole experience could not be explained by a reduction to its elements.

There are several founders of Gestalt psychology, each of which made a unique contribution to the field. Wertheimer studied philosophy and psychology and received his Ph.D. under Oswald Külpe. He was reportedly a passionate lecturer, and with the rise of the Nazis he was one of the earliest refugees to come to America, where he worked at the New School for Social Research. Kurt Koffka earned his Ph.D. under Karl Stumpf, and one year later began to work with Wertheimer and Köhler. He also came to America, teaching as a visiting professor before going to Smith College in Northampton, Massachusetts. Wolfgang Köhler was the main spokesperson for the Gestalt movement. He went to Tenerife in 1913 to study chimpanzees, but World War I began 6 months later and stranded him there. He published this work in the book *The Mentality of Apes* (1917), and was able to return to Germany in 1920.

Outside of some visiting professor work at Clark University, he stayed in Germany until 1935 when he left because of the Nazi regime. He had been vocally critical of the Nazis and had been threatened by them. He taught at Swarthmore College in Pennsylvania and stayed there for the duration of his career.

Gestalt psychology was, in Germany, a revolutionary challenge to Wundtian psychology. One of the Gestalt research findings was the idea of perceptual constancy. For example even though an opening door projects an image of a rectangle becoming a trapezoid, we perceive a constant shape. "The perception is a whole, a Gestalt, and any attempt to analyze or reduce it to elements will destroy it." The Gestalt psychologists also did research to determine how we go about organizing what we perceive, and determined that perceptual organization happens instantly. Principles for perceptual organization include: proximity (items grouped together we perceive as belonging together), continuity (we connect items that are actually disconnected), similarity (items that are similar on some quality we perceive as belonging together), closure (we complete incomplete pictures), simplicity (tending to see certain figures such as squares and circles), and figure/ground (seeing objects as figures separated from their background).

Additional areas of research include Köhler's studies of the problem solving ability of apes on Tenerife. Original source material from his *The Mentality of Apes* (1927) focus largely on Sultan, Köhler's "smartest ape." Köhler believed that Sultan displayed insight, which is in stark contrast to the conditioning described by the behaviorists. Kohler was especially critical of Thorndike's trial-and-error learning paradigm, and believed that Thorndike's experimental conditions were too artificial and did not allow Thorndike's animals to view the full apparatus (the full latch mechanism or the whole maze).

In 1945, Wertheimer published *Productive Thinking in Humans*, in which "he applied Gestalt principles of learning to creative thinking in humans." He argued that a teacher must present problems as a whole to allow the student to make connections and develop solutions. He challenged traditional educational practices like rote learning and memorization, because they were less effective than insight learning and eliminated creative thinking. The Gestalt psychologists also attempted to isolate the physical areas of the brain responsible for human perception. They developed the idea of isomorphism, which is "the doctrine that there is a correspondence between psychological or conscious experience and the underlying brain experience."

"By the mid-1920's, the Gestalt movement was a coherent, dominant, and forceful school of thought in Germany." When the Nazi's came to power, however, they showed a contempt for intellectualism that caused many scholars to leave Germany and many came to the United States. Gestalt had been introduced to the United States but did not spread quickly. Several reasons were at play, including: the peak of behaviorism, Gestalt literature being limited to the German language, the belief that Gestalt applied only to perception, the founders went to small colleges in the U.S., and the main opposition to Gestaltian thought (Wundt) was not present in the United States. To resolve these issues, the Gestalt psychologists took aim at behaviorism, attacking its reductionism (to response units) and disregard for consciousness. Meanwhile, in Nazi Germany, the remaining Gestalt psychologists, "like all German universities at the time," focused on research to help the war effort.

One person whose ideas were related to Gestalt psychology and who applied the idea of the force fields in physics to psychology was Kurt Lewin. Lewin received his Ph.D. under Carl Stumpf and received training in psychology as well as mathematics and physics. He eventually fled Nazi Germany and settled in the University of Iowa.

Lewin believed that "a person's psychological activities occur within a kind of psychological field, which he called the life space," which includes all events (past, present, and future) that could affect the person. The life space has positive and negative valences, barriers, and vectors of direction. In this way, Lewin's theory is a theory of motivation, explaining why people do, or don't do, certain things. One early test of Lewin's theory was done by his student, Bluma Ziegarnik, who gave subjects a list of tasks. Some subjects were allowed to complete all tasks, while some were interrupted before completion. Those who were interrupted remembered uncompleted tasks better. From these results, Lewin suggested that a state of tension arises due to having unfinished tasks. Lewin was also interested in social psychology where he concentrated on group dynamics. In a famous study performed by Lewin, boys were assigned to a leader exhibiting one of three leadership styles (authoritarian, democratic, and laissez-faire), and he found that the style of leadership significantly affected how the boys behaved. His interest in social psychology also drew attention to social action research and promoted social change. By conducting empirical studies, Lewin transformed the nature of social problem solving.

Gestalt psychology was criticized for being too vague (they countered that they were incomplete, not vague) and for being "too occupied with theory at the expense of research." They were also criticized because their research was not quantitatively analyzed or experimentally controlled. That said, "the Gestalt movement left an indelible imprint on psychology and influenced work on perception, learning, thinking, personality, social psychology, and motivation."

Outline

I.   A Sudden Insight
- A. Wolfgang Köhler studied apes on the island Tenerife
- B. Ape learning is not because of trial and error
- C. Köhler did not train the apes, he wanted to see how they would solve problems
- D. Example: an ape named Nueva
  1. picked up a stick Köhler put in her cage, played with it, lost interest
  2. 10 minutes later fruit placed out of her reach, outside of cage
  3. she tried to reach it, whimpered, threw herself on the ground
  4. minutes later, she looks at stick, stops whining, uses stick to get fruit
  5. an hour later fruit placed, Nueva lost little time retrieving it
- E. Köhler: Nueva's movements are goal-oriented, not stumbled on accidentally

II.   The Gestalt Revolt
- A. Gestalt revolution in Germany took place around the same time as behaviorist revolution in U.S.
  1. 1912: Watson begins attack on Wundt and Titchener
  2. Thorndike and Pavlov: animal research having impact
  3. Psychoanalysis 10 years old
  4. Gestalt and behaviorist revolutions independent of one another
     a. both started by opposing Wundt's focus on sensory elements
     b. ended up opposing each other
        (1) value of consciousness
            (a) Gestalt psychologists accepted it
            (b) behavioral psychologists refused it entirely
        (2) Gestalt psychologists criticized behaviorists' attempts to reduce the science to atoms and elements
- B. Began as a protest against Wundtian psychology

C. Gestalt criticisms of Wundt's approach
   1. elementistic nature of Wundt's psychology
      a. sensory elements as inert atoms
      b. only combination is by mechanical associations
         (1) Gestalt: criticized this as "brick-and-mortar" psychology
            (a) brick = elements
            (b) mortar = process of association
      c. we see whole objects (chair, book), not sensory elements (brightness, hue)
   2. Wundt: perception of objects is a mere summation of elements into a bunch of elements
   3. Gestalt: the combination of sensory elements produces something novel (similar to Wundt's creative synthesis); the whole is different from the sum of its parts
D. Gestalt believes there's more to perception than meets the eye
   1. perception goes beyond the sensory elements
   2. example: the perception of a book is not just a dark, red parallelogram→ the book itself is meaningful
   3. these elements are more than physical data coming to the sense organs
III. Antecedent Influences on Gestalt psychology
   A. Kant (1724-1804)
      1. the meaningful organization of sensory elements
      2. is not a mechanical process of association
      3. mind creates a unitary experience by taking "raw data" of perception and creating coherent elements
   B. Brentano (1838-1917)
      1. psychology should study the act of experiencing
      2. introspection as artificial: favored less rigid and more direct methods of observation
      3. approach similar to eventual Gestalt approach
   C. Mach (1838-1916)
      1. a physicist
      2. discussed spatial (e.g., geometric figures) and temporal (e.g., melodies) patterns
         a. considered them to be sensations
         b. independent of their elements
      3. perception of an object does not change when our orientation to it changes; i.e., angle, direction (similar to later Gestalt idea of perceptual constancies)
   D. von Ehrenfels (1859-1932)
      1. there exist qualities of experience not explained as combinations of elementary sensations
         a. called these qualities Gestalt qualitäten (form qualities)
         b. perceptions based on more than amalgamation of separate sensations
         c. same melody (form quality) even when played in different keys
      2. mind creates a new element as it operates on the sensory elements
      3. Wertheimer, a student of von Ehrenfel, considered von Ehrenfels' work the most important antecedent of and stimulation for the Gestalt movement

E. William James
    1. opposed elementism: regarded elements of consciousness as artificial abstractions
    2. people perceive wholes, not collections of sensations
    3. Koffka and Köhler studied James's work while Stumpf's students

F. Phenomenology (Stumpf's introspective method): "...an approach to knowledge based on an unbiased description of immediate experience as it occurs, not analyzed or reduced to elements."
    1. uncorrected observation
    2. experience not reduced into elements
    3. involves naïve experience of common sense
    4. untrained observers

IV. The Changing Zeitgeist in Physics

A. Physics Zeitgeist toward end 19th century moving away from atomism (reduction of everything to atoms) to force fields (consideration of what atoms create)

B. Fields of force: "Regions or spaces traversed by lines of force, such as of a magnet or electric current."
    1. magnetism as typical example: iron shavings around any magnet form a distinctive pattern although not touched by the magnet
    2. fields possess properties of spatial extension and pattern
    3. fields believed to be novel structural entities, not summations of elements or particles

C. Physicists' descriptions of fields and organic wholes: authentication for
    1. Kohler: background in physics and studied with Max Planck
        a. saw connection between field physics and Gestalt wholes
        b. Gestalt psychology as an application of field physics to parts of psychology
    2. Watson: no training in the new physics
        a. continued reductionism of old physics
        b. views compatible with previous atomism

V. The Phi Phenomenon: A Challenge to Wundtian Psychology

A. A product of Wertheimer's 1910 research
    1. research idea: seeing movement when no actual physical motion occurs
    2. phi phenomenon: "The illusion that two stationary flashing lights are moving from one place to another."
        a. Koffka and Köhler served as subjects
        b. subject: apparent movement
        c. apparatus: tachistoscope to project light through 2 slits
            (1) 1st slit vertical
            (2) 2nd slit 20-30 degrees from the vertical
        d. procedure: project light sequentially
            (1) long (200+ milliseconds) interval: subjects saw two successive lights
            (2) short interval: subjects saw two continuous lights
            (3) optimal (60 milliseconds) interval: subjects saw a single light that appeared to move back and forth between the slits
            (4) Wertheimer called the latter an "impression of movement"
        e. the sensory elements are different than the whole experience

3. explanations
    a.   Wertheimer
        (1) apparent motion is as elementary as a sensation
        (2) yet different from a sensation or series of sensations
        (3) did not need explanation
        (4) could not be reduced to anything simpler
    b.   Wundt
        (1) introspection of stimulus could only produce two successive points of light—a trained observer would be able to reduce the experience into these elements
        (2) no observer could do what Wundt proposed
4. fact: the whole experience (apparent movement) different from the sum of parts (two stationary slits)
5. challenged the associationistic, elementistic psychology of Wundt
    1912: Wertheimer published results in article "Experimental Studies of the Perception of Movement" (formal start of Gestalt school)

VI.   Max Wertheimer (1880-1943)
    A. Background
        1. studied law at University of Prague, changed to philosophy
        2. attended lectures by von Ehrenfels
        3. studied philosophy and psychology at University of Berlin
        4. 1904: Ph.D. from University of Würzburg with Külpe
        5. Position at University of Frankfurt to research and lecture; professorship at Frankfurt (1929)
        6. World War I: military research on listening devices for submarines and harbor fortifications
        7. 1920's=most productive research on Gestalt psychology (University of Berlin)
        8. Good lecturer: vivid imagery, stimulating, passionate
        9. 1921: Koffka, and Köhler, assisted by Kurt Goldstein and Hans Gruhle, founded the journal *Psychological Research* (official publication of Gestalt psychology)
      10. 1933: arrives in NYC; associated with the New School for Social Research
      11. 1994 (after his death): University of Frankfurt established the Max Wertheimer Lecture Series
      12. influences Maslow (developed self-actualization and humanistic school)

VII.   Kurt Koffka (1886-1941)
    A. Most inventive of all Gestalt founders
    B. Background
        1. interest in science and philosophy
        2. 1909: Ph.D. from University of Berlin with Stumpf
        3. 1910: began association with Wertheimer and Köhler at University of Frankfurt
        4. 1911-1924: Koffka accepted a position at the University of Giessen→ work with brain damaged and asphasic patients
    C. 1922: "Perception: An Introduction to Gestalt-Theorie" published in American journal *Psychological Bulletin*
        1. described Gestalt psychology's basic concepts and research results and implications
        2. 1st introduction to Gestalt theory for U.S. psychologists

3. "perception" in title led to misunderstanding that was the sole interest of Gestalt psychologists
4. Gestalt movement actually had a broader concern
   a. cognitive processes, i.e., problems of thinking and learning
   b. all aspects of conscious experience
D. 1921: publishes *The Growth of the Mind*, about developmental child psychology; became successful in Germany and in the U.S.
E. 1927: Professor at Smith College until his death
F. 1935: Principles of Gestalt psychology
   1. difficult to read
   2. therefore, not the definitive treatment of Gestalt that he intended

VIII. Wolfgang Köhler (1887- 1967)
A. Most prolific promoter of Gestalt
B. Background
   1. trained in physics with Max Planck
   2. convinced that
      a. Gestalten (forms or patterns) occur in psychology as well as in physics
      b. psychology must become allied with physics
   3. 1909: Ph.D. from University of Berlin with Stumpf
C. Career
   1. 1913-1920: journey to Tenerife (Canary Islands) to study the behavior of chimpanzees
   2. unable to leave because of WWI
   3. suggested that Köhler may have been a German spy and broadcasted from his home about the movement of allied ships
      a. no proof either way
   4. 1917: The Mentality of Apes
      a. after publication, became bored with animal research
      b. paranoid that he no longer notices behaviors as easily
   5. 1920: return to Germany, donated chimps to zoo but soon died because of change in climate
   6. 1922: succeeded Stumpf as Professor of Psychology at University of Berlin
      a. probable reason for prestigious appointment: publication of *Static and Stationary Physical Gestalts* (1920)
      b. suggested Gestalt theory as general law of nature
   7. mid 1920s: divorced wife, married young student, broke off contact with the 4 children of his prior marriage, developed tremor that increased when angry
   8. 1929: published *Gestalt Psychology*, comprehensive account of Gestalt movement
   9. 1935: left Germany due to anti-Nazi activities
      a. criticized regime in classroom lectures
      b. only non-Jewish psychologist in Germany to publicly protest firing of Jewish scholars
      c. most instructors and students actively backed the Nazi regime
      d. leaders of the German Psychological Society went even further, firing Jewish journal editors, lauding Hitler, and proclaiming the Jews "evil influence"
   10. emigrated to U.S. to teach at Swarthmore College

11. published books

12. edited Gestalt journal Psychological Research

13. 1957: Distinguished Scientific Contribution Award from APA

14. 1959: president of APA

IX. The Nature of the Gestalt Revolt

A. In German psychology: heretical and a rebellion directly against Wundt

B. Demanded complete revision of psychology

C. Research

1. Wertheimer: apparent movement

2. perceptual constancy: "A quality of wholeness or completeness in perceptual experience that does not vary even when the sensory elements change."

3. all perceptual experience: there exists a wholeness not found in any of the component parts

4. the character of the perception differs from the character of the sensory stimulation

5. attempts at analysis destroy the perception or whole (aka Gestalt)

D. *Gestalt* is an unclear description of the movement

E. Two meanings of Gestalt noted by Köhler (1929)

1. shape or form as a property of objects

2. a whole or concrete entity that has one of its attributes a specific shape or form

3. therefore, "Gestalt" refers to both objects and to their characteristic forms

4. the term is not restricted to visual or sensory fields

5. can refer to learning, thinking, emotions, and behavior

6. extends to all of psychology

F. Gestalt psychologists include the entire province of psychology

X. Gestalt Principles of Perceptual Organization

A. 1923: Wertheimer's principles published in an article

1. perceive objects as wholes, not clusters of sensations

2. perceptual organization occurs instantly and is spontaneous and inevitable

3. brain as a dynamic system; all active elements interact

4. specific organizational principles:

a. proximity, continuity, similarity, closure, simplicity (prägnanz or good form), and figure/ground

5. organizing principles not dependent on either higher mental processes or past experience

6. organizing principles instead are present in the stimuli themselves

a. called these peripheral factors

7. Gestalt psychologists focus more on peripheral factors of perceptual organization than on learning or experience

XI. Gestalt Studies of Learning: Insight and the Mentality of Apes

A. Intelligence of chimpanzees demonstrated in ability to solve problems

B. Apparatus: animal's cages, convenient objects (i.e., cage bars, sticks, bananas, boxes)

C. Köhler's interpretation of results

1. in terms of the whole

2. in terms of the relationships among the various stimuli

D. Original Source Material: From Köhler's (1927) The Mentality of Apes

1. Focuses on

a. the personalities of his subjects

b. the individual differences he observed

2. Method
    a.   no formal experimental design
    b.   no pre- and post-test measures
    c.   no formal experimental treatments or control groups
    d.   no statistical analyses
    e.   he simply described his observations

E. Comment
  1. Einsicht or insight (Köhler) and ideational learning (Yerkes)
  2. insight versus trial-and-error learning
  3. insight studies support
    a.   molar (Gestalt) versus molecular (behavioristic) view
    b.   learning involves a reorganization of the psychological environment

XII.   Productive Thinking in Humans
A. Based on book by Wertheimer published posthumously (1945)
B. Thinking as done in terms of wholes
  1. the learner regards the situation as a whole
  2. the teacher must present the situation as a whole
  3. problem solving: the whole problem must dominate the parts
    a.   at different ages
    b.   at various levels of problem difficulty
C. The principle of the solution: when problems are presented in meaningful wholes they are easier to learn and remember; can be applied to other situations
D. Köhler argued against mentalistic drills and rote learning
  1. interferes with the transfer principles
  2. material like names and dates can be learned through association and strengthened by repetition
  3. leads to mechanical performance, not creative thinking
  4. insight learning much more useful

XIII.   Isomorphism
A. Theory about underlying neurological correlates of perceived Gestalts
  1. Gestalt: view the cortex as a dynamic system
    a.   active elements interact
  2. associationists: brain is passive
    a.   incapable of actively organizing sensory elements received
    b.   incapable of modifying sensory elements received
B. Werthheimer
  1. brain activity is a configural, whole process
  2. apparent and actual motion experienced identically
  3. therefore, cortical processes for the two must be similar
  4. isomorphism: "The doctrine that there is a correspondence between psychological or conscious experience and the underlying brain experience."
C. Köhler (1920): *Static and Stationary Physical Gestalts*; extended Wertheimer's position
  1. cortical processes are similar to fields of force
  2. fields of neuronal activity due to electromechanical processes in the brain that are the response of sensory impulses

XIV.   The Spread of Gestalt psychology
A. Mid-1920's
  1. a coherent and dominant school in Germany

GESTALT PSYCHOLOGY

2. one of the world's largest research laboratories
3. *Psychological Research*, widely read and respected
B. 1933 Nazi regime: anti-intellectualism in Germany, shift of Gestalt psychology to the United States
C. Koffka and Köhler visited the United States to lecture at universities and conferences
D. Slow acceptance in the United States
   1. behaviorism was at its peak
   2. a language barrier
   3. belief that Gestalt psychology dealt solely with perception
   4. Wertheimer, Köhler, and Koffka at small colleges without graduate programs, thus no graduate research assistants
   5. Gestalt focus of protest (Wundt) no longer of concern in U.S.
XV. The Battle With Behaviorism
   A. Gestalt criticisms of its new target: behaviorism
      1. reductionistic and atomistic
      2. deals with artificial abstractions (S-R units)
      3. denies the validity of introspection
      4. eliminates consciousness
      5. would make psychology no more than a collection of animal research
      6. conflicts between proponents of the two schools: increasingly emotional and personal
XVI. Gestalt Psychology in Nazi Germany
   A. The founders fled, but students of Gestalt remained
   B. They continued research, focusing on vision and depth perception
   C. Kohler's Psychological Institute remained open
   D. Like all German universities, lack of openness to intellectual thought, focus on research to help war effort
XVII. Field Theory: Kurt Lewin (1890-1947)
   1. field relationships are the trend in late 19th-century science (i.e., physics)
   2. field theory: "Lewin's system using the concept of fields of force to explain behavior in terms of one's field of social influences."
   3. extended beyond the orthodox Gestalt framework to include human needs, personality, and social influences on behavior
   B. Lewin's life
      1. studied mathematics and physics at German universities
      2. 1914: PhD at University of Berlin with Stumpf
      3. research: human motivation and behavior within its total context
         a. early career: research on association and motivation
         b. middle career: field theory
         c. later career: social psychology and group dynamics
      4. 1929: presented field theory to American psychologists at International Congress of Psychology at Yale
   C. The life space
      1. "His overall conception of psychology was practical, focusing on social issues that affect how we live and work."
      2. the psychological field of the individual (aka life space)
         a. encompasses all past, present, and future events that may affect a given person
         b. each of the above events may determine behavior in a given situation

394   CHAPTER 12

      c.   life space= person's needs as an interaction with environment

      d.   degrees of development as a function of the amount and kind of experience we have accumulated

  3. sought a mathematical model

      a.   interested in the single case

      b.   statistics not useful

      c.   used topology, a form of geometry, to diagram life space

      d.   within a topological map

          (1) vector (arrow): direction of a person's movement toward goal

          (2) valence (weighted + or –): values of objects in the life space

          (3) barrier: vertical line

      e.   his diagrams: sometimes called "blackboard psychology"

D. Motivation and the Zeigarnik effect

  1. Lewin proposed state of balance or equilibrium

      a.   between the person and her or his environment

      b.   disturbance in equilibrium produces tension

      c.   resultant movement is attempt to restore the balance

      d.   behavior = cycle of tension (need) states followed by activity and relief

  2. research study: subjects were given a list of tasks but were interrupted before completion

      a.   Lewin's predictions:

          (1) A tension-system develops when subjects are given a task to perform.

          (2) When the task is completed, the tension is dissipated.

          (3) If the task is not completed, the persistence of tension results in a greater likelihood that the subjects will recall the task.

  3. the Zeigarnik effect: "The tendency to recall uncompleted tasks more easily than completed tasks."

E. Social psychology

  1. Lewin's interest in it began in 1930s

      a.   pioneering contributions

      b.   sufficient to justify high status in history of psychology

      c.   outstanding feature: group dynamics

          (1) applied to individual and group behavior

          (2) psychological field: person + his/her environment

          (3) social field: group + its environment

          (4) concurrent social entities

          (5) group behavior: function of the total field situation at a given time

             (a) classic experiment

               (i) effects of authoritarian, democratic, and laissez-faire leadership styles on behavior of boys

               (ii) authoritarian style: aggressive behavior

               (iii)democratic style: friendly with more tasks completed

      d.   social action research

          (1) study of social problems

          (2) goal: implementing change

           (3) problems studied: integrated housing, equal opportunity, prejudice reduction

     e.   sensitivity training groups (T-groups)

           (1) target participants: educators and businessmen/women

           (2) goal: reduce intergroup conflict; develop individual potential

           (3) forerunner of the encounter groups of 1960s/1970s

XVIII. Criticisms of Gestalt psychology

  A. Basic criticisms

    1. Organization of perceptual processes accepted as fact rather than studied scientifically; no room for refuting

    2. Gestalt position is vague

    3. Basic concepts and terms are not defined with sufficient rigor

    4. Too preoccupied with theory at the expense of research and empirical support

    5. Research lacks adequate controls

    6. Its unquantified data elude statistical analysis

    7. Gestalt experimental work is inferior to that of the behaviorists

    8. insight learning: not replicable

    9. poorly defined physiological assumptions

  B. Gestalt rebuttals

    1. a young science's explanation and definitions are necessarily incomplete

    2. incomplete is not the same vague

    3. has from the beginning emphasized experimentation

    4. has engendered a considerable amount of research

    5. qualitative results take precedence over quantitative ones

    6. Gestalt research is exploratory

    7. Gestalt research is within a different framework than the behaviorists'

    8. Gestalt speculations about physiological assumptions are a tentative but useful adjunct to their system

XIX. Contributions of Gestalt psychology

  A. Permanent imprint on psychology

  B. Influenced work in "perception, learning, thinking, personality, social psychology, and motivation

  C. Retained its identity, not absorbed by the mainstream as was behaviorism

  D. Focus on consciousness

    1. fostered interest in consciousness as a legitimate problem for psychology

    2. centered on phenomenology, not on the Wundt/Titchener elements of consciousness

    3. recognizes consciousness cannot be studied with the precision and objectivity the behaviorists demand

    4. phenomenological approach to psychology accepted more by European than by U.S. psychologists

    5. this phenomenology influenced humanistic psychology movement in U.S.

Lecture prompts/Discussion topics for chapter twelve

- What might be some real-life applications for the Zeigarnik effect?
- Should Gestalt be considered a school of psychology? Do you think it would still be a cohesive school if the 3 founders had gone to colleges with graduate programs/students?
- For much of psychology, animals are used as subjects. But don't animals have different senses than we do? Do you think this affects the way they "think"?

Internet Resources for chapter twelve

Classics in the History of Psychology: Perception: an introduction to Gestalt-theorie
http://psychclassics.yorku.ca/Koffka/Perception/perception.htm

This is the full-text article that Kurt Koffka wrote to introduce Gestalt theory to the United States. It is the title of this article that led American psychologists to mistakenly believe that Gestalt dealt with perception only.

Kohler's work on insight learning
http://www.pigeon.psy.tufts.edu/psych26/kohler.htm

This is a nifty page that summarizes Kohler's insight learning. It has some photos of some of the apes solving problems in Tenerife, and has links leading to such things as Kohler's written criticism of Thorndike's puzzle box approach.

Kurt Lewin: groups, experiential learning and action research
http://www.infed.org/thinkers/et-lewin.htm

This page gives much more information about Lewin's work, particularly work not mentioned in the text, such as Lewin's organizational change model and his action research.

Phi Phenomenon
http://www.yorku.ca/eye/balls.htm

This page gives an example of apparent movement using stationary balls. It resembles the Phi phenomenon described by Wertheimer.

Apparent Movement
http://www.michaelbach.de/ot/col_lilacChaser/index.html

This website is another example of apparent movement, as demonstrated by the Phi phenomenon. This link also lets you play a bit with the speed of the movement; in general the faster the blinking, the more compelling the apparent movement.

Biography: Max Wertheimer
http://psychology.jrank.org/pages/653/Max-Wertheimer.html

This page has a variety of information about Wertheimer, including some suggestions for further reading.

Potential answers to chapter twelve discussion questions

1. Explain the differences between the Gestalt and behaviorist revolts against Wundtian psychology.
The behaviorist revolts against Wundtian psychology were against the fundamental method and scope of Wundt's system. Wundt strove to understand conscious processes. Behaviorism (particularly radical behaviorism) rejected the study of conscious processes. The Gestalt psychologists also studied conscious processes, but they revolted against Wundt because of Wundt's attempts to reduce those processes to their elements instead of examining them as a whole. The Gestalt psychologists believed that the elements will not give you full information about the experience taken as a whole.

2. What did the Gestalt psychologists mean by the expressions "the whole is different from the sum of its parts" and "there is more to perception than meets the eye"?
Gestalt psychologists believed that conscious experience needed to be studied in its wholeness. This is summarized in both phrases.

3. If you looked at a book on a table and said, "I see a book on the table," what error would you be committing, according to Titchener?
Titchener believed this to be an error in introspection, called the stimulus error.

4. Describe the antecedent influences on Gestalt psychology.
Gestalt thought began with the philosopher Immanuel Kant who discussed the idea that the mind actively organizes perceptions. Franz Brentano thought that psychology should "study the act of experiencing." Ernst Mach discussed how the shapes of objects may appear to change (as we move around a table, for example) but we perceive them as constants. Mach's work was extended by Christian Von Ehrenfels (who taught Max Wertheimer, one of Gestalt's founders). William James discussed that "people see objects as wholes, not as bundles of sensations." Another precursor was the philosophical movement "Phenomenology", which was the study of experiences as they happen.

5. How did the Zeitgeist in physics change toward the end of the nineteenth century? How did that change influence Gestalt psychology?
The Zeitgeist of the time contributed to the development of Gestalt psychology. As physics was "becoming less atomistic" and concentrating on "fields of force," the scientific focus shifted to an analyses of wholes rather than parts. Köhler, one of the founders of the Gestalt movement, made the connection between the fields of force movement in physics and the Gestalt movement in psychology, suggesting that both were progressive movements whereas the behaviorist school was a return to elementism.

6. What is the phi phenomenon? How is it produced? Why couldn't the phi phenomenon be explained by Wundt's psychology?
Gestalt began with Max Wertheimer who was struck with an idea while he was on a train; he wished to study instances where people see motion when there is actually no motion occurring. This was later called the phi phenomenon, and it could not be explained by Wundtian thought. Two lights presented side-by-side appeared to create movement. With Wundt, introspectionists would report two individual lights, but that would not explain why motion was perceived and an essential piece of the experience would be missing.

7. Why did some people mistakenly assume that Gestalt psychology dealt only with perception?

This arose from an article written by Koffka called "Perception: An Introduction to the Gestalt-Theories" published in an American journal that was intended to introduce Gestalt to America. This wording led the American audience to believe that Gestalt theory was strictly about perception. The name Gestalt was also ambiguous, and left little clarity about the definition of the field.

8. Describe some of the principles of perceptual organization.

The Gestalt psychologists did research to determine how we go about organizing what we perceive, and determined that perceptual organization happens instantly. Principles for perceptual organization include: proximity (items grouped together we perceive as belonging together), continuity (we connect items that are actually disconnected), similarity (items that are similar on some quality we perceive as belonging together), closure (we complete incomplete pictures), simplicity (tending to see certain figures such as squares and circles), and figure/ground (seeing objects as figures separated from their background).

9. How do studies of perceptual constancies support the Gestalt viewpoint?

One of the Gestalt research findings was the idea of perceptual constancy; for example even though an opening door projects an image of a rectangle becoming a trapezoid, we perceive a constant shape. "The perception is a whole, a Gestalt, and any attempt to analyze or reduce it to elements will destroy it."

10. Why has the word _Gestalt_ caused problems for the movement?

"Unlike functionalism or behaviorism, the term does not clearly denote what the movement stands for. Also, it has no precise English-language counterpart," and has been defined as "form," "shape," or a "concrete entity."

11. Give an example of Köhler's research on insight on the island of Tenerife.

Sultan, the ape that Köhler called the "smartest," stacked two boxes (one on top of the other) in order to reach a banana that was hung too high to be reached.

12. How does insight learning differ from the trial-and-error learning described by Thorndike?

Köhler believed that Sultan and the other apes displayed insight, an immediate cognition, that allowed the problem at hand to be solved. This is in stark contrast to the conditioning described by the behaviorists, wherein learning occurs slowly over through time with successive approximations. Kohler was especially critical of Thorndike's trial-and-error learning paradigm, and believed that Thorndike's experimental conditions were too artificial and did not allow Thorndike's animals to view the full apparatus (the full latch mechanism or the whole maze). Insight learning suggests a consciousness and mind—and implies that animals, like humans, understand the problem and set out to solve it purposefully.

13. How did Wertheimer apply Gestalt principles of learning to creative thinking in humans?

Wertheimer published _Productive Thinking in Humans_ (1945) in which "he applied Gestalt principles of learning to creative thinking in humans." In the book he argued that a teacher must present problems as a whole to allow the student to make connections and develop solutions. In addition, he believed that rote learning and memorization were ineffective compared to insight learning.

14. How does isomorphism relate perception to underlying neurological correlates?
The Gestalt psychologists attempted to isolate the processes in the brain that caused humans to perceive the way we do. They developed the idea of isomorphism, "The doctrine that there is a correspondence between psychological or conscious experience and the underlying brain experience."

15. What factors impeded the acceptance of Gestalt psychology in the United States?
Gestalt had been introduced to the United States but did not spread quickly. Several reasons were at play, including: the peak of behaviorism, Gestalt literature being limited to the German language, the belief that Gestalt applied only to perception, the founders went to small colleges in the U.S., and the main opposition to Gestaltian thought (Wundt) was not present in the United States. To resolve these issues, the Gestalt psychologists took aim at behaviorism, attacking its reductionism (to response units) and disregard for consciousness. Meanwhile, in Nazi Germany, the remaining Gestalt psychologists, "like all German universities at the time," focused on research to help the war effort.

16. On what grounds has Gestalt psychology been criticized?
Gestalt psychology was criticized for being too vague (they countered that they were incomplete, not vague) and for being "too occupied with theory at the expense of research." They were also criticized because their research was not quantitatively analyzed or experimentally controlled.

17. On what grounds did Gestalt psychologists criticize behaviorism?
Gestalt psychologists then took aim at behaviorism, and attacked its reductionism (to response units) and its lack of "recognition of consciousness."

18. Describe Lewin's concept of a field theory and tell how it was influenced by physics.
Lewin believed that "a person's psychological activities occur within a kind of psychological field, which he called the life space," which includes all events (past, present, and future) that could affect the person. The life space has positive and negative valences, barriers, and vectors of direction. Physics was moving toward field theory as well.

19. How does field theory deal with motivation and with social psychology? What is social action research?
Field theory describes "at any given moment a person's possible goals and the paths leading to them." A person seeks a state of balance, and any imbalances lead to tension with the person becoming motivated to reduce that tension. For Lewin's social psychology, the social context (the group) becomes a part of a person's field. Social action research is the idea of doing research about social problems with the aim of helping those problems.

20. In what ways did Gestalt psychology affect psychology as a whole?
"The Gestalt movement left an indelible imprint on psychology and influenced work on perception, learning, thinking, personality, social psychology, and motivation."

Key terms from chapter twelve

- **Closure** Gestalt principle that says that we complete incomplete pictures
- **Continuity** Gestalt principle that says that we connect items in space or tiem that are actually disconnected
- **Field theory** Kurt "Lewin's system using the concept of fields of force to explain behavior in terms of one's field of social influences."
- **Fields of force** an idea from physics, the idea that space is crossed with lines of force
- **Figure/Ground** seeing objects as figures separated from their background
- **Insight** "Immediate apprehension or cognition
- **Isomorphism** The Gestalt "doctrine that there is a correspondence between psychological or conscious experience and the underlying brain experience."
- **Life space** the psychological "past, present, and future events that may affect us"
- **Perceptual constancies** "a quality of wholeness or completeness in perceptual experience that does not vary even when the sensory elements change."
- **Phenomenology** "a doctrine based on an unbiased description of immediate experience just as it occurs."
- **Phi phenomenon** "the illusion that two stationary flashing lights are moving from one place to another."
- **Proximity** Gestalt principle that says that we perceive as belonging together items grouped together in space or time
- **Stroboscope** A toy that projects a series of images to create the illusion of movement, and is the first piece of research equipment purchased by Max Wertheimer
- **Similarity** Gestalt principle that says that we perceive as belonging together items that are similar on some quality
- **Simplicity** Gestalt principle that says that we tend to see certain figures such as squares and circles
- **Sultan** The name of what Köhler describes as the "most intelligent ape" at his Tenerife research facility
- **Zeigarnik effect** "the tendency to recall uncompleted tasks more easily than completed tasks."

ESSAY

1. What people and which of their ideas were antecedent influences on Gestalt psychology? In what way did the changing zeitgeist in physics affect this emerging school of thought?

   ANS:
   Answer not provided.

   PTS: 1   MSC: WWW

2. Describe Köhler's "insight" learning and Thorndike's law of effect. What is(are) the major difference(s) between the two?

   ANS:
   Answer not provided.

   PTS: 1

3. What was the central thrust or point of Max Wertheimer's book on productive thinking? What is productive thinking? Describe his approach to problem solving as well as his views on mechanical drill and rote learning.

   ANS:
   Answer not provided.

   PTS: 1   MSC: WWW

4. Describe the various contextual forces that interfered with Gestalt psychology's having a major impact in the United States.

   ANS:
   Answer not provided.

   PTS: 1

5. What are the major contributions of Gestalt psychology to psychology as a discipline?

   ANS:
   Answer not provided.

   PTS: 1

MULTIPLE CHOICE

6. Gestalt psychology started as a movement opposed to ____.
   a. functionalism
   b. behaviorism
   c. Wundt's approach
   d. Titchener's system
   e. structuralism

   ANS: C   PTS: 1   REF: The Gestalt Revolt
   MSC: WWW

7. The Gestalt protest against Wundt's system focused on his ____.
   a. elementism
   b. denial of will
   c. notion of imageless thought
   d. use of introspection
   e. determinism

   ANS: A   PTS: 1   REF: The Gestalt Revolt

8. Köhler reported that he was "shocked" by ____.
   a. the phi phenomenon
   b. the primates' insight learning
   c. Wundt's notion that psychological facts are composed of inert atoms
   d. Thorndike's law of effect
   e. Watson's behaviorism

   ANS: C   PTS: 1   REF: The Gestalt Revolt

9. The Gestalt school's major difference with behaviorists was over the ____.
   a. existence of the phi phenomenon
   b. utility of the concept of consciousness
   c. utility of the concept of perception
   d. experimental method
   e. use of introspection

   ANS: B   PTS: 1   REF: The Gestalt Revolt

10. Which of the following statements indicates how Gestalt psychology and behaviorism treated the study of consciousness?
    a. Gestalt psychology rejected the existence of consciousness. Behaviorism accepted the study of consciousness and claimed it can be analyzed into stimulus-response associations.
    b. Both Gestalt psychology and behaviorism accepted the study of consciousness. However, Gestalt psychology did not believe that consciousness could be analyzed into mental elements whereas behaviorism accepted the possibility of analyzing consciousness into part processes.
    c. Both Gestalt psychology and behaviorism rejected the study of consciousness in psychology.
    d. Gestalt psychology accepted the study of consciousness but criticized the attempt to analyze it into elements. Behaviorism refused to acknowledge the existence of consciousness.
    e. None of the choices are correct.

    ANS: D   PTS: 1   REF: The Gestalt Revolt
    MSC: WWW

11. The Gestalt psychologists referred to Wundt's system as ____.
    a. structuralism
    b. elementism
    c. brick and mortar psychology
    d. voluntarism
    e. elementary psychology

    ANS: C   PTS: 1   REF: The Gestalt Revolt

12. Gestalt psychologists believed that ____.
    a. less is more
    b. there is less to perception than meets the eye
    c. more is less
    d. there is more to perception than meets the eye
    e. All of the choices can be true, depending on the situation.

    ANS: D   PTS: 1   REF: The Gestalt Revolt

13. The essence of the Gestalt system is found in the work of the philosopher ____.
    a. Kant
    b. Leibnitz
    c. La Mettrie
    d. Locke
    e. James Mill

    ANS: A   PTS: 1   REF: Antecedent Influences on Gestalt Psychology

14. Contrary to the notion of a passive mind, as portrayed by the British empiricists, the German philosopher Kant held that the mind ____.
    a. is a stream of consciousness
    b. actively organizes sensory information into a coherent experience
    c. actively organizes sensory information according to a mechanical process of association
    d. is sensitive to perceptions, not sensations
    e. All of the choices are correct.

    ANS: B   PTS: 1   REF: Antecedent Influences on Gestalt Psychology

15. For Brentano, the subject matter of psychology was ____.
    a. sensations
    b. perceptions
    c. temporal patterns
    d. associations
    e. experiences

    ANS: E   PTS: 1   REF: Antecedent Influences on Gestalt Psychology

16. For Mach, sensations are ____.
    a. temporal
    b. dependent on the elements of which they are composed
    c. spatial
    d. independent of the elements of which they are composed
    e. illusory

    ANS: D   PTS: 1   REF: Antecedent Influences on Gestalt Psychology

17. The notion of Gestalt quälitaten was offered by ____.
    a. Brentano
    b. von Ehrenfels
    c. Mach
    d. Wertheimer
    e. Lewin

    ANS: B   PTS: 1   REF: Antecedent Influences on Gestalt Psychology

18. For the school of Gestalt psychology, "form" was ____.
    a. something that existed outside of sensation
    b. a creation of the mind
    c. dependent on the elements
    d. an artificial abstraction
    e. All of the choices are correct.

    ANS: B   PTS: 1   REF: Antecedent Influences on Gestalt Psychology

19. The unbiased description of immediate experience as it occurs is ____.
    a. mediate experience
    b. an unarticulated insight
    c. a temporal form
    d. the phi phenomenon
    e. phenomenology

    ANS: E   PTS: 1   REF: Antecedent Influences on Gestalt Psychology
    MSC: WWW

20. In what way was the phi phenomenon a challenge to Wundt's system?
    a. The phi phenomenon could not be reduced to its basic elements.
    b. Specially trained observers proved that the empirical methods used to prove the phi phenomenon were more applicable to their perceptions than that of Wundt's introspective method.
    c. Although it contradicted Wundt's reductionistic theory, Wundt adequately demonstrated that the phenomenon could be reduced to basic elements.
    d. The phi phenomenon demonstrated the existence of consciousness in humans.
    e. None of the above.

    ANS: A   PTS: 1
    REF: The Phi Phenomenon: A Challenge to Wundtian Psychology

21. Concurrent with the rise of Gestalt psychology, the Zeitgeist in physics was embracing ____.
    a. positivism
    b. operationism
    c. phenomenology
    d. field theory
    e. topology

    ANS: D   PTS: 1   REF: The Changing Zeitgeist in Physics

22. Complete the following analogy: Field of force: _____ :: _____ : Psychology.
    a. Physics; Gestalts
    b. Biology; Consciousness
    c. Anatomy; Behaviorism
    d. Physiology; Psyche
    e. Geography; Introspection

    ANS: A   PTS: 1   REF: The Changing Zeitgeist in Physics

23. Who was a subject in Wertheimer's research on the perception of apparent movement?
    a. His son, Michael
    b. Koffka
    c. Köhler
    d. Koffka **and** Köhler
    e. Wundt

    ANS: D   PTS: 1
    REF: The Phi Phenomenon: A Challenge to Wundtian Psychology

24. "Apparent movement" is another term for _____.
    a. Gestalt quälitaten
    b. existentialism
    c. extensity
    d. the phi phenomenon
    e. vectors

    ANS: D   PTS: 1
    REF: The Phi Phenomenon: A Challenge to Wundtian Psychology

25. How did Wertheimer explain the phi phenomenon?
    a. He did not; he said it did not need explanation.
    b. He could not.
    c. He explained it in terms of the speed of the flashing of the lights.
    d. He described it in terms of the principle of proximity.
    e. He described it in terms of the principle of continuity.

    ANS: A   PTS: 1
    REF: The Phi Phenomenon: A Challenge to Wundtian Psychology

26. Maslow's notion of self-actualization was partially based on _____.
    a. the Gestalt principles of good closure and continuity
    b. phenomenology
    c. the application of principles of fields of force to personality development
    d. the personal characteristics of Max Wertheimer
    e. Lewin's topology

    ANS: D   PTS: 1   REF: Max Wertheimer (1880-1943)
    MSC: WWW

27. The Gestalt system was introduced to American scholars by _____.
    a. Wertheimer
    b. Koffka
    c. Köhler
    d. Lewin
    e. von Ehrenfels

    ANS: B   PTS: 1   REF: Kurt Koffka (1886-1941)

28. One of the major reasons that Gestalt psychology failed to become popular in the United States apparently was ____.
   a. the animosity toward the Germans that was provoked by events of World War I
   b. its coincidental association with the rise of the Nazi regime
   c. American scholars' belief that Gestalt theory had only to do with perception
   d. because it was vociferously opposed by Titchener and Watson
   e. its focus on consciousness when Watson was criticizing the concept

   ANS: C   PTS: 1   REF: The Spread of Gestalt Psychology

29. The Gestalt psychologists initially chose to focus on perception ____.
   a. to challenge Wundtian psychology directly
   b. because research on insight was dependent on vision
   c. in order to confront the inadequacies of introspection directly
   d. because isomorphism was not applicable to learning
   e. because Gestalt principles of organization applied only to the narrow fields of sensation and perception

   ANS: A   PTS: 1
   REF: The Phi Phenomenon: A Challenge to Wundtian Psychology

30. ____ was the spokesman for the Gestalt movement who studied the thinking processes of chimpanzees, left Germany because of his anti-Nazi activities, came to the United States, and eventually became president of the American Psychological Association.
   a. Max Wertheimer
   b. Kurt Goldstein
   c. Kurt Koffka
   d. Wolfgang Köhler
   e. Kurt Lewin

   ANS: D   PTS: 1   REF: Wolfgang Köhler (1887-1967)
   MSC: WWW

31. The connection between certain aspects of Gestalt psychology and principles and terms of physics reflects ____.
   a. Köhler's training in physics
   b. the impact of Bridgman's work on operationism
   c. a lack of alternative systems from which to draw vocabulary
   d. Lewin's topologies
   e. Wertheimer's fascination with stroboscopes

   ANS: A   PTS: 1   REF: The Changing Zeitgeist in Physics

32. Perhaps the best known of the books written by the Gestalt psychologists, *The Mentality of Apes*, ____.
   a. was the result of the influence of Darwin's theory of evolution
   b. documented animals' purposeful behaviors to solve problems
   c. aided in the discovery of perceptual constancies
   d. is an example of the application of field theory to the behavior of monkeys
   e. demonstrates the influence of the functionalist school and its emphasis on adaptation

   ANS: B   PTS: 1
   REF: Gestalt Studies of Learning: Insight and the Mentality of Apes

33. The leaders of the _____ immediately supported the Nazi regime and proclaimed the "evil influence" of the Jews.
    a. Gestalt movement
    b. German Psychological Society
    c. Anti-Defamation League
    d. None of the choices are correct.
    e. All of the choices are correct.

    ANS: B   PTS: 1   REF: Wolfgang Köhler (1887-1967)

34. In Germany, the Gestalt protest of Wundt's system was _____.
    a. welcomed by colleagues at German universities who were annoyed at the limitations of Wundt's system but unable to challenge it
    b. considered to be heresy
    c. welcomed by the Nazi party because it was a direct assault on the power of the German university system and the German intelligentsia
    d. welcomed by the Nazi party because it led to the emigration of a number of influential Jewish intellectuals from Germany
    e. All of the choices are correct.

    ANS: B   PTS: 1   REF: The Nature of the Gestalt Revolt

35. A(n) _____ is a quality of wholeness or completeness in perceptual experiences that does not vary even when the actual sensory elements change.
    a. Gestalt
    b. illusion
    c. perceptual constancy
    d. state of consciousness
    e. insight

    ANS: C   PTS: 1   REF: Gestalt Principles of Perceptual Organization

36. The importance of perceptual constancies in the Wundt versus Gestalt debate was that the experience supported _____.
    a. Wundt's findings that replication of experimental introspection methods provided the same or similar data
    b. Wundt's position that forms can always be reduced to constant elements (sensations and feelings)
    c. Wundt's findings that analysis of an experience does not distort it
    d. the Gestalt position that "completeness" of an experience is not altered when the actual sensory components of the experience are altered
    e. the Gestalt finding that unless the animal changes an element of the problem, it cannot "see" (perceive) the solution

    ANS: D   PTS: 1   REF: The Nature of the Gestalt Revolt
    MSC: WWW

37. The Gestalt psychologists argued that reduction to the elements of experience _____.
    a. are products of reflection
    b. are products of abstraction
    c. are remote from immediate experience
    d. do not and cannot explain a perception
    e. All of the choices are correct.

    ANS: E   PTS: 1   REF: The Nature of the Gestalt Revolt

38. The notion that form is a property of objects is ____.
    a. a definition of "Gestalt"
    b. a criterion for the phi phenomenon
    c. necessary for the occurrence of insight learning
    d. unique to the sensory field
    e. *a priori*

    ANS: A   PTS: 1   REF: The Gestalt Revolt

39. The basic premise of the Gestalt principles of perception is that perceptual organization is ____.
    a. a reflex
    b. an instinct
    c. innate
    d. learned
    e. constant

    ANS: C   PTS: 1   REF: Gestalt Principles of Perceptual Organization

40. The Gestalt principles of organization ____.
    a. depend on higher mental processes
    b. depend on past experiences
    c. are present in the stimuli themselves
    d. are central factors
    e. did not receive research support

    ANS: C   PTS: 1   REF: Gestalt Principles of Perceptual Organization

41. Wertheimer defined "peripheral factors" as ____.
    a. those that distort perceptions
    b. those that determine whether a component is figure or ground
    c. those that influence perception
    d. those that mediate experiences
    e. the organizing principles present in the stimuli

    ANS: E   PTS: 1   REF: Gestalt Principles of Perceptual Organization
    MSC: WWW

42. Köhler's basic criterion for intelligence was ____.
    a. the ability to solve problems
    b. the ability to mimic the humans in their environment
    c. the speed with which subjects solve problems
    d. the number of trial-and-error attempts the subject made
    e. whether the subject required a reinforcer to solve a problem

    ANS: A   PTS: 1
    REF: Gestalt Studies of Learning: Insight and the Mentality of Apes

43. Köhler argued that solving a problem requires ____.
    a. experience with the tools available in the perceptual field
    b. a restructuring of the perceptual field
    c. opposable thumbs
    d. critical thinking skills
    e. transfer of training

    ANS: B   PTS: 1
    REF: Gestalt Studies of Learning: Insight and the Mentality of Apes

44. Köhler's research on Tenerife ____
    a. invoked a pre-test/post-test design to assess learning
    b. required the use of domesticated animals
    c. used the systematic manipulation of problem difficulty
    d. required an anthropomorphic approach
    e. was analyzed based solely on his descriptions of incidents

    ANS: E   PTS: 1
    REF: Gestalt Studies of Learning: Insight and the Mentality of Apes

45. In the original source material from *The Mentality of* Apes, Köhler argued that "a particular difficulty must lie in the ____."
    a. role of instincts
    b. lack of direction of some subjects
    c. role of imitation
    d. role of genius
    e. problem itself

    ANS: E   PTS: 1
    REF: Gestalt Studies of Learning: Insight and the Mentality of Apes

46. According to Köhler, insight involves ____.
    a. the learning of a stimulus-response association
    b. the learning of a connection between a response and reinforcement
    c. an immediate apprehension or cognition of relationships
    d. the ability to use intuition to solve problems
    e. All of the choices are correct.

    ANS: C   PTS: 1
    REF: Gestalt Studies of Learning: Insight and the Mentality of Apes

47. Pavlov ____.
    a. replicated Köhler's work on Tenerife with the same results
    b. did not attempt to replicate Köhler's work because it was nonsensical
    c. replicated Köhler's work but found it to be "chaotic"
    d. did not attempt to replicate Köhler's work because it made perfect sense
    e. revised his own system as a result of Köhler's work

    ANS: C   PTS: 1
    REF: Gestalt Studies of Learning: Insight and the Mentality of Apes

48. The spontaneous understanding of a phenomenon is called ____.
    a. problem solving
    b. *Einsicht*
    c. *Einfall*
    d. über-Ich
    e. Seele

    ANS: B   PTS: 1
    REF: Gestalt Studies of Learning: Insight and the Mentality of Apes

49. Köhler's findings occurred simultaneously with ____ discovery of ____.
    a. Wertheimer's; productive thinking
    b. Thorndike's; the law of effect
    c. Yerkes'; the army Beta test
    d. Wertheimer's; isomorphism
    e. Yerkes'; ideational learning

    ANS: E   PTS: 1
    REF: Gestalt Studies of Learning: Insight and the Mentality of Apes

50. Köhler argued that trial-and-error learning ____.
    a. overlooked the small units of S-R connections the animal acquired on each trial
    b. was a condition of vicarious learning
    c. was a consequence of vicarious learning
    d. was a consequence of not allowing the subject to see the whole situation
    e. was especially useful because of its application of reinforcement

    ANS: D   PTS: 1
    REF: Gestalt Studies of Learning: Insight and the Mentality of Apes

51. From the Gestalt perspective, insight requires that one ____.
    a. perceive the relationships between the components of the problem or issue
    b. deconstruct the component elements of a problem
    c. be able to distinguish the figure from the ground
    d. have familiarity with at least half of the components of the issue or problem
    e. have some capacity for communication either directly or through sign language

    ANS: A   PTS: 1
    REF: Gestalt Studies of Learning: Insight and the Mentality of Apes
    MSC: WWW

52. In the Gestalt view, learning entails ____.
    a. rote memorization
    b. a restructuring of the psychological environment
    c. transfer of training
    d. the principles of prägnanz and figure/ground
    e. reinforcement

    ANS: B   PTS: 1
    REF: Gestalt Studies of Learning: Insight and the Mentality of Apes

53. Wertheimer's basic premise for productive thinking was that _____.
    a. the whole problem must dominate the parts
    b. the learner must be given all the necessary tools for solving the problem
    c. rote learning is *not* learning; it is memorization
    d. the principles of solutions must be understood, not just situation-specific or problem-specific solutions
    e. both the whole problem must dominate the parts **and** the principles of solutions must be understood, not just situation-specific or problem-specific solutions

    ANS: E   PTS: 1   REF: Productive Thinking in Humans

54. For Wertheimer, rote memorization and/or rote learning _____.
    a. had the fastest decay period
    b. was inefficient compared to insight learning
    c. was an effective way to learn
    d. was appropriate only for those of below-average intelligence
    e. None of the choices are correct.

    ANS: B   PTS: 1   REF: Productive Thinking in Humans

55. Wertheimer suggested that brain activity is _____.
    a. a "configural whole process"
    b. incongruent with conscious experience
    c. rather like fields of force
    d. is placed "on edge" when insight occurs
    e. None of the choices are correct.

    ANS: A   PTS: 1   REF: Isomorphism

56. The Gestalt psychologists maintained that a correspondence called _____ exists between perceptual activity and brain activity.
    a. continuity
    b. isomorphism
    c. similarity
    d. closure
    e. the Zeigarnik effect

    ANS: B   PTS: 1   REF: Isomorphism

57. It is known that before an eye movement or a finger movement occurs, it is possible to record altered activity in a specific cerebral cortex area. The Gestaltists would argue that this is support for the principle of _____.
    a. *Einsicht*
    b. cerebral sign Gestalt
    c. isomorphism
    d. quasimorphism
    e. equimorphism

    ANS: C   PTS: 1   REF: Isomorphism
    MSC: WWW

58. The thrust of Gestalt psychology's attack on behaviorism focused on the latter's ____.
    a. exclusive use of animal subjects
    b. denial of perception
    c. reductionism
    d. notion of intervening variables
    e. focus on learning

    ANS: C   PTS: 1   REF: The Spread of Gestalt Psychology

59. The term *field theory* was applied to whose system?
    a. Gestalt psychology's
    b. Wertheimer's
    c. Koffka's
    d. Köhler's
    e. Lewin's

    ANS: E   PTS: 1   REF: Field Theory: Kurt Lewin (1890-1947)

60. The focus of Lewin's system was on ____.
    a. motivation
    b. learning
    c. psychophysics
    d. behavior within its total physical context
    e. behavior exclusive of its social context

    ANS: A   PTS: 1   REF: Field Theory: Kurt Lewin (1890-1947)

61. The construct of the life space describes ____.
    a. the person's psychological field
    b. behavior in a given situation
    c. the person's adaptation to physical barriers
    d. a topological field
    e. the interaction of vectors

    ANS: A   PTS: 1   REF: Field Theory: Kurt Lewin (1890-1947)

62. According to Lewin, life space ____.
    a. is another term for locus of control
    b. refers only to the physical environment in which a person lives
    c. represents the goals a person has in life
    d. corresponds to all the events that can influence a person's behavior
    e. is similar to sensitivity training

    ANS: D   PTS: 1   REF: Field Theory: Kurt Lewin (1890-1947)

63. Like Skinner, Lewin argued that ____.
    a. a mathematical model was the ultimate goal of psychology
    b. the individual person should be the focus of study
    c. the "whole" of the environment and S-R contingencies must be considered in the functional analysis of behavior
    d. statistics were not useful
    e. behavior should be the focus of behaviorism

    ANS: D   PTS: 1   REF: Field Theory: Kurt Lewin (1890-1947)
    MSC: WWW

64. An analysis of an overt behavior in Lewin's system requires a consideration of ____.
    a. vectors
    b. barriers
    c. goals
    d. valences
    e. All of the choices are correct.

    ANS: E   PTS: 1   REF: Field Theory: Kurt Lewin (1890-1947)

65. When Gestalt psychology was in its infancy, which school(s) of thought was/were already established?
    a. behaviorism
    b. functionalism
    c. psychoanalysis
    d. A and C only.
    e. All of the above.

    ANS: A   PTS: 1   REF: The Gestalt Revolt

66. The observation that an undone task is remembered until completed is an illustration of ____.
    a. goals
    b. insight
    c. vectors
    d. valences
    e. the Zeigarnik effect

    ANS: E   PTS: 1   REF: Field Theory: Kurt Lewin (1890-1947)

67. An early test of Lewin's tension theory was done by Zeigarnik who discovered that humans ____.
    a. suffer depression when they experience constant failures
    b. better remember an unusual item in a series of items
    c. tend to remember unfinished tasks better than finished ones
    d. use phenomenology when the introspect
    e. sometimes show less insight than do apes

    ANS: C   PTS: 1   REF: Field Theory: Kurt Lewin (1890-1947)

68. The most outstanding feature of Lewin's social psychology is ____.
    a. sensitivity dynamics
    b. group dynamics
    c. the social field
    d. leadership styles
    e. psychological action research

    ANS: B   PTS: 1   REF: Field Theory: Kurt Lewin (1890-1947)

69. Psychologists attacked which aspect of Gestalt psychology?
    a. the lack of rigor in its definitions
    b. its preoccupation with theory
    c. its qualitative results and lack of statistical analysis
    d. poorly defined physiological assumptions
    e. All of the choices are correct.

    ANS: E   PTS: 1   REF: Criticisms of Gestalt Psychology

70. Perhaps the major contribution of Gestalt psychology to contemporary systems was the _____.
   a. focus on perception
   b. focus on the principles of perceptual organization
   c. legitimization of conscious experiences
   d. similarity between Gestalt insight learning and Freud's notion of insight
   e. precision of its methodology

   ANS: C   PTS: 1   REF: Contributions of Gestalt Psychology

TRUE/FALSE

71. The Gestalt protest arose in opposition to Titchener's structuralism.

   ANS: F   PTS: 1   REF: The Gestalt Revolt
   MSC: WWW

72. The physicist who most influenced Gestalt psychology was Mach.

   ANS: T   PTS: 1   REF: Antecedent Influences on Gestalt Psychology

73. The greatest stimulus for Gestalt psychology are Müller's Gestalt quälitaten.

   ANS: F   PTS: 1   REF: Antecedent Influences on Gestalt Psychology

74. The psychologist who most directly influenced the basic tenets of Gestalt psychology was Ebbinghaus.

   ANS: F   PTS: 1   REF: Antecedent Influences on Gestalt Psychology
   MSC: WWW

75. The Zeitgeist in physics at the time Gestalt psychology was founded was "fields of force."

   ANS: T   PTS: 1   REF: The Changing Zeitgeist in Physics

76. Wertheimer's "impression of movement" was the phi phenomenon.

   ANS: T   PTS: 1   REF: The Changing Zeitgeist in Physics

77. Wertheimer did not explain perceived movement but instead simply accepted it.

   ANS: T   PTS: 1   REF: The Changing Zeitgeist in Physics

78. A major challenge Wundt and his associates failed to meet was the reduction of the phi phenomenon.

   ANS: T   PTS: 1   REF: The Changing Zeitgeist in Physics

79. Maslow's self-actualized person concept was based partly on Lewin.

   ANS: F   PTS: 1   REF: Max Wertheimer (1880-1943)

80. Unfortunately, Gestalt psychology was unable to extend its work beyond the area of perception.

ANS: F   PTS: 1   REF: Kurt Koffka (1886-1941)
MSC: WWW

81. According to Gestalt psychology, perceptual organization is instantaneous.

ANS: T   PTS: 1   REF: Gestalt Principles of Perceptual Organization

82. The characteristics of the organism that influence perception are peripheral factors.

ANS: F   PTS: 1   REF: Gestalt Principles of Perceptual Organization

83. Yerkes' discovery of insight was labeled "ideational learning."

ANS: T   PTS: 1
REF: Gestalt Studies of Learning: Insight and the Mentality of Apes

84. Insight learning requires a restructuring of the perceptual field.

ANS: T   PTS: 1
REF: Gestalt Studies of Learning: Insight and the Mentality of Apes

85. Although acclaimed for his work on static and stationary physical Gestalts, Koffka is better known for his work on insight learning.

ANS: F   PTS: 1   REF: Kurt Koffka (1886-1941)
MSC: WWW

86. The contemporary emphasis on critical thinking is a restatement of Wertheimer's productive thinking idea.

ANS: T   PTS: 1   REF: Productive Thinking in Humans

87. The notion of isomorphism reflects the idea that brain activity is a Gestalt.

ANS: T   PTS: 1   REF: Isomorphism

88. One reason Gestalt psychology did not influence American psychology in the 1930s was that its criticisms of Wundt's system were no longer necessary.

ANS: T   PTS: 1   REF: The Spread of Gestalt Psychology

89. The term *field theory* is associated with Wertheimer's work on brain-behavior relationships.

ANS: F   PTS: 1   REF: Field Theory: Kurt Lewin (1890-1947)

90. Lewin's concepts of force, valence, and vector were borrowed from physiology.

ANS: F   PTS: 1   REF: Field Theory: Kurt Lewin (1890-1947)

91. The basis of Lewin's concept of motivation is equilibrium.

    ANS: T   PTS: 1   REF: Field Theory: Kurt Lewin (1890-1947)
    MSC: WWW

92. Lewin's major impact on psychology was his system of personality theory.

    ANS: F   PTS: 1   REF: Field Theory: Kurt Lewin (1890-1947)

93. Lewin's social action research involved the study of relevant social problems from the point of view of change.

    ANS: T   PTS: 1   REF: Field Theory: Kurt Lewin (1890-1947)

94. Some critics claim that the Gestalt psychologists were too occupied with research at the expense of theory.

    ANS: F   PTS: 1   REF: Criticisms of Gestalt Psychology

95. The impact of the phenomenological thrust of Gestalt psychology can be seen in contemporary humanistic psychology.

    ANS: T   PTS: 1   REF: Contributions of Gestalt Psychology

Chapter 13

Psychoanalysis: The Beginnings

As a 7 year old child, Sigmund Freud dreamed that his mother was being taken by bird-like creatures. Upon waking, the image affected Freud so much that it stayed with him for the rest of his life. Thirty years later, he evaluated the meaning of the dream and determined that it revealed an unconscious longing to have sexual relations with his mother. Freud then developed a system called psychoanalysis for the treatment of abnormal behavior, which has since become widely popular. Freud equates the impact of his work to the impact of the work of Copernicus and Darwin because of its revolutionary ideas. His system began in 1895 when his first book was published. Unlike the other systems discussed so far, Freud's system grew outside of academia and is not a "pure" science.

Although psychoanalysis was developed as a means of treatment, Freud's system has a breadth of theoretical grounding that is mainly based on the unconscious. The idea of the unconscious was not novel, but Freud introduced a scientific way of examining it. The unconscious was first elaborated on by Gottfried Leibnitz in the early 1700's and later refined by Freidrich Herbart 100 years later. Fechner also speculated about the unconscious, and compared the mind to an iceberg (most of which lies beneath the surface and is influenced by unobservable forces). Fechner came up with the "pleasure principle, psychic energy, and aggression," all of which Freud later adopted. The idea of the unconscious was also popular and pervasive in the late 1800's in media and literature (e.g., *Dr. Jekyll and Mr. Hyde*).

Because Freud's system cannot be compared to academic psychology, it can only be considered a branch in the history of mental health treatment. Beginning in 2000 B.C., mental disorders were considered demonic possession and those with disturbances were treated humanely through magic and prayer. However, with the rise of Christianity in the fourth century, those with mental disorders started being tortured and put to death (such victims were considered possessed or guilty of witchcraft). By the 18th century imprisonment was the only treatment available. Those who advocated for the humane treatment of the mentally disturbed include Juan Vives (1500's Spain), Philippe Pinel (early 1800's France), and Dorothea Dix (mid- to late-1800's U.S.). Two camps disagreed about whether mental disorders were somatic ("brain lesions, under-stimulated nerves") or psychic ("emotional or psychological" etiology). Psychoanalysis grew in opposition to those who aligned with the somatic argument.

During this time, the Emmanuel movement was gaining steam in the United States (1906 to 1910), which also endorsed the idea that the mind was the source of mental disorder. The movement involved talk therapy, or psychotherapy, performed by religious leaders using the power of suggestion and moral authority to urge parishioners to behave righteously. Hypnosis had also been present before Freud, and began "mesmerism." Franz Mesmer thought that he could use magnetism to heal the body and mind and reverse mental illness. For some time he and his treatment were influential in Europe. Mesmer's system was reviewed scientifically by a committee who found no substance to Mesmer's claim, but his ideas remained popular in Europe and the United States. Later, James Braid "called the trancelike state neuro-hypnology, from which the term hypnosis was eventually derived." Hypnosis was used by Jean Charcot and Pierre Janet in Paris with mentally disturbed individuals. This emphasized the psychic causes of mental illness, instead of the somatic causes.

Author Frank Sulloway's research on Freud revealed that he was heavily influenced by Darwin's work. Darwin had discussed such things as "the significance of dreams,...and the importance of sexual arousal." He also posited that there is a continuity between childhood and adulthood, and that the sex drive appears in infancy. Freud later said that Darwinian theory is an integral part of psychoanalytic training. Other influences on Freud's thinking were the physiologists (like Helmholtz), the permissive sexual climate of Vienna at the time, Aristotle's concept of catharsis, and the idea of dream symbolism.

Sigmund Freud was born in what is now known as the Czech Republic, and when Freud was 4 his family moved to Vienna, where he spent 80 years of his life. He feared his father, who was strict, and felt great love for his mother. His feelings towards his parents were later articulated in the Oedipus complex, which suggests that all young boys are jealous of their fathers and have romantic love for their mothers. His mother doted on him and believed he was destined for greatness. He was given special treatment compared to his seven siblings, yet he still resented them. Being academically inclined, he came to speak eight languages, some of which he taught himself.

Freud pursued medicine because he wanted a "career in scientific research," and took classes in biology and philosophy. While at the university, he experimented with cocaine (which was not illegal) and enthusiastically gave it to his friends, family, and patients. His endorsement and writings on cocaine were "later held partly responsible for the epidemic of cocaine use in Europe and the United States that lasted well into the 1920's." Freud received his M.D. in 1881 and entered private medical practice because he needed the money (although he had wished for an academic job). He and Martha Bernays married after a four-year engagement. Although he had little time to spend with his new family, he was jealous of anyone receiving attention from his wife (even her own family).

In Vienna, Freud befriended Josef Breuer and they would sometimes discuss their patients. One of Breuer's cases was the infamous Anna O, who suffered from "hysterical complaints including paralysis, memory loss, mental deterioration, nausea, and disturbances of vision and speech." Her symptoms started when she was caring for her dying father. Breuer treated her with hypnosis (which reduced her symptoms) and saw her every day for about a year, but Breuer stopped the sessions at his wife's request. Later records tell us that Anna O. was Bertha Pappenheim, and that Breuer's sessions did not cure her illness. Later Bertha becomes "a social worker and feminist." This case introduced Freud to the "talking cure" that became a hallmark of his therapy.

In 1885 Freud spent a few months in Paris working with Charcot, who emphasized the importance that sex played in his hysterical patients and who used hypnosis as treatment. This introduced Freud to the techniques of catharsis and hypnosis. Although he retained the former method, he became disillusioned with the benefits of hypnosis, claiming that it could not provide long-term cures. He then developed the therapeutic technique called "free association" where the patient is encouraged to say everything that comes to mind. Freud found that often the things that were said related to childhood events and to sexuality, both of which become prominent in his system.

The beginning of psychoanalysis is the publication of *Studies on Hysteria* (1895) by Freud and Breuer, which was well received. The book marked a rift between the authors because of Freud's insistence on emphasizing sex as the root of neuroses, and a few years later their friendship was dissolved.

Freud presented a paper to a scientific society in 1896 in which he argued that most women are sexually abused as children by an adult figure, often the father. The paper was not well received because the dominant theories were based on somatic causes of neuroses, and Freud was criticized for his questionable methods. Freud reversed his position a year later, claiming that in *most* cases the childhood seduction experiences his patients described were not real experiences, but fantasy. There is some controversy about whether Freud changed this position to make his system more acceptable.

Freud himself had sexual difficulties. "He considered the sex act degrading" and gave up sex when he was 41, blaming the fact that his wife could easily conceive and that he wanted no more children. "He had occasionally experienced impotence," and believed that sex was an animalistic drive that was of no use to him. As his theory would predict, he later developed neuroses and attributed the behaviors to the sex drive. To reduce his ailments, Freud psychoanalyzed himself through dream analysis. He then "realized the considerable hostility he felt toward his father," the "sexual longings for his mother," and "sexual wishes toward his eldest daughter." He later wrote *The Interpretation of Dreams* (1900) based on this analysis, which is "now considered his major work." He was a prolific writer and soon introduced the "Freudian slip" in the book *The Psychopathology of Everyday Life* (1901).

Freud's system flourished and he attracted many followers. He was soon intolerant of anyone who disagreed with him. In 1909, he and Carl Jung were invited to speak at Clark University by G. Stanley Hall. His talks were well received, he met many prominent American psychologists, and shortly afterward psychoanalytic associations began forming in the United States. Freud's students began to revise his system, which caused breaks between them and Freud; Alfred Adler left in 1911 and Jung two years later. Freud was diagnosed with mouth cancer in 1923 "and underwent 33 operations to remove portions of his palate and upper jaw." Freud left Vienna for England in 1938 when it became clear that his life was in danger because of the Nazi regime. He died in England in 1939, having received a purposeful overdose of morphine because of the pain from his cancer. The authors include an excerpt from Freud's first lecture at Clark, in which he describes the Anna O. case.

When using psychoanalysis as a therapeutic system, Freud found that patients would come to a point during free association where they would stop. He called this resistance and attributed it to thoughts that were "too shameful to be faced." Because of this phenomenon, he formulated the idea of repression (forcefully excluding unwanted thoughts from consciousness). Another key aspect to his therapeutic system was dream analysis. Freud believed that dreams have a surface story line (manifest content) but also a "hidden or symbolic meaning" (latent content). The latent content of a dream implies one's secret desires. Freud was less interested in helping patients and more interested in case-study research in order to build his theory. Although Freud was trained in scientific methods, his system was built on the case study method.

As a system of personality, Freud's system included a variety of topics that other psychologists did not address. For example, Freud believed that humans had driving forces such as death instincts (destructive and aggressive forces) and life instincts ("hunger, thirst, sex"). The energy of the life instinct was the libido. Freud's saw personality as having three components: the id (which is primitive and unconscious and operated under the pleasure principle), the ego (the mediator between the external world and the id), and the superego (an internalized parent/voice of morality). Such between the three aspects of personality causes anxiety and therefore tension, which is reduced by using defense mechanisms.

Freud "became one of the first theorists to emphasize the importance of child development" and "believed that the adult personality was formed almost completely by age five. He developed his psychosexual stage theory, which posits that all children pass through the same psychosexual stages in development. If a given stage was resolved then the child would pass into the next stage normally. However, too much or too little satisfaction of a stage would stunt development and cause adult personality problems. For example, in the anal stage, children who refuse to expel feces grow to be adults who are "anal retentive" and will be compulsively clean and neat. The stages include: oral, anal, phallic (when the Oedipus complex arises), latent, and genital. In this way, Freud believed that all adult disorders were caused by childhood experiences.

Freud's system was deterministic in that he "believed that all mental events, even dreams, are predetermined; nothing occurs by chance or free will."

Psychoanalysis was eschewed by American academic psychologists, particularly during World War I "when virtually everything German was considered suspect." At the same time, his ideas were being included in psychology textbooks even though behaviorism was the prevailing thought. "But by the 1930's and 1940's psychoanalysis had captured public attention," which irritated academicians because psychoanalysis was being equated with academic psychology. To fight this, academic psychologists tested psychoanalytic theory.

The scientific studies on psychoanalysis revealed support for "1. some characteristics of the oral and anal personality types, 2. castration anxiety, 3. the notion that dreams reflect emotional concerns, and 4. aspects of the Oedipus complex in boys." There was no support found for "1. dreams satisfy symbolically repressed wishes and desires, 2. in resolving the Oedipus complex, boys identify with the father and accept his superego standards out of fear, 3. women have an inferior conception of their bodies, have less severe superego standards than men, and find it more difficult to achieve an identity, and 4. personality is formed by age 5 and changes little after that." Other research has supported the idea of the unconscious influencing "thoughts, emotions, and behavior," and the presence and use of some of the defense mechanisms and the Freudian slip.

Eventually many ideas from psychoanalysis were absorbed into psychology. For example, in the 1950's and 1960's, "behaviorists [were] translating psychoanalytic terminology into the language of behavior."

Psychoanalysis has been criticized because Freud's data collection was unsystematic. Because he worked from notes written after the therapy sessions, data may have been forgotten or reinterpreted. Some critics believe that Freud may have guided patients with suggestions. Another criticism is that his sample was small and limited generalizability. Also, "there are discrepancies between Freud's notes on the therapy sessions and the published case histories supposedly based on those notes." A last criticism is that Freud never attempted to verify if his patients were telling the truth.

Those criticisms aside, Freud argued that his system "was scientific and that he had amassed ample proof to support his conclusions." Psychoanalysis has declined as a form of therapy because of the large and necessary commitment of time and money. Drug and other therapies have increased, largely because of their expediency and effectiveness. There is no doubt, however, that Freud's system had an incredible impact on the ideas and systems of psychology. It was also accepted by the general public. Even as recently as 2005 the British Broadcasting Company "produced a four-hour television documentary about Freud's influence in Western society."

Outline

I.   The Mommy Track
    A. A boy dreams of his mother being carried by bird-like creatures, not sure if she was dead or alive
    B. 30 years later the dream is still emotional to the dreamer, Sigmund Freud
    C. Freud analyzes the symbolic content
        1. recalls a childhood friend who liked to talk about sex and used slang term "Vögeln" (sexual intercourse)
        2. says dream represents his unconscious sexual longing for his mother

II.   The Development of Psychoanalysis
    A. Freud's place in history
        1. "Psychoanalysis" and "Sigmund Freud": known all over world
        2. Freud recognizable to general public
        3. Cover of Time magazine: 3 times, once 60 years after death
        4. Recently revered on 150th anniversary of his birth (2006)
        5. Pivotal person in history of civilization
        6. Changed the way we think of ourselves
    B. Three great shocks to the collective human ego (Freud, 1917)
        1. Copernicus: earth not center of universe
        2. Darwin: humans not a distinctive species
        3. Freud: unconscious forces rather than rational thought drive our lives
    C. Chronological overlap with other schools of thought
        1. 1895
            a.   formal beginning of psychoanalysis
            b.   Wundt: age 63
            c.   Titchener: age 28
            d.   functionalism: beginning to thrive in U.S.
            e.   Watson: age 17
            f.   Wertheimer: age 15
        2. 1939
            a.   Freud's death
            b.   Wundtian psychology, structuralism, and functionalism were past
            c.   Gestalt psychology: in the process of transplantation
            d.   behaviorism was dominant
    D. Schools other than psychoanalysis
        1. shared an academic heritage
        2. owed much to Wundt
        3. concepts and methods refined in laboratories, libraries, and lecture halls
        4. concerned with topics such as sensation, perception, and learning
        5. attempted to maintain a pure science
    E. Psychoanalysis
        1. not a school of thought directly comparable to the others
        2. not a "pure" science; no academic/research foundation
        3. arose from medicine and psychiatry
        4. subject matter is abnormal behavior of "mentally ill"
        5. not mainstream in subject matter, methods, and goals
        6. primary method is clinical observation (rather than controlled experiments)
        7. deals with the unconscious

F. Idea of unconscious forces
    1. not accepted by Wundt and Titchener
        a. not amenable to study using introspection
        b. cannot be reduced to sensory elements
    2. functionalists disregarded it
        a. James briefly acknowledged unconscious processes
        b. 1904: Angell devoted a mere 2 pages to topic in text
        c. 1921: Woodworth dealt with subject as postscript
    3. Watson: no use for either the unconscious or consciousness
    4. Freud: brought concept of the unconscious to psychology

III. Antecedent Influences on Psychoanalysis
  A. Theories of the unconscious mind: philosophical speculations
    1. Leibnitz's (1646-1716) monadology: "theory of psychic entities, called monads, which are similar to perceptions"
        a. the monads
            (1) individual elements of all reality (not physical atoms)
            (2) not composed wholly of matter
            (3) each is an psychic entity that is not perceived by itself
            (4) each, while mental, has some properties of physical matter
            (5) when enough are grouped together, an extension (expansion) results
            (6) similar to perceptions
        b. mental events: the activity of the monads
            (1) have different degrees of consciousness: from completely unconscious to completely conscious
                (a) petites perceptions
                    (i) smaller amount of consciousness,
                        (a) e.g., individual drops of water
                        (b) each drop not consciously perceived
                    (ii) conscious realization of petites perceptions = apperception
                        (a) e.g., sound of waves breaking on the beach
                        (b) enough drops collected = apperception
    2. Johann Friedrich Herbart (1776-1841)
        a. Unconscious (Leibnitz) sharpened to idea of threshold of consciousness (Herbart)
        b. ideas influence each other in terms of the mechanics of forces
            (1) ideas below = unconscious
                (a) to rise above the conscious level of awareness
                    (i) an idea must be compatible with ideas already in consciousness
                (b) inhibited ideas
                    (i) ideas forced out of consciousness due to incompatibility with other conscious ideas
                    (ii) exist below threshold
                    (iii) result in conflict as they fight to become conscious

3. Gustav Fechner
    a.   also used threshold concept
    b.   mind= iceberg (influenced Freud)
        (1) much of mind is unconscious (concealed below surface of water)
        (2) is influenced by unobservable forces
    c.   1860: Elements of Psychophysics
        (1) influenced psychoanalysis as well as experimental psychology
        (2) Freud quoted from Fechner
        (3) Freud took ideas from Fechner
            (a) pleasure principle
            (b) psychic energy
            (c) importance of aggression
4. 1880's Europe: ideas about the unconscious
    a.   a part of the intellectual climate
    b.   a fashionable topic of conversation
    c.   book called *Philosophy of the Unconscious*: 9 editions attest to its popularity
5. Freud claimed did not originate the unconscious, only a way to scientifically study it

B. Early ideas about psychopathology
  1. psychoanalysis was not in competition with academic psychology (Wundtian, functionalism, etc.)
  2. Freud revolted against trends in the treatment of mental disorders
  3. history of treatment of mental disorders
    a.   2000 B.C. Babylonians: mental illness = possession by demons
        (1) treated humanely
        (2) used magic and prayer
    b.   Hebrew cultures: mental illness = punishment for sin
        (1) used magic and prayer to treat it
    c.   Greek philosophers: mental illness = disordered thought processes
        (1) used persuasive, healing power of words to treat it
    d.   4th century Christianity: mental illness = possession by evil spirits
        (1) treatment for next 1000 years: torture and execution
        (2) 15th century + next 300 years: Inquisition
            (a) rigorous hunt for heresy and witchcraft
            (b) searched out symptoms of mental disorder
            (c) severely punished any symptoms of mental disorder
    e.   18th century view: mental illness = irrational behavior
        (1) confined mentally ill in institutions comparable to jails
        (2) no longer put to death
        (3) no treatment offered
        (4) patients sometimes displayed in public like zoo animals
        (5) some chained, restrained, hooked on a wall
        (6) their "prisons" called lunatic asylums
  4. More humane treatments
    a.   Juan Luis Vives (1492-1540)
        (1) Spanish scholar
        (2) called for sensitive and caring treatment

(3) language and geographic obstacles restricted his sympathetic views to Spain

    b.   Philippe Pinel (1745-1826)

        (1) mental illness is a biological phenomenon to be treated by natural-science methods

        (2) freed patients from chains

        (3) listened to their problems

        (4) maintained precise case histories

        (5) maintained careful records of cure rates

        (6) number of "cured" patients increased

    c.   changes in United States and Europe

        (1) chains removed from patients

        (2) mental illness became a research topic

        (3) patients as machines that need to be fixed when broken.

        (4) instruments used to aid "repair" of patients

    d.   Dorothea Dix (1802-1887)

        (1) leading reformer of U.S. insane asylums

        (2) very religious

        (3) depressed

        (4) actively worked to establish Pinel's reforms all over U.S.

        (5) self-described advocate of the mentally ill

    e.   Benjamin Rush (1745-1813)

        (1) 1st practicing psychiatrist in U.S.

        (2) signed Declaration of Independence

        (3) started 1st hospital for treatment of emotional disturbances

        (4) mechanistic forms of treatment

            (a) hypothesis: some irrational symptoms due to excess or deficit of blood

            (b) solution: drain or infuse with blood

        (5) devised revolving chair: rapidly rotate patients at high speed until they faint

        (6) used type of shock treatment: plunged patients into ice water

        (7) first tranquilizing technique: restrained in a chair; pressure to head via wooden blocks held by vise

        (8) methods appear extreme to us but were used to relieve sickness rather than merely institutionalizing patients and ignoring them or worse

    f.   two major schools of thought in psychiatry

        (1) somatic: causes of abnormal behavior are physical, e.g., brain lesions or "understimulated" or "tight" nerves

            (a) dominant view

            (b) supported by Kant

        (2) psychic: causes of abnormal behavior are emotional or psychological

    g.   psychoanalysis: a revolt against the somatic orientation

C. The Emmanuel Movement

    1. Emmanuel Church Healing Movement

    2. fostered psychic approach to mental illness in U.S.

    3. advocated psychotherapy

4. focus on talk therapy increased salience of psychological causes of mental illness to both general public and therapeutic community
5. originator: Elwood Worcester
   a. rector of Emmanuel Church, Boston, Massachusetts
      (1) Ph.D. in philosophy and psychology from University of Leipzig
      (2) studied under Wundt
6. height of movement: 1906-1910
7. talk therapy sessions
   a. both individual and group
   b. led by religious leaders from different denominations
   c. methods: power of suggestion and moral authority
   d. goal: appropriate course of patient behavior
8. outcome of movement
   a. widespread popularity
   b. magazine articles
   c. best-selling book on "scientific psychotherapy": Religion and Medicine: the Moral Control of Nervous Disorders (Worcester and 2 co-authors).
   d. opposition to ministers as psychotherapists from medical community and clinical psychologists (e.g., Witmer and Münsterberg)
   e. warm welcome for Freud/psychoanalysis in 1909 U.S. visit
   f. talk therapy = part of Zeitgiest

D. Hypnosis
   1. advanced emerging focus on psychological causes of mental illness
   2. Franz Anton Mesmer (1734-1815)
      a. Viennese physician
      b. scientist
      c. dramatic promoter
      d. central concept: animal magnetism
         (1) "mysterious, murky force"
         (2) origin: magnetic energy in body
         (3) process: penetrate objects and influence them from afar
         (4) effects: include healing of mental disorders through re-establishing equilibrium between magnetic levels of patient and the environment
         (5) development of methodology
            (a) patient grips metal bars, reverses illness
            (b) transfer to Mesmer's magnetism to patients by his touch or stroke
         (6) verdict of medical community: he's a quack
         (7) as a result of investigations, Mesmer escaped to Switzerland
         (8) mesmerism became very popular in U.S.
   3. James Braid (1795-1860)
      a. called trancelike conditions neurohypnology, later known as hypnosis
      b. meticulous work
      c. contempt for overstated claims
      d. impact: lent scientific respectability to study of hypnosis

4. Jean Martin Charcot (1825-1893)
   a. French physician
   b. worked with insane women at Salpêtrière, a Paris hospital
   c. found hypnosis an effective treatment of hysterical patients
   d. used medical terminology in descriptions of symptoms and use of hypnosis
   e. work primarily neurological, not psychological
5. Pierre Janet (1859-1947)
   a. Charcot's student
   b. director of psychological laboratory at Salpêtrière
   c. rejected conception of hysteria as somatic
   d. hypothesized that mental phenomena (e.g., memory impairment or unconscious forces) are causes
   e. used hypnosis as the method of treatment
   f. influenced Freud
   g. significance of Charcot's and Janet's work with the mentally ill
      (1) psychiatrists began changing from somatic to psychic point of view
      (2) treatment of emotional disturbances: focus on mind, not body
      (3) in U.S. and Europe, psychotherapy was a widespread idea by time of Freud's 1st book

E. The influence of Charles Darwin
   1. 1979: *Freud: Biologist of the Mind* by Frank J. Sulloway
      a. studied books in Freud's library, including those by Darwin
      b. all Darwin's works read by Freud, who made marginal notes
      c. enormous influence on Freud
      d. Darwinian theory is essential to psychoanalysis training
   2. ideas from Darwin
      a. unconscious mental processes/conflicts
      b. the significance of dreams
      c. the hidden symbolism of certain behaviors
      d. the importance of sexual arousal
      e. notion of continuity in emotional behavior from childhood to adulthood
      f. evidence of the sex drive appears in infants 7 weeks old
      g. humans are driven by biological forces of love and hunger
   3. ideas from Romanes
      a. elaboration on developmental continuity in emotional expression from childhood to adulthood
      b. idea that sex drive appears as young as 7 weeks
   4. ideas from Krafft-Ebing
      a. sexual gratification and self-preservation the only human instincts
   5. cumulative effect: in adhere to Darwin's leadership, scientists acknowledged sex as a fundamental human drive/motivation

F. Additional influences
   1. from Freud's university training
      a. mechanistic orientation of Ernst Brücke, his major professor
      b. prevailing determinist attitude reflected in Freud's concept of psychic determinism

2. receptive Zeitgeist led to interest in Freud's concepts
    a. 19th century Vienna
       (1) generally permissive toward sex
       (2) Freud and neurotic upper-middle-class women: more sexually inhibited
       (3) Victorian England and Puritan U.S.: not as stereotypically prim, proper, and inhibited as sometimes portrayed
       (4) 1880s-1890s: from sublimation of sex to overt expression
    b. sexual interest evident in everyday life and scientific research
       (1) sexologists: study human sexuality not as sin but as an integral part of the natural world
       (2) research published on: sexual pathologies, infantile sexuality; suppression of sexual impulses and its mental/ physical consequences
       (3) sex drive is present in children as young as 3
          (a) Adolf Patze, Germany: 1845
          (b) Henry Maudsley, Great Britain: 1867
       (4) Psychopathia Sexualis (Krafft-Ebing, 1886)
       (5) Albert Moll (1897)
          (a) Viennese physician
          (b) childhood sexuality
          (c) the child's love for the parent of the opposite sex
       (6) Moritz Benedickt
          (a) Viennese neurologist and colleague of Freud
          (b) cures with hysterical women
             (i) patients talked about their sex lives
       (7) Alfred Binet: published on sexual perversions
       (8) libido: a term already in use
3. catharsis
    a. already a popular concept
    b. 1890: more than 140 publications in German
4. Freud's concepts about dreams
    a. anticipated in the literature of philosophy and physiology
    b. already studied by Charcot, Janet, and Krafft-Ebing
5. Freud's genius: his ability to weave the threads of ideas and trends into a tapestry of a coherent system

IV. Sigmund Freud (1856-1939) and the Development of Psychoanalysis
  A. Background
    1. born in Freiburg, Moravia (now Pribor, Czech Republic)
    2. moved to Vienna when four; lived there approximately 80 years
    3. much of his theory is autobiographical
       a. father 20 years older than mother
          (1) strict, authoritarian
          (2) both feared and loved by Freud
       b. mother
          (1) protective, loving
          (2) Freud emotionally attached to her
          (3) she was enormously proud of him, giving him preferential treatment

   c. Oedipus complex is autobiographical
      (1) fear of father
      (2) sexual attraction to mother
  4. as a young student
    a. early signs of intellectual ability
    b. accordingly given special treatment and privileges
    c. entered high school a year early and graduated at 17 with distinction
  5. university career
    a. Darwin's theory: elicited an interest in science
    b. 1873: began study of medicine at University of Vienna
      (1) goal: research, not practice
      (2) eight years to get his degree: took courses outside of medical curriculum, e.g., philosophy
      (3) initially concentrated on biology: eel testicle morphology
        (a) inconclusive findings
        (b) sexually related topic
      (4) moved to physiology: the spinal cord of the fish
        (a) 6 years in physiological institute
      (5) experimented with cocaine
        (a) not illegal
        (b) use: for self, friends and family, medical patients
        (c) enthusiastically maintained it ameliorated his depression and indigestion
        (d) called it a miracle drug; thought it would lead to his fame
        (e) Carl Koller, a colleague, learned of drug through Freud; used it to anesthetize eye during surgery
        (f) Koller gained the recognition Freud craved for introducing the drug as medicine
        (g) Freud's article on cocaine benefits is in part responsible for its widespread use in U.S. and Europe during the 1920s
          (i) for rest of career downplayed his initial approval
          (ii) evidence that he used it until middle age
      (6) wished for appointment in academic research lab
        (a) Brücke, his professor and director of the physiological lab where Freud trained, dissuaded him
          (i) used financial grounds
          (ii) would take years to obtain professorship
          (iii)Freud too poor to provide for himself in interim
      (7) taking Brücke's advice, Freud took medical exams for private practice
  6. 1881: earned M.D. and started clinical neurology practice
    a. did not like his work
    b. money kept him going
    c. engaged to Martha Bernays
      (1) several wedding dates postponed due to finances
      (2) when did marry, they pawned their watches and borrowed money to pay costs

d.   4 year engagement to Martha
      (1) highly jealous of her attention
      (2) wanted to be center of her affection
      (3) wanted her to renounce her family
      (4) spent little time with her or their children
      (5) vacationed alone or with sister-in-law Minna (only one who could keep up with him while hiking and sightseeing)

B. The case of Anna O.
  1. Josef Breuer (1842-1935)
     a.   famous for study of respiration
     b.   discovered the functioning of the semicircular canals
     c.   made friends with the younger Freud
     d.   successful, experienced father figure who lent money and gave advice to Freud
     e.   discussed patient cases with Freud, including Anna O.
  2. Anna O.
     a.   her case crucial to development of psychoanalysis
     b.   21 years old
     c.   intelligent, attractive
     d.   wide range of hysterical symptoms
     e.   symptoms first manifested while nursing her dying father with whom she had romantic love for
     f.   Breuer began with hypnosis
       (1) when Anna talked about symptoms connected with specific experiences, symptoms abated
       (2) daily sessions for one year
       (3) Anna's called the sessions: "chimney sweeping" and "the talking cure"
       (4) repulsive acts recalled under hypnosis
       (5) reliving the experiences under hypnosis ameliorated the symptoms
     g.   positive transference
       (1) Breuer's wife jealous of emotional bonds connecting her husband and Anna
       (2) Anna transferring her love for her father to love for her therapist
     h.   Breuer terminated the therapy
     i.   distorted data of history: the false pregnancy myth
       (1) hours after learning that her therapy had ended, Anna felt labor pains from hysterical childbirth
       (2) Breuer ended the pregnancy through hypnosis
       (3) for a type of second honeymoon, Breuer took wife to Venice
       (4) Breuer's wife becomes pregnant
     j.   known fact: none of Breuer children was conceived at alleged time
     k.   Anna O. (Bertha Pappenheim) allegedly not cured by Breuer
       (1) institutionalized
       (2) spend hours under portrait of father, talking about visiting his grave
       (3) exhibited a myriad of symptoms, including severe facial pain
       (4) morphine prescribed by Breuer for facial pain

l.   new evidence about Bertha Pappenheim's (Anna O's)

          (1) symptoms were mild and therapy with Breuer helped

          (2) somehow overcame emotional problems

          (3) became social worker and feminist

          (4) proponent of education for women

          (5) published short stories and women's rights play

          (6) honored on German postage stamp

m.   Anna O. case introduced Freud to the method of catharsis, the talking cure

C. The sexual basis of neurosis

   1. 1885: Freud received a mini-grant to study with Charcot

       a.   trained in hypnosis to treat hysteria

       b.   Charcot became another father-figure

       c.   attracted to Charcot's daughter; imagined career advancement through marrying her

       d.   informed by Charcot of the function of sex in hysteria

   2. upon return to Vienna, Rudolph Chrobak, gynecologist, reinforced possible link between sex and emotional problems

       a.   referred Freud to a women suffering anxiety attacks

       b.   anxiety would only be relieved when she knew the whereabouts of her physical pain

       c.   caused by husband's impotency (marriage not consummated after 18 years)

       d.   Freud adopted methods of hypnosis and catharsis

   3. Freud became dissatisfied with hypnosis

       a.   relieved some symptoms but not effective as a long-term

       b.   patients vary in ability to be hypnotized

       c.   retained catharsis as a treatment method

       d.   developed the method of free association

   4. free association: "a psychotherapeutic technique in which the patient says whatever comes to mind."

       a.   goal of psychoanalysis: bring repressed memories into conscious awareness

       b.   repressed memories: the source of abnormal behavior

   5. free association material

       a.   Freud: stream of consciousness talking is not random

       b.   the experiences recalled are predetermined

       c.   cannot be consciously censored

       d.   the nature of the conflict forces the material out to be articulated to therapist

       e.   its roots were in early childhood

       f.   much of it concerned sexual matters

       g.   1898: "...the most significant causes of neurotic illness are to be found in factors arising from sexual life"

D. Studies on hysteria

   1. 1895: Studies on Hysteria written by Breuer and Freud

       a.   the formal beginning of psychoanalysis (term 1st used by Freud one year later)

       b.   contained papers by both authors plus case histories, including that of Anna O.

       c.   mostly favorable reviews throughout Europe

2. conflicts between Breuer and Freud
   a.   Breuer reluctant to publish
   b.   not convinced, as was Freud, that sex is the sole cause of neurosis
   c.   Breuer felt Freud had insufficient evidence
   d.   disagreement between them led to estrangement
3. Freud's position
   a.   believed he was right; therefore no need for additional data
   b.   concerned that delay in publication might result in others laying claim to same ideas
   c.   reveal Freud's ambition
4. Breuer concerned with Freud's dogmatic attitudes
   a.   complete break between the two within a few years
   b.   Freud resentful
   c.   but gave Breuer written credit as a pioneer in hysteria treatment
   d.   upon Breuer's death in 1925, a considerably mellowed Freud wrote a perceptive obituary and sent a sympathy letter to Breuer's son

E. The childhood seduction controversy
1. Freud viewed sex as the key cause of neurosis
2. believed a normal sex life precludes neuroses
3. 1896 paper: based on free-association data, reported in a paper that patients exposed childhood seduction traumas often caused by the father or other older family member
   a.   his conclusion: sexual/seductive traumas caused adult neurotic behavior
   b.   patients very tentative when describing the incident
4. paper was received with skepticism
   a.   Krafft-Ebing: described it as a "scientific fairy tale"
   b.   Freud response: "said his critics were asses and could go to hell."
   c.   general conclusion by historians: negative reaction caused by audience shock and anger about suggestion of frequent child abuse
   d.   Esterson (2002): negative reaction caused by
       (1) prevailing belief in somatic causes of emotional problems
       (2) belief that Freud's methods were unreliable
   e.   outcome: paper not the success that Freud hoped for
5. 1897: Freud reversed his position
   a.   the seduction scenes were fantasies
   b.   patients believed they were real experiences
   c.   fantasies sexual in nature, so sex remained the root of the problem
   d.   Freud: sex remained the cause of neurosis
6. 1984: Jeffrey Masson, briefly director of Freud Archives, wrote that Freud lied
   a.   sexual abuse of Freud's patients actually occurred
   b.   Freud called them fantasies to make his theory more agreeable to professionals and laymen
   c.   Masson's claims denounced by most scholars
       (1) Freud's position: *some* sexual abuse had actually happened; yet not *all* reported incidents were true
   d.   contemporary data: child sexual abuse more frequent than professionals agree to
   e.   whether Freud deliberately suppressed the truth is undetermined

7. 1930's Ferenczi determined there were real acts of sexual abuse
    a. 1932 psychoanalytic meeting, Freud unsuccessfully attempted to keep Ferenczi from speaking
    b. led the resistance to Ferenczi's standpoint
8. other possible reason for reversal: if Freud's initial seduction theory was true, his father, like all fathers might be guilty of abuse

F. Freud's own sex life
1. held a negative attitude toward sex
2. experienced sexual difficulties
    a. intermittent impotence
    b. at times refrained from sex because disliked the available birth control methods, condoms and coitus interruptus
3. sexuality a dangerous, animal need
4. age 41: gave up sex and blamed wife
5. resented her fertility, pregnancy sickness, refusal of sex except for procreation
6. attracted to beautiful women who became his students in inordinate numbers
7. Freud became "a textbook example of his theory
    a. his sexual frustrations emerged as neuroses
    b. year he gave up sex had "odd states of mind"
    c. fears of death, travel, open spaces
8. diagnosed self as suffering from anxiety neurosis and neurasthenia as a consequence of sexual tension
9. Krüll, 1986: "Freud's theory of actual neurosis is thus a theory of his own neurotic symptoms"
10. Freud decided that he required psychoanalysis and analyzed himself using his dreams

G. Dream analysis
1. lesson from patients: dreams a rich source of information providing clues to causes of disorder
2. his deterministic belief that everything has a cause led him to look for unconscious sources of the meaning in dreams
3. dream analysis: "A psychotherapeutic technique involving interpreting dreams to uncover unconscious conflicts."
4. emergent themes
    a. hostility toward father
    b. childhood sexual attraction to mother
    c. sexual wishes regarding eldest daughter
5. result: the basis of his theory
6. two-year duration of self-analysis
7. 1900: *The Interpretation of Dreams*
    a. the culmination of Freud's self-analysis
    b. his major work
    c. outlined the Oedipus complex
    d. for the most part favorably reviewed
    e. read by Carl Jung, who adopted psychoanalysis
8. Freud embraced dream analysis as a psychoanalytic technique
9. continued to analyze his own dreams at the end of each day
    a. not much sexual content, contrary to his assertion that dreams can reveal infantile sexual desires

          b.   ambition was a significant dream theme, but was not a personal trait he accepted

H. The Pinnacle of Success

    1. 1901: *The Psychopathology of Everyday Life*

        a.   Freudian slip: "An act of forgetting or a lapse in speech that reflects unconscious motives or anxieties."

        b.   occur in everyday life

        c.   appear to be casual but signal inner motives

    2. 1902: began weekly psychoanalytic discussion group with students

        a.   included Jung and Adler

        b.   most viewed as neurotic themselves

        c.   discussed own problems as well as those of others

        d.   Freud would brook no disagreement about the role of sexuality in the genesis of emotional problems

        e.   those who deviated were expelled

    3. 1905: *Three Essays on the Theory of Sexuality*

    4. 1909: Freud and Jung invited by G. Stanley Hall to Clark University's 20th anniversary

    5. Freud lectured; received honorary doctorate in psychology

    6. self-described in lectures as scientist and therapist with significant findings

    7. James, Titchener, and Cattell were among the leading American psychologists with whom he met

    8. 1909/1910: publication of the Clark lectures in the *American Journal of Psychology*, with numerous translations

    9. his work discussed at American Psychological Association meeting

        a.   Americans very receptive to idea of unconscious mind

        b.   had been introduced to concept by writings of Canadian H. Addington Bruce

        c.   Freud critical of America

    10. 1911: the break with Adler

    11. 1914: the break with Jung

    12. 1923: diagnosis of cancer, followed by 33 surgeries in 16 years, continues to smoke 20 cigars a day

    13. 1933: public burning of Freud's books by the Nazis

    14. 1934: Nazi obliteration of psychoanalysis in Germany

    15. 1938: Anna Freud arrested and detained by the Nazis

    16. move to Paris, then London

    17. 1939: death by overdose of morphine injected by Dr. Max Schur who had promised not to let Freud suffer

I. Original source material on psychoanalysis from Freud's first lecture at Clark University, September 9, 1909

    1. modest introduction

    2. discusses the following regarding Breuer's patient, Anna O.

        a.   Breuer's role in the development of psychoanalysis

        b.   Anna's symptoms

        c.   differentiation between symptoms of hysteria and those resulting from organic lesions

        d.   genesis of symptoms

(1) Anna tended for her father during illness that led to his death

(2) she herself fell ill while caring for him

(3) suffered from absences during which she muttered words to herself

e. hypnotic treatment

(1) Breuer repeated Anna's words to her while she was hypnotized expressed her emotions during the absences

(2) for several hours afterward was symptom-free

(3) she called the treatment "talking cure" or "chimney sweeping"

(4) gives an example of apparent hydrophobia stemming from an encounter with her disliked governess and the latter's dog who drank water from a glass

(5) describes Breuer's meticulous efforts to replicate the treatment

f. Freud deduces that symptoms of psychic traumas determined by exposure to original sources/repeating the trauma; later traumas must be cleared away before original can be dealt with

g. Freud's conclusion: "Our hysterical patients suffer from reminiscences. Their symptoms are the remnants and the memory-symbols of certain traumatic experiences."

V. Psychoanalysis as a method of treatment

A. Patients reached point of being unable or unwilling to continue

1. Freud called these points resistances: "a blockage or refusal to disclose painful memories during a free-association session."

2. served as protection against emotional pain

3. pain indicated closeness to problem genesis

4. necessitated further probing on the part of the therapist

B. Repression (based on resistances): "The process of barring unacceptable ideas, memories, or desires from conscious awareness, leaving them to operate in the unconscious mind."

1. job of therapist: bring repressed material back to conscious awareness

2. to do so, patient and therapist must have a close personal relationship

3. therefore, transference was essential to therapeutic process

4. one goal: wean patients from childlike dependency on therapist to function as adults

C. Dream analysis

1. dreams represent a disguised satisfaction of repressed desires

2. a dream's essence is wish fulfillment

3. two dream levels

a. manifest content: conscious dream recollection

b. latent content: underlying meaning

(1) symbolism unique to the individual

(2) but some common symbols

(3) indicate secret desires

4. not all dreams are caused by emotional conflicts; some caused by room temperature or overeating before bedtime

5. not all dreams contain repressed or symbolic material

D. Freud had no passion for helping

1. little personal interest in his system's potential therapeutic value

2. goal: the explanation of the dynamics of human behavior

3. viewed the techniques of association and dream analysis as research tools for data collection

4. therapeutic value was secondary
5. was described as an indifferent therapist; sometimes would fall asleep during sessions
6. sometimes allowed his dog, Jofi, to participate in therapy sessions
E. Freud's system
1. unlike traditional experimental psychology of his time in both content and method
2. developed without experimental approach or statistics; used free association, dream analysis, and case histories instead
3. nonetheless, believed by him to be scientific
4. Freud believed his cases and self-analysis provided ample support for his theories
5. based on evidence formulated, revised, and extended by Freud who was sole interpreter
6. guided by Freud's own critical abilities
7. Freud insisted only psychoanalysts who abided by his methods could judge its scientific worth
8. rarely responded to his critics
9. "Psychoanalysis was his system, and his alone."
VI. Psychoanalysis as a System of Personality
A. Freud explored otherwise ignored areas
1. unconscious motivating forces
2. conflicts among those forces
3. effects of the conflicts on behavior
B. Instincts: "mental representations of internal stimuli (such as hunger) that motivate personality and behavior."
1. propelling or motivating forces
2. biological forces that release mental imagery
3. are not inherited predispositions
   a. Did not use the German Instinkt: innate drives in animals
   b. Did use the German Trieb: human impulse or driving force
      (1) not inherited predispositions
      (2) more exactly, sources of stimulation within the body
      (3) goal: to remove or reduce the stimulation through behavior, e.g., eating, drinking, sexual intercourse
4. two types of instincts
   a. the life instinct (e.g., hunger, thirst, sex)
      (1) relate to self-preservation and survival of the species
      (2) manifested in libido: "the psychic energy that drives a person toward pleasurable thoughts and behaviors"
   b. the death instinct (e.g., suicide, hatred, aggression)
      (1) destructive force
      (2) can be directed inward or outward
      (3) appeared autobiographical
      (4) supposedly a response to personal experience of cancer, war horror, and family deaths, but new research refutes this
      (5) he did have awareness of own aggressiveness and capacity to hate
      (6) bitterness and irrevocability with which he severed relationships with dissenting colleagues

(7) aggression-as-motivator acceptable but death instinct not accepted by psychoanalysts

C. Levels of personality
    1. early conception: two parts of mental life, conscious and unconscious
        a. conscious part like tip of iceberg
           (1) small and insignificant
           (2) a superficial representation of the total personality
        b. unconscious part like the huge, submerged part of iceberg
           (1) vast and powerful
           (2) contains the instincts; driving forces of behavior
    2. revised conception: conscious/unconscious distinction replaced by id, ego, superego representation
        a. id (Es or "it"): "The source of psychic energy and the aspect of personality allied with the instincts."
           (1) corresponds more or less to earlier unconscious
           (2) the most primitive and least accessible part of personality
           (3) includes sexual and aggressive instincts
           (4) "cauldron full of seething excitations" (Freud)
           (5) irrational, unrelenting passions and blind cravings
           (6) unaware of reality
           (7) operates in accord with the pleasure principle
               (a) goal: reduce tension
               (b) methods: seek pleasure; avoid pain
           (8) contains basic psychic energy (libido)
           (9) ultimately, to satisfy needs and balance tension, interactions with the external world become necessary
        b. ego (Ich or "I"): "The rational aspect of personality responsible for controlling the instincts."
           (1) represented by the tip of the iceberg; the visible aspect of self
           (2) the mediating agent between id and the external world
           (3) goal: to facilitate their interaction
           (4) represents rational thought, reason
           (5) Freud himself used term "ego" infrequently; did not like it
           (6) is aware of reality and manipulates it to regulate id
           (7) operates in accord with the reality principle: restraining id urges until suitable object is located which fills the need and thus reduces tension
           (8) derives its power from id, cannot exist independent of id
        c. superego (über-Ich or "above I"): "The moral aspect of personality derived from internalizing parental and societal values and standards."
           (1) develops when child incorporates rules of behavior from caregivers
           (2) develops in response to a system of rewards and punishments
           (3) two parts of superego
               (a) conscience: child's incorporation of what the caretakers (as representatives of society) think is wrong and punishable
               (b) ego-ideal: child's incorporation of what the caretakers consider to be acceptable and worthy of reward
           (4) represents morality

PSYCHOANALYSIS: THE BEGINNINGS   437

(5) goal: perfection

(6) attempts to completely inhibit id

3. represents a conflict model of personality: unremitting struggle among id, ego, and superego

D. Anxiety

1. indicates ego is stressed or threatened

2. three types of anxiety

a. objective anxiety: fear of actual dangers

b. neurotic anxiety: derivative of objective anxiety; fear of punishment for expressing id impulses

c. moral anxiety: derivative of objective anxiety; fear of one's conscience, expressed through guilt or shame

d. anxiety produces tension which motivates a person to reduce it

e. defense mechanisms: "Behaviors that represent unconscious denials or distortions of reality but which are adopted to protect the ego against anxiety."

(1) protective devices developed by the ego for coping/self-protection

(2) unconscious

(3) distort reality

(4) examples: Denial, Displacement, Projection, Rationalization, Reaction Formation, Regression, Repression, Sublimation

E. Psychosexual stages of personality development: "In psychoanalytic theory, the developmental stages of childhood centered on erogenous zones."

1. neuroses arise from childhood experiences

2. Freud emphasizes the importance of child development

3. by age 5: adult personality almost completed

4. children are autoerotic: sensual pleasure derives from stimulation of bodies erogenous zones

5. each stage focuses on a different erogenous zone

6. inadequate (too little or too much) stimulation at a given stage leads to adult behaviors tied to that stage

a. oral stage

(1) erogenous zone = mouth

(2) birth to age 2

(3) primary source of sensual pleasure is stimulation of the mouth through sucking, biting, swallowing

(4) inadequate stimulation: adult with habits focused on the mouth, e.g., smoking or eating or exhibiting behaviors such as undue optimism or sarcasm

b. anal stage

(1) erogenous zone = anus

(2) age 2 to 4

(3) primary source of sensual pleasure is stimulation of the anus through expelling or withholding feces

(4) issue: control; obeying or disobeying parents' wishes

(5) inadequate stimulation: adult who is messy, dirty, wasteful (anal-expulsive) or one who is exceedingly neat, clean, compulsive (anal-retentive)

c.   phallic stage
       (1) erogenous zone = genitals
       (2) age 4 to 5
       (3) primary source of sensual pleasure is stimulation of the genitals through fondling or exhibition or through sexual fantasies
       (4) occurrence of Oedipus complex: "At ages 4 to 5, the unconscious desire of a boy for his mother and the desire to replace or destroy his father."
       (5) in general: child attracted to opposite sex parent and fearful of the rival same sex parent
       (6) resolution of the complex: identification with same sex parent; socially acceptable form of affection for opposite sex parent
       (7) attitudes toward the opposite sex that develop persist into adulthood
       (8) child assumes the same-sex parent's superego standards if identification is complete
d.   latency stage
       (1) no erogenous zone
       (2) age 5-12
e.   genital stage
       (1) erogenous zone = genitals
       (2) onset of puberty
       (3) heterosexual behavior is prominent
       (4) love/marriage, work, parenthood

VII.   Mechanism and Determinism in Freud's System
    A. Strict mechanist and determinist
       1. in agreement with structuralists and behaviorists
       2. no free will
       3. every action has a cause
       4. both unconscious and conscious motives are causal
       5. principles of natural science can explain all phenomena
       6. by using term psychoanalysis, Freud was signaling the importance of the analytic methods used in physics and chemistry
    B. 1895: Freud's conception of scientific psychology
       1. all phenomena reducible to the principles of physics
       2. mental phenomena are built on neurophysiological processes and reflect their characteristics
       3. goal of psychology: to represent mental processes quantitatively as states of specified matter
       4. project never completed but reflected throughout his later work in adaptations from physics (e.g., mechanics, electricity, and hydraulics)
       5. abandoned project because could not study human personality using techniques of physics and chemistry
       6. however, maintained positivist and mechanist positions yet remained willing to alter them when they became too constraining
VIII. Relations Between Psychoanalysis and Psychology
    A. Psychoanalysis for the most part outside the mainstream of psychology
       1. 1924: Journal of Abnormal Psychology
          a.   complaints about the number of papers on the unconscious

                    b.   next 20 years: few articles on psychoanalysis accepted for journal
                            publication
        B. Criticism by academic psychologists
                1. 1916: all things German were distrusted because of Germany's wartime
                    aggression
                2. Christine Ladd-Franklin: psychoanalysis as product of "undeveloped German mind"
                3. Robert Woodworth: psychoanalysis as "uncanny religion"
                4. J. B. Watson: psychoanalysis as "voodooism"
                5. James McKeen Cattell: Freud as living in a world of dreams populated by
                    sexually perverted orgies
        C. Psychology textbooks
                1. early 1920's books included some of Freud's ideas
                2. defense mechanisms, the unconscious mind, and dream analysis attracted
                    important attention
                3. as a whole, in the heyday of behaviorism, psychoanalysis was ignored
        D. 1930's and 1940's psychoanalysis
                1. popular with the general public because of sex, violence, and hidden motives
                2. often confused with mainstream psychology
        E. The academics' response
                1. experimental tests of psychoanalytic concepts
                    a.   claimed to have verified inferiority of psychoanalysis to
                            experimental psychology
                    b.   showed the public experimental psychology was relevant
                2. 1950's and 1960's
                    a.   behaviorist's translation of psychoanalytic concepts into
                            behavioristic terms
                    b.   psychology incorporated many of Freud's concepts [unconscious
                            motivation, pivotal nature of childhood experience, use of defense
                            mechanisms]
IX.   The Scientific Validation of Psychoanalytic Concepts
        A. More valid tests of Freudian concepts followed the more unconvincing studies of the
        1930s and 1940s
        B. Major analysis of 25,00 studies from psychology and other relevant disciplines
                1. difficult to experimentally test some concepts: e.g., id, ego, superego, libido
                2. some support for
                    a.   aspects of oral and anal personality
                    b.   castration anxiety
                    c.   dream reflect emotional concern
                    d.   aspects of the Oedipus complex
                3. no support for
                    a.   satisfaction of repressed motives, wishes, desires through dreams
                    b.   link between male Oedipal complex resolution and identification
                            with and acceptance of superego standards of father through fear
                    c.   inferiority of women's bodily conceptions, morality, and sense of
                            identity
                    d.   personality is formed by age 5 and changes little after that
        C. Later research and perspectives
                1. support for of the role of unconscious processes on thoughts, emotions, and
                    behaviors

    2. cognitive psychology: affirms existence of mental processes outside of conscious awareness

    3. support for defense mechanisms and Freudian slips

D. Most important learning: some psychoanalytic concepts can be operationally defined and tested by scientific methods

X. Criticisms of Psychoanalysis

A. General

    1. Freud's methods of data collection

       a. conditions were unsystematic and uncontrolled

       b. data consisted of what Freud recollected

       c. Freud may have reinterpreted patients' words

       d. Freud may have recalled and recorded primarily the material consistent with his theses

       e. discrepancies exist between Freud's notes and the published case histories

       f. Freud destroyed most of his data (patient files)

       g. only six case histories were published, and none provides compelling support

       h. accuracy of patient's reports not corroborated

    2. undisclosed reasoning process and method for deriving inferences and making generalizations from data

       a. data not quantified or analyzed statistically

       b. small and unrepresentative sample

       c. not possible to determine their reliability

    3. the power of suggestion

       a. Freud may have used coercive techniques

       b. May elicit or implant false memories

    4. Freud's views on women

       a. penis envy: lack of penis as cause of women's alleged weak superegos and feelings of bodily inferiority

         (1) Karen Horney's defection and ultimate retort: men have womb envy

       b. verdict by contemporary analysts:

         (1) Freud's views regarding psychosexual development of women unproven and wrong

         (2) social forces must be taken into consideration

    5. criticisms by neo-Freudians

       a. the denial of free will

       b. the focus on past behavior and exclusion of hopes and goals for the future

       c. theory based on neurotics, not on normal people

B. Consequences: rise of alternative theories and increasing divisiveness within psychoanalysis

XI. Contributions of Psychoanalysis

A. Despite concerns about scientific adequacy, which exist for all theories, psychoanalysis has been accepted by its advocates on the basis of other types of evidence

    1. the experimental method is not the sole method for discovery

    2. intuitive plausibility is another criterion

B. Strong impact on American academic psychology

1. attention to Freudian concepts continues at a high level
2. interest in psychoanalytic therapy has decreased both in terms of clients and of trained analysts
   a.   Freudian therapy: expensive, long-term investment
   b.   alternative therapies: less expensive, briefer
   c.   contextual forces: cost-cutting of health management organizations and development of psychoactive drugs
C. Enormous impact on popular culture
D. Misinterpretation of Freud's message about sex: did not advocate sexual freedom but instead thought that inhibition of the sex drive was essential for the continuation of civilization
E. Regardless of his intention, Freud's emphasis on sex led in part to increase in sexual liberation and to the popularity of his ideas
F. Notwithstanding concerns about lack of scientific accuracy and methodological problems, Freudian psychology vitally affected contemporary psychology

Lecture prompts/Discussion topics for chapter thirteen

- At the beginning of class, before any lecture, pass out slips of paper and ask students to write down one thing they would do if they had a cloak of invisibility for 48 hours. Be sure they do not put their names on the paper, then collect the papers and set them aside. Later in the lecture I discuss the difference between finding support for a theory and the idea of falsifiability. I ask them for ideas to test the presence of the Id, which generates some interesting discussions usually surrounding the fact that one would have to remove the ego and the superego from a person's personality. At that point, I tell them that's what I did with the cloak of invisibility question, then I read the slips one by one. Most of the slips will deal with either stealing or spying, which I argue is the Id. Then I ask how I could prove that Id does NOT exist, which cannot be done because the Id is not a falsifiable construct.
- Have students discuss: Is Freud's system "psychology"? Why or why not? Has he done psychology more harm or more good?

Internet Resources for chapter thirteen

The Freud Museum in London
http://www.freud.org.uk/
    Information about this museum includes on the site some exhibit information, information about Freud's live in London after he left Vienna, and an online store where one can purchase Freud-related goods.

The New York Psychoanalytic Society and Institute
http://www.psychoanalysis.org/
    This is the oldest psychoanalytic organization in the United States, and was founded by Abraham Brill. The site gives a little history information about the organization as well as current psychoanalytic thought.

Sigmund Freud Archives
http://www.freudarchives.org/
>This is a cataloging of, according to the site, over 45,000 items including such things as "Sigmund Freud's psychoanalytic and personal papers, his correspondence, photos, records, memorabilia, etc."

Sigmund Freud: Conflict and Culture (online exhibit at the Library of Congress website)
http://www.loc.gov/exhibits/freud/
>This is a fantastic site that has a variety of nice details about Freud's life, including a wide variety of photographs.

Time 100: Sigmund Freud
http://www.time.com/time/magazine/article/0,9171,991227,00.html
>This website lists Time magazine's 100 most important people of the 20th century (published 1999), with Freud listed as one of the most influential Scientists/Thinkers.

Potential answers to chapter thirteen discussion questions

1. According to Freud, what were the three great shocks in history that were delivered to the collective human ego?
"The first was when Copernicus...showed us that the earth was not the center of the universe but merely one of many planets revolving around the sun. The second revelation came...when Charles Darwin demonstrated that we are not a unique and separate species with a privileged place in creation but only a higher form of animal species that evolved from lower forms of animal life. And Freud administered the third shock by proclaiming that we are not the rational rulers of our lives but are under the influence of unconscious forces of which we are unaware and over which we have little, if any, control."

2. Describe the historical development of psychoanalysis relative to the other schools of thought in psychology.
Unlike the other systems discussed so far, Freud's system grew outside of academia and is not a science. Furthermore, its focus is psychopathology which was not a focus of the other systems. A last difference is Freud's focus on the unconscious, an idea ignored by all but a few psychologists (William James is one who did discuss the unconscious).

3. What was the role of the unconscious in structuralism, functionalism, and behaviorism?
"Wundt and Titchener did not accept the idea of unconscious forces in their systems because it is impossible to apply the method of introspection to the unconscious. Therefore, since the unconscious cannot be introspected, it cannot be reduced to sensory elements. The functional psychologists, with their exclusive focus on consciousness, had no use for the unconscious mind, although James did admit to the notion of unconscious processes." "Of course, Watson had no more room in his system of behaviorism for the unconscious than he did for consciousness."

4. Describe the theories of the unconscious developed by Leibnitz and Herbart.
The idea of the unconscious was first developed by Gottfried Leibnitz in the early 1700's and was called monadology. "Leibnitz believed that mental events (which are composed of the activity of monads) had different degrees of consciousness." The example given in the book is the idea that

a wave crashing on the beach is perceived, but the individual drops that make up the waves are below conscious perception. This theory was later refined by Freidrich Herbart 100 years later. Herbart believed that ideas that are below the level of consciousness will not be allowed to rise unless they are compatible with what is in consciousness.

5. Discuss two major sources of influence on the psychoanalytic movement.

One influence was the shift in the treatment of mentally ill members of society: from punishment/institutionalization to treatment/curing. This shift occurred under the mechanistic premise that mental illness was not a disease but instead a deficit that could be fixed. Another influence was the evolutionary work of Charles Darwin. A book published in 1979 by Frank Sulloway makes the argument that Darwin was much more influential on Freud than was previously believed. Sulloway looked at books from Freud's library and found extensive notes in Freud's handwriting in the margins. "Darwin discussed several ideas that Freud later made central issues in psychoanalysis, including unconscious mental processes and conflicts, the significance of dreams, the hidden symbolism of certain behaviors, and the importance of sexual arousal."

6. How were mentally ill persons dealt with before the time of Freud?

Beginning in 2000 B.C., mental disorders were considered demonic possession and those with disturbances were treated humanely through magic and prayer. However, with the rise of Christianity in the fourth century, those with mental disorders started being tortured and put to death (such victims were considered possessed or guilty of witchcraft). By the 18th century, imprisonment was the only treatment available. Those who advocated for the humane treatment of the mentally disturbed include Juan Vives (1500's Spain), Philippe Pinel (early 1800's France), and Dorothea Dix (mid- to late-1800's U.S.).

7. In what ways was Freud influenced by Mesmer and by Charcot?

Hypnosis had been present before Freud, and began with "mesmerism." Franz Mesmer thought that magnetism could health the body and mind, and for some time he and his treatment were influential in Europe. Patients would come in and be treated with magnets and would appear to be healed. Mesmer's system was reviewed scientifically by a committee, who found no substance to Mesmer's claim, but his ideas remained popular in Europe and the United States. Later, James Braid "called the trancelike state neuro-hypnology, from which the term hypnosis was eventually derived." Hypnosis is later used by Jean Charcot in Paris with hysteric individuals, and he taught his student Pierre Janet to do the same. This helps to shift the belief of the cause of mental disorders from somatic to psychic.

8. What was the Emmanuel Movement? How did it influence the acceptance of psychoanalysis in the United States?

The Emmanuel movement became popular in the United States "from about 1906 to 1910." It began in a church in Boston by a church rector named Elwood Worcester. Essentially this was psychotherapy performed by church officials using the power of suggestion. It popularized the notion of talk therapy. This was very popular and helped the acceptance of psychoanalysis because both endorsed the idea that the mind was the source of mental disorder.

9. Discuss the influences of evolutionary theory and of the notion of mechanism on the development of psychoanalysis.

Darwin had discussed such things as "unconscious mental processes and conflicts, the significance of dreams, the hidden symbolism of certain behaviors, and the importance of sexual arousal," which went on to Freud's theory of personality. Additionally, Darwin had some ideas about child development that used in Freud's conception of sexual drives and child development. "During Freud's university training, he was exposed to the idea of mechanism, as represented by the physiologists, including Helmholtz. They had united to take the position that there are no forces active within the organism other than the common physical and chemical ones." This later influenced Freud's attempts at making psychoanalysis a "pure science" by adopting methods and terms from physics and chemistry.

10. In what ways was psychoanalysis influenced by Freud's own childhood experiences and by his own views on sexuality?

Freud both feared and loved his father, who was a strict disciplinarian. His mother doted on him and believed he was destined for greatness and favored him over her other children. Freud felt great love for his mother. Later one of the components of his system is the Oedipus complex, which describes little boys falling in love with their mothers and seeing their fathers as romantic rivals. In addition, Freud's own inadequacies led him to give up sex, which eventually led to neurotic symptoms. He built his concepts of sex drive on these experiences.

11. Why was the case of Anna O. of such importance in Freud's thinking?

This case introduced Freud to the "talking cure" that became a hallmark of his therapy. He was also introduced to the methods of catharsis and hypnosis. In addition, her case study was the foundation of his theories about sex drive and neurosis.

12. What was the controversy about Freud's view of childhood seduction experiences?

Freud presented a paper to a scientific society in 1896 in which he argued that most women are sexually abused as children by an adult figure, often the father. The paper was not well received because the common theory at the time attributed mental illness to somatic causes. In addition, Freud's methods were subject to scrutiny. "About a year later, Freud reversed his position. Now he claimed that in most cases the childhood seduction experiences his patients described were not real," but were a product of fantasy. There is some controversy about whether Freud changed this position to make his system more acceptable, thereby suppressing what he believed to be the truth.

13. Describe the psychosexual stages of development.

Freud "became one of the first theorists to emphasize the importance of child development" and "believed that the adult personality was formed almost completely by age 5. He developed his psychosexual stage theory in which children pass through stages in their development. He thought that children could receive too much, too little, or just enough satisfaction at each stage, which would cause adult personality characteristics. For example, in the anal stage, children who refuse to expel feces grow to be adults who are "anal retentive" and will be compulsively clean and neat. The stages in order are: oral (birth-2 years, satisfaction from the mouth), anal (satisfaction from the anus, coinciding with toilet training), phallic (around age 4, this when the Oedipus complex arises), latent (from 5-12 years), and genital (puberty begins, heterosexual relationships develop).

14. Define repression, instinct, id, ego, and superego. What are the life instincts and the death instinct?

Repression involves forcefully excluding unwanted thoughts from consciousness. Freud believed that humans had driving forces such as death instincts (destructive and aggressive forces) and life instincts ("hunger, thirst, sex"). Freud's conception of the personality included the id (which is primitive and unconscious and operated under the pleasure principle), the ego (the mediator between the external world and the Id), and the superego (an internalized parent/voice of morality). "

15. What is the therapeutic significance of free association, of resistances, and of repression?
With free association, patients say whatever comes to mind, with the idea that such things will give clues about what is in the person's unconscious. Freud found that patients would come to a point while they were engaging in free association where they would stop. He called this resistance and he said this happened because the thoughts were "too shameful to be faced." It is at this point that Freud believed "the analytic process was closing in on the source or the problem and that the analyst should continue to probe that line of thought." He later referred to this process as repression, which involves forcefully excluding unwanted thoughts from consciousness.

16. In what ways do Freud's proposed levels of personality differ from one another? Why are they so often in conflict?
The id, ego, and superego are in conflict because they are driven by different motivations. While the id is driven by the pleasure principle, the ego is driven by social expectations and conditioning. The ego is designed to resolve the conflict between the two; however, anxiety often results from the pressure inherent to the equation. is the anxiety, or tension, is reduced by using defense mechanisms.

17. What is the relationship between psychoanalysis and mainstream academic psychology?
Psychoanalysis was eschewed by American academic psychologists, particularly during World War I "when virtually everything German was considered suspect." At the same time, his ideas were being included in psychology textbooks even though behaviorism was the prevailing thought. "But by the 1930's and 1940's psychoanalysis had captured public attention," which irritated academicians because psychoanalysis was being identified as psychology. To fight this, academic psychologists tested psychoanalytic theory, and in the 1950's and 1960's the "behaviorists [were] translating psychoanalytic terminology into the language of behavior." Eventually many ideas from psychoanalysis were absorbed into psychology.

18. How did Freud attempt to explain mental processes in mechanistic and deterministic terms?
Freud's system was deterministic in that he "believed that all mental events, even dreams, are predetermined; nothing occurs by chance or free will." Freud attempted to develop his system using "the principles of physics" and later one can see in his "writings the ideas and terminology he adopted from physics, especially mechanics, electricity, and hydraulics."

19. Describe the results of attempts to test Freudian concepts experimentally.
Some of his ideas received support, and others did not. The scientific studies on psychoanalysis revealed that there was evidence of support for "1. some characteristics of the oral and anal personality types, 2. castration anxiety, 3. the notion that dreams reflect emotional concerns, and 4. aspects of the Oedipus complex in boys." There was no support found for the ideas that "1. dreams satisfy symbolically repressed wishes and desires, 2. in resolving the Oedipus complex, boys identify with the father and accept his superego standards out of fear, 3. women have an inferior conception of their bodies, have less severe superego standards than men, and find it more difficult to achieve an identity, and 4. personality is formed by age 5 and changes little after that." Other research has supported the idea of the unconscious influencing "thoughts, emotions, and behavior," and the presence and use of some of the defense mechanisms and the Freudian slip.

20. What criticisms have been made of Freud's methods for collecting data? How did Freud believe his concepts should be tested?

Psychoanalysis has been criticized because his data collection was unsystematic (he worked from notes written after the therapy sessions) he probably forgot information or reinterpreted it. Some critics believe that Freud may have guided patients with suggestions. Another criticism is that his sample was small and of limited generalizability. Also, "there are discrepancies between Freud's notes on the therapy sessions and the published case histories supposedly based on those notes." A last criticism is that Freud never attempted to verify if his patients were telling the truth. Freud believed that the only people capable of testing psychoanalysis were those who had been trained in it.

21. What, in general, has been the impact of psychoanalysis on psychology and on popular culture?

Psychoanalysis has declined as a form of therapy because of the large and necessary commitment of time and money. Drug and other therapies have increased, largely because of their expediency and effectiveness. There is no doubt, however, that Freud's system had an incredible impact on and was accepted by the general public. Even as recently as 2005 the British Broadcasting Company "produced a four-hour television documentary about Freud's influence in Western society."

He "remains the most frequently cited individual in the psychology research literature," and the APA's Psychoanalysis division is "the sixth largest of all the APA's divisions."

22. Do you believe that Freud was correct when he included himself in the list of the three people who changed the world?

Perhaps, but Freud's impact has been far greater outside of psychology that within it. Given the criterion "people who have changed the world" I'd have to say yes, but if the criterion was "people who have changed psychology" I'd have to say no.

Key terms from chapter thirteen

- **Anxiety** This occurs "when the ego is being threatened", and there are three types; objective anxiety (from real dangers in the world), neurotic anxiety (fear of being punished for expressing impulses), and moral anxiety (fear of experiencing guilt or shame).
- **Catharsis** "The process of reducing or eliminating a complex by recalling it to conscious awareness and allowing it to be expressed."
- **Defense mechanisms** "Behaviors that represent unconscious denials or distortions of reality but which are adopted to protect the ego against anxiety."
- **Dream analysis** The technique whereby dreams are analyzed for their hidden and symbolic content in order to detect unconscious conflicts.
- **Ego** "The rational aspect of personality responsible for controlling the instincts."
- **The Emmanuel movement** Begun by Elwood Worcester, a church rector, these were forms of talk therapy that swept through and became popular in America and predated Freud's visit to Clark University in 1909.
- **Free association** The "technique in which the patient says whatever comes to mind."
- **Freudian slip** "An act of forgetting or a lapse in speech that reflects unconscious motives or anxieties."
- **Id** "The source of psychic energy and the aspect of personality allied with the instincts."

- **Instincts** Freud's definition is that these are "mental representations of internal stimuli (such as hunger) that motivate personality and behavior."
- **Latent content** The symbolic content of a dream, in contrast to the manifest content which is the story line of the dream.
- **Libido** "To Freud, the psychic energy that drives a person toward pleasurable thoughts and behaviors."
- **Manifest content** The story line of a dream, in contrast to the latent content which is the symbolic content.
- **Monadology** "Leibnitz's theory of psychic entities, called monads, which are similar to perceptions."
- **Oedipus complex** "At ages 4 to 5, the unconscious desire of a boy for his mother and the desire to replace or destroy his father."
- **Petites perceptions** Leibnitz's conception of unconsciousness, which later influenced Freud.
- **Pleasure principle** The force which guides the Id, which seeks pleasure and avoids pain.
- **Psychosexual stages** "In psychoanalytic theory, the developmental stages of childhood centering on erogenous zones." The stages in order are: oral (birth-2 years, satisfaction from the mouth), anal (satisfaction from the anus, coinciding with toilet training), phallic (around age 4, this when the Oedipus complex arises), latent (from 5-12 years), and genital (puberty begins, heterosexual relationships develop).
- **Repression** "The process of ejecting or excluding from consciousness any unacceptable ideas, memories, and desires, leaving them to operate instead in the unconscious."
- **Resistance** "A blockage or refusal to disclose painful memories during a free-association session."
- **Superego** "The moral aspect of personality derived from internalizing parental and societal values."
- **Transference** A process where "a patient responds to the therapist as if the therapist were a significant person (such as a parent) in the patient's life."

TESTBANK

ESSAY

1. Describe each of the three great shocks to the collective human ego suggested by Freud.

   ANS:
   Answer not provided.

   PTS: 1

2. Compare and contrast psychoanalysis with structuralism, functionalism, Gestalt psychology and behaviorism according to their (a) chronology, (b) heritage, and (c) subject matter.

   ANS:
   Answer not provided.

   PTS: 1

3. Name and describe the two basic orientations toward the treatment of mental illness, giving examples from the historical development of each. Which orientation did Charcot support? Janet? Freud?

   ANS:
   Answer not provided.

   PTS: 1

4. What was the influence of Charles Darwin and evolutionary theory on Freud's theory? Name three additional *external* influences on Freud's work, discussing one of them in detail.

   ANS:
   Answer not provided.

   PTS: 1

5. In addition to external influences on the development of psychoanalysis there were also major *internal* influences from Freud's life experiences and his psychological problems. Identify and discuss three of these internal influences, providing the link between each and its appearance within the theory.

   ANS:
   Answer not provided.

   PTS: 1   MSC: WWW

6. Describe the case of Anna O, drawing on information from both the textbook summary by Schultz and Schultz and from the Original Source Material by Freud.

   ANS:
   Answer not provided.

   PTS: 1

7. Describe the childhood seduction controversy, including Freud's vacillating attitude toward it as well as toward sex. What was his eventual self-analysis with regard to his attitude and personal sexual difficulties and by what method did he deal with them?

ANS:
Answer not provided.

PTS: 1   MSC: WWW

8. Psychoanalysis is both a method of treatment and a system of personality. Select one of these two perspectives and describe it, including the central concepts within it.

ANS:
Answer not provided.

PTS: 1

9. Describe the role of mechanism and determinism in Freud's system.

ANS:
Answer not provided.

PTS: 1

10. To what extent has there been scientific validation of psychoanalytic concepts? For which concepts is there the most research support and for which the least?

ANS:
Answer not provided.

PTS: 1

11. What was Freud's central method of collecting data? What are the five deficiencies of this method according to Schultz and Schultz?

ANS:
Answer not provided.

PTS: 1

12. What have been the central contributions of Freudian psychoanalysis to modern psychology?

ANS:
Answer not provided.

PTS: 1

13. According to Freud, the "third shock" to the collective human ego was the realization ____.
    a. that humans are not the rational commanders of their lives
    b. of id forces
    c. of conscious forces of behavior
    d. that laws of association predict human behavior
    e. that psychoanalysis is the only way to resolve mental illness

    ANS: A   PTS: 1   REF: The Development of Psychoanalysis

14. At the time of Freud's death, the dominant form of American psychology was ____.
    a. functionalism
    b. behaviorism
    c. Gestalt psychology
    d. humanistic psychology
    e. cognitive psychology

    ANS: B   PTS: 1   REF: The Development of Psychoanalysis
    MSC: WWW

15. A basic difference between psychoanalysis and the other systems of psychology was that ____.
    a. the other systems had an academic background and a focus on pure science
    b. psychoanalysis had only consciousness as its subject matter
    c. psychoanalysis did not hypothesize physical or physiological referents
    d. the other systems were not grounded in a natural science
    e. psychoanalysis came from Germany

    ANS: A   PTS: 1   REF: The Development of Psychoanalysis

16. The primary method of psychoanalysis was ____.
    a. the experimental method
    b. systematic experimental introspection
    c. psychosynthesis
    d. clinical observation
    e. extirpation of the unconscious

    ANS: D   PTS: 1   REF: The Development of Psychoanalysis

17. A topic addressed by psychoanalysis and essentially ignored by the other schools of psychology was ____.
    a. dynamic psychology
    b. childhood influences on later behavior
    c. a central organizing mechanism as a determinant of behavior
    d. the unconscious
    e. sex as the only motive or drive

    ANS: D   PTS: 1   REF: The Development of Psychoanalysis

18. Wundt's system dealt only with consciousness because ____.
    a. the unconscious has only one element (feelings)
    b. the unconscious cannot be reduced to basic elements
    c. the unconscious cannot be introspected
    d. the *a priori* knowledge of the unconscious cannot be distinguished from empirical knowledge
    e. he posited that the unconscious is a pseudo-problem

    ANS: C   PTS: 1   REF: The Development of Psychoanalysis

19. Monads were defined as ____.
    a. the sexual organs of humans
    b. unextended psychic entities
    c. extended physical realities
    d. individual elements of all reality, similar to perceptions
    e. components of the unconscious

    ANS: D   PTS: 1   REF: Antecedent Influences on Psychoanalysis

20. The creator of monadology was ____.
    a. Kant
    b. Leibnitz
    c. La Mettrie
    d. Watson
    e. Aristotle

    ANS: B   PTS: 1   REF: Antecedent Influences on Psychoanalysis
    MSC: WWW

21. "Little perceptions" were ____.
    a. apperceived
    b. below consciousness
    c. just noticeable differences
    d. absolute thresholds
    e. subtle impulses

    ANS: B   PTS: 1   REF: Antecedent Influences on Psychoanalysis

22. The concept of threshold of consciousness is attributed to ____.
    a. Leibnitz
    b. Herbart
    c. Weber
    d. Fechner
    e. Freud

    ANS: B   PTS: 1   REF: Antecedent Influences on Psychoanalysis

23. For Herbart, like James Mill, ideas influence one another ____.
    a. mechanically
    b. chemically
    c. physically
    d. physiologically
    e. above the absolute threshold

    ANS: A   PTS: 1   REF: Antecedent Influences on Psychoanalysis

24. According to Herbart, if a new idea is incompatible with pre-existing ideas, the new idea will be _____.
    a. remembered
    b. forgotten
    c. denied
    d. inhibited
    e. rationalized

    ANS: D   PTS: 1   REF: Antecedent Influences on Psychoanalysis

25. Which of the following is an original idea created by Freud, and not his predecessors?
    a. hypnosis
    b. the unconscious
    c. the mind as an iceberg
    d. All of the above.
    e. None of the above.

    ANS: E   PTS: 1   REF: Antecedent Influences on Psychoanalysis

26. The analogy that the mind is like an iceberg, with its bulk hidden from view (unconscious), is attributed to _____.
    a. Leibnitz
    b. Herbart
    c. Darwin
    d. Fechner
    e. Freud

    ANS: D   PTS: 1   REF: Antecedent Influences on Psychoanalysis

27. The notion of the pleasure principle was borrowed by Freud from _____.
    a. Aristotle
    b. Watson
    c. Leibnitz
    d. Darwin
    e. Fechner

    ANS: E   PTS: 1   REF: Antecedent Influences on Psychoanalysis

28. Freud claimed that his discovery was _____.
    a. the unconscious mind
    b. a way to scientifically study the unconscious mind
    c. the importance of aggression
    d. the importance of early childhood experiences
    e. All of the choices are correct.

    ANS: B   PTS: 1   REF: Antecedent Influences on Psychoanalysis

29. "A new movement requires something to revolt against"; Freud opposed the current trends in _____.
    a. philosophy
    b. psychophysics
    c. behavioral psychology
    d. applied psychology
    e. the treatment of mental disorders

    ANS: E   PTS: 1   REF: Antecedent Influences on Psychoanalysis
    MSC: WWW

PSYCHOANALYSIS: THE BEGINNINGS   453

30. The first person to argue for the humane treatment of the mentally ill was ____.
    a. Freud
    b. Pinel
    c. Vives
    d. Rush
    e. Dix

    ANS: C   PTS: 1   REF: Antecedent Influences on Psychoanalysis

31. By the 18th century, abnormal behavior was deemed to be ____.
    a. punishment for sin
    b. due to cognitive defects
    c. natural phenomena
    d. irrational behavior
    e. wholly physical

    ANS: D   PTS: 1   REF: Antecedent Influences on Psychoanalysis

32. The spirit of mechanism in relation to the treatment of mental illness portrayed mentally ill persons as ____.
    a. merely needing to be repaired
    b. "having a screw loose"
    c. defective
    d. possessed by evil spirits
    e. needing a religious conversion to Christianity

    ANS: A   PTS: 1   REF: Antecedent Influences on Psychoanalysis

33. The person who most strongly influenced humane reforms for the mentally ill in the United States was ____.
    a. Freud
    b. Pinel
    c. Vives
    d. Rush
    e. Dix

    ANS: E   PTS: 1   REF: Antecedent Influences on Psychoanalysis

34. The first psychiatrist in formal practice in the United States was ____.
    a. Freud
    b. Pinel
    c. Vives
    d. Rush
    e. Dix

    ANS: D   PTS: 1   REF: Antecedent Influences on Psychoanalysis

35. Rush's treatment techniques reflect ____.
    a. mechanistic theory
    b. the somatic approach
    c. what he thought were "humane" treatment innovations
    d. early crude attempts at shock therapy and sedation
    e. All of the choices are correct.

    ANS: E   PTS: 1   REF: Antecedent Influences on Psychoanalysis
    MSC: WWW

36. By the era of Freud's medical training, the dominant view in psychiatry about the cause of mental illness was _____.
    a. psychic determinism
    b. psychic mechanism
    c. psychophysiological
    d. psychosomatic
    e. somatic

    ANS: E   PTS: 1   REF: Antecedent Influences on Psychoanalysis

37. The psychic approach to mental illness was encouraged in the U.S. by _____.
    a. medical doctors
    b. the Red Cross
    c. Emmanuel Church Healing movement
    d. the Ecumenical Council of Churches
    e. None of the choices are correct.

    ANS: C   PTS: 1   REF: Antecedent Influences on Psychoanalysis

38. Franz Anton Mesmer contributed to which of the following?
    a. He taught statistical methods.
    b. He believed he was curing mental and physical illness by using magnetism.
    c. He used the term neurohypnology to describe his clinical treatment.
    d. He disputed the use of hypnosis.
    e. None of the choices are correct.

    ANS: B   PTS: 1   REF: Antecedent Influences on Psychoanalysis

39. The techniques of Mesmer _____.
    a. were investigated and he was discredited
    b. often involved convulsions
    c. were investigated and he was discredited **and** often involved convulsions
    d. have, for the most part, been accepted by modern psychology
    e. were actually unrelated to hypnosis

    ANS: C   PTS: 1   REF: Antecedent Influences on Psychoanalysis
    MSC: WWW

40. Hypnosis garnered some scientific respectability through the work of _____.
    a. Mesmer on hysteria
    b. Braid on neurohypnology
    c. Braid on neurology
    d. Gall on hysteria
    e. Charcot on psychotherapy

    ANS: C   PTS: 1   REF: Antecedent Influences on Psychoanalysis

41. Who was the first to argue that hysteria did not have a physical basis?
    a. Janet
    b. Charcot
    c. Freud
    d. Rush
    e. Mesmer

    ANS: A   PTS: 1   REF: Antecedent Influences on Psychoanalysis

PSYCHOANALYSIS: THE BEGINNINGS   455

42. A major theme of Freud's system, borrowed from Darwin, was the ____.
    a. importance of the sex drive throughout life
    b. recapitulation theory
    c. notion that sexual gratification was the only human instinct
    d. variability hypothesis
    e. physical inferiority of females

    ANS: A   PTS: 1   REF: Antecedent Influences on Psychoanalysis

43. The concept of childhood sexuality can be traced to ____.
    a. Aristotle
    b. Romanes
    c. Darwin
    d. Patze
    e. All except Aristotle

    ANS: E   PTS: 1   REF: Antecedent Influences on Psychoanalysis

44. Freud's espousal of mechanism has been traced to the influence of ____.
    a. Helmholtz
    b. Galton
    c. G. E. Müller
    d. Brücke
    e. Romanes

    ANS: D   PTS: 1   REF: Antecedent Influences on Psychoanalysis

45. The attitude toward sex in the Vienna of the Victorian era was ____.
    a. permissive and open
    b. publicly repressed but actually fraught with sexual perversions
    c. publicly repressed but marked by an incomparable degree of child prostitution
    d. permissive only in the middle class
    e. repressive only among the aristocracy

    ANS: A   PTS: 1   REF: Antecedent Influences on Psychoanalysis

46. Which of the following topics had already been discussed before Freud?
    a. infantile sexuality
    b. libido
    c. catharsis
    d. the importance of dreams
    e. All of the choices are correct.

    ANS: E   PTS: 1   REF: Antecedent Influences on Psychoanalysis

47. Charcot and Janet had practiced ____ prior to Freud's work on the same idea.
    a. infantile sexuality
    b. libido
    c. catharsis
    d. hypnosis
    e. All of the choices are correct.

    ANS: D   PTS: 1   REF: Antecedent Influences on Psychoanalysis

48. In common with functionalism and behaviorism, psychoanalysis bears the influences of _____.
    a. mechanism
    b. determinism
    c. Fechner's work
    d. Darwin's theory
    e. All of the choices are correct.

    ANS: E   PTS: 1   REF: Antecedent Influences on Psychoanalysis

49. Freud's interest in a scientific strategy to acquiring knowledge has been attributed to his reading of _____.
    a. Helmholtz
    b. G. E. Müller
    c. Darwin
    d. Fechner
    e. Charcot

    ANS: C   PTS: 1   REF: Antecedent Influences on Psychoanalysis

50. Freud's early research was in _____.
    a. biology and physiology
    b. medicine and philosophy
    c. neurology and psychiatry
    d. medicine and psychophysics
    e. medicine and hypnosis

    ANS: A   PTS: 1
    REF: Sigmund Freud (1856-1939) and the Development of Psychoanalysis

51. Freud's infamous use of cocaine _____.
    a. has been exaggerated
    b. was limited to the period in which he published on its utility in medicine
    c. extended to middle age
    d. was limited to his research trips to Paris in his early career
    e. both has been exaggerated **and** was limited to the period in which he published on its
       utility in medicine

    ANS: C   PTS: 1
    REF: Sigmund Freud (1856-1939) and the Development of Psychoanalysis

52. Breuer's fame was _____.
    a. dependent on the case of Anna O
    b. dependent on his association with Freud
    c. established by his discovery of the functioning of the semicircular canals
    d. established by his use of the "talking cure" and catharsis
    e. both dependent on the case of Anna O and on his association with Freud

    ANS: C   PTS: 1
    REF: Sigmund Freud (1856-1939) and the Development of Psychoanalysis

PSYCHOANALYSIS: THE BEGINNINGS   457

53. In the case of Anna O., the recollections she revealed while under hypnosis involved _____.
    a. ideas or experiences she found disgusting
    b. a positive transference
    c. the exacerbation of her conversion symptoms
    d. All of the choices are correct.
    e. None of the choices are correct.

    ANS: A   PTS: 1
    REF: Sigmund Freud (1856-1939) and the Development of Psychoanalysis

54. Freud's use of hypnosis was a direct consequence of _____.
    a. the case of Anna O
    b. his association with Breuer
    c. a research grant to study with Charcot
    d. his training with Brücke
    e. his association with Breuer and a research grant to study with Charcot

    ANS: E   PTS: 1
    REF: Sigmund Freud (1856-1939) and the Development of Psychoanalysis
    MSC: WWW

55. Currently known data fragments indicate that Freud was first apprised of the role of sexuality in hysterical symptoms by _____.
    a. Charcot
    b. Breuer
    c. Brücke
    d. Krafft-Ebing
    e. Janet

    ANS: A   PTS: 1
    REF: Sigmund Freud (1856-1939) and the Development of Psychoanalysis

56. The goal of Freud's therapies was to _____.
    a. investigate the "false memory" syndrome
    b. determine the incidence and prevalence of childhood sexual experiences in adult psychiatric patients
    c. refine the techniques of free association and dream analysis
    d. make the unconscious conscious
    e. All of the choices are correct.

    ANS: D   PTS: 1
    REF: Sigmund Freud (1856-1939) and the Development of Psychoanalysis

57. The beginning of psychoanalysis is considered to be indicated by the publication of _____.
    a. *Studies on Hysteria*
    b. *The Interpretation of Dreams*
    c. *The Psychopathology of Everyday Life*
    d. *Three Essays on the Theory of Sexuality*
    e. the Freud-Fliess letters

    ANS: A   PTS: 1
    REF: Sigmund Freud (1856-1939) and the Development of Psychoanalysis

58. Freud proposed that neurotic behavior did **not** develop in persons who ____.
    a. had never been seduced
    b. led a normal sex life
    c. experienced the seduction trauma before the phallic stage
    d. experienced the seduction trauma before the superego emerged
    e. were raised by sexually open and permissive parents

ANS: B   PTS: 1
REF: Sigmund Freud (1856-1939) and the Development of Psychoanalysis

59. Freud argued that whether an event happened in childhood ____.
    a. is irrelevant
    b. must be determined
    c. is not the determinant of neuroses in adults
    d. is less important than the patient's belief that it occurred
    e. can be determined only by hypnotherapy

ANS: D   PTS: 1
REF: Sigmund Freud (1856-1939) and the Development of Psychoanalysis

60. Freud's self-analysis was precipitated by ____.
    a. his sexual affairs outside of his marriage
    b. the worsening of his own neurotic symptoms
    c. the death of his father
    d. the death of his daughter
    e. his being abandoned by Jung, Adler, and other important dissidents

ANS: B   PTS: 1
REF: Sigmund Freud (1856-1939) and the Development of Psychoanalysis
MSC: WWW

61. Freud proposed that ____.
    a. dreams result from something in the patient's conscious mind
    b. nothing in a dream is without a cause
    c. dreams were a rich source of intellectual but not emotional material
    d. dreams could be completely without meaning
    e. dreams were unrelated to the underlying causes of a disturbance

ANS: B   PTS: 1
REF: Sigmund Freud (1856-1939) and the Development of Psychoanalysis

62. As a result of Freud's analysis of his own dreams, he recognized ____.
    a. sexual longings toward his mother
    b. sexual wishes toward his daughter
    c. the outlines of the Oedipus complex
    d. hostility toward his father
    e. All of the choices are correct.

ANS: E   PTS: 1
REF: Sigmund Freud (1856-1939) and the Development of Psychoanalysis

63. Freud's major work is considered to be ____.
   a. *Studies on Hysteria*
   b. *The Interpretation of Dreams*
   c. *The Psychopathology of Everyday Life*
   d. *Three /Essays on the Theory of Sexuality*
   e. *The Ego and the Mechanisms of Defense*

   ANS: B   PTS: 1
   REF: Sigmund Freud (1856-1939) and the Development of Psychoanalysis

64. In 1909, Freud ____.
   a. completed his self-analysis
   b. developed the concept of the thanatos
   c. received an honorary doctorate in psychology from Clark University
   d. expelled Jung from his circle of associates
   e. was diagnosed as having cancer

   ANS: C   PTS: 1
   REF: Sigmund Freud (1856-1939) and the Development of Psychoanalysis

65. The American public was primed for Freud's work because of ____:
   a. the publicity generated by Masson's and Malcolm's works on the seduction theory
   b. the popularity of the functionalists, especially its tenets on the unconscious
   c. Bruce's seven books and some five dozen magazine articles on the unconscious
   d. its familiarity with the work of Hall and its enthusiasm for anything he introduced into the young psychology
   e. its literacy in the German language, which enabled people to read Freud in the original

   ANS: C   PTS: 1
   REF: Sigmund Freud (1856-1939) and the Development of Psychoanalysis

66. Freud underwent a vasectomy ____.
   a. because he found sex so repulsive
   b. as part of a cancer treatment
   c. as a result of his self-analysis
   d. as part of a mid-life crisis
   e. both because he found sex so repulsive and as a result of his self-analysis

   ANS: B   PTS: 1
   REF: Sigmund Freud (1856-1939) and the Development of Psychoanalysis

67. Psychoanalysis was eradicated in Germany by ____.
   a. the Wundtians and Gestalt psychologists alike
   b. the Nazi party
   c. Adler and Jung, the dissidents of Freud
   d. the blitz at the hands of the Allies in World War II
   e. Freud's move to London

   ANS: B   PTS: 1
   REF: Sigmund Freud (1856-1939) and the Development of Psychoanalysis

68. Freud died as the result of _____.
    a. pernicious anemia
    b. cancer
    c. cocaine abuse
    d. a morphine overdose - administered at his request by his physician *[handwritten]*
    e. congestive heart failure, undetected because of the focus on his cancer

ANS: D   PTS: 1
REF: Sigmund Freud (1856-1939) and the Development of Psychoanalysis
MSC: WWW

69. According to Freud in his first lecture at Clark University, psychoanalysis originated with _____.
    a. himself
    b. Fechner
    c. Breuer
    d. Kant and Leibnitz
    e. the British associationists

ANS: C   PTS: 1
REF: Sigmund Freud (1856-1939) and the Development of Psychoanalysis

70. In the material presented at Clark University, Freud said that while hypnotized, Anna O. _____.
    a. described the mental images that controlled her thoughts
    b. developed new symptoms to replace the old ones
    c. recalled repugnant details of her dreams
    d. was able to describe the sources of her slips of the tongue
    e. could describe her dreams with remarkable clarity

ANS: A   PTS: 1
REF: Sigmund Freud (1856-1939) and the Development of Psychoanalysis

71. During his Clark University lecture, Freud proposed that psychic traumas are _____.
    a. the result of the child's witnessing the primal scene
    b. "the royal road to the unconscious"
    c. affect-laden events
    d. solely the result of seduction in early childhood
    e. All of the choices are correct.

ANS: C   PTS: 1
REF: Sigmund Freud (1856-1939) and the Development of Psychoanalysis

72. At the conclusion of his Clark University lecture, Freud stated that "hysterical patients suffer from _____."
    a. seduction traumas
    b. hysterical symptoms
    c. regression to infantile sexuality
    d. reminiscences
    e. psychic innovations

ANS: D   PTS: 1
REF: Sigmund Freud (1856-1939) and the Development of Psychoanalysis

73. Freud found that the free association method ____.
    a. operated freely
    b. did not always operate freely because of resistance
    c. was identical with dream analysis
    d. required catharsis of strangulated affect
    e. did not occur during countertransference

    ANS: B   PTS: 1   REF: Psychoanalysis as a Method of Treatment

74. ____ is an unconscious inability to bring into conscious awareness memories that are too shameful or painful to be faced.
    a. resistance
    b. recession
    c. rationalization
    d. regression
    e. projection

    ANS: A   PTS: 1   REF: Psychoanalysis as a Method of Treatment

75. ____ is the process of forcefully ejecting or excluding from consciousness any unacceptable ideas, memories, and desires.
    a. Reciprocity
    b. Repression
    c. Rationalization
    d. Regression
    e. Projection

    ANS: B   PTS: 1   REF: Psychoanalysis as a Method of Treatment

76. Freud's overriding goal was to ____.
    a. avoid practicing medicine
    b. have an academic research career
    c. describe and explain the dynamics of human behavior
    d. discover and develop an effective treatment methodology
    e. analyze and overcome his own neuroses

    ANS: C   PTS: 1   REF: Psychoanalysis as a Method of Treatment

77. Freud's investigative approach was ____.
    a. experimental
    b. to consider evidence as he alone interpreted it
    c. to present evidence to his disciples for joint analysis and consensus of interpretation
    d. reliable, despite its flaws
    e. valid, despite its flaws

    ANS: B   PTS: 1   REF: Psychoanalysis as a Method of Treatment

78. Freud conceived of *Instinkts* as ____.
    a. fundamental drives
    b. unique to animals
    c. libidinal
    d. defined in Darwin's *Origin of Species*
    e. defined by Romanes

    ANS: B   PTS: 1   REF: Psychoanalysis as a System of Personality

79. *Triebs* were, in Freud's system, ____.
    a. humans' motivating forces
    b. unique to animals
    c. unique to the phallic stage
    d. the root of neurosis
    e. similar to Einfall

    ANS: A   PTS: 1   REF: Psychoanalysis as a System of Personality

80. Self-preservation as a major human motive was expressed by Freud in his notion of the ____.
    a. *Instinkts*
    b. *Triebs*
    c. *Einfall*
    d. *libido*
    e. *Uber-Ich*

    ANS: D   PTS: 1   REF: Psychoanalysis as a System of Personality
    MSC: WWW

81. Freud's view of instincts is that they are ____.
    a. overrated
    b. inherited predispositions
    c. innate behaviors
    d. grouped into three general categories
    e. sources of stimulation and motivation within the body

    ANS: E   PTS: 1   REF: Psychoanalysis as a System of Personality

82. In his system of personality, Freud replaced the conscious/unconscious distinction with the concept of ____.
    a. soul
    b. petites perceptions
    c. monads
    d. id, ego, and superego
    e. the pleasure principle

    ANS: D   PTS: 1   REF: Psychoanalysis as a System of Personality

83. According to Freud, the biological, need-related part of everyone's personality is the ____.
    a. id
    b. superego
    c. ego
    d. ego-ideal
    e. conscience

    ANS: A   PTS: 1   REF: Psychoanalysis as a System of Personality

84. Fear of being the victim of a violent crime while visiting a gang-infested area in the United States is an example of ____.
    a. libido
    b. thanatos
    c. neurotic anxiety
    d. moral anxiety
    e. objective anxiety

    ANS: E   PTS: 1   REF: Psychoanalysis as a System of Personality

85. In Freud's system, personality development is built on the _____.
    a. psychosexual stages
    b. adequacy of the defense mechanisms
    c. efficacy of the ego
    d. reality principle
    e. resolution of the phallic stage

    ANS: A   PTS: 1   REF: Psychoanalysis as a System of Personality
    MSC: WWW

86. The Oedipal conflict occurs during the _____ stage of development.
    a. anal
    b. genital
    c. phallic
    d. oral
    e. latency

    ANS: C   PTS: 1   REF: Psychoanalysis as a System of Personality

87. Freud's position on reductionism was that _____.
    a. it obscures the dynamics of the personality
    b. it obscures the source of the psychic traumas
    c. all phenomena can be reduced to the principles of psychology
    d. all phenomena can be reduced to the principles of physics
    e. it destroys the Gestalt whole

    ANS: D   PTS: 1   REF: Mechanism and Determinism in Freud's System

88. Freud proposed that the aim of psychology was to _____.
    a. describe human behavior
    b. represent mental processes as quantitatively determined states
    c. adhere to a strict mechanistic approach
    d. eventually apply the methods of experimentation to his system of psychoanalysis
    e. All of the choices are correct.

    ANS: B   PTS: 1   REF: Mechanism and Determinism in Freud's System

89. By the 1930s and 1940s, psychoanalysis _____.
    a. as a whole was generally ignored by academic psychology
    b. was seen as a threat to the stature and dominance of behaviorism
    c. was perceived by American academics to be a variation of Gestalt psychology
    d. was wholeheartedly embraced by the American public
    e. as both a domain of study and as a therapy was confined to Germany

    ANS: D   PTS: 1   REF: Relations between Psychoanalysis and Psychology

90. The response of scientific psychology to psychoanalysis by the 1950s and 1960s was to _____.
    a. submit Freud's notions to observation
    b. continue to rail against the concept of "unconscious"
    c. bar it from discourse at the most prestigious universities
    d. reframe Freud's concepts in behavioral terms
    e. totally absorb Freud into the mainstream and remove the menace psychoanalysis posed

    ANS: D   PTS: 1   REF: Relations between Psychoanalysis and Psychology

91. Experimental research on Freudian theory has shown that ____.
    a. some of his concepts are testable by the methods of science
    b. some support for unconscious influences
    c. evidence for some Freudian concepts
    d. some concepts have resisted attempts at scientific validation
    e. All of the choices are correct.

ANS: E   PTS: 1
REF: The Scientific Validation of Psychoanalytic Concepts

92. The analyst ____ broke with Freud over his claim that women feel inferior to men.
    a. Karen Horney
    b. Carl Jung
    c. Lou Andreas-Salome
    d. Alfred Adler
    e. Anna Freud

ANS: A   PTS: 1   REF: Criticisms of Psychoanalysis

TRUE/FALSE

93. Sigmund Freud believed that his system was one of three great shocks to Western civilization.

ANS: T   PTS: 1   REF: The Development of Psychoanalysis

94. The schools of psychology arising concurrent with Freud's system were distinct from his in their attempt to maintain a pure science.

ANS: T   PTS: 1   REF: The Development of Psychoanalysis

95. The primary methods of psychoanalysis are the clinical methods of extirpation.

ANS: F   PTS: 1   REF: The Development of Psychoanalysis

96. Wundt and Titchener rejected the unconscious as subject matter because it could not be studied experimentally.

ANS: T   PTS: 1   REF: The Development of Psychoanalysis
MSC: WWW

97. Kant's construct of apperception is comparable to Freud's notion of consciousness.

ANS: F   PTS: 1   REF: Antecedent Influences on Psychoanalysis

98. Freud claimed to have discovered a method for studying the human unconscious.

ANS: T   PTS: 1   REF: Antecedent Influences on Psychoanalysis

99. The major conceptions of mental illness in the 19th century were the psychic and the mental.

ANS: F   PTS: 1   REF: Antecedent Influences on Psychoanalysis

100. Neurohypnology was given scientific credibility by Janet.

ANS: F   PTS: 1   REF: Antecedent Influences on Psychoanalysis

101. Janet proposed that hysteria was caused by mental phenomena.

ANS: T   PTS: 1   REF: Antecedent Influences on Psychoanalysis

102. Freud called his theory "unconscious determinism."

ANS: F   PTS: 1   REF: Antecedent Influences on Psychoanalysis
MSC: WWW

103. Among the concepts Freud borrowed from Darwin was the significance of dreams.

ANS: T   PTS: 1   REF: Antecedent Influences on Psychoanalysis

104. Freud's doctrine of psychic determinism was influenced by the physiologist Brücke.

ANS: T   PTS: 1   REF: Antecedent Influences on Psychoanalysis

105. Among Freud's few original ideas was the notion of catharsis.

ANS: F   PTS: 1   REF: Antecedent Influences on Psychoanalysis

106. The Freudian concept of dream symbolism can be traced to Freud's childhood.

ANS: F   PTS: 1
REF: Sigmund Freud (1856-1939) and the Development of Psychoanalysis

107. Freud's use of cocaine was limited to research and some careless affairs while still a young man.

ANS: F   PTS: 1
REF: Sigmund Freud (1856-1939) and the Development of Psychoanalysis
MSC: WWW

108. The first patient treated with psychoanalysis proved its effectiveness with her complete recovery.

ANS: F   PTS: 1
REF: Sigmund Freud (1856-1939) and the Development of Psychoanalysis

109. Freud's primary method of analysis was free association.

ANS: T   PTS: 1
REF: Sigmund Freud (1856-1939) and the Development of Psychoanalysis

110. Freud's break with Breuer was the result of the positive transference Anna O. developed for Freud while Breuer was on vacation.

ANS: F   PTS: 1
REF: Sigmund Freud (1856-1939) and the Development of Psychoanalysis
MSC: WWW

111. Freud initially proposed that neurotic behavior in adults was the result of positive transference with the parent of the opposite sex.

ANS: F   PTS: 1
REF: Sigmund Freud (1856-1939) and the Development of Psychoanalysis

112. A contemporary Freud scholar has argued that "opposition to the seduction theory claim was based...on the grounds that findings obtained by means of Freud's clinical procedures were unreliable."

ANS: T   PTS: 1
REF: Sigmund Freud (1856-1939) and the Development of Psychoanalysis

113. Freud's position that childhood seduction was imaginary was disputed in the 1930s by Ferenczi.

ANS: T   PTS: 1
REF: Sigmund Freud (1856-1939) and the Development of Psychoanalysis
MSC: WWW

114. Freud himself held a positive attitude toward sex.

ANS: F   PTS: 1
REF: Sigmund Freud (1856-1939) and the Development of Psychoanalysis

115. Freud's neurotic symptoms marked the development of dream analysis, his technique of self-analysis.

ANS: T   PTS: 1
REF: Sigmund Freud (1856-1939) and the Development of Psychoanalysis

116. The most prevalent theme in Freud's dreams was ambition.

ANS: T   PTS: 1
REF: Sigmund Freud (1856-1939) and the Development of Psychoanalysis

117. Breuer, not Freud, coined the phrase "the talking cure".

ANS: F   PTS: 1
REF: Sigmund Freud (1856-1939) and the Development of Psychoanalysis

118. Freud hypothesized that almost all the symptoms of hysteria are residuals of psychic traumas, i.e., reminiscences.

ANS: T   PTS: 1
REF: Sigmund Freud (1856-1939) and the Development of Psychoanalysis

119. Freud posited that there are three types of instincts: the life instinct, the death instinct, and the sex instinct.

ANS: F   PTS: 1   REF: Psychoanalysis as a System of Personality

120. Freud did not distinguish between animal instincts and human drives or impulses.

ANS: F   PTS: 1   REF: Psychoanalysis as a System of Personality

121. Freud hypothesized that the three components of the human psyche are *Es, Ich,* and *Trieb*.

ANS: F   PTS: 1   REF: Psychoanalysis as a System of Personality

122. Freud's term for what is known as the superego was *Einfall*.

ANS: F   PTS: 1   REF: Psychoanalysis as a System of Personality

123. Freud's system was deterministic and mechanistic.

ANS: T   PTS: 1   REF: Mechanism and Determinism in Freud's System

124. Freud followed through on his intention to model psychology after physics.

ANS: F   PTS: 1   REF: Mechanism and Determinism in Freud's System

125. A major criticism of Freud's data is that there are discrepancies between his notes on the therapy sessions and the published case histories.

ANS: T   PTS: 1   REF: Criticisms of Psychoanalysis

Chapter 14

Psychoanalysis: After the Founding

Abraham Maslow's relationship with his mother deviated greatly from the Oedipal relationship Freud would have predicted. As a child, Maslow brought home two kittens and his mother immediately clobbered them to death. His father was of no help, as he was always away drinking and womanizing. In short, his childhood was a miserable experience. His mother so adversely affected him that he said that "The whole thrust of my life-philosophy…and all my research and theorizing, has its roots in a hatred for and revulsion against everything she stood for." Maslow's was one of the systems that rose in reaction to Freud's psychoanalysis. Such systems began only 20 years after the founding of psychoanalysis, and were not well tolerated by Freud. These systems each differed in how they revised Freud's original thinking.

One prominent neo-Freudian was Freud's youngest child, Anna Freud, who became the only of his children to follow in his footsteps. She reported having an unhappy childhood, although she was her father's favorite child. "She became interested in [her father's] work," and 8 years later went into analysis with him for four years (for which he was heavily criticized). Her work focused on "the development and extension of psychoanalytic theory and its application to the treatment of emotionally disturbed children." Sigmund "took pride in Anna's work." One revision to Freud's work was her redefining the "ego functioning independently of the id."

Another branch of neo-Freudian thought was Object Relations theory, which emphasized "the social and environmental influences on personality, particularly within the mother-child interaction." Melanie Klein, an Object Relations theorist, focused on the social and cognitive (not sexual) aspects of the mother-child relationship particularly during the first 6 months of the child's life. She posits that the breast is the child's first part-object and is regarded as either hostile or satisfying depending on how satisfied the id is. The mother, the child's first whole object, is similarly regarded as good or bad. In this way, the first six months of life sets the child up for how it will interact with other objects (people) in its life.

One of the most influential of the neo-Freudians was Carl Jung, who at one time Freud called "my successor and crown prince." Jung later developed what he called analytic psychology. Jung had an unhappy childhood with a father given to rages and an emotionally disturbed mother. He obtained an M.D. in 1900 and established his own clinical practice before becoming interested in Freud's system. After reading *The Interpretation of Dreams*, Jung contacted Freud and they corresponded for a year before they finally met. A close mentorship and friendship ensued. "In 1911, at Freud's insistence, and despite opposition from the Viennese members, Jung became the first president of the International Psychoanalytic Association." He wrote *The Psychology of the Unconscious* (1912), which established differences between his and Freud's systems. That same year they terminated their personal correspondence, and in 1914 Jung resigned from the association.

One of the major differences between Jung's analytic theory and Freud's psychoanalysis is that Jung dismissed the importance Freud placed on sex. Some theorists believe that this is because Jung had a normal sex life while Freud had many insecurities concerning sex. In addition, Jung broadened the definition of libido to refer to life energy, not just in terms of sexual energy. Furthermore, for Jung, "personality was not fully determined by experiences during the first five years of childhood but could be changed throughout one's lifetime." Lastly, Jung added "a new dimension" to the unconscious, which he called the collective unconscious.

According to Jung, we have a personal unconscious and a collective unconscious. The personal unconscious contains "memories, impulses, wishes, faint perceptions, and other experiences in a person's life that have been suppressed or forgotten." The collective unconscious "contains inherited experiences of human and prehuman species." Within the collective unconscious are "inherited tendencies called archetypes...that dispose a person to behave not unlike ancestors who confronted similar situations." Jung developed these by investigating and finding similar myths and symbols across cultures. The four most frequently occurring archetypes are the persona (the mask we present to others), anima/animus (characteristics of the opposite sex), shadow (a dark, animalistic part), and—most importantly—the self (the balance we strike within our unconscious).

Jung's theory of personality involves the concepts of introversion (contemplative and introspective) and extraversion (sociable and confident in social situations). Other personality types he developed were thinking ("provides meaning and understanding"), feeling ("weighing and valuing"), sensing ("perception of physical objects"), and intuiting ("perceiving in an unconscious way").

Although Jung's system "influenced such diverse fields as religion, history, art, and literature," it has been largely ignored by experimental psychology. Strong evidence has resulted from testing Jung's theories empirically and created of the word-association test , the Myers-Briggs Type Indicator, and the Maudsley Personality Inventory. Thus, the "concepts of introversion and extraversion are widely accepted in psychology today."

Around the turn of the century, social sciences like sociology and anthropology were emerging, emphasizing the thorough influence of social environments on human personality and behavior. This American Zeitgeist applied pressure on Freud's tradition system and inspired younger psychoanalysts, like Alfred Adler and Karen Horney, to make revisions.

Alfred Adler had a "childhood...marked by illness, jealousy of an older brother, and rejection by his mother." At both home and school, his childhood was marked by feelings of inferiority. He received his M.D. in 1895 and practiced medicine. In 1902 he joined Freud's "weekly discussion groups" and later began to form his own personality theory. A rift began between them and they broke off with acrimony in 1911. He named his system individual psychology, which soon became popular in America.

Adler's system differed from Freud's in several ways. "Adler believed that human behavior is determined largely by social forces, not biological instincts." Adler also thought that Freud put too much emphasis on the importance of sex, and instead focused more on conscious (rather than unconscious) processes. Furthermore, Adler saw personality as being unified and motivated by "an overriding goal...[of reaching] perfection." Finally, "Adler argued that there was no biological reason, such as Freud's concept of penis envy, for any alleged sense of inferiority women might feel," and such feelings were driven instead by inequitable social forces.

Adler believed that a feeling of inferiority was the universal motivating force for humans, which leads us to compensate by overcoming obstacles. If we cannot overcome obstacles, we form "an inferiority complex, which renders the person incapable of coping with life's problems." Although our goal of perfection is universal, how we strive for the goal is not. Adler calls these differences the style of life, which become fixed by age 4 or 5. Adler believed that we have "creative power of the self" in which we shape our own destiny.

One social variable Adler became interested in is the effect of birth order on personality development. He believed that oldest, middle, and youngest children have different social environments, which in turn produce different personality traits. Oldest children become dethroned when the second and subsequent children are born and they become "insecure and hostile." Middle children, he believed, would be "ambitious, rebellious, and jealous." Youngest children "were likely to be spoiled and predisposed toward behavior problems."

Because Adler's system is more optimistic than Freud's it was "warmly received by scholars." However, critics contested that Adler's system was too simple. In addition, criticisms about how Freud collected data from his patients also applies to Alder. Some of Adler's system has received empirical support, particularly research on birth order.

Karen Horney also made changes to Freud's system. She, like many other psychoanalysts before her, had an unhappy childhood. Horney spent her adolescence in a "frantic search for the love and acceptance she lacked at home." She obtained her M.D. in 1913, "married, gave birth to three daughters…and became increasingly depressed." She had several affairs and eventually divorced her husband. She underwent Freudian analysis, but it did not help her so she engaged in a self-analysis. Eventually she became formally trained in psychoanalysis, came to the United States in 1932, became disillusioned with Freudian psychoanalysis, and founded her own institute.

"Horney disputed Freud's view that personality depends on unchanging biological forces. She denied the preeminence of sexual factors, challenged the validity of the Oedipal theory, and discarded the concepts of libido and the three-part structure of personality. However, she did accept unconscious motivation and the existence of emotional, non-rational motives. Counter to Freud's belief that women are motivated by penis envy, Horney argued that men are motivated by womb envy: jealousy of women for their ability to give birth." These ideas were the foundations for the women's rights movement and for feminist psychology.

Horney founded the concept of basic anxiety, which is the result of social and environmental forces in a person's childhood. Basic anxiety is a result of unfulfilling relationships with parents or caregivers. It may lead to three personality types that attempt to deal with the anxiety: the compliant personality (seeks approval, affection), the detached personality (seeks independence, perfection), and the aggressive personality (seeks power, exploitation). Horney believed that neurotic individuals had "a false picture of the personality or self" which she called the idealized self-image. However, Horney's system is optimistic in proposing that these personality types are not universal or inevitable. They can be prevented by parental warmth, loving, and caring in childhood.

Horney's system, like Adler's, was praised for its optimism (in contrast to Freud's determinism). Similar to Adler and Freud, Horney built her system based on her clinical observations, which were subject to the same criticisms of validity and reliability. Her work received renewed attention with the women's movement, and indeed Horney was the first to write about a "feminine psychology" in 1922.

In the 1960's a new school of thought in psychology, called humanism rose in opposition to the two prevailing schools: psychoanalysis and behaviorism, both of which were deemed mechanistic and dehumanizing. "Humanistic psychology emphasized human strengths and positive aspirations, conscious experience, free will (rather than determinism), the fulfillment of human potential, and a belief in the wholeness of human nature." Some of the foundation of humanism was provided by Brentano and Külpe, and to some extent James and the Gestalt psychologists. Humanism grew out of the Zeitgeist of the 1960's, which included a focus on pleasure and hedonism and a protest against mechanism and materialism. Two humanist psychologists that this chapter focused on are Abraham Maslow and Carl Rogers.

Maslow had an unhappy childhood, but received his Ph.D. in psychology in 1934. He began his professional career as a Watsonian behaviorist, but became disenchanted with what he saw as behaviorism's limitations. After World War II began, he was motivated to study "models of the best of human nature," and believed that "people are capable of more noble behaviors than hatred, prejudice, and war." Using these ideas, Maslow examined a small sample of individuals whom he believed achieved the highest level of self-actualization, in order to determine what differentiated them from the normal population. His new idea had difficulty being taken seriously by colleagues and getting published (behaviorism was still at its peak), but he was eventually recognized and "was elected president of the APA" in 1967.

Maslow believed that we all were capable of self-actualization, the highest state in Maslow's hierarchy of needs. However, before one is capable of self-actualization, the needs in the lower part of the hierarchy must be satisfied (including physiological, safety, belongingness, and esteem from others).

To achieve self-actualization, one needs to have a supportive and loving childhood, and the two basic needs must be satisfied within the first two years of life. According to Maslow, people who reach self-actualization "are almost always middle-aged or older and account for less than 1% of the population." The authors include an excerpt from Maslow's *Motivation and Personality* (1970) in which he elaborates on 3 of the 11 hallmarks of self-actualized individuals: a continued freshness of appreciation for the things around them, peak experiences, and social interest.

Maslow's ideas have been criticized because of the small sample size he used. In his defense, Maslow said that this was because there are so few self-actualized people. His system has received some empirical support, and enthusiastic support from his followers both inside and outside psychology. It also served as the basis for positive psychology.

Another humanist, Carl Rogers, is best known for his person-centered therapy techniques. Rogers grew up in a house with very restrictive rules. The lonely boy was jealous of his older brother and turned to reading "incessantly." At the age of 22, while attending a Christian student conference in China, "he finally freed himself from his parents' fundamentalist code and adopted a more liberal philosophy of life." He "received his Ph.D. in clinical and educational psychology in 1931" and later worked as a clinician for college students.

For Rogers, all people strive toward self-actualization, but this can be hindered if a person did not receive unconditional positive regard from his or her mother in childhood. Conditional positive regard can pose problems, because children internalize the conditions of worth and grow to fear rejection. The best case scenario for psychological health is unconditional positive regard. The idea of the fully-functioning person is similar to Maslow's self-actualized person (which Rogers acknowledged). Rogers' person-centered therapy was developed just as veterans were returning from World War II and needed clinical therapy. He was elected president of APA in 1946 and won numerous awards.

"The humanistic psychology movement became formalized with its own journal, association, and division of the APA. The Journal of Humanistic Psychology began in 1961, the American Association for Humanistic Psychology in 1962, and the Division of Humanistic Psychology of the APA in 1971. The Humanistic Psychologist became the division's official journal in 1989, and in 1986 the humanistic psychology archive was established at the University of California at Santa Barbara." However, even humanists believe that humanism never fully formed as a school of psychology because it was never accepted into mainstream psychology. This might be because humanists largely worked in clinical settings rather than academic institutions. This might also be because by the time humanism rose against psychoanalysis and behaviorism, those two schools had begun to lose power; humanism had no school against which to revolt. Despite this, it has had an impact on contemporary psychology with the current positive psychology movement.

In 1998 then-president of APA Martin Seligman called for psychologists to focus on positive aspects of humans rather than the traditional focus on negative aspects. Since then, numerous studies and books have been published focusing on positive psychology, and even journals have been started beginning in 2000 called *Journal of Happiness* studies, and in 2006 the *Journal of Positive Psychology*.

Several empirical studies have found that happiness has broad implications for one's life. Material things do not make a person happy, although a lack of money and resources can make a person unhappy. Good health also does not create happiness, but bad health can create unhappiness. There seem to be no differences on happiness between men and women. Married people reported higher levels of happiness than unmarried/divorced/widowed people. In addition, happiness is correlated with high levels of job success and productivity. Although positive psychology has its roots in humanism, it is different in that its findings are based on scientific research. Current psychologists do not see positive psychology as a separate school, but rather a general shift in focus for all of psychology.

Outline

I. When Life hands you Lemons…
   A. A lonely boy brings home stray kittens, mother kills them
   B. Boy is Abraham Maslow, hated mother, did not love her as Oedipus complex predicts
   C. Maslow has nightmarish childhood: "it's a wonder I'm not a psychotic"
   D. No friends, father was aloof, drank, womanized
   E. Mother openly rejected Maslow
   F. All Maslow's work "has its roots in a hatred for and revulsion against everything she stood for"
   G. As a teen, felt inferior because of big nose, scrawny build
   H. Immersed himself in books
   I. As adult received adoration and admiration for his ideas

II. Competing Factions
   A. Splintered movement
      1. within 20 years of its founding
      2. Freud never again spoke to the rebels
   B. Three major groups of subsequent theorists
      1. Neo-Freudians who elaborated on Freud: Anna Freud, Melanie Klein, and Heinz Kohut
      2. Orthodox Freudians who became dissenters: Carl Jung, Alfred Adler and Karen Horney
      3. Protesters against both psychoanalysis and behaviorism: Abraham Maslow and Carl Rogers

III. The Neo-Freudian and Ego Psychology
   A. In general
      1. adhered to Freud's central premises
      2. modified selected aspects
   B. Major change: expansion of the concept of the ego
      1. more independent of the id
      2. has its own energy
      3. has functions separate from the id
      4. is free of the conflict produced by id pressures
   C. Influences on Freudian personality theory
      1. de-emphasize biological forces
      2. emphasize social and psychological forces
      3. minimize the import of infantile sexuality
      4. minimize the import of the Oedipus complex

IV. Anna Freud (1895-1982)
   A. Her life
      1. the youngest of Freud's six children; not a welcomed child at birth
      2. mother's least preferred daughter

PSYCHOANALYSIS: AFTER THE FOUNDING   473

3. became her father's favorite child
4. early interest in her father's work
   a. attended meetings of the Vienna Psychoanalytic Society from the age of 14
5. age 22: began four-year analysis with her father (criticized as incestuous)
6. age 29: read her first scholarly paper to the Vienna Psychoanalytic Society
   a. "Beating fantasies and daydreams" (1924)
      (1) presented as a case history but in reality about herself
      (2) gained her admission into the Society
7. courted by many but unmarried
8. developed intense friendship with Dorothy Tiffany Burlingham and acted as second mother to her kids
9. nursed her father when he developed cancer
10. devoted her life to the psychoanalysis of emotionally disturbed children

B. Child Analysis
   1. 1927: *Introduction to the Technique of Child Analysis*
      a. considered children's relative immaturity
      b. considered children's lack of verbal skills
      c. innovative methods
         (1) the use of play materials
         (2) the observation of the child in the home
   2. London
      a. opened a clinic
      b. established a psychoanalytic training center (now the Ana Freud Centre in London)
   3. 1936: *The Ego and the Mechanisms of Defense*
      a. elaborated and clarified the use of defense mechanisms that protect ego from anxiety
      b. remains a core work in ego psychology
      c. gave mechanisms a more precise definition and example from her analysis of children
   4. 1945: publication of first of eight volumes of The Psychoanalytic Study of the Child
   5. substantially revised orthodox psychoanalytic theory
   6. expanded the role of the ego

C. Comment
   1. 1940s: ego psychology became the primary American form of psychoanalysis
   2. neo-Freudians
      a. translated, simplified, and operationally defined concepts
      b. encouraged experimental investigation of the hypotheses
      c. modified psychoanalytic psychotherapy (Steele, 1985)
   3. fostered a conciliatory relationship with academic psychology

V. Object Relations Theories
A. Object: Freud's term "to refer to any person, object, or activity than can satisfy an instinct"
   1. mother's breast: 1st object infant's world to gratify an instinct
   2. primary object: mother (comes to be an instinct-gratifying object)
   3. later, other people also become such objects

B. Theory focus: interpersonal relationships with objects
    1. contrasts with Freud's focus on the actual instinctual drives
    2. highlighted social and environmental effects within the mother-child relationship
    3. personality created early in infancy through nurturing relationships
    4. most crucial concern in personality development: ability and need of child to establish an independent identity apart from the mother and to develop relationships with other objects (persons)

C. Melanie Klein (1882-1960)
    1. unwanted child
    2. depressed throughout life from feelings of rejection
    3. alienated by her own adult daughter (who later became an analyst)
    4. daughter maintains that her brother committed suicide because of mother
    5. theory focuses on the deep, emotional mother-infant bond (especially within first 6 months)
    6. describes that bond in social-cognitive, not sexual, terms
    7. breast becomes a satisfying or hostile part-object, depending on its degree of id gratification
    8. whole objects, including the mother, are similarly defined as satisfying or hostile
    9. nature of infant-mother social bond in the first 6 months of life generalizes to all child-object relationships

VI. Carl Jung (1875-1961)
A. For a brief time served as Freud's surrogate son and heir to the psychoanalytic throne
B. 1914: split with Freud to develop own approach called analytical psychology
C. Jung's life
    1. unhappy, lonely childhood
    2. father: temperamental, clergyman who lost faith
    3. mother: emotionally unstable with history of family mental illness
    4. Jung: lack of trust in others for the rest of his life
    5. turned from logical world to dream, fantasies, and the unconscious
    6. made decisions based on what his unconscious told him in dreams
    7. 1900: MD from University of Basel
        a. interested in psychiatry
        b. first job with Eugen Bleuler, working with schizophrenics
    8. 1905: appointed lecturer in psychiatry at University of Zurich
        a. married wealthy heiress
        b. resigned position to write, do research, and have a private practice
    9. private practice
        a. patients faced him in comfortable chair rather than lying on couch
        b. occasional meetings on his sailboat
        c. sometimes sang to patients, at other times was rude
        d. professional reputation established before he met Freud
    10. interest in Freud's work
        a. 1900: read The Interpretation of Dreams
        b. 1906: began correspondence with Freud
        c. 1907: first meeting lasted 13 hours; 20 years difference in age
    11. personal relationship with Freud
        a. intensely close relationship contains elements of Oedipal complex

      b.   Jung reported sexual experience at age 18, father figure made sexual advances and Jung rejected them

      c.   may have led to the rejection of Freud later

      d.   rebels against older men trying to dominate him

12. work with Freud

      a.   1909: lectures at Clark University with Freud

      b.   1911: first president of the International Psychoanalytic Association

          (1) Freud insisted

          (2) Viennese members opposed it

          (3) an issue: Jung was not Jewish

      c.   1912: *The Psychology of the Unconscious*

          (1) Jung had never been uncritical of Freud

          (2) however, tenets in this book differed in major ways from Freud

          (3) expected this book would strain his relationship with Freud

          (4) the relationship was terminated

13. 1914: Jung resigned from International Psychoanalytic Association

14. age 38: severe emotional problems for 3-year period

      a.   thought he was losing his mind

      b.   unable to conduct any type of intellectual work

      c.   suicidal; kept gun next to bed

      d.   continued treating patients

      e.   similar to Freud's personal life crisis

          (1) at midlife

          (2) treatment: explore the unconscious

          (3) analyzed his own dreams, among other stimuli (but not in the systematic way Freud did)

          (4) a time of immense creativity

      f.   led to the development of his personality theory→ decided that personality was not shaped during childhood but in middle age

      g.   resolved crisis but still exhibited unusual behavior

15. highly productive; continued to write and develop system for the rest of his 86 years of life

D. Analytical psychology

1. autobiographical influences, particularly with regard to views of about sex

      a.   Oedipus complex not relevant to his childhood experience

      b.   no major adult sexual difficulties

      c.   preferred company of women

      d.   had affairs

          (1) theorists say: because Jung had a normal sex life, sex played a minimal role in his system; because Freud had insecurities, sex was the center of his system

      e.   isolation as child reflected in his theoretical focus on inner growth rather than social relationships

      f.   sex plays a minimal role in explaining human motivation

2. libido

      a.   major difference with Freud's theory

      b.   for Jung, is a generalized life energy rather than the sexual energy depicted by Freud

c. the energy expresses itself in growth, reproduction, and other critical processes and events
3. forces that influence personality
    a. Freud: people are victims of their childhoods
    b. Jung:
       (1) one is partly shaped by goals/hopes/aspirations for the future
       (2) personality can be changed throughout life rather than be shaped during the first 5 years of life
4. unconscious mind
    a. added the component of the collective unconscious: inherited experience of the human species and its animal ancestors

E. The collective unconscious
1. personal unconscious: "The reservoir of material that once was conscious but has been forgotten or suppressed."
    a. comprised all suppressed or forgotten experiences
    b. not a deep level of unconscious
    c. unconscious experiences can easily be brought into awareness
2. complexes
    a. groups of experiences in the personal unconscious
    b. are manifested by a preoccupation with some idea
    c. the preoccupation/idea influences behavior
    d. is a smaller personality formed within the whole
3. collective unconscious: "The deepest level of the psyche; it contains inherited experiences of human and prehuman species."
    a. deeper level than the personal unconscious
    b. unknown to the person
    c. contains cumulative experiences of prior generations and animal ancestors
    d. consists of universal evolutionary experiences
    e. forms the basis of personality

F. Archetypes: "Inherited tendencies within the collective unconscious that dispose a person to behave similarly to ancestors who confronted similar situations."
1. inherited tendencies within the collective unconscious
2. innate determinants of mental life
3. predispose one to behave in a manner like one's ancestors
4. four common archetypes
    a. persona
       (1) social mask
       (2) characterizes what we want others to think of us
       (3) may not correspond to our actual personality
    b. anima/animus
       (1) arise from primitive past of the human species
       (2) each person has some of the characteristics of the opposite sex
       (3) comes through association with the opposite sex throughout history
       (4) anima: feminine characteristics in men
       (5) animus: masculine characteristics in women
    c. shadow
       (1) our darker side

(2) all immoral, passionate, and unacceptable desires

(3) pushes us to behave in ways we ordinarily find unacceptable

(4) source of spontaneity, creativity, insight, and deep cmotion

    d.   self

(1) most important archetype

(2) integrates all aspects of the unconscious

(3) provides unity and stability to the personality

(4) a drive or force toward self-actualization (harmony and completeness)

(5) self-actualization cannot occur prior to middle age (30-40)

    e.   midlife crucial to personality development

(a) a natural time of transition

(b) personality undergoes necessary and beneficial changes

G. Introversion and extraversion (attitudes)

    1. extravert

        a.   libido directed outside the self

        b.   strongly influenced by forces in the environment

        c.   is sociable and self-confident

    2. introvert

        a.   libido directed inward

        b.   resistant to external influences

        c.   is contemplative, introspective, less confident in relations with others and the external world, less sociable

    3. opposing attitudes

        a.   exist in all of us to some degree

        b.   no one is a total extravert or total introvert

        c.   dominant attitude at a given moment can be influenced by experience

H. Psychological types: The functions and attitudes

    1. four functions of personality: thinking, feeling, sensing, intuiting

        a.   rational modes or pairs: involve reason and judgment in decision-making

(1) thinking: provides meaning and understanding

(2) feeling: process of weighing and valuing

        b.   nonrational modes or pairs: ways of perceiving the world

(1) sensing: conscious perception of physical objects

(2) intuiting: perceiving in an unconscious way

    2. functions represent ways in which one orients one's self

        a.   to the external objective world

        b.   to one's internal subjective world

    3. for each pair of functions, only one can be dominant at a given time

    4. eight psychological types

        a.   combinations of dominant functions and attitudes

        b.   examples include "extraverted thinking type" or "introverted intuiting type"

I. Comment

    1. Jung's work influenced: religion, history, art, and literature

    2. Jung's analytical psychology ignored by scientific psychology

a. many of his books had no English translation until 1960s
b. writing was "convoluted" and organization unclear
c. his disregard for scientific methods and research designs repulsed experimentalists
    (1) Jung's mystical and seemingly theological ideas even less acceptable than Freudian concepts
    (2) reliance on observation and interpretation was similar to Freud's and less acceptable than controlled studies in the lab
3. lasting and continuing influence on psychology
    a. Word-association Test
        (1) 100 words used to elicit emotions
        (2) measured time to respond to word, as well as physiological responses
        (3) designed to measure emotional intensity of stimulus words
    b. Myers-Briggs Type Indicator
        (1) personality test assessing the psychological types
        (2) widely used for research and application in counseling and personnel settings
    c. Eysenck's Maudsley Personality Inventory
        (1) assesses the attitudes of introversion and extraversion
    d. research using both tests has given empirical support for the Jungian concepts underlying them
    e. other concepts such as the collective unconscious have been more difficult to operationalize and study scientifically
4. concept of self-actualization anticipated humanistic psychology
5. concept of midlife crisis as necessary to personality development
6. still possible to receive formal training as a Jungian analyst
7. avenues for formal communication among Jungians
    a. Society of Analytical Psychology
    b. Journal of Analytical Psychology

VII. Social Psychological Theories: The Zeitgeist Strikes Again
A. Revised conception of human nature
1. rise of anthropology, sociology and other social sciences
2. de-emphasis of biological factors (popular in physics and biology)
3. emphasis on social and environmental influences
4. psychoanalysts question whether taboos and neurotic symptoms Freud described were universal
5. turned to social science explanation of behavior, which was supported by American Zeitgeist
6. Adler and Horney (Freudian dissenters) look at interpersonal relationships' effects on personality formation and human behavior, especially in childhood

VIII. Alfred Adler (1870-1937)
A. Most salient facts
1. broke with Freud in 1911
2. thought to be the 1st advocate of taking a social psychological view within psychoanalysis
3. social interest a key concept in his theory
4. a string quartet was named for him
B. His life

1. wealthy Viennese family
2. childhood marked by illness, sibling rivalry, rejection by mother, feelings of inadequateness and unattractiveness, and learning difficulties
    a. no experience of an Oedipus complex
3. worked diligently to become popular and do well in school
    a. core of his system: inferiority feelings and compensating for weaknesses are autobiographical in nature, as he himself noted
4. 1895: MD from University of Vienna
    a. specialty in ophthalmology; practiced general medicine
    b. later went into psychiatry
5. 1902: joined Freud's weekly discussion group
    a. openly criticized the emphasis on sexual factors
    b. 1910: named president of the Vienna Psychoanalytic Society by Freud in an attempt to reconcile their differences
6. 1911: relationship with Freud terminated with bitterness
7. 1914-1918: World War I army physician
8. postwar: organized child guidance clinics
9. 1920's: developed his system called individual psychology
    a. individual psychology: "Adler's theory of personality; it incorporates social as well as biological factors."
10. numerous visits to United States
    a. professor of medical psychology at the Long Island College of Medicine in New York
    b. extremely popular as a person, a writer, and a speaker
11. 1934: professor of medical psychology at Long Island College of Medicine
12. 1937: died in Scotland during a demanding speaking tour
    a. Freud remained bitter about him
C. Individual psychology
    1. social forces, not biological instincts, are the central causes of human behavior
    2. social interest: "Adler's conception of an innate potential to cooperate with other people to achieve personal and societal goals."
        a. develops through learning experiences in infancy
    3. personality determinants
        a. minimizes the role of sex in personality development
        b. focuses on conscious rather than unconscious determinants
        c. future goals have greater effect than past events
    4. stressed wholeness and uniformity of personality
        a. single driving force
        b. toward one overriding goal: superiority
    5. striving for superiority (meaning perfection) permeates the personality
        a. a dominant life goal
        b. exemplifies total self-realization
        c. innate, vigorous, and universal
        d. evident in every aspect of the personality
    6. women no different than men in terms of real or imagined inferiority
        a. thought that Freud's theory of inferiority of women was a male myth propagated through self-interest
        b. social forces, not innate predispositions, contribute to any inferiority feelings of women
        c. champion of equal rights for women

D. Inferiority feelings
1. generalized sense of inferiority motivates compensatory behavior
   a. originally conceived as stemming from physical imperfection
   b. extended to involve any real or imagined handicap of any type
2. infant's dependence on others and helplessness arouse sense of inferiority
3. lifelong push-pull between inferiority feelings and striving for superiority
4. lead to achievements and the continued improvement of society
5. inferiority complex: "A condition that develops when a person is unable to compensate for normal inferiority feelings."

E. Style of life
1. represents the different and unique ways each person strives for superiority (perfection)
2. involves behaviors uses by the person to compensates for actual or perceived inferiority
3. set at ages 4 to 5 (importance of early life experiences)
4. resistant to change thereafter
5. serves as perspective through which subsequent experiences are viewed
6. person can consciously construct a life style of choice

F. The creative power of the self
1. person has ability to fashion his/her personality in a manner consistent with his/her unique style of life
2. similar to soul: human essence which is dynamic and productive
3. person can actively and consciously use inherited and learned abilities and experiences to form an attitude toward his/her life and fate

G. Birth order: the different social experiences of the oldest, youngest, and middle children result in different personalities and coping mechanisms
1. oldest: insecure and hostile (because of being center of attention than being dethroned)
2. middle: ambitious, rebellious, and jealous (because trying to surpass the first)
3. youngest: likely to be spoiled and predisposed toward behavior problems (because they are the center of attention)

H. Comment
1. in contrast to Freud, Adler presents an optimistic picture of humans who can shape their own destinies no matter what genetic or childhood obstacles they face
2. criticisms
   a. superficial
   b. common sense concepts (others found same ideas "shrewd and insightful")
   c. system is too simple (simplicity viewed by Adler and others as a virtue)
   d. experimental psychologists have same concerns with Adlerian methods as they do with those of Freud and Jung
      (1) observations of patients neither replicable nor verifiable
         (a) not obtained under controlled conditions
         (b) not systematic
         (c) patients' reports not corroborated
      (2) did not explain methods of analysis and conclusion

3. contributions
    a.   rescarch on his birth order concept
    b.   effects of early memories on adult style of life
    c.   influence on ego psychology
        (1) emphasis on social forces; also influenced Horney
        (2) focus on unity of personality
    d.   creative power of self: influenced Maslow
    e.   stress on social variables: influenced Rotter
    f.   attention to social and cognitive variables in tune with contemporary psychology
    g.   continuation of published research
        (1) Adlerian journal Individual Psychology
        (2) Other, European journals
    h.   existence of Adlerian training institutes world-wide
    i.   current use of his theory in counseling and parenting

IX.   Karen Horney (1885-1952)
A. Overview
    1. one of 1st feminists
    2. trained as a Freudian analyst
    3. intended to extend Freud's work, not replace it
B. Horney's life
    1. born in Hamburg, Germany
    2. childhood experiences influenced her system
        a.   father
            (1) religious, gloomy
            (2) captain of a ship
            (3) much older than Horney's mother
            (4) disparaged Karen's attractiveness and intelligence
        b.   mother
            (1) liberal
            (2) full of life
            (3) hated husband
            (4) married to avoid spinsterhood
            (5) rejected Karen
            (6) treated older brother as special
        c.   lack of parental love is the impetus for her autobiographical concept of basic anxiety: "Horney's conception of pervasive loneliness and helplessness, feelings that are the foundation of neuroses."
    3. adolescence: crushes and fervent pursuit of love and acceptance
    4. 1913: MD from University of Berlin, despite father's opposition
    5. married; had 3 daughters (2 analyzed by Melanie Klein)
    6. progressively more depressed
    7. marital difficulties
    8. physical problems: crying spells, stomach pains, chronic fatigue, compulsive behaviors, suicidal thoughts, inability to work
    9. had affairs
    10. divorced husband
    11. ceaseless search for approval
    12. most lasting affair with Erich Fromm, another analyst

13. distraught by end of the affair, she entered psychoanalysis
14. turned to self-analysis when formal analysis failed: "she concluded that by studying medicine and engaging in promiscuous sexual behavior, she was acting more like a man than like a woman"
15. lifelong search for love
16. 1914-1918: training as orthodox psychoanalyst at Berlin Psychoanalytic Institute
17. became faculty member at Institute and started private practice
18. published on problems of female personality, delineating her differences with Freudian theory
19. 1932: associate director of Chicago Institute for Psychoanalysis
20. taught at and later broke with New York Psychoanalytic Institute
21. founded and served as head of American Institute of Psychoanalysis
22. remained head of American Institute until her death

C. Disagreements with Freud
1. opposed view that personality depends on unchangeable biological influence
2. denied the primacy of sex in personality formation
3. disputed Oedipal theory
4. rejected the concept of libido
5. rejected the Freudian three-part (id, ego, superego) structure of personality
6. accepted only unconscious motivation and existence of emotional, non-rational factors
7. opposed Freud's tenet that women are motivated by penis envy
8. posited that men are instead motivated by womb envy and have to hold women down through "denying women equal rights, limiting their opportunities, and downgrading their efforts to achieve" in order to promote the false idea of natural superiority
9. contrasting views of human nature as viewed by Horney
   a. Freud: pessimist, skeptic with regard to human decency and growth potential, humanity destined to suffer or destroy
   b. Horney: optimistic, believer in human potential and decency, humans capable of change

D. Basic anxiety
1. primary idea in Horney's theory
2. feelings of isolation and helplessness in a hostile world
3. results from parents' behaviors toward the child (i.e., dominance, lack of protection and love, and erratic behavior)
4. not innate
5. basic motivation: need for safety and freedom from fear
6. personality
   a. develops in early childhood
   b. continues to change throughout life
   c. focus on parental behavior as determinants
   d. child development NOT universal
   e. personality depends on cultural, social, and environmental variables

E. Neurotic needs
1. parent-child relationship fosters basic anxiety
2. child respond by developing strategies to cope with this anxiety and its concomitant defenselessness and uncertainty

3. neurotic need
   a. a coping strategy that has become a permanent part of personality
   b. a mode of defense against anxiety
   c. examples: affection, achievement, and self-sufficiency
4. Horney identified 10 neurotic and later grouped them into 3 trends
   a. the compliant personality: movement toward others for affection, approval, domination in order to feel secure
   b. the detached personality: movement away from others to gain independence and faultlessness and withdraw from contact
   c. the aggressive personality: movement against others to gain power and status and aggress against others
5. all are unrealistic way to deal with anxiety
   a. generate conflict through their incompatibility
   b. are too inflexible to permit alternative behaviors
   c. if deep-rooted, will exacerbate one's problems
   d. permeate all aspects of our personality, behavior, and relationships

F. The idealized self-image
   1. false picture of self
   2. masks and denies true self
   3. leads to belief that one is a better person than one really is
   4. neurotic conflicts
      a. neither innate nor inevitable
      b. arise from undesirable situations in childhood
      c. could be prevented with warmth, understanding, and love in child's home life

G. Comment
   1. Horney's optimism greeted with pleasure
   2. described personality using social rather than innate variables
   3. supporting evidence
      a. clinical observations of patients
         (1) non-replicable, non-validated, unsystematic
         (2) non-experimental
      b. her system engendered little research
   4. renewed popularity with the woman's movement
   5. major contribution: writings on feminine psychology

X. The Evolution of Personality Theory: Humanistic Psychology
   A. Some 15 to 20 theories represent were derived in some respect from Freudian psychoanalytic theory
   B. Like Wundt, Freud presented a system of thought that both brought followers and motivated revolt
   C. Freudian theory was a point of revolt, not a base, for humanistic psychology
   D. Humanistic psychology (Maslow and Rogers) = Third Force (supplants other two forces: behaviorism and psychoanalysis)
   E. Basic themes
      1. emphasis on the positive rather than the negative in human traits and goals
      2. focus on conscious experience
      3. belief in free will
      4. confidence in unity of human personality

F. Antecedent influences on humanistic psychology
    1. Brentano: argued for study of function, not structure of consciousness; criticized mechanistic and reductionistic approaches
    2. Külpe: conscious experience cannot be reduced to elementary forms
    3. James: argued against mechanistic approach; focus on consciousness as a "whole"
    4. Gestalt psychology: focus on the conscious experience as a whole and its emergent quality, not on parts
    5. Adler, Horney:
        a. conscious as well as unconscious determinants of personality and behavior humans capable of free will and have capacity to shape themselves the present and future are important determinants along with the past
    6. the Zeitgeist: the 1960s
        a. protest against Western mechanism and materialism
        b. focus on personal fulfillment
        c. belief in human perfectibility
        d. emphasis on
            (1) the present
            (2) hedonism
        e. tendency to self-disclose
        f. valuing feelings over reasoning

G. The nature of humanistic psychology
    1. protested behaviorism
        a. narrow, inflexible, unfruitful
        b. deterministic and mechanistic
        c. objectification, quantification, and reduction of humans to animal-like S-R components
    2. protested Freudianism
        a. also deterministic and mechanistic
        b. minimization of consciousness
        c. only studied neurotics and psychotics
    3. protested psychology's
        a. focus on mental illness
        b. tendency to ignore human strengths and virtues
        c. disregarded joy, contentment, ecstasy, kindness, and generosity
    4. intent: a serious study of neglected areas

XI. Abraham Maslow (1908-1970)
A. Overview
    1. spiritual father of humanistic psychology
    2. strongest influence in initiating the movement
    3. garnered academic respectability for the movement
    4. goal: to understand the highest achievements of which humans are capable
    5. studied a small sample of psychologically outstanding people to determine how they differ from average people

B. His life
    1. born in Brooklyn
    2. unhappy childhood, escaped through study and books
    3. at Cornell University, horrid first course in psychology taught by Titchener

4. transferred to the University of Wisconsin; PhD in 1934
5. initially an enthusiastic behaviorist
6. personal experiences demonstrated limitations of behaviorism
7. influenced by contact with European psychologists in United States (Adler, Horney, Koffka, and Wertheimer)
8. Wertheimer and Benedict: prototypes of human nature—both self-actualizing
9. affected by World War II: resolved to devote himself to developing a psychology that would deal with the highest human ideals in order to show humans were capable of more than just hatred and violence
10. early attempts to humanize psychology while teaching at Brooklyn College
    a. ostracized by behaviorists and avoided by colleagues
    b. liked by students
    c. major journals refused to publish his work
11. 1951-1969, Brandeis University
    a. refined theory
    b. published popular books
    c. elected APA president
    d. became celebrity
    e. hero to counterculture movement
    f. compensated for his childhood feelings of inferiority

C. Self-actualization: "The full development of one's abilities and the realization of one's potential."
    1. characteristics
        a. innate predisposition
        b. the highest human need
        c. involves active use of all of one's traits and talents
        d. involves the growth and realization of one's potential
    2. the hierarchy of needs
        a. physiological
        b. safety
        c. belonging and love
        d. esteem
        e. self-actualization
    3. research focus: characteristics shared by self-actualized persons
    4. research method: analysis of biographies and other information of people such as Albert Einstein, Eleanor Roosevelt, and George Washington Carver
    5. self-actualized persons: free of neurosis, middle-aged or older
    6. tendencies common to self-actualizers
        a. "objective perception of reality;
        b. a full acceptance of their own nature;
        c. a commitment and dedication to some kind of work;
        d. simplicity and naturalness of behavior;
        e. a need for autonomy, privacy, and independence;
        f. intense mystical or peak experiences;
        g. empathy with and affection for humanity;
        h. resistance to conformity;
        i. a democratic character structure;
        j. an attitude of creativeness, and
        k. a high degree of what Adler termed social interest."

7. prerequisites for self-actualization
    a.   adequate childhood love
    b.   meeting of physiological and safety needs in first two years
D. Original Source Material on Humanistic Psychology from *Motivation and Personality* (1970)
    1. characteristics of self-actualizers
        a.   continued freshness of appreciation
           (1) repeated sense of naive awe and delight of life's experiences and beauty
           (2) comes sporadically at unforeseen moments
           (3) individual differences in the content (music, nature, children) of what is perceived as beautiful
           (4) does not emanate from commonly considered sources of happiness such as going to a party or receiving money
        b.   the peak (mystic) experience
           (1) previously described by William James
           (2) strong, chaotic, pervasive emotions
           (3) similarity between mystic experiences and some subjects' descriptions of sexual orgasms
               (a) boundless possibilities
               (b) mixture of power and helplessness
               (c) feelings of ecstasy and amazement
               (d) freedom from time and space
               (e) sense of transformation
           (4) both are natural, not religious, experiences
           (5) can vary in intensity
           (6) mild peak experiences occur often during a week
           (7) intense peak experiences accompanied by self-transcendence
        c.   social interest (gemeinschaftsgefuehl)
           (1) German word invented by Alfred Adler
           (2) deep feeling of appreciation for and empathy with others even if they exhibit shortcomings
           (3) identification with humankind
           (4) Adler's "older-brotherly attitude"
E. Comment
    1. criticism
        a.   small sample sizes preclude generalizability
        b.   subjects selected according to Maslow's subjective criteria
        c.   terms are ambiguous and inconsistently defined
    2. rebuttal: no other way to study self-actualization; perceived work as preliminary and would one day be confirmed
    3. limited empirical support
        a.   some characteristics of self-actualizers confirmed
        b.   order of needs in hierarchy corroborated
           (1) people who do not satisfy safety, belongingness, and esteem needs more likely to be neurotic
           (2) positive correlation between self-reported esteem and self-confidence and competence
        c.   most of theory has no research support

4. concept of self-actualization intuitively popular

5. broad impact: applied in business, education, medicine, and psychotherapy

6. some of his ideas found in positive psychology movement

XII. Carl Rogers (1902-1987)

A. Overview

    1. developed person-entered therapy

        a. client is responsible for change

        b. assumes one can consciously and rationally alter one's thoughts and behavior

    2. personality theory

        a. focuses on a single motive factor (akin to self-actualization)

        b. subject population: students treated at campus counseling centers

        c. rejected Freudian idea of unconscious restraints

        d. personality formed by the present and how it is consciously perceived

B. Roger's life

    1. born in Oak Park, Illinois

    2. parents: strict fundamentalist religious views, suppression of emotion

    3. Rogers: parental views held him in a "vise"; eventually rebelled

    4. a solitary child: turned to reading

    5. relied on his own experiences

    6. family considered his overly sensitive and nervous

    7. age 12: family moved to a farm; Rogers interest in nature, agriculture and science kindled

    8. age 22: attended Christian student conference in China; freedom from parents' belief system; assumed more liberal views

    9. new beliefs became cornerstones of his theory

        a. people must rely on their own interpretation of events

        b. people can consciously and actively strive to improve

    10. 1931: Ph.D. in clinical and educational psychology from Teachers College at Columbia University

    11. 1st 9 years of career counseling delinquent and needy children

    12. 1940: begins academic career; taught and developed his theory at Ohio State, University of Chicago, and University of Wisconsin

    13. nervous breakdown during which he felt "deeply certain of my complete inadequacy as a therapist, my worthlessness as a person, and my lack of any future in the field of psychology"

    14. Roger's clinical and theoretical base: college students undergoing counseling

        a. young

        b. bright

        c. articulate

        d. problems of adjustment rather than severe psychiatric disorders

    15. subjects very different from Freud's or that of others in private practice

C. Self-actualization

    1. a drive

        a. the major motive in personality

        b. innate

        c. can be helped or hindered by childhood experiences and learning

2. mother-child relationship: key to actualization
    a. important for its effect on the child's sense of self
    b. positive regard: "The unconditional love of a mother for her infant."
    c. with positive regard, child will have a healthy personality
    d. if mother's love is conditional on proper behavior (conditional positive regard) then child internalizes her attitude
        (1) develops conditions of worth: feels praiseworthy only when acts in parentally approved ways
        (2) tries not to behave in disapproved ways
        (3) true self remains undeveloped
        (4) in order to avoid rejection, curtails aspects of self
    e. conditional reward
3. most important precursor: unconditional positive regard
    a. love and acceptance regardless of child's behavior
    b. leads to self-acceptance rather than conditions of worth
    c. no part of self need be repressed
    d. self-actualization becomes possible
4. epitome of psychological health
5. similar to Maslow's concept of self-actualization
6. Rogers differs to some extent from Maslow on the characteristics of the psychologically healthy person, listing the following
    a. "an openness to, and freshness of appreciation of, all experience;
    b. a tendency to live fully in every moment;
    c. the ability to be guided by their instincts rather than by reason or the opinions of others;
    d. a sense of freedom in thought and action;
    e. a high degree of creativity; and
    f. the continual need to maximize one's potential."
7. Rogers: the person is continually in the process of actualizing rather than actualized
8. 1961: *On becoming a person*: emphasis on spontaneity, flexibility, continued growth

D. Comment
1. major impact on psychology
2. acceptance fostered in part by end of World War II
    a. large number of veterans need to adjust to daily life
    b. demand for more therapists and quickly-learned therapy
    c. psychoanalysis required an M.D. and several years of specialization
    d. Roger's person-centered therapy simpler, had less prep time
3. found broader application, not just therapy, but self-image enhancement
    a. used in training for managers
    b. used to train clinical psychologists, social workers, and counselors
4. over 50 journals and 200 organizations promote person-centered therapy
5. 1960s: part of human potential humanistic psychology movements
6. 1946: President of the American Psychological Association
7. APA Distinguished Scientific Contribution Award
8. APA Distinguished Professional contribution award

XIII. The Fate of Humanistic Psychology
    A. Formalization of movement
        1. 1961: Journal of Humanistic Psychology
        2. 1962: American Association for Humanistic Psychology
        3. 1971: became a division of APA
        4. 1986: humanistic psychology archive started at University of California at Santa Barbara
        5. 1989: The Humanistic Psychologist became journal of the APA Division of Humanistic Psychology
    B. Some characteristics of a school of thought
        1. definition of psychology different than those of behaviorism and psychoanalysis
        2. passionate conviction
    C. Not a school in eyes of the humanists themselves
        1. "failed experiment" (Cunningham)
        2. "perceived as having little importance" (Rogers)
    D. Not a part of the mainstream of psychological thought
        1. practitioners in private practice rather than academia
        2. comparatively little research and few publications
        3. no graduate training programs
        4. ill-timed attacks on the psychoanalytic and behaviorism, schools already in decline
    E. Contributions
        1. within psychoanalysis, strengthened the idea that one can consciously and freely change
        2. indirectly facilitated the return of the experimental study of consciousness
        3. added to endorsement of changes already occurring in psychology
        4. impact on 21st century psychology
XIV. Positive Psychology
    A. Continued humanistic theme of studying the best characteristics of humans
    B. 1998: Martin Seligman, APA president
        1. noted preponderance of attention to negative (e.g., anxiety and aggression) as compared with positive (e.g., altruism and honesty) influences
        2. called for more positive framework for studying the nature and potential of humans
        3. sounded like Maslow 30 years earlier
    C. eager response to Seligman
        1. constant stream of research and publications
        2. 2000: special issue of the *American Psychologist* on positive psychology followed year later by 4 articles on "Why Positive Psychology is necessary"
        3. 2001: area had largest increase in number of publications for last forty years 2002: Seligman's book *Authentic Happiness: Using the New Positive Psychology to Realize Your Potential for Lasting Fulfillment* well received by psychologists and the public at large
        4. 2005: Time magazine publishes 40-page special on Seligman and colleagues work
        5. 2006: *Journal of Positive Psychology* begins
        6. positive topics now covered in contemporary psychology textbooks

D. Research on Positive Psychology
   1. Happiness
      a. joy happiness and well-being less dependent on money, more dependent on feeling respected, control of one's life, close friends and family
      b. however, lack of economic resources and security can lead to unhappiness
      c. hedonistic treadmill: "both positive and negative events will affect our level of happiness only temporarily, after which we revert to our normal level of hedonic neutrality"
      d. "The more people endorse materialistic goals, the less happy and satisfied they are with life"
   2. Health & happiness
      a. good health not essential, but poor health can reduce happiness
      b. seemingly unrelated to gender
      c. well-being improves with age, except when there are serious health problems or physical limitations in old age
      d. happier people live longer
   3. Interpersonal relationships and happiness
      a. married people happier than unmarried/divorced/widowed people
   4. Self-esteem and happiness
      a. high happiness positively correlated with self-concept, internal locus of control, extraversion, and conscientiousness
      b. high happiness negatively correlated with neuroticism
   5. Race/ethnicity and happiness
      a. older African Americans who had experienced discrimination less happy than those who had no such experience
      b. Black college students with stronger connection to Black community happier
   6. Success and happiness
      a. people high in subjective well-being more likely to get job interviews
      b. more likely to be evaluated positively by supervisors
      c. superior performance and productivity
      d. handle managerial jobs better
E. Comment
   1. Contrasting views that positive psychology is legacy of humanistic psychology versus a mere repackaging
   2. Differences between positive and humanistic psychology as well as between positive psychology and psychoanalysis
      a. positive psychology rests on controlled, mainly experimental research
   3. Viewed as an extension of, not replacement for other positions
   4. Conceptualizations and methods to the study the human condition are very different than Freud's
XV. The Psychoanalytic Tradition in History
A. Multiplicity of views and positions
B. Some are psychoanalytic only in the sense that they are not in the behavioral-experimental tradition of mainstream psychology

C. Psychoanalysis more splintered, with more sub-schools than behaviorism
D. Remains an important, evolving school

Lecture prompts/Discussion topics for chapter fourteen

- So many of these people acknowledged that their theories were derived from autobiographical experiences. Do you think this is a good or a bad thing?
- Put this quote on the board before discussing humanism and ask students which systems are being addressed in the quote and specifically where: "Man is aware…Man has choice…Man is intentional", from Bugental, *The third force in psychology*, Journal of Humanistic Psychology, 1964, pg. 26

Internet Resources for chapter fourteen

Alfred Adler Institute of San Francisco & Northwestern Washington
http://pws.cablespeed.com/~htstein/
This is the home page for one of the many Adler associations. This homepage has a Web link to video clips of Adler speaking a bit about his system.

Carl Rogers
http://www.nrogers.com/carlrogers.html
A tribute site devoted to Carl Rogers that was developed by his daughter Natalie. This site contains a timeline of his life, a biography, links, and other information about Rogers.

C. G. Jung Institute of Zurich
http://www.junginstitut.ch/main/Show$Id=1102.html
This site offers information about Jung's system and life, as well as gives information about training in Jung's system.

Martin Seligman's webpage at the University of Pennsylvania
http://www.psych.upenn.edu/~seligman/
This page contains more information about Seligman's work on positive psychology, including some links to full-text writings.

Maslow: A Theory of Human Motivation
http://psychclassics.yorku.ca/Maslow/motivation.htm
This is a full text version of the paper in which Maslow introduces his hierarchy of needs.

Potential answers to chapter fourteen discussion questions

1. What personal experiences influenced Maslow's approach to psychology?
The chapter begins with a story from Abraham Maslow which illustrated the cruelty of his mother, the aloofness of his father, and the misery of his childhood. His mother so adversely affected him that he said that "The whole thrust of my life-philosophy…and all my research and theorizing, has its roots in a hatred for and revulsion against everything she stood for." His was one example of an autobiographical system.

2. In what ways did the neo-Freudians change Freudian psychoanalysis?
The neo-Freudians saw the ego as having "a more extensive role," including "the ideas that the ego was more independent of the id, possessed its own energy not derived from the id, and had functions separate from the id." "Neo-Freudian analysts also suggested that the ego was free of the conflict produced when id impulses pressed for satisfaction." Finally, the neo-Freudians emphasized "social and psychological forces" while de-emphasizing biological forces.

3. How did the changing Zeitgeist in social science influence the later development of psychoanalysis?
Around the turn of the century a multitude of disciplines were doing work that showed that people are heavily influenced by their social environments. For example, anthropological studies showed that there were some cultures for which incest was not taboo. This Zeitgeist applied pressure on Freud's system to change, and the younger psychoanalysts felt freer to make such revisions.

4. Describe Anna Freud's relationship with her father. What changes did she introduce into psychoanalysis?
Freud's youngest child, Anna Freud, was the only of his children to follow in his footsteps. She reported having an unhappy childhood, although she was her father's favorite child. "She became interested in [her father's] work" when she was 14, and 8 years later went into analysis with him for four years (for which he was heavily criticized). Her work focused on "the development and extension of psychoanalytic theory and its application to the treatment of emotionally disturbed children." Sigmund "took pride in Anna's work." One revision to Freud's work was her redefining the "ego functioning independently of the Id," which has later been called Ego psychology and marks many of the neo-Freudians.

5. To what does the word *object* refer in *object relations theory*?
"Freud used the word "object" to refer to any person, object, or activity that can satisfy an instinct." "Object relations theories focus on the interpersonal relationships with these objects, whereas Freud focused more on the instinctual drives themselves. Thus, object relations theorists emphasize the social and environmental influences on personality, particular within the mother-child interaction."

6. How did the approach of Melanie Klein differ from Freudian psychoanalysis?
Melanie Klein focused on the social and cognitive (not sexual) aspects of the mother-child relationship particularly during the first 6 months of the child's life. Whereas object relations theorists such as Klein focus on the interpersonal relationships with objects (e.g., the mother), Freudian psychoanalysts focused more on the instinctual drives themselves. Thus, object relations theorists emphasize the social and environmental influences on personality, particular within the mother-child interaction. They also believe that personality is formed in infancy by the nature of that relationship, at an earlier age than Freud proposed.

7. In what ways did Jung's life experiences influence his analytical psychology?
Some of the differences between Jung and Freud are that Jung did not include the Oedipus complex, and he insisted that he was not attracted to his "fat and unattractive" mother. Jung did not have the inhibitions about sex that Freud did, in fact he appeared to have had many sexual relationships with women, which probably led to him dismissing the importance Freud placed on sex. Jung broadened the definition of libido to include other life-affirming activities besides sex.

8. Describe the Jungian concepts of the collective unconscious and the archetypes.
The collective unconscious "contains inherited experiences of human and prehuman species." Within the collective unconscious are "inherited tendencies called archetypes...that dispose a person to behave not unlike ancestors who confronted similar situations." Jung developed these by investigating and finding similar myths and symbols across cultures. The most frequently occurring archetypes are persona (the mask we present to others), anima/animus (characteristics of the opposite sex), and shadow (a dark, animalistic part), but the most important one is self (the balance we strike within our unconscious).

9. How did Jung's analytical psychology differ from Freudian psychoanalysis?
Some of the differences between Jung and Freud are that Jung did not include the Oedipus complex and dismissed the importance Freud placed on sex. Jung broadened the definition of libido to include other life-affirming activities besides sex. Furthermore, for "Jung, personality was not fully determined by experiences during the first five years of childhood but could be changed throughout one's lifetime." Lastly, Jung added "a new dimension" to the unconscious, which he called the collective unconscious.

10. On what issues did Adler and Freud disagree?
Adler's system differed from Freud's in several ways. "Adler believed that human behavior is determined largely by social forces, not biological instincts." Adler also thought that Freud put too much emphasis on the importance of sex, and focused more on conscious (rather than unconscious) processes. Furthermore, Adler saw the personality as being unified and motivated by "an overriding goal...[of reaching] perfection", not broken up into Id, Ego, and Superego. Finally, "Adler argued that there was no biological reason, such as Freud's concept of penis envy, for any alleged sense of inferiority women might feel" and such feelings were driven instead by inequitable social forces.

11. Explain what Adler meant by "style of life." According to Adler's theory, how do inferiority feelings develop?
Adler believed that a feeling of inferiority was the universal motivating force for humans which leads us to compensate by overcoming obstacles. If we cannot overcome obstacles, we form "an inferiority complex, which renders the person incapable of coping with life's problems." Although our goal of perfection is universal, how we strive for the goal is not. Adler calls these different ways to behave the style of life, which become fixed by age 4 or 5.

12. What lasting contributions to psychology have been made by Jung and by Adler?
Jung had a larger impact outside of psychology, but within psychology he did create the word-association test which is used in clinical work, and his personality types have been developed into the Myers-Briggs Type Indicator. The "concepts of introversion and extraversion are widely accepted in psychology today." Adler's impact can be seen in his birth order theory, as well as his insistence of the influence of social variables on the individual.

13. How were Horney's views of personality influenced by her childhood experiences?
Karen's mother rejected her "in favor of the first-born brother, whom Karen envied simply for being a boy, and her father belittled her appearance and intelligence. As a result, she felt inferior, worthless, and hostile...This lack of parental love fostered what Horney later called 'basic anxiety'." Later in life, Horney exhibited behaviors designed to seek love and companionship. In psychoanalysis, one therapist believed this was because she longed for the love of a dominant authority figure such as her father.

14. In what ways did Freud and Horney differ in their views of feminine psychology?
Freud believed that women had penis envy, and Horney countered that men had womb envy (jealousy at the inability to give life). Horney said that because of womb envy, men engaged in behaviors (unconsciously) "designed to harass and belittle women." Freud set back feminine psychology with his masochistic theory while Horney laid the ground work for the development of feminine psychology.

15. Explain Horney's concepts of basic anxiety, neurotic needs, and idealized self-image.
With Horney, a person can have basic anxiety, which is the result of social and environmental forces in a person's childhood, and is primarily created by interactions with parents or caregivers. If this anxiety develops, the person takes on behaviors that are driven by neurotic needs and are reflected in one of three ways; the compliant personality ("need for approval, affection", the detached personality ("need for independence, perfection), and the aggressive personality ("need for power, exploitation). Horney believed that neurotic individuals had "a false picture of the personality or self," which she called the idealized self-image.

16. On what grounds did the humanistic psychologists criticize behaviorism and psychoanalysis?
Humanists revolted against the determinism and mechanism of both behaviorism and psychoanalysis, and saw psychoanalysis as focusing on the worst of human nature. They believed behaviorism was too reductionistic while psychoanalysis was too narrow in scope.

17. Compare the views of Maslow and Rogers on self-actualization and the characteristics of the psychologically healthy person.
For Maslow, self-actualized people "are free from neuroses" and have the following characteristics: "1. an objective perception of reality, 2. a full acceptance of their own nature, 3. a commitment and dedication to some kind of work, 4. simplicity and naturalness of behavior, 5. a need for autonomy, privacy, and independence, 6. intense mystical or peak experiences, 7. empathy with and affection for all humanity, 8. resistance to conformity, 9. a democratic character structure, 10. an attitude of creativeness, and 11. a high degree of what Adler termed social interest." "Rogers's conception, by his own admission, is similar in principle to Maslow's, although they differ somewhat on the characteristics of psychologically healthy people.
To Rogers, psychologically healthy or fully functioning persons have the following qualities: 1. an openness to, and a freshness of appreciation of, all experience; 2. a tendency to live fully in every moment; 3. the ability to be guided by their instincts rather than by reason or the opinions of others; 4. a sense of freedom in thought and action; 5. a high degree of creativity; and 6. the continual need to maximize their potential.

18. On what grounds have the theories of Maslow and Rogers been criticized?
Maslow's ideas have been criticized because of the small sample size, although Maslow said that this was a function of there being so few self-actualized people. Rogers' theory has been criticized because of his "lack of specificity about the innate potential for self-actualization and the acceptance of subjective conscious experiences to the exclusion of unconscious influences."

19. For what reasons did humanistic psychology fail to reach its goal of transforming psychology?
Humanism never fully formed as a school of psychology, and this was recognized by the humanists. This might be because humanists largely worked in clinical settings rather than academic institutions. This might also be because by the time humanism rose against

psychoanalysis and behaviorism, those two schools had begun to lose power; humanism had no school against which to revolt.

20. In your opinion, will the positive psychology movement have a more lasting influence on the field than the humanistic psychology movement did? Why or why not?

At the moment, positive psychology has already had a lasting influence on psychology, but by re-focusing the field to emphasize human achievement rather than human deficits. Because humanism never was accepted into mainstream psychology, it was never able to accomplish that goal. Positive psychology however, has been widely used in popular culture and become a lasting part of art, literature, media, and the American lifestyle.

21. What factors have been shown to affect subjective well-being? What other factors do you think can affect happiness?

Several empirical studies have found that happiness has broad implications for one's life. Material things do not make a person happy, although a lack of money and resources can make a person unhappy. Good health also does not create happiness, but bad health can create unhappiness. There seem to be no differences on happiness between men and women. Married people reported higher levels of happiness than unmarried/divorced/widowed people. In addition, happiness is correlated with high levels of job success and productivity.

Key terms from chapter fourteen

- **Analytical psychology** The term Jung used for his system of thought.
- **Anima/Animus** In Jung's system, the archetypes reflecting the characteristics of the opposite sex within us. Anima is "feminine characteristics in man" and Animus is "masculine characteristics in woman."
- **Archetypes** In Jung's system, "inherited tendencies within the collective unconscious that dispose a person to behave similarly to ancestors who confronted similar situations."
- **Basic Anxiety** In Horney's system, the "pervasive loneliness and helplessness, feelings that are the foundation of neuroses."
- **Collective Unconscious** In Jung's system, "the deepest level of the psyche; it contains inherited experiences of human and prehuman species."
- **Extroversion** In Jung's system, the libido is directed outward to make a person "sociable and self-confident in a variety of situations."
- **Individual Psychology** The name of Adler's system, which "incorporated social as well as biological factors."
- **Inferiority complex** In Adler's system, "a condition that develops when a person is unable to compensate for normal inferiority feelings."
- **Introversion** In Jung's system, the libido is directed inward to make a person "contemplative, introspective, and resistant to external pressures."
- **Neurotic needs** In Horney's system, a behavioral strategy arising from neuroses. These include three broad trends: the compliant personality ("need for approval, affection", the detached personality ("need for independence, perfection), and the aggressive personality ("need for power, exploitation).
- **Object** For Freud, "any person, object, or activity that can satisfy an instinct" and becomes a focus later for Object Relations theorists

- **Persona** In Jung's system, the archetype that is "the mask each of us wears when we come in contact with other people."
- **Personal Unconscious** In Jung's system, "the reservoir of material that once was conscious but has been forgotten or suppressed."
- **Positive psychology** A new focus, charged by Martin Seligman, to study positive aspects of being human instead of focusing on negative aspects.
- **Positive regard** In Roger's system, "the unconditional love of a mother for her infant."
- **Psychological types** The ways we "orient ourselves to the" world. They are: thinking ("provides meaning and understanding"), feeling ("weighing and valuing"), sensing ("perception of physical objects"), and intuiting ("perceiving in an unconscious way").
- **Self** In Jung's system, the archetype that balances "all aspects of the unconscious".
- **Self-actualization** In Maslow's system, "the full development of one's abilities and the realization of one's potential."
- **Shadow** In Jung's system, the archetype that is "the animalistic part of personality", but is also the "wellspring of spontaneity, creativity, insight, and deep emotion."
- **Social Interest** Adler's "innate potential to cooperate with other people to achieve personal and societal goals."

TESTBANK

ESSAY

1. Identify and discuss three changes that the neo-Freudians introduced within psychoanalysis. How did the neo-Freudians differ from the dissenters?

ANS:
Answer not provided.

PTS: 1

2. What role did Anna Freud play within the psychoanalytic movement? Describe her relationship with her father and the ways in which she expanded his system.

ANS:
Answer not provided.

PTS: 1

3. How did Sigmund Freud define the term *object*? What are the general differences in theoretical focus between Freud and the object relations theorists? Briefly describe the mother-child bond from the viewpoints of (a) Melanie Klein and (b) Heinz Kohut.

ANS:
Answer not provided.

PTS: 1

4. Identify and discuss at least three basic differences between Jung's analytical psychology and Freud's psychoanalysis.

   ANS:
   Answer not provided.

   PTS: 1

5. Compare and contrast Freud and Jung's conceptions of the unconscious mind. Within Jungian theory, define/describe collective unconscious, archetypes, and the relationship between the two. Name at least four of the archetypes discussed by Schultz and Schultz; describe two of them in detail.

   ANS:
   Answer not provided.

   PTS: 1   MSC: WWW

6. Describe at least three of the fundamental differences between Adler's individual psychology and Freud's psychoanalysis.

   ANS:
   Answer not provided.

   PTS: 1

7. The personal experience of a theorist can impact his or her choice of central personality concepts. A central concept for Adler was *inferiority* feelings while Horney concentrated on *basic anxiety*. Define and describe each concept and discuss possible links between it and the life circumstances and experiences of the theorist who proposed it.

   ANS:
   Answer not provided.

   PTS: 1   MSC: WWW

8. Identify and discuss at least three of the disagreements that Horney had with Freud.

   ANS:
   Answer not provided.

   PTS: 1

9. Describe the evolution and antecedent influences on humanistic psychology. What is its current status in psychology?

   ANS:
   Answer not provided.

   PTS: 1

10. Describe the similarities and differences between the concepts of self-actualization as developed by Maslow and Rogers.

    ANS:
    Answer not provided.

    PTS: 1

11. What is positive psychology as proposed by Seligman? In what ways is it similar to and different from humanistic psychology?

    ANS:
    Answer not provided.

    PTS: 1

MULTIPLE CHOICE

12. Just as with Wundt's experimental psychology, within _____ years of its founding, Freud's system was splintering.
    a. 2
    b. 10
    c. 20
    d. 30
    e. 50

    ANS: C   PTS: 1   REF: Competing Factions

13. The essential difference between those who are classified as dissenters and those who are classified as carrying on in the Freudian tradition is that the dissenters _____.
    a. expanded and elaborated on Freud's system
    b. developed their own theories during Freud's lifetime
    c. identified themselves as Freudians
    d. were centrally concerned with ego development or object relations
    e. None of the choices are correct.

    ANS: B   PTS: 1   REF: Competing Factions
    MSC: WWW

14. Which of the following psychotheorists is NOT considered a neo-Freudian?
    a. Adler
    b. Jung
    c. Anna Freud
    d. Horney
    e. None of the choices are correct; they are all considered neo-Freudian.

    ANS: E   PTS: 1   REF: Competing Factions

15. The ego psychologists emphasized the influence of ____ while de-emphasizing the role of ____.
    a. parents; biological forces
    b. conscious forces; unconscious forces
    c. conscious forces; social forces
    d. social forces; biological forces
    e. the superego; the id

    ANS: D   PTS: 1   REF: The Neo-Freudians and Ego Psychology

16. The ego psychologists amended Freud's original position by emphasizing that the ____.
    a. ego is derived from the id
    b. ego is servant to the superego
    c. id is servant to the ego
    d. ego can carry out some functions independently of the id
    e. None of the choices are correct.

    ANS: D   PTS: 1   REF: The Neo-Freudians and Ego Psychology

17. Anna Freud's pioneering work was ____.
    a. on the id
    b. on the mechanisms of motivation
    c. on child analysis
    d. realized only after her father's death and her self-analysis
    e. the founding of a clinic for training psychology teachers

    ANS: C   PTS: 1   REF: Anna Freud (1895-1982)

18. Play therapy, a standard technique of contemporary psychotherapy with children, was introduced by ____.
    a. Melanie Klein
    b. Anna Freud
    c. Karen Horney
    d. Helene Deutsch
    e. Erik Erikson

    ANS: B   PTS: 1   REF: Anna Freud (1895-1982)

19. Anna Freud's most important revision of orthodox psychoanalysis ____.
    a. was called conservative psychoanalysis
    b. was called reformed psychoanalysis
    c. was to focus on the middle age crisis
    d. was to clarify the defense mechanisms
    e. None of the choices are correct.

    ANS: D   PTS: 1   REF: Anna Freud (1895-1982)

20. Which branch of psychoanalysis did Anna Freud found?
    a. orthodox psychoanalysis
    b. ego psychology
    c. object relations analysis
    d. analytical psychology
    e. individual psychology

    ANS: B   PTS: 1   REF: Anna Freud (1895-1982)

21. In order to achieve their goal of making psychoanalysis a part of scientific psychology, the ego psychologists ____.
    a. modified psychoanalytic psychotherapy
    b. operationally defined Freud's constructs
    c. pursued the experimental study of psychoanalytic hypotheses
    d. All of the choices are correct.
    e. None of the choices are correct.

ANS: D   PTS: 1   REF: Anna Freud (1895-1982)

22. Freud used the word "object" to refer to any ____.
    a. person, object, or activity that can satisfy an instinct
    b. person, object, or activity that can influence personality development
    c. thing, entity, or item existing in the external world
    d. thing, entity, or item existing in the internal world
    e. physical object in the world that can become a fetish

ANS: A   PTS: 1
REF: Object Relations Theories: Melanie Klein (1882-1960)

23. Object relations theorists emphasize the ____ influences on personality
    a. instinctual
    b. evolutionary
    c. social and environmental
    d. personal, political, and developmental
    e. innate

ANS: C   PTS: 1
REF: Object Relations Theories: Melanie Klein (1882-1960)

24. In contrast to Freud, object relations theorists believe that personality is formed ____.
    a. in middle age
    b. during the first 6 months of life
    c. in adolescence, roughly 12-18 years of age
    d. throughout the life span
    e. in early childhood, roughly 3-7 years of age

ANS: B   PTS: 1
REF: Object Relations Theories: Melanie Klein (1882-1960)

25. According to object relations theorists, the most critical developmental issue is for the child is ____.
    a. to continue a relationship with the primary object (the mother) while maintaining a strong sense of self and develop relations with other objects
    b. to form a lasting attachment that becomes foremost for the child
    c. to form a sense of self, then a sense of the primary object (mother), then a sense of other objects (people)
    d. to break free from the primary object (the mother) in order to establish a strong sense of self and develop relations with other objects (people)
    e. None of the choices are correct.

ANS: D   PTS: 1
REF: Object Relations Theories: Melanie Klein (1882-1960)

26. Melanie Klein described the mother-infant relationship in ____.
    a. terms of play therapy
    b. relationship to psychopathology
    c. social-cognitive terms
    d. intellective terms
    e. sexual terms

    ANS: C   PTS: 1
    REF: Object Relations Theories: Melanie Klein (1882-1960)

27. Klein suggested that the ____ is the first part-object for the child.
    a. father
    b. doctor
    c. mother
    d. doctor's hand
    e. mother's breast

    ANS: E   PTS: 1
    REF: Object Relations Theories: Melanie Klein (1882-1960)

28. If a part-object satisfies an id instinct, it is judged by the baby to be ____.
    a. whole
    b. part of the mother
    c. part of the father
    d. good
    e. bad

    ANS: D   PTS: 1
    REF: Object Relations Theories: Melanie Klein (1882-1960)   MSC: WWW

29. Upon birth, the infant relates to ____ objects. When the infant's world expands, they then relate to ____ objects. Eventually the infant will relate to ____ objects.
    a. part; whole; all
    b. all; part; whole
    c. part; all; whole
    d. All of the choices are possible orders.
    e. None of the choices are correct.

    ANS: A   PTS: 1
    REF: Object Relations Theories: Melanie Klein (1882-1960)

30. For Klein, the adult personality is rooted in the nature of the mother-child relationship in the first ____ of life.
    a. month
    b. three months
    c. six months
    d. year
    e. two years

    ANS: C   PTS: 1
    REF: Object Relations Theories: Melanie Klein (1882-1960)

31. Klein's theory believes that the initial social interaction between mother and child ____.
    a. will affect the child's personality later in life
    b. will be generalized to all relationships in the child's life
    c. is important for child development
    d. All of the above.
    e. None of the above.

    ANS: D   PTS: 1
    REF: Object Relations Theories: Melanie Klein (1882-1960)

32. Freud wanted ____ to take over the psychoanalytic school.
    a. Anna Freud
    b. Jung
    c. Maslow
    d. Watson
    e. Adler

    ANS: B   PTS: 1   REF: Carl Jung (1875-1961)

33. Like Freud, Jung's theory ____.
    a. was autobiographical
    b. focused on sex
    c. discounted the role of outside influences
    d. emphasized the importance of the collective consciousness
    e. None of the above.

    ANS: A   PTS: 1   REF: Carl Jung (1875-1961)

34. Which of the following is NOT one of the archetypes common to all humans?
    a. persona
    b. anima
    c. animus
    d. warrior
    e. shadow

    ANS: D   PTS: 1   REF: Carl Jung (1875-1961)
    MSC: WWW

35. One of Jung's main criticisms is that ____.
    a. he did not adhere to Freud's vision
    b. his theory of personality is not empirically sound
    c. his theory was copied from the earlier work of Anna Freud
    d. analytical psychology cannot be applied to field outside of psychology
    e. his theory has flawed methods

    ANS: E   PTS: 1   REF: Carl Jung (1875-1961)

36. Jung's theoretical system is known as ____.
    a. individual psychology
    b. neoanalytic psychology
    c. analytical psychology
    d. identity psychology
    e. postmodern psychoanalysis

    ANS: C   PTS: 1   REF: Carl Jung (1875-1961)

37. For Jung, dream analysis was ____.
    a. a lifelong practice for resolving personal crises
    b. a method of which he was skeptical
    c. the sole method of psychotherapy that he used
    d. replaced by his system of analytical psychology
    e. the source of his concepts of archetypes and the collective unconscious

    ANS: A   PTS: 1   REF: Carl Jung (1875-1961)

38. While Jung was writing ____, he anticipated the break with Freud.
    a. *The Interpretation of Dreams*
    b. *The Psychology of the Unconscious*
    c. *Psychic Conflicts in a Child*
    d. *Man and His Symbols*
    e. *Individual Psychology*

    ANS: B   PTS: 1   REF: Carl Jung (1875-1961)

39. Freud selected Jung to be the first president of the International Psychoanalytic Association because ____.
    a. like himself, Jung was not German
    b. Jung was not Jewish
    c. Jung was an established psychiatrist
    d. Jung was younger
    e. he strongly desired a reconciliation with Jung

    ANS: B   PTS: 1   REF: Carl Jung (1875-1961)

40. Like Freud, Jung ____.
    a. had several extramarital affairs
    b. had an Oedipal relationship with his youngest daughter
    c. gave up sex at about age 40
    d. experienced a profound and lengthy emotional crisis at about age 40
    e. and his theory were deeply affected by his relationship with his father

    ANS: D   PTS: 1   REF: Carl Jung (1875-1961)

41. For Jung, the Oedipus complex was ____.
    a. an object relations approach
    b. irrelevant
    c. dependent upon the infant's libidinal drives
    d. part of the "Good Mother" and "Evil Mother" archetypes
    e. described in terms of the primeval forces of the collective unconscious

    ANS: B   PTS: 1   REF: Carl Jung (1875-1961)

42. For Jung, sexuality was ____.
    a. problematic
    b. one of several needs that required satisfaction
    c. heterosexual from birth
    d. not heterosexual
    e. All of the choices are correct.

    ANS: B   PTS: 1   REF: Carl Jung (1875-1961)

43. Jung proposed that libido ____.
    a. is a generalized life force
    b. is unrelated to sex
    c. reflects the major role sex played in his own life
    d. has its roots in the collective unconscious
    e. drives the archetypes

    ANS: A   PTS: 1   REF: Carl Jung (1875-1961)

44. Jung proposed that personality is shaped by ____.
    a. childhood experiences
    b. experiences which occur throughout one's life
    c. one's goals, expectations, and ambitions
    d. the past
    e. All of the choices are correct.

    ANS: E   PTS: 1   REF: Carl Jung (1875-1961)
    MSC: WWW

45. Jung's concept of the personal unconscious ____.
    a. is quite unique and very different from any of Freud's conceptualizations
    b. is at a very deep level, unknown to the individual
    c. contains individual experiences that have been suppressed or forgotten
    d. includes the conscious plus the unconscious
    e. includes the archetypes

    ANS: C   PTS: 1   REF: Carl Jung (1875-1961)

46. Jung described patterns of emotions and memories with common themes in the personal unconscious as
    ____.
    a. personality
    b. persona
    c. complexes
    d. shadow
    e. basic anxieties

    ANS: C   PTS: 1   REF: Carl Jung (1875-1961)

47. For Jung, a preoccupation with an idea that influences behavior is evidence of ____.
    a. a fixation
    b. an archetype
    c. the shadow
    d. the personal conscious
    e. a complex

    ANS: E   PTS: 1   REF: Carl Jung (1875-1961)

48. According to Jung, our individual storehouse of repressed memories, impulses, and wishes is the ____.
    a. unconscious
    b. preconscious
    c. collective unconscious
    d. personal preconscious
    e. personal unconscious

    ANS: E   PTS: 1   REF: Carl Jung (1875-1961)

49. According to Jung, in our _____, we retain experiences of our ancestors, animal and human.
    a. personal unconscious
    b. collective unconscious
    c. anima/animus
    d. shadow
    e. archetypes

    ANS: B   PTS: 1   REF: Carl Jung (1875-1961)

50. Darwin's theory of evolution is best reflected in the Jungian concept of _____.
    a. personal unconscious
    b. collective unconscious
    c. introversion
    d. extraversion
    e. self

    ANS: B   PTS: 1   REF: Carl Jung (1875-1961)
    MSC: WWW

51. Within the personal unconscious, patterns of emotions and memories with common themes are called
    _____.
    a. archetypes
    b. the collective unconscious
    c. attitudes
    d. functions
    e. complexes

    ANS: E   PTS: 1   REF: Carl Jung (1875-1961)

52. In Jung's system, the experiences that form the basis of personality are part of the _____.
    a. personal unconscious
    b. anima/animus
    c. shadow
    d. collective unconscious
    e. persona

    ANS: D   PTS: 1   REF: Carl Jung (1875-1961)

53. For Jung, innate determinants of one's mental life are the _____.
    a. *Instinkts*
    b. *Triebs*
    c. archetypes
    d. style of life
    e. monads

    ANS: C   PTS: 1   REF: Carl Jung (1875-1961)

54. The _____ is/are often experienced in the form of emotions associated with significant life events or reaction to extreme danger.
    a. feeling function
    b. collective unconscious
    c. personal unconscious
    d. belief in evolution
    e. archetypes

    ANS: E   PTS: 1   REF: Carl Jung (1875-1961)

55. The most animalistic aspect of one's personality, according to Jung, is the ____.
    a. *Triebs*
    b. Instinkts
    c. animus/anima
    d. repressions
    e. shadow

    ANS: E   PTS: 1   REF: Carl Jung (1875-1961)

56. For Jung, the ____ archetype is the source of spontaneity and creativity.
    a. shadow
    b. *Triebs*
    c. anima/animus
    d. persona
    e. self

    ANS: A   PTS: 1   REF: Carl Jung (1875-1961)

57. In Jung's system, the self is ____.
    a. a drive toward self-actualization
    b. manifested in the persona
    c. manifested in the shadow
    d. heavily influenced by the anima/animus
    e. manifested in the four functions

    ANS: A   PTS: 1   REF: Carl Jung (1875-1961)

58. Jung called the two basic attitudes within the person ____.
    a. anima and animus
    b. introversion and extraversion
    c. thinking and feeling
    d. sensing and intuiting
    e. judging and sensing

    ANS: B   PTS: 1   REF: Carl Jung (1875-1961)
    MSC: WWW

59. For Jung, the ways in which we orient ourselves to both the external (objective) and internal (subjective) world are found in the ____.
    a. attitudes
    b. functions
    c. psychological types
    d. persona
    e. self

    ANS: C   PTS: 1   REF: Carl Jung (1875-1961)

60. For the most part, Jung's ideas have not influenced the field of ____.
    a. religion
    b. literature
    c. psychology
    d. history
    e. art

    ANS: C   PTS: 1   REF: Carl Jung (1875-1961)

PSYCHOANALYSIS: AFTER THE FOUNDING   507

61. A component of the Zeitgeist at the beginning of the 20th century that influenced some dissenters within psychoanalysis was the ____.
    a. American notion of manifest destiny
    b. close of the Victorian era
    c. atrocities of World War I
    d. women's movement (the suffragettes)
    e. recognition of the influence of social forces

    ANS: E   PTS: 1
    REF: Social Psychological Theories: The Zeitgeist Strikes Again

62. Alfred Adler and Karen Horney claimed that human behavior is determined by ____.
    a. interpersonal relationships to which the individual has been exposed, particularly in childhood
    b. biological forces such as inheritance
    c. traumas, especially those which have been experienced in infancy
    d. political systems such as socialism and capitalization
    e. None of the choices are correct.

    ANS: A   PTS: 1
    REF: Social Psychological Theories: The Zeitgeist Strikes Again

63. As he himself acknowledged, Adler's childhood experiences are a direct reflection of his concept of ____.
    a. individual psychology
    b. social interest
    c. birth order
    d. inferiority
    e. basic anxiety

    ANS: D   PTS: 1   REF: Alfred Adler (1870-1937)

64. Child guidance clinics in the Vienna school system were established by ____.
    a. Witmer
    b. A. Freud
    c. S. Freud
    d. Klein
    e. Adler

    ANS: E   PTS: 1   REF: Alfred Adler (1870-1937)

65. One of Adler's criticisms of psychoanalysis was of its focus on ____.
    a. sexual factors in personality development
    b. unconscious determinants of behavior
    c. biological instincts
    d. All of the choices are correct.
    e. None of the choices are correct.

    ANS: D   PTS: 1   REF: Alfred Adler (1870-1937)

66. Adler held that behavior is determined primarily by ____.
    a. social factors
    b. unconscious factors
    c. complexes
    d. the id
    e. basic anxiety

    ANS: A   PTS: 1   REF: Alfred Adler (1870-1937)

67. Like Jung but unlike Freud, Adler thought that ____ could influence present behavior.
    a. social interest
    b. reinforcement
    c. social forces
    d. future goals
    e. style of life

    ANS: D   PTS: 1   REF: Alfred Adler (1870-1937)

68. In Adler's system, a motivating force in behavior based on actual or perceived defects is(are) ____.
    a. inferiority feelings
    b. social interest
    c. striving for superiority
    d. the style of life
    e. the creative power of the self

    ANS: A   PTS: 1   REF: Alfred Adler (1870-1937)
    MSC: WWW

69. Inferiority feelings, according to Adler, develop in ____.
    a. those with a manifest intellectual or physical defect
    b. those who are pampered by the parents and/or siblings
    c. those who are rejected by the mother
    d. the earlier born rather than the later born in the family
    e. everyone

    ANS: E   PTS: 1   REF: Alfred Adler (1870-1937)

70. "Striving for superiority," in Adler's system, ____.
    a. is universal
    b. takes a unique form in each of us
    c. is a response to learned feelings of inferiority
    d. serves to assuage basic anxiety
    e. is universal **and** takes a unique form in each of us

    ANS: E   PTS: 1   REF: Alfred Adler (1870-1937)

71. For Adler, ____ involves the behaviors used to compensate for feelings of inferiority.
    a. striving for superiority
    b. personality
    c. inferiority complex
    d. style of life
    e. creative power of the self

    ANS: D   PTS: 1   REF: Alfred Adler (1870-1937)

PSYCHOANALYSIS: AFTER THE FOUNDING   509

72. Adler's concept of the creative power of the self reflects his rejection of ____.
    a. determinism
    b. positivism
    c. mentalism
    d. the concept of soul
    e. operationism

    ANS: A   PTS: 1   REF: Alfred Adler (1870-1937)

73. Which of the following statements is NOT true of Adler's theory?
    a. Adler proposed that birth order is important in the development of personality.
    b. Adler developed the concept of social interest, the innate human potential to cooperate with other people to achieve personal and societal goals.
    c. Adler developed the concept of inferiority complex.
    d. Adler speculated that basic personality types involving introversion and extraversion are formed early in life.
    e. Adler believed that we strive for superiority.

    ANS: D   PTS: 1   REF: Alfred Adler (1870-1937)

74. Freud criticized Adler's system as ____.
    a. inappropriately ignoring the seduction theory
    b. inadequately describing childhood development
    c. based on case studies rather than systematic observation
    d. unscientific
    e. being too simple

    ANS: E   PTS: 1   REF: Alfred Adler (1870-1937)

75. Which aspect of Adler's system has led to the most research?
    a. the inferiority complex
    b. striving for superiority
    c. birth order
    d. archetypes
    e. womb envy

    ANS: C   PTS: 1   REF: Alfred Adler (1870-1937)
    MSC: WWW

76. The core of Horney's system reflects ____.
    a. her unsatisfactory relationship with her parents
    b. a preoccupation with sexuality
    c. the fixation of personality in early childhood
    d. neurotic needs that mark the personal crisis that occurs at about age 40
    e. her belief in the importance of biology in determining personality

    ANS: A   PTS: 1   REF: Karen Horney (1885-1952)

77. In Horney's system, the central idea is ____.
    a. basic anxiety
    b. the need for freedom from fear
    c. the neurotic needs
    d. the idealized self-image
    e. the inferiority complex

    ANS: A   PTS: 1   REF: Karen Horney (1885-1952)

78. When the child responds to anxiety arising from parental actions by using unchanging behavioral strategies, he/she is exhibiting _____.
    a. a neurotic need
    b. compliance
    c. detachment
    d. the idealized self-image
    e. the style of life

    ANS: A   PTS: 1   REF: Karen Horney (1885-1952)

79. Horney called a false picture of oneself _____.
    a. a neurotic need
    b. compliance
    c. detachment
    d. the style of life
    e. the idealized self-image

    ANS: E   PTS: 1   REF: Karen Horney (1885-1952)

80. When Hillary Rodham Clinton remarked that not all women are content to stay home and bake cookies, she was restating a position stated earlier by _____.
    a. Anna Freud
    b. Melanie Klein
    c. Karen Horney
    d. Alfred Adler
    e. Christiana Morgan

    ANS: C   PTS: 1   REF: Karen Horney (1885-1952)

81. In general, the designation "third force" applies to _____.
    a. Skinner's behaviorism
    b. the neo-Freudians
    c. Gestalt psychology
    d. humanistic psychology
    e. social learning theories

    ANS: D   PTS: 1
    REF: The Evolution of Personality Theory: Humanistic Psychology

82. The component(s) of the Zeitgeist of the 1960s in the United States that were manifested in humanistic psychology was(were) _____.
    a. rebellion against the older order
    b. a focus on personal fulfillment
    c. an emphasis on the present
    d. None of the choices are correct.
    e. All of the choices are correct.

    ANS: E   PTS: 1
    REF: The Evolution of Personality Theory: Humanistic Psychology

PSYCHOANALYSIS: AFTER THE FOUNDING   511

83. The humanistic psychologists insisted on the study of ____.
    a. motivation
    b. needs
    c. neglected aspects of human nature
    d. one's style of life
    e. life-span development

    ANS: C   PTS: 1
    REF: The Evolution of Personality Theory: Humanistic Psychology

84. The spiritual father of humanistic psychology is considered to be ____.
    a. Wertheimer
    b. Titchener
    c. May
    d. Maslow
    e. Rogers

    ANS: D   PTS: 1   REF: Abraham Maslow (1908-1970)

85. Maslow renounced behaviorism because it ____.
    a. did not reveal how to alter human behaviors
    b. did not reveal information on motivation
    c. was not relevant for enduring human issues
    d. was artificial and rarefied
    e. relied too heavily on the concept of free will

    ANS: C   PTS: 1   REF: Abraham Maslow (1908-1970)
    MSC: WWW

86. For Maslow, the major motivating force is ____.
    a. self-actualization
    b. learning
    c. love fulfillment
    d. money
    e. None of the choices are correct.

    ANS: A   PTS: 1   REF: Abraham Maslow (1908-1970)

87. To become self-actualized, one must first satisfy basic needs in the ____.
    a. hierarchy of needs in humans
    b. university catalog
    c. the book, *Motivation and Personality*
    d. first ten years of life
    e. list of tendencies of self-actualizers

    ANS: A   PTS: 1   REF: Abraham Maslow (1908-1970)

88. The majority of Maslow's research was ____.
    a. experimental
    b. on normal subjects
    c. on locating those whom he judged to be self-actualized
    d. on describing the attributes of those he deemed self-actualized
    e. All of the choices are correct.

    ANS: D   PTS: 1   REF: Abraham Maslow (1908-1970)

89. In the selection from *Motivation and Personality*, Maslow describes the _____ of self-actualizing people.
    a. continuous search for new, exciting experiences
    b. ability to experience boredom
    c. dissatisfaction with everyday life
    d. continued freshness of appreciation
    e. eleven characteristics

    ANS: D   PTS: 1   REF: Abraham Maslow (1908-1970)

90. Maslow called the intensification of experiences felt with emotions such as wonder and awe _____.
    a. clues of possible psychopathology
    b. objective expressions
    c. a spiritual encounter
    d. a peak experience
    e. None of the choices are correct.

    ANS: D   PTS: 1   REF: Abraham Maslow (1908-1970)

91. The feeling of identification with mankind is reflected in Maslow's concept of _____.
    a. peak experience
    b. social interest
    c. freshness of appreciation
    d. hierarchy of needs
    e. human identification

    ANS: B   PTS: 1   REF: Abraham Maslow (1908-1970)

92. Maslow's data and research methodology have been criticized because of a(n) _____.
    a. use of subjective criteria
    b. small sample of subjects
    c. ambiguous and inconsistent use of terms
    d. All of the choices are correct.
    e. None of the choices are correct.

    ANS: D   PTS: 1   REF: Abraham Maslow (1908-1970)

93. Maslow _____ with the criticism that his research _____.
    a. disagreed; lacked scientific vigor
    b. agreed; lacked scientific vigor
    c. disagreed; used too many subjects
    d. disagreed; used objective criteria
    e. agreed; was very good

    ANS: B   PTS: 1   REF: Abraham Maslow (1908-1970)

94. Most research on Maslow's theory has _____.
    a. supported some characteristics of self-actualizers.
    b. provided some support for the order of needs in the hierarchy of needs.
    c. confirmed it.
    d. supported the self-actualization theory only for those in industry.
    e. supported some characteristics of self-actualizers **and** provided some support for the order of needs in the hierarchy of needs.

    ANS: E   PTS: 1   REF: Abraham Maslow (1908-1970)

95. Rogers's approach is _____.
   a. experimental
   b. applicable to the noncriminal as well as the criminal
   c. person-centered
   d. based on pure research rather than applied
   e. All of the choices are correct.

   ANS: C   PTS: 1   REF: Carl Rogers (1902-1987)

96. The view that individuals must guide their lives by their own interpretation of events rather than by the beliefs of others is a fundamental principle of whose system?
   a. Murray
   b. Rogers
   c. Maslow
   d. Miller
   e. Neisser

   ANS: B   PTS: 1   REF: Carl Rogers (1902-1987)

97. Roger's clinical experience during the time he was developing his theory was with _____.
   a. schizophrenics
   b. college students
   c. the seriously emotionally disturbed
   d. everyday people
   e. incarcerated men

   ANS: B   PTS: 1   REF: Carl Rogers (1902-1987)

98. The basic human motivation in Rogers's system is _____.
   a. the drive to actualize the self
   b. food and water
   c. authenticity
   d. freedom from fear
   e. tension (need) reduction

   ANS: A   PTS: 1   REF: Carl Rogers (1902-1987)

99. In Rogers's formulation, the urge toward self-actualization is _____.
   a. innate
   b. influenced by learning
   c. influenced by childhood experience
   d. All of the choices are correct.
   e. None of the choices are correct.

   ANS: D   PTS: 1   REF: Carl Rogers (1902-1987)

100. Rogers called the unconditional love of a mother for her infant _____.
   a. positive self-esteem
   b. positive regard
   c. conditional positive regard
   d. psychological regard
   e. None of the choices are correct.

   ANS: B   PTS: 1   REF: Carl Rogers (1902-1987)

101. The consequence of conditional positive regard is ____.
    a. learning that some behaviors will bring rejection
    b. the imposition of conditions of worth on others
    c. the failure to acquire empathy
    d. the existential crisis
    e. to preclude self-actualization

    ANS: A   PTS: 1   REF: Carl Rogers (1902-1987)

102. It is the judgment of humanistic psychologists themselves that they ____.
    a. did not become a formal school of thought
    b. successfully established themselves as a school of thought
    c. never became formalized within the American Psychological Association
    d. did not offer a definition of psychology distinct from that of behaviorism and
       psychoanalysis
    e. lacked the passion of their convictions

    ANS: A   PTS: 1   REF: The Fate of Humanistic Psychology

103. Which of the following appears to have interfered with humanistic psychology's becoming part of the
    mainstream of psychological thought?
    a. Humanism's ideas were untestable.
    b. Because it was a reflection of the rebellion of the 1960s and 1970s, the traditional, more
       conservative psychologists rejected it.
    c. Its adherents were in private practice, not training graduate students, and were less likely
       to engage in systematic research and publication.
    d. Its therapies had such a high casualty rate.
    e. It was ahead of its time, that is, more a reflection of the Zeitgeist of the 1980s than of the
       1960s.

    ANS: C   PTS: 1   REF: The Fate of Humanistic Psychology
    MSC: WWW

104. One of the strongest influence the humanistic systems exerted on psychology was the ____.
    a. use of videotapes and audiotapes as sources of data for analysis
    b. use of co-therapists
    c. restoration of the study of consciousness to psychology
    d. focus on the functional analysis of behavior
    e. attempt to operationally define concepts and to test them experimentally

    ANS: C   PTS: 1   REF: The Fate of Humanistic Psychology

105. The humanistic theme that psychologists should study the best as well as the worst of human
    characteristics was reinstated by ____.
    a. neurotics
    b. positive psychology
    c. hippies
    d. everyday people
    e. All of the choices are correct.

    ANS: B   PTS: 1   REF: The Fate of Humanistic Psychology

106. The positive psychology movement was initiated by ____.
   a. Miller
   b. Cunningham
   c. Rogers
   d. Seligman
   e. Maslow

   ANS: D   PTS: 1   REF: Positive Psychology

107. The question, "*How has it happened that the social sciences view...human strengths and virtues...while weakness and negative motivations...are viewed as authentic?*" was asked by ____.
   a. Miller
   b. Cunningham
   c. Rogers
   d. Seligman
   e. Maslow

   ANS: D   PTS: 1   REF: Positive Psychology

108. The 1998 call for positive psychology has ____.
   a. not as yet had time to be reflected in research and publications but the potential is promising
   b. resulted in a strong increase in number of publications dealing with positive emotions
   c. not been well-received
   d. largely covered concepts introduced by Freud
   e. None of the choices are correct.

   ANS: B   PTS: 1   REF: Positive Psychology

109. In the research on the characteristics of happy people, the happiest people ____.
   a. have a lot of money
   b. are physically attractive
   c. have mediocre health
   d. are unmarried
   e. are more successful and productive

   ANS: E   PTS: 1   REF: Positive Psychology

110. According to Schultz and Schultz, positive psychology "may represent the most enduring legacy of ____."
   a. Rogers
   b. Maslow
   c. humanistic psychology
   d. psychoanalysis
   e. None of the choices are correct.

   ANS: C   PTS: 1   REF: Positive Psychology

111. The major difference between positive psychology and both humanistic psychology and psychoanalysis is that positive psychologists tend to use ____ while the other two approaches tend to use ____.
   a. subjective case histories; rigorous experimental methods
   b. rigorous experimental methods; subjective case histories
   c. correlational designs; survey methods
   d. survey methods; correlational designs
   e. None of the choices are correct.

   ANS: B   PTS: 1   REF: Positive Psychology

112. Freud encouraged his followers to make changes in his original system so that it would be improved.

    ANS: F   PTS: 1   REF: Competing Factions
    MSC: WWW

113. The ego psychologists, dissenters, and humanists all derived their ideas by elaborating on or opposing Freud's work.

    ANS: T   PTS: 1   REF: Competing Factions

114. The ego psychologists focused on the analysis of the ego's responses to the id rather than the whole psyche.

    ANS: F   PTS: 1   REF: The Neo-Freudians and Ego Psychology
    MSC: WWW

115. The neo-Freudians focused on the influence of psychosocial factors rather than on the sexual determinants of behavior.

    ANS: T   PTS: 1   REF: The Neo-Freudians and Ego Psychology

116. A major factor in Freud's relationship with Jung was that Jung had analyzed Anna Freud and uncovered her fantasies of being beaten.

    ANS: F   PTS: 1   REF: Anna Freud (1895-1982)

117. Anna Freud's major contributions were in the area of child analysis.

    ANS: T   PTS: 1   REF: Anna Freud (1895-1982)
    MSC: WWW

118. The major work on the defense mechanisms was by Adler.

    ANS: F   PTS: 1   REF: Anna Freud (1895-1982)

119. The theory of object relations was among Anna Freud's contributions to psychoanalysis.

    ANS: F   PTS: 1   REF: Anna Freud (1895-1982)

120. Freud used the word "object" to refer to any person, object, or activity that can satisfy an instinct.

    ANS: T   PTS: 1
    REF: Object Relations Theories: Melanie Klein (1882-1960)

121. Object relations theorists emphasize the social and environmental influences on personality.

    ANS: T   PTS: 1
    REF: Object Relations Theories: Melanie Klein (1882-1960)   MSC: WWW

122. Breaking completely away from the mother is unhealthy for the infant according to object relations theorists.

    ANS: F   PTS: 1
    REF: Object Relations Theories: Melanie Klein (1882-1960)

123. According to object relations theorists, the most critical developmental issue is for the child to continue a very close relationship with the primary object (the mother) while maintaining a strong sense of self and develop relations with other objects (people).

    ANS: F   PTS: 1
    REF: Object Relations Theories: Melanie Klein (1882-1960)   MSC: WWW

124. Melanie Klein's object relations theory focused on the intense emotional bond between mother and child, particularly during the first six months of a child's life.

    ANS: T   PTS: 1
    REF: Object Relations Theories: Melanie Klein (1882-1960)

125. Carl Jung was the neo-Freudian who invented ego psychology.

    ANS: F   PTS: 1   REF: Carl Jung (1875-1961)

126. Several of Jung's practices in the treatment of clients are questionable from an ethical point of view.

    ANS: T   PTS: 1   REF: Carl Jung (1875-1961)

127. Freud apparently wanted Jung to be the first president of the International Psychoanalytic Association because Jung was Jewish.

    ANS: F   PTS: 1   REF: Carl Jung (1875-1961)

128. Jung's midlife crisis led to a resolution of his sexual neuroses.

    ANS: F   PTS: 1   REF: Carl Jung (1875-1961)

129. For Jung, libido is a generalized energy rather than a sexual drive.

    ANS: T   PTS: 1   REF: Carl Jung (1875-1961)

130. Unlike Freud, Jung believed thoughts about the future affected current behavior.

    ANS: T   PTS: 1   REF: Carl Jung (1875-1961)

131. Jung referred to the archetypes as the "gods" of the unconscious.

    ANS: T   PTS: 1   REF: Carl Jung (1875-1961)

132. Jung said that the archetypes are learned through one's life experiences.

    ANS: F   PTS: 1   REF: Carl Jung (1875-1961)

133. In Jung's system, the source of spontaneity and creativity is the archetype called "self".

    ANS: F   PTS: 1   REF: Carl Jung (1875-1961)

134. For Jung, the period crucial to personality development is midlife.

    ANS: T   PTS: 1   REF: Carl Jung (1875-1961)

135. Horney's system is called analytical psychology.

    ANS: F   PTS: 1   REF: Carl Jung (1875-1961)

136. For Adler, the determining force in behavior is social interest.

    ANS: T   PTS: 1   REF: Alfred Adler (1870-1937)

137. In Adler's system, an inferiority complex leads to continuous improvement.

    ANS: F   PTS: 1   REF: Alfred Adler (1870-1937)

138. Like Freud, Jung, and Adler, Horney's beliefs about personality development are congruent with her personal experience.

    ANS: T   PTS: 1   REF: Karen Horney (1885-1952)

139. Horney proposed that neurotic needs are normal coping strategies so long as they do not become complexes.

    ANS: F   PTS: 1   REF: Karen Horney (1885-1952)

140. In Horney's system, the healthy person models an idealized self-image.

    ANS: F   PTS: 1   REF: Karen Horney (1885-1952)

141. Humanistic psychology is called the "third force" because it was anticipated that it would replace the two existing main forces, behaviorism and psychoanalysis.

    ANS: T   PTS: 1
    REF: The Evolution of Personality Theory: Humanistic Psychology

142. Among its intellectual ancestors, humanistic psychology includes Brentano, Külpe, and James.

    ANS: T   PTS: 1
    REF: The Evolution of Personality Theory: Humanistic Psychology

143. A driving force in the development of humanistic psychology was that behaviorism and psychoanalysis ignored unique aspects of humanity.

    ANS: T   PTS: 1
    REF: The Evolution of Personality Theory: Humanistic Psychology

144. Maslow was an ardent behaviorist but was deeply affected by his relationship with European psychologists who had fled Nazi Germany.

    ANS: T   PTS: 1   REF: Abraham Maslow (1908-1970)

145. Consistent with Jung's hypothesis, the self-actualizing person in Maslow's system is middle-aged or older.

ANS: T   PTS: 1   REF: Abraham Maslow (1908-1970)

146. For Maslow, the self-actualizing person has an objective perception of reality.

ANS: T   PTS: 1   REF: Abraham Maslow (1908-1970)

147. Rogers's argued that one's personality is shaped by how one perceives the present.

ANS: T   PTS: 1   REF: Carl Rogers (1902-1987)

148. Rogers's hypothesized that the child who receives unconditional positive regard will necessarily repress certain aspects of the self.

ANS: F   PTS: 1   REF: Carl Rogers (1902-1987)

149. Whereas Rogers's described the fully functioning person as peaked, Maslow focused on the concept of the self-actualizing person.

ANS: F   PTS: 1   REF: Carl Rogers (1902-1987)

Chapter 15

Contemporary Developments in Psychology

The chapter begins with the story of the great chess champion, Garry Kasparov, losing his first match in a dramatic and emotional story to an unnamed opponent. Kasparov's loss came as a surprise to the world, and to himself. After days of arduous chess matches, he expressed terror and fear, which he later attributed to the fact that he could no longer understand the logic that his opponent was using against him. The relevance of this example to contemporary psychology will be revealed later in the chapter.

The rise and fall of different schools of thought had a dramatic impact on the way modern psychology looks and functions. As the focus of psychology changed from structuralism to functionalism, and then to Gestalt psychology, psychoanalysis and behaviorism, so did the subject matter. As a result of a return to the study of consciousness, the two newest movements in psychology are cognitive psychology and evolutionary psychology. Because of the power of behaviorism, consciousness was neglected as a proper focus of psychology. That changed in the mid-1970's when McKeachie, in his APA presidential address, noted "that psychology was changing and that the new conception included a refocus on consciousness."

The precursors of cognitive psychology begin with the Greek philosophers Plato and Aristotle. Other influences include structuralists (like Wundt), functionalists, and behaviorists (like Guthrie and Tolman). The Gestalt psychologists also helped the cognitive movement by reintroducing consciousness. In addition, the work of Jean Piaget, who studied the cognitive development of children, helped broaden the subject matter of psychology.

The American Zeitgeist also served to help cognitive psychology emerge, drawing from changes in the field of physics. A new way of thinking in physics occurred with the idea that there is no way to objectively observe the world. Observations will include subjective material from the observer. This "rejection of an objective, mechanistic subject matter and [the]…recognition of subjectivity" allowed the conscious experience to once again become an acceptable focus for psychologists. There was no revolt, no dramatic shift, and no charismatic leadership marking the beginning of cognitive psychology (in stark contrast to Watson's behaviorism and several other schools of thought). Rather, the change occurred slowly. The two people whose work can be considered groundbreaking are: George Miller and Ulrich Neisser.

George Miller received a master's degree in speech from the University of Alabama and went on to become a professor of psychology. He went to Harvard and received his Ph.D. in psychology working on vocal communication. At that time he "accepted the behaviorist school of thought, noting that he had little choice because behaviorists held the leadership positions." By the 1950's, Miller began to work on problems in cognitive psychology and published the famous article: "The magical number seven, plus or minus two: Some limits on our capacity for processing information." In the article, he postulates that humans can only process 7 (plus or minus 2) "chunks" of information at a given time. This reflects not only his interest in conscious processes, but the term "processing information" is derived from his interest in computer models of human thought. In 1960, Miller and colleague Jerome Bruner, founded the Center for Cognitive Studies at Harvard University. "Researchers at the center investigated a wide range of topics: language, memory, perception, concept formation, thinking, and developmental psychology." Miller later became president of APA (1969) and has won numerous awards for his work promoting and contributing to cognitive theory.

Another influential cognitive psychologist, Ulrich Neisser, switched his studies from physics to psychology after taking one class taught by George Miller. He received his bachelor's degree at Harvard, his master's under Wolfgang Köhler at Swarthmore, and his Ph.D. at Harvard in 1956. He then published *Cognitive Psychology* (1967), which was "a landmark in the history of psychology." With this book, he was deemed the "father of cognitive psychology." Later, he criticized cognitive psychology because of its narrow focus and reliance on laboratory rather than real-life settings.

Similar to how clocks and automata have in the past served as models for studying people, computers began to serve as the model for human behaviors according to cognitive psychology. "It is the program (the software), not the computer itself (the hardware), that serves as the explanation for mental operations." In this way, human cognitive functions were likened to data servers. The first calculating machines were the ones designed by Babbage and Hollerith. In World War II a machine was desperately needed to do a very large amount of calculations for artillery rounds. To solve this problem, the ENIAC machine was created, which was physically massive and made up of thousands of vacuum tubes, resistors, etc. After ENIAC, computers evolved and became smaller and more powerful. Eventually people began to ask if these computers were capable of intellectual functioning. Artificial intelligence became the goal of technology.

In an attempt to compare the human brain to the capacities of artificial intelligent of the time, Alan Turing defined the Turing test, which asks whether a person can be persuaded "that the computer with which he or she is communicating is really another person, not a machine." He used an interrogator to ask questions of two parties, one being a computer, in order to assess which respondent was in fact human. He concluded that it is possible for a machine to deceive a human when programmed to do so.

One critic of the Turing test is the philosopher John Searle, who discussed the Chinese room problem. "Imagine you are sitting at a desk. In the wall in front of you are two slots. Slips of paper appear one at a time from the slot on the left. Each paper contains a group of Chinese characters. Your job is to match by shape the set of symbols with those in a book. When you find the matching set, you are directed to copy another set of symbols from the book onto a piece of paper and feed the paper through the slot on the right." Searle says that to the person feeding in the slips of paper, you look like you know Chinese, but the reality is that you are just mechanically responding using the codebook. With Searle's problem, the Turing test becomes insufficient to determine whether a machine is "thinking."

In the chess match mentioned at the beginning of the chapter, Kasparov was playing against a computer called Deep Blue, which was programmed by IBM to play chess. This shows that the processing of a computer, though similar to that of a human, is still not yet as advanced.

Cognitive psychology has affected just about every aspect of psychology. Although sometimes likened to behaviorism, there are still differences between cognitive psychology and behaviorism. "First, cognitive psychologists focuses on the process of knowing rather than merely responding to stimuli." Second, cognitive psychologists study "how the mind structures or organizes experience" while behaviorists do not believe "that the mind...possesses inherent organizational abilities." Third, cognitive psychologists believe that we actively engage with our environment and make choices about which stimuli to attend to, while behaviorists see us as passively responding to environmental stimuli.

One field that has re-emerged within cognitive psychology is cognitive neuroscience, whose aim is to map the functions of the brain and find out "how brain functions give rise to mental activity." This began with Gall, Flourens, and Broca in the 1700's and 1800's "using methods such as extirpation and electrical stimulation." Modern methods include using electroencephalogram (EEG), computerized axial tomography (CAT), magnetic resonance imagery (MRI), and positron emission tomography (PET) technologies—all of which capture an aspect of brain functioning in conscious subjects using computer imagery. Research within cognitive neuroscience gives an idea of types of societal problems the area aims to address. In 2006, a paralyzed 25-year-old man was able to do such things as move a cursor on a computer and open email by using only an electrode that had been placed in his motor cortex. This field is called neuroprosthetics and gives hope to disabled individuals.

Cognitive psychology has reintroduced introspection as a research method, although attempts have been made to increase objectivity and quantifiability. Even so, it is still subject to errors from socially desirable responses as well as from processes that occur below conscious awareness. Now researchers are attempting to access unconscious cognition, which many believe has a profound impact on our conscious thoughts and behavior. The modern focus on unconscious cognition is different from the Freudian conception, which is why modern cognitive psychologists prefer the term "nonconscious". It is here that information is processed (rather than being a seat of "repressed desires and memories").

With cognitive psychology, animal cognition has once again become an appropriate focus for psychologists. Those that study such cognition say that animals can form "cognitive maps, sense the motives of others, plan by taking into account past experiences, understand the concept of numbers, and solve problems through the use of reason." This field is still quite controversial. For example, one experiment attempts to find the existence of animal personality. This field began with two psychologists who studied "44 red octopuses at the aquarium in Seattle, Washington." Their conclusions are that the octopuses differed reliably on three dimensions of personality: activity, reactivity, and avoidance. They believe this to be indicative of the existence of animal personality. Such research has grown to include "a variety of animals including fish, spiders, farm animals, hyenas, chimps, and dogs."

As a movement, cognitive psychology has had a revolutionary and profound impact. In the 1970's through the mid-1990's seven journals have been created that continue to publish cognitive studies. An attempt to unify a number of sciences has been named cognitive science. Even so, Skinnerian psychologists and others oppose cognitive psychology because of disagreements about cognitive topics and how to define terms, and because of a lack of focus on such things as motivation and emotion. Cognitive psychology appears to be a new school of thought, and we may eventually talk about cognitivism, but only time will tell.

Another new branch of psychology is evolutionary psychology, which "is based on the assumption that people with certain behavioral, cognitive, and affective tendencies were more likely to survive and bear and raise children." This theory suggests that humans are "predisposed at birth to certain ways of behaving as shaped by evolution." One of the movement's founders, David Buss, calls it "one of the most important scientific revolutions we've ever had in the history of psychology." The term "evolutionary psychology" was coined by William James who predicted that one day psychology would be based on evolution. James believed that a wide range of behaviors were instinctive.

Although these ideas are antithetical to Watsonian behaviorism (in which all things are learned), there is some empirical evidence to support evolutionary psychology. For example, the instinctual drift discovered by Breland and Breland demonstrated that certain behaviors are difficult to extinguish even with reinforcement. Another example comes from Martin Seligman, who showed that it is more difficult to condition people to become fearful of neutral stimuli ("such as a car or screwdriver") compared to other stimuli for which fear would serve an evolutionary purpose (such as snakes, spiders, and heights).

Cognitive psychology served as an antecedent to evolutionary psychology because of a focus on how consciousness has evolved over time. A final precursor to the field was the book by E. O. Wilson called *Sociobiology: A New Synthesis* (1975) in which he discusses the important influence of heredity on behavior. This book received great praise and criticism—so much criticism that the term sociobiology is not used and in its place is used evolutionary psychology.

Evolutionary psychology is criticized by Skinnerian psychologists, but also by individuals who believe that evolutionary psychology is deterministic (its proponents say it is not deterministic, that not all behaviors are hereditary). Other critics say that evolutionary psychology is not testable, because it requires understanding primitive people who lived "hundreds of generations" ago.

Outline

I.   Chess champion capitulates to cunning computer
    A. Garry Kasparov was acknowledged as the greatest chess player in history
    B. undefeated
    C. in a rematch, the usual unflappable Kasparov begins to break down emotionally
    D. he wins first game
    E. signs of confusion and terror begin during the second game
    F. emotional breakdown caused by the fact that he could no longer see the logic that his opponent was using against him
    G. second and third games end in draw
    H. fourth won by opponent
    I. fifth game, the next day ends in a draw
    J. Kasparov resigns the sixth game on the following day, after only 19 moves played, shocks onlookers
    K. attributes resignation and fear to the fact that he encountered something her could not understand

II. Schools of Thought in Perspective
    A. Earlier schools (except psychoanalysis) absorbed into mainstream
    B. Structuralism
        1. established science of psychology
        2. obtained its independence from philosophy
    C. Functionalism
        1. permeates modern American psychology
    D. Gestalt: influenced
        1. traditional areas: learning, perception, thinking
        2. applied areas: clinical and social
    E. Behaviorism
        1. profound impact
        2. maintained its identity despite factions
    F. Psychoanalysis
        1. profound impact
        2. maintained its identity despite factions
    G. Behaviorism and psychoanalysis firmly opposed
        1. in definitions of problems
        2. in approaches to problems
    H. Humanistic Psychology
        1. growth of positive psychology movement
    I. New fields: Cognitive and evolutionary psychology

III. The Cognitive Movement in Psychology
    A. History
        1. 1913: Watson demanded the rejection of all references to consciousness
        2. 1976: McKeachie's APA presidential address: psychology's image of human nature was becoming human and refocusing on consciousness
        3. 1978: article called "Consciousness (Natsoulas) published in *American Psychologist*
        4. 1979: "Behaviorism and the Mind: A (Limited) Call for a Return to Introspection" (Lieberman) published in *American Psychologist*
        5. textbooks revised and courses offered to reflect these changes
        6. psychology has moved beyond Watson and Skinner
    B. Antecedent influences on cognitive psychology
        1. ancient interest in consciousness: Plato and Aristotle work on thought processes
        2. more modern influence: British empiricists and associationists
        3. Wundt: perhaps the forerunner of cognitive psychology; emphasis on mind's creative activity
        4. structuralism and functionalism: elements and functions of consciousness
        5. behaviorism: outright dismissal of consciousness for 50 years
        6. return to consciousness: 1950's
        7. neobehaviorists
            a. Guthrie at end of career: decried mechanism and reductionism; stimuli must be described perceptually or cognitively (1959)
            b. Tolman: his purposive psychology acknowledged importance of cognitive and intervening variables; play a part in the weakening of the S-R approach
        8. Gestalt psychology: kept interest in consciousness alive
        9. Piaget: work on cognitive stages of development in children
            a. "clinical method of interviewing children and his insistence on highly detailed note-taking during the interviews were seen as a major inspiration for the famous Hawthorne studies of industrial workers in the 1920s"
            b. helped broaden the range of behavior for which cognitive psychology can be applied
    C. The changing Zeitgeist in physics
        1. rejection of the mechanistic model of the universe
        2. attempts to bridge the gap between observer and observed (i.e., Einstein, Niels Bohr, and Werner Heisenberg)
        3. shift of focus of scientific investigation
            a. from an independent and objectively knowable universe
            b. to one's own observation of that universe
        4. modern scientists: participant observers; no longer detached observers
        5. modern physics: objective knowledge is really subjective
        6. restoration of the role of conscious experience in acquiring knowledge
        7. scientific psychology resisted the new physics for at least 50 years
    D. The founding of cognitive psychology
        1. change was slow
        2. no "flashpoint" in contrast to Watson's paper
        3. no single founder

4. two scholars contributed groundbreaking work: George Miller and Ulric Neisser

IV.   George Miller (1920-   )
    A. His life
        1.   majored in speech and English
        2.   as a graduate student, taught 16 sections of introductory psychology
        3.   1941: master's in speech from University of Alabama
        4.   1946: PhD from Harvard, began studying psycholinguistics
        5.   1951: Language and Communication
        6.   behaviorism
            a.   Miller accepted it as the primary school (had no choice)
            b.   investigated statistical learning theory, information theory, and computer-based models of the mind
            c.   mid-1950s: determined behaviorism was inadequate
        7.   rebellious nature helped him rebel against the confines of behaviorism
        8.   1956: classic article "The Magical Number Seven, Plus or Minus Two: Some Limits on our Capacity for Processing Information"
            a.   suggests that humans can only process seven (plus or minus two) "chunks" of information at a given time
            b.   significant because it deals with a conscious action while other psychologists were only looking at behaviors
            c.   "processing information" influenced by a computer-based model for the mind
    B. The Center for Cognitive Studies
        1.   Harvard University
        2.   purpose: to investigate the human mind
        3.   cognition defined by what it was not (not behaviorism)
        4.   cognitive psychology: an accretion rather than a revolution
            a.   slow growth and accumulation
            b.   evolutionary
            c.   a return to commonsense psychology
        5.   wide range of topics investigated: "language, memory, perception, concept formation, thinking, and developmental psychology."
        6.   1969: American Psychological Association president
        7.   APA Distinguished Scientific Contribution Award
        8.   1991: National Medal of Science
        9.   2003: APA's Outstanding Lifetime Contribution to Psychology Award

V.   Ulric Neisser (1928-   )
    A. His life
        1.   born in Kiel, Germany; came to the United States at age 3
        2.   at Harvard University: a physics major, switched to psychology
        3.   influenced by Miller and by Koffka's *Principles of Gestalt Psychology* (1935)
        4.   1950: bachelor's from Harvard
        5.   master's at Swarthmore with Köhler
        6.   1956: PhD from Harvard
        7.   behaviorist (had no choice)
        8.   first position at Brandeis, with Maslow as department head
            a.   opportunity to pursue his interest in cognitive psychology
            b.   Maslow unsuccessful at convincing him to study humanism

claimed cognitive psychology is the "third force" (rather than humanism)

        9. 1967: *Cognitive Psychology*, which becomes landmark book
- a. attempt to define a new approach
- b. made him the "father" of cognitive psychology

      10. 1976: *Cognition and Reality*
- a. dissatisfied with cognitive psychology
  - (1) the narrowing of the cognitive position
  - (2) the reliance on artificial laboratory situations for data
  - (3) lack of generalizability
  - (4) reliance on lab and not real-world settings
  - (5) does not solve practical problems
- b. conclusion: cognitive psychology could contribute little

      11. became a vocal critic of cognitive psychology

VI. The Computer Metaphor
- A. Computer replaced clock as the model of the mind
  1. agent for the overthrow of behaviorism in America
  2. operations of computer are liken to cognitive processes
  3. symbols and data are the current language for information processing, reasoning, problem solving
- B. Focus on the program (software), not the hardware (computer)
- C. Of interest to cognitive psychologists
  1. focus: how the mind processes information
  2. goal: the discovery of patterns of thinking (programs)
- D. Computer, like the clock, is a machine
- E. The Development of the Modern Computer
  1. Antecedents: work of Charles Babbage and Henry Hollerith in developing machines that could think
  2. Goal: to develop a machine capable of the rapid calculations, based on mathematical tables, need to accurately fire cannons and other artillery
  3. Result: Electronic Numerical Integrator And Calculator (ENIAC)

VII. Artificial Intelligence
- A. Is the intelligence of the computer the same as that of the human?
- B. Initially, idea eagerly accepted
- C. 1950 Turing test: Can a subject interacting with a computer be persuaded that he/she is communicating instead with a human?
  1. method: an interrogator questions two parties (one is a computer) to determine which is AI.
  2. computer designed to manipulate and deceive to make interrogator believe it is human
- D. Criticism of Turing Test: John Searle
  1. used the example of Chinese Room problem to show deficit of Turning test
  2. method: if you are asked to copy symbols that are written in Chinese, and manage to do so, you may look like you know Chinese when in fact you do not.
  3. a physical product is not indicative of knowledge or intelligence
  4. whether or not one understands Chinese, rote following of instructions, not thinking, is involved
  5. computer programs that appear to "think" do not understand to any greater degree than subjects in the Chinese Room problem

E. Explanation of Garry Kasparov loss:
  1. opponent was Deep Blue (gigantic IBM computer)
  2. Kasparov: "Instead of a computer that thought and played like a human, with human creativity and intuition, [the programmers] got one that played like a machine, systematically evaluating 200 million possible moves on the chess board per second and winning with brute number-crunching force"
  3. tied the computer 3-3 (yet quit after that)
  4. shows that computers cannot (yet) attain the same type of intelligence as humans

VIII. The Nature of Cognitive Psychology
  A. Cognitive factors a consideration in nearly every area
  B. Differs from behaviorism
    1. focus on the process of knowing
      a. *knowing* rather than responding
      b. important factors: mental processes and events
      c. emphasizes mind, not behavior
      d. behaviors are sources for inferences
    2. interest in how the mind structures or organizes experience
    3. the person actively and creatively arranges the stimuli received from the environment
  C. Cognitive Neuroscience
    1. 18th & 19th Centuries: Gall, Flourens, Broca map brain functions
    2. cognitive neuroscience = today's equivalent
    3. amalgam of cognitive psychology and neurosciences
    4. goals: effects of brain functions on mental activity and correlations between types of information processing and specified brain regions
    5. tools: advanced imaging systems
      a. electroencephalogram (EEG): measure electrical activity in parts of brain
      b. computerized axial tomography (CAT) scans: comprehensive brain cross-sections
      c. magnetic resonance imagery (MRI): 3-D brain images
      d. positron emission topography (PET): scan: live pictures of cognitive activities
    6. new research (2006): 25-year-old paralyzed man
      a. electronic sensors placed into motor cortex
      b. sensors interfaced with a computer
      c. demonstrates that human brain was able to control a computer, a television, a robot
      d. could move computer's cursor
        (1) open email
        (2) move objects with robotic arm
        (3) play simple video game
        (4) draw crude circle on screen
      e. this new field called neuroprosthetics
        (1) hope for people with disabilities to interact with their environments

D. The role of introspection
   1. attempts to quantify introspective reports
      a.   increase objectivity and ability to do statistical analyses
      b.   retrospective phenomenological assessment
   2. Wilson (2003): conscious states revealed by introspection "often good predictors of people's behavior"
   3. Some form of introspection "most frequently used research method in contemporary psychology", still has limitations
      a.   social desirability influencing reports
      b.   some thoughts are not available: in unconscious
E. Unconscious cognition
   1. cognitive psychologists agree: unconscious does more than we thought it did
      a.   most of our thinking and information processing
      b.   operates more quickly and efficiently than conscious mind
   2. the new unconscious or nonconscious
      a.   not the same as Freud's concept
      b.   more rational than emotional
      c.   different than being unaware, sleep, or comatose
      d.   form an integral part of learning
   3. studies of unconscious thought (deliberation-without-attention)
      a.   purchasing decisions more creative and diverse
      b.   led to more satisfying purchases than did conscious deliberation
   4. subliminal perception and subliminal activation
      a.   stimulation presented below conscious awareness
      b.   stimuli "activate conscious processes"
      c.   shows we are influenced by things we can't see or hear
F. Animal cognition
   1. cognitive revolution returned consciousness to animals
   2. since 1970's, how animals "encode, transform, compute, and manipulate" information
   3. focus: information processing
   4. animal memory is complex and flexible
   5. some processing shown to be similar to humans
   6. studies on: space, time, number, and cause/effect processing
   7. studies use a wide variety of animals
   8. animals can form cognitive maps, sense others' motives, plan by taking past experiences into account, understand numbers, and problem solve using reason
   9. criticisms
      a.   some say cannot yet compare human to animal mind
      b.   behavioral psychologists continue to reject the notion
G. Animal personality
   1. early 1990's, two psychologists study 44 red octopuses
      a.   keepers saw different personalities in them
      b.   psychologists observed using 3 experimental situations
      c.   found 3 factors: activity, reactivity, avoidance
      d.   they said this was personality

2. since then other studies have shown support for animal personality
    a. variety: "fish, spiders, farm animals, hyenas, chimps, and dogs"
    b. example: mice, chimps, elephants, and dolphins showed empathy
3. evidence of more similarity between humans and animals

IX. Current Status
  A. Consciousness reclaimed its former importance
  B. Cognitive psychology is a success
    1. eight journals since 1970 for just cognitive research
    2. Jerome Bruner and Roger Sperry speak to the profound impact of cognitive psychology
    3. its impact is felt by many areas: linguistics, anthropology, philosophy, computer sciences, artificial intelligence, neuroscience
  C. "Cognitive science"
    1. multidisciplinary: a combination of diverse fields
    2. some psychology departments have been renamed cognitive science departments
    3. use of experimental methods praised (similar to behaviorism)
  D. Criticisms
    1. opposed by behaviorists
    2. lack of agreement on concepts
    3. considerable confusion about terminology and definitions
    4. overemphasis on cognition
       a. ignoring other influences such motivation and emotion
       b. becoming fixated on thought processes
  E. Contributions and status of cognitive psychology
    1. widely accepted in psychology today
    2. recent analysis shows the "primacy of cognitive psychology"
    3. has achieved some features of a school of thought
       a. multiple journals
       b. laboratories
       c. professional organizations and meetings
       d. body of research and terminology
       e. convinced followers
    4. can speak of cognitivism

X. Evolutionary psychology
  A. as biological animals, humans have been programmed (wired) through evolution to behave and process information in a manner that increases the likelihood of survival and reproduction
  B. survival of the fittest
  C. humans who defended territory, nurtured children, and strove for domination are more likely to produced viable offspring
  D. those evolutionary traits will be passed on
  E. biology influences human development as much as and perhaps more than learning and social and cultural forces
  F. four fundamental questions
    1. How did the human mind evolve?
    2. How is it designed and organized?
    3. What are its functions?
    4. How does it interact with environmental stimuli to effect behavior?

G. wide-ranging field that encompasses many disciplines: animal behavior, biology, genetics, neuropsychology, and evolutionary theory

H. David Buss, founder, believes it is like a revolution

I. antecedent influences on evolutionary psychology
   1. Charles Darwin
      a. integral to any psychological theory involving evolution
   2. Herbert Spencer and his survival of the fittest concept
   3. William James 1st to use term in *The Principles of Psychology*
      a. instincts drive behaviors, some are animalistic
      b. some include: parenting skills, love, sociability, and pugnacity (the tendency to quarrel and fight)
   4. genetic determinants anathema to orthodox behaviorists
   5. evidence supporting such determinants found in research
      a. the Brelands (IQ zoo)
      b. Harlow (cloth-mother versus wire-mother monkey experiments)
      c. Seligman demonstrates it is easier to condition people to fear naturally dangerous stimuli than to fear neutral ones: called this fact biological preparedness (positive psychology)
   6. cognitive psychology: mind, like the computer, needs to be programmed
   7. evolutionary psychology specified ways in which the design of the mind led to survival and reproduction

J. the influence of sociobiology
   1. 1975: biologist Edward O. Wilson published the seminal book *Sociobiology: A New Synthesis*
      a. defined sociobiology as "the systematic study of the biological basis of all social behavior."
      b. controversy erupted because of several implications
         (1) humans are not created equal
         (2) genetic, not cultural, influences may determine behavior
         (3) suggests unchangeable nature of human behavior
         (4) division of labor based on sex, ethical behavior, tribalism, male dominance, territorial aggression, etc., defined as elements of human nature
      c. sociobiology became extremely negative term
      d. to avoid stigma, association of proponents called themselves the Human Behavior and Evolution Society
      e. in psychology, the term evolutionary psychology sidestepped the negativity

K. current status of evolutionary psychology
   1. socially acceptable and popular
   2. drawn substantial criticism, particularly
      a. from environmentalists
      b. from those who say the breadth of the field make it difficult to form and test meaningful hypotheses

XI. Comment
   A. cognitive and evolutionary psychologies, as with all schools of thought, have supporters and detractors
   B. due to relative newness, they have not reached the point to determine final impact and value

Lecture prompts/Discussion topics for chapter fifteen

- Can machines 'think'? Can they imitate human intelligence? What would a machine have to do in order to be called intelligent?
- Is there a way to show that another person's brain is something more than Searle's Chinese room? How would you do that?
- I put this quote on the board, ask students what a silicon brain might mean, ask them if they think it is possible, and ask them if they think it is desirable. "In 1981 Robert Jastrow, director of the Goddard Institute for Space Studies, predicted that "around 1995, according to current trends, we will see the silicon brain as an emergent form of life, competitive with man", The Post-Human World, *Science Digest*. (January/February 1981), p. 144

Internet Resources for chapter fifteen

Animal Cognition and Learning
http://www.pigeon.psy.tufts.edu/psych26/
> Dr. Robert Cook at Tufts University offers a course on animal cognition, this website provides a very large amount of information about the topic for his students and, luckily, us as well.

Center for evolutionary psychology
http://www.psych.ucsb.edu/research/cep/
> This Web site has a very large library of information about evolutionary psychology. If you click on the research link you will find a wide variety of full-text articles grouped by categories.

Cognitive Neuroscience Society
http://www.cogneurosociety.org/
> From their Web site: "The Cognitive Neuroscience Society (CNS) is committed to the development of mind and brain research aimed at investigating the psychological, computational, and neuroscientific bases of cognition." The site has some interesting information in their past newsletters, which reflect the very wide variety of topic areas cognitive neuroscientists study.

The Magic Number Seven
http://www.musanim.com/miller1956/
> This is a full text copy of Miller's famous paper, and has a link to Miller's webpage at Princeton University, where he is a professor emeritus.

20 questions
http://20q.net/
> This is an artificial intelligence engine that plays 20 questions and frequently wins. It is useful bring this Web site up during class after discussing what might distinguish human thought from machine thought. Often students will say that humans learn and machines don't, but this program does learn from previous trials.

Potential answers to chapter fifteen discussion questions

1. Describe the accomplishments, failures, and ultimate fates of the major schools of thought in psychology.

"Each of the schools of thought in psychology developed, prospered for a time, and then—with the exception of psychoanalysis—became part of mainstream contemporary psychological thought." Although structuralism "has left little direct imprint on psychology as we know it today," it promoted psychology as a discipline separate from philosophy. Functionalism's impact can be seen in the application of psychology to solve real-world problems. Gestalt succeeded in opposing elementalism, and making conscious processes a legitimate topic for psychology. The greatest impact, though, has been from behaviorism and psychoanalysis, both of which have remained separate and distinct schools of thought (although there is much disagreement within both schools). Cognitive psychology arose to challenge these schools of thought and address areas that they neglected, specifically the conscious experience.

2. What were the precursors of cognitive psychology?

Because of the power of behaviorism as a force in psychology, for many years consciousness was not deemed a proper focus of psychology. That changed in the mid-1970's when McKeachie, in his APA presidential address, noted "that psychology was changing and that the new conception included a refocus on consciousness." The precursors of cognitive psychology begin, of course, with the Greek philosophers and must also include Wundt, the structuralists and the functionalists, but also the behaviorists Guthrie and Tolman. Other influences on cognitive psychology include the Gestalt psychologists and the work of Jean Piaget who studied the cognitive development of children.

3. How did the changing Zeitgeist in physics influence cognitive psychology?

The Zeitgeist served to help cognitive psychology emerge, drawing from changing attitudes in the field of physics about the objectivity of the human experience. A new way of thinking in physics occurred with the idea that there is no way to objectively observe the world. Observations will include subjective material from the observer. This "rejection of an objective, mechanistic subject matter and [the]…recognition of subjectivity" allowed conscious experience to once again become an acceptable focus for psychologists. This change introduced the participant observer as the scientist who both actively participates in the research and simultaneously measures the phenomena. In addition, the Zeitgeist introduced social science to the world, with the advent of sociology and psychology, and allowed for the possibility of social influences on scientific studies.

4. What were the early signs of a cognitive revolution in psychology?

There was no dramatic shift or leadership marking cognitive psychology (this is in stark contrast to Watson's behaviorism), rather the change occurred slowly. The authors include two people whose work can be considered groundbreaking: George Miller and Ulrich Neisser. Miller along with Jerome Bruner, founded the Center for Cognitive Studies at Harvard University. Neisser published Cognitive Psychology (1967) which was "a landmark in the history of psychology."

5. What personal factors motivated Miller and Neisser?

Both felt forced to "accept" behaviorism for a while, because behaviorism was the prevailing thought, and behaviorists held powerful positions and resources within psychology. They each were personally dissatisfied with behaviorism as the "answer" in psychology. Miller began developing the basis of cognitive psychology when he found the study of behaviorism did not address the question of how thinking occurs. He later trained Neisser, and together they founded cognitive psychology and the methods of empirical research involved in its practice.

6. In what ways did cognitive psychology differ from behavioral psychology?

"First, cognitive psychologists focuses on the process of knowing rather than merely responding to stimuli." Second, cognitive psychologists study "how the mind structures or organizes experience" while the behaviorists do not believe "that the mind...possesses inherent organizational abilities." Third, cognitive psychologists believe that we actively engage with our environment and make choices about which stimuli to attend to, while behaviorists see us as passively responding to environmental stimuli.

7. What does the term "ecological validity" mean?

In 1976, Ulirch "Neisser published *Cognition and Reality* (1976), which expressed dissatisfaction with the narrowing of the cognitive position and its reliance on laboratory situations instead of real-world settings from which to collect data. He insisted that the results of psychological research should have ecological validity. By that he meant that they should be generalizable to situations beyond the confines of the laboratory. In addition, Neisser insisted that cognitive psychologists should be able to apply their findings to practical problems, helping people deal with the everyday issues in their work and in their lives. Thus, Neisser had become disillusioned, concluding that the cognitive psychology movement had little to contribute to psychology's understanding of how people cope."

8. Discuss the shift from clocks to computers as metaphors for the mind.

Just as clocks and automata have in the past served as models for studying people, computers served as the model for cognitive psychology. "It is the program (the software), not the computer itself (the hardware), that serves as the explanation for mental operations."

9. What practical need in World War II led to the development of the modern computer? What was ENIAC?

In World War II a machine was desperately needed to do a very large amount of calculations for artillery rounds. These computations were being done by hand, but there were so many variables that went into the calculations that human computations could not keep up.

The ENIAC (Electronic Numerical Integrator and Calculator) machine was created, which was the first modern computer. It was physically very large and made up of thousands of vacuum tubes, resistors, etc. and required several large fans to keep the machine and room from overheating.

10. What did the most famous chess match of the twentieth century tell us about the ability of machines to think?

The great chess champion, Garry Kasparov, lost his first match in a dramatic and emotional story to a computer called Deep Blue, but the computer was only doing what it was programmed to do. This shows the immense capabilities of machines to simulate human thought. However, because the champion tied the machine 3-3, it is still a fact that humans are of superior intelligence to machines.

11. How are the Turing Test and the Chinese Room problem used to examine the proposition that computers can think?

Alan Turing defined the Turing test, which is if a person can be persuaded "that the computer with which he or she is communicating is really another person, not a machine."

One critic of the Turing test is the philosopher John Searle, who discussed the Chinese room problem. "Imagine you are sitting at a desk. In the wall in front of you are two slots. Slips of paper appear one at a time from the slot on the left. Each paper contains a group of Chinese

534   CHAPTER 15

characters. Your job is to match by shape the set of symbols with those in a book. When you find the matching set, you are directed to copy another set of symbols from the book onto a piece of paper and feed the paper through the slot on the right." Searle says that to the person feeding in the slips of paper, you look like you know Chinese, but the reality is that you are just mechanically responding using the codebook. With Searle's problem, the Turing test becomes insufficient to determine whether a machine is "thinking."

12. Discuss three ways in which cognitive psychology differs from behaviorism.
Cognitive psychology has affected just about every aspect of psychology, although there are still differences between cognitive psychology and behaviorism. "First, cognitive psychologists focuses on the process of knowing rather than merely responding to stimuli." Second, cognitive psychologists study "how the mind structures or organizes experience" while the behaviorists do not believe "that the mind...possesses inherent organizational abilities." Third, cognitive psychologists believe that we actively engage with our environment and make choices about which stimuli to attend to, while behaviorists see us as passively responding to environmental stimuli.

13. Describe cognitive neuroscience and the techniques used to map the brain.
One field that has re-emerged with a new name is cognitive neuroscience, whose aim is to map the functions of the brain and find out "how brain functions give rise to mental activity." Modern methods include using electroencephalogram (EEG), computerized axial tomography (CAT), magnetic resonance imagery (MRI), and positron emission tomography (PET) technologies, all of which capture an aspect of brain functioning in conscious subjects. These techniques also all use computerized imaging to capture a realistic image of how and when the brain functions.

14. How does cognitive neuroscience relate to earlier attempts to explain brain functioning?
The mapping of brain functions started with Gall, Flourens, and Broca in the 1700's and 1800's "using methods such as extirpation and electrical stimulation." These earlier methods provided the theoretical basis of modern cognitive neuroscience, but without modern technology, our current abilities to see how the mind works would not be possible.

15. What is neuroprosthetics and how does it involve cognitive neuroscience?
An example of neuroprosthetics is the case of a paralyzed 25-year-old man who was able to do such things as move a cursor on a computer and open email by using only an electrode that had been placed in his motor cortex. This field gives disabled individuals hope to have the same physical capacities that others have.

16. What are the limitations to the use of introspection in cognitive psychology?
It is still subject to errors from socially desirable responses as well as from processes that occur below conscious awareness.

17. In what ways does the current version of the cognitive unconscious differ from the Freudian view of the unconscious?
The modern focus on unconscious cognition is different from the Freudian conception, which is why modern cognitive psychologists prefer the term "nonconscious". It is here that information is processed (rather than being a seat of "repressed desires and memories").

18. Describe the current view of animal cognition.
Animal cognition has once again become an appropriate focus for psychologists. Those that study such cognition say that animals can form "cognitive maps, sense the motives of others, plan by taking into account past experiences, understand the concept of numbers, and solve problems through the use of reason."

19. In your opinion, are animals capable of cognitive activities, or are we attributing human functions to them that they do not really possess?
Long answer: That's difficult to say. The problem is that animals cannot report to us their conscious experiences, which is the only way we know that other people experience consciousness (as long as their brain is not Searle's Chinese room). If we chose to not use self-report and relied on observation to get information about conscious processes, I believe we would find that humans and animals are very similar and we could not attribute cognition to one and not the other.

Short answer: I am a pet owner, so of course I think they think: Yes!

20. How does evidence favoring the existence of personality in animals support Darwin's notion of evolution and the field of evolutionary psychology?
If animals do have distinctive individual personalities as the evidence suggests, this supports Darwin and evolutionary psychology because there is now very little that separates humans from animals; we have all undergone the same process.

21. Describe what is meant by the terms "embedded cognition" and "cognitive overload."
A recent extension of cognitive psychology called embedded cognition recognizes that there are physical aspects of cognition revealed in brain activity and in sensation and perception. It follows, then, that perceptual and motor response systems affect, direct, and often determine the cognitive processes that occur in the mind. Another important topic in cognitive psychology is cognitive overload, which deals with that familiar activity known as multitasking. Research has shown that college students who were exposed to a variety of electronic images and tasks performed poorly.

22. What is the present status of cognitive psychology?
As a movement, cognitive psychology has had a revolutionary and profound impact. In the 1970's through the mid-1990's seven journals have been sustained which publish cognitive studies. An attempt to unify a number of sciences has been named cognitive science. Cognitive psychology appears to be a new school of thought, and we may eventually talk about cognitivism, but only time will tell.

23. Describe the relationship between evolutionary psychology and cognitive psychology. Which one draws upon the other?
Evolutionary psychology draws upon cognitive psychology. Because the cognitive movement used the computer as a metaphor for human thinking, the idea came about that the mind would therefore need to be programmed. This program occurs, according to the evolutionary psychologists, in the process of evolution selecting those traits of consciousness that provide a better fit to the environment.

24. In your opinion, has psychology reached the stage of a unified paradigm that unites all the different approaches to psychology? Do you think evolutionary psychology is likely to be the final stage in the fractious and fragmented history of the field?

No, in fact I believe we are more fragmented than ever. Just look at the differences between the APA and the APS and the type of research they support. I also do not think evolutionary psychology will be the last school. As technology gets better and better, I believe that cognitive neuroscience has the best last shot of making psychology the natural science it has wished to be.

Key terms from chapter fifteen

- **Biological preparedness** The idea proposed by Martin Seligman that it is easier to condition fear to naturally occurring dangers such as snakes and heights than to neutral objects like a car or a pencil, this supports evolutionary psychology
- **Chinese room** John Searle's answer to the Turing test: a machine can seem to an observer to be understanding (or "thinking") but in reality may simply be processing coded information using a set of given commands
- **Cognitive Neuroscience** A new field, mapping brain functioning and determining how the brain creates conscious experience
- **Cognitive Science** the perspective that joins a multitude of sciences to study conscious experience: cognitive psychology, linguistics, anthropology, philosophy, computer sciences, artificial intelligence, and the neurosciences
- **Deep Blue** The computer manufactured by IBM that defeated the then-undefeated master chess player Garry Kasparov.
- **Nonconscious** the term preferred instead of unconscious (which connotes Freudian psychoanalytic thought) to describe the information processing that occurs outside of conscious awareness
- **Turing Test** Proposed by Alan Turing, a way to determine if machines can think: can a person tell whether they are interacting with a person or machine?

ESSAY

1. How did each of the major schools of thought shape psychology as a discipline? What is their current status within the field?

   ANS:
   Answer not provided.

   PTS: 1

2. Describe the antecedents of the cognitive movement in psychology, including the early indications within the field that a new school of thought was emerging and the role of the changing zeitgeist in physics in influencing it.

   ANS:
   Answer not provided.

   PTS: 1   MSC: WWW

3. Describe the nature of the founding of cognitive psychology, the roles played by Miller and Neisser in developing it, and the major contributions of each.

   ANS:
   Answer not provided.

   PTS: 1

4. In what ways is the computer an appropriate metaphor for cognitive psychology? Explain the concept of artificial intelligence and the significance of the chess games between Garry Kasparov and Deep Blue in terms of determining whether artificial intelligence is equivalent to human intelligence.

   ANS:
   Answer not provided.

   PTS: 1   MSC: WWW

5. Describe the distinctions between early approaches and contemporary cognitive approaches to introspection, unconscious cognition, and animal cognition.

   ANS:
   Answer not provided.

   PTS: 1

6. What is the current status of cognitive psychology?

   ANS:
   Answer not provided.

   PTS: 1

7. Describe evolutionary psychology and the four fundamental questions it addresses.

   ANS:
   Answer not provided.

   PTS: 1

8. Describe the antecedent and sociobiological influences on evolutionary psychology and its current status within psychology.

   ANS:
   Answer not provided.

   PTS: 1

MULTIPLE CHOICE

9. Garry Kasparov was ____.
   a. president of the Russian Psychological Association
   b. one of the founders of cognitive psychology
   c. the greatest chess player in history
   d. celebrated for his phenomenal work in artificial intelligence
   e. a minor player on the world stage

   ANS: C   PTS: 1   REF: Chess Champion Capitulates to Cunning Computer

10. In his match against the "cunning opponent," why did Kasparov exhibits signs of fear and confusion?
    a. Because he was playing against a computer that could challenge him intellectually.
    b. Because he couldn't help thinking about the rapid fall of the Soviet Union.
    c. Because he was trying to trick his opponent into thinking he had won.
    d. Because, after winning five straight games, he was tired.
    e. Because he saw a basic flaw in the reasoning of his opponent.

    ANS: A   PTS: 1   REF: Chess Champion Capitulates to Cunning Computer

11. Which of the following schools made substantial contributions to psychology's evolution?
    a. Gestalt psychology
    b. structuralism
    c. functionalism
    d. behaviorism
    e. All of the choices are correct.

    ANS: E   PTS: 1   REF: Schools of Thought in Perspective

12. There are no structural psychologists left in the United States. However, structural psychology was a success because it _____.
    a. discovered metal elements that compose consciousness
    b. helped to establish psychology as an independent science
    c. was able to perfect the method of introspection as a means to explore the nature of consciousness
    d. discovered the phi phenomenon which shows that mentality has the job of trying to interpret reality from sensory inputs
    e. None of the choices are correct.

    ANS: B   PTS: 1   REF: Schools of Thought in Perspective
    MSC: WWW

13. Of all the schools of psychology initiated by 1930, only behaviorism and psychoanalysis _____.
    a. have maintained their identities
    b. have been absorbed into the mainstream
    c. have been phased out of contemporary psychology
    d. maintained a focus on the pseudo-problem of consciousness
    e. are the primary schools of thought in contemporary psychology

    ANS: A   PTS: 1   REF: Schools of Thought in Perspective

14. The imperative that "psychology must discard all references to consciousness" was the command of _____.
    a. Dewey
    b. Angell
    c. Watson
    d. Skinner
    e. Seligman

    ANS: C   PTS: 1   REF: The Cognitive Movement in Psychology
    MSC: WWW

15. In McKeachie's opinion, the return of consciousness to psychology signaled a change in favor of _____ psychology.
    a. operational
    b. mechanistic
    c. humanistic
    d. cognitive
    e. behavioral

    ANS: D   PTS: 1   REF: The Cognitive Movement in Psychology

16. Cognitive psychology is concerned with _____.
    a. reducing mental processes to the activity of the brain
    b. the study of all mental processes such as perception, learning, memory, and problem solving
    c. the analysis of behavior into stimulus-response associations
    d. the explanation of behavior using external stimuli as causes
    e. human cognition only

    ANS: B   PTS: 1   REF: The Cognitive Movement in Psychology

17. In terms of its antecedent influences, cognitive psychology represents a return to _____.
    a. the early attempts at a science of the mind and consciousness
    b. the type of speculations engaged in by philosophers
    c. introspection
    d. the active role of the perceiver
    e. All of the choices are correct.

    ANS: E   PTS: 1   REF: The Cognitive Movement in Psychology

18. Guthrie argued that the behaviorists were unable to deal with _____.
    a. the phi phenomenon
    b. sign Gestalts
    c. the meaningfulness of a stimulus to the organism
    d. Hull's construct of excitatory potential
    e. why the rat runs the maze the *first* time

    ANS: C   PTS: 1   REF: The Cognitive Movement in Psychology

19. Tolman's contribution to the decline of S-R psychology was the _____.
    a. concept of cognitive maps
    b. Gestalt principles of organization
    c. concept of habit strength
    d. work on eyelid conditioning
    e. concept of self-efficacy

    ANS: A   PTS: 1   REF: The Cognitive Movement in Psychology
    MSC: WWW

20. Bridgman's response to behaviorism's radical operationism was to recommend the use of _____.
    a. introspection
    b. experimentation
    c. animals
    d. operational definitions
    e. Gestalt principles of organization

    ANS: A   PTS: 1   REF: The Cognitive Movement in Psychology

21. The "new" Zeitgeist in physics is characterized by _____.
    a. chaos theory
    b. Berkeley's argument that objective knowledge is subjective knowledge
    c. the notion that the objective universe is unknowable
    d. the notion of relativity
    e. the use of magnetic resonance as an index of conscious processes

    ANS: B   PTS: 1   REF: The Cognitive Movement in Psychology

22. This person's work on cognitive stages of development was not widely accepted under behaviorism, was welcomed by cognitive theorists, and finally was rewarded by mainstream psychology when he became the first European psychologist to receive the APA Distinguished Scientific Contribution Award.
    a. Carnap
    b. Piaget
    c. Binet
    d. Heisenberg
    e. Köhler

    ANS: B   PTS: 1   REF: The Cognitive Movement in Psychology

23. The founder of cognitive psychology was ____.
    a. Tolman
    b. Guthrie
    c. Miller
    d. Neisser
    e. There was no single founder.

    ANS: E   PTS: 1   REF: The Cognitive Movement in Psychology

24. Both Miller and Neisser were once behaviorists because of their ____.
    a. undergraduate work at Yale University
    b. undergraduate work with Hull at the University of Iowa
    c. undergraduate work at Cornell, which left them no choice
    d. graduate work at Harvard, which left them no choice
    e. None of the choices are correct.

    ANS: D   PTS: 1   REF: George Miller (1920-)
    MSC: WWW

25. The founders of the Center for Cognitive Studies ____.
    a. defined their position in opposition to the behaviorists
    b. did not know what cognition really meant
    c. located their facility at Harvard
    d. All of the choices are correct.
    e. None of the choices are correct.

    ANS: D   PTS: 1   REF: George Miller (1920-)

26. The definition of "cognition" at the Center for Cognitive Studies was ____.
    a. in terms of sign Gestalts
    b. in terms of the stream of consciousness reported by the *Einfall* technique
    c. whatever introspectors reported
    d. focused on Köhler's insight learning phenomenon
    e. whatever behaviorism was not

    ANS: E   PTS: 1   REF: George Miller (1920-)

27. Neisser's career was influenced by ____.
    a. Miller
    b. Koffka
    c. Köhler
    d. Maslow
    e. All of the choices are correct.

    ANS: E   PTS: 1   REF: Ulric Neisser (1928-)

28. The field of cognitive psychology was inaugurated by ____.
    a. Tolman's purposive behaviorism
    b. Piaget's work on cognitive development
    c. Miller's work in psycholinguistics
    d. Neisser's book on cognitive psychology
    e. Köhler's and Koffka's books

    ANS: D   PTS: 1   REF: Ulric Neisser (1928-)

29. Neisser's definition of "cognitive" basically involves terms from the metaphor of ____.
    a. clockworks
    b. information processing
    c. psychoanalysis
    d. Tolman's cognitive psychology
    e. neurolinguistic programming

    ANS: B   PTS: 1   REF: Ulric Neisser (1928-)

30. For Neisser, "everything a human being might possibly do" is the ____.
    a. focus of behaviorism
    b. focus of humanistic psychology
    c. parallel to neurolinguistic programming
    d. definition of cognition
    e. definition of psychology

    ANS: D   PTS: 1   REF: Ulric Neisser (1928-)

31. By 1976, Neisser concluded that cognitive psychology ____.
    a. was the dominant school in psychology
    b. had little to contribute to psychology
    c. was distorted by the research in real-life settings
    d. was being supplanted by the information processing model
    e. had reached Kuhn's paradigm stage

    ANS: B   PTS: 1   REF: Ulric Neisser (1928-)
    MSC: WWW

32. In the computer metaphor, cognitive processes are represented by ____.
    a. input
    b. output
    c. storage and retrieval
    d. the software program
    e. the chip

    ANS: D   PTS: 1   REF: The Computer Metaphor

33. The very first "thinking" machines, used for calculations, were developed by ____.
    a. Babbage and Hollerith
    b. IBM
    c. DaVinci
    d. Neisser
    e. Skinner

    ANS: A   PTS: 1   REF: The Computer Metaphor

34. The modern age of computers in the 20th century was initiated by ____.
    a. Babbage and Hollerith
    b. IBM
    c. the need for artillery firing tables in World War II
    d. Neisser
    e. None of the choices are correct.

    ANS: C   PTS: 1   REF: The Computer Metaphor

35. The question "Can computers think?" is a question about ____.
    a. human intelligence
    b. the essence of life
    c. artificial intelligence
    d. introspection
    e. cognitive neuroscience

    ANS: C   PTS: 1   REF: Artificial Intelligence

36. The principle purpose of the Turing Test is to determine if ____.
    a. an interrogator can distinguish a computer from a human
    b. a grand tour of Europe is necessary
    c. computers can calculate mathematical problems
    d. computers can translate Chinese into English
    e. people are as smart as computers

    ANS: A   PTS: 1   REF: Artificial Intelligence
    MSC: WWW

37. Many cognitive scientists came to believe that computers ____.
    a. cannot pass the Turing test
    b. are the same as humans when it comes to thinking
    c. can simulate intelligence without being intelligent
    d. have self-awareness
    e. None of the choices are correct.

    ANS: C   PTS: 1   REF: Artificial Intelligence

38. The point of Searle's Chinese room problem was to show that ____.
    a. Chinese is a difficult language to learn
    b. machines and humans use the same thinking strategies
    c. machines can and do display "thinking"
    d. machines can pass the Turing test and still not be "thinking"
    e. None of the choices are correct.

    ANS: D   PTS: 1   REF: Artificial Intelligence

39. The general consensus was that Deep Blue was ____.
    a. not thinking even if it behaved as if it were
    b. thinking just like a human
    c. a very convincing joke carefully planned by oceanographers
    d. smarter than humans
    e. an illusion

    ANS: A   PTS: 1   REF: Artificial Intelligence

40. Kasparov believed he was _____.
    a. the winner by a knockout
    b. the loser on all counts
    c. representing the human race
    d. overweight
    e. underweight

    ANS: C   PTS: 1   REF: Artificial Intelligence

41. The inclusion of cognitive factors in the theories of _____ altered American behaviorism.
    a. Skinner and Tolman
    b. Kasparov and Tolman
    c. Bandura and Rotter
    d. Watson and Yerkes
    e. Seligman and Maslow

    ANS: C   PTS: 1   REF: The Nature of Cognitive Psychology
    MSC: WWW

42. The study of cognitive factors is confined to research in(on) _____.
    a. basic psychology
    b. applied psychology
    c. social psychology
    d. clinical psychology
    e. None of the choices are correct; cognitive psychology affects almost all of psychology.

    ANS: E   PTS: 1   REF: The Nature of Cognitive Psychology

43. Cognitive psychology differs from behaviorism because cognitive psychologists _____.
    a. believe that people actively and creatively arrange environmental stimuli
    b. are interested in how the mind organizes experience
    c. focus on the process of knowing, not just on responses to stimuli
    d. All of the choices are correct.
    e. None of the choices are correct.

    ANS: D   PTS: 1   REF: The Nature of Cognitive Psychology

44. Cognitive psychologists view organizational abilities as _____ whereas behaviorists do not.
    a. innate
    b. haphazard
    c. organized
    d. learned
    e. None of the choices are correct.

    ANS: A   PTS: 1   REF: The Nature of Cognitive Psychology

45. The discipline representing a hybrid of cognitive psychology and the neurosciences is called _____.
    a. cognitive neuropsychology
    b. cognitive neuroscience
    c. neuro-cognitive psychology
    d. neuro-psychological science
    e. None of the choices are correct.

    ANS: B   PTS: 1   REF: The Nature of Cognitive Psychology

46. Which of the following imaging techniques are providing scientists with exceptional detail in mapping the brain?
    a. magnetic resonance imagery (MRI)
    b. positron emission tomography (PET)
    c. computerized axial tomography (CAT)
    d. All of the choices are correct.
    e. None of the choices are correct.

    ANS: D   PTS: 1   REF: The Nature of Cognitive Psychology

47. Acceptance of conscious experiences led cognitive psychologists to take another look at the first research method of scientific psychology, the _____ method.
    a. psychophysics
    b. introspection
    c. trial and error
    d. experimental
    e. correlational

    ANS: B   PTS: 1   REF: The Nature of Cognitive Psychology

48. One contemporary approach to introspection is called retrospective _____.
    a. observation
    b. subjective observation
    c. phenomenological assessment
    d. subjective retrospection
    e. experimental introspection

    ANS: C   PTS: 1   REF: The Nature of Cognitive Psychology
    MSC: WWW

49. Wilson has concluded that the self-report of conscious processes _____.
    a. is worthless
    b. is retrospection, not introspection
    c. is mediate experience, not immediate experience
    d. often predicts people's behaviors
    e. addresses a pseudo-problem

    ANS: D   PTS: 1   REF: The Nature of Cognitive Psychology

50. The technique of subliminal perception as used in cognitive psychology research has _____.
    a. been discounted as fraud
    b. been discounted as a pseudo-problem
    c. suggested that learning occurs primarily at a conscious level
    d. suggested that "mental aspects" of learning occur at a nonconscious level
    e. suggested that Freud's conceptualizations of unconscious influences on behavior are better accounted for by subliminal activation

    ANS: D   PTS: 1   REF: The Nature of Cognitive Psychology

51. The cognitive psychologists' focus on cognitive processes has meant that using animals as subjects is ____.
    a. inappropriate
    b. only useful with regard to using primates
    c. impossible because animal cognition is a pseudo-problem
    d. fruitful in cognitive psychology
    e. limited to only the simplest stimuli

    ANS: D   PTS: 1   REF: The Nature of Cognitive Psychology
    MSC: WWW

52. The idea that animals have personality is ____.
    a. something that has received some research support
    b. scoffed at by cognitive psychologists
    c. impossible to determine with cognitive psychology
    d. has received no research support
    e. None of the choices are correct.

    ANS: A   PTS: 1   REF: The Nature of Cognitive Psychology

53. The behaviorists' response to the advent of cognitive psychology has been to ____.
    a. attack it by operationally defining the cognitive concepts, as they did when threatened by psychoanalysis
    b. attack it by subjecting the cognitive psychologists' constructs and hypotheses to experimentation
    c. undermine the impact of cognitive psychology by redefining its constructs in terms of observable stimuli and responses
    d. undermine the impact of cognitive psychology by absorbing its terms and tenets into the mainstream, which behaviorism dominates
    e. hold fast to their position that consciousness (and thus cognitive psychology) should be rejected as a key subject matter

    ANS: E   PTS: 1   REF: The Nature of Cognitive Psychology

54. *Cognitive science* is a term that ____.
    a. was adopted by the cognitive psychologists to unify seemingly dissimilar fields
    b. was adopted to reflect the interdisciplinary nature of its domains of study
    c. distinguishes cognitive research in the natural sciences from cognitive research in psychology
    d. distinguishes cognitive psychology from such areas as linguistics, anthropology, and philosophy, which also use the term *cognitive* in their contemporary writings
    e. was adopted by the cognitive psychologists to unify seemingly dissimilar fields **and** was adopted to reflect the interdisciplinary nature of its domains of study

    ANS: E   PTS: 1   REF: The Nature of Cognitive Psychology

55. Even those psychologists who support cognitive psychology point out that there ____.
    a. remains considerable confusion about terminology and definitions
    b. are few concepts on which the majority of cognitive psychologists agree
    c. is really nothing that is truly cognitive
    d. remains considerable confusion about terminology and definitions and are few concepts on which the majority of cognitive psychologists agree
    e. None of the choices are correct.

    ANS: D   PTS: 1   REF: The Nature of Cognitive Psychology
    MSC: WWW

56. Ulric Neisser suggested that cognition is a narrow, sterile approach to the field of psychology because it
____.
   a. only uses the experimental method
   b. has no emotion
   c. doesn't deal with complex motivations
   d. has no emotion and doesn't deal with complex motivations
   e. All of the choices are correct.

   ANS: E   PTS: 1   REF: The Nature of Cognitive Psychology

57. Which branch of psychology is the most recently developed approach?
   a. behavioral psychology
   b. evolutionary psychology
   c. cognitivism
   d. psychoanalysis
   e. All of the choices are correct.

   ANS: B   PTS: 1   REF: Evolutionary Psychology

58. The basic principle of evolutionary theory is that ____.
   a. humans are biological creatures that have been programmed by evolution to behave, think,
      and learn in ways that have fostered species survival
   b. evolution specifically determines how we behave, think, and learn
   c. the process of evolution combines with the learning process to assist humans in adapting
      to their environment and finding a cultural niche in which to progress and prosper
   d. reinforcements in the environment shape behavior
   e. All of the choices are correct.

   ANS: A   PTS: 1   REF: Evolutionary Psychology

59. Evolutionary psychologists assert that ____.
   a. we are predisposed at birth to certain ways of behaving as shaped by evolution
   b. we are shaped as much if not more by learning than by biology
   c. genes cannot shape behavior
   d. social and cultural forces have very little influence on our behavior
   e. None of the choices are correct.

   ANS: A   PTS: 1   REF: Evolutionary Psychology

60. Which of the following is **not** one of the four fundamental questions dealt with by evolutionary
psychology?
   a. What explains the current nature of the human mind?
   b. What are the components, parts, and processes of the mind and how are they designed and
      organized?
   c. What accounts for the present nature of the human behavior?
   d. What are the functions of the mind?
   e. In what ways do stimuli from the environment interact with the genetically determined
      predispositions of the mind to determine behavior?

   ANS: C   PTS: 1   REF: Evolutionary Psychology

61. Evolutionary psychology owes a debt to ____.
   a. Darwin
   b. James
   c. Spencer
   d. All of the choices are correct.
   e. None of the choices are correct.

   ANS: D   PTS: 1   REF: Evolutionary Psychology

62. When behaviorism dominated psychology from 1913 to around 1960, the idea that any behavior might be determined genetically was ____.
   a. considered but not focused upon
   b. anathema
   c. fairly widely accepted
   d. an underlying force hidden behind most research
   e. None of the choices are correct

   ANS: B   PTS: 1   REF: Evolutionary Psychology

63. The behaviorist premise that all behavior is learned was challenged by ____.
   a. the Brelands' work on instinctual drift
   b. Harlow's work with monkey-mothers
   c. Seligman's work on biological preparedness
   d. All of the choices are correct.
   e. None of the choices are correct.

   ANS: D   PTS: 1   REF: Evolutionary Psychology

64. The idea that although phobias are learned through classical conditioning, some fears that were adaptive to our ancestors are learned more easily is called ____.
   a. instinctual drift
   b. biological preparedness
   c. evolutionary psychology
   d. positive psychology
   e. learning psychology

   ANS: B   PTS: 1   REF: Evolutionary Psychology

65. The cognitive movement was ____.
   a. an antecedent of evolutionary psychology
   b. a force against which evolutionary psychology rebelled
   c. enthusiastic about the work of Wilson on sociobiology
   d. suppressed shortly after its arrival by evolutionary psychology
   e. All of the choices are correct.

   ANS: A   PTS: 1   REF: Evolutionary Psychology

66. Evolutionary psychologists argue that the cognitive revolution ____.
   a. did not go far enough
   b. had little relevance for their work
   c. omitted the source and purpose of our information-processing capability
   d. did not go far enough and omitted the source and purpose of our information-processing capability
   e. All of the choices are correct.

   ANS: E   PTS: 1   REF: Evolutionary Psychology

67. A book entitled *Sociobiology: A New Synthesis* written by _____ was a contemporary force for evolutionary psychology.
    a. Seligman
    b. the Brelands
    c. Wilson
    d. Schultz
    e. Buss

    ANS: C   PTS: 1   REF: Evolutionary Psychology

68. The thesis of sociobiology challenged the assumption that _____.
    a. humans are irrational
    b. everyone is created equal
    c. biological forces alone foster or limit human development
    d. All of the choices are correct.
    e. None of the choices are correct.

    ANS: B   PTS: 1   REF: Evolutionary Psychology

69. The term sociobiology _____
    a. is now an accepted part of evolutionary psychology
    b. has been absorbed by the cognitive psychologists and used in the term "sociocognitivism"
    c. is used at meetings of the Human Behavior and Evolution Society
    d. has such a negative connotation that it has been dropped from use
    e. was coined by William James

    ANS: D   PTS: 1   REF: Evolutionary Psychology

70. Evolutionary psychology _____.
    a. incorporated the work of Wilson
    b. is very popular
    c. deals with psychological mechanisms that are programmed into humans because they were successful in human history
    d. All of the choices are correct.
    e. None of the choices are correct.

    ANS: D   PTS: 1   REF: Evolutionary Psychology

71. Criticisms of evolutionary psychology _____.
    a. include learning theorists
    b. point to the broad range of behavior with which it deals
    c. point to the difficulty of testing the theory in any significant manner
    d. All of the choices are correct.
    e. None of the choices are correct.

    ANS: D   PTS: 1   REF: Evolutionary Psychology

72. All approaches to psychology have _____.
    a. areas of vulnerability
    b. critics
    c. contributed to the development of the discipline as a whole
    d. All of the choices are correct.
    e. None of the choices are correct.

    ANS: D   PTS: 1   REF: Evolutionary Psychology

73. One criticism of evolutionary psychology is the idea that there might be biological determinants of behavior and therefore no free will. How is this criticism answered by evolutionary psychologists?
a. As uncomfortable as it may feel, it is true.
b. Not all behaviors are determined by genes.
c. Most psychologists say there is no free will (including Skinner).
d. The environment has little influence on behavior.
e. Evolutionary psychologists left this criticism unanswered.

ANS: B   PTS: 1   REF: Evolutionary Psychology

74. According to Schultz and Schultz, when a movement within psychology becomes a formalized school, the only way its momentum can be stopped is by its _____.
a. success
b. complete disintegration
c. flexibility
d. over-reliance on its founder
e. misdeeds

ANS: A   PTS: 1   REF: Evolutionary Psychology

TRUE/FALSE

75. Garry Kasparov lost his fighting spirit while playing against a computer.

ANS: T   PTS: 1   REF: Chess Champion Capitulates to Cunning Computer
MSC: WWW

76. All the schools of thought in psychology named as such in the textbook have become part of mainstream thought in the discipline.

ANS: F   PTS: 1   REF: Schools of Thought in Perspective

77. While each school attained success in its own way, some make little contribution to psychology's evolution.

ANS: F   PTS: 1   REF: Schools of Thought in Perspective

78. A few structuralists of Titchener's type remain in contemporary psychology as a minority within cognitive psychology.

ANS: F   PTS: 1   REF: Schools of Thought in Perspective
MSC: WWW

79. Compared with the other schools, structuralism dominated psychology for a considerable period of time.

ANS: F   PTS: 1   REF: Schools of Thought in Perspective

80. Unlike structuralism, functionalism has continued as a distinct school of thought.

ANS: F   PTS: 1   REF: Schools of Thought in Perspective

81. The functional viewpoint has changed the nature of psychology.

ANS: T   PTS: 1   REF: Schools of Thought in Perspective

82. The Gestalt school transformed psychology in the manner anticipated by its founders.

    ANS: F   PTS: 1   REF: Schools of Thought in Perspective

83. The effects of behaviorism and psychoanalysis on psychology have been profound.

    ANS: T   PTS: 1   REF: Schools of Thought in Perspective

84. Skinner's psychology is best viewed as the last stage in the development of psychology.

    ANS: F   PTS: 1   REF: Schools of Thought in Perspective

85. Humanistic psychology failed to make an impact as a separate school of thought within psychology.

    ANS: T   PTS: 1   REF: Schools of Thought in Perspective

86. For decades, introductory psychology textbooks described the functioning of the brain but refused to discuss any conception of the mind.

    ANS: T   PTS: 1   REF: Schools of Thought in Perspective
    MSC: WWW

87. Cognitive psychology came into being suddenly.

    ANS: F   PTS: 1   REF: The Cognitive Movement in Psychology

88. The behaviorists Tolman and Guthrie are considered precursors to cognitive psychology.

    ANS: T   PTS: 1   REF: The Cognitive Movement in Psychology

89. Bridgman, the father of operationism, argued that introspection is necessary.

    ANS: T   PTS: 1   REF: The Cognitive Movement in Psychology

90. Contemporary physics has rejected the notion of subjectivity in science.

    ANS: F   PTS: 1   REF: The Cognitive Movement in Psychology

91. Miller and Neisser said they became behaviorists because they had no choice.

    ANS: T   PTS: 1   REF: The Cognitive Movement in Psychology

92. Miller wrote about the magic number 7, plus or minus 2.

    ANS: T   PTS: 1   REF: George Miller (1920-)

93. Miller's and Bruner's Center for Cognitive Studies studied whatever was not behaviorism.

    ANS: T   PTS: 1   REF: George Miller (1920-)
    MSC: WWW

94. Neisser's influential book was called "Behavior of Organisms."

ANS: F   PTS: 1   REF: Ulric Neisser (1928-)

95. Cognitive psychology has replaced the clockwork metaphor with the computer metaphor.

ANS: T   PTS: 1   REF: The Computer Metaphor

96. Whereas the early mechanists reduced the human mind to gears, levers, and pulleys, cognitive psychologists reduced the mind to software and binary bits.

ANS: T   PTS: 1   REF: The Computer Metaphor

97. The Turing test was one way to judge whether a computer could think.

ANS: T   PTS: 1   REF: Artificial Intelligence

98. In response to Searle's "Chinese room", Turing developed the "Turing test" which became the definitive test of whether a machine can think.

ANS: F   PTS: 1   REF: Artificial Intelligence
MSC: WWW

99. Scientists can use machines, such as MRI and PET, to produce images of what is going on while someone "thinks."

ANS: T   PTS: 1   REF: The Nature of Cognitive Psychology

100. The text authors discuss the case of a paralyzed young man who can move a computer cursor by using his thoughts.

ANS: T   PTS: 1   REF: The Nature of Cognitive Psychology

101. Introspection has finally been abolished in psychology today.

ANS: F   PTS: 1   REF: The Nature of Cognitive Psychology

102. Modern cognitive psychologists have determined that the unconscious mind actually does much of our thinking.

ANS: T   PTS: 1   REF: The Nature of Cognitive Psychology

103. The modern cognitive idea called "nonconscious" is much like Freud's "unconscious" in that both are ruled by repressed desires and memories.

ANS: F   PTS: 1   REF: The Nature of Cognitive Psychology

104. The research in subliminal processing shows that we can absorb information that we can't see or hear.

ANS: T   PTS: 1   REF: The Nature of Cognitive Psychology

105. A part of research in cognitive psychology is on animal personality.

ANS: T   PTS: 1   REF: The Nature of Cognitive Psychology

106. Cognitive psychology is showing the signs of beginning to decline as a school of thought.

ANS: F   PTS: 1   REF: The Nature of Cognitive Psychology

107. Evolutionary psychology is an approach that assumes that some behaviors are genetically determined.

ANS: T   PTS: 1   REF: Evolutionary Psychology

108. The term "evolutionary psychology" was coined by William James.

ANS: T   PTS: 1   REF: Evolutionary Psychology

109. "Biological preparedness" refers to an animal's tendency to eat when hungry and drink when thirsty.

ANS: F   PTS: 1   REF: Evolutionary Psychology

110. E.O. Wilson's book on sociobiology was immediately and universally embraced.

ANS: F   PTS: 1   REF: Evolutionary Psychology